THE

P O E M S

OF

RICHARD CRASHAW

Oxford University Press, Ely House, London W. 1

GLASGOW NEW YORK TORONTO MELBOURNE WELLINGTON
CAPE TOWN SALISBURY IBADAN NAIROBI LUSAKA ADDIS ABABA
BOMBAY CALCUTTA MADRAS KARACHI LAHORE DACCA
KUALA LUMPUR HONG KONG

FIRST EDITION 1927
SECOND EDITION 1957
REPRINTED 1966
PRINTED LITHOGRAPHICALLY IN GREAT BRITAIN
AT THE UNIVERSITY PRESS, OXFORD
FROM CORRECTED SHEETS OF THE FIRST EDITION

LORETO.   From an engraving published in 1853

THE

POEMS

English Latin and Greek

OF

RICHARD CRASHAW

Edited by L. C. MARTIN

Second Edition

OXFORD

At the Clarendon Press

TO
D. M. M.

PREFACE TO SECOND EDITION

SINCE 1927, when Crashaw's poems were first included in this series, a good deal of fresh information about them and about their author has come to light, and in this second edition a number of corrections and additions have been made. Some parts of the introduction have been rewritten. Nearly all the rest of the new material is in the form of additional notes on pp. xcii–xciv. An index of titles is added on pp. 475–6.

I wish here to underline all the acknowledgements which I made in the preface of 1927, now reprinted, remembering especially the generous help given by the late Professor Edward Bensly in numerous notes on Crashaw's Latin usages and affiliations. I wish also to record my continued and much increased indebtedness to the late Canon F. E. Hutchinson, for many helpful comments on the edition of 1927.

My obligations to other scholars are acknowledged at the relevant places. It is fitting, however, that in thanking all of them I should make special mention of Professor Austin Warren, for his valuable contributions to knowledge of this poet's life and work.

Dr. J. G. McManaway kindly sent me a microfilm of a manuscript in the Folger Shakespeare Library containing poems by Crashaw.

The plate facing p. 315 has been made from a manuscript in the Pierpont Morgan Library, New York, with the Library's kind permission.

L. C. M.

PREFACE TO FIRST EDITION

THE chief purpose of this volume is to provide a reliable account of the text and canon of Richard Crashaw's complete works, and to make it easier than it has hitherto been to appreciate the qualities and follow the development of his mind and art. With it there goes no attempt to guide the reader in the assignment of praise or blame. The more striking merits of Crashaw's poetry have often been described, and his place among the more considerable poets of his time is now so well established as hardly to call for repeated definition here. Neither does it seem necessary any longer to apologize for what used to be censured as his 'faults' of taste and expression. Attempts to read the literature of the seventeenth century in the spirit in which it was written are often more whole-hearted now than they used to be; and with no very violent effort of sympathy and imagination the modern student will be able to understand and enjoy some of the features of Crashaw's art which the eighteenth and nineteenth centuries were wont to deplore. But it is among the requisites of any closer study, such as this volume is intended to facilitate, that the text on which it is based should not only supply the most accurate possible record of what the poet wrote, but by its convenient disposition serve as a mirror to his growing and changing nature as thinker and as artist—in either or in both of which respects previous editions of Crashaw have usually been a good deal to seek.

The circumstances are somewhat peculiar. Crashaw was anything but a prolific writer, even considering his early death, but he was clearly given to revising, recasting, and amplifying such portions of his works as seemed worth the trouble. Between the first, second, and third published volumes of his English poems the differences are often substantial and striking; and it seems obvious that the method generally followed hitherto of crystallizing the text into a single form and leaving its evolution to be gathered from foot-notes is not the most helpful that could be devised.

The plan which has been adopted in the present edition should be clear enough from the textual introduction, but it may be shortly premised here that the two main stages discernible in the text of some of the most important English poems, corresponding to the first edition (*Steps to the Temple . . . With other Delights of the Muses*, 1646) and the much altered and extended second edition of the same work (1648) find their counterpart in the present volume in what may be described as corrected reprints, aiming at true texts, of the first edition and of *Carmen Deo Nostro*, the collection published in Paris in 1652 and consisting almost entirely of ' divine ' poems which had been revised for the edition of 1648 or had appeared there for the first time. The Paris edition has been followed for these poems, rather than that of 1648, because although in general it conforms closely to the 1648 text it also contains some new and undoubtedly authentic alterations and additions—one of the finest examples of Crashaw's invention, for example, appearing here for the first time [1]; and further because the peculiar conditions and features of its production place it among the most interesting and valuable volumes of English poetry published during the seventeenth century. The text of the first edition (1646) has been adopted for poems reprinted in 1648 with little or no alteration, as well as for the early form of poems which in the second edition were much changed, because on the whole, and as often happened in the seventeenth century, the first edition was more carefully and characteristically produced. The poems which in the present volume are printed twice are with hardly any exception poems which had been so much changed between 1646 and 1648 that to print one text only and indicate the variants by means of foot-notes would be to give less than its due prominence to a very important aspect of Crashaw's work ; and the method of double

---

[1] Lines 93–108 of ' The Flaming Heart ' (see p. 326 below).

presentation has the further advantage that it holds the foot-notes within convenient bounds, restricting them very largely to cross-references which may facilitate comparison and to the recording of manuscript variants, which have the usual and strong claim to attention that they seem often to point back to a still earlier stage of composition than that enshrined in the first published edition. The MSS. usually conform most closely to the text of 1646, which has therefore in most instances been taken as the basis of collation.

Between the two sections of the present edition thus corresponding to the editions of 1646 and 1652 will be found the few poems which are peculiar to the edition of 1648. The Latin and Greek epigrams published in 1634 and 1670 precede the poems from the volume of 1646, and after *Carmen Deo Nostro* are printed certain additional Latin, Greek, and English poems, chiefly from manuscript sources. Of the MSS. the most important are British Museum Add. MSS. 40176 and 33219, and Harleian 6917; and Bodleian MS. Tanner 465, all of which contain material not found elsewhere. From MS. Tanner 465 five poems are now, it is believed, printed for the first time. MS. Harleian 6917 yields the fine Epithalamium, which was not printed or claimed for Crashaw until it appeared in the *London Mercury*, June 1923, p. 159 sqq.; and the reader's attention is specially drawn to the introductory notes on these MSS.

The attempt has been made to represent accurately each of the original editions on which, successively, the present one is based, preserving their essential features and recording all departures from them in the foot-notes, with the following exceptions :

(1) long ' ſ ' and devices like ' õ ' for ' om ' or ' q̃ ' for ' que ' are abandoned throughout the text ;

(2) errors of spacing, wrong founts, and turned letters are corrected silently, these including the frequent use of ' à ' for ' a ', ' th- ' for ' th' ' in the Paris edition of 1652. On the other hand, the faults or inconsistencies of accentuation in Latin and Greek verses have not been eradicated.

Seventeenth-century variants of any genuine significance,

in printed editions as well as in MSS., are recorded in the
foot-notes, together with suggestions of modern editors
which have been found interesting or helpful, but not the
numerous misprints occurring in the volume of 1648, except
where that volume, being the only authority, has been used
as the basis of the text; and not, again, manuscript
variants merely and obviously due to hasty or ignorant
copying. The foot-notes also usually take no account of
variant spellings.

'Significant variants', however, are understood to include many instances of variant punctuation, both in
printed and in manuscript versions. To record all differences of punctuation whatever would of course unduly
encumber the apparatus, but in the unavoidable necessity
of making selections consistency has been aimed at, the
general rule observed being only to note instances where the
variant stop could have had a special emphasizing or
explanatory shade of significance for the seventeenth-
century reader. Where the foot-notes give no contrary
indication it must be assumed that the other printed texts
and the MSS. concerned agree or are of similar import, or
again (as frequently in the MSS.) that there is no punctuation at all.

It was hoped that it might also be possible to record the
variant usage of italics in the printed editions, corresponding
to the manuscript convention of writing certain words and
phrases in a larger hand for the sake of emphasis. But this
again would have tended to overweight the foot-notes and
the intention was in general abandoned. In some more
striking instances, however, where the printed editions use
no italics but a MS. distinguishes a word or a phrase, the
circumstance has been recorded. The convention has also
been observed in printing the poems for which MSS. are
the only authority.

The materials for a biography of Crashaw are a little less
exiguous than they were fifty years ago, when Grosart
published his edition, and though the reconstruction of
details in the poet's experience must remain largely a

matter of conjecture, the new facts and documents which have come to light since Crashaw's life was written for the *Dictionary of National Biography* are perhaps considerable enough to justify, as a setting for them, a restatement of the more important of those which were earlier available. This edition is the first to include a copy of Crashaw's letter written from Leyden in 1644 and of the Queen's letter introducing him to the Pope in 1646.[1]

The notes at the end of the volume are intended to supplement the biography, to elucidate obscurity, to supply where necessary evidence of authorship, and to provide illustrative material such as may throw light on the influences which went to make Crashaw's poetry what it was.

It is a pleasure to own my indebtedness and express my gratitude to all those who have assisted me with their information or counsel, and of whom some are mentioned at the relevant points. Other obligations fall to be acknowledged here. The value of the help given by Professor E. Bensly in regard to Crashaw's Latin and Greek verses, and the generosity of the giving, could hardly be overstated. His scholarly tact and wide knowledge of medieval and Renaissance as well as of ancient Latin and Greek have been placed unreservedly at my service and have given me far more confidence than I could otherwise have felt in attempting to define this difficult part of the text. I cannot claim that the result is such as Professor Bensly would have secured himself ; I am sure that most of what is good in it is due to him. It is specially gratifying to recall various peculiarities of word or phrase which by classical standards might seem to require emendation, but which have been shown to accord with medieval or later practice and therefore allowed to stand. Professor Bensly has also supplied many Greek and Latin parallels given in the Commentary. Particular thanks are also due to Lord Denbigh, for the loan of his copy of *Carmen Deo Nostro*,

---

[1] This letter was first printed in full in *Secentismo e Marinismo in Inghilterra* (1925) by Dr. Mario Praz, who obtained this and other material from the present editor.

for permission to reproduce as a frontispiece the portrait, by Gerbier, of Susan, first Countess of Denbigh, and for other accommodations ; to Lady Elizabeth and Lady Victoria Feilding, for kind assistance given at Newnham Paddox ; to Mr. J. Burford Leonard, for his loan of the original MS. of the letter by Crashaw of which a reproduction faces p. xxx; to Mr. Geoffrey Keynes, for lending copies of early editions ; to Mr. Everard Meynell, for useful bibliographical matter ; to Dr. T. Walker, for information relative to Crashaw's life at Peterhouse and for access to the College Records ; to Mr. D. Nichol Smith, Professor Garrod, and Professor D. A. Slater, who have seen different portions of the text and made very valuable suggestions for its improvement ; to Dr. Mario Praz, for parallels from Marino ; to the Librarian of the Santa Casa, the Rev. P. Dalmonte, for the text of the documents at Loreto given in Appendix II; to the officials of the British Museum, Bodleian Library, Cambridge University Library, and the Library of Trinity College, Dublin, for their unfailing kindness and facilitations; and to the Secretary and Staff of the Clarendon Press, for much friendly interest and advice. I have received assistance of various kinds from the Rev. Professor W. Lock, of Christ Church, the Rev. F. E. Hutchinson, Professor H. J. C. Grierson, Mr. R. Flower, Miss E. Cruwys Sharland, Mr. Percy Simpson and Mr. G. Thorn Drury. Special thanks are due to the last-mentioned scholar for his scrutiny of my Introduction, and for the material embodied in several items of the Commentary. I am also greatly indebted to my wife for help in the collation of MSS., and for many other valuable services. For any errors or shortcomings which may be found in this edition I am alone responsible.

L. C. MARTIN.

LIVERPOOL.

CONTENTS

Contents.

PLATES

INTRODUCTION

I. BIOGRAPHY

1. 1612–1631. *London and Yorkshire.*

ALTHOUGH in the Admission Book of Pembroke College, Cambridge, Richard Crashaw is no doubt correctly described as ' natus Londini ', since at the time of his birth his father, William Crashaw, was preacher at the Temple, the Crashaw family had for generations before this been settled in Yorkshire. The more original form of the name, Crawshaw, is still of fairly common occurrence in that county and is even to be found at the present day in the neighbourhood of Handsworth, Sheffield, where William Crashaw was born in 1572. The researches of Dr. Grosart at the parish church of Handsworth showed that William Crashaw's father and grandfather were both apparently named Richard, and that Richard Crashaw, the grandfather of the poet, died in 1585.

William Crashaw entered St. John's College, Cambridge, on May 1, 1591. The date of his first graduation is not recorded, but on January 19, 1594, he succeeded to the Bishop of Ely's Fellowship at the same college, being nominated by the queen in the temporary vacancy of the bishopric. He proceeded M.A. in 1595 and subsequently took the degree of B.D. How long he resided at Cambridge is not known, but he maintained for many years his relations with St. John's, and his memory is secured there by the collection of his own books which, apparently, he induced the Earl of Southampton to buy and present to the college library.[1]

His will at Somerset House begins with a statement of the various places with which he had been pastorally connected after he left Cambridge : ' I William Crashawe, Bachelor in Divinitye Preacher of Gods worde. First at Bridlington then at Beverley in Yorkshire afterwards at the Temple Since then Pastor of the Church of Ag: Burton· in the diocese of Yorke.

[1] Article in the college magazine, *The Eagle*, Dec. 1901, quoting letters from William Crashaw kept at St. John's.

Nowe Pastor of that too greate Parishe of Whitechappell in the Suburbs of London. . . .' It is not possible to give exact dates for his tenure of these various cures, but it is known that he was appointed Preacher to the Temple in February 1604–5,[1] about eight years before his son was born. During those years he was occupied not only as a preacher but as a writer and a collector of books, becoming famous as a Puritan controversialist, and assembling what must have been one of the finest private theological libraries of the time. At the Temple, where as he said one could enjoy 'the most comfortable and delightful company for a scholler, that (out of the Universities) this Kingdom yields',[2] he remained at least until 30 August 1613, when he signed Sir Thomas Cuming's 'Album Amicorum' (British Museum Add. MS. 17083, f. 145 v.) as 'Gul. Crashavius verbi div. ap. Templar. london praedic:'. On March 23, 1614, however, he writes to St. John's College about his books, giving as his address 'Ag. Burton',[3] so that evidently by that date he had obtained the living to which his right had earlier been disputed (see *D.N.B.* art. William Crashaw). It is probable that he was reinstated here as a result of his (undated) petition to the king, now in the British Museum (Royal MS. 17. B. ix), in which he requests facilities for compiling 'A discoverye of popy[s]he Corruption requiringe A kingely reformation . . .' and asks that with a view to the necessary leisure he may be restored to a 'litle vicharage' of which he had been dispossessed 'in ye last yeare of the Queene'. On November 13, 1618, he was instituted to the living of St. Mary Matfellon, Whitechapel,[4] where he remained until his death in 1626.

He was twice married, but the year of his first marriage and the identity of his first wife remain unknown in spite of careful inquiry, and approximations of date have to suffice. The *terminus a quo* is provided in a Jesuit answer of 1612 to some of William Crashaw's recent attacks on the Church of Rome; this was *The Overthrow of the Protestants Pulpit-Babels, Convincing their Preachers of Lying & Rayling, to make the Church*

---

[1] F. A. Inderwick, *Calendar of the Inner Temple Records*, ii, p. 9. Information kindly supplied by Mr. P. J. Wallis.

[2] Quoted from *Romish Forgeries*, 1606, by A. Warren, *Richard Crashaw*, p. 212.

[3] Authority in note on p. xv.

[4] A copy of the official document recording his induction is in Bodl. MS. Rawl. 377, f. 335.

of Rome seeme mysticall Babell. Particularly confuting VV. Crashawes Sermon at the Crosse, printed as the patterne to iustify the rest. . . . Togeather with a discouery of M. Crashawes spirit : and an Answere to his Iesuites Ghospell. By I. R. Student in Diuinity. . . M.DC.XII. On p. 321 of this work the writer mentions a sermon preached by William Crashaw on February 21, 1609/10 (published in 1610) on the subject of Virginia, and addressing its author suggests that he might have been glad for some ministers ' to forsake their Benefices, and goe to *Virginia* in person, that you might have stepped into one of their roomes with your wife, whom perchance then you had in hart if not in house (for you married not long after) . . .'.

Richard Crashaw, apparently the only issue of this marriage, seems to have been born towards the end of 1612 or early in 1613. He is described in the Admission Book of Pembroke College, Cambridge, as ' annos habens 18 ' on July 6, 1631, and from the obituary publication in honour of William Crashaw's second wife, to be quoted below, it appears that he was baptized eight years before October 1620, though the ' eight years ' are doubtless only approximate. The date of the first wife's death is unknown, but the second marriage took place in 1619. This is shown both by the registers of All Hallows, Barking, and in the volume of *Marriage-licences granted by the Bishop of London* (Harleian Society, vol. xxvi, 1887) :

[1619]
May 8 Mr William Crashawe, Clerk, B.D., of St Mary, White-chapel, Widower, 42, & Elizabeth Skynner, of same, Spinster, 26, dau. of Anthony Skynner, of same, Gent., who consents ; at All Hallows Barking.

This second wife died about October 4, 1620, soon after which there appeared *The Honovr of Vertve. or The Monument erected by the sorowfull Husband, and the Epitaphes annexed by learned and worthy men, to the immortall memory of that worthy Gentle-woman Mrs Elizabeth Crashawe. Who dyed in child-birth, and was buried in Whit-Chappell : Octob. 8. 1620. In the 24 yeare of her age.* . . . [n. d.]. The reference to Richard Crashaw's baptism occurs on p. A 3 verso of this publication, where it is stated that ' The Funerall Sermon was made by

Doctor *Vsher* of *Ireland*, then in *England*, and now Lord Bishop of *Meath*, in *Ireland*. It was her owne earnest request to him, that he would preach at the Baptisme of her Sonne, as he had eight yeares afore, being then also in *England*,[1] at the Baptisme of her husbands elder sonne '. The only other reference to the future poet is in the tribute which is made to Elizabeth Crashaw's ' singular motherly affection to the child of her predecessor '.

Richard Crashaw's godfather was his namesake Richard Crashaw, Master of the Goldsmiths' Company (see p. xx, below).[2]

William Crashaw's will, dated June 10, 1622, was proved on October 16, 1626,. by Robert Dixon, the other executor appointed being ' my sonne Richarde ', who was then only about fourteen years of age. No special legacy is made to him in the will and he was no doubt otherwise provided for, though it seems clear that his portion was not very large. His father had never been a rich man, and in the petition to the king already mentioned William Crashaw speaks of ' havinge spent my patrimonye in bookes, and my time in perusinge them '; and though he subsequently married one who according to *The Honovr of Vertve* was ' like to be of great estate, and therefore much sought after by yong gallants and rich heires ', it is not known that he derived any great pecuniary benefit from the step. But beyond its various worldly dispositions the will contains a solemn asseveration of the faith which both in the pulpit and in his published works William Crashaw had so often and so zealously upheld, and of which his son's later career was to provide so explicit a denial :

I accounte Poperie (as nowe it is) the heape and chaos of all

---

[1] Biographies of Ussher state that he was in England in the early months of 1613 (N.S.): actually Ussher wrote letters from London between September 1612 and April 1613 (A. Warren, op. cit., p. 210).

[2] This is no doubt the Richard Crashaw referred to in *Epigrammatum Hecatontades Dvæ. Authore R. B. Londoni . . . 1627. Hecatontas Altera* No. 11 is inscribed ' *Ad virum probatissimum, Richardum Crashaw Ciuem Londinensum* ' and runs as follows :

> Nesciat, ut manuum quid agat tua dextra, sinistra,
>   Pauperibus quando des eleemosynas,
> Aut aliud pietatis agas.opus ; acta, docente
>   Christo hoc, testantur te didicisse tua.
> A te sentit opem miser, ignoratque ferentem,
>   Munera das, & dans munera nullus eris.

heresies and the channell whereinto the fowlest impieties & heresies y^t have byne in the christian Worlde have runn and closelye emptied themselues· I beleeue the Popes seate and power to be the power of the greate Antechrist and the doctrine of the Pope (as nowe it is) to be the doctrine of Antechriste. yea that doctrine of Divells prophecied of by the Apostle and that the true and absolute Papist soe livinge and dyeinge debarrs himself of salvation for oughte that we knowe, . . .

William Crashaw's real and characteristic though not strikingly eminent gifts as a writer had often been employed in works of devotional as well as of controversial intent,[1] and in these his deep and earnest piety may be unmistakably discerned. Some of them are in verse, which is by no means wanting in movement and inspiration, and it is of interest to observe that Richard Crashaw apparently read it with care and admiration, since he occasionally re-echoes it in his own poetry. The poem, in particular, at the end of his father's *Manuall for true Catholickes* . . ., called ' The Conclusion, with a devout and holy prayer ' was probably remembered both for its rhythm and its phraseology by Richard Crashaw when he wrote his version of Psalm xxiii (see the notes to that poem, p. 435, below).

It was not, apparently, before 1629 that Crashaw entered the Charterhouse, and where he first went to school is not known. His earliest biographer, Lloyd (*Memoires*, &c., 1668),[2] speaks of his having been under the protection of two lawyers, Sir Henry Yelverton and Sir Randolph Crew, of whom it is to be noted that the latter became a governor of the Charterhouse in 1628. The minutes of an Assembly of Governors, under the date July 2, 1629, contain a list of boys passed for admission successively as places fell void, and ' Richard Crosshow ' is thirteenth in the list with a note ' no exception to his age '.[3] The only other relevant entry in the school

---

[1] See the list of his works given in the *D.N.B.*, article William Crashaw.

[2] The two first published biographies, or rather approaches to a biography, of Crashaw, Lloyd's, and Wood's in *Fasti Oxonienses*, ii, col. 4 (ed. Bliss, 1820) are given in Appendix II. Both are scrappy and rhetorical, drawing upon the Preface to *Steps to the Temple* for some flamboyant phrases, and Lloyd's is certainly not accurate in all its details. But their contact with Crashaw's time gives them thus much authority.

[3] This probably means that Crashaw was over the age at which ' gown-boys ' or Foundation Scholars were admitted ; or else it is

records is one dated July 11, 1631, to the effect that ' Richard Crasshowe ' was sent as exhibitioner to Pembroke College, Cambridge.

Lloyd gives much credit to Robert Brook, who was Head Master of the Charterhouse from 1628 to 1643, for laying the foundations of Crashaw's future proficiency as a writer, by prescribing exercises imitative of ' the choicest Orators and Poets ' ; and Crashaw himself pays a tribute to his former master in the address to Brook prefixed to the Latin epigrams published in 1634. But whether any of the poems which are preserved were written during his boyhood must remain doubtful. It seems at least probable that some of them belong to his school days, more especially some of the epigrams. In *Charterhouse : Old and New* [1] (1910, p. 14) an old rule under the Founder's will is mentioned which ' used to provide that the Foundation Scholars in the highest form should every Sunday set up in the Great Hall four Greek and four Latin verses apiece upon any part of the second lesson appointed for the day, for the Master of the Hospital or any stranger to view '. The English poems, again, in MS. Tanner 465, on the Gunpowder Treason and on the King's Coronation, which are marked by a violence of tone and striving after effect, of some-what youthful quality, may well have been written before he went to Cambridge. The same is possibly true of some of the Latin verses preserved in MS. Tanner 465, and of the version of Psalm xxiii, which has a childlike simplicity besides recalling the style of William Crashaw's poem mentioned above.[2]

Just before he left school Richard Crashaw became the heir to certain property and to twenty pounds in money left him by his godfather, the Richard Crashaw who was Master of the Goldsmiths' Company and who appears to have died on June 2, 1631. The relevant portion of the will, as quoted in *Notes and Queries*, Ninth Series, vi, July 28, 1900 (p. 64), is as follows :

> Item I give and bequeath unto Richard Crashawe my godsonn sonne of Willyam Crashawe late of White Chappell preacher

a proviso lest he should become over age by the time a vacancy occurred. It should be added that the records only refer to ' gown-boys ' and not to the other Carthusians, who were boarders. I am indebted to the Master of the Charterhouse for this information.

[1] By A. P. Eardley Wilmot and E. C. Streatfeild.

[2] See the note on the chronological order of Crashaw's poems, p. xc, below.

my house and two gardens without Bishopps gate against the
Spitle, and my house att Bassing Hall in London, and my house
at Mortelacke in the countie of Surrey, To hould the same to
the said Richard Crashawe and his heires for his better maine-
tenance and education in learning and for the good respecte
which I beare unto his father, And also I give to my said God
sonne twentie poundes in money to buie him bookes or other
thinges needfull.

II. 1631–1643. *Cambridge.*

Richard Crashaw was matriculated at Cambridge as a
pensioner on March 26, 1632, but the entry in the Admission
Book of Pembroke College is as follows :

> Julii 6. 1631 Richardus Crashawe Gulielmi pr⟨e⟩sbyteri filius
> natus Londini annos hens 18, admissus est ad 2ᵃᵉ mensæ ordinem
> sub tutela Mʳˡ Tourney.

In September 1631, the death of Dr. Samuel Brooke, of
Trinity College, occurred ; in October that of Dr. Mansell,
President of Queens' College, and of William Herrys, Fellow
of Pembroke ; and the elegiac poems written by Crashaw for
these occasions are the first of a series belonging to the early
years of his residence. There is of course no reason to suppose
that any friendship or personal feelings were involved in his
relations with these fairly prominent figures. But the fact
of his writing these funeral verses so soon after his arrival
shows that he went to Cambridge with a mature talent for original composition and that he may, like Cowley, have brought
with him a certain repute. It was also in October 1631 that
he was elected to the Greek Scholarship at Pembroke, the
duties of which included the making of Latin and Greek
verses on scriptural themes.[1] Many of the Latin epigrams
which Crashaw published in 1634 were probably written to
meet this requirement. 1634 was the year also in which he
took the degree of B.A.

Up to this date and indeed right up to the appearance in
1646 of his *Steps to the Temple*, the known writings of Crashaw
give no evidence of strong Romanist inclinations. The third
poem ' on the Gunpowder-Treason ' (p. 387, below) is thoroughly Protestant in its denunciation of Papal truculence,
and the Latin 'epigram on the shadow of St. Peter (p. 19,

---

[1] See A. Warren, ' Crashaw's *Epigrammata Sacra* ', *J.E.G.P.*, xxxiii,
1934, pp. 233–9, and the same writer's *Richard Crashaw*, 1939, pp. 22–3
and 215–16.

below), still suggests an attitude of somewhat satirical criticism towards the Roman claims. Moreover, his reference, in the prose address to the reader, p. 14, below, l. 25, to the 'Acygniani' (the anagram for the Jesuits or Ignatians employed in Barclay's *Euphormionis Satyricon* (1603–7), seems to indicate that a spirited though polite resistance was being made to Jesuit propaganda. But his High Anglicanism was clearly well developed by 1634. The epigrams are preceded by complimentary verses to his tutor, Tournay, a notable High-Churchman, and to Laney, then the Master of Pembroke, who is praised for his zeal in restoring beauty to the college chapel and to its worship. In the following year, too, Crashaw contributed his prefatory poem to Shelford's *Five pious and learned Discourses, . . .* Cambridge 1635, in which the doctrine of Justification by Faith is impugned as it had already been by Tournay,[1] and in which another Protestant theory, accepted by Crashaw's father, that the Pope is Antichrist, is also called in question (see Crashaw's poem, p. 137, below, and the note thereto, p. 139).

It was probably in the year 1635, too, that Crashaw was elected to his Fellowship at Peterhouse, then perhaps the most important focus at Cambridge of Laudian High-Churchmanship. John Cosin had succeeded Matthew Wren as Master in 1634. Crashaw's formal admission is dated 20 November 1636,[2] but according to contemporary habit this may well have followed by as much as a year or more his entry upon his duties. The new chapel, consecrated in 1632 and in full use from that date, was not yet complete in all its details; and as early as July 1635 the college records (Box 'Collegium' R 9) show that Crashaw was concerned in its embellishment. About this time there are several items recording the purchase, among other things, of 'frames' (which are credibly though not certainly picture-frames) and on July 30:

Item one Bill for work done about ye organ, vestry, altars, dayles[3] for ye gallery, frames for Mr Crashaw[4] &c 4 10 1

[1] Dr. Ward, Master of Sidney Sussex, reported Tournay's defection to Ussher in 1634. See Ussher, *Works*, ed. Elrington, vol. xv, pp. 579–80. Quoted p. 425, below.

[2] See Appendix II, p. 418, below.   [3] i. e. (deal) boardings.

[4] For Crashaw's interest in the graphic arts see the Preface to *Steps to the Temple*, p. 76, l. 58; and A. Warren, *Richard Crashaw*, pp. 28–9.

Crashaw is also described as ' Coll. S. Pet. Socius ' in *Carmen Natalitium, etc.*, published in 1635 (see foot-notes to p. 161, below). It is likely to have been about this time that he wrote the two Latin poems, first published in 1648, appealing for the assistance which Peterhouse needed for the completion of its new buildings, ' Votiva Domus Petrensis Pro Domo Dei ' and ' In cæterorum Operum difficili Parturitione Gemitus '.

The date of Crashaw's ordination is unknown but the *Ely Episcopal Records*[1] show that he was Curate of Little St. Mary's in 1639. This is the church which adjoins Peterhouse and which served as the college chapel prior to the building of the new one; and Crashaw's connexion with it is attested again in the Preface to *Steps to the Temple* (1646):

> *Reader, we stile his Sacred Poems*, Stepps to the Temple, *and aptly, for in the Temple of God, under his wing, he led his life in St.* Maries *Church neere St.* Peters *Colledge .*

Lloyd extols his preaching. ' Those thronged Sermons on each Sunday and Holiday, that ravished more like Poems . . . scattering not so much Sentences [as] Extasies '[2] have not come down to us but the description is credible enough. Crashaw could have distinguished himself in this way either as Curate of Little St. Mary's or as College Catechist, another office which he held towards the end of his Cambridge days. After leaving the University he spoke regretfully of the 'little contentfull kingdom' which his Fellowship had meant for him, and it is easy to see how satisfying the life at Peterhouse must have been to one of his enthusiastic yet retiring nature. All his gifts would be happily employed in the teaching and writing, the ministrations and the friendships,[3] which this appointment brought with it.

Among the first pupils assigned to him was Ferrar Collet,[4] younger brother of Mary Collet and nephew of Nicholas Ferrar, the founder of the Anglican community at Little

---

[1] Ed. A. Gibbons, 1891, p. 227. For further particulars see A. Warren, 'Crashaw, "Catechist and Curate"', *Mod. Philology*, xxxii, 1935, pp. 261–9, and the same writer's *Richard Crashaw*, pp. 40–2. Crashaw was described later by the queen as 'ayant esté Ministre en Angleterre' (see p. xxxiii). [2] See p. 416.

[3] e.g. with Joseph Beaumont, Fellow of Peterhouse 1636–44, who calls him 'my onely worthy self' (see p. xxxix).

[4] 'Maii 16, 1636. Farrer Collet Huntingtoniensis admissus est ad secundam mensam sub tutelâ Dni Crashaw.' T. A. Walker, *Admissions to Peterhouse*, 1912, p. 55.

Gidding. This is one of the first signs of Crashaw's connexion with that community ;[1] but that the relationship was of earlier origin is suggested by the fact that Crashaw had already written the commendatory poem published with the translation of Lessius' *Hygiasticon*, 1634 (see p. 156, below), this work having been a favourite with Nicholas Ferrar, who may well have encouraged Crashaw to write in its praise. The translation from Barclay's *Argenis* (' No roofes of gold o're riotous tables shining ', see p. 338, below), also probably written with Little Gidding in mind, is perhaps of later date. The first published statement of the connexion is that made in *Memoirs of the Life of Mr. Nicholas Ferrar. By P. Peckard, D.D. . . . Cambridge . . . MDCCXC.*, where with reference to the vigils which were kept at Little Gidding it is said (p. 243) that ' Several religious persons both in the neighbourhood, and from distant places, attended these watchings : and amongst these the celebrated Mr. Rich. Crashaw, Fellow of Peterhouse, who was very intimate in the family, and frequently came from Cambridge for this purpose, and at his return often watched in Little St. Mary's Church near Peterhouse '. This is a good though late authority, being based largely on family tradition, but now that Crashaw's letter, written in 1643/4 to one of the Ferrar family, has come to light, the intimacy of which Peckard speaks is seen to have been deeper than could before have been surmised.

When the conflict between the King and Parliament broke out—it is foreshadowed in the verses which Crashaw added in 1640 to the poem originally called ' A Panegyrick. Upon the birth of the Duke of Yorke ' (see p. 176, below)—Crashaw's sympathies, as was to be expected, showed themselves to be pronouncedly and more than sentimentally royalist. A docu-

---

[1] Another is Sancroft's note on the epitaph on Nicholas Ferrar, junior (as quoted in MS. Tanner 88, fo. 2) ' by Mr Crashaw, I thinke '. Cp. Hearne, *Caii Vindiciæ*, p. 810. The epitaph is attributed by Nicholas Ferrar's brother John to ' Mr. Mark Frank, once fellow of Pembroke Hall in Cambridge '. See J. E. B. Mayor, *Cambridge in the Seventeenth Century. Part I. Nicholas Ferrar. 1855.*, p. 144. There is, however, another and a shorter Latin epitaph of Nicholas Ferrar, the elder, in existence, which may be by Crashaw and of which Sancroft may have heard. It was published in the *Church Quarterly Review* (Oct. 1921, pp. 59–60) from a manuscript source by the Rev. H. Skipton, with the suggestion that Sancroft may have confused the two epitaphs. There is no positive evidence, however, of Crashaw's authorship.

ment is preserved in the Treasury at Peterhouse from which it appears that he was one of several Fellows who joined their forces to guarantee a loan of sixty pounds to the king in July 1642.[1] But as the situation grew worse in the eastern counties (Cambridge was itself occupied by the rebels in the spring of 1643) Crashaw must have realized that his own position was threatened; and like other College Fellows he may well have decided soon not to remain in Cambridge, where he might lose his post at once on refusing to accept the Covenant. He was not in fact ejected until April 1644 (see pp. xxxi–xxxii); but there is evidence that he ceased to live in college, and he may have left Cambridge too, early in the preceding year.[2] As was to be expected, the Parliamentary Commissioners, implementing the Act of 28 August 1643 ('Monuments of Superstition or Idolatry to be demolished'[3]) gave a good deal of attention to the scenes of Crashaw's former activities. At Peterhouse, it appears from William Dowsing's Diary,[4] 'We pulled down 2 mighty great Angells with Wings, & divers other Angells, & the 4 Evangelists & Peter with his Keies, over the Chapell Dore, & about a hundred Chirubims & Angells & divers Superstitious Letters in gold'; at Little St. Mary's[5] 'We brake down 60 Superstitious Pictures, Some Popes & Crucyfixes & God the father sitting in a chayer & holding a Glasse in his hand'. Where Crashaw was during this visitation is unknown, but it is quite likely that he had retired first to Little Gidding.

III. 1643–1649. *Leyden, (?) Oxford, Paris,*
Rome, Loreto.

The next definite news of Crashaw is that he is in Holland in February 1643/4, in circumstances that witness very clearly to the closeness of his relationship with the Little Gidding community. The evidence for this is the letter already referred to above, the only piece of English prose from Crashaw's hand known to exist[5], and a document of the greatest interest for the light which it throws upon his character and temperament and upon his situation and feelings

---

[1] See copy of this and of the succeeding document, pp. 418–19.
[2] See A. Warren, 'Crashaw's Residence at Cambridge', *T.L.S.*, 3 Nov. 1932, p. 815.
[3] H. Scobell, *A Collection of Acts and Ordinances* . . . 1658, Cap. 17.
[4] As given in Cooper's *Annals of Cambridge*, iii, p. 364.
[5] Ibid., p. 366.
[6] Apart from titles and (probably) the dedication on p. 231.

at this very critical moment of his life. The letter has been preserved among other original documents belonging to descendants of the Ferrar family ; it is now in the possession of the University Library, Cambridge, and was first published in an article entitled 'Richard Crashaw and Mary Collet' contributed to the *Church Quarterly Review*, vol. lxxiii, No. 146, January 1912, p. 358, by Miss E. Cruwys Sharland. The handwriting, though cramped and hurried, is almost certainly Crashaw's; and the personal references, with the signature 'R. C.', point unmistakably to his authorship.

It appears that Crashaw has been for some little time at Leyden and that a lady who may have been Mary Collet, the niece of Nicholas Ferrar and, since 1632, the 'Mother'[1] of the Community, is also there ; but that for reasons which are not stated and which may have been of a political or religious nature, he is no longer allowed to see her. How Mary Collet, if indeed it was she, came to visit Holland at this time, or why Crashaw accompanied or joined her there does not appear. It does not follow necessarily from anything said in the letter that she had gone primarily on his behalf. Evidently she had an uncle in Leyden (and it will be remembered that the Ferrars were of Flemish descent), into whose house Crashaw had earlier been admitted with her. Crashaw, however, now writes (possibly either to John Ferrar, the brother and biographer of Nicholas, or to Mary Collet's father) to inform him that these relations have been broken off and to propose a plan by which Crashaw hopes to do a service, to derive some profit still from his Fellowship, and perhaps to secure the reversion of his office in happier times. The plan is to send in a formal resignation of the Fellowship in favour of his friend and former pupil, Ferrar Collet, who was now a By-Fellow, and who if appointed to Crashaw's post would have the usual right to let part of the accommodation which went with it and thus be in a position to place at Crashaw's disposal the 'chamber-income' of which he stood in so much need.

The final paragraph of the letter tells of more intimate things. In it Crashaw anticipates and seeks to remove the

---

[1] See *The Story Books of Little Gidding*, by E. C. Sharland, 1899, p. 164. It is difficult to think of any one else whom Crashaw could describe as ' my mother ' with equal fitness.

anxiety which he thinks his news will naturally arouse, assuring his friend that he is not yet ' purposed for fixing '. This may, of course, only refer, as the immediate context might imply, to the choice of an abiding city or a fixed occupation ; but the tone of the whole paragraph, with the apology for what seems to the writer ' a defect at least a disproportion of my weak soul to seuerer courses ' and the suggestion that delay will be in the nature of a relief to his correspondent, point to the conclusion that he is rather, or also, thinking of religious settlement and perhaps of the discipline which monastic life, for example, would impose. It is not hard to believe that his troubles were already encouraging him to take the step, which he must have taken by 1646, of seeking admission into the Roman Communion.

It is not known whether the practical object of this letter was served. Ferrar Collet, with several others, was himself turned out of Peterhouse on January 3, 1644/5, for refusing to accept the Covenant.[1] But the preservation of the letter, seeing that it was to be destroyed ' if nothing to this purpose ' suggests that something may have been attempted or even done, at least for the time.[2] The following is the text of the letter : [3]

Dear S^r

For all ye mystery of that my Monopoly of England confessed on both hands in my pretious mothers transplantation hither, there yet remaines so much behind as leaues mee cares enough to keep mee company here. God knows I cary about me ye mind and thoughts of some great landed man, and think my share in the hazards of Englands to be no small one. Can any man deny him that name and ye consequent cares of a great Rich man who

[1] J. Bass Mullinger, *The University of Cambridge*, vol. iii, p. 282.

[2] Such an expedient would not be without parallel. Of Robert Quarles it is recorded that ' on his appointment to a Peterhouse Fellowship he wrote privately to the dispossessed Joseph Beaumont, acquainting him with his intention to hand over to the latter all the pecuniary profits of the office ; a promise which he faithfully fulfilled '. (T. A. Walker, *Peterhouse*, p. 112.)

[3] The letter is written on a single sheet, $11\frac{4}{5} \times 7\frac{3}{8}$ in., 76 ll. recto and 29 verso. There is therefore much cramping and the readings are not all quite certain. But all the instances in which the text given here differs from that already published have had very careful consideration, and all the points that still remain doubtful are noted. Bracketed letters are missing in the manuscript, owing to wear at the right-hand ends of lines. See plate facing p. xxx. I am here indebted to Mr. R. Flower, of the British Museum, for assistance.

is able to number to himself two reall friends. And lo ! so
much lands at least haue I left in England or wheresoeuer your
self and yᵉ dear enclosed name haue or shall haue being. But
that which is yᵉ comfort shall I say, or yᵉ more care, is that these
pretious particulars of my Estate, which make yᵉ very totall
of my friendly Essence, are rather moueable goods indeed then
firme and fixed lands. And whome shall I ask of what hand but
yʳ owne shall I call for an account what is become of so much of
mee ? And how comes it then that you giue me so little accompt
10 of this great Stewardship, (not of those inconsiderable imperti-
nences in this comparison, which yet are otherwise yᵉ short and
the long of all I haue in the world of which your self-injurious
curtesy hath giuen you yᵉ worthles and almost thankles custody,
not of those nothings I say but) of the totall sum of me in my
morall being. I mean your self. Your wonted noblenes in this
writing liberality has exposed you to a more suffering censure in
this behalf. For me besides my supposed and well experienced
deficiency and disproportion in this expectation (and in fine you'l
say if one fault must go for yᵉ deprecation of another and yᵉ
20 constancy of a crime may be called its excuse if you haue of late
less heard of me then euen of me you could expect, I ly under
a speciall difficulty of what or rather how to writ. There has
hapned in my condition of residence a chang so little expected
by you I know and to mee so litle pleasant as puts me to't eu'en
for expression. It was you say a word welcome to your embraces
yᵗ which told you I was still yᵉ same. And how shall I do to
obtrude yᵉ same to a beleife with you when I shall haue told you
I that I am now not onely not with my mother but a stranger to
her and haue been these 2 months. But I must make hast to
30 correct and heal if I can these ill sauouring phrases. Let me
resume that word and I will see if I can qualify it. Did I say I am
become a stranger to her ? I should haue sayd to her house.
Did I say to *her* house. I should haue sayd to her Uncles. Some
mystery there is you'l think in yᵉ matter, and tis best suffer it to
be so till further oportunity may be of better satisfaction by
freer discourse then at this distan[ce.] I say no more but that
you beware yᵉ least suspition of ought upon my noble mothers
part unworthy of he[r] self or wherefore she too may not plead
still yᵉ same. And what is that to say but yᵉ gentlest kindes[t]
40 most tender-hearted and liberall handed soul I think this day
aliue ? And I would she had no more of the affliction then yᵉ

1 lo !] *perhaps* lo.   6 Essence] *This reading, instead of ' gaines ',
was only arrived at after long consideration of the peculiarities of Crashaw's
hand ; but it seems fairly certain. For the meaning see O.E.D. art.
Essence,* 5.   10 Stewardship,] *comma uncertain.*   11 comparison,] *comma uncertain.*   21 expect,] *comma uncertain.*   28 l
that I] *The first ' I ' is perhaps for ' ay '—or it may have been intended
to erase it.*   33 house.] *The stop is uncertain.*

faut of this busines falling to her share. In sum̄ (and that
I may make my transition to yᵉ more pertinent part of my letter
and leaue bemoaning whats past to looke forward to what lyes
yet perhaps under our providence) she hath in all this matter so
demeaned her self, that I find my self still foulded in and round
wrapped about with a still encreasing ty of inextricable engage-
ments, which grow so fast and gaine so upon mee that I am put
to a perpetuall but ineffectuall projection with my self what
possible mean to imagine which might in any measure speak for
mee, not yᵉ deed but yᵉ desire of a soul that is ashamed to be quite 10
left behind in curtesy. This pressure hath put mee to a Resolution
of this enclosed Resignation of my part in Peter house to my
mothers Brother as far as it may be by your most confidently
presumed asistance seruiceable to yᵉ purpose. How little is don
in doing this I know and yet perhaps but partly nether that is how
nee[r] I am to yᵉ having nothing to resigne. But I haue hope &
not unjust, me thinkes yᵗ yᵉ wisdome if not yᵉ curtesy of the
Colledg will be easily by you (& his tutor Mr B. for of you two at
least I take a totall assurance of your utmost endeauours in the
thing, and how farr those two lines may stretch if need be in any 20
kinde of collaterall help, though it were needfull to be fetched euen
as far as from Court I must needs comfort my self to remember
that they will be easily I say perswaded to accept of a less deserv-
ing son of their owne society then this we propose, rather then
whome tis like they will haue obtruded from a broad. The onely
killing danger of this honest designe seemes to me to be delay.
But your diligent hands do I chuse as an antidote for that Nether
shall I need so much as to intimate to your carefull loue that you
look this matter proue not meerly my loss without gaine to him.
I haue I assure you no desire to be absolutely and irrespectiuely 30
rid of my beloued Patrimony in St Peter. No man then my self
holds more high the humble scepter of such a little contentfull
kingdom. And as safely may I say no man more unprouided of
any present course. And withall neither am I so extreemly an
Antipodes of Desperation to your better boding soule that I
haue no hope of a brighter side that may break out from this
great black cloud that now blotts yᵉ whole face of our Horison.
And as I am not an obtinate Heretick to your hopes, so am I as
firm as any in beleiffe that the hoped Resurrection of Royalty,
(if we may so humble those holy phrases) wilbe likewise a Restitu- 40
tion of all things. And that in yᵉ meantime our poor inheritances
wilbe but more proudly deposited in the hands of such potent

10 mee,] (?) mee   12 Peter house] *perhaps* Peterhouse   15
nether] *perhaps* nether,   25 a broad] *perhaps* abroad   27 that]
perhaps that.   29 meerly] *perhaps* meerely   31 Peter.] *The stop is
uncertain.*   34 am I] *preceded by* I a *erased.*   38 am I] *The MS. has* I
am I *but the first ' I ' appears to be erased.*   39 Royalty] *preceded by* Rialty
erased.

usurpers. But this mean time may proue so much time that all put together I chuse rather the present comfort and content of my friends certaine accomodation (if it may be) then the uncertainty at least of my future fruition and restauration Why the matter may not be fecible enough, falling into so friendly hands, if it can but opportunely step in between yᵉ opposition of the invaders, my short and shallow providence can not perceiue. Otherwise as I sayd I am sure of your no want of vigilancy to looke to the abolishing of this script, that it may be nothing if nothing to this
10 purpose.

Now Sʳ after yᵉ former Narration of what is past in the chang of my Condition here and this present Resignation for what remaines of my future subsistence with you, I know well your watchfull loue and natiue sagacity will soon sharpen your suspition to a mighty suspense what these two symptomes must spell in mee. Between that Remoueuall and this Resignation, or rather between these two Resignations myn of my fellowship and my mothers of mee, (but Hers I dare say as unwilling as mine is willing) wᵗ is likely think my friends to be yᵉ result. Why Ile
20 tell you. Nothing but a third resignation of all to God. His good pleasure his gratious providence, yᵉ one for yᵉ end, the other for yᵉ way and meanes to it, into these do I desire to resolue my totall self. I confess this last peece of my persecution the very sorest I yet haue suffered, in my exclusion and compleat excomunicãon from my gratious mother to whome I had so holy and happy adherence, & in whome I tresured up to my self as much as you could wish (I need say no more of sacred satis-faction and Catholick contentation, my extrusion and exhæredita-tion hence, I say has been such a concussion of mee such a disloca-
30 tion of my whole condition, as puts mee into yᵉ greatest exigence both spirituall and temporall I was euer cast into. And to those that were the workers of this I cannot chuse so oft as I think of it and see my self in this plight but giue the palme and asscrib yᵉ very perfection (as I sayd) in all my persecutions. They whoso-euer they were, of all men are the onely that haue hit me right (say I) & found yᵉ way to use mee as I am worthy. And this I thank God is yᵉ worst I say of them. But what now remaines to be don with this desolate thing, this that is left of mee ; what must I doe ? what must I bee ? If I must be any thing of religious
40 being, here I must not be. To be left thus at this Athens alone (Leyden I mean where yet I am my spirit will not support it I may on with yᵉ borrowed stile of yᵉ sacred text and say I so wholly see the people giuen to Idolatry. you guest I mean the

2 together] *perhaps* together,   4 restauration] *perhaps* restaura-tion. *The paper is torn.*   13 you,] *comma uncertain.*   27 more] *parenthesis not closed.*   32 this] *perhaps* this,   chuse] *perhaps* chuse,   41 am] *parenthesis not closed.*

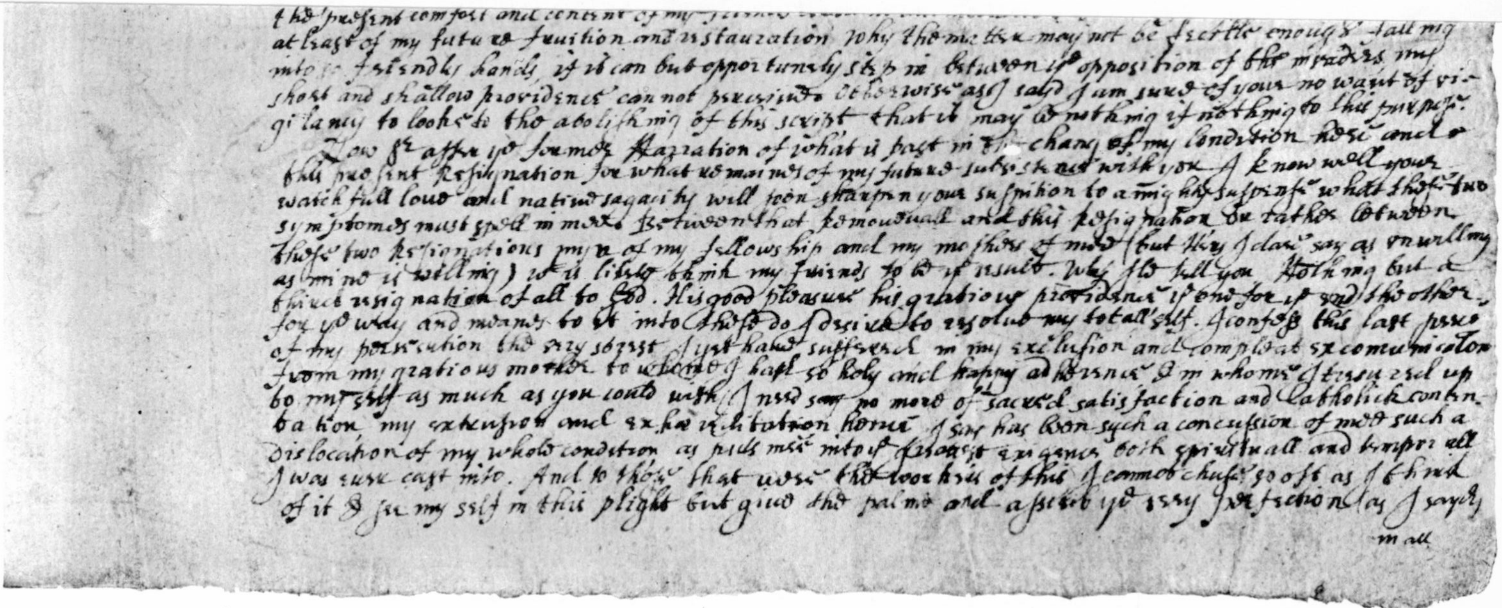
the present comfort and content of my ...
at least of my future fruition and restauration why the matter may not be fertile enough to fall in
into so friendly hands if it can but opportunely step in between the opposition of the invaders my
short and shallow providence cannot prescribe Otherwise as I said I am sure of your no want of vigilancy to looke to the abolishing of this secret that it may be nothing if nothing to the purpose.
Now Sr after the former relation of what is past in the change of my condition here and
this present Resignation for what remaines of my future subsistence with you I know well your
watchfull love and native sagacity will soon sharpen your suspition to a mighty suspence what those two
symptomes must spell or make Between that removeall and this resignation or rather between
those two Resignations mine of my fellowship and my mothers of mee (but they I dare say as unwilling
as mine is willing) what is likely think my friends to be the result. Why Sr to tell you Nothing but a
direct resignation of all to God. His good pleasure his gratious providence the end for the one and the other
for the way and meanes to it into those do I desire to resolve my totall self. I confesse this last peece
of my persecution the very sorest I yet have suffered in my exclusion and compleat excommunication
from my gratious mother to whome I had so holy and happy adherence & in whome I treasured up
to my self as much as you could wish I need say no more of sacred satisfaction and Catholick contem-
tation my extension and exhibition here I say has been such a concussion of mee such a
dislocation of my whole condition as puts mee into the greatest exigence both spirituall and temporall
I was ever cast into. And to those that were the workers of this I cannot chuse so oft as I think
of it & see my self in this plight but give the palme and ascribe the very perfection (as I sayd)
in all

THE LETTER WRITTEN AT LEYDEN 20 February 1643/4

God of this world, Gaine, but I dare say you guest not that To
make it a meer Athens indeed they haue set up in the great
church of St Peter here the plaine Pagan Pallas, Cap a pee, with
speare and Helmet, & Owl & all, in the place of saints at least
which heretofore it seemes usurped the window. So that for me
I am either not scholler enough or not Pagan enough for this
place. Besides I must see something euen for shame But that
I am not yet so desperate to your desires of further suspence,
I assure you or rather confes to you, for though t'will pleas you
better perhaps tis more a fault I fear, a defect at least a dispropor- 10
tion of my weak soul to seuerer courses, I am not at present
purposed for fixing. Nay I am so wretched that I am sometimes
euen carefull for some meanes whereby to maintaine my trauells
so as to keep me up from a necessity of engagement whethersoeuer
I goe. For this purpose what of mine your merciful loue and
diligence can procure for mee (you know the Partys wilbe
seasonably welcome. And so much more missed is that which by
your letter I might haue long ere now looke to haue Receiued by
Mr. Tollys sending. My chamber incomb may be perhaps somewhat more readily payd mee if I may haue the same successor 20
thereto. How our neighbours do if well were a welcom hearing.
How Mr. Haward. How my poore goods but aboue all how your
self S^r the much worthier half of

Your poore friend. R C.

My good and gratious mother guilty of nothing to me
Feb: 20   wards but so great a share in my deserued sorrow, seekes
 1643   to be remenber to you and your prayers, with and affection worthee of her self.

You shall not be angry, and Mr. Collet I know will not that
while I writ I changed so much of ye circumstance as rather to put 30
the Resignation into his mothers hands and his who will be less
partiall procurers perhaps of my desires in this.

Six days after this letter was written, the Earl of Manchester, administering the 'Ordinance for regulating the
University of Cambridge, and for removing scandalous
ministers in the seven Associated Counties' issued an order
to the effect that the Fellows, Scholars, and Officers of Peterhouse were to be resident on March 10 'to give an account
of such things as should be demanded'. On March 13
Cosin was expelled from the Mastership 'for opposing the

---

6 shame] *perhaps* shame.   12 carefull] *perhaps* care full   15
Partys] *parenthesis not closed.*   23 worthier] *preceded by* better *erased.*
26–7 with . . . self] *It seems likely that a word is to be supplied between* with
and and. *It will be seen that the word* 'an', *partly underlined, occurs
between* of *and* her; *and it seems most likely that erasure was intended.*

proceedings of Parliament, and other scandalous acts '. On
April 8, 1644, ' Mr. Tolly, Mr. Beaumont, Mr. Pennyman,
Mr. Crashaw, and Mr. Comyn ', not being resident when sum-
moned, were ejected from their Fellowships, and their suc-
cessors were appointed on June 11 of the same year.[1]

Whether Crashaw ever returned to England, and if so at what
date, are questions which as yet admit of no certain answer; but
if he did return—and this seems rather more than possible—
it would be natural for him at this time to seek shelter at
Oxford. There the Court had been established since July 1643,
and there, until April 17, 1644, he would have an opportunity
of meeting Susan, first Countess of Denbigh, to whom he was to
acknowledge an ' immortall obligation ' (see page 231, below).
On that date, however, the Countess of Denbigh left Oxford
for Exeter with Queen Henrietta Maria, to whom she was
First Lady of the Bedchamber, and thence proceeded with the
queen to France.[2] Wood's statement that Crashaw was incorporated at Oxford in 1641 is confessedly based on hearsay ;
but it is very possible that the fact is true and the date incor-
rect ; and further, it is intimated clearly in the letter from the
queen recommending Crashaw to the Pope in 1646 that he had
been a member of both English universities, and, less clearly,
that he went to France direct from England. There is therefore considerably more than a shadow of justice in the claim
that Crashaw was of Oxford as well as of Cambridge, though
the evidence, attractive as it may be to Oxford *alumni*, hardly
amounts to proof.

The queen's dispatch from Paris, of September 7, 1646,
affords the next certain date in Crashaw's life. The statement
in it that he had ' vescú prés d'un an aupres de moy ' need not
be understood as conflicting with Wood's assertion that he
was presented to the queen through the agency of Cowley, who
is said to have gone to Paris as secretary to Lord Jermyn in
1646.[3] But it seems quite as likely that on Crashaw's removal
to Paris some time in 1645 he made or renewed acquaintance
with the Countess of Denbigh, and that she had at least had

[1] T. A. Walker, *Peterhouse* (1935), pp. 57–8. See also the document
(IV) cited in Appendix II, p. 419, below.

[2] A good account of the first Countess of Denbigh is given in *Royalist
Father and Roundhead Son*, 1915, by Cecilia, Countess of Denbigh.

[3] See *D.N.B.*, art. A. Cowley.

SUSAN, FIRST COUNTESS OF DENBIGH

*From the painting by Gerbier now owned by
the present Earl of Denbigh*

a hand in bringing him to the queen's notice. The queen's recommendation is copied *literatim* from the Roman Transcripts (Series I, Bundle 93) in the Public Record Office.

Tressaint Pere.

Le Sieur Crashau ayant esté Ministre en Angleterre et nourri dans les Universitez de ce païs parmy des gens tres esloignez des sentiments de nostre Sainte Religion, s'est toutes fois par la Lecture et son estude rendu Catholique ; et pour en jouïr plus paisiblement l'exercice, s'est transporté en deçà, et vescú prés d'un an aupres de moy, ou par le bon exemple de sa vie il a beaucoup edifié tous ceux qui ont conversé avec luy : Ce qui m'a convié s'en allant presentem̃ á Rome d'escrire ce mot á vostre S̝.̲ pour la prier de le considerer comme une personne de qui les Catholiques Anglois ont conceu de grandes esperances, et que J'estime beaucoup, et de luy departir ses graces, et faveurs aux occasions qui se presenteront. Ce que J'estimẽãy parmi les autres obligations particulieres que J'ay á V.S. Et sur ce Je prie Dieu Tressaint Pere qu'il conserve V.S. longues années pour le bien et utilité de Son Esglise.

De S̝ Germain en Laye[1] ce 7 Septembre 1646.

Vre[1] tres devotte fille

Henriette Marie R.

Foris

A nostre Tressaint Pere

le Pape

If the statements are correct that Crashaw had been in France for about a year in September 1646 and that he had gone there to practise his new faith in greater peace and security, the date of his acceptance of it must go back to 1645, and may even be earlier. It seems unlikely that he would have written the poem 'On the Assumption' (*Steps to the Temple*, 1646) long before he joined the Roman Church, as this doctrine is not recognized in any Anglican formularies of the time ; on the other hand there is nothing in the poem to suggest that the step had been taken very recently.

While in Paris Crashaw, according to Wood, 'being a meer Scholar and very shiftless', was sought out and helped by Cowley. The friendship is likely to have begun at Cambridge and it was probably there that Crashaw wrote the verses 'Upon two greene Apricockes sent to Cowley by Sir Crashaw', in which Cowley's youthful *Poetical Blossomes* (1633) are warmly praised and contrasted with Crashaw's imperfect harvest. When or where the two poets wrote their brilliant controversy

[1] Layé . . . Vré in the Transcript.

on Hope (see pp. 143–5) is unknown, nor can it be stated which of them took the initiative in employing irregular verse for lyrical poetry, though some of Crashaw's experiments in this kind (as in 'On the Assumption') were in print ten years before Cowley's *Pindaric Odes* were published. The volume containing the Odes, *Poems,* 1656, contained also Cowley's famous elegy on Crashaw, in which Cowley shows how deeply he had been impressed by his friend's genius and character, by the 'Poet and Saint' whose Christian virtues could amply redeem any waywardness of religious faith. 'His *life* was in the right'.

In Paris Crashaw would make or renew acquaintance also with Thomas Car, Founder and Confessor of the Monastery of Canonesses of St. Augustin at Paris;[1] and the publication of *Carmen Deo Nostro,* addressed to the Countess of Denbigh, and afterwards (in 1652) produced in Paris with Car's introductory verses,[2] is likely to have been planned before Crashaw left France.

The journey to Rome seems to have been undertaken without delay, but it was more than a year before the queen's recommendation produced any solid result, and then apparently only owing to official protests, if indeed the Pope had anything to do with the slight advancement that Crashaw secured. Significant evidence of the queen's waning influence at Rome is provided by the memoranda which her representative there, Sir Kenelm Digby, addressed to the Pope in 1647, deploring the neglect of her cause and her requests ; and one of these memoranda (dated November 20) indicates that by this time Crashaw was reduced to great poverty, and that his health was already suffering. After representing that nothing had been done for Thomas Vane, formerly a royal chaplain, on behalf of whom the queen had sent an introduction similar to Crashaw's on September 4, 1646,[3] and who is now described as 'ridotto . . . in somma povertà per l'amor di Dio ', the document[4] proceeds :

> Et il simil si puo dire de S.r Ricardo Crescia (il dotto figliolo del famoso heretico dell' istesso nome) il quale venuto à i piedi

---

[1] See *D.N.B.,* art. Thomas Carre (Miles Pinkney).
[2] See below, p. 233.
[3] Public Record Office, loc. cit.
[4] As given in the Roman Transcripts in the Public Record Office Series I, bundle 94, p. 251, from *Archivio Vaticano Politicorum* T. 16.

di V. Sta con simili raccommandationi non ha ancora ricevuto
pur minimo sussidio dalla liberalità et carità di V. Sta in un
anno di tempo, che è stato in questa Corte travagliato altretanto
da gravi et pericolose infermità, quanto da estrema necessità
et mancamenti per sovvenire à esse.

It must have been soon after this, however, that Crashaw
obtained a post under Cardinal Palotto, for it was in 1647,
apparently, that he was found in that service by Dr. John
Bargrave, who in his MS. published in 1867 for the Camden
Society—*Pope Alexander the Seventh and the College of Cardinals* (edited by James Craigie Robertson, p. 37) sums up in
a few lines (written in 1662) the remaining two years of
Crashaw's life :

> When I went first of my four times to Rome, there were four
> revolters to the Roman Church that had been fellows of Peter-
> house in Cambridge with myself. The name of one of them was
> Mr. R. Crashaw, who was of the Seguita (as their term is ; that
> is, an attendant, or one of the followers,) of this Cardinal ; for
> which he had a salary of crowns by the month (as the custom
> is), but no diet. Mr Crashaw infinitely commended his Cardinal,
> but complained extremely of the wickedness of those of his
> retinue ; of which he, having the Cardinal's ear, complained
> to him. Upon which the Italians fell so far out with him that
> the Cardinal, to secure his life, was fain to put him from his
> service, and procuring him some small imploy at the Lady's of
> Loretto ; whither he went in pilgrimage in summer time, and,
> overheating himself died in four weeks after he came thither,
> and it was doubtful whether he were not poisoned.[1]

The account of Crashaw at this stage of his career given in
*Legenda lignea : with an Answer to Mr. Birchley's Moderator.
(Pleading for a Toleration of Popery.) And a Character of some
hopefull Saints Revolted to the Church of Rome . . . London . . .*

In the Archives of the See of Westminster (MSS. *Archiv. Westmon.*,
vol. xxx, No. 100) there is a somewhat later translation of this document with title : *The Negotiation of the Honble Sr Kenelm Digby Resident
for ye late Queen at Rome . . . Faithfully translated out of the Italian
Manuscript*, in which the passage relating to Crashaw runs as follows :
The same may be sayd of Mr Richard Crashaw (the learned son of
a famous Heretic of the same name) who having cast himself at the
feet of yor Holiness with ye like recomendations, has not in a years
time of his continuance at this Court (tho' assaulted on ye one hand
by many grievous and dangerous infirmities, on ye other hand with
extream wants and necessities) receav'd from ye munificence &
charity of yor Holiness wherewith to redress them.
[1] In Cowley's elegy the disease is described as a fever.

1653 [1] (chap. xxxvii, p. 169) is more prejudiced, and obviously not very well informed, since no mention is made of Crashaw's death, but it may preserve some truth in its details.

> Master *Crawshaw* (Son to the *London* Divine) and sometimes Fellow of St. *Peter* house in *Cambridge*) is another slip of the times, that is, transplanted to *Rome*. This peevish sillie Seeker glided away from his Principles in a Poetical vein of fancy, and impertinent curiosity ; and finding that Verses, and measur'd flattery took, and much pleas'd some female wits, *Crawshaw* crept by degrees into favour and acquaintance with some Court-Ladies, and with the gross commendations of their parts and beauties (burnisht and varnisht with some other agreeable adulations) he got first the estimation of an innocent, harmless Convert ; and, a purse being made by some deluded, vain-glorious Ladies, and their friends, the Poet was dispatch'd in a Pilgrimage to *Rome*, where if he had found in the See Pope *Urban* the eighth, instead of Pope *Innocent*, he might possibly have received a greater quantity, and a better number of Benedictions ; For *Urban* was as much a pretender to be Prince, and Oecumenical patron of Poets, as head of the Church ; but *Innocent* being more harsh and dry, the poor small Poet *Crawshaw*, met with none of the generation and kindred of *Mæcænas*, nor any great blessing from his Holiness, which misfortune puts the pitiful wier-drawer to a humor of admiring of his own raptures : and in this fancy (like *Narcissus*) he is fallen in love with his own shadow, conversing with himself in verse, and admiring the birth of his own brains ; he is onely laughed at, or (at most) but pitied by his new Patrons, who conceiving him unworthy of any preferments in their Church, have given him leave to live (like a lean swine almost ready to starve) in a poor Mendicant quality ; and that favour is granted, only because *Crawshaw* can rail as satyrically and bitterly at true Religion in Verse, as others of his grain and complexion can in Prose, and loose discourses : this fickle shuttlecock so tost with every changeable puff and blast, is rather to be laughed at, and scorned for his ridiculous levity, than imitated in his sinfull and notorious Apostacy and Revolt.

And an anecdote of Crashaw recorded by Sir Robert Southwell in a letter written from Rome, December 23, 1660, and now among the manuscripts belonging to the Marquis of Egmont,[2] tells the same story of failure and disappointment, the touch of ironical humour attributed to Crashaw offering no real

---

[1] Altered to 1652 in ink in British Museum copy.

[2] *Hist. MSS. Comm.*, Report on the MSS. of the Earl of Egmont, vol. i, part ii, p. 616.

opposition to what we otherwise know of his character, though
the story is probably not free from invention.

> The last night one was telling me the life and death of your
> famous Cambridge wit, Crasshaw, who coming here to the last
> Pope Innocent, declared his condition and abilities, and that
> he had left all for the Roman Church, so in fine expecting to
> meet with a happy maintenance here, the Pope gave him but
> twenty pistoles, with which departing very ill satisfied, he told
> the person that presented him, certainly if the Roman church
> be not founded upon a rock, it is at least founded upon some-
> thing which is as hard as a rock. He after, by the favour of
> a Cardinal, got a place of two hundred crowns a year, but in
> a short time after died.
>
> The English wits do think that if they turn, and come hither,
> they shall be courted as princes ; which is a sad mistake, for
> it is well if they get a livelihood.[1]

Whatever truth there may be in Bargrave's assertion as to
the reasons which led to Crashaw's appointment at Loreto,
it is a fact that on April 28, 1649, he was admitted by proxy
in the degree of ' beneficiatus '[2] to a vacancy, in the gift of
Cardinal Palotto, at the Cathedral of the Santa Casa. The
formal documents at Loreto referring to Crashaw, which are

---

[1] The same letter speaks of the duties and way of living of the
servants of Cardinals :

I have now had some opportunity of seeing Rome and viewing the
magnificence of the Pope's Court, which certainly is the most absolute
model of punctuality and method of any other in the world ; for
each Cardinal going to the palace has all his train of coaches and
livery men, in so precise an equipage, that their whole pomp falls
under the eye at one view. There is no straggling of servants or
other disorder here, for each person, even to the least, has all the
rules of his duty at his fingers' ends, and obeys them with a kind of
agility, nay, the servants here are so versed in the points of ceremony
and honour that belongs to their Cardinal in respect of others, that
upon rencounter of coaches in the street they instruct what measure
of respect is to be showed, or what state to be kept, in respect of the
way or pre-eminence, for such are the punctilios of this place, which
in another country would be ridiculous. There is no expense here
but what is designed for ostentation and show, for you shall have
a Cardinal that in the morning went to the Court with a train of
fifty coaches, return home, disband all his company, and only have
one pigeon for dinner, with a few herbs and fruit. Perhaps he has
one servant that there attends him, but all the rest eat abroad, and
the greatest wages that any gentleman of their attendance has is ten
crowns a month.

[2] The third of the four degrees maintained at Loreto. ' Beneficiatus '
corresponds to ' mansionarius ' at other churches. In a marginal note
to Cowley's elegy the office is described as that of a ' Canon '.

given in full in Appendix II, pp. 420–4, below, show that he died there on August 21 in the same year, and was buried ' in tumulo sacerdotum '.[1]

Of the two editions of *Steps to the Temple*, &c., which had appeared since Crashaw left England (1646 and 1648), the second contained much material that was not included in the first. The volume published in 1652, *Carmen Deo Nostro*, adds little to that which appeared in 1648, but the additions include some of the finest lines Crashaw ever wrote (ll. 93–108 of ' The Flaming Heart '). The last publication in the seventeenth century to contain new material in English by Crashaw appears to have been the *Letter* (? 1653) given on pp. 348–50, below—an amplified version of the address to the Countess of Denbigh published in *Carmen Deo Nostro* ' Perswading her to Resolution in Religion & to render her selfe without further delay into the Communion of the Catholick Church.' Here again Crashaw is at his best, in the congenial task of reconciling argument, wit, and poetry. Whether his powers had reached their full maturity or not they had lost none of their youthful freshness and impetus. His obvious affinities with other poets of his time, English and continental, need not obscure from us the gifts which he shared with the greater poets of all time, the warmth and eagerness of spirit, the wealth of imagery, the 'sense of musical delight'. Crashaw represents a special phase in the history of European poetry, but he also transcends it.

IV. *Contemporary and Posthumous Fame.*

It was perhaps owing in some measure to Cowley's famous elegy ' On the Death of Mr. Crashaw ' and to Pope's criticism in his letter to Henry Cromwell (December 17, 1710) that Crashaw was less completely forgotten in the first century and a half after his death than might have been expected from the fate of some hardly less distinguished contemporaries. During his lifetime he seems to have enjoyed no very wide reputation. Within the limited Cambridge circle in which he moved from 1631 to 1643 he must clearly have been highly esteemed ; but a much more general recognition could hardly be attained

---

[1] The ' tumulus sacerdotum ' no longer exists.

Biography. xxxix

before the publication of *Steps to the Temple*, &c., in 1646, and this was only three years before he died.

The first public reference to his work seems to have been that made in the course of a review of pagan and Christian poets occurring in Canto IV of *Psyche : or Loves Mysterie In XX Canto's : ... By Joseph Beaumont, ... London M.D.C.XL.VIII*, where two stanzas (Nos. 94 and 95, p. 48) are devoted to Crashaw and to an expression of regret that he can no longer help the writer with criticism of his verses.[1] Stanza 93 praises Gregory of Nazianzen.

94

And by this soul-attracting Pattern, *Thou*,
My onely worthy self, thy Songs didst frame :
Witnesse those polish'd *Temple-Steps*, which now
Whether thou wilt or no, this Truth proclaim,
  And spight of all thy Travels, make't appear
  Th'art more in England, than when thou wert here.

95

More unto Others ; but not so to Me
Of old acquainted with thy secret worth :
What half-lost I endure for want of Thee
The World will read in this mis-shapen *Birth* :
  Fair had my *Psyche* been, had she at first
  By thy kinde-censuring hand been dress'd and nurst.

Various references belonging to the next few years indicate that Crashaw's repute grew with some vigour. In both Carier's *Missive to King James*, reissued in 1649 with a Preface by N. Strange, and Birchley's *Christian Moderator* (1652) he is described as ' well-knowne for his excellent Poems '. Two lines (11–12) of his ' Know you faire on what you looke ' are quoted in the 1650 and subsequent editions of *Wit's Recreations* by way of introduction to a part of Vaughan's ' The Resolve '. In 1651 ' Jo. Leigh, Esquire ', in a commendatory

---

[1] There is a good deal of evidence of the close association of the two poets in Beaumont's shorter performances, which often reproduce Crashaw's characteristic thoughts, sentiments, and imagery. See *The Minor Poems of Joseph Beaumont*, ed. Eloise Robinson (1914), where some verbal parallels are noted. Some of the more striking of these are quoted in the Commentary at the end of the present volume. But the influence seems pervasive. It is worth noting, too, that two of Beaumont's poems ' Ascension—The Hymn ' and ' The Sheepherd ' are described in Beaumont's MS. as ' Sett to 5 Parts for voices & violls. by R. C.'— who may well have been Crashaw. Compare *Steps to the Temple*, Preface, p. 76, l. 57, below.

poem prefixed to the volume of Cartwright's dramas and poems, refers to Crashaw among authors whose works had been published by Humphrey Moseley :

> Then learned CRASHAVV'S *Muse proves to the eye*
> Parnassus *lower than Mount* Calvary :

and in the same year appeared Clement Barksdale's *Nympha Libethris, Or The Cotswold Muse*, with its lines on ' Herbert and Crashaw ' : [1]

> When into Herbert's temple I ascend
> By Crashaw's steps, I do resolve to mend
> My lighter verse, and my low notes to raise,
> And in high accent sing my Maker's praise.
> Mean while these sacred poems in my sight
> I place, and read, that I may learn to write.

In the MS. of *An English Traveler's First Curiosity, or The Knowledge of his owne Country*, by Henry B[elasyse], 1657 (*Hist. MSS. Comm.*, Var. Coll. II, 1903, p. 194), Crashaw appears in very highly distinguished company : ' What nation can shew more refined witts then those of our Ben, our Shakespeare, our Baumont, our Fletcher, our Dunn, our Randol, our Crashew, our Cleveland, our Sidney, our Bacon, &c.' And some passages in *Paradise Lost* quoted in the Commentary at the end of the present edition seem to show that Milton had been interested by Crashaw's translation from Marino, ' Sospetto d'Herode ' (p. 109, below).

But the early tributes to Crashaw's genius came to their most eloquent expression in the resonant couplets of Cowley's fine poem, first published in 1656 :

> *Poet* and *Saint* ! to thee alone are given
> The two most sacred *Names* of *Earth* and *Heav'en*
> The hard and rarest *Union* which can be
> Next that of *Godhead* with *Humanitie* . . .

Soon after this, other signs of admiration, less effusive but perhaps not less convincing, began to appear [2]. In 1658 there was published *The Upright Man And His Happy End : Opened and Applyed In A Sermon Preached at the Funerals Of the Honourable Francis Pierrepont, Esq; . . . By John Whitlock, M.A. . . .* and on fol. G 3 verso of this work a poem is

---

[1] Quoted from Brydges' reprint, 1816.
[2] Mr. Percy Simpson kindly drew my attention to the two following instances.

begun which is a tissue of appropriations from Crashaw's verses ' Upon the Death of the most desired Mr. Herrys '. The identity of the appropriator is unknown, but his retribution was swiftly prepared for him. Thomas Shipman's *Carolina : or, Loyal Poems* . . . London. 1683 contains, on p. 29, ' The Plagiary. 1658. *Upon* S. C. *a* Presbyterian *Minister, and Captain, stealing* 48 *Lines from* Crashaw's *Poems to patch up an* Elegy *for Mr* F. P.', in which the action of ' S. C.' is arraigned as

> Impudent Theft, as ever was exprest,
> Not to steal Jewels only, but the Chest.
> Not to nib bits of *Gold* from *Crashaw's* Lines,
> But swoop whole Strikes together from his Mynes !

A different kind of tribute was paid by one John Lidyat, in 1675. A copy of Crashaw's works, as published in 1670 (No. 7 in the list given below, p. lii), is extant [1] in which the separate title-page to *Carmen Deo Nostro* is missing and the general title-page replaced by another, specially printed, and modelled on the abstracted title-page to *Carmen Deo Nostro : Sacred Poems Collected, Corrected, Augmented, Most Humbly Presented, To My Valentine Mrs. Margaret Neal By her most devoted servant John Lidyat Death and Absence differ only in this, That Absence is but a Short Death, and Death a long Absence. Who takes every acquaintance for a Friend, is like him who takes every Pebble Stone for a Diamond.—Dedicated in the year M.DCLXXV.* [2]

Meanwhile the account of Crashaw in Lloyd's *Memoires* (see Appendix II, p. 415, below) had appeared, to be followed by *The Lives Of the most Famous English Poets, or the Honour of Parnassus ;* . . . *Written by William Winstanley, Author of the English Worthies.* . . . *London.* . . . 1687., which contains (pp. 161–162) a section on Crashaw as rhapsodical as Lloyd's paragraph, describing him as ' This devout Poet, the Darling of the *Muses*, whose delight was the fruitful Mount *Sion*, more than the barren Mount *Pernassus* . . . a religious pourer forth of his divine Raptures and Meditations, in smooth and pathetick Verse. His Poems consist of three parts, . . . *Steps to the Temple,* . . . charming the ear with a holy Rapture. The

---

[1] It was offered for sale in 1905 ; and first described fully in the *Library* for Jan. 1917, p. 77, by Mr. Hugh C. H. Candy.

[2] John Lidyat has not been identified, and it must be left to surmise by what process the alteration was made. Lidyat may have been a printer.

Second part, *The delights of the Muses, . . .* ; such rich pregnant Fancies as shewed his Breast to be filled with *Phoebean* Fire. The third and last part *Carmen Deo Nostro, . . .* all which bespeak him,

The learned Author of Immortal Strains.'

The first piece of real and considered criticism of Crashaw is that contained in Pope's letter to Henry Cromwell, December 17, 1710 (ed. Elwin and Courthope, vol. vi, pp. 116–18), a descant on the theme that Crashaw is ' one of those whose works may just deserve reading '. Pope reserved his highest commendation for the incidental beauties of Crashaw's poetry, and showed his sincerity by borrowing some of them.[1] Yet, in spite of the interest which may have been stimulated by even the faint praise of such an authority, Crashaw's work was with much truth to be described as ' sinking into utter oblivion ' in the course of the eighteenth century.[2] No place was found for him in Johnson's *Lives of the Poets*, and the mention of him in the Life of West is perhaps a greater honour for both West and Cowley (who is quoted) than for Crashaw.[3] Some references in the *Gentleman's Magazine* [4] revealed a deep ignorance of the original publications of Crashaw's works that was shared in large measure by the first makers of Crashaw reprints.

Once fairly begun, however, the recovery was not slow (see the list of eighteenth- and nineteenth-century editions, p. lxxxii, sqq., below). Shelley was probably acquainted with Crashaw's poetry ; [5] and it is not the least of Crashaw's honours that a part (ll. 43–64) of the ' Hymn to St. Teresa ' (p. 132, below) was acknowledged to have been constantly in the mind of Coleridge ' whilst writing the second part of *Christabel* ; if, indeed, by some subtle process they did not suggest the first thought of the whole poem '.[6]

---

[1] See article ' Crashaw ' in Index to Pope's *Works*, ed. Elwin and Courthope.

[2] Anderson, in *The Works of the British Poets*, 1795.

[3] ' Crashaw is now not the only maker of verses to whom may be given the two venerable names of *Poet* and *Saint*.'

[4] Aug. 1785, pp. 630–1, Nov. 1793, p. 1,001.

[5] See notes by D. F. McCarthy in *Notes and Queries*, II. v. 449, &c. ; and a note by L. C. Martin in the *Modern Language Review*, vol. xi (1916), p. 217.

[6] *Table Talk*, Oxford Edition, 1917, p. 441.

II. TEXT AND CANON

THE works of Richard Crashaw existed in the seventeenth century in the following different forms :

(1) poems printed singly in volumes of occasional verse or in books to which they were prefixed by way of commendation ;

(2) six volumes devoted to Crashaw's work alone and containing fresh material of varying quantity ; and probably three [1] volumes consisting only of republished material ; and

(3) manuscripts, belonging as a rule to the period before the editions appeared.

Of the early editions of Crashaw only one was published while he lived in England. Of the manuscripts seen by the present editor none contains any poem in Crashaw's handwriting. British Museum Add. MS. 40176, a collection of the *Epigrammata Sacra*, has an autograph dedication in Latin prose (see pp. lvi and 2–3). A portion of the manuscript described on p. xciii is probably autograph. The other MSS., usually miscellanies containing selections of different lengths, are copies, at removes probably of varying distance from the original. The MSS. are open to the usual suspicions, but it seems likely that their variants often preserve true readings or represent Crashaw's own retouchings. The relations of the MSS. to the printed editions and to the present text are indicated in the following bibliography; and the authenticity of 'doubtful' poems, especially those which have not been printed before, is discussed in connexion with the MSS. in which they are found. Arguments in favour of genuineness are supported by parallels quoted in the commentary.

A. EARLY PRINTED EDITIONS [2]

1. *Epigrammatum Sacrorum Liber . . . Cantabrigiae . . .* 1634. (Title-page reproduced on p. 5, below.) ¶1, title-page, verso blank ; ¶2–8, prefatory matter ; A–E 8 in eights, epigrams. Collated with the edition of 1670 (No. 6 below) and with the

---

[1] See Nos. 7, 8, and 9 in the following list, pp. lii and liv, below; No. 9 is undated.

[2] The poems printed singly are given in a list in the section on the chronological order of Crashaw's works, pp. lxxxvii–lxxxviii, below.

MS. versions in the British Museum and the Library of Trinity College, Dublin respectively (Nos. 10 and 11 below).

Two of the epigrams in this edition are also given, with Greek translations, in a series of seven epigrams published at the end of *Horæ Subsecivæ* : seu Prophetiæ *Jonæ* et Historiæ *Susannæ* Paraphrasis Græca Versibus Heroicis. Authore *H. Stubbs ex Æde Christi, Oxoniæ.* (London, 1651). This supplement is preceded by the notice ' Ne subsequentes Paginæ vacarent, visum est adnectere Miscellanea quædam Epigrammata è *Randolpho, Crashawo,* &c. Græcè reddita. The variants to these two epigrams (viz. ' Christe, loquutus eras ', p. 26, below and ' Infantis fore te ', p. 31, below) are recorded in the foot-notes. The same series contains three epigrams, also in Latin and Greek, obviously translated from Crashaw's English ones (' Let it no longer be a forlorne hope ', ' Two went to pray ? ' and ' Could not once blinding me ', pp. 85, 89, 102, below) unless the Latin versions are Crashaw's own originals. Other Latin versions of two of these three epigrams are in this 1634 edition (' Ille niger sacris ', p. 17, below, and ' En duo Templum adeunt ', p. 15, below) but it is not impossible that Crashaw made the versions thus preserved in the volume by Henry Stubbs (or Stubbe) and subsequently suppressed them. Of the other (' Crudelis, nonne suffecit ') no other early Latin version appears to exist. The three Latin epigrams in question are given in the Commentary, in connexion with their English representatives. See pp. 434–5, below.

The volume of 1634 is on the whole carefully printed, and though not perfect in this respect may well have been seen through the press by Crashaw himself, since he was then in residence at Cambridge. A few mistakes in the chapter or verse numbers preceding the epigrams have been corrected in the present edition.

Designated ' 34 ' in the footnotes.

2. *Steps to the Temple. Sacred Poems, With other Delights of the Muses . . . London . . . 1646.* (Title-pages reproduced on pp. 73 and 147, below). A 1, blank ; A 2, title-page ; A 3–6, prefatory matter ; B–G 11 in twelves, poems and index. Second title-page F 3 recto.

Entered on the Stationers' Register June 1, 1646, as ' a booke

called Stepps to the Temple, sacred poems, &c, by Rich:
Crashaw '.

Collated with the editions of 1648, 1652, and 1670 (Nos. 3, 4,
and 7, below) and with MSS. A few trifling differences between
the British Museum copy and the Bodleian copy of this issue
are recorded in the foot-notes.

Much of the textual interest of this volume lies in the fact
that it preserves the early form of many poems which afterwards appeared in a much revised form in the volumes of 1648
and 1652, but it has also been followed in the present edition
for the poems which were reprinted in 1648 with little or no
alteration, because of its careful printing and characteristic
and expressive punctuation. One poem in this collection
which although reprinted in 1648 is, for reasons given in the
notes, almost certainly not by Crashaw has been omitted here
and placed in Appendix I, of poems probably spurious (see
p. 410, below). With this exception the volume of 1646 is
reproduced bodily though not *literatim*, and without following
the original order, which was due to a printer's error signalized
in a stop-press notice facing p. 1 :

> Reader, there was a sudden mistake ('tis too late to recover
> it) thou wilt quickly find it out, and I hope as soone passe it over,
> some of the humane Poems are misplaced among the Divine.

The rectification of this mistake is not difficult, the originally
intended order being fairly clear from the grouping of subjects
and from the order in the corrected second edition of 1648.
The actual order of the poems in the 1646 edition may be seen
from the list of contents, pp. 199–201, below.

The admission of this probably spurious poem and the
unknown editor's reference to Crashaw as ' now dead to us '
would make it fairly certain that Crashaw was not immediately
responsible for the form in detail of this volume, were there not
already reason to believe that he had been in Paris for some
time when it appeared. But though he cannot, therefore, have
seen it through the press a MS. containing some slight improvements upon the MSS. still extant seems to have been used,
though probably not an autograph MS., not all of very recent
transcription, and not in every respect reliable. That much
of it may have gone back at least as far as to 1635 is suggested
by the fact that the poem beginning ' Brittaine ! the mighty

Oceans lovely Bride, ' (see p. 176, below) refers to nothing later than the birth of the Princess Elizabeth in that year, although a longer form had been printed in a Cambridge collection (*Voces Votivae*, &c.) in 1640. And the occasional imperfection of the printer's copy may be illustrated by ll. 17–18 of the poem ' On a foule Morning . . .' (see p. 182, below) where the edition of 1646, followed by that of 1648, reads

> ˙ Shall rise in a sweet Harvest ; which discloses
> To every blushing Bed of new-borne Roses.

for which latter line MS. Tanner seems to supply the true reading :

> Two euer blushing beds of new blowne roses.

Mistakes of this kind might of course be made by a printer, especially if he were setting up from dictation ; but in this instance the reading of 1646 is repeated in Add. MS. 33219 (No. 13, below), which is itself probably derived entirely from an early MS. and not even partly from a printed edition, though not from the same MS. as that used by the printer. It is, therefore, very likely that the printer's copy contained the same error. Such circumstances would be explicable if, as Add. MS. 40176 seems to show, Crashaw was in the habit of employing a scrivener who was occasionally puzzled and over-come by the poet's not too legible handwriting, and whose makeshifts were not always observed and corrected. But though it has thus seemed indispensable to depart here and there from the 1646 text in favour of a MS. (especially Tanner 465, q.v. p. lxi, below) or later printed variant, a good array of examples might also be quoted, and may be gathered from the foot-notes, of the superiority of the readings of 1646 over the readings of the MSS. And one plausible, though by no means certain, explanation of the textual questions which thus arise would be that when the edition of 1646 was pro-posed, Crashaw hastily went over a MS. of fairly early origin, improving and adding to it without correcting all its errors of transcription.

Designated ' 46 ' in the foot-notes.

3. *Steps to the Temple, Sacred Poems. With The Delights of the Muses . . . The second Edition wherein are added divers*

pieces not before extant . . . *London* . . . 1648. (Title-pages and engraving reproduced on pp. 204–5, 213, below.) The engraving which should precede the title-page is absent in some copies. A 1, title-page; A 2–4, prefatory matter; B–F 12 in twelves, poems and index + title-page to *The Delights of the Muses.* Fresh pagination then begins; A–C 12 in twelves, poems; two leaves without signature, index to *The Delights of the Muses.*

Collated with the editions of 1646, 1652, and 1670 (Nos. 2, above, 4 and 7, below). Examples of trifling differences between the British Museum copy and the present editor's copy of this issue are given in the foot-notes. There are many more.

In this edition, which is on the whole much less attractively printed than that of 1646, several poems, as stated on the title-page, appeared for the first time and several already published in the first edition were amplified to the dimensions which they usually retain in *Carmen Deo Nostro* (1652). By 1648 Crashaw had probably been absent from England for three years; but the supposition that he had written, for him, a good deal between 1646 and 1648 seems a likely one, and, though some of the material appearing here for the first time no doubt represents gleanings from the Cambridge period (especially the poems in Latin), the religious and devotional verse now first published seems likely to have been very largely of recent composition. No fresh MS. appears to have been used for the poems which were here reprinted without substantial change. A few obvious misprints in the text of 1646 are corrected, but some others are introduced and the punctuation is frequently altered in a more modern and less expressive direction. On the other hand, for many consecutive pages, perhaps entrusted to an inexperienced but careful compositor, both the punctuation and the spelling of 1646 are followed almost exactly. This text has only been used as a basis for poems which are peculiar to this volume. See pp. 211, 229, below for the original lists of contents.

Designated ' 48 ' in the foot-notes.

4. *Carmen Deo Nostro, Te Decet Hymnvs Sacred Poems,* . . . *At Paris,* . . . *M.DC.LII.* (Title-page reproduced on p. 231 below.) a i, title-page; a ii–iv, prefatory matter, to end of poem addressed to the Countess of Denbigh; A–R 1 in fours + one leaf recto only, without page-number or signature, poems.

Collated with the editions of 1646, 1648, and 1670 (Nos. 2, 3 above, 7 below).

This is a carefully and in the circumstances a well-produced volume, containing some important matter never before published, but consisting chiefly of poems either first printed in 1648 or first printed there in their altered and expanded forms. It is reprinted here entirely, with due corrections. The numerous misprints which it contains are yet not more numerous than might have been expected from its having been set up by a foreign compositor with probably little knowledge of English and perhaps none at all. The sign ' y ' for ' th ' in the MS. caused him a good deal of confusion. Crashaw had now been dead for about three years and the volume was no doubt seen through the press by Thomas Car (see p. xxxiv above), who contributes two prefatory poems.

Thomas Car's ambiguous words about 'the pictures in the following Poemes which the Authour first made with his owne hand' can be taken to mean that Crashaw was the original artist of all the twelve engravings. That this was not the case seems clear both from the inequalities of style and technique which the engravings present, and from the fact that several of them are marked 'I. Messager excud.' or ' Messager excud.' Jean Messager was a printer and publisher of engravings whose business, according to Nagler, *Neues allgemeines Kunstler-Lexicon* (1840), flourished between 1615 and 1631. An engraving from his studio of later date (1637) has been seen in the Bibliothèque Nationale, but it seems difficult to believe that he engraved these drawings in the first instance for Crashaw's volume, especially as their style is in general more characteristic of the first than of the second quarter of the century. And if he executed some he might equally well have done the rest. One, that heading the poem ' In the Holy Nativity ' (see p. 247, below), bears the initials I. G. and comprises a couplet in *French*. Nevertheless it seems probable that at least the two engravings heading respectively the poem addressed to the Countess of Denbigh (p. 236, below) and ' The Weeper ' (p. 308, below) represent Crashaw's own drawings.

Different copies of this issue occasionally vary in respect of these engravings. One of the two British Museum copies lacks them altogether. In the Bodleian copy the engraving usually preceding 'The Himn, O Gloriosa Domina' (see p. 302, below) is replaced by another, as follows:

The engraving reproduced on p. 254 below from the Bodleian copy sometimes appears without its framework and with other varieties of detail.

Designated '52' in the footnotes.

5. *A Letter from Mr. Crashaw to the Countess of Denbigh, Against Irresolution and Delay in matters of Religion . . . London.* (Title-page reproduced on p. 347, below.) Size $8\frac{1}{4} \times 6\frac{3}{8}$ in. Two leaves only. Poem begins on verso of title-page (p. 1) and ends on A 2 verso (p. 3).

The copy of this work in the British Museum, with the date 1653 added in ink in a contemporary hand, is believed to be unique.[1] The Letter is a longer form of the poem first published in *Carmen Deo Nostro* (1652), from which it also differs greatly in the lines common to both versions.

6. *Richardi Crashawi Poemata et Epigrammata . . . Editio Secunda, Auctior et emendatior . . . Cantabrigiae . . .* 1670. (Title-page reproduced on p. 65, below.) A 1, title-page; A 2–B 2, prefatory matter and 'poemata'; B 3 recto, title-page to Epigrams; B 3 verso–B 6 recto, 'Lectori'; B 6 verso–F 8 in eights, epigrams.

[1] G. Thomason, to whom it belonged, has added 'Sept: 23' above the year date.

Pfal. 137. 2.

In conspectu Angelorum psallam tibi et adorabo
ad Templum sanctam tuum.

STEPS
TO THE
TEMPLE,
THE
DELIGHTS
OF THE
MUSES,
AND
CARMEN
DEO NOSTRO.

By *Ric. Crashaw,* fometimes Fellow of *Pembroke Hall,* and late Fellow of *St Peters
Colledge* in *Cambridge.*

The 2d *Edition.*

In the *SAVOY,*
Printed by *T. N.* for *Henry Herringman* at the
Blew Anchor in the *Lower Walk* of the
New Exchange. 1670.

Collated with the editions of 1634, 1646, and 1648 (nos. 1, 2, and 3, above). The 1648 edition of *Steps to the Temple* apparently supplies the 'poemata', printed here, with emendations, between the dedicatory poem beginning ' O mihi ' and the poem headed ' Lectori ', in the following order ; and with the following headings :

The additions to the epigrams consist of five in Latin, of which the two following are also in MS. Tanner 465 (No. 12, below) :

> Improba turba tace. Mihi tam mea vota propinquant, (p. 69, below)
> O ut ego angelicis fiam bona gaudia turmis, (p. 70, below)

and of Greek versions of nine which had already been published in Latin in 1634. The Greek immediately follows the Latin in each instance.

Only one emendation of the earlier text has been found, apart from trifling differences of punctuation.

Designated ' 70L ' in the foot-notes.

7. *Steps to the Temple, The Delights Of The Muses, and Carmen Deo Nostro. By Ric. Crashaw, . . . The 2ᵈ Edition. In the Savoy, . . . 1670.* (Title-page and engraving reproduced above.) Engraving faces A 1, title-page ; A 2–8, prefatory matter and index ; B–O 7 in eights, poems with separate title-page to *The Delights of the Muses* at F 8 (reproduced opposite) ; and separate title-page to *Carmen Deo Nostro* at K 5.[1]

Collated with the editions of 1646, 1648, and 1652 (Nos. 2, 3, and 4, above).

This volume is a reprint of the editions of 1646 and 1652, and its claim to be the ' second edition ' is no doubt made in ignorance of the genuine second edition (1648). It thus has

[1] For the strange treatment of this by John Lidyat in 1675, see p. xli, above.

THE
DELIGHTS
OF THE
MUSES.
OR,

*Other Poems written on several
occasions.*

By RICHARD CRASHAVV.

Mart. *Dic mihi quid melius defidiofus agas.*

---

no independent authority and it is not very carefully produced ; it sometimes prints twice, for example, a poem that occurs in both its originals, though without intention ; and its occasional abbreviations of titles, made in the interests of convenience and economy, have not all seemed worth recording. On the other hand, its deviations of stopping, &c., are sometimes to the point, and are then noted.

Designated ' 70 ' in the foot-notes.

8. *Richardi Crashawi Poemata et Epigrammata, Quae scripsit Latina & Græca, Dum Aulæ Pemb. Alumnus fuit, Et Collegii Petrensis Socius. Editio Secunda, Auctior & emendatior. . . . Cantabrigiæ, Ex Officina Joan. Hayes, Celeberrimæ Academiæ Typographi.* 1674. *Prostant venales apud Joann. Creed.*

This is a re-issue with fresh title-page (reproduced opposite) of the volume (No. 6, above) published in 1670.

9. (Recorded in Grosart's edition, 1872, vol. ii, p. viii—not seen by present editor.)

' The 1670 edition of the " Steps ", &c. . . . was re-issued with an undated title-page as " The Third Edition. London. Printed for Richard Bently, Jacob Tonson, Francis Saunders, and Tho. Bennet." It is from the same type, and identical in every way except the fresh title-page, with the (so-called) " 2ᵈ Edition ".'

B. MANUSCRIPTS

10. British Museum Add. MS. 40176.

Size 5½ × 3⅘ in., 59 leaves, bound in vellum.

This MS. was acquired by the Museum in February 1922, and consists of what appears to be an early draft of the volume published in 1634 (No. 1, above) ; it may, however, have been designed for circulation in MS. form. It has a general title-page ' Sacroru˜ Epigramãtum Liber.', and it contains all the epigrams which were printed in 1634, with the addition of six which were not printed, but which are also found in MS. Tanner 465 (No. 12, below) ; and of which the following are the first lines :

Jam cedant, veteris cedant miracula saxi,
Candide rex campi, cui floris eburnea pompa est,
Ergo ille, Angelicis o sarcina dignior alis,
Arma, viri l (ætheriam quocunǫ sub ordine pubem
Ipsos naturæ thalamos sapis, imaǫ rerum
Credo quidem. sed & hoc hostis te credidit ipse

Richardi Crashawi

POEMATA
ET
EPIGRAMMATA,

Quæ scripsit Latina & Græca,

Dum *Aula Pemb.* Alumnus fuit,

Et

Collegii *Petrensis* Socius.

Editio Secunda, Auctior & emendatior.

Εἵνεχεν ἐυμαθίης πινυτόφρονος, ἦν ὁ Μελιχρὺς
Ἤσκησεν, Μυσῶν ἄμμυγα καὶ Χαείτων.   Ἀνθολ.

CANTABRIGIÆ,

Ex Officina *Joan. Hayes,* Celeberrimæ Academiæ
Typographi. 1674.
Prostant Venales apud *Joann. Creed.*

The variant readings in the epigrams in this MS. are not very numerous, but they suggest that it is of earlier date than the MS. used by the printer.

The chief interest of this MS. lies in its dedication, which is quite different from that published, and which, as appears from a comparison of the handwriting with that of Crashaw's signatures at Peterhouse, Cambridge, and of the letter quoted above, p. xxvii, was written and signed by the poet himself, the rest of the volume, except the title-page, also inscribed by Crashaw, being in another hand, possibly that of a professional scrivener. The following is a reproduction of the signature:

What seems to be another specimen of Crashaw's handwriting occurs in the MS. described on p. xciii; but that of Add. MS. 33219 (No. 13, below), which was once, on the confident affirmation of Grosart, thought to be an autograph MS., is altogether different.

The order of the epigrams in the MS. differs somewhat from the published order. In the MS. they run as follows:

The first eight in 1634, then Jam cedant, veteris cedant miracula saxi—Gutta brevis nummi (vitæ patrona senilis)—Aspice (namque novum est) ut ab hospite pendeat hospes—Ferte sinus, ô ferte : cadit vindemia cœli—Ille niger sacris exit (quam lautus !) ab undis—Ecce hic peccator timidus petit advena templum—Dic mihi, quò tantos properas, puer auree, nummos—Non modò vincla, sed & mortem tibi, Christe, subibo—Candide rex campi, cui floris eburnea pompa est—Ille Deus, Deus : hæc populi vox unica : tantum—the five next following in 1634—Dum linquunt Christum (ah morbus !) sanantur euntes :—En redeunt, lacrymasque breves nova gaudia pensant :—I miser, inque tuas rape non tua tempora curas—Ah satis, ah nimis est : noli ultra ferre magistrum—Uno oculo ? ah centum potiùs mihi, millia centum :—the thirteen next following in 1634—Arma, viri ! (ætheriam quocunque sub ordine pubem—Ipsos naturæ thalamos sapis, imáque rerum—Credo quidem. sed & hoc hostis te credidit ipse—Fundite ridentes animas ; effundite cœlo—the seven next following in 1634—Ergo ille, Angelicis ô sarcina dignior alis—Esse levis quicunque voles, onus accipe Christi—Ecce vagi venit unda cibi ; venit indole sacra—the three next following in 1634—Tu matutinos prævertis, sancta, rubores (for the second time) —Ergò istis socium se peccatoribus addit—the fifty-one next following in 1634—Quantumcunque ferox tuus hic (Petre) fulminat ensis—Felices animæ ! quas cœlo debita virtus—Vox jam missa suas potuit

jam tangere metas—Felix, qui potuit tantæ post nubila noctis—Noli
altum sapere (hoc veteres voluere magistri)—Illa domus stabulum ? non
est (Puer auree) non est—Felix ! ergò tuæ spectas natalia dextræ—Illa
manus lavat unda tuas, vanissime Judex—Sive oculos, sive ora vocem
tua vulnera ; certe—Christum, quod misero facilis peccata remittit—
Saxa ? illi ? quid tam fœdi voluere furores—Nasceris, en ! tecumque
tuus (Rex auree) mundus—Scilicet & tellus dubitat tremebunda : sed
ipsum hoc—His oculis (nec adhuc clausis coiere fenestris—Tu piscem si,
Christe, velis, venit ecce, suumque—Tu contra mundum dux es meus,
optime Jesu—Vadit (Io !) per aperta sui penetralia cœli—Tu qui adeo
impatiens properasti agnoscere Christum—Ergo mihi salvete mei, mea
gaudia, luctus—O Grex, o nimium tanto pastore beatus—Jam cœli
circum tonuit fragor : arma, minasque—Ah nimis est, illum nostræ
vel tradere vitæ—Ad cœnam voco te (domini quod jussa volebant)—
the twenty next following in 1634—Nulla (precor) busto surgant mihi
marmora : bustum—thence to the end as in 1634.

Designated ' A4 ' in the foot-notes.

11. Trinity College Dublin MS. F. 4. 28 (659).

Size 7¼ × 5¾ in.

A seventeenth-century MS. containing Latin poems of a
religious nature and other matter, including a list of ' Lord
Chancellors &c. of Ireland ', in which the latest year recorded
appears to be 1688. ' Classis F ' of the Dublin MSS. is described
in the Catalogue by Monck Mason as ' ex dono Reverendi admodum viri, Johannis Stearne, Episcopi Cloghorensis, honoratis:
nostri Vice-Cancellarii ; A. D. 1741— '. On p. 2 there is a
bookplate with crest and motto and ' Thomas Madden of
the Inner Temple London Esq. descended of the Maddens
formerly of Maddenton in Wiltshire, who are now seated at
Rousky Castle in the County of Fermanagh in the Kingdome
of Ireland '.

Pages 38–68 contain ' Christiania Epigrammata ' of unknown authorship. Crashaw's Latin epigrams begin on p. 73,
with heading : ' Epigrammata Divina Siue Occurrentia
Quaedam ex X! Uitâ et Quatuor Euangelijs decerpta.~'
Crashaw is not mentioned by name. The epigrams published
in 1634 are then given entire, up to and including l. 16 of the
penultimate epigram beginning ' Ah tamen Ipse roga '. They
are numbered and divided into two parts, each with separate
numbering, the first epigram in the second part (headed
' Secunda Pars Epig: Divin: ') being that which begins ' Ulmum
vitis' (p. 41, below). This epigram is followed by that beginning
'Saxa? illi' (p. 42, below) ; otherwise the order of the epigrams
in the MS. is that of the printed edition.

This MS. betrays much carelessness and ignorance in its copyist, with full evidence of which it has not seemed worth space to encumber the foot-notes. There is, besides, very little punctuation, and the MS. seldom follows the printed edition in the use of brackets. On the other hand, it appears to have been derived from another MS. and not from the printed text, and it contains some variant readings which may well represent, however dimly, a true though earlier stage of composition, and these have been generously recorded.

Designated ' D ' in the foot-notes.

12. Bodleian MSS. Tanner 465 and 466.

Size of Tanner 465, 7⅝ ×5⅝ in. 110 leaves.

Size of leaves in Tanner 466 various. Crashaw's poems occur in two sections of the book, viz. fos. 1–38, measuring 6¼ ×8¾ in., and fos. 154–173, measuring 8 × 6 in.

A collection of poems by various seventeenth-century writers, but mainly by Crashaw, in the handwriting and formerly in the possession of Archbishop Sancroft, who lived in Cambridge as student and Fellow of Emmanuel College from 1633 to 1651.

On fo. 38 verso of Tanner 466 the serial number *465* is given, together with the following description, applying also to what is now Tanner 465 : ' Poemata varia Lat: & Angl: Quorum plurima scribuntur Manu Gul. Sancroft olim Coll: Eman: Cantabr. Soc: deinde Arch: Epi Cantuar.' There is no sure indication of the date or dates at which the transcriptions were made, and the poems copied seem to belong to the period of Crashaw's residence both at Pembroke and Peterhouse, though chiefly at the former. (See the section on the chronological order of Crashaw's works, p. lxxxvii, below.)

On the front page of Tanner 465 there is a list of contents which begins as follows : ' Mʳ Crashaw's poëms transcrib'd frõ his own Copie, before they were printed ; among wᶜʰ are some not printed. Latin, on yᵉ Gospels√ p. 7. On other Subjects. p. 39. 95. 229. English sacred poëms p. 111. on other subjects— 39. 162. 164.√ 167√. 196. 202.√ 206. 223.√ Suspetto di Herode. translated frõ Cav. Marino. p. 287√.'

In this list the tick ' √ ', which has sometimes been printed as a ' v ', signifies ' cetera ' and seems, for the most part, to be

used as the abbreviation 'sqq.' is used now. Of the 110 leaves
in Tanner 465, fos. 1–96 correspond to the old pagination referred
to in the list, extending on both sides of the leaves up to p. 300,
there being numerous gaps. All the pages mentioned, however,
are still in the volume, except 287. 'Suspetto di Herode'[1] is in
Tanner 466, in two copies, fos. 154–63 and 164–73, of which
the second gives the original page-numbers 287, 288, 289, and
then stops paging. Beyond this Tanner 466 only contains three
poems by Crashaw, and these are also in Tanner 465, viz. :

> On the proud banks of great Euphrates flood
> Happy Me ! Oh happie Sheep !
> O te, te nimis, & nimis beatum,

The opening paragraph in the list, referring to Crashaw
alone, is followed by an index of other poems, sometimes with
their authors' names, e. g. :

T. R.   On Good Friday. p. 130—Idem ad Amica~ p. 166

Sr H. Wotton, on ye Q of Bohemia, you meaner Beauties p. 161.
Ask me no more 195.

Per· Cornwallis on W^m. Henshaw of E. C. 200 on Wm Carr of E.C.
201. On a Friend. On a Cobbl^er 205. N. Culverwell on Mr Hol-
dens Death 207. Dr Goad on ye Death of K. James. p. 231. On
Felton hanging in chains. On an Infant 234. On Y^e Lady Parker
235. On Xpher Rouse Esq. 234. On Hobson ye Carrier 235. . . .

MSS. Tanner 465 and 466, it will be seen, are of the highest
importance both for the poems by Crashaw printed in the
seventeenth century and for those not then printed, Tanner 465
being in most instances the only authority for the unpublished
pieces.

The following is a list of first lines of poems which occur in
Tanner 465 and which were also published during the seventeenth century, the lines preceded in the list by their MS. page-
numbers and followed by their page-numbers in the present
edition. In the text of the MS. the headings of poems by
Crashaw are sometimes followed by the initials ' R. C.' or the
designation ' R. Crashaw ', and these are distinguished in the
present list by an asterisk. In the MS. a stroke has usually
been drawn through the poems which were published.

---

[1] This has not been noticed by previous editors.

As regards the textual authority of these poems and their relationship to the text of 1646, there is no reason to doubt that, as stated in the index, they were derived from Crashaw's ' own Copie ' ; but it does not, of course, follow that the latter was in Crashaw's handwriting or that it was the same copy which was ultimately sent to the printer. As already pointed out in connexion with the volume printed in 1646, the MS. then used by the printer, while agreeing in its general outlines with the

Tanner MSS., appears to contain some improvements on them, though here and there the readings of these MSS. are certainly to be preferred and have occasionally been adopted in the present text. A notable instance of this superiority, in addition to that already quoted, occurs in ' Sospetto d'Herode ' [1], stanza 51, l. 1, where the MS. supplies the three missing words of a curious gap, all modern editions hitherto having been obliged either to rely on guesswork or to follow the seventeenth-century editions in reading a blank, indicated by a line. In two or three other places, too, the MS. versions of this poem restore sense where it has hitherto been lacking ; of which a good instance may be found in stanza 48, ll. 2–4. Here the edition of 1646, followed by all editors, reads

> The fields fair eyes saw her and saw no more
> But shut their flowery lids ; for ever Night
> And Winter strow her way.

and the MS., with evident reason, punctuates l. 3

> But shut their flowery lids for ever.   Night

The general character of this MS. seems to confirm the impression that several copies of a collection of English poems by Crashaw were in circulation before 1646, with mistakes in them which the poet himself could hardly have made, and which were possibly due to faulty copying on the part of a scrivener ; and that perhaps, as occasion offered, Crashaw retouched these copies in accordance with his latest inspiration, without, as a rule, noticing the copyist's errors and with anything but business-like consistency. It may thus well be that Tanner 465 and 466, Add. MS. 33219 (No. 13, below), and the published text of 1646 were all derived from separate copies.

The following is a list of the poems in MS. Tanner 465 which were not printed in the seventeenth century and which have hitherto been attributed to Crashaw by modern editors (beginning with Grosart) chiefly on the evidence of the index or of the fact that the initials ' R. C.' or ' R. Cr.' are attached to them in the text.

It must be noted, however, at the outset, that the index contains some mistakes ; e. g. in the extract quoted above the page-number following the entry ' On Yᵉ Lady Parker ' should be ' 233 ', not ' 235 ' ; that following the entry ' On an Infant '

[1] See foot-note to p. lix ; also pp. lxxxii–lxxxiii.

should be ' 232 ', not ' 234 '. Again, the poem beginning 'Ask me no more ', on p. 195, is attributed to Sir H. Wotton instead of to Carew, and the mistake is repeated in the text. It must not, therefore, be too lightly concluded that poems attributed to Crashaw in the index or by means of initials in the body of the MS. are necessarily by him, though if the internal or other evidence does not conflict, the assignment by initials may carry a good deal of weight. And, on the other hand, the prevailing uncertainty of the index may afford an additional reason for ascribing to Crashaw any poems which on internal grounds alone may seem likely to be from his hand.

In this list, besides asterisks indicating that the poems in question are assigned to Crashaw by initials, a cross preceding a MS. page-number signifies that the page-number is mentioned in the MS. index of Crashaw's poems quoted above.

Page nos. in MS.	Poems.	Page nos. in present edn.
†7–22	The Latin poems given in their MS. order below	352–378 and 411–413
†39–44	,, ,, ,, ,, ,,	
46–52	,, ,, ,, ,, ,,	
†95	Posuit sub istâ (non gravi) caput terrâ . . .	378
96	Ergo iterum in lacrymas, & saevi murmura planctûs .	379
119	And is he gone, whom these armes held but now ? .	379
123	Soe I may gaine thy death, my life I'le giue . .	381
129	Come, braue soldjers, come, & see	381
130	Æternall loue ! what 'tis to loue thee well, . .	381
†164	Little=buzzing=wanton elf	413
176	*The bird, that's fetch't from Phasis floud, . .	382
177–8	*Shame of thy mother soyle ! ill-nurtur'd tree ! .	382
180–1	I sing Impiety beyond a name :	384
181–3	Reach me a quill, pluckt from the flaming wing .	386
183–4	Grow plumpe, lean Death ; his Holinesse a feast .	387
185–6	Sound forth, cælestiall Organs, lett heauens quire .	389
186–7	Strange Metamorphosis ! It was but now . .	390
190–2	Bright starre of Majesty, oh shedd on mee, . .	391
†196	*Bright Goddesse, (whether Joue thy father be ; .	392
†202–3	Hath aged winter, fledg'd with feathered raine, .	394
205	Hee's dead : Oh what harsh musicks there . .	393
229	Stay, silver=footed Came, striue not to wed . .	395

It will appear from these two lists together that pp. 7–65, allowing for the missing pp. 23–38, are occupied entirely by Latin poems, of which a good number were published, either in Latin or in English translations, among Crashaw's works during his lifetime, and there seems to be no reason, as a general rule, to reject the rest. Three poems, however, provide exceptions to this rule, those of which the first lines are respectively

> Dum vires refero vomitûs, & nobile munus,
> Quid facis ? ah ! tam perversâ quid volvitur irâ ?
> Sordes ô tibi gratulamur istas,

The Latin burlesque poem by W. Hawkins, to which the last two of these poems refer, *En Priscianus verberans et vapulans*, has for its theme an incident that occurred at Hadleigh School, in Suffolk, where Hawkins was Master, and was first published in 1632. This edition included five prefatory lines (fo. A 2 verso) signed ' Gaguinus Nash Magister Artium '. The same work was published with additions in 1634, with title *Nisus verberans et vapulans*, and in this volume Nash's verses are supplemented by two lines (39 and 40) from the first of the two poems in question attributed to Crashaw (one word only is changed), and fourteen lines from different parts of the second (with several variants). The contribution is signed ' Gaguinus Nash, *Mag. Art. Aulae Pembr. Socius* '. It seems likely that Nash offered Hawkins both poems and that Hawkins exercised rights of censorship in the interests of space. There is no apparent reason why Crashaw should have been concerned, and the theme is not one which could be expected to appeal to him. This applies no less strongly to the poem ' Dum vires refero vomitûs, et nobile munus ', the composition of which would have been very much at variance with the spirit and the tone of Crashaw's works as they are otherwise known. These three poems are therefore placed in Appendix I (*Poems probably spurious*).

Pages 66–94 of the MS. are blank or missing or occupied by poems definitely and credibly attributed to other writers than Crashaw.

Page 95 has the Latin poem in honour of Dr. Brooke, followed on p. 96 by the poem on Dr. Mansell, which may be fairly ascribed to Crashaw by its position and by the fact that it is not attributed to any one else in the MS. Pages 97–102 are blank and the succeeding pages to 110 inclusive are missing. Pages 111–34 consist of a group of English poems, all published as Crashaw's in the seventeenth century with the exception of a single epigram ascribed in the Index to ' T. R.' and in the text to ' T. Randolph ' (i. e. ' On Good Friday ', p. 130), and of the four ' not printed ' poems occurring on pp. 119, 123, 129, and 130. For the authenticity of these four poems the internal evidence is very strong apart from their incidence in this large group of poems which is clearly attributable to Crashaw. From p. 134 to p. 163 the succession of Crashaw's poems is a good deal broken up by poems definitely and no doubt fairly ascribed to other authors or to ' Anon '.

Page 164, containing only the poem ' Upon a Gnat burnt in a Candle ' is given to Crashaw in the index and has therefore been printed as Crashaw's by several modern editors. It is true that it is not ascribed to any one else in either index or text ; but even so there is fairly strong evidence, both external and internal, against its authenticity. In the first place the poem occurs in another Bodleian MS. (Rawl. poet. 147, pp. 14–15), where it is attributed in both index and text to one ' Thomas Vincent, Coll. Trin.'. And the comparatively awkward, jerky prosody and the absence of any imagery characteristic of Crashaw strengthen faith in the relatively unknown Vincent's claim to the authorship. This poem has therefore in the present edition been placed in Appendix I.

From p. 165 onwards it will be noticed that the initials ' R. Cr.' are much more frequently attached in the MS. to poems by Crashaw, all the poems from pp. 165–79 being so distinguished except the poem on p. 166 ascribed to Randolph. This section includes two poems unpublished in the seventeenth century (pp. 176–8) in which the internal evidence does not conflict with the initials,[1] and this applies also to the poem on p. 196 which is placed to Crashaw's account in both text and index. There is no reason, again, to doubt the index on the score of pp. 202–3, containing the elegy on Mr. Stanninow, who is also celebrated in *Steps to the Temple*, the elegy in the MS. being full of very characteristic imagery. For the remaining eight in the serial list given above (pp. 180–92, 205, and 229) it will be seen that the external evidence is on the whole negative, i.e. neither index nor text definitely gives them to Crashaw, nor are they definitely ascribed to another hand, with the possible exception of the poem on p. 205, which is indexed separately though the index is non-committal as to its authorship. See pp. lxxiii and 393.

---

[1] The poem on p. 176 also occurs in Add. MS. 33219.

As the chief evidence, therefore, for these poems being from the hand of Crashaw must be derived from the poems them-selves, it is well to be sure at the outset as to the kinds of test that are likely to give reasonable satisfaction.

It is obvious that close parallels, amounting to whole phrases or lines, between these more doubtful poems and other poems printed contemporaneously in Crashaw's works, may carry considerable weight, but they can only be admitted as evidence after due allowance has been made for the existence of a stock of conventional images and turns of phrase, upon which any poet of this time would be apt to draw, and for the very general habit of plagiarism, at every stage between un-conscious reminiscence and intentional appropriation. In the circumstances it could easily happen that a close and obvious parallel, though valuable as confirmatory evidence, might have much less weight by itself than when combined with parallels which are verbally more distant, but which show how on two similar occasions the poet's mind has reacted in the same way, passing through similar associations without necessarily adopting the same phraseology. And it will be an added advantage if both these kinds of parallel can be supplemented by considerations of prosody, of characteristic poetic gesture, of predilection for certain *kinds* of imagery, all these factors pointing, though with varying certainty, in the direction of a single author.

In Crashaw, as distinguished from the majority of his con-temporaries, the reader learns to expect a considerable sureness and consistency of touch in the management of the seven-, eight-, and ten-syllabled lines, with much successful variety of stress, with numerous rhetorical and dramatic pauses, and with a well-marked faculty for building up the separate sen-tences into a well-rounded verse-paragraph, often culminating with epigrammatic effect at the close. The poem ' On a foule Morning, being then to take a journey ', published in 1646, affords a fair example of Crashaw's average prosody :

> Where art thou Sol, while thus the blind-fold Day
> Staggers out of the East, looses her way
> Stumbling on Night ? Rouze thee Illustrious Youth,
> And let no dull mists choake the Lights faire growth.
> Point here thy Beames ; ô glance on yonder flockes,
> And make their fleeces Golden as thy lockes.

Vnfold thy faire front, and there shall appeare
Full glory, flaming in her owne free spheare.
Gladnesse shall cloath the Earth, we will instile
The face of things, an universall smile.   10
Say to the Sullen Morne, thou com'st to court her
And wilt command proud *Zephirus* to sport her
With wanton gales : his balmy breath shall licke
The tender drops which tremble on her cheeke ;
Which rarifyed, and in a gentle raine
On those delicious bankes distill'd againe
Shall rise in a sweet Harvest ; which discloses
Two euer blushing beds of new-borne Roses.
Hee'l fan her bright locks teaching them to flow,
And friske in curl'd *Mæanders* : Hee will throw   20
A fragrant Breath suckt from the spicy nest
O'th pretious *Phœnix*, warme upon her Breast.
Hee with a dainty and soft hand, will trim
And brush her Azure Mantle, which shall swim
In silken Volumes ; wheresore're shee'l tread,
Bright clouds like Golden fleeces shall be spread.
    Rise then (faire blew-ey'd Maid) rise and discover
Thy silver brow, and meet thy Golden lover.
See how hee runs, with what a hasty flight
Into thy Bosome, bath'd with liquid Light.   30
Fly, fly prophane fogs, farre hence fly away,
Taint not the pure streames of the springing Day,
With your dull influence, it is for you,
To sit and scoule upon Nights heavy brow ;
Not on the fresh cheekes of the virgin Morne,
Where nought but smiles, and ruddy joyes are worne.
Fly then, and doe not thinke with her to stay ;
Let it suffice, shee'l weare no maske to day.

This poem also illustrates some other qualities of Crashaw's
style ; the peculiar lightness, energy, and limpidity of expression—the ' nimble raptures ' of which he speaks in another
poem ; the comparative simplicity of thought, though the
early training in the school of epigram sometimes shows its
effect ; and the employment of imagery which though often
conventionally extravagant practically never fails to justify
itself by a genuinely sensuous quality, favourable to strong
contrasts of light and shade and colour, and appealing almost
as much to the faculties of smell and touch as to the faculty of
vision. The latter sense, however, is the most vigorously exercised, the peculiar pictorial effect recalling Crashaw's known
addiction to the arts of ' Drawing, Limning and Graving '

(Preface to *Steps to the Temple*). The poem also contains some of Crashaw's favourite images, the metaphorical use of ' swim ' (l. 24), for example—and of ' bath'd ' (l. 30). The phœnix (l. 22) is, of course, no *rara avis* in seventeenth-century poetry, but it certainly occurs in Crashaw's works with distinctive frequency. But the most common and characteristic of all Crashaw's images is that of ' the tear ' (compare l. 14), which in its various associations of rain, rivers, seas, pearls, diamonds, milk, cream, and stars, is contemplated by Crashaw so insistently as to suggest the origin of its fascination in some unusually deep-seated mental bias.

This published poem may now be compared with one of the ' doubtful ' poems from the MS., the second of the two on the king's coronation :

Strange Metamorphosis ! It was but now
The sullen heauen had vail'd its mournfull brow
With a black maske : the clouds with child by greife
Traueld th' Olympian plaines to find releife.
But at the last (having not soe much powe'r
As to refraine) brought forth a costly shower
Of pearly drops, & sent her numerous birth
(As tokens of her greife) unto the earth.
Alas, the earth, quick drunke with teares, had reel'd
From of her center, had not Joue vpheld   10
The staggering lumpe : each eye spent all its store,
As if heereafter they would weepe noe more.
Streight from this sea of teares there does appeare
Full glory flaming in her owne free sphære.
Amazed Sol throwes of his mournful weeds,
Speedily harnessing his fiery steeds,
Up to Olympus stately topp he hies,
From whence his glorious rivall hee espies.
Then wondring starts, & had the curteous night
Withheld her vaile, h' had forfeited his sight.   20
The joyfull sphæres with a delicious sound
Affright th' amazed aire, & dance a round
To their owne Musick, nor (vntill they see
This glorious Phœbus sett) will quiet bee.
Each aery Siren now hath gott her song,
To whom the merry lambes doe tripp along
The laughing meades, as joyfull to behold
Their winter coates couer'd with flaming gold.
Such was the brightnesse of this Northerne starre,
It made the Virgin Phœnix come from farre   30

To be repaird : hither she did resort,
Thinking her father had remou'd his court.
The lustre of his face did shine soe bright,
That Rome's bold Eagles now were blinded quite,
The radiant darts, shott from his sparkling eyes,
Made euery mortall gladly sacrifice
A heart burning in loue ; all did adore
This rising sunne. their faces nothing wore,
But smiles, & ruddy joyes, & at this day
All melancholy clowds vanisht away.   40

It will be observed that l. 14 of this poem exactly repeats
l. 8 of the other, and that ll. 38–9 correspond closely to l. 36
of the other. But as already suggested it is possible to give
too much weight to facts of this kind, striking though they may
be. The line repeated verbatim, at least, was worth stealing,
and the evidence needs to be confirmed by parallelism of a less
simple nature and by reference to qualities which both poems
may share with other works known to be by the same poet.
It would be of no avail, further, to point to similarities arising
from the use of classical personifications, or from the use of the
hackneyed similitude about the sun dispelling the clouds of
grief or the mists of dullness ; or from the presence in both poems
of the ubiquitous Phœnix. It is rather in the details of the
pictures, in small points of style and imagery closely woven into
the texture of the thought that parallels of more persuasive
force are likely to be found. Thus it may be noticed that in the
first of the two quoted poems the ' blindfold day ' is delayed
and made to *stagger* from its course as a result of the unusual
obscurity, though in the end the *sullen* morn consents to wear
no *mask*. In the second it is the ' sullen heauen ' which has
' vail'd its mournfull brow with a black maske ', and the earth
that ' staggers ' from its centre under the excessive load of grief
discharged from the sky. Again, in the first poem, l. 6, as a
result of the sun's appearance, the fleeces of the flocks are to
become as golden as the sun's own beams. In the second, l. 26,
the appearance of the sun's royal rival will enable the lambs, or
the meadows—and in the close association of ideas it hardly
matters which—' to behold their winter coates couer'd with
flaming gold '. Furthermore, the second poem shows the same
easy flow of verse and diction, the characteristic afflatus,
the epigrammatic flavour, the cult of luxurious imagery, and

contains, in ll. 6–12, a riot of similitudes based on the thought of tears.

It is clear that none of these factors alone could properly carry conviction as to the authorship of the second poem ; but their accumulated weight seems at least sufficient to justify its continued inclusion in editions of Crashaw's works, if not once for all to dispel the mists of doubt. And if this poem be included it may go in company with the four that immediately precede it in the MS., viz. three on the Gunpowder Plot and the first of the two on the king's coronation, and also the poem on the birth of the Princess Elizabeth which comes next after the coronation poems, and the poem on p. 229 of the MS., on the death of Dr. Porter ; for all of which, evidence, hardly less arresting, of Crashaw's authorship is adduced in the notes at the end of this volume.

The discussion and the illustration of the internal evidence for Crashaw's authorship of these poems have been prolonged here partly because the present edition is the first to include five poems from this MS. to which similar criteria have been applied and in regard to which the evidence, though not as finally decisive as could be wished, is yet as strong as such evidence can usually be, depending as it does not on one or two different factors only, but, as with the poems already considered, on several.

The following are the titles of the five poems in question :

	Page nos. in MS.		Page nos. in present edn.
(1)	200	On the death of Wm Henshaw, student in Emān. Coll.	401
(2)	201	An Elegy upon the death of Mr Wm Carre, student in Emān: Colledge	402
(3)	233	An Elegy on the death of the Lady Parker . .	403
(4)	234	An Elegy upon the death of Mr. Christopher Rouse Esquire	404
(5)	235	An Epitaph	405

The present editor's notice and suspicion had already fallen upon (5) with its ' watry pearls from each kind eye ' (l. 6), when his attention was very kindly drawn by Mr. E. J. O'Brien, of Forest Hill, Oxford, to this, to (4), the long elegy which immediately precedes the epitaph and of which the epitaph is presumably a continuation, and to (1). This led to a fuller and more careful consideration of all the poems in the

MS. not there definitely attributed to Crashaw, and to the decision to print in a special section these three and the two others on what is virtually internal evidence alone, this seeming to demand their provisional inclusion in the Crashaw canon until they can be finally shown to proceed from another hand, or from another hand unguided by Crashaw.

It has to be admitted that there is some serious external evidence against Crashaw's authorship, in that all the first four poems (and as already indicated No. 5 is apparently an appendage to No. 4) are listed in the index apart from the initial section pertaining to Crashaw (see the sections of the index quoted above, p. lix), and two of them (Nos. 1 and 2) are, both in the index and in the text, attributed to another author ' Peter Cornwallis '. Furthermore, these two poems occur again in another Bodleian MS., Rawl. poet. 147 (which contains also No. 3 and the poem on the death of Dr. Porter occurring on p. 229 of Tanner 465—both unassigned to any author) and there again they are ascribed to ' Cornwallis '.[1] As against this, however, it may be recalled :

(1) That the MS. as a whole is devoted primarily to Crashaw.

(2) That the index is both faulty and incomplete.

(3) That in at least one instance the compiler erred as to the authorship of a poem, attributing Carew's ' Ask me no more ' to Sir Henry Wotton.

(4) That the ascription to Peter Cornwallis might have arisen from Cornwallis's having claimed them whereas in fact he had appropriated them, or obtained Crashaw's assistance in writing them or induced Crashaw to write them for him.

(5) That Cornwallis is otherwise apparently unknown as a poet, whereas if the ascription to him is correct he is the author of two poems which not only recall features of Crashaw's style and imagery but which vie intrinsically with that writer's best achievements in the elegiac form.

(6) That although with poets of solid contemporary standing, like Donne and Ben Jonson, minute and frequent points of similarity might conceivably arise from obsequious imitation, Crashaw could have had no such repute at the age of twenty as would lead to his being followed as closely as he appears to be

[1] There was a Philip (not Peter) Cornwallis at Emmanuel College between 1631 and 1634.

by the author of the elegies on Henshaw and Carre, both of whom died in 1633.

The second of these two poems provides the more obvious though not necessarily the most convincing kind of parallel suggestive of Crashaw's authorship, containing as it does in ll. 25–6, almost exactly, the line which has already been shown to be common to the two poems last quoted—'Full glory flaming in her own free Sphere '. Lines 35–6 again are almost exactly repeated in another of Crashaw's published poems, the second elegy on Mr. Herrys (p. 170, below), ll. 59–60 :

> Spare him Death, o spare him then,
> Spare the sweetest among men.

But there are a good number of more minute features suggestive of Crashaw's hand both in this and in the other four poems, and so far as these indications have seemed definable they are illustrated in the notes at the end of this volume. A few may also be exemplified here, as :

In (1), phrases like ' the liquid jewel of a tear ' l. 24, ' our wat'ry eyes ' l. 27, compared with numerous phrases of similar import and feeling in Crashaw's works.

In (2) ll. 17–18 :

> And in spite of the sick steames
> And lazy foggs of death, his beames

compared with ll. 29–30 of ' Temperance ' (p. 343, below) :

> A soul, whose intellectuall beames
> No mists doe mask, no lazy steames.

In (3) the turn of phrase, with inversion in the second line, in ll. 11–12 :

> Nor can my humble fancy soare so high
> As was her Excellence

compared with ll. 17–18 of the poem ' Upon the Birth of the Princess Elizabeth (see p. 391, below) :

> And though these humble lines soare not soe high
> As is thy birth . . .

In (4) apart from the fine and characteristic imagery maintained throughout, small points like the use of ' I mean ' in ll. 29 and 36. Compare ' The Weeper ', stanza 1, ll. 5–6, p. 79, below) :

> I meane
> Thy faire Eyes sweet *Magdalene*

and the first poem on the king's coronation, l. 31 (p. 389, below) :

> I meane those three great starres . . .

Or, again, the fondness for the double adjective shown in ll. 1, 7, and 12. A study of Crashaw's works, and perhaps especially of his early works, will suggest that this frequency is characteristic ; often the double adjective occurs, as in l. 1 here, at the beginning of a line, the first adjective consisting of one syllable and the second of two, or three by 'equivalence', e.g. ' Rich liberal Heaven ', ' Fair, flowery Name ', ' Sly lurking Treason ', ' Black dismal Horror ', ' Poor meagre Horror ', ' Dark, dusty Man ', ' Dull, sluggish Isle '.

And in (5) l. 4 :

> Which now makes Abram's bosom fine

compared with ' The Weeper ', stanza 2, l. 6 :

> What ever makes Heavens fore-head fine.

There remains the elegy on p. 205 of the MS. See p. 393. This has hitherto figured only in Grosart's edition, and is re-admitted here because the internal evidence (especially the imagery, the epigrammatic flavour, and the fluent expression in ll. 4–5), although on the whole less strong than in the poems considered above, seems to warrant its inclusion in an edition where, if error is unavoidable, it is desired to err rather upon the inclusive side than otherwise.

Other poems in this MS. which seemed to call for consideration have been considered, and though there are several which cannot be assigned to any particular author there appears to be no positive reason for assigning them to Crashaw, and they are therefore excluded from this edition. It is unfortunate that no greater certainty seems attainable at present.

Designated ' T ' in the foot-notes, ' T5 ' and ' T6 ' distinguishing, where necessary, MSS. Tanner 465 and 466 ; ' TA ' and ' TB ' distinguishing the two copies of ' Sospetto d'Herode ' in Tanner 466.

13. British Museum Add. MS. 33219.

Size 6½ × 4 in. 50 leaves, numbered in pencil. No original page numbers. Four blank sheets precede and twelve follow the numbered leaves. One blank sheet between fos. 1 and 2 ; two between fos. 12 and 13. The whole bound in silvered silk.

This collection, though without date or indication of its origin or first ownership, seems for reasons given below in the section on the chronological order of Crashaw's poems, likely to contain only poems written before 1635, and may therefore with some plausibility be assigned approximately to that date. It also contains nothing known to be by any one but Crashaw. It gives the impression of having been designed as a gift to a lady ; and since the two dedicatory poems which are chiefly responsible for this impression are certainly in Crashaw's style, it is possible, though by no means certain, that Crashaw was himself the donor. At the same time it is quite clear that the volume, though so catalogued, is not in Crashaw's handwriting. This had long been suspected from the strange verbal errors which the MS. contains and which could hardly all have been made by the poet himself ; and the suspicion becomes certainty when the MS. is compared with the signatures at Peterhouse or with the other known specimens of Crashaw's autograph.

While seeming indubitably to preserve some true early readings, this MS. sometimes shares the errors of the printed editions, and its relation to Crashaw's original MS., for the reason already suggested on p. xlvi, above, is almost certainly not direct and is possibly less close than that of MS. Tanner 465.

This MS. is the only source of the two dedicatory poems with which it commences and of the translation from Grotius, ' O thou the span of whose Omnipotence '. The following are the first lines of its contents, the three poems not found elsewhere marked ' † '.

Page nos. in MS.	Poems.	Page nos. in present edn.
†1	At th' Iuory Tribunall of your hand	397
†1–1 v	Though now 'tis neither May nor June . . .	397
2	(*General heading* : Diuine Epigrams.) . . .	85
	Each blest drop on each blest limme . . .	85
	The Worlds light shines, shine as it will . .	97
	Lett it no longer bee a forlorne hope . . .	85
	See here an easy feast that knowes no wound . .	86
2 v	Two Mites, two drops, (yet all her house and land) .	86
	Tell me, bright Boy. tell me my golden lad ! .	86
	Now Lord, or neuer they'le beleeue on thee . .	88
	Under thy shadow may I lurke a while	87
	Thy hands are wash't. but ô the Water's spilt . .	88
3	What euer story of their cruelty	86
	Here where our Lord once layd his head . . .	86

Designated ' *A3* ' *in the foot-notes.*

14. British Museum MSS. Harleian 6917 and 6918.

Size $7\frac{7}{8} \times 5\frac{3}{4}$ in. No. 6917, 105 leaves ; No. 6918, 102 leaves and slightly stouter paper. The handwriting of No. 6917 is apparently continued in No. 6918, with modifications perhaps due to the advance of years, and it may be that the two MSS. were once united, though the pagination is not continuous. There is a note on fo. 2 verso of No. 6917, in Edward Harley's hand, to the effect that the book is ' out of Lord Somers Library ' ; but of the earlier ownership of these MSS. there appears to be no indication beyond the name on the initial page of No. 6918, ' Peter Calfe '. Calfe appears to be the author of several poems at the end of No. 6918, one of which has a clear reference to the year 1659 ; but the writing is obviously different from that of the major portion of that MS. and it seems unlikely that Calfe was the first owner.

The two volumes contain a large collection of English poems,

chiefly of the seventeenth century. No. 6917 seems to be of
the earlier compilation, and to judge by the poems selected and
by the evidence of their references to external events its transcriptions were made somewhere between 1630 and 1645. Carew,
Herrick, Randolph, Corbet, and King are among the principal
authors represented. At fo. 54 (p. 99) begins a selection of
six poems which, although not there assigned to any writer,
were all published in the first edition of *Steps to the Temple*
(1646). Between the fifth and the sixth of these intervene the
satirical verses on Sir John Suckling, attributed to Sir John
Mennis,[1] and Suckling's ' The Reply '. The following are the
first lines of Crashaw's poems :

Page nos. in MS.	Poems.	Page nos. in present edn.
99	What succour can I hope my muse will send	183
101	Where art thou, Sol, while thus the blindfold day	181
102	faithlesse, and fond mortalitie .	166
103	A Brooke whose streame so great so good .	175
103	To these whom death againe did wedd	174
107	Who ere she bee	195

Of these poems it will be seen from the notes to the present
edition that the third and the fourth were probably both
written in 1631, and it is very probable that all of them belong
to the undergraduate stage of Crashaw's career (1631–4) and
were copied about that time. (Cp. the heading to the first of
these six poems as copied in Add. MS. 22118 : ' Crosh: To
ye Deane on occasion of sleeping chappell '.)

The variant readings presented by these two MSS. are on the
whole slight and do not call for special comment here.

The six poems which are indisputably Crashaw's are immediately (beginning on fo. 52, p. 95) preceded by the Epithalamium which was in 1927 for the first time included in an
edition of Crashaw's works and which seems never to have been
printed until 1923.[2] Its authorship is attributed to Crashaw
on the general principles indicated in the discussion of MS. Tanner 465 (pp. lxvi–lxxiii, above), and for the particular reasons
of parallel, &c., given in the notes to this poem on pp. 462–3,
below. No poem between pp. 400 and 409 is ascribed to Crashaw
with the same confidence that is felt in regard to this one.

[1] See Suckling, *Works*, ed. A. Hamilton Thompson, 1910, p. 74.
The verses were printed in *Wit and Drollery*, 1656, p. 44.
[2] *London Mercury*, June, pp. 159 sqq., ed. L. C. Martin.

MS. Harleian 6918 contains only one poem by Crashaw, that beginning ' Deare Hope ; Earth's dowry, and heauens debt '. This is on fo. 80 verso, and the poem by Cowley to which it is an answer precedes it, beginning on fo. 80. (See p. 345, below). *Designated ' H ' in the foot-notes.*

15. British Museum Add. MS. 22118.

Size 6¾ × 4 in.   49 leaves.

This volume contains miscellaneous poems (by Randolph, Carew, Corbet, &c.). The date at which the transcriptions were made is uncertain, but it is probable that nearly all the poems by Crashaw belong to the undergraduate period of his residence at Cambridge and were copied then or soon after. The ' Panegyric ' addressed to the queen, for example, ' Brittaine ! yᵉ mightye Oceans louely bride ' is in the earlier form in which it appears in the edition of 1646 (and in which the latest reference is to the birth of the Princess Elizabeth in 1635), not the form to which it was amplified for *Voces Votivæ* (1640) and published in the 1648 edition of *Steps to the Temple.* The following are the first lines of the poems by Crashaw, which extend, with interruptions, from fo. 10 to fo. 29 verso. They are usually ascribed to him by the designation ' Crosh: '.

Page nos. in MS.	Poems.	Page nos. in present edn.
23	What succour can I hope my Muse will send	183
24	Brittaine ! yᵉ mightye Oceans louely bride	176
27	Where art thou Sol ? while thus yᵉ blindfold day	181
28	How life & death in thee	93
33	Now westward Sol had spent yᵉ richest beames	149
40	I would bee marryed, yett would haue no wife	183
51	Goe now with some daringe drugge	156
58	This reuerend shadow caste yᵗ setting Sun,	163
58	High mounted on an Aunt Nanus yᵉ tall	161
59	Happy mee, O happye sheepe	102
62	Siste paululum uiator, vbi longum sisti necesse sit	164

Designated ' A2 ' in the foot-notes.

16. British Museum Add. MS. 34692.

Size 7⅔ × 3³⁄₁₀ in.   33 leaves.

The major portion of this MS. is occupied by a sermon by ' Thom. Lenthall ' in defence of the divine right of kings and by the preface thereto dated ' Pemb: Hall: Cal: July: Aᵒ 1642://:'. The sermon is followed by two of Crashaw's poems, preceded by an emblematic page (fo. 26 recto) comprising Crashaw's couplet

> Live IESU Live & lett it bee
> My life to dye for love of thee

(see p. 78, below). The first lines of the two succeeding poems are 'Loe heere a little Volume but large booke' (fo. 26 verso, see p. 126, below) with 'R: Crashaw Coll: Petren:' at the end, and 'Harke she is called the parting hower is come' with 'Rob: Crashaw: A: Pet: Artib: Magistr:' at the end (p. 139 below).

Designated 'A34' in the foot-notes.

17. British Museum MS. Sloane 1925.

Size $5\frac{1}{2} \times 3\frac{1}{2}$ in.   75 leaves.

The contents of this note-book are described on the title-page as 'Poems Characters Proverbs Sentences Historicall Remarques Tales'. There is no clear indication of date. The selections from Crashaw's works begin at fo. 17 and are continued to fo. 27, but for the most part they consist only of extracts, 2–7 lines long. Two of the epigrams in English are given in full on fo. 25 : 'Each blest drop on each blest limme' and 'See here an easy feast y^t knows no wound', but for the rest the only poem quoted entire is 'Musicks Duell'. The excerpts were probably taken from another MS. containing Crashaw's early work. The following are the first lines of poems from which they are derived :

> Now westward Sol had spent ye richest bea[mes]
> What bright soft thing is this ?
> Haile, *Sister Springs,*
> Welcome my Griefe, my Ioy; how deare's
> Each blest drop on each blest limme,
> See here an easie Feast y^t knows no wound
> Well Peter dost thou wield thy active sword,
> Thou hast the art on't *Peter*; and canst tell
> Rise, Heire of fresh Eternity,
> Come wee Shepheards who have seene
> Who ere shee bee,
> Rise then, immortall maid ! *Religion* rise!
> I would be married but I'de haue no wife,
> Where art thou Sol, while thus the blind-fold Day
> Passenger who e're thou art,
> Death, what dost ? ô hold thy Blow,
> A plant of noble stemme, forward and faire,
> To see both blended in one flood

Designated 'S' in the foot-notes.

18. British Museum Add. MS. 22603.

Size 6⅘ × 4¼ in. 72 leaves.

This volume contains numerous seventeenth-century extracts from Cleveland, Herrick, Lovelace, &c.; Clement Paman is strongly represented. There is only one poem by Crashaw, 'An Elegie on a Scholler' ('ffaythlesse and fond mortalitie') concluding with l. 30, 'Theyr Cadence is Rhetoricall' (p. 166, below).

Designated 'A226' in the foot-notes.

19. Bodleian MS. Rawl. poet. 142.

Size 8⅛ × 5½ in. 84 leaves.

Among the extracts in this volume are two items by Crashaw (1) part of 'The Weeper', and (2) 'The Teare'. As usual in the MSS. the version of 'The Weeper', so far as it goes, conforms more closely to the 1646 than to the 1648 text, and the copy may well have been made during the Cambridge period (pp. 79 and 83, below).

Designated 'R' in the foot-notes.

20. Bodleian MS. Rawl. poet. 147.

Size 5½ × 4⁹⁄₁₀ in. 140 leaves.

This large collection contains the following poems of which the authorship is uncertain (see pp. lxiii–lxxiii, above):

Page nos. in MS.		*Page nos. in present edn.*
14	Sylly Buzzing wanton Elfe	413
37	Hee's dead. Oh what harsh Musick's there . .	393
38	Here in deaths Closett (Reader) know . .	405
40	Can such perfection fade ? Can virtue dye . .	403
42	Death hath drawn our golden Carre	402
50	See a sweete streame of Helicon	401

It also comprises the two following which may, on the evidence of MS. Tanner 465 (No. 12, above), be more confidently attributed to Crashaw.

Page nos. in MS.

38	Stay syluer-footed Chame, striue not to wed (see p. 395, below).
69	Hath aged winter fledg'd wᵗʰ feather'd rayne (see p. 394, below).

Designated 'R7' in the foot-notes.

21. British Museum Add. MS. 18044.

Size 6⁷⁄₁₀ × 4⅖ in. 188 leaves.

A note-book comprising 'Collections out of seuerall Authors

by Marmaduke Raudon Eboriensis 1662   Hodsden '. All
the material of the Crashaw selections is to be found in the text
of *Carmen Deo Nostro* (1652), to which few variants are presented ; it seems likely that these are due to another hand than
Crashaw's and that the MS. is derived from the printed book
and not from another MS. Indeed this is almost certain from
its inclusion of the Latin verses ('Sum pulcher' etc.) attached
to one of the engravings printed in 1652, probably not by
Crashaw at all. The extracts begin· at fo. 7 verso, with the
general heading ' Out of Crashawes Poemes ' and then ' The
office of the Holy Crosse ' (see p. 263, below). This is followed
by twelve of the poems.

Designated ' A1 ' in the foot-notes.

22. Bodleian MS. 31037 (Eng. misc. e. 13, known as ' Dr.
Lynnet's Commonplace Book ').

Size $7\frac{4}{5} \times 5\frac{1}{2}$ in. 31 leaves.

This contains only ' To y^e reader on Lessius hygiasticon '
(see pp. 156 and 342, below), probably derived from one of the
editions of that work published in 1634 and 1636.

23. British Museum Add. MS. 11258.

Size $7\frac{5}{8} \times 6$ in. 41 leaves.

. This is a collection chiefly of late seventeenth- and also of
eighteenth-century extracts ; and it contains, of Crashaw's,
only the version of Martial's epigram ' Four Teeth thou had'st
that rank'd in goodly State ' (p. 188, below).

24. Folger Shakespeare Library MS. 267.1, a book of miscellaneous extracts formerly owned by Bertram Dobell. It contains many passages and a few complete poems by Crashaw
written in a contemporary hand by a compiler who sometimes
appears to introduce his own readings. His main or only
source was probably the edition of 1648 ; the error therein,
' habit ' for ' hasty ' (see p. 240, l. 50), is repeated. At one time
the MS. had been lent to G. Thorn Drury, who supplied the
variants given in 1927. These remain (see pp. 89, 309 sqq., and
319). The passage cited on p. 319 *may* come from a separate
source. But the variants as a whole seem unauthoritative and
are not recorded. A microfilm of the MS. (omitting its pages
of shorthand) is in the University Library at Liverpool.

Designated 'Dobell' (as before) in the foot-notes.

25. Pierpont Morgan Library. See p. xciii.

C. MODERN EDITIONS

The modern editing of Crashaw's works may be said to date from the year 1785, with the publication of :

Poetry By Richard Crashaw. With Some Account of the Author ; and an Introductory Address to the Reader, By Peregrine Phillips.
This is a small volume (5¾ × 3½ in., pp. xxiv, 158) containing a selection clearly derived from the reprint published in 1670 (No. 7 above), without reference to the other original editions or to any MSS.

Two years later Headley's *Select Beauties of Ancient English Poetry* (1787), vol. i, pp. 49 sqq., included ' The Alarm of SATAN, with the Instigation of HEROD ', being stanzas 5–66 of ' Sospetto d'Herode '. This is followed by the note ' Translated from Marino, by R. Crashaw, Edit. 1670 '.

The first edition to claim completeness was that included in Anderson's *A Complete Edition of the Poets of Great Britain . . . London.* (The second title-page gives place and date : Edinburgh . . . *Anno* 1793.) Poems by Crashaw are given in vol. iv (pp. 707–54) and it is stated in the introductory notice that ' His whole works, reprinted from the edition in 1648, are now, for the first time, received into a collection of classical English poetry '. The bibliographical notes show that the editor had seen neither the volume of 1646 nor that of 1652 (Nos. 2 and 5, above), but since he quotes ll. 93–108 of ' The Flaming Heart ' (see p. 326, below) he presumably had seen a copy of the 1670 edition (No. 7, above). A few Latin epigrams are included, doubtless from the volume of 1634 or from that of 1670 (Nos. 1 and 6, above). No other sources seem to have been utilized and the edition is of no great interest. . The claim of completeness is not justified, even for the edition of 1648, and the original order of the poems in that volume is abandoned.

The next edition was that contained in vol. vi of Chalmers's *The Works of the English Poets . . . in twenty-one volumes . . . London . . .* 1810. In this again the text appears to be based on the edition of 1648, and the editor has the distinction of being the first to fill up the blank in stanza 51, l. 1 of ' Sospetto d'Herode '. The reading ' proud usurping Herod ', for which there is no other authority and which is clearly the result of a guess, persisted in the two editions of ' Sospetto d'Herode ' which came next, and which are no doubt based entirely on Chalmers's text. These are : (1) in *The Works of the British Poets. With Lives of the Authors by Ezekiel Sanford . . . Philadelphia . . .* 1819. ' Sospetto d'Herode ' occupies pp. 191–212 of vol. i and is the only poem by Crashaw represented. (2) *The Suspicion of Herod, Being The First Book of The Murder of the Innocents. Translated from the Italian By Richard Crashaw . . . Printed by Bournes Jun., Brothers, Church Street, Kensington. MDCCCXXXIV.*

A good number of years now elapsed before the next edition : *The Poetical Works of Richard Crashaw and Quarles' Emblems. With Memoirs and Critical Dissertations, by the Rev. George Gilfillan . . . Edinburgh . . . M.DCCC.LVII.* This was issued again in Cassell's Library Edition of British Poets (n. d.). It appears to be based, independently of earlier modern reprints, only upon the edition of 1670 (No. 7, above).

Since then, (to take no further account of selections) there have been three editions aiming at and claiming completeness, including the poems in Latin. These are :

(1) *The Complete Works of Richard Crashaw, Canon of Loretto. Edited by William B. Turnbull, Esq. . . . London . . .* 1858.

In the preface to this volume it is stated that ' In preparing the present edition, the first that contains the whole of Crashaw's writings known, I have carefully examined and collated all the earlier ones '. It must be admitted, however, that there is no very great evidence of this process, and far too much reliance seems to be placed on the reprint of 1670 (No. 7, above). Turnbull's edition is of little value now that so many poems by Crashaw have been rescued from MSS., of which Turnbull takes no notice. It is also very careless. Many of the numerous misprints in the text are recorded with savage triumph by Grosart, though Grosart had much less ground for self-satisfaction than this action implied.

(2) *The Complete Works of Richard Crashaw. For the first time collected and collated with the original and early editions, and much enlarged . . . Edited by the Rev. Alexander B. Grosart . . . Printed for Private Circulation.* 1872.

The chief merits of this edition are its inclusion of a freshly compiled biography, with many new facts, and of numerous poems derived from MSS. and not printed before ; its use of MSS. to correct mistakes in the original texts, and its great advance upon previous reprints in bibliographical investigation and description. Grosart not only states but shows that he has seen all the original editions, and he succeeded in tracking down the poems which had been published before they were collected in 1646. Unfortunately, having secured his material he proceeded in his own edition to shuffle it confusingly together, arranging the poems in a way that makes it difficult to see at once from what original volumes they are taken ; and the text itself has but little consistency of plan, no effort being made to show the evolution of the poems existing in more than one form. Perhaps the limits of Grosart's want of judgement in this respect are reached where he cheerfully mixes the two versions of ' The Weeper ', incorporating in the revised version of 1648 and 1652 the stanzas which are peculiar to the text of 1646. The apparatus is very incomplete, and the volumes as a whole carry many marks of the carelessness and haste with which they must have been compiled. It was typical of Grosart that having discovered Add. MS. 33219, he hailed as ' hitherto unprinted and unknown ' two poems which he prints himself elsewhere in his own edition from the original printed texts.

It seems fair to say of this edition that it is as good and as bad as Grosart's editions were wont to be ; it did some useful work in its own time and still retains a little value. But it falls very far below the standards of conscientious modern editing.

(3) *Richard Crashaw Steps to the Temple Delights of the Muses and other Poems The text edited by A. R. Waller . . . Cambridge : at the University Press* 1904.

This edition, which has the great merit that it follows a consistent though hardly a perfect plan, and which considered as a mere reprint is more reliable than any of its predecessors, is yet marred by too many signs of hasty editing to be thoroughly serviceable. In the preface it is stated that ' The text of 1648 has been followed but only those poems have been printed which were not revised at a later date for the

volume entitled *Carmen Deo Nostro,* 1652 . . . The text of the
first edition . . . 1646, has been collated with that of 1648, and
both texts with that of *Carmen Deo Nostro,* and the verbal
alterations, omissions and additions in these three texts will
be found in the Appendix, this course being deemed more
satisfactory than to form an eclectic text by guesswork '.

Were it possible to be content with a single text of the more
extensively revised poems, there might be little to object to in
the method proposed here, provided : (1) that all the obvious
misprints in the original texts are corrected and no fresh ones
introduced ; (2) that the variants are not only recorded but
adopted where they are necessary to the sense ; and (3) that
the variants are recorded fully, clearly, and conveniently. In
all these respects, however, Waller's edition fails, sometimes
seriously—the absence of numbered lines, in particular, combined with the dismissal of the apparatus to the Appendix,
causing much difficulty. And then, as already maintained,
the static presentation of a changing text like Crashaw's cannot
be satisfactory. The different phases must be shown in their
proper order and contexts ; and any edition that merges in an
Appendix of critical notes a fine poem like the second version
of the appeal to the Countess of Denbigh (see p. 348, below)
can hardly be said to treat its material with fairness and
respect. The bibliographical note prefixed to this volume is
not adequate to the material.

LIST OF PRINCIPAL SIGLA USED IN FOOT-NOTES,
IN NUMERICAL AND ALPHABETICAL ORDER

34	= *Epigrammatum Sacrorum Liber* .	1634	(No. 1, p. xliii)
46	= *Steps to the Temple, &c.* . .	1646	(No. 2, p. xliv)
48	= *Steps to the Temple, &c.* . .	1648	(No. 3, p. xlvi)
52	= *Carmen Deo Nostro* . . .	1652	(No. 4, p. xlvii)
70	= *Steps to the Temple, &c., with Car-*		
	men Deo Nostro . . .	1670	(No. 7, p. lii)
70L	= *Richardi Crashawi Poemata et Epi-*		
	grammata	1670	(No. 6, p. xlix)
A1	= Brit. Mus. Add. MS. 18044		(No. 21, p. lxxx)
A2	= ,, ,, ,, 22118		(No. 15, p. lxxviii)
A226	= ,, ,, ,, 22603		(No. 18, p. lxxx)
A3	= ,, ,, ,, 33219		(No. 13, p. lxxiii)
A34	= ,, ,, ,, 34692		(No. 16, p. lxxviii)
A4	= ,, ,, ,, 40176		(No. 10, p. liv)
D	= Trinity College, Dublin, MS. F. 4. 28 (659)		(No. 11, p. lvii)
Dobell.	See No. 24, p. lxxxi.		
H	= Brit. Mus. MSS. Harleian 6917 and 6918		(No. 14, p. lxxvi)
R	= Bodleian MS. Rawl. poet. 142		(No. 19, p. lxxx)
R7	= ,, ,, ,, ,, 147		(No. 20, p. lxxx)
S	= Brit. Mus. MS. Sloane 1925		(No. 17, p. lxxix)
Stubbe.	See p. xliv.		
T	= Bodleian MSS. Tanner 465 and 466, *T5* and		
	T6 distinguishing the two MSS. where		
	necessary ; *T*A and *T*B distinguishing the		
	two copies of *Sospetto d'Herode* in *T6*		(No. 12, p. lviii)

The meanings of other abbreviations used here and there will be clear from their immediate contexts in the foot-notes.

III. THE CHRONOLOGICAL ORDER
OF CRASHAW'S POEMS

The order in which Crashaw's poems were written is a question that only admits of safe settlement in respect of those which can be referred to definite occasions, and these are a minority. But though to the rest no precise date can be assigned with any confidence there are considerations which justify the rough arrangement of many of them in groups corresponding to broadly definable stages in the poet's career and development ; and it may be helpful to set these considerations down.

First, however, it will be convenient to supply in chronological order a list of the poems which were composed for definite and identifiable occasions, or of which the publication separately from volumes devoted to Crashaw's works alone supplies a date that will serve as a *terminus ad quem*. The evidence for the dates assigned will be found in the foot-notes to the poems in question or in the Commentary. The poems attributed to Crashaw for the first time in this edition are marked with an asterisk.

Poems.	Dates.	Page nos. in present edn.
Upon Bishop Andrewes his Picture before his Sermons	Publ. 1631	163
Honoratiss° D° Rob° Heath . .	1631	376
An Epitaph. Upon Doctor Brooke . .	1631	175
In reū. Dr̄ē Brooke. Epitaphium .	1631	378
In obitum Rev. V. Dr̄ᶦˢ Mansell .	1631	379
Epitaphium in Dominum Herrisium .	1631	164
Upon the Death of Mr. Herrys .	1631	167
In Eundem Scazon . . .	1631	214
Upon the Death of the most desired Mr. Herrys	1631	168
Another	1631	170
His Epitaph	1631	172
In Natales Mariæ Principis .	1631	375
In faciem Augustiss. Regis à morbillis integram	Publ. 1632	190
On the Frontispiece of Isaacsons Chronologie explained (Or Thus) . .	Publ. 1633	191
Rex Redux	Publ. 1633	193
Ad Reginam	Publ. 1633	187
Upon the Duke of Yorke his Birth .	1633	176
In praise of Lessius his rule of health	Publ. 1634	156

Apart from these more certain assignments, the relative chronology of many poems may be gathered, in widely varying degrees of precision, from indications such as the following :

(1) A hint of date may sometimes be taken from a MS. intimation. Thus if at the head or the foot of a poem Crashaw is described as of ' Aul. Penb.' or of ' Coll. Petren.' there is some reason to suppose that the poem was written during his attachment to the society mentioned. Or again, when in MS. Tanner 466 the date ' Nov. 25 1637 ' is placed prominently on the title-page to the translation from ' Sospetto d'Herode ' it seems likely that the date is taken from the original MS. and refers to the time of composition rather than to that of transcription.

(2) The subjects of Crashaw's poems sometimes afford a suggestion of chronology even though assignment to a particular year can hardly seem justified. Thus the poems on ' the King's Coronation ' are, from their subject, scarcely likely to have been written in the first instance much later than February 1626 ; but though precocity such as this would imply was not unparalleled in the seventeenth century it must also be allowed that these poems may have been written, possibly as school exercises, some time after the event which they celebrate and that they may even have been revised before they were distributed or lent at Cambridge. In juxtaposition

with these two poems in the MS. occur the three poems ' On
yᵉ Gunpowder-Treason ', which for other reasons, to be indicated below, are also likely to have been written first at a very
early date. Several of the secular Latin poems and of the
Latin epigrams might also well have been written as school
exercises (see p. xx, above).

Again it is to be expected that religious or devotional subjects would tend to exclude secular ones after 1635, when
Crashaw left Pembroke College to take up his connexion with
Peterhouse and its chapel. It is to be noted that in the list
given above of the more confidently datable poems only four
are later than 1635, and that of these all are formal congratu-
latory addresses to the queen, and the last and longest an
amplification of material almost certainly initiated as early as
1633; and it seems fair to assume that this diminution is due
to the claims of other occupations and interests, which if they
left him leisure for writing at all would naturally lead him to
write ' divine ' poetry rather than poetry of any other kind.
It is worth remember ng, too, with regard to poetry on amatory
subjects, that the acceptance of a Fellowship meant the
acceptance also of celibacy during its tenure, so that even the
' not impossible she ' of a famous poem which for other reasons
seems likely to have been written before 1635 might tend to
fall outside the range of poetical subjects after that date.

(3) The MS. selections from Crashaw's works often contain
a large percentage of occasional poems which are assignable
only to very early dates. And where there is reason to suppose
that the MS., or the relevant part of it, was copied all at one
time, it seems fair to surmise, so long as it is not concluded,
that the poems not so datable in the same series are also of
early composition. Evidence of this kind may at least have
a good deal of confirmatory weight, and it was partly on
account of this that it seemed worth while to give a list of the
poems occurring in each MS. For example, reference to p.
lxxvii, above, will show that in MS. Harleian 6917 two of the six
poems known to be by Crashaw belong to the year 1631. If
the Epithalamium occurring in the same MS. is his, the latest
date assignable to any poem in the series is still, apparently,
only 1635, and the poems which cannot be dated may well be
contemporaneous or earlier. Similarly, the range of assignable

dates in Add. MS. 22118 is 1631–5 and the MS. also contains two of the poems given in MS. Harleian 6917, so that confirmatory evidence is available, for these at least, that they belong to the same period. But the most useful MS. in this connexion is Add. MS. 33219. It seems to be an anthology, compiled for a lady, of Crashaw's best work in English up to date, whatever the date was, and it was evidently all copied out at one time. The occasional verse which it contains ranges from 1631 to 1634, the panegyric poem beginning ' Britain ! the mighty Oceans lovely bride ! ' (see p. 176, below) showing clearly by the omission in the MS. of the relevant lines that ' the Lady Elizabeth ' was not yet born when the poem was written in that form. Add. MS. 33219 also contains all the English poems in MS. Harleian 6917 (except the Epithalamium) and in Add. MS. 22118, and in so far as 1634 may be regarded as a date-limit for the composition of all the poems occurring here—and on the whole the inference seems fairly just—a *terminus ad quem* is found for many of Crashaw's best-known pieces first published in 1646, including ' The Weeper ', ' Musicks Duell ', ' Wishes. To his (supposed) Mistresse ', and the ' divine' epigrams. It will be noticed that no poem in this MS. gives evidence that any very pronounced High Anglican or Roman doctrines had been accepted ; and indeed, apart from the ' Assumption ' poem contained in MSS. Tanner 465 and Add. MS. 34692 (where it is followed by the designation ' Rob: Crashaw: A: Pet: Artib: Magister:') poems of such doctrinal import are not found in MS. form except in Add. MS. 18044, where they seem to be derived from the volume published in 1652.

(4) The argument from the internal evidence of style and literary influence is perhaps the most hazardous of all, but here again confirmatory evidence is sometimes supplied. Thus the assignment of an early date to the English epigrams seems to be supported by their occasional reflection of the works of William Crashaw [1] (see the notes to the Epigrams, pp. 434–5, below) ; and the same influence seems to be discernible not only in the style but in the religious bias of the third poem on

---

[1] The fact, however, that with only three exceptions there are Latin versions by Crashaw of all the English epigrams, while the Latin epigrams are much more numerous, suggests that the latter were written first.

the ' Gunpowder-Treason ' (see p. 387, below—' his Holinesse
a feast Hath now præpar'd '), and the theory that the Gunpowder-Treason poems are more or less contemporaneous
with those on the king's coronation thus receives some partial
confirmation.   The notes to the version of Psalm xxiii
(p. 435, below) will suggest that the example of William
Crashaw was not forgotten when it was written, and the
simplicity of the style lends support to the supposition of an
early date.

If the argument from the contents of Add. MS. 33219 has
any value it would appear that the Italian influence comes in
early, since that MS. contains the short translations from Ceba
and Marino (see pp. 188 and 190, below), and ' The Weeper ', in
which Marino's influence may be traced ; and the same influence may also be looked for elsewhere among comparatively
early poems, as, if the date in the MS. version of the translation
from ' Sospetto d' Herode ' is to be trusted, Crashaw was still
interested in Marino in 1637.   This is of course precarious
evidence, and so is the occurrence of echoes from Crashaw in
the verse of Joseph Beaumont (or vice versa) ; but this perhaps mutual influence of the two English poets would be most
likely to affect works written during the association of Crashaw and Beaumont as contemporary Fellows of Peterhouse.
The works of St. Teresa, with their atmosphere of rapturous
devotion, seem to have come in Crashaw's way somewhat
later than the Italian influence.   His friend and colleague
Joseph Beaumont, in a Latin oration delivered at Cambridge
in 1638, speaks of St. Teresa with great enthusiasm but indicates
that her writings had not hitherto been well known there—
' nomen vobis inauditum, credo ' (Warren, *Richard Crashaw*, p.
44) ; and ' The Flaming Heart ', with its title probably borrowed
from that of St. Teresa's autobiography as translated into
English and published in 1642, did not appear until the second
edition of *Steps to the Temple* (1648).

The poems which were added to *Steps to the Temple* in 1648
show that, apart from the continued preoccupation with
' divine ' subjects and the continued and perhaps increased
fostering of an exalted religious sense, Crashaw's style was now
developing away from the clearly apprehended imagery and
precise metrical forms of his earliest poetry towards a freer

verse and more complex metaphorical utterance, in which
the images, as in Shakespeare's later style, seem to follow
each other in quicker succession, without always being clearly
conceived or fully exploited ; and these are criteria which
again may be used as confirmatory tests in determining the
period of any poem (such as that ' On the Assumption ') which
was published in the volume of 1646 but which it seems reasonable, on other grounds, to assign to a later date than the
majority of the poems in that volume.

It seems hardly worth space to embark upon a detailed
chronological list in which so much would needs be conjectural ;
but if account be taken of all the considerations advanced
above there would seem to be some semblance of authority for
the following loose and hypothetical grouping, which together
with the safer list already given may serve at least as a basis for
future and more precise estimates.

Periods.	*Groups.*
Up to 1630.	Poems on the Gunpowder-Treason and the King's Coronation. Some of the Latin and English epigrams. Translations of Psalms xxiii and cxxxvii.
Up to 1635.	Latin epigrams published in 1634. Some of the Latin secular poems comprised in the editions of 1646 and 1648. All the English poems in Add. MS. 33219.
1637.	' Sospetto d' Herode.'
1635–45.	Latin poems on Peterhouse and its chapel. ' In the Glorious Assumption.' ' Lo here a little volume.' Teresa poems.
1645–8	Most of the additions in English in the volume of 1648.
1647–9	Those additions to the ' divine ' poems which appear for the first time in *Carmen Deo Nostro* (1652), and the amplified version of the introductory poem in that volume published separately in (?) 1653 (see p. xlix above, No. 5).

IV. ADDITIONAL NOTES

Page xliii, l. 3. *poems printed singly*. These, as a rule, were collected
and reprinted in Crashaw's own volumes; but possibly there is an
exception in *Justa Edovardo King naufrago*, Cambridge, 1638, wherein,
as observed by Miss Ruth C. Wallerstein in her *Richard Crashaw, A
Study in Style and Poetic Development* (Madison, 1935), p. 26, the Latin
verses on pp. 23–4 signed ' R.C.' may well be by Crashaw.

Pages xlvi–xlvii. On the relations between the texts of 1646 and 1648
see an article by J. C. Maxwell in *Philological Quarterly*, April, 1950,
pp. 216–20.

Page 38, l. 24. *Nympha pudica, &c.* A. Warren (*Richard Crashaw*,
p. 226) cites an epigram by Benlowes on the miracle at Cana in that
writer's *Sphinx Theologica*, p. 51, beginning 'Candida Lympha fuit,
sed et illa rubescere coepit'. The date of Benlowes's work was 1636, not

1626 as sometimes given. See Harold Jenkins, *Edward Benlowes*, 1952, pp. 127–8 (footnote). So Crashaw's epigram may have been written first.

Page 126. *On a prayer booke.* A. F. Allison in *R.E.S.* xxiii, 1947, pp. 34–42, suggests that this poem is influenced by St. Teresa's *El Castillo Interior* and also by George Herbert and Thomas Carew; and that the influence of *El Castillo Interior* can be found again in the three poems on St. Teresa and in 'A Song of Divine Love' (p. 327).

Page 131. *In memory of the . . . Lady Madre de Teresa.* A manuscript of this poem with 'An Apologie' (p. 136) was acquired by the Pierpont Morgan Library, New York, in 1951 and was described by me in *T.L.S.*, 18 April 1952, p. 272. The manuscript is attached to a copy of *Las Obras de la S. Madre Teresa de Iesus . . . Primera parte que contiene su Vida* (Antwerp, 1630); and its most important feature is the lengthy title, which has several differences from that given in *52*, including the addition of nine concluding lines; this title is in a deliberately formal handwriting which is very probably Crashaw's own. See plate facing p. 315 and specimens of Crashaw's hand on p. lvi and facing pp. xxx and xxxi. The alterations made at ll. 104, 130–1, and 145 are apparently in the same hand. The text of the poem and of 'An Apologie' is in a different hand from that of the alterations. Some of the unaltered readings (see notes below on ll. 1, 5, 20, 80, 104, 130, 145, and 156) are not found in any of the printed versions and may represent an earlier stage of composition; but many of the unaltered readings are found again in *48* and *52*. The variants from the text of *46* (not including all those of punctuation) are as follows: 1 absolute.   5 Men ripe of growth,   8 into   9 Name. To   11 great: 15 has . . . ye name   18 spent, 20 Love with Death   25 has   37 dares   39 reason;   48 diadem.   49 She'l offer   50 (With Christ's Name in't)   53 For him 80 sacred breath.   91 lov'd. And   93 The fair'st, & firstborn   94 Seraphim   104 that she   104 still may die *erased*: thus may neuer leaue to dy *substituted (the reading of 48 and 52)*   120 tell. Suffice 130 she(?) *erased*: Reueal'd LIFE *substituted*   131 her *erased*: his *substituted*   happy *inserted over a caret between* thy *and* lipps   134 joys   136 Those . . . heavn *bracketed*   145(?) Shall inclose thy radiant brows. *erased heavily and replaced by printed reading*   147 sit   153 that late   156 rare lines   177 them to (*omitting* first) 179 shalt   180 setts

There are also four marginal notes, probably in the same hand as that of the alterations. Three (against ll. 47, 94, and 198) refer the reader to St. Teresa's autobiography (chaps. i, xxix, and xx), and one (against l. 173) to the Life by Ribera.

A photograph of the manuscript has been placed in the University Library, Liverpool.

Page 136. *An Apologie for the precedent Hymne.* See note to p. 322 on the altered title in *52*. In the manuscript described above the Apology is separated from the Hymn by a space, but has no heading. There are the following variants from the text of 1646: 12 heer ly   16 a blood   26 own *erased*: warm *substituted in the hand responsible for the alterations in the Hymn*   21 soe're   28 scorn the dust   35 soule. Some   39 Where dwells (*reading not in printed texts*)   41 youth, life   42 mixtures (*reading not in printed texts*)

Page 190. *Out of the Italian (second poem).* The original was unknown until Professor M. Praz found it in Alfredo Obertello's *Madrigali italiani in Inghilterra*, 1949, p. 105. See *T.L.S.*, 21 Oct., 1949, p. 681. The poem is by Valerio Marcellini and was set to music by Luca Marenzio (*Il quarto libro de' madrigali a cinque voci*, Venice, 1584, no. xviii). The text is as follows:

Sapete, amanti, perché ignudo sia,
Perché fanciullo, e perché cieco Amore ?
Perché mentre l'angelica armonia
Della mia bella donna intento udia,
Per gran dolcezza uscito di sé fuore
Perdé la veste, il senno, gl'occh' e 'l core.

Page 216. *Bulla.* Cf. Erasmus, *Adagia*, II. iii. 48: 'Homo bulla. Proverbium hoc admonet, humana vita nihil esse fragilius, nihil fugacius, nihil inanius. Est enim bulla tumor ille inanis, qui visitur in aquis momento temporis enascens simul et evanescens. . . .'

Page 236. *Non vi*, l. 3. *'Tis loue alone, &c.* The letters which can be read on the key in the engraving include A M O and R.

Page 236. *To the . . . Countesse of Denbigh, &c.* The step which Crashaw recommends was taken in 1651. See E. E. Phare, 'The Conversion of Crashaw's Countess of Denbigh', *Cambridge Rev.*, 2 Dec. 1932, pp. 147–9.

Page 283. *Sancta Maria Dolorum.* With passages in this and other poems ('An Apologie' and 'The Flaming Heart') A. F. Allison, in *R.E.S.*, xxiv, 1948, pp. 295–302, compares passages in *Le Traité de l'Amour de Dieu*, 1616, by St. François de Sales (translated by Crashaw's friend, Thomas Car, 1630. See note to p. 235, l. 16).

Page 322. Heading] *as hauing been writt when the author was yet among the protestantes.* As observed by Professor A. Warren in *T.L.S.*, 16 Nov. 1935, p. 746, this addition to the original title is misleading and may be the work of Crashaw's editor, Thomas Car. There is no reference in the poem to Crashaw's former protestantism. He first apologizes to St. Teresa for praising her in his 'weak and worthlesse song', and then, in a plea for international Christian charity, justifies himself to his own countrymen for praising St. Teresa even though she was a Spaniard.

Page 326, l. 95. *eagle . . . doue.* Cf. the eagle–dove imagery in St. Teresa's autobiography, end of ch. xx (transl. *The Flaming Hart*, 1642, p. 274): 'she is not yet, become so true an Eaglet, of this swift, and strong Eagle, which bred her, as that she can be able to looke earnestly vpon this Sunne . . . but when she lookes in, vpon her self, her eyes are stopped vp, with clay; and so this poore Doue, is blind. . . .' Cf. also Donne, 'The Canonization', l. 22: 'And wee in us finde the Eagle and the Doue.'

Page 327. *A Song.* This poem occurs in Bodl. MS. Don. c. 57, f. 35ᵛ, with the following variants: 2 see thy   8 may still   10 to be still so   13–14:

O welcome high & Heavenly art
of life & death in one poore heart

Page 393. *Upon the death of a freind.* See pp. lxv and lxxiii.

Page 399, ll. 52–4. *The Water blush'd, &c.* Cf. p. 38, Epigram 4. Grotius has:

Undae liquentis ebrios potus bibit
Galilaea pubes.

Page 399, l. 55. *gate.* Gat, obtained.

Page 407, ll. 74–6. *faint denyings, &c.* Perhaps a reminiscence of Beaumont and Fletcher's *The Maydes Tragedy*, I. i. 247–8;

Stay, and confound her teares and her shrill cryings;
Her weake denials, vows, and often dyings.

EPIGRAMMATUM

SACRORUM LIBER

Amplissimi et ornatissimi nominis viro,
Custodi nostro dignissimo,
custodiam cælestem.[1]

TUUM ecce (vir amplissime) sacratissimum nomen aperire
sibi ausus est libellus iste ; in lucem suam magìs an in
vmbram nescio. neque vero habet quo se excuset nisi id quod
& ipsum excusatione indiget ; nimirum non tam esse audacis
Musæ robustam fiduciam, quàm teneræ adhuc & infantis pænè
lasciuientem proterviam quæ illam sub oculos tuos ac si in
quoddam augustissimi secreti adytum simplici quidem æstu
officiosi amoris ludentem quasi & exultantem impulit. Et
satis hinc habebit profectò, vnde se istius saltem laudis nomine
commendare posteritati possit ; quòd simplicis utcunque, 10
rudis, & implumis, legitimæ tamen nec degeneri indole exsur-
gentis infantiæ argumenta dederit ; ex eo nimirum quòd
rectà adeò se recipere norit ad Apollinem suum. Quidni verò
liceat et mihi, cum hoc fætu meo qualicunque, venire in
partem publici illius & auspicatissimi radii, quo intimè pene-
tras in omnem hujus familiæ tuæ angulum ; qui quidem nullus
est tam obscurus suâque nocte ignobilis, quin suum te sentiat
& fateatur Phæbum. O interim beatos nos (juvat enim
fælicitate nostrâ ad jactantiam etiam frui. juvat orbis invidiæ
tantisper indulgere) ô nos beatos ! qui proprium audemus & 20
nostrum dicere suaue illud sed & verendum sydus oris tui te
plenissimi & virtutum tuarum (quarum tamen luci vmbram
modestiæ offundens, minùs fervido quidem sed dulci multo
magis radio nobis eas dispensat, et in tantum nostris quasi
parcit oculis) sydus inquam illud cujus ab auspicijs nostræ
influxu nunquam non pacatissimo temperantur dies, nec nisi
serenos experiuntur & Apollineos soles. Nos verò tantæ &
tam audacis felicitatis nobis conscij, non possumus profectò
nostra non timere gaudia. sed et ipse jampridem indignatur
orbis, communisque rerum publicarum status queritur sub 30
angustijs privatæ virtutis castigari ingentem tuum Genium ;
neque vero patiens esset tam diu te sibi deberi fastigioque te
jamdudum expectanti, nisi numen ipsi Joui tam prudentiâ
quam potentiâ proximum, viam tibi in hoc strauisset modò,
teque in sphæra tui capaciore explicare jam nunc cæpisset ;
vnde tandem te tuarum virtutum splendor (reluctante tuâ

10 commendare] commendre *A 4* (*letter missing through wear of MS.
at edge*)   33 ipsi] ipso *A 4*

[1] The autograph dedication prefixed to Crashaw's *Epigrammatum
Sacrorum Liber* in Brit. Mus. Add. MS. 40176 and printed for the first
time in 1927 ; see p. lvi above.

quantumcunque modestiâ) elevabit te in apicem meritis tuis
tam minorem, quam majorem votis (—nec vanus vatem me
finxit Apollo.) Enimverò hoc ipsum cuj non spondebat omen
illud divinitùs indultum, quod te a domesticorum sacrorum 40
curâ ad aras majores transtulit ? Placeant sibi suarum
sordium pulchritudine, pij nimirum isti & religiosi homines,
quo nescio quam sacrorum illuviem amant, ipsosque (proh
pudor !) cælites, & sacro-sanctos numinis ritus deducere in consortium squalloris sui (barbari homines) non erubescunt :
pergant credere se ad illas aras litare posse, quarum & ipsi
quidem vota dedignantur exaudire ; orantium scilicet, & quasi
supplices manus (frustra) tendentium, velint a se horrorem
illum abstergere, vultusque elegantes, lucidos, augustos, suos
demum sibi reddere. apud nos interim sub tuis (vir sanctissime) 50
auspicijs amæniori facie Religio se spectandam indulget. comit
se pulcherrima dea ; suosque jam ornatiore curâ distinguens
radios, majestatem suam venustate etiam commendari quærit.
nimirum ad oris tui exemplum, vbi severitatis reverentiam
ita demulcet amænitas, vt pulcherrimo demonstret argumento,
quàm bene possit amabile quid esse, & sanctum simul. ecce
autem dum suum sacris sedibus nitorem restituis, dum in
rebus divinis ornandis totus es ; splendorem quem sacris suis
attulisti modò, gratum numen in te refudit ; et æquissimâ
vice quasi repercussis in te tuis honoribus, redijsti ab aris tuis 60
ipse excultus donarijs. adeò res auctas nostri sacelli sacrarium
rependit regium ; et qui illud ornasti benignissimè, ab altero
justissimè exornaris invicem. Sed tuam nolo vltrà onerare
modestiam, nec etiam Epistolæ meæ : cui jampridem pudo-
rem feci, dum has laudum tuarum partes ei viderer velle
assignari, quæ quidem provocare possint anhelum Panegyrico
spiritu oratorem, et etiam obruere. Augeat te sibi Deus
optimus maximus diuque te (vir egregie) nobis nostræque, tibi
verò tuæque felicitati æternum servet. tu interim hoc qualicunque murmure infantis Musæ patere tibi demulceri non 70
quidem censorias, sed paternas aures. eumque quem prono
semper sydere tantillo mihi indulsisti radium, ornare porrò et
fouere digneris.

Tuorum minimorum minimus

Ri: Crashaw.

---

46 posse,] *the comma after* ' posse' *is perhaps a semicolon*　54 ex-
emplum] exemlum *A 4*　50 sanctissime)] *there is a comma after this*
word which the bracket perhaps deletes.　68 *the brackets seem to delete*
commas　72 indulsisti] indulsi *A 4*

EPIGRAM-
MATUM
SACRORUM
LIBER.

CANTABRIGIÆ,
Ex Academiæ celeberrimæ
typographeo. 1634.

REVERENDO ADMODUM
VIRO
BENJAMINO LANY
SS. Theologiæ Professori,

Aulæ Pembrochianæ Custodi dignissimo,

ex suorum minimis

minimus

R. C.

custodiam cœlestem

P.

SUus est & florum fructus; quibus fruimur, si non utiliùs, delicatiùs certé. Neque etiam rarum est quòd ad spem veris, de se per flores suos quasi pollicentis, adultioris anni, ipsiúsque adeò Autumni exigamus fidem. Ignoscas igitur (vir colendissime) properanti sub ora Apollinis sui, primǽque adolescentiæ lasciviâ exultanti Musæ. Teneræ ætatis flores adfert, non fructus seræ : quos quidem exigere ad seram illam & sobriam maturitatem, quam in fructibus expectamus meritò, durum fuerit ; forsan & ipsâ hac præcoci importunitate suâ placituros magís : Tibi præsertim quem paternus animus 10 (quod fieri solet) intentum tenet omni suæ spei diluculo, quò tibi de tuorum indole promittas aliquid. Ex more etiam eorum, qui in præmium laboris sui pretiúmque patientiæ festini, ex iis quæ severunt ipsi & excoluerunt, quicquid est flosculi prominulum, primâ quasi verecundiâ auras & apertum Jovem experientis arripiunt avidè, saporémque illi non tam ex ipsius indole & ingenio quàm ex animi sui affectu, foventis in eo curas suas & spes, affingunt. Patere igitur (reverende Custos) hanc tibi ex istiusmodi floribus corollam necti ; convivalem veró : nec aliter passuram Sydus illud oris tui 20 auspicatissimum nisi (quâ est etiam amœnitate) remissiore

(Heading) R. C.] R. CRASHAW *70L*

radio cùm se reclinat, & in tantum de se demit. Neque sanè
hoc scriptionis genere (modò partes suas satìs præstiterit) quid
esse potuit otio Theologico accommodatius, quo nimirum res
ipsa Theologica Poëticâ amœnitate delinita majestatem suam
venustate commendat. Hoc demum quicquid est, amare
tamen poteris ; & voles, scio : non ut magnum quid, non ut
egregium, non ut te dignum denique, sed ut tuum : tuum
summo jure ; utpote quod è tua gleba, per tuum radium, in
manum denique tuam evocatum fuerit. Quod restat hujus 30
libelli fatis, exorandus es igitur (vir spectatissime) ut quem
sinu tam facili privatum excepisti, eum jam ore magìs publico
alloquentem te non asperneris. Stes illi in limine, non
auspicium modò suum, sed & argumentum. Enimvero
Epigramma sacrum tuus ille vultus vel est, vel quid sit docet ;
ubi nimirum amabili diluitur severum, & sanctum suavi
demulcetur. Pronum me vides in negatam mihi provinciam ;
laudum tuarum, intelligo : quas mihi cùm modestia tua
abstulerit, reliquum mihi est necessariò ut sim brevis : imò
verò longus nimiúm ; utpote cui argumentum istud abscissum 40
fuerit, in quo unicè poteram, & sine tædio, prolixus esse. Vale,
virorum ornatissime, neque dedigneris quòd colere audeam
Genii tui serenitatem supplex tam tenuis, & (quoniam numen
quoque hoc de se non negat) amare etiam. Interim verò da
veniam Musæ in tantum sibi non temperanti, quin in hanc
saltem laudis tuæ partem, quæ tibi ex rebus sacris apud nos
ornatis meritissima est, istiusmodi carmine involare ausa sit,
qualicunque,

S *Alve, alme custos Pierii gregis :*
    Per quem erudito exhalat in otio ;
     Seu frigus udi captet antri, 50
      Sive Jovem nitidósque soles.

Non ipse custos pulchrior invias
    Egit sub umbras Æmonios greges ;
     Non ipse Apollo notus illis
      Lege suæ meliore cannæ.

Tu si sereno des oculo frui ;
    Sunt rura nobis, sunt juga, sunt aquæ,
     Sunt plectra dulcium sororum ;
      (Non alio mihi nota Phœbo) 60

30 evocatum] evocata 34 *corrected in ink to* evocatū *in three copies
seen.* 60 *There should perhaps be a stop after Phœbo) as ' nota '
refers to ' plectra ' in l. 59 and a new sentence follows.*

*Crashaw's
own view
of ornamentation
see White
pp 230–1*

Te dante, castos composuit sinus ;
Te dante, mores sumpsit ; & in suo
    Videnda vultu, pulverémque
        Relligio cinerémque nescit.

Stat cincta dignâ fronde decens caput :
Suósque per te fassa palàm Deos,
    Comísque, Diva, vestibúsque
        Ingenium dedit ordinémque.

Jámque ecce nobis amplior es modò
Majórque cerni.   Quale jubar tremit   70
    Sub os ! verecundúsque quantâ
        Mole sui Genius laborat !

Jam qui serenas it tibi per genas,
Majore cœlo Sydus habet suum ;
    Majórque circum cuspidatæ
        Ora comit tua flos diei.

Stat causa.   Nempe hanc ipse Deus, Deus,
Hanc ara, per te pulchra, diem tibi
    Tuam refundit, obvióque
        It radio tibi se colenti.   80

Ecce, ecce ! sacro in limine, dum pio
Multúmque prono poplite amas humum,
    Altaria annuunt ab alto ;
        Et refluis tibi plaudit alis

Pulchro incalescens officio, puer
Quicunque crispo sydere crinium,
    Vultúque non fatente terram,
        Currit ibi roseus satelles.

Et jure.   Nam cùm fana tot inviis
Mœrent ruinis, ipsáque (ceu preces   90
    Manúsque, non decora supplex,
        Tendat) opem rogat, heu negatam !

Tibi ipsa voti est ara sui rea.
Et solvet.   O quàm semper apud Deum
    Litabis illum, cujus aræ
        Ipse preces priùs audiisti !

Venerabili viro Magistro *Tournay*,

Tutori suo summè observando.

MEssis inauravit Cereri jam quarta capillos,
   Vitis habet Bacchum quarta corona suæ,
Nostra ex quo, primis plumæ vix alba pruinis,
   Ausa tuo Musa est nidificare sinu.
Hîc nemus, hîc soles, & cœlum mitius illi :
   Hîc sua quod Musis umbra vel aura dedit.
Sedit ibi secura malus quid moverit Auster,
   Quæ gravis hybernum vexerit ala Jovem.
Nescio quo interea multùm tibi murmure nota est :
   Nempe sed hoc poteras murmur amare tamen.   10
Tandem ecce (heu simili de prole puerpera) tandem
   Hôc tenero tenera est pignore facta parens.
Jámque meam hanc sobolem (rogo) quis sinus alter haberet ?
   Quis mihi tam noti nempe teporis erat ?
Sed quoque & ipsa Meus (de te) meus, improba, tutor
   (Quàm primùm potuit dicere) dixit, erit.
Has ego legitimæ, nec lævo sydere natæ
   Non puto degeneres indolis esse notas ;
Nempe quòd illa suo patri tam semper apertos,
   Tam semper faciles nôrit adire sinus.   20
Ergò tuam tibi sume : tuas eat illa sub alas :
   Hoc quoque de nostro, quod tuearis, habe.
Sic quæ Suada tuo fontem sibi fecit in ore,
   Sancto & securo melle perennis eat.
Sic tua, sic nullas Siren non mulceat aures,
   Aula cui plausus & sua serta dedit.
Sic tuus ille (precor) Tagus aut eat objice nullo,
   Aut omni (quod adhuc) objice major eat.

Ornatissimo viro Præceptori suo colen-

dissimo, Magistro *Brook.*

O *Mihi qui nunquam nomen non dulce fuisti*
   Tunc quoque cùm domini fronte timendus eras !
Ille ego pars vestri quondam intactissima regni,
   De nullo virgæ nota labore tuæ,
Do tibi quod de te per secula longa queretur
   Quòd de me nimiùm non metuendus eras :
Quòd tibi turpis ego torpentis inertia sceptri
   Tam ferulæ tulerim mitia jura tuæ.
Scilicet in foliis quicquid peccabitur istis,
   Quod tua virga statim vapulet, illud erit.   10
Ergò tibi hæc pœnas pro me mea pagina pendat.
   Hîc agitur virgæ res tibi multa tuæ.
In me igitur quicquid nimis illa pepercerit olim,
   Id licet in fœtu vindicet omne meo.
Hîc tuus inveniet satìs in quo sæviat unguis,
   Quódque veru docto trans obeliscus eat.
Scilicet hæc mea sunt ; hæc quæ mala scilicet : ô si
   (Quæ tua nempe forent) hîc meliora forent !
Qualiacunque, suum nôrunt hæc flumina fontem.
   (Nilus ab ignoto fonte superbus eat)   20
Nec certè nihil est quâ quis sit origine.   Fontes
   Esse solent fluvii nomen honórque sui.
Hic quoque tam parvus (de me mea secula dicant)
   Non parvi soboles hic quoque fontis erat.
Hoc modò & ipse velis de me dixisse, Meorum
   Ille fuit minimus.   Sed fuit ille meus.

LECTORI.

Salve. Jámque vale. Quid enim quis pergeret ultrá ?
Quà jocus & lusus non vocat, ire voles ?
Scilicet hîc, Lector, cur noster habebere, non est ;
Delitiis folio non faciente tuis.
Nam nec Acidalios halat mihi pagina rores ;
Nostra Cupidineæ nec favet aura faci.
Frustra hinc ille suis quicquam promiserit alis :
Frustra hinc illa novo speret abire sinu.
Ille è materna meliùs sibi talia myrto ;
Illa jugis meliùs poscat ab Idaliis.   10
Quærat ibi suus in quo cespite surgat Adonis,
Quæ melior teneris patria sit violis.
Illinc totius Floræ, verísque, suíque
Consilio, ille alas impleat, illa sinus.
Me mea (casta tamen, si sit rudis) herba coronet :
Me mea (si rudis est, sit rudis) herba juvat.
Nulla meo Circæa tument tibi pocula versu :
Dulcia, & in furias officiosa tuas.
Nulla latet Lethe, quam fraus tibi florea libat,
Quam rosa sub falsis dat malè fida genis.   20
Nulla verecundum mentitur mella venenum :
Captat ab insidiis linea nulla suis.
Et spleni, & jecori foliis bene parcitur istis.
Ah malè cum rebus staret utrumque meis.
Rara est quæ ridet ; nulla est quæ pagina prurit :
Nulla salax, si quid nôrit habere salis.
Non nudæ Veneres : nec, si jocus, udus habetur :
Non nimiùm Bacchus noster Apollo fuit.
Nil cui quis putri sit detorquendus ocello ;
Est nihil obliquo quod velit ore legi.   30
Hæc coràm, atque oculis legeret Lucretia justis :
Iret & illæsis hinc pudor ipse genis.
Nam neque candidior voti venit aura pudici
De matutina virgine thura ferens :
Cùm vestis nive vincta sinus, nive tempora fulgens,
Dans nive flammeolis frigida jura comis,
Relligiosa pedum sensim vestigia librans,
Ante aras tandem constitit ; & tremuit.
Nec gravis ipsa suo sub numine castior halat
Quæ pia non puras summovet ara manus.   40

Tam Venus in nostro non est nimis aurea versu :
　Tam non sunt pueri tela timenda dei.
Sæpe puer dubias circum me moverat alas ;
　Jecit & incertas nostra sub ora faces.
Sæpe vel ipse sua calamum mihi blandus ab ala,
　Vel matris cygno de meliore dedit.
Sæpe Dionææ pactus mihi serta coronæ ;
　Sæpe, Meus vates tu, mihi dixit, eris.
I procul, i cum matre tua, puer improbe, dixi :
　Non tibi cum numeris res erit ulla meis.　　　　　50
Tu Veronensi cum passere pulchrior ibis :
　Bilbilicisve queas comptiùs esse modis.
Ille tuos finget quocunque sub agmine crines :
　Undique nequitiis par erit ille tuis.
Ille nimis (dixi) patet in tua prælia campus :
　Heu nimis est vates & nimis ille tuus.
Gleba illa (ah tua quam tamen urit adultera messis)
　Esset Idumæo germine quanta parens !
Quantus ibi & quantæ premeret Puer ubera Matris !
　Nec cœlos vultu dissimulante suos.　　　　　60
Ejus in isto oculi satìs essent sydera versu ;
　Sydereo matris quàm bene tuta sinu !
Matris ut hic similes in collum mitteret ulnas,
　Inque, sinus niveos pergeret, ore pari !
Utque genis pueri hæc æquis daret oscula labris !
　Et bene cognatis iret in ora rosis !
Quæ Mariæ tam larga meat, quàm disceret illîc
　Uvida sub pretio gemma tumere suo !
Staret ibi ante suum lacrymatrix Diva Magistrum :
　Seu levis aura volet, seu gravis unda cadat ;　　　70
Luminis hæc soboles, & proles pyxidis illa,
　Pulchriùs unda cadat, suaviùs aura volet.
Quicquid in his sordet demum, luceret in illis.
　Improbe, nec satìs est hunc tamen esse tuum ?
Improbe cede puer : quid enim mea carmina mulces ?
　Carmina de jaculis muta futura tuis.
Cede puer, quà te petulantis fræna puellæ ;
　Turpia quà revocant pensa procacis heræ ;
Quà miseri malè pulchra nitent mendacia limi ;
　Quà cerussatæ, furta decora, genæ ;　　　　　80
Quà mirere rosas, alieni sydera veris ;
　Quas nivis haud propriæ bruma redempta domat.

Cede puer (dixi, & dico) cede improba mater :
Altera Cypris habet nos ; habet alter Amor.
Scilicet hîc Amor est. Hîc est quoque mater Amoris.
Sed mater virgo. Sed neque cæcus Amor.
O puer ! ô Domine ! ô magnæ reverentia matris !
Alme tui stupor & relligio gremii !
O Amor, innocuæ cui sunt pia jura pharetræ ;
Nec nisi de casto corde sagitta calens ! 90
Me, puer, ô certâ, quem figis, fige sagittâ.
O tua de me sit facta pharetra levis.
Quódque illinc sitit & bibit, & bibit & sitit usqué ;
Usquè meum sitiat pectus, & usquè bibat.
Fige, puer, corda hæc. Seu spinis exiguus quis,
Seu clavi aut hastæ cuspide magnus ades ;
Seu major cruce cum totâ ; seu maximus ipso
Te corda hæc figis denique. Fige puer.
O metam hanc tuus æternum inclamaverit arcus :
Stridat in hanc teli densior aura tui. 100
O tibi si jaculum ferat ala ferocior ullum,
Hanc habeat triti vulneris ire viam.
Quique tuæ populus cunque est, quæ turba, pharetræ ;
Hic bene vulnificas nidus habebit aves.
O mihi sis bello semper tam sævus in isto !
Pectus in hoc nunquam mitior hostis eas.
Quippe ego quàm jaceam pugnâ bene sparsus in illâ !
Quàm bene sic lacero pectore sanus ero !
Hæc mea vota. Mei sunt hæc quoque vota libelli.
Hæc tua sint Lector ; si meus esse voles. 110
Si meus esse voles ; meus ut sis, lumina (Lector)
Casta, sed ô nimiùm non tibi sicca precor.
Nam tibi fac madidis meus ille occurrerit alis,
(Sanguine, seu lacrymâ diffluat ille suâ :)
Stipite totus hians, clavísque reclusus & hastâ :
Fons tuus in fluvios desidiosus erit ?
Si tibi sanguineo meus hic tener iverit amne,
Túne tuas illi, dure, negabis aquas ?
Ah durus ! quicunque meos, nisi siccus, amores
Nolit ; & hîc lacrymæ rem neget esse suæ. 120
Sæpe hîc Magdalinas vel aquas vel amaverit undas ;
Credo nec Assyrias mens tua malit opes.

121 *undas*] *ignes conj. Bensly*

Scilicet ille tuos ignis recalescet ad ignes ;
Forsan & illa tuis unda natabit aquis.
Hîc eris ad cunas, & odoros funere manes :
Hinc ignes nasci testis & indè meos.
Hîc mecum, & cum matre sua, mea gaudia quæres :
Maturus Procerum seu stupor esse velit ;
Sive per antra sui lateat (tunc templa) sepulchri :
Tertia lux reducem (lenta sed illa) dabit.   130
Sint fidæ precor ah (dices) facilésque tenebræ ;
Lux mea dum noctis (res nova !) poscit opem.
Denique charta meo quicquid mea dicat amori,
Illi quo metuat cunque, fleátve, modo,
Læta parùm (dices) hæc, sed neque dulcia non sunt :
Certè & amor (dices) hujus amandus erat.

SI nimium hîc promitti tibi videtur, Lector bone, pro eo cui
satisfaciendo libellus iste futurus fuerit; scias me in istis non
ad hæc modò spectare quæ hîc habes, sed ea etiam quæ olim
(hæc interim fovendo) habere poteris. Nolui enim (si hactenus
deesse amicis meis non potui, flagitantibus à me, etiam cum
dispendii sui periculo, paterer eos experiri te in tantum favorém-
que tuum) nolui, inquam, fastidio tuo indulgere. Satìs hîc habes
quod vel releges ad ferulam suam (neque enim maturiores sibi
annos ex his aliqua vendicant) vel ut pignus plurium adultiorúm-
que in sinu tuo reponas. Elige tibi ex his utrumvis. Me interim 10
quod attinet, finis meus non fefellit. Maximum meæ ambitionis
scopum jamdudum attigi : tunc nimirum cùm qualecunque hoc
meum penè infantis Musæ murmur ad aures istas non ingratum
sonuit, quibus neque doctiores mihi de publico timere habeo, nec
sperare clementiores ; adeò ut de tuo jam plausu (dicam ingenuè
& breviter) neque securus sim ultrà neque solicitus. Prius tui,
quisquis es Lector, apud me reverentia prohibet ; de cujus judicio
omnia possum magna sperare : posterius illorum reverentia non
sinit, de quorum perspicacitate maxima omnia non possum mihi
non persuadere. Quanquam ô quàm velim tanti me esse in quo 20
patria mea morem istum suum deponere velit, genio suo tam non
dignum ; istum scilicet quo, suis omnibus fastiditis, ea exosculatur
unicè, quibus trajecisse Alpes & de transmarino esse, in pretium
cessit ! Sed relictis hisce nimis improbæ spei votis, convertam
me ad magistros Acygnianos ; quos scio de novissimis meis verbis
(quanquam neminem nominârim) iratos me reliquisse : bilem
verò componant ; & mihi se hoc debere (ambitioso juveni verbum
tam magnum ignoscant) debere, inquam, fateantur : quòd
nimirum in tam nobili argumento, in quo neque ad fœtida de
suis Sanctis figmenta, neque ad putidas de nostris calumnias 30
opus habeant confugere, de tenui hoc meo dederim illorum
magnitudini unde emineat. Emineat verò ; (serius dico) Sciántque
me semper se habituros esse sub ea, quam mihi eorum lux major
affuderit, umbrâ, placidissimè acquiescentem.

126 *testis*] testis, 34

EPIGRAMMATA
SACRA.

Luc. 18.

Pharisæus & Publicanus.

EN *duo Templum adeunt* (*diversis mentibus ambo :*)
Ille procul trepido lumine signat humum :

It gravis hic, & in alta ferox penetralia tendit.
Plus habet hic templi ; *plus habet ille* Dei.

Matth. 21. 7.

In Asinum Christi vectorem.

* ILle *suum didicit quondam objurgare magistrum :*
Et quid ni discas tu celebrare tuum ?

Mirum non minùs est, te jam potuisse tacere,
Illum quàm fuerat tum potuisse loqui.

* BALAAMI Asinus.

Luc. 4.

Dominus apud suos vilis.

EN *consanguinei ! patriis en exul in oris*
Christus ! & haud alibi tam peregrinus erat.

Qui socio demum pendebat sanguine latro,
O consanguineus *quàm fuit ille magìs !*

Joann. 5.

Ad Bethesdæ piscinam positus.

QUis *novus hic refugis incumbit Tantalus undis,*
Quem fallit toties tam fugitiva salus ?

Unde hoc naufragium felix ? medicæque procellæ ?
Vitáque, tempestas quam pretiosa dedit ?

2·1 *No foot-note D A4*   4·3 *medicæque*] medicæuè *D*

JOANN. 20.

Christus ad Thomam.

S *Æva fides ! voluisse meos tractare dolores ?*
Crudeles digiti ! sic didicisse Deum ?

Vulnera, nè dubites, vis tangere nostra : sed eheu,
Vulnera, dum dubitas, tu graviora facis.

MATTH. 16. 25.

Quisquis perdiderit animam suam meâ causâ, inveniet eam.

I *Vita ; I, perdam : mihi mors tua, Christe, reperta est :*
(Mors tua vita mihi est ; mors tibi, vita mea)

Aut ego te abscondam Christi (mea Vita) sepulchro.
Non adeò procul est tertius ille dies.

JOANN. 20. I.

Primo mane venit ad sepulchrum MAGDALENA.

T *U matutinos prævertis, sancta, rubores,*
Magdala ; sed jam tum Sol tuus ortus erat.

Jámque vetus meritò vanos Sol non agit ortus,
Et tanti radios non putat esse suos.

Quippe aliquo (reor) ille, novus, jam nictat in astro,
Et se nocturnâ parvus habet faculâ.

Quàm velit ô tantæ vel nuntius esse diei !
Atque novus Soli Lucifer ire novo !

JOANN. 6.

Quinque panes ad quinque hominum millia.

E *N mensæ faciles, redivicáque vulnera cœnæ,*
Quæque indefessâ provocat ora dape !

Aucta Ceres stupet arcanâ se crescere messe.
Denique quid restat ? Pascitur ipse cibus.

2·2 *mihi est A4* : *mea est 34*   3 (*Heading*) MAGDALENA] Magdalis
A4 (first copy of epigram)   3·7 *tantæ*] tanti *D*

A c t. 8.

Æthiops lotus.

ILle niger *sacris exit* (*quàm lautus !*) *ab undis :*
   Nec frustra Æthiopem *nempe* lavare *fuit.*

Mentem quàm niveam piceæ cutis umbra fovebit !
   Jam volet & nigros sancta Columba lares.

L u c. 18. 13.

Publicanus procul stans percutiebat pectus suum.

ECce *hic peccator timidus petit advena templum ;*
   Quódque audet solum, pectora mœsta ferit.

Fide miser ; pulsáque fores has fortiter : illo
   Invenies templo *tu* propiore *Deum.*

M a r c. 12. 44.

Obolum Viduæ.

GUtta brevis nummi (vitæ patrona senilis)*
   E digitis stillat non dubitantis anûs :

Istis multa vagi spumant de gurgite census.
   Isti abjecerunt *scilicet ; Illa* dedit.

L u c. 10. 39.

MARIA verò assidens ad pedes ejus, audiebat eum.

ASpice (namque novum est) ut ab hospite pendeat hospes !*
   Huic ori parat ; hoc sumit ab ore cibos.

Túne epulis adeò es (soror) officiosa juvandis,
   Et sinis has (inquit) MARTHA, *perire dapes ?*

A c t. 2.

In SPIRITÛS sancti Descensum.

FErte sinus, ô ferte : cadit vindemia cœli ;*
   Sanctáque ab æthereis volvitur uva jugis.

Felices nimiùm, queîs tam bona musta bibuntur ;
   In quorum gremium lucida pergit hyems !

1·3 *fovebit*] fovebat *D*   1·4 volet & nigros] volet, et nigros *A 4*
2·2 *Quódque audet solum*] bracketed *A 4*   2·4 propiore] meliore *A 4*
3 (*Heading*) 'Obolum Viduæ.] in Viduæ Obolũ *D*   4·1 *pendeat*]
penderet *D*

En caput ! en ut nectareo micat & micat astro !
Gaudet & in roseis viva corona comis !

Illis (ô Superi ! quis sic neget ebrius esse ?)
Illis, nè titubent, dant sua vina faces.

Luc. 15. 13.

Congestis omnibus peregrè profectus est.

DIc mihi, quò tantos properas, puer auree, nummos ?
 Quorsum festinæ conglomerantur opes ?
Cur tibi tota vagos ructant patrimonia census ?
 Non poterunt siliquæ nempe minoris emi ?

Act. 21. 13.

Non solùm vinciri sed & mori paratus sum.

NOn modò vincla, sed & mortem tibi, Christe, subibo,
 Paulus ait, docti callidus arte doli.
Diceret hoc aliter : Tibi non modò velle ligari,
 Christe, sed & *solvi nempe paratus ero.

  * Phil. 1. 23. τὴν ἐπιθυμίαν ἔχων εἰς τὸ ἀναλύσαι.

Act. 12. 23.

In Herodem σκωληκόβρωτον.

ILle Deus, Deus : hæc populi vox unica : tantùm
 (Vile genus) vermes credere velle negant.
At citò se miseri, citò nunc errâsse fatentur ;
 Carnes degustant, Ambrosiámque putant.

Matth. 14.

Videns ventum magnum, timuit, & cùm cœpisset demergi, clamavit, &c.

PEtre, cades, ô, si dubitas : ô fide : nec ipsum
 (Petre) negat fidis æquor habere fidem.
Pondere pressa suo subsidunt cætera : solum
 (Petre) tuæ mergit te levitatis onus.

 2 (Heading) est.] est Prodigus D   3 (Heading) solùm] modo D
4 (Heading) σκωληκόβρωτον] ab Angelo percussŭ D   5 (Heading)
clamavit] clamabat D   Heading in A4 : Mat. 14 | In S: Petrum
mergi incipientĕ 5·1 dubitas] dubites D

A c t. 8. 18.

Obtulit eis pecunias.

Q*Uorsum hos hîc nummos profers ? quorsum, impie Simon ?*
  Non ille hîc Judas, *sed tibi* Petrus *adest.*

Vis emisse Deum ? *potiùs (precor) hoc age, Simon,*
  Si potes, ipse priùs dæmona vende tuum.

A c t. 5. 15.

Umbra S. Petri medetur ægrotis.

C*Onveniunt alacres* (sic, sic juvat ire sub umbras)
  Atque umbras *fieri (creditis ?)* umbra *vetat.*

O Petri umbra potens ! quæ non miracula præstat ?
  Nunc quoque, Papa, tuum sustinet illa decus.

M a r c. 7. 33, 36.

Tetigit linguam ejus, &c.——& loquebatur——
& præcepit illis nè cui dicerent : illi verò
eò magìs prædicabant.

C*Hriste, jubes muta ora loqui ; muta ora loquuntur :*
  Sana tacere jubes ora ; nec illa tacent.

Si digito *tunc usus eras, muta ora resolvens ;*
  Nónne opus est totâ *nunc tibi, Christe,* manu ?

L u c. 10. 32.

Sacerdos quidam descendens eâdem viâ,
vidit & præteriit.

S*Pectásne (ah!) placidísque oculis mea vulnera tractas ?*
  O dolor! ô nostris vulnera vulneribus !

Pax oris quàm torva tui est ! quàm triste serenum !
  Tranquillus miserum qui videt, ipse facit.

2·1 umbras] umbris *D*　　2·3 *O Petri*] Petri *D*　　3·3 digito] digitis
A 4

L u c. 17.

Leprosi ingrati.

*D*Um linquunt Christum (ah morbus !) sanantur euntes :
  Ipse etiam morbus *sic medicina fuit.*

At sani Christum (mens ah malesana !) relinquunt :
  Ipsa etiam morbus sic medicina *fuit.*

M a t t h. 6. 34.

Nè soliciti estote in crastinum.

*I*Miser, inque tuas rape non tua tempora curas :
  Et nondum natis perge perire malis.

Mî querulis satìs una dies, satìs angitur horis :
  Una dies lacrymis mî satìs uda suis.

Non mihi venturos vacat expectare dolores :
  Nolo ego, nolo hodie crastinus esse miser.

M a t t h. 9. 9.

A telonio Matthæus.

*A*H satìs, ah nimis est : noli ultrà ferre magistrum,
  Et lucro domino turpia colla dare.

Jam fuge ; jam (Matthæe) feri fuge regna tyranni :
  Inque bonam *felix i fugitive* *crucem.

* *CHRISTI* scilicet.

L u c. 7.

Viduæ filius è feretro matri redditur.

*E*N redeunt, lacrymásque breves nova gaudia pensant :
  Bísque illa est, uno in pignore, facta parens.

Felix, quæ magìs es nati per funera mater !
  Amisisse, *iterum cui* peperisse *fuit.*

MATTH. 18.

Bonum intrare in cœlos cum uno oculo, &c.

UNo oculo? *ah centum potiùs mihi, millia centum :*
 Nam quis ibi, in cœlo, quis satìs Argus *erit ?*
Aut si oculus mihi tantùm unus conceditur, unus
 Iste oculus fiam totus & omnis ego.

LUC. 14.

Hydropicus sanatur.

IPse suum pelagus, morbóque immersus aquoso*
 Qui fuit, ut lætus nunc micat atque levis !
Quippe in vina iterum Christus (puto) transtulit undas ;
 Et nunc iste suis ebrius est ab aquis.

LUC. 2. 7.

Non erat iis in diversorio locus.

ILli non locus est ? Illum ergò pellitis ? Illum ?*
 Ille Deus, *quem sic pellitis ; ille* Deus.
O furor ! humani miracula sæva furoris !
 Illi non locus est, quo sine nec locus est.

LUC. 16.

In lacrymas Lazari spretas à Divite.

FElix ô ! lacrymis (ô Lazare) ditior istis,*
 Quàm qui purpureas it gravis inter opes !
Illum cùm rutili nova purpura vestiet ignis,
 Ille tuas lacrymas quàm volet esse suas !

MATTH. 26. 65.

Indignatur Caiphas Christo se confitenti.

TU Christum, Christum quòd non negat esse, lacessis :*
 Ipsius hoc crimen, quod fuit ipse, *fuit.*
Téne Sacerdotem credam ? Novus ille Sacerdos,
 Per quem impunè Deo non licet esse Deum.

2 *Heading in* D : Melius est intrare Cælos quam̃ uno Occulo &ct
2·2 *lætus*] lætens D   3·4] Illi non est locus quo sine nec est locus D

JOANN. 12. 37.

Cùm tot signa edidisset, non credebant in eum.

NOn tibi, Christe, fidem tua tot miracula præstant :
    (O verbi, ô dextræ dulcia regna tuæ !)

Non præstant ? neque te post tot miracula credunt ?
    Mirac'lum, qui non credidit, ipse fuit.

MARC. 1. 16.

Ad S. Andream piscatorem.

QUippe potes pulchrè captare & fallere pisces !
    Centum illîc discis lubricus ire dolis.

Heus bone piscator ! tendit sua retia Christus :
    Artem inverte, et jam tu quoque disce capi.

JOANN. 1. 23.

Ego sum vox, &c.

VOx ego sum, dicis : tu vox es, sancte Joannes ?
    Si vox es, genitor cur tibi mutus erat ?

Ista tui fuerant quàm mira silentia patris !
    Vocem non habuit tunc quoque cùm genuit.

ACT. 12.

Vincula sponte decidunt.

QUi ferro Petrum cumulas, durissime custos,
    A ferro disces mollior esse tuo.

Ecce fluit, nodîsque suis evolvitur ultro :
    I fatue, & vinc'lis vincula pone tuis.

---

2 (Heading) Ad S.] in Sanct: D   S.] D⁻ A4   4·2 disces]
discis D   4·3 suis] satis D   ultro] ultrà A4

In diem omnium Sanctorum.

R E V. 7. 3.

Nè lædite terram, neque mare, neque arbores,
quousque obsignaverimus servos Dei
nostri in frontibus suis.

NUsquam immitis agat ventus sua murmura ; nusquam
  Sylva tremat, crispis sollicitata comis.
Æqua Thetis placidè allabens ferat oscula Terræ ;
  Terra suos Thetidi pandat amica sinus :
Undique Pax effusa piis volet aurea pennis,
  Frons bona dum signo est quæque notata suo.
Ah quid in hoc opus est signis aliunde petendis ?
  Frons bona sat lacrymis quæque notata suis.

In die Conjurationis sulphureæ.

QUàm bene dispositis annus dat currere festis !
  Post Omnes Sanctos, Omne scelus sequitur.

Deus sub utero virginis.

ECce tuus, Natura, pater ! pater hic tuus, hic est :
  Ille, uterus matris quem tenet, ille pater.
Pellibus exiguis arctatur Filius ingens,
  Quem tu non totum (crede) nec ipsa capis.
Quanta uteri, Regina, tui reverentia tecum est,
  Dum jacet hîc, cælo sub breviore, Deus !
Conscia divino gliscunt præcordia motu
  (Nec vehit æthereos sanctior aura polos)
Quàm bene sub tecto tibi concipiuntur eodem
  Vota, & (vota cui concipienda) Deus !   10
Quod nubes alia, & tanti super atria cæli
  Quærunt, invenient hoc tua vota domi.
O felix anima hæc, quæ tam sua gaudia tangit !
  Sub conclave suo cui suus ignis adest.

1 (*Heading*) obsignaverimus . . . suis.] obsignavimus servos Dei. *D*
1·1 *agat*] dabit *D*   1·3 *ferat*] dabit *D*   1·4 *pandat*] pandit *D*
1·5 *volet*] volat *D*   1·7 *Ah*] At *D*   2 *Heading in D* : in diem
Sulphureæ Conjurationis   3·4 (*crede*) *nec*] scilicet *A 4*   3·7
motu] motu. *A 4*   3·8 *polos*)] polos.) *A 4*

Corpus amet (licet) illa suum, neque sydera malit :
Quod vinc'lum est aliis, hoc habet illa domum.

Sola jaces, neque sola ; toro quocunque recumbis,
Illo estis positi túque tuúsque toro.

Immo ubi casta tuo posita es cum conjuge conjunx,
(Quod mirum magìs est) es tuus ipsa torus. 20

A c t. 7. 16.

Ad Judæos mactatores Stephani.

F*Rustra illum increpitant, frustra vaga saxa : nec illi*
Grandinis (heu sævæ !) dura procella nocet.

Ista potest tolerare ; potest nescire : sed illi,
Quæ sunt in vestro pectore, saxa nocent.

R e v. 1. 9.

D. Joannes in exilio.

E*Xul, Amor Christi est : Christum tamen invenit exul :*
Et solitos illîc invenit ille sinus.

Ah longo, æterno ah terras indicite nobis
Exilio, Christi si sinus exilium est.

M a t t h. 2.

Ad Infantes Martyres.

F*Undite ridentes animas ; effundite cœlo :*
Discet ibi vestra (ô quàm bene !) lingua loqui.

Nec vos lac vestrum & maternos quærite fontes :
Quæ vos expectat lactea tota via est.

L u c. 2.

Quærit Jesum suum beata Virgo.

A*H, redeas miseræ, redeas (puer alme) parenti ;*
Ah, neque te cœlis tam citò redde tuis.

Cœlum nostra tuum fuerint ô brachia, si te
Nostra suum poterunt brachia ferre Deum.

2·3 *tolerare ;*] tolerare ista *D*   5 (*Heading*) Jesum suum]
Jesũ *D*   5·3 *brachia,*] brachia : *A 4*

Matth. 8.

Non sum dignus ut sub tecta mea venias.

IN tua tecta Deus veniet : tuus haud sinit illud
Et pudor, atque humili in pectore celsa fides.

Illum ergò accipies quoniam non accipis *: ergò*
In te *jam veniet, non* tua tecta, *Deus.*

Matth. 27. 12.

Christus accusatus nihil respondit.

NIl ait : *ô sanctæ pretiosa silentia linguæ !*
Ponderis ô quanti res nihil *illud erat !*

Ille olim, verbum *qui* dixit, *& omnia* fecit,
Verbum non dicens *omnia nunc* reficit.

Luc. 2.

Nunc dimittis.

SPésne meas tandem ergò mei tenuêre lacerti ?
Ergò bibunt oculos lumina nostra tuos ?

Ergò bibant ; possíntque novam sperare juventam :
O possint senii non meminisse sui !

Immo mihi potiùs mitem mors induat umbram
(Esse sub his oculis si tamen umbra potest)

Ah satis est. Ego te vidi (puer auree) vidi :
Nil post te, nisi te (Christe) videre volo.

Luc. 8.

Verbum inter spinas.

SÆpe Dei verbum sentes cadit inter ; & atrum
Miscet spina procax (ah malè juncta !) latus.

Credo quidem : nam sic spinas ah scilicet inter
Ipse Deus Verbum tu quoque (Christe) cadis.

4·1 *atrum*] illi *A 4*

L u c. 14. 5.

Sabbatum {
Judaicum,
&
Christianum.

R*Es eadem vario quantum distinguitur usu !*
Nostra hominem *servant sabbata ; vestra* bovem.
Observent igitur (pacto quid justius isto ?)
Sabbata nostra homines, *sabbata vestra* boves.

M a r c. 10. 52.

Ad verbum Dei sanatur cæcus.

C*Hriste, loquutus eras (ô sacra licentia verbi !)*
Jámque novus cæci fluxit in ora dies.
Jam, credo, * Nemo est, sicut Tu, *Christe,* loquutus :
Auribus? immo oculis, *Christe, loquutus eras.*

* Joann. 7. 46.

M a t t h. 11.

Onus meum leve est.

E*Sse levis quicunque voles, onus accipe Christi :*
Ala tuis humeris, non onus, illud erit.
Christi onus an quæris quàm sit grave ? scilicet, audi,
Tam grave, ut ad summos te premat usque polos.

J o a n n. 6.

Miraculum quinque panum.

E*Cce vagi venit unda cibi ; venit indole sacrâ*
Fortis, & in dentes fertilis innumeros.
Quando erat invictæ tam sancta licentia cœnæ ?
Illa famem *populi pascit, &* illa *fidem.*

1 (*Heading*) Sabbatum &c. . . .] Sabatũ Christianũ | et | Judaicũ : *D*   1·3 *Observent*] Obseruant *D*   2 (*Heading*) MARC.] MATTH. *34 etc.*   (*Heading*) Dei] Dom[1]. *A4*   *Heading in Stubbe (see Introd., p. xliv, above) : Loquente Deo caecus videt.* Matth. 10. 52   2·1 *licentia*] potentia *Stubbe*   2·3 *asterisk in D but no note. Neither asterisk nor note in A4*   3·3 *sit D A4 70L : est 34, in some copies altered in ink to ' sit '*   3·4 *premat*] premet *D*   4 *Heading in A4* : Cænæ miraculum.

JOANN. 8. 52.

Nunc scimus te habere dæmonium.

AUt Deus, aut saltem dæmon tibi notior esset,
  (Gens mala) quæ dicis dæmona habere Deum.

Ignorâsse Deum poteras, ô cæca : sed oro,
  Et patrem poteras tam malè nôsse tuum ?

In beatæ Virginis verecundiam.

IN gremio, quæris, cur sic sua lumina Virgo
  Ponat ? ubi meliùs poneret illa, precor ?

O ubi, quàm cælo, meliùs sua lumina ponat ?
  Despicit, at cœlum sic tamen illa videt.

In vulnera Dei pendentis.

O Frontis, lateris, manuúmque pedúmque cruores !
  O quæ purpureo flumina fonte patent !

In nostram (ut quondam) pes non valet ire salutem,
  Sed natat ; in fluviis (ah !) natat ille suis.

Fixa manus ; dat, fixa : pios bona dextera rores
  Donat, & in donum solvitur ipsa suum.

O latus, ô torrens ! quis enim torrentior exit
  Nilus, ubi pronis præcipitatur aquis ?

Mille & mille simul cadit & cadit undique guttis
  Frons : viden' ut sævus purpuret ora pudor ?   10

Spinæ hôc irriguæ florent crudeliter imbre,
  Inque novas sperant protinus ire rosas.

Quisque capillus it exiguo tener alveus amne,
  Hôc quasi de rubro rivulus oceano.

O nimiùm vivæ pretiosis amnibus undæ !
  Fons vitæ nunquam verior ille fuit.

1·2 *dicis*] uis D   3·1 *lateris*] laterum D   3·10 *purpuret*] purpurat D

Matth. 9. 11.

Quare cum Publicanis manducat Magister vester?

E*Rgò* istis *socium se peccatoribus addit ?*
 Ergò istis *sacrum non negat ille latus ?*
Tu, Pharisæe, rogas Jesus cur fecerit istud ?
Næ dicam : Jesus, *non* Pharisæus, *erat.*

Matth. 28.

Ecce locus ubi jacuit Dominus.

I*Psum,* Ipsum *(precor) ô potiùs mihi (candide) monstra :*
 Ipsi, Ipsi, *ô lacrymis oro sit ire meis.*
Si monstrare locum *satìs est, & dicere nobis,*
 En, Maria, hîc tuus en, hîc jacuit Dominus ;
Ipsa ulnas monstrare meas, & dicere possum,
 En, Maria, hîc tuus en, hîc jacuit Dominus.

Luc. 17.

Leprosi ingrati.

L*Ex jubet ex hominum cœtu procul ire* leprosos :
 At mundi *à Christo cur abiêre procul ?*
Non abit, at sedes tantùm mutavit in illis ;
 Et lepra, quæ fuerat corpore, mente sedet.
Sic igitur dignâ vice res variatur ; & à se
 Quàm procul antè homines, nunc habuêre Deum.

Joann. 20.

In cicatrices quas Christus habet in se adhuc superstites.

Q*Uicquid* spina *procax, vel stylo* clavus *acuto,*
 Quicquid purpureâ scripserat hasta *notâ,*
Vivit adhuc tecum : sed jam tua vulnera non sunt :
 Non, sed vulneribus sunt medicina meis.

1·3 *fecerit*] fecit *D* 4 (*Heading*) habet] habuit *D* 4·1 *stylo*
clavus] clauus stylo *D*

Act. 5.

Æger implorat umbram D. Petri.

*P*Etre, tua lateam paulisper (Petre) sub umbra :
  Sic mea me quærent fata, nec invenient.

Umbra dabit tua posse meum me cernere solem ;
  Et mea lux umbræ sic erit umbra tuæ.

Luc. 24. 39.

Quid turbati estis ? Videte manus meas & pedes, quia ego ipse sum.

*E*N me, & signa mei, quondam mea vulnera ! certè,
  Vos nisi credetis, vulnera sunt & adhuc.

O nunc ergò fidem sanent mea vulnera vestram :
  O mea nunc sanet vulnera vestra fides.

Act. 12.

In vincula Petro sponte delapsa, & apertas fores.

*F*Erri non meminit ferrum : se vincula Petro
  Dissimulant : nescit carcer habere fores.

Quàm bene liber erit, carcer quem liberat ! *ipsa*
  Vincula quem solvunt, *quàm bene tutus erit !*

Act. 19. 12.

Deferebantur à corpore ejus sudaria, &c.

*I*Mperiosa premunt morbos, & ferrea fati
  Jura ligant, Pauli lintea tacta manu.

Unde hæc felicis laus est & gloria lini ?
  Hæc (reor) è Lachesis pensa fuêre colo.

3 (*Heading*) Petro] Petri *D*   3·3] Quā bene liber erat carcer
liberabat et ipsa *D*   3·4 solvunt] solvent *A 4*

JOANN. 15.

Christus Vitis ad Vinitorem Patrem.

EN serpit tua, purpureo tua palmite vitis
　　Serpit, & (ah !) spretis it per humum foliis.
Tu viti succurre tuæ, mi Vinitor ingens :
　　Da fulcrum ; fulcrum da mihi : quale ? crucem.

ACT. 26. 28.

Penè persuades mihi ut fiam Christianus.

PEnè ? quid hoc penè est ? Vicinia sæva salutis !
　　O quàm tu malus es proximitate boni !
Ah ! portu qui teste perit, bis naufragus ille est ;
　　Hunc non tam pelagus, quàm sua terra premit.

Quæ nobis spes vix absunt, crudeliùs absunt :
　　Penè fui felix, Emphasis est miseri.

JOANN. 3. 19.

Lux venit in mundum, sed dilexerunt homines magis tenebras quàm lucem.

LUce suâ venit ecce Deus, mundóque refulget :
　　Pergit adhuc tenebras mundus amare suas.
At Stygiis igitur mundus damnabitur umbris :
　　Pergit adhuc tenebras mundus amare suas ?

LUC. 16.

Dives implorat guttam.

O Mihi si digito tremat & tremat unica summo
　　Gutta ! ô si flammas mulceat una meas !
Currat opum quocunque volet levis unda mearum :
　　Una mihi hæc detur gemmula, Dives ero.

1·3 *mi*] mihi *D*　　1·4 *quale ?* crucem.] quale ✝ *D*　　2 (*Heading*)
persuades mihi] me persuadeas *D*　　2·2 *tu malus es*] malus tu es *D*
3 (*Heading*) sed . . . lucem.] sed dilexerant Tenebras Homines magis
quaˆ Lucem *D*　　4 (*Heading*) guttam] Guttulã *D*　　4·4 *mihi
hæc*] mihi *D*

JOANN. 3. 4.

Quomodo potest homo gigni qui est senex?

DIc, Phœnix unde in nitidos novus emicat annos ;
Plaudit & elusos aurea penna rogos ?

Quis colubrum dolus insinuat per secula retro,
Et jubet emeritum luxuriare latus ?

Cur rostro pereunte suam prœdata senectam
Torva ales, rapido plus legit ore diem ?

Immo, sed ad nixus quœ stat Lucina secundos ?
Natales seros unde senex habeat.

Ignoras, Pharisœe ? sat est : jam credere disces :
Dimidium fidei, qui bene nescit, habet.   10

MARC. II. 13.

Arbor Christi jussu arescens.

ILle jubet : procul ite mei, mea gloria, rami :
Nulla vocet nostras ampliùs aura comas.

Ite ; nec ô pigeat : nam vos neque fulminis ira,
Nec trucis ala Noti verberat : Ille jubet.

O vox ! ô Zephyro vel sic quoque dulcior omni !
Non possum Autumno nobiliore frui.

LUC. I. 18.

Zacharias minùs credens.

INfantis fore te patrem, res mira videtur ;
Infans interea factus es ipse pater.

Et dum promissi signum *(nimis anxie) quœris,*
Jam nisi per signum *quœrere nulla potes.*

1·1 *annos*] ales *D*   2·1 *mei,*] ite *D*   2·3 *fulminis ira*] verbera
Cauri *A4*   2·4 *ala*] ira *A4*   *verberat*] fulminet *A4*   2·5 *vel sic
quoque*] vel si quo *D*   3 (*Heading*) 18.] 12. 34 etc.   3·2
es] est *D*   3·3 *Et*] Nam *Stubbe*

JOANN. 3.

In aquam baptismi Dominici.

Felix ô, sacros cui sic licet ire per artus !
Felix ! dum lavat hunc, ipsa lavatur aqua.

Gutta quidem sacros quæcunque perambulat artus,
Dum manet hîc, gemma est ; dum cadit hinc, lacryma.

LUC. 13. 11.

Mulieri incurvatæ medetur Dominus, indignante Archisynagogo.

IN proprios replicata sinus quæ repserat, & jam
Dæmonis (infelix !) nil nisi nodus erat,

Solvitur ad digitum Domini : sed strictior illo
Unicus est nodus ; cor, Pharisæe, tuum.

MATTH. 22. 46.

Neque ausus fuit quisquam ex illo die eum ampliùs interrogare.

CHriste, malas fraudes, Pharisaica retia, fallis :
Et miseros sacro discutis ore dolos.

Ergò tacent *tandem, atque invita silentia servant :*
Tam bene non aliter te potuêre loqui.

MATTH. 20. 20.

S. Joannes matri suæ.

O Mihi cur dextram, *mater, cur, oro,* sinistram
Poscis, ab officio mater iniqua tuo ?

Nolo manum *Christi* dextram *mihi, nolo* sinistram :
Tam procul à sacro non libet esse sinu.

1·1 *licet*] libet *D*   2 (*Heading*) incurvatæ] incuivatæ *34*   Archi-
synagogo] Archisynagogâ *A 4*

MATTH. 4.
Si Filius Dei es, dejice te.

NI *se dejiciat Christus de vertice Templi,*
  Non credes quòd sit Filius ille Dei.
At mox te humano de pectore dejicit : heus tu,
  Non credes quòd sit Filius ille Dei ?

LUC. 19. 41.
Dominus flens ad Judæos.

DIscite vos miseri, venientes discite flammas ;
  Nec facite ô lacrymas sic periisse meas.
Nec periisse tamen poterunt : mihi credite, vestras
  Vel reprimet flammas hæc aqua, vel faciet.

LUC. 18. 11.
Nec velut hic Publicanus.

IStum ? *vile caput ! quantum mihi gratulor, inquis,*
  Istum quòd novi tam mihi dissimilem !
Vilis at iste abiit sacris acceptior aris :
  I nunc, & jactes hunc tibi dissimilem.

ACT. 9. 3.
In Saulum fulgore nimio excæcatum.

QUæ lucis tenebræ ? *quæ nox est ista diei ?*
  Nox nova, quam nimii luminis umbra facit !
An Saulus fuerit cæcus, vix dicere possum ;
  Hoc scio, quòd captus lumine Saulus erat.

LUC. 10. 23.
Beati oculi qui vident.

CUm Christus nostris ibat mitissimus oris,
  Atque novum cæcos jussit habere diem,
Felices, oculos qui tunc habuêre, vocantur ?
  Felices, & qui non habuêre, voco.

2 (*Heading*) Dominus] Deus *A4*   5 (*Heading*) vident] vident
&c: *A4*   5·2 *novum*] novam *A4*   5·3 oculos *A4 D* : oculus
34   5·4 *A4 distinguishes the.line*

Luc. 7. 15.

Filius è feretro matri redditur.

E Rgóne tam subitâ potuit vice flebilis horror
  In natalitia candidus ire toga ?
Quos vidi, matris gemitus hos esse dolentis
  Credideram ; gemitus parturientis erant.

Matth. 11. 25.

In seculi sapientes.

E Rgóne delitias facit, & sibi plaudit ab alto
  Stultitia, ut velit hâc ambitione peti ?
Difficilisne adeò facta est, & seria tandem ?
  Ergò & in hanc etiam quis sapuisse potest ?
Tantum erat, ut possit tibi doctior esse ruina ?
  Tanti igitur cerebri res, periisse, fuit ?
Nil opus ingenio ; nihil hâc opus Arte furoris :
  Simpliciùs poteris scilicet esse miser.

Luc. 4. 29.

In Judæos Christum præcipitare conantes.

D Icite, quæ tanta est sceleris fiducia vestri ?
  Quod nequiit dæmon, id voluisse scelus ?
Quod nequiit dæmon scelus, id voluisse patrare !
  Hoc tentare ipsum dæmona (credo) fuit.

Rev. 12. 9.

In Draconem præcipitem.

I Frustra truculente ; tuas procul aurea rident
  Astra minas, cœlo jam bene tuta suo.
Túne igitur cœlum super ire atque astra parabas ?
  Ascensu tanto non opus ad barathrum.

2 (Heading) sapientes corrected to sapientem A4   2·4 Ergò &]
Ergone D   2·5 doctior] ditior D   4 (Heading) 12.] 7. 34 etc.
4·3 parabas] parabis D   4·4 ad] est corrected to ad A4

L U C. 1.

Beatæ Virgini credenti.

Miraris (quid enim faceres ?) sed & hæc quoque credis :
Hæc uteri credis dulcia monstra tui.
En fidei, Regina, tuæ dignissima merces !
Fida Dei fueras filia ; mater eris.

M A R C. 12.

Licétne Cæsari censum dare ?

Post tot Scribarum (Christe) in te prælia, tandem
Ipse venit Cæsar : Cæsar in arma venit.
Pugnant terribiles non Cæsaris ense, sed ense
Cæsare : quin Cæsar vinceris ipse tamen.
Hoc quoque tu conscribe tuis, Auguste, triumphis.
Sic vinci dignus quis nisi Cæsar erat ?

M A T T H. 9.

In tibicines & turbam tumultuantem
circa defunctam.

Vani, quid strepitis ? nam, quamvìs *dormiat *illa,*
Non tamen è somno est sic revocanda suo.
Expectat solos Christi sopor iste susurros :
Dormit ; nec dormit omnibus *illa tamen.*

* Vers. 24. Non enim mortua est puella, sed dormit.

M A T T H. 4. 19.

Piscatores vocati.

Ludite jam pisces secura per æquora : pisces
Nos quoque (sed varia sub ratione) sumus.
Non potuisse capi, vobis spes una salutis :
Una salus nobis est, potuisse capi.

1 *(Heading)* LUC. 1.] LUC. 2. *34:* LUC: *A4* *Heading in D :* In
Beatã Uirginĕ Credentem 1·1 *sed &·*] sed *D* 2·5 *conscribe*]
scribe *D* 3·1 dormiat] dormitat *D. No note or asterisk A4*
3·4] *Dormit enim ; sed* Non Omnibus *illa tamen.* 7oL 4 *Head-*
ing in D : In Piscatores Uocatos *(Heading)* 4. *A4:* 6. *34* 4·1
secura] secure *D* 4·4 *potuisse capi.*] *A4 distinguishes*

M A R C. 12.

Date Cæsari.

CUncta Deo debentur : habet tamen & sua Cæsar ;
　Nec minus indè Deo est, si sua Cæsar habet.

Non minus indè Deo est, solio si cætera dantur
　Cæsareo, Cæsar cùm datur ipse Deo.

M A T T H. 21. 7.

Dominus asino vehitur.

ILle igitur vilem te, te dignatur asellum,
　O non vecturâ non bene digne tuâ ?

Heu quibus haud pugnat Christi patientia monstris ?
　Hoc, quòd sic fertur, hoc quoque ferre fuit.

L U C. 21. 27.

Videbunt Filium hominis venientem in nube.

IMmo veni : aërios (ô Christe) accingere currus,
　Inque triumphali nube coruscus ades.

Nubem quæris ? erunt nostra (ah !) suspiria nubes :
　Aut sol in nubem se dabit ipse tuam.

J O A N N. 20.

Nisi digitum immisero, &c.

IMpius ergò iterum clavos ? iterum impius hastam ?
　Et totum digitus triste revolvet opus ?

Túne igitur Christum (Thoma) quò vivere credas,
　Tu Christum faceres (ah truculente !) mori ?

Act. 7.

Ad Judæos mactatores S. Stephani.

Quid datis (*ah miseri !*) *saxis nolentibus iras ?*
Quid nimis in tragicum præcipitatis opus ?

In mortem Stephani se dant invita : sed illi
Occiso faciunt sponte suâ tumulum.

Sancto Joanni, dilecto discipulo.

TU fruere ; *augustóque sinu caput abde (quod ô tum*
Nollet in æterna se posuisse rosa)

Tu fruere : & sacro dum te sic pectore *portat,*
O sat erit tergo me potuisse vehi.

Matth. 2.

In lactentes Martyres.

VUlnera natorum qui vidit, & ubera matrum,
Per pueros fluviis (ah !) simul ire suis ;

Sic pueros quisquis vidit, dubitavit, an illos
Lilia cælorum diceret, anne rosas.

Matth. 1. 23.

Deus nobiscum.

NObiscum Deus *est ? vestrum hoc est (hei mihi !) vestrum :*
Vobiscum Deus *est, ô asini atque boves.*

Nobiscum non est : nam nos domus aurea sumit :
Nobiscum Deus est, & jacet in stabulo ?

Hoc igitur nostrum *ut fiat (dulcissime Jesu)* ·
Nos dandi stabulis, vel tibi danda domus.

1 (*Heading*) Act. 7.] Act. 8. *34*   S. Stephani] Stephani
D   1·4 *faciunt*] *corrected to* faciunt *A4*   3·1 *vidit*] videt *D*
4·1 *vestrum hoc*] verbum hoc *D*   4·3 *nos*] non *D*

Christus circumcisus ad Patrem.

H*as en primitias nostræ (Pater) accipe mortis ;*
  (Vitam ex quo sumpsi, vivere dedidici)
Ira (Pater) tua de pluviâ gustaverit istâ :
  Olim ibit fluviis hoc latus omne suis.

Tunc sitiat licèt & sitiat, bibet & bibet usqué :
  Tunc poterit toto fonte superba frui.

Nunc hastæ *interea possit præludere* culter :
  Indolis in pœnas spes erit ista meæ.

In Epiphaniam Domini.

N*On solitâ contenta dies face lucis Eoæ,*
  Ecce micat radiis cæsariata novis.

Persa sagax, propera : discurre per ardua Regum
  Tecta, per auratas marmoreásque domus :

Quære ô, quæ intepuit Reginæ purpura partu ;
  Principe vagitu quæ domus insonuit.

Audin' Persa sagax? Qui tanta negotia cœlo
Fecit, Bethlemiis vagiit in stabulis.

L u c. 2. 49.

Ecce quærebamus te, &c.

T*E quæro misera, & quæro :* tu nunc quoque tractas
  Res Patris : Pater *est unica cura tibi :*

Quippe quòd ad pœnas tantùm & tot nomina mortis,
  Ad luctum & lacrymas (hei mihi !) mater ego.

J o a n n. 2.

Aquæ in vinum versæ.

U*Nde rubor vestris, & non sua purpura lymphis ?*
  Quæ rosa mirantes tam nova mutat aquas ?

Numen (convivæ) præsens agnoscite Numen :
  Nympha pudica Deum vidit, & erubuit.

  1·1 *primitias*] *A 4 distinguishes*   1·3 *gustaverit istâ*] gustaverat
ipsâ *D*   1·8 *pœnas*] Pugnas *D*   3·1 *nunc*] tunc *D*
3·2 Pater] Patris *D*   4 *Heading in D :* In Aquâ ad Vinũ
versam *D*   4·4 *vidit*] noscit *D*

Matth. 8. 13.

Absenti Centurionis filio Dominus absens medetur.

Q*Uàm tacitis inopina salus illabitur alis !*
Alis, quas illi vox tua, Christe, dedit.

Quàm longas vox ista manus habet ! hæc medicina
Absens, & præsens *hæc medicina fuit.*

Marc. 4. 40.

Quid timidi estis ?

T*Anquam illi insanus faceret sua fulmina ventus !*
Tanquam illi scopulos nôrit habere fretum !

Vos vestri scopuli, vos estis ventus & unda :
Naufragium cum illo qui metuit, meruit.

Luc. 2.

Nunc dimittis.

I*Te mei (quid enim ulteriùs, quid vultis ?) ocelli :*
Leniter obductis ite superciliis.

Immo & adhuc & adhuc, iterúmque iterúmque videte ;
Accipite hæc totis lumina luminibus.

Jámque ite ; & tutis ô vos bene claudite vallis :
Servate hæc totis lumina luminibus.

Primum est, quòd potui te (Christe) videre : secundum,
Te viso, rectà jam potuisse mori.

Matth. 13. 24.

In segetem sacram.

E*Cce suam implorat, demisso vertice, falcem :*
Tu segeti falcem da (Pater alme) suam.

Tu falcem non das ? messem tu (Christe) moraris ?
Hoc ipsum falx est : hæc mora messis erit.

3·1 *enim*] vultis *D*   3·8 *rectà*] statim *D*   4·2 *suam*] tuam *D*

Luc. 7. 37.

Cœpit lacrymis rigare pedes ejus, & capillis
extergebat.

UNda sacras sordes lambit placidissima : flavæ
Lambit & hanc undam lucida flamma comæ.
Illa per has sordes it purior unda ; simúlque
Ille per has lucet purior ignis aquas.

Luc. 18. 41.

Quid vis tibi faciam ?

QUid volo (Christe) rogas ? quippe ah volo, Christe, videre :
Quippe ah te (dulcis Christe) videre volo.
At video ; *fideique oculis te nunc quoque figo :*
Est mihi, quæ nunquam est non oculata, fides.
Sed quamvìs videam, *tamen ah volo (Christe) videre :*
Sed quoniam video (Christe) videre volo.

Matth. 15. 21.

Christus mulieri Canaaneæ difficilior.

VT pretium facias dono, donare recusas :
Usquè rogat supplex, tu tamen usquè negas.
Hoc etiam donare fuit, donare negare.
Sæpe dedit, quisquis sæpe negata dedit.

Luc. 11. 27.

Beatus venter & ubera, &c.

ET quid si biberet Jesus vel ab ubere vestro ?
Quid facit ad vestram, quòd bibit ille, sitim ?
Ubera mox sua & Hic (ô quàm non lactea !) pandet :
E nato Mater *tum bibet ipsa suo.*

2 (Heading) Luc. 18. 41.] Luc: *A4*   2·6 videre volo] *A4 distin-*
guishes   4 (Heading) 11. 27.] 2 *70L*   4·2 facit] est *D*
4·3] Huic quoꝗ quando suum vber erit (suum et huic erit uber) *A4*

JOANN. 15. 1.

In Christum Vitem.

*U*Lmum vitis amat (quippe est & in arbore flamma,
   Quam fovet in viridi pectore blandus amor :)
Illam ex arboribus cunctis tu (Vitis) *amâsti,*
   Illam, quæcunque est, quæ crucis arbor *erat.*

JOANN. 16. 20.

Vos flebitis & lamentabimini.

*E*Rgò mihi salvete mei, mea gaudia, luctus :
   Quàm charum (ô Deus) est hoc mihi flere meum !
Flerem, ni flerem : Solus tu (dulcis Iesu)
   Lætitiam donas tunc quoque quando negas.

JOANN. 10.

In gregem Christi Pastoris.

O Grex, ô nimiùm tanto Pastore beatus !
   O ubi sunt tanto pascua digna grege ?
Nè non digna forent tanto grege pascua, Christus
   Ipse suo est Pastor, pascuum *& ipse gregi.*

In vulnera pendentis Domini.

*S*Ive oculos, sive ora *vocem tua vulnera ; certè*
   Undique sunt ora (heu !) undique sunt oculi.
Ecce ora ! ô nimiùm roseis florentia labris ! ·
   Ecce oculi ! sævis ah madidi lacrymis !
Magdala, quæ lacrymas solita es, quæ basia sacro
   Ferre pedi, sacro de pede sume vices.
Ora *pedi sua sunt, tua quò tibi basia reddat :*
   Quò reddat lacrymas scilicet est oculus.

3·4 pascuum &] Pasculum *D*   4·2 *heu*] eheu *D*   4·6 *vices*]
vires *D*

MARC. 2.
Paralyticus convalescens.

CHristum, *quòd misero facilis peccata remittit,*
  Scribæ blasphemum *dicere non dubitant.*
Hoc scelus ut primùm Paralyticus audiit ; irâ
Impatiens, lectum sustulit atque abiit.

JOANN. 8. 59.
Tunc sustulerunt lapides.

SAxa ? illi ? quid tam fædi voluêre furores ?
  Quid sibi de saxis hi voluêre suis ?
Indolem, & antiqui agnosco vestigia patris :
Panem de saxis hi voluêre suis.

In resurrectionem Domini.

NAsceris, en ! tecúmque tuus (Rex auree) mundus,
  Tecum * virgineo *nascitur è tumulo.*
Tecum in natales properat natura secundos,
Atque novam vitam te novus orbis habet.

Ex vita (Sol alme) tua vitam omnia sumunt :
Nil certè, nisi mors, cogitur indè mori.

At certè neque mors : nempe ut queat illa sepulchro
(Christe) tuo condi, mors volet ipsa mori.

  * Joann. 19. 41. ἐν ᾧ οὐδέπω οὐδεὶς ἐτέθη.

MATTH. 28. 17.
Aliqui verò dubitabant.

SCilicet & tellus * dubitat tremebunda : sed ipsum hoc,
  Quòd tellus dubitat, vos dubitare vetat.
Ipsi custodes vobis, si quæritis, illud
Hoc ipso dicunt, * dicere quòd nequeunt.

  * Vers. 2. σεισμὸς ἐγένετο μέγας.
  * Vers. 4. ἐσείσθησαν οἱ τηροῦντες καὶ ἐγένοντο ὡσεὶ νεκροί.

2·1 *Saxa ? illi ? quid tam fædi*] Saxa tibi tã fœdi *D*   2·2 *sibi*]
tibi *D*   3·2 *No note or asterisk D A 4*   3·7 *At*] Ac *D*
4·1, 4 *No notes or asterisks D A 4*

J o a n n. 20. 20.

In vulnerum vestigia quæ ostendit Dominus,
ad firmandam suorum fidem.

H *Is oculis (nec adhuc clausis coïêre fenestris)*
Invigilans nobis est tuus usus amor.

His oculis nos cernit amor tuus : his & amorem
(Christe) tuum gaudet cernere nostra fides.

L u c. 7. 19.

Mittit Joannes qui quærant à Christo, an is sit.

T *U qui adeò impatiens properâsti agnoscere Christum,*
Tunc cùm claustra uteri te tenuêre tui,

Tu, quis sit Christus, rogitas ? & quæris ab ipso ?
Hoc tibi vel mutus dicere quisque potest.

J o a n n. 18. 10.

In Petrum auricîdam.

Q *Uantumcunque ferox tuus hic (Petre) fulminat ensis,*
Tu tibi jam pugnas (ô bone) non Domino.

Scilicet in miseram furis implacidissimus aurem,
Perfidiæ testis nè queat esse tuæ.

M a r c. 3.

Manus arefacta sanatur.

F *Elix ! ergò tuæ spectas natalia dextræ,*
Quæ modò spectanti flebile funus erat.

Quæ nec in externos modò dextera profuit usus,
Certè erit illa tuæ jam manus & fidei.

1 *(Heading)* quæ . . . fidem] ab Jesu ostensa ad firmandam ffidem *D*
2 *(Heading)* Luc. 7.] Luc. 17. 34 *etc.* 3·3–4 *omitted in D*
3·4 *A4 distinguishes the line* ' 4·4 *erit*] erat *D*

MATTH. 27. 24.

In Pontium malè lautum.

ILla manus lavat unda tuas, vanissime Judex :
Ah tamen illa scelus non lavat unda tuum.

Nulla scelus lavet unda tuum : vel si lavet ulla,
O volet ex oculis illa venire tuis.

MATTH. 17. 27.

In piscem dotatum.

TU piscem si, Christe, velis, venit ecce, suúmque
Fert pretium : tanti est vel periisse tibi.

Christe, foro tibi non opus est ; addicere nummos
Non opus est : ipsum se tibi piscis emet.

JOANN. 16. 33.

Ego vici mundum.

TU contra mundum dux es meus, optime Jesu ?
At tu (me miserum !) dux meus ipse jaces.

Si tu, dux meus, ipse jaces, spes ulla salutis ?
Immo, ni jaceas tu, mihi nulla salus.

In ascensionem Dominicam.

VAdit (Io !) per aperta sui penetralia cœli :
It cœlo, & cœlum fundit ab ore novum.

Spargitur ante pedes, & toto sidere pronus
Jam propiùs Solis Sol bibit ora sui.

At fratrì debere negans sua lumina Phœbe,
Aurea de Phœbo jam meliore redit.

Hos, de te victo, tu das (Pater) ipse triumphos :
Unde triumphares, quis satìs alter erat ?

---

1 *(Heading)* Pontium] Pontiũ: Pilat: *D*   3·3 *ulla*] nulla *D*
4·8 *erat*] erit *D*

In descensum Spiritûs sancti.

JAm cœli circùm tonuit fragor : arma, minásque
    Turbida cum flammis mista ferebat hyems.

Exclamat Judæus atrox ; Venit ecce nefandis,
    Ecce venit meriti fulminis ira memor.

Verùm ubi composito sedit fax blandior astro,
    Flammáque non læsas lambit amica comas ;

Judæis, fulmen quia falsum apparuit esse,
    Hoc ipso verum nomine fulmen erat.

J O A N N. 3. 16.

Sic dilexit mundum Deus, ut Filium morti traderet.

AH nimis est, illum nostræ vel tradere vitæ :
    Guttula quod faceret, cur facit oceanus ?

Unde & luxuriare potest, habet hinc mea vita :
    Amplè & magnificè mors habet unde mori.

L u c. 14. 19.

Juga boum emi.

AD cœnam voco te (domini quod jussa volebant)
    Tu mihi, nescio quos, dicis (inepte) boves.

Imò vale, nobis nec digne nec utilis hospes !
    Cœna tuos (credo) malit habere boves.

A c t. 14.

D. Paulum, verbo sanantem claudum, pro Mercurio Lystres adorant.

QUis Tagus hic, quæ Pactoli nova volvitur unda ?
    Non hominis vox est hæc : Deus ille, Deus.

Salve, mortales nimiùm dignate penates !
    Digna Deo soboles, digna tonante Deo !

O salve ! quid enim (alme) tuos latuisse volebas ?
    Te dicit certè vel tua lingua Deum.

Laudem hanc haud miror : Meruit facundus haberi,
    Qui claudo promptos suasit habere pedes.

1·5 *sedit*] sedeat *D*   1·8 *erat*] erit *D*

In S. Columbam ad Christi caput sedentem.

C*Ui* sacra *sydereâ* volucris *suspenditur alâ ?*
     Hunc nive plùs niveum cui dabit illa pedem ?

Christe, tuo capiti totis se destinat auris,
     Quà ludit densæ blandior umbra comæ.

Illîc arcano quid non tibi murmure narrat ?
     (*Murmure mortales non imitante sonos*)

Sola avis hæc *nido hoc non est indigna cubare :*
     Solus nidus hic *est hâc bene dignus ave.*

A c t. 12.

In fores Divo Petro sponte apertas.

Q*Uid juvit clausisse fores (bone janitor) istas ?*
     Et Petro claves *jam liquet esse suas.*

Dices, Sponte patent : Petri ergò hoc scilicet ipsum
     Est clavis, Petro clave quòd haud opus est.

L u c. 15. 2.

Murmurabant Pharisæi, dicentes, Recipit peccatores & comedit cum illis.

A*H malè, quisquis is est, pereat ! qui scilicet istis*
     Convivam (sævus !) non sinit esse suum.

Istis cùm Christus conviva adjungitur, istis
     O non conviva est Christus, at ipse cibus.

M a t t h. 15.

In trabem Pharisaicam.

C*Edant, quæ, rerum si quid tenue atque minutum est,*
     Posse acie certâ figere, vitra dabunt.

Artis opus miræ ! Pharisæo en optica trabs *est,*
     Ipsum (vera loquor) quâ videt ille nihil.

JOANN. 9. 22.

Constituerunt ut si quis confiteretur eum esse
Christum, synagogâ moveretur.

INfelix, *Christum* reus *es quicunque colendi !*
   O reus infelix ! quàm tua culpa gravis !
Tu summis igitur, summis damnabere *cœlis :*
   O reus infelix ! quàm tua pœna gravis !

MATTH. 20. 20.

De voto filiorum Zebedæi.

SIt tibi (*Joannes*) *tibi sit* (*Jacobe*) *quod optas :*
   Sit tibi dextra *manus ; sit tibi* læva *manus.*
Spero, alia in cœlo est, & non incommoda, sedes :
   Si neque læva *manus ; si neque* dextra *manus.*
Cœli hanc aut illam *nolo mihi quærere partem :*
   O, cœlum, cœlum *da* (*Pater alme*) *mihi.*

JOANN. 6.

Ad hospites cœnæ miraculosæ quinque panum.

VEscere pane tuo : *sed & (hospes) vescere Christo :*
   Est panis pani scilicet ille tuo.
Tunc pane hoc CHRISTI rectè satur (hospes) abibis,
   Panem ipsum CHRISTUM si magìs esurias.

JOANN. 16. 33.

De Christi contra mundum pugna.

TUne, miser ? tu (*Mundus ait*) *mea fulmina contra*
   Ferre manus, armis cùm tibi nuda manus ?
I lictor ; manibúsque audacibus injice vinc'la :
   Injecit lictor vincula, & arma dedit.

1 *Heading in D*: Si quis fateretur X:ᵗᵘ Synagoga expellatur
1·1 *es*] est *D*   2·1 *tibi sit*] sit tibi *D*   2·3 *cœlo*] Cælis *D*
2·5 *quærere*] credere *D*   3 (*Heading*) quinque panum] *omitted in A 4*
3·3 *Tunc*] Tum *A 4*   *satur*] sapit *D*   3·4 *ipsum CHRISTUM*]
Christum ex hoc *A 4*   4 *Heading in D*: De Pugna Saluatoris contra
mundũ   De . . . pugna] Ego vici mundum *A 4*   4·4 *vincula*]
Uincla *D*

A c t. 9. 29.

Græci disputatores Divo Paulo mortem machinantur.

E*Uge argumentum !* sic disputat : *euge sophista !*
  Sic pugnum Logices stringere, sic decuit.
Hoc argumentum in causam quid (Græcule) dicit?
  Dicit, te in causam dicere posse nihil.

L u c. 22. 26.

Qui maximus est inter vos, esto sicut qui minimus.

O *Bone, discipulus Christi vis maximus esse ?*
  At verò fies hâc ratione minor.
Hoc sanctæ ambitionis iter (mihi crede) tenendum est,
  Hæc ratio ; Tu, nè sis minor, esse velis.

L u c. 19. 41.

In lacrymantem Dominum.

V*Obis (Judæi) vobis hæc volvitur unda ;*
  Quæ vobis, quoniam spernitis, ignis erit.
Eia faces (Romane) faces ! seges illa furoris,
  Non nisi ab his undis, ignea messis erit.

M a t t h. 2.

Christus in Ægypto.

H*Unc tu (Nile) tuis majori flumine monstra :*
  Hunc (nimis ignotum) *dic caput esse tibi.*
Jam tibi (Nile) tumes : jam te quoque multus inunda :
  Ipse tuæ jam sis lætitiæ fluvius.

M a t t h. 9.

In cæcos Christum confitentes, Pharisæos abnegantes.

N*E mihi, tu (Pharisæe ferox) tua lumina jactes :*
  En cæcus ! Christum cæcus at ille videt.
Tu (Pharisæe) nequis in Christo cernere Christum :
  Ille videt cæcus ; cæcus es ipse videns.

1·2 *pugnum*] Pugnâ *D*   1·3 *dicit*] dicat *D*   4·2 *dic*] ait *D*
5 (*Heading*) Pharisæos abnegantes] et Pharisæos negantes *D*   5·3
(*Pharisæe*) *nequis*] nequis, ô Pharisæe *A 4*   5·4 *A 4 distinguishes the line*

Matth. 16. 24.

Si quis pone me veniet, tollat crucem & sequatur me.

Ergò sequor, sequor *en! quippe & mihi crux mea, Christe, est:*
   Parva quidem ; sed quam non satìs, ecce, rego.
Non rego? non parvam hanc? ideo neque parva putanda est.
   Crux magna est, parvam non bene ferre crucem.

Luc. 5. 28.

Relictis omnibus sequutus est eum.

Quas Matthæus opes, *ad Christi jussa, reliquit,*
   Tum primùm verè cœpit habere suas.
Iste malarum est usus opum bonus, unicus iste ;
   Esse malas homini, quas bene perdat, opes.

Matth. 23. 29.

Ædificatis sepulchra Prophetarum.

SAnctorum in tumulis quid vult labor ille colendis?
   Sanctorum mortem non sinit ille mori.
Vane, Prophetarum quot ponis saxa sepulchris,
   Tot testes lapidum, queis periêre, facis.

Marc. 3.

In manum aridam quâ Christo mota est miseratio.

PRende (miser) Christum ; *& cum Christo prende salutem :*
   At manca est (dices) dextera : prende tamen.
Ipsum hoc, in Christum, manus est : hoc prendere Christum est,
   Quâ Christum prendas, non habuisse manum.

Ad D. Lucam medicum.

NUlla mihi (Luca) *de te medicamina posco,*
   Ipse licèt medicus sis, licèt æger ego :
Quippe ego in exemplum fidei dum te mihi pono,
   Tu, medice, ipse mihi es tu medicina mea.

1 *Heading in D*: Si Quis Pone veniat tollat Crucĕ &ct: 2.2
Tum] Tunc *D*   3 (*Heading*) 23. 25. 34 *etc.*   4 *Heading in D*:
In manum aridam a Christo sanatā   4.2 *dices*] dicis *D*

917.9   E

Luc. 14. 4.

Hydropicus sanatus, Christum jam sitiens.

PEllitur indè sitis ; sed & hinc sitis altera surgit :
　Hinc sitit ille magìs, quò sitit indè minús.

Fælix ô, & mortem poterit qui temnere morbus !
　Cui vitæ ex ipso fonte sititur aqua !

In cœtum cœlestem omnium Sanctorum.

FElices animæ ! quas cælo debita virtus
　Jam potuit vestris inseruisse polis.

Hoc dedit egregii non parcus sanguinis usus,
　Spésque per obstantes expatiata vias.

O ver ! ô longæ semper seges aurea lucis !
　Nocte nec alternâ dimidiata dies !

O quæ palma manu ridet ! quæ fronte corona !
　O nix virgineæ non temeranda togæ !

Pacis inocciduæ vos illîc ora videtis :
　Vos Agni dulcis lumina : vos——Quid ago ?　　10

Matth. 8. 13.

Christus absenti medetur.

VOx jam missa suas potuit jam tangere metas ?
　O superi ! non hoc ire sed îsse fuit.

Mirac'lum fuit ipsa salus (bene credere possis)
　Ipsum, mirac'lum est, quando salutis iter.

Joann. 9.

Cæcus natus.

FElix, qui potuit tantæ post nubila noctis
　(O dignum tantâ nocte !) videre diem :

Felix ille oculus, felix utrinque putandus ;
　Quòd videt, & primùm quòd videt ille Deum.

　1 (*Heading*) jam sitiens] sitiens *D*　　1·1 *hinc*] hic *D*　　2·10
Quid ago] quod Ego *D*　　4 (*Heading*) Joann. 9.] *omitted in A4*

MATTH. 9.
Et ridebant illum.

LUctibus in tantis, Christum ridere vacabat?
 Vanior iste fuit risus, an iste dolor?
Luctibus in tantis hic vester risus, inepti,
 (Credite mî) meruit maximus esse dolor.

MATTH. 11. 25.
In sapientiam seculi.

NOli altum sapere (*hoc veteres voluêre magistri*)
 Nè retrahat lassos alta ruina gradus.
Immo mihi dico, Noli sapuisse profundum :
 Non ego ad infernum me sapuisse velim.

In stabulum ubi natus est Dominus.

ILla domus stabulum ? *non est (Puer auree) non est :*
 Illa domus, quâ tu nasceris, est stabulum ?
Illa domus toto domus est pulcherrima mundo ;
 Vix cœlo dici vult minor illa tuo.

Cernis ut illa suo passim domus ardeat auro ?
 Cernis ut effusis rideat illa rosis ?

Sive aurum non est, nec quæ rosa rideat illîc ;
 Ex oculis facile est esse probare tuis.

ACT. 7.
S. Stephanus amicis suis, funus sibi curantibus.

NUlla (*precor*) *busto surgant mihi marmora : bustum*
 Hæc mihi sint mortis conscia saxa meæ.

Sic nec opus fuerit, notet ut quis carmine bustum,
 Pro Domino (*dicens*) *occidit ille suo.*

Hic mihi sit tumulus, quem mors dedit ipsa ; meíque
 Ipse hic martyrii *sit mihi* martyrium.

1·1 *vacabat*] uacabant D   1·2 *an iste*] an ille D   3·8
tuis] suis D   4 (*Heading*) ACT. 7.] ACT. 8. *34 : omitted in* A4
S. Stephanus . . . curantibus.] Sepulchralia S.[1] Stephani A4

E 2

In D. Joannem, quem Domitianus ferventi oleo (illæsum) indidit.

I*Llum (qui, toto currens vaga flammula mundo,*
  Non quidem Ioannes, ipse sed audit amor)
Illum ignem extingui, bone Domitiane, laboras ?
Hoc non est oleum, *Domitiane,* dare.

In tenellos Martyres.

A*H qui tam propero cecidit sic funere, vitæ*
  Hoc habuit tantùm, possit ut ille mori.
At cujus Deus est sic usus funere, mortis
  Hoc tantùm, ut possit vivere semper, habet.

Matth. 4. 24.

Attulerunt ei omnes malè affectos, dæmoniacos, lunaticos——& sanavit eos.

C*Ollige te tibi (torve Draco) furiásque facésque,*
  Quásque vocant pestes nox Erebúsque suas :
Fac colubros jam tota suos tua vibret Erinnys ;
  *Collige, collige te fortiter, ut——*pereas.

Luc. 2.

Tuam ipsius animam pertransibit gladius.

Q*Uando habeat* gladium *tua, Christe, tragœdia nullum,*
  Quis fuerit gladius, *Virgo beata, tuus?*
Námque nec ulla aliàs tibi sunt data vulnera, Virgo,
  Quàm quæ à vulneribus sunt data, Christe, tuis.
Forsan quando senex jam caligantior esset,
  Quod Simeon gladium *credidit,* hasta *fuit.*
Immo neque hasta *fuit, neque* clavus, *sed neque* spina :
  Hei mihi, spina *tamen,* clavus, *&* hasta *fuit.*
Nam queiscunque malis tua, Christe, tragœdia crevit,
  Omnia sunt gladius, *Virgo beata, tuus.*   10

1·1 *qui,*] qui in *D*   2·1 *cecidit*] accidit *D*   3 (*Heading*)
lunaticos——] *omitted in D*   3·4 *ut*——pereas] ——ut pereas *A* 4
4 (*Heading*) ipsius] *omitted in D*   4·3 *sunt data*] data sunt *D*
4·8 *tamen,*] *omitted in D*

In sanguinem circumcisionis Dominicæ.
Ad convivas, quos hæc dies apud nos solennes habet.

H*Eus conviva ! bibin' ? Maria hæc, Mariæque puellus,*
  Mittunt de prælo musta bibenda suo.

Una quidem est (toti quæ par tamen unica mundo)
  Unica gutta, suo quæ tremit orbiculo.

O bibite hinc ; quale aut quantum vos cunque bibistis,
  (Credite mî) nil tam suave bibistis adhuc.

O bibite & bibite ; & restat tamen usquè bibendum :
  Restat, quod poterit nulla domare sitis.

Scilicet hîc, mensura sitis, mensura bibendi est :
  Hæc quantum cupias vina bibisse, bibis.   10

L U C. 2.

Puer Jesus inter Doctores.

F*Allitur, ad mentum qui pendit quemque profundum,*
  Ceu possint læves nil sapuisse genæ.

Scilicet è barba malè mensuratur Apollo ;
  Et bene cum capitis stat nive, mentis hyems.

Discat, & à tenero disci quoque posse magistro :
  Canitiem capitis *nec putet esse* caput.

J O A N N. 2.

Ad Christum, de aqua in vinum versa.

S*Igna tuis tuus hostis habet contraria signis :*
  In vinum tristes tu mihi vertis aquas.

Ille autem è vino lacrymas & jurgia ducens,
  Vina *iterum in tristes (hei mihi !) mutat* aquas.

---

1 (*Heading*) quos . . . habet] *omitted in A4*   1·5 *hinc*] hic *D*
1·9 *hîc*] hæc *D*   2·6 *putet*] putat *D A4*   3 (*Heading*) JOANN. 2.]
omitted in D

L u c. 2.

Christus infans Patri sistitur in templo.

AGnus eat, ludátque (licet) sub patre petulco ;
  Cúmque sua longùm conjuge turtur agat.
Conciliatorem *nihil hîc opus ire per* agnum :
  Nec tener ut volucris non sua fata ferat.
Hactenus exigua hæc, quasi munera, lusimus ; hæc quæ
  Multum excusanti sunt capienda manu.
Hoc Donum est ; de quo, toto tibi dicimus ore,
  Sume Pater : *meritis hoc tibi sume suis.*
Donum hoc est, hoc est ; quod scilicet audeat ipso
  Esse Deo dignum : scilicet ipse Deus.   10

M a t t h. 8.

Leprosus Dominum implorans.

CRedo quòd ista potes, velles modó : sed quia credo,
  Christe, quòd ista potes, credo quòd ista voles.
Tu modò, tu faciles mihi, Sol meus, *exere vultus ;*
  Non poterit radios nix mea *ferre tuos.*

M a t t h. 8.

Christus in tempestate.

QUòd fervet tanto circum te, Christe, tumultu,
  Non hoc ira maris, Christe, sed ambitio est.
Hæc illa ambitio est, hoc tanto te rogat ore,
  Possit ut ad monitus, Christe, tacere tuos.

A c t. 16. 21.

Annunciant ritus, quos non licet nobis suscipere,
cùm simus Romani.

HOc Cæsar tibi (Roma) tuus dedit, armáque ? solis
  Romanis igitur non licet esse piis ?
Ah, meliùs, tragicis nullus tibi Cæsar in armis
  Altus anhelanti detonuisset equo ;

                    ferat
    1·4 *ferat*] premat *D*   1·9–10 *quod scilicet audeat ipso Esse*]
lautũ qᵈ scilicet ipso Esset *D*   2·3 *Tu modò*] En modo *D*
2·4 *poterit*] Potuit *D*   3·1 *fervet tanto*] tanto fervet *A 4*
4 (*Heading*) nobis . . . Romani] nobis suscipere Romanis *D*

Nec domini volucris *facies horrenda per orbem*
  Sueta tibi in signis torva venire tuis :

Quàm miser ut staret de te tibi (Roma) triumphus,
  Ut tantâ fieres ambitione nihil.

Non tibi, sed sceleri vincis : proh laurea tristis !
  Laurea, Cerbereis aptior umbra comis !   10

Tam turpi vix ipse pater diademate Pluto,
  Vix sedet ipse suo tam niger in solio.

De tot Cæsareis redit hoc tibi (Roma) triumphis :
  Cæsareè, *aut (quod idem est)* egregiè *misera es.*

M ATT H. 4.

Hic lapis fiat panis.

ET fuit : *ille lapis (quidni sit dicere ?) panis,*
  Christe, fuit : panis sed tuus *ille fuit.*

Quippe, Patris cùm sic tulerit suprema voluntas,
  Est panis, panem non habuisse, tuus.

M ATT H. 15.

Mulier Canaanitis.

QUicquid *Amazoniis dedit olim fama puellis,*
  Credite : Amazoniam *cernimus ecce* fidem.

Fœmina, tam fortis fidei ? jam credo fidem esse
  Plus quàm grammaticè fœminei generis.

L uc. ii.

Deus, post expulsum Dæmonem mutum, maledicis Judæis os obturat.

UNâ *penè operâ duplicem tibi Dæmona frangis :*
  Iste quidem Dæmon mutus ; *at ille* loquax.

Scilicet in laudes (quæ non tibi laurea surgit ?)
  Non magìs hic loquitur, *quàm* tacet *ille tuas.*

4 *(Heading)* Deus] D⁸ *A4*   4·2 *ille*] iste *D*

J o a n n. 6.

Dicebant, Verè hic est propheta.

POst tot quæ videant, tot quæ miracula tangant,
   Hæc & quæ gustent (Christe) dabas populo.

Jam Vates, Rex, & quicquid pia nomina possunt,
   Christus erat : vellem dicere, venter erat.

Namque his, quicquid erat Christus, de ventre repleto
   Omne illud vero nomine venter erat.

J o a n n. 10. 22.

Christus ambulabat in porticu Solomonis, & hyems erat.

BRuma fuit? non, non : ah non fuit, ore sub isto :
   Si fuit ; haud anni, nec sua bruma fuit.

Bruma tibi vernis velit ire decentior horis,
   Per sibi non natas expatiata rosas.

At, tibi nè possit se tam bene bruma negare,
   Sola hæc, quam vibrat gens tua, *grando vetat.

          * Vers. 31. sustulerunt lapides.

M a t t h. 28.

Dederunt nummos militibus.

NE miles velit ista loqui, tu munera donas ?
   Donas, quod possit, cùm tacet ipse, loqui.

Quæ facis à quoquam, pretio suadente, taceri ;
   Clariùs, & dici turpiùs ista facis.

Beatæ Virgini.

De salutatione Angelicâ.

XΑῖρε suum *neque Cæsareus jam nuntiet ales ;*
  Xαῖρε tuum *pennâ candidiore venit.*

Sed taceat, qui Xαῖρε tuum *quoque nuntiat, ales ;*
  Xαῖρε meum *pennâ candidiore venit.*

Quis dicat mihi Xαῖρε meum *magè candidus autor,*
  Quàm tibi qui dicit candidus ille tuum ?

Virgo, rogas, quid candidius quàm candidus ille
  Esse potest ? Virgo, quæ rogat, esse potest.

Xαῖρε tuum (*Virgo*) *donet tibi candidus ille ;*
  Donas candidior tu mihi Xαῖρε meum.   10

Xαῖρε meum *de* Xαῖρε tuo *quid differat, audi :*
  Ille tuum dicit, *tu* paris (*ecce*) *meum.*

Pontio lavanti.

N*On satìs est cædes, nisi stuprum hoc insuper addas,*
  Et tam virgineæ sis violator aquæ ?

Nympha quidem pura hæc & honesti filia fontis
  Luget, adulterio jam temerata tuo.

Casta verecundo properat cum murmure gutta,
  Nec satìs in lacrymam se putat esse suam.

Desine tam nitidos stuprare (ah, desine) rores :
  Aut dic, quæ miseras unda lavabit aquas.

In die Passionis Dominicæ.

T*Amne ego sim tetricus ? valeant jejunia : vinum*
  Est mihi dulce meo (nec pudet esse) cado.

Est mihi quod castis, neque prelum passa, racemis
  Palmite virgineo protulit uva parens.

1·6 *qui dicit*] quæ dicat *34 etc.*   2·1 *hoc insuper*] desuper *A 4*
3·1 *sim*] sum *D*   3·3 neque prelum] nec prelo *D*

Hoc mihi (ter denis sat enim maturuit annis)
Tandem ecce è dolio præbibit hasta suo.

Jámque it ; & ô quanto calet actus aromate torrens !
Acer ut hinc aurâ divite currit odor !

Quæ rosa per cyathos volitat tam viva Falernos ?
Massica quæ tanto sydere vina tremunt ?   10

O ego nescibam ; atque ecce est Vinum *illud* amoris :
Unde ego sim tantis, unde ego par cyathis ?

Vincor : & ô istis totus propè misceor auris :
Non ego sum tantis, non ego par cyathis.

Sed quid ego invicti metuo bona robora vini ?
*Ecce est, quæ validum diluit, *unda, merum.*

* Joh. 19. & continuò exivit sanguis & aqua.

In die Resurrectionis Dominicæ.

Venit ad sepulchrum Magdalena ferens aromata.

Q*Uin & tu quoque busta tui Phœnicis adora ;*
   Tu quoque fer tristes (*mens mea*) *delitias.*

Si nec aromata sunt, nec quod tibi fragrat amomum ;
(Qualis Magdalinâ est messis odora manu)

Est quod aromatibus præstat, quod præstat amomo :
Hæc tibi mollicula, hæc gemmea lacrymula.

Et lacryma est aliquid : *neque frustra Magdala flevit :*
Sentiit hæc, lacrymas non nihil esse suas.

His illa (& tunc cùm Domini caput iret amomo)
Invidiam capitis fecerat esse pedes.   10

Nunc quoque cùm sinus huic tanto sub aromate sudet,
Plus capit ex oculis, quo litet, illa suis.

Christe, decent lacrymæ : decet isto rore rigari
Vitæ hoc æternum mane, tuúmque diem.

1·7 *& ô*] et *D*   1·8 *Acer ut*] Quamꝗ acer *A4*   2 (*Heading*) In die] In Diem *D*   2 (*Heading*) Venit . . . aromata] Magdalena fert Aromata ad Sepulchrũ Jesu *D*   2·13 *decet isto*] decent ipso *D*

L u c. 24.

In cicatrices Domini adhuc superstites.

ARma vides ; arcus, pharetrámque, levésque sagittas,
   Et quocunque fuit nomine miles Amor.

His fuit usus Amor : sed & hæc fuit ipse ; suúmque
   Et jaculum, & jaculis ipse pharetra suis.

Nunc splendent tantùm, & deterso pulvere belli
   E memori pendent nomina magna tholo.

Tempus erit tamen, hæc iræ quando arma, pharetrámque
   Et sobolem pharetræ spicula tradet Amor.

Heu ! quâ tunc animâ, quo stabit conscia vultu,
   Quum scelus agnoscet dextera quæque suum ?   10

Improbe, quæ dederis, cernes ibi vulnera, miles,
   Quâ tibi cunque tuus luserit arte furor.

Seu digito suadente tuo mala Laurus inibat
   Temporibus ; sacrum seu bibit hasta latus :

Sive tuo clavi sævùm rubuêre sub ictu ;
   Seu puduit jussis ire flagella tuis.

Improbe, quæ dederis, cernes ibi vulnera, miles :
   Quod dederis vulnus, cernere, vulnus erit.

Plaga sui vindex clavósque rependet & hastam :
   Quóque rependet, erit clavus & hasta sibi.   20

Quis tam terribiles, tam justas moverit iras ?
   Vulnera pugnabunt (Christe) vel ipsa tibi.

J o a n n. 14.

Pacem meam do vobis.

BElla vocant : arma (ô socii) nostra arma paremus
   Atque enses : nostros scilicet (ah !) jugulos.

Cur ego bella paro, cùm Christus det mihi pacem ?
   Quòd Christus pacem dat mihi, bella paro.

Ille dedit (nam quis potuit dare certior autor ?)
   Ille dedit pacem : sed dedit ille suam.

1·11 *cernes*] cernis *D*   1·15 *sævùm rubuêre*] durum ingemuere *A 4*
2·4 *dat*] det *D*

Act. 9.

In D. Paulum illuminatum simul & excæcatum.

Q*Uæ, Christe, ambigua hæc* bifidi *tibi gloria* teli *est,*
  Quod simul huic oculos abstulit, atque dedit ?
Sancta dies animi, hac oculorum in nocte, latebat ;
  Te ut possit Paulus cernere, cæcus erat.

Joann. 15.

Ego sum via. Ad Judæos spretores Christi.

O *Sed nec calcanda tamen : pes improbe pergis ?*
  Improbe pes, ergò hoc cœli erat ire viam ?
Ah pereat (Judæe ferox) pes improbus ille,
  Qui cœli tritam *sic facit esse* viam.

Matth. 2.

In nocturnum & hyemale iter infantis Domini.

E*Rgò viatores teneros, cum Prole Parentem,*
  Nox habet hos, queîs est digna nec ulla dies ?
Nam quid ad hæc Pueri vel labra, genásve Parentis ?
  Heu quid ad hæc facient oscula, nox & hyems ?
Lilia ad hæc facerent, faceret rosa ; quicquid & halat
  Æterna Zephyrus qui tepet in viola.
Hi meruêre, quibus vel nox sit nulla ; vel ulla
  Si sit, eat nostrâ puriùs illa die.
Ecce sed hos quoque nox & hyems clausêre tenellos :
  Et quis scit, quid nox, quid meditetur hyems ? 10
Ah nè quid meditetur hyems sævire per Austros !
  Quæque solet nigros nox mala ferre metus !
Ah nè noctis eat currus non mollibus Euris !
  Aspera nè tetricos nuntiet aura Notos !

2 *Heading in A4* : Joh: 15. | (Ad Judæos spretores Ch:[1]) | Ego sum via.
3 *(Heading)* & hyemale] *omitted in A4*   3 *Verses arranged in*
quatrains, not couplets, in D   3·8 *nostrâ*] nostro *D*   3·10, 11
meditetur] meditatur *D*

Heu quot habent tenebræ, quot vera pericula secum !
Quot noctem dominam, quantáque monstra colunt !

Quot vaga quæ falsis veniunt ludibria formis !
Trux oculus ! Stygio concolor ala Deo !

Seu veris ea, sive vagis stant monstra figuris ;
Virginei satìs est hinc, satìs indè metûs. 20

Ergò veni ; totóque veni resonantior arcu,
(Cynthia) prægnantem clange procul pharetram.

Monstra vel ista, vel illa, tuis sint meta sagittis :
Nec fratris jaculum certior aura vehat.

Ergò veni ; totóque veni flagrantior ore,
Dignáque Apollineas sustinuisse vices.

Scis bene quid deceat Phœbi lucere sororem :
Ex his, si nescis, (Cynthia) disce genis.

O tua, in his, quantò lampas formosior iret !
Nox suam, ab his, quantò malit habere diem ! 30

Quantùm ageret tacitos hæc luna modestior ignes !
Atque verecundis sobria staret equis !

Luna, tuæ non est rosa tam pudibunda diei :
Nec tam virgineo fax tua flore tremit.

Ergò veni ; sed & astra, tuas age (Cynthia) turmas :
Illa oculos pueri, quos imitentur, habent.

Hinc oculo, hinc astro ; at parili face nictat utrumque ;
Ætheris os, atque os æthereum Pueri.

Aspice, quàm bene res utriusque deceret utrumque !
Quàm bene in alternas mutua regna manus ! 40

Ille oculus cœli hôc si staret in æthere frontis ;
Sive astrum hoc Pueri, fronte sub ætherea.

Si Pueri hoc astrum ætherea sub fronte micaret,
Credat & hunc oculum non minùs esse suum.

Ille oculus cœli, hoc si staret in æthere frontis,
Non minùs in cœlis se putet esse suis.

Tam pulchras variare vices cum fronte Puelli,
Cúmque Puelli oculis, æther & astra queant.

22 *clange*] plange *A 4*   25 *flagrantior*] fragrantior *D*   27
quid] quod *D*   28 *Ex his, si nescis,*] Vel si nescis, ab his *A 4*   37 *at*]
ac *D*   41 *si*] seu *A 4*

Astra quidem vellent ; vellent æterna pacisci
   Fœdera mutatæ sedis inire vicem.   50

Æther & *ipse* (licèt numero tam dispare) vellet
   Mutatis oculis tam bona pacta dari.

Quippe iret cœlum quantò melioribus astris,
   Astra sua hos oculos si modò habere queat !

Quippe astra in cœlo quantum meliore micarent,
   Si frontem hanc possint cœlum habuisse suum.

Æther & astra velint : frustra velit æther, & astra :
   Ecce negat Pueri frons, oculíque negant.

Ah neget illa, negent illi : nam quem æthera mallent
   Isti oculi ? aut frons hæc quæ magìs astra velit ?   60

Quid si aliquod blandâ face lenè renideat astrum ?
   Lactea si cœli térque quatérque via est ?

Blandior hic oculus, roseo hôc qui ridet in ore ;
   Lactea frons hæc est térque quatérque magis.

Ergò negent, cœlúmque suum sua sydera servent :
   Sydera de cœlis non bene danda suis.

Ergò negant : séque ecce sua sub nube recondunt,
   Sub tenera occidui nube supercilii :

Nec claudi contenta sui munimine cœli,
   Quærunt in gremio Matris ubi lateant.   70

Non nisi sic tactis ubi nix tepet illa pruinis,
   Castáque non gelido frigore vernat hyems.

Scilicet iste dies tam pulchro vespere tingi
   Dignus ; & hos soles sic decet occidere.

Claudat purpureus qui claudit vesper Olympum ;
   Puniceo placeas tu tibi (*Phœbe*) toro ;

Dum tibi lascivam Thetis auget adultera noctem,
   Pone per Hesperias strata pudenda rosas.

Illas nempe rosas, quas conscia purpura pinxit ;
   Culpa pudórque suus queîs dedit esse rosas.   80

Hos soles, niveæ noctes, castúmque cubile,
   Quod purum sternit per mare virgo Thetis ;

---

50 *vicem*] viã *D*   57 *velit*] velint *D*   61 *lenè*] bene
D   67 *negant*] negent *D*   71 *ubi*] qua *A4*   72 *Castáque*]
Casta ubi *A4*   80 *suus*] suis *D*   *esse rosas*] illa rosis *D*   82
sternit A4 : sternet *34*

Hos, sancti flores ; hos, tam sincera decebant
  Lilia ; quæque sibi non rubuêre rosæ.

Hos, decuit sinus hic ; ubi toto sydere proni
  Ecce lavant sese lacteo in oceano.

Atque lavent : tandémque suo se mane resolvant,
  Ipsa dies ex hoc ut bibat ore diem.

J O A N N. 16. 26.

Non dico, me rogaturum Patrem pro vobis.

AH tamen Ipse roga : *tibi scilicet ille roganti*
  Esse nequit durus, nec solet esse, Pater.

Ille suos omni facie te figit amores ;
  Inque tuos toto effunditur ore sinus.

Quippe, tuos spectans oculos, se spectat in illis ;
  Inque tuo (Jesu) se fovet ipse sinu.

Ex te metitur sese, & sua numina discit :
  Indè repercussus redditur ipse sibi.

Ille tibi se, te ille sibi par nectit utrinque :
  Tam tuus est, ut nec sit magìs ille suus. 10

Ergò roga : Ipse roga : *tibi scilicet ille roganti*
  Esse nequit durus, nec solet esse, Pater.

Illum ut ego rogitem ? Hôc (eheu) non ore rogandum ;
  Ore satìs puras non faciente preces.

Illum ego si rogitem, quis scit quibus ille procellis
  Surgat, & in miserum hoc quæ tonet ira caput ?

Isto etiam forsan veniet mihi fulmen ab ore :
  (Sæpe isto certè fulmen ab ore venit)

Ille unâ irati forsan me cuspide verbi,
  Uno me nutu figet, & interii : 20

Non ego, non rogitem : mihi scilicet ille roganti
  Durior esse potest, & solet esse, Pater.

Immo rogabo : nec ore meo tamen : immo rogabo
  Ore meo (Jesu) scilicet ore tuo.

87 *tandémque suo*] donec roseo *A* 4   *resolvant*] resoluent *D*
2·13 *ut ego*] eheu ut *D*   2·16 *is the concluding line in D*

In die Ascensionis Dominicæ.

USque etiam nostros Te (Christe) tenemus amores?
 Heu cœli quantam hinc invidiam patimur!

Invidiam patiamur: habent sua sydera cœli;
 Quæque comunt tremulas crispa tot ora faces;

Phœbênque & Phœbum, & tot pictæ vellera nubis;
 Vellera, quæ roseâ Sol variavit acu.

Quantum erat, ut sinerent hâc unâ nos face ferri?
 Una sit hîc: sunt (& sint) ibi mille faces.

Nil agimus: nam tu quia non ascendis ad illum,
 Æther * descendit (Christe) vel ipse tibi.   10

  * Act. 1. Nubes susceptum eum abstulit.

FINIS.

10 *A 4 distinguishes the line*

Richardi Crashawi

POEMATA

ET

EPIGRAMMATA,

Quæ scripsit Latina & Græca,

Dum *Aulæ Pemb.* Alumnus fuit,

Et

Collegii *Petrensis* Socius.

Editio Secunda, Auctior & emendatior.

Εἵνεκεν ἐυμαθίης πινυτόφρον⊙, ἥν ὁ Μελιχρὸς
Ἤσκησεν, Μυσῶν ἄμμιγα ϰ̀ Χαρίτων.   Ἀνθολ.

CANTABRIGIÆ,

Ex Officina *Joan. Hayes,* Celeberrimæ Academiæ
Typographi. 1670.

Ἄνδρες, ἰδού, (ἑτέροισι νόοις) δύω ἱρον ἐσῆλθον·
Τήλοθεν ὀρρωδεῖ κεῖνος ὁ φρικαλέος,
Ἀλλ' ὁ μὲν ὡς σοβαρὸς νηοῦ μυχὸν ἐγγὺς ἱκάνει·
Πλεῖον ὁ μὲν νηοῦ, πλεῖον ὁ δ' εἶχε θεοῦ.

Κερματίοιο βραχεῖα ῥάνις, βιότοιο τ' ἀφαυρῆς
Ἕρκος, ἀποστάζει χειρὸς ἀπὸ τρομέρας.
Τοῖς δὲ ἀνασκιρτᾷ πολὺς ἀφρὸς ἀναίδεος ὄλβου·
Οἱ μὲν ἀπόρριπτον· κεῖνα δέδωκε μόνον.

Φαίδιμε, μοὶ αὐτὸν μᾶλλόν μοι δείκνυθι αὐτόν.
Αὐτός μου, δέομαι, αὐτὸς ἔχη δάκρυα.
Εἰ δὲ τόπόν μοι δεικνύναι ἅλις ἐστὶ, καὶ εἰπεῖν
Ὧδε τεὸς Μαριὰμ (ἤνιδε) κεῖτο ἄναξ.
Ἀγκοίνάς μου δεικνύναι δύναμαι γε, καὶ εἰπεῖν
Ὧδε τεὸς Μαριὰμ (ἤνιδε) κεῖτο ἄναξ.

Οὐρανοῦ ἐκτύπησε βρόμος· πόλεμον καὶ ἀπειλὰς
Ἦγε τρέχων ἄνεμος σὺν φλογὶ σμερδαλέῃ.
Αὖεν Ἰουδαῖος. μιαρὰ στυγερῶν τὰ κάρηνα
Ἔφθασε τῆς ὀργῆς τὸ πρέπον οὐρανίης.
Ἀλλὰ γαληναίῳ ὅτε κεῖται ἥσυχον ἄστρῳ
Φλέγμα, καὶ ἀβλήτους λείχε φιλὸν πλοκαμούς,
Ἐκθαμβεῖ. ὅτι γὰρ κείνοις οὔκ ἦεν ἀληθής,
Νυνὶ ἐτεὸν διότι τῷδε κεραυνὸς ἔῃ.

1 Ἄνδρες, ἰδού, &c. Follows epigram beginning 'En duo Templum'
(see p. 15, above)   2 Κερματίοιο &c. Follows epigram beginning
'Gutta brevis' (see p. 17, above)   3 Φαίδιμε, &c. Follows epigram
beginning 'Ipsum, Ipsum (precor)' (see p. 28, above)   4 Οὐρανοῦ &c.
Follows epigram beginning 'Jam cœli' (see p. 45, above)   4·2
σμερδαλέῃ] σμιρδαλέῃ 70L

F 2

Πῆ ταχυεργὸς ἄγει πτέρυγ' ἀστερόεσσαν ἐρετμὸς ;
  Ἦ τινὶ κεῖνα φέρει τὴν πόδα χιονέην ;

Χριστὲ τεῇ κεφαλῇ πάσαις πτερύγεσσιν ἐπείγει·
  Πῆ σκιά τοι δασίοις παίζε μάλα πλοκάμοις.

Ποῖά σοι ἀρρήτῳ ψιθυρίσματι κεῖν' ἀγορεύει ;
  Ἄρρητ', οὐκ ἠχῆς ἶσα μὲν ἀνδρομέης.

Μοῦνα μὲν ἠδ' ὄρνις καλιᾶς ἐστ' ἄξια ταύτης·
  Ἄξια δ' ὄρνιθος μοῦνα μὲν ἡ καλιά.

Οὐδὲν ἐγὼ, Λουκᾶ, παρά σου μοι φάρμακον αἰτῶ,
  Κἂν σὺ δ' ἰατρὸς ἔῃς, κἂν μεν ἐγὼ νοσερός.

Ἀλλ' ἐν ὅσῳ παράδειγμα πέλεις μοι πίστιος, αὐτὸς,
  Αὐτὸς ἰατρὸς, ἐμοὶ γ' ἐσσὶ ἀκεστορίη.

Οἶκος ὅδ' ἐστ' αὔλη. οὐ μή.   τεὸς οἶκος, Ἰησοῦ,
  Ἐν θ' ᾧ τὺ τίκτῃ αὔλιον οὐ πέλεται.

Οἴκων μὲν πάντων μάλα δὴ κάλλιστος ἐκεῖνος·
  Οὐρανοῦ οὐδὲ τεοῦ μικρότερος πέλεται.

Ἤνιδε κεῖνο νεῷ δῶμ' ἐμπυρίζετο χρύσῳ,
  Ἤνιδε κεῖνο νεοῖς δῶμα ῥόδοισι γελᾷ.

Ἦν ῥόδον οὐχὶ γελᾷ, ἢν οὐδὲ τε χρύσον ἐκεῖθεν·
  Ἐκ σου δ' ὀφθαλμῶν ἐστὶν ἐλεγχέμεναι.

Ἄρτος ἔην τοι δῆτ' (εἰπεῖν θέμις ἐστὶν) ἐκεῖνος
  Χριστέ τοι ἄρτος ἔην καὶ λίθος· ἀλλὰ τεός.

Ἦν οὕτως τοῦ πατρὸς ἐῇ μεγάλου τὸ θέλημα
  Ἄρτος ὅτ' οὐκ ἦν τοι, Χριστὲ, τοι ἄρτος ἔην.

1 Πῆ ταχυεργὸς, *&c. Follows epigram beginning ' Cui sacra ' (see
p. 46, above)*   2 Οὐδὲν ἐγὼ, *&c. Follows epigram beginning ' Nulla
mihi ' (see p. 49, above)*   3 Οἶκος *&c. Follows epigram beginning
' Illa domus ' (see p. 51, above)*   3·1 τεὸς] σεὸς *70L*   4 Ἄρτος
&c. Follows epigram beginning ' Et fuit ' (see p., 55 above)   4·3
Ἦν] Ἤη *70L*

Ν Υ῀ν ἔτι ἡμέτερον σε, Χριστὲ, ἔχομεν τὸν ἔρωτα ;
    Οὐρανοῦ οὖν ὅσσον τὸν φθόνον ὡς ἔχομεν·

'Αλλὰ ἔχωμεν. ἔχει ἑὰ μὲν τὰ δ' ἀγάλματα αἰθήρ·
    Ἄστρατε, καὶ Φοῖβον, καὶ καλὰ τῶν νεφέλων.

῞Οσσον ἔην, ἡμῖν ὄφρ' εἴη ἐν τόδε ἄστρον ;
    Ἄστρον ἐν ἡμῖν ἦ· εἰσι τοι ἄστρ' ἕκατον.

Πάντα μάτην. ὅτι Χριστὲ συ οὐκ ἀνάβαινες ἐς αὐτὸν,
    Αὐτὸς μὲν κατέβη οὐρανὸς εἰς σε τεός.

L u c. 18.

Cæcus implorat Christum.

I Mproba turba tace. Mihi tam mea vota propinquant,
    Et linguam de me vis tacuisse meam ?

Tunc ego tunc taceam, mihi cùm meus ille loquetur :
    Si nescis, oculos vox habet ista meos.

O noctis miserere meæ, miserere ; per illam
    In te quæ primo riserit ore, diem.

O noctis miserere meæ, miserere ; per illam
    Quæ, nisi te videat, nox velit esse, diem.

O noctis miserere meæ, miserere ; per illam
    In te quam fidei nox habet ipsa, diem.   10

Hæc animi tam clara dies rogat illam oculorum :
    Illam, oro, dederis ; hanc mihi nè rapias.

Ν Υκτ' ἐλέησον ἐμήν. ἐλέησον. ναί τοι ἐκεῖνο
    Χριστὲ ἐμοῦ ἦμαρ, νὺξ ὅ γ' ἐμεῖο ἔχει.

'Οφθαλμῶν μὲν ἐκεῖνο, Θεὸς, δέεται τόδε γνώμης.
    Μή μοι τοῦτ' αἴρῃς, δός μοι ἐκεῖνο φάος.

Νῦν ἔτι &c. Follows epigram beginning 'Usque etiam' (see p. 64,
above)   1·4 Φοῖβον] φοῖβον 70L   2 Luc. 18. &c. Altered form in T.
See p. 362, below. Greek not in T   2·14 ὅ γ'] ὅδ' 70L

L U C. 15. 4.

Quis ex vobis si habeat centum oves, & perdiderit
unam ex illis ... &c.

O*Ut ego angelicis fiam bona gaudia turmis,*
Me quoque sollicito quære per arva gradu.

Mille tibi tutis ludunt in montibus agni,
Quos potes haud dubiâ dicere voce tuos.

Unus ego erravi quò me meus error agebat,
Unus ego fuerim gaudia plura tibi.

Gaudia non faciunt, quæ nec fecêre timorem ;
Et plus, quæ donant ipsa peric'la, placent.

Horum, quos retines, fuerit tibi latior usus.
De me, quem recipis, dulcior usus erit. 10

Ε Ἰς μὲν ἐγὼ, ἦ μου πλάνη περιῆγεν, ἄλημι·
῀Εις δὲ τοι σῶς ἔσομαι γηθοσύναι πλέονες.

Ἀμνὸς ὁ μή ποιῶν φόβον, οὐ ποιεῖ δέ τε χάρμα.
Μείζων τῶν μὲν, ἐμοῦ χρεῖα δὲ γλυκυτέρη.

Herodi D. Jacobum obtruncanti.

N*Escis Jacobus quantum hunc tibi debeat ictum,*
Quæque tua in sacrum sæviit ira caput.

Scilicet ipso illi donâsti hoc ense coronam,
Quo sacrum abscideras scilicet ense caput.

Abscissum pensare caput quæ possit abundè,
Sola hæc tam sæva & sacra corona fuit.

Ε Ν μὲν, Ἰάκωβε, κεφαλὴν τοι ξίφος ἀπῆρεν,
῀Εν τόδε καὶ στέφανον ξίφος ἔδωκε τεόν.

Μοῦνον ἀμείβεσθαι κεφαλὴν, Ἰάκωβε, δύναιτο
Κεῖνος ὅδ' ὡς καλὸς μαρτυρίου στέφανος.

Luc. 15. 4. &c. *Altered form in* T. *See p.* 357, *below. Greek not in* T
(*Heading*) Luc. 15. 4.] Luc. ix. T *with no further heading* 1·1 ut ego]
ego vt T 1·5 agebat,] abegit: T 1·8 ipsa peric'la,] ipsa, periĉla T
1·9 Horum] Ex his T 1·10 De] Ex T

MATTH. 20. 34.

Cæci receptis oculis Christum sequuntur.

ECce manu impositâ Christus nova sidera ponit.
  Sectantur patriam sidera fida manum.

Hæc manus his, credo, cælum est. Hæc scilicet astra
  Suspicor esse, olim quæ geret ille * manu.

* Revel. 1. 16.

ΧΕὶρ ἐπιβαλλομένη Χριστοῦ ἐπίβαλλεν ὀπωπῶν
  Ἄστρα. ὀπηδεύει κεῖνά γε χειρὶ Θεοῦ.

Χεὶρ αὕτη τούτοις πέλεν οὐρανός. ἄστρα γὰρ ὅιμαι,
  Ἐν χερὶ ταῦτ᾽ ὄισει Χριστὸς ἔπειτα ἑῇ.

LUC. 19. 4.

Zachæus in Sycomoro.

QUid te, quid jactas alienis fructibus, arbor?
  Quid tibi cum foliis non (Sycomore) tuis?

Quippe istic ramo qui jam tibi nutat ab alto,
  Mox è divinâ vite racemus erit.

ΤΙ´πτ᾽ ἐπικομπάζεις κενεόν; ξεινῷ δὲ τε καρπῷ,
  Καὶ φύλλοις σεμνὴ μὴ, συκόμωρε, τεοῖς;

Καί γαρ ὅδ᾽ ἐκκρημνὴς σοῦ νῦν μετέωρος ἀπ᾽ ἔρνους,
  Ἀμπέλου ὁ κλαδὼν ἔσσεται οὐρανίου.

FINIS.

STEPS
TO THE
TEMPLE.
Sacred Poems,

With other Delights of the MUSES.

By RICHARD CRASHAW, *sometimes of* Pembroke *Hall, and
late Fellow of S.* Peters *Coll.
in* Cambridge.

Printed and Published according to Order.

LONDON,
Printed by *T. W.* for *Humphrey Moseley*, and
are to be sold at his shop at the Princes
Armes in St. *Pauls* Church-
yard. 1646

The Preface to the Reader.

Learned Reader,

THe *Authors friend, will not usurpe much upon thy eye:*
This is onely for those, whom the name of our Divine Poet
hath not yet seized into admiration, I dare undertake, that what
Jamblicus (*in vita* Pythagoræ) *affirmeth of his Master, at his*
Contemplations, these Poems can, viz. *They shal lift thee*
Reader, some yards above the ground: and, as in Pythagoras
Schoole, every temper was first tuned into a height by severall
proportions of Musick; and spiritualiz'd for one of his weighty
Lectures; So maist thou take a Poem hence, and tune thy soule
by it, into a heavenly pitch; and thus refined and borne up upon 10
the wings of meditation, in these Poems thou maist talke freely
of God, and of that other state.

Here's Herbert's *second, but equall, who hath retriv'd Poetry*
of late, and return'd it up to its Primitive use; Let it bound
back to heaven gates, whence it came. Thinke yee, St. Augustine
would have steyned his graver Learning with a booke of Poetry,
had he fancied their dearest end to be the vanity of Love-Sonnets,
and Epithalamiums? No, no, he thought with this, our Poet,
that every foot in a high-borne verse, might helpe to measure the
soule into that better world: Divine Poetry; *I dare hold it,* 20
in position against Suarez *on the subject, to be the Language of*
the Angels; it is the Quintessence of Phantasie and discourse
center'd in Heaven; 'tis the very Outgoings of the soule; 'tis
what alone our Author is able to tell you, and that in his owne
verse.

It were prophane but to mention here in the Preface those
under-headed Poets, Retainers to seven shares and a halfe;
Madrigall fellowes, whose onely businesse in verse, is to rime
a poore six-penny soule, a Subburb sinner into hell;—May

3 *admiration,*] admiration. *48*   11 *meditation, 48: meditation. 46*
17 *their*] its *48*   29 *Subburb*] Subburd *46*

such arrogant pretenders to Poetry vanish, with their prodigious 30
issue of tumorous heats and flashes of their adulterate braines,
and for ever after, may this our Poet fill up the better roome of
man. Oh! *when the generall arraignment of Poets shall be, to*
give an accompt of their higher soules, with what a triumphant
brow, shall our divine Poet sit above, and looke downe upon
poore Homer, Virgil, Horace, Claudian ? &c. *who had amongst*
them the ill lucke to talke out a great part of their gallant Genius,
upon Bees, Dung, froggs, and Gnats, &c. and not as himselfe here,
upon Scriptures, divine Graces, Martyrs and Angels.

Reader, we stile his Sacred Poems, Stepps to the Temple, *and* 40
aptly, for in the Temple of God, under his wing, he led his life
in St. Maries *Church neere St.* Peters *Colledge : There he lodged*
under Tertullian's *roofe of Angels : There he made his nest more*
gladly then David's *Swallow neere the house of God : where like*
a primitive Saint, he offered more prayers in the night, then
others usually offer in the day ; There, he penned these Poems,
Stepps *for happy soules to climbe heaven by.*

And those other of his pieces intituled, The Delights of the
Muses, *(though of a more humane mixture) are as sweet as they*
are innocent. 50

The praises that follow are but few of many that might be
conferr'd on him, hee was excellent in five Languages (besides
his Mother tongue) vid. Hebrew, Greek, Latine, Italian, Spanish,
the two last whereof hee had little helpe in, they were of his owne
acquisition.

Amongst his other accomplishments in Accademick (as well
pious as harmlesse arts) hee made his skill in Poetry, Musicke,
Drawing, Limming, graving, (exercises of his curious invention
and sudden fancy) to bee but his subservient recreations for
vacant houres, not the grand businesse of his soule. 60

To the former Qualifications I might adde that which would ·
crowne them all, his rare moderation in diet (almost Lessian
temperance) hee never created a Muse out of distempers, nor with
our Canary scribblers) cast any strange mists of surfets before
the Jntelectuall beames of his mind or memory, the latter of which,
hee was so much a master of, that hee had there under locke and
key in readinesse, the richest treasures of the best Greeke and
Latine Poets, some of which Authors hee had more at his com-
mand by heart, then others that onely read their workes, to retaine
little, and understand lesse. 70

57 Poetry, 48 : Poetry 46   63 with] (with 48

Enough Reader, I intend not a volume of praises, larger then his booke, nor need I longer transport thee to thinke over his vast perfections, I will conclude all that I have impartially writ of this Learned young Gent. (now dead to us) as hee himselfe doth, with the last line of his Poem upon Bishop Andrews *Picture before his Sermons*

Verte paginas.

—Look on his following leaves, and see him breath.

The Authors Motto.

Live Jesus, Live, and let it bee
My life to dye, for love of thee.

The Weeper.

1   HAile *Sister Springs*,
Parents of Silver-forded rills !
Ever bubling things !
Thawing Christall ! Snowy Hills !
Still spending, never spent ; I meane
Thy faire Eyes sweet *Magdalene.*

2   Heavens thy faire Eyes bee,
Heavens of ever-falling stars,
Tis seed-time still with thee
And stars thou sow'st whose harvest dares
Promise the earth ; to countershine
What ever makes Heavens fore-head fine.

3   But wee are deceived all,
Stars they are indeed too true,
For they but seeme to fall
As Heavens other spangles doe :
It is not for our Earth and us,
To shine in things so pretious.

4   Vpwards thou dost weepe,
Heavens bosome drinks the gentle streame.
Where th' milky rivers meet,
Thine Crawles above and is the Creame.
Heaven, of such faire floods as this,
Heaven the Christall Ocean is.

The Weeper. For altered and extended version of this poem in 52 (and 48) see p. 308, below. 48 inserts after title the couplet 'Loe where a wounded heart etc.', which in 52 precedes the poem on a separate page. This couplet (only) is also in A1. Complete MS. versions in T A3. R gives stanzas 10–end, except 17 and 20, followed by 'The Teare'. Several preceding pages in R are torn out. S gives sts. 10, 11, 13 after 'The Teare', and then the couplet

         I'le weepe, and weepe, and will y^rfore
         Weepe, cause I can weepe no more.

Cp. p. 95, 4·3–4. For MS. Dobell see foot-notes p. 308 sqq.
   1·2 Silver-forded] *So also* 48 : syluer-footed *52 T*   2·5 earth ;] earth, *48* : earth *52 70 T A3*   3·1 wee are] we're *70* : w'are *T* : we are *48* : we'are *52*   3·2 they are indeed] indeed they are *48 52* : they're indeed *70*   4·3 meet] creepe *48 52 T A3*   4·4 Crawles] floates *48 52* 4·5–6 *Cp. 52*   4·5 floods as this,] floods, as these, *T*

5   Every morne from hence,
   A briske Cherub something sips
    Whose soft influence
   Adds sweetnesse to his sweetest lips.
  Then to his Musicke, and his song
  Tastes of this breakefast all day long.

6   When some new bright guest
   Takes up among the stars a roome,
    And Heaven will make a feast,
   Angels with their Bottles come ;
  And draw from these full Eyes of thine,
  Their Masters water, their owne Wine.

7   The dew no more will weepe,
   The Primroses pale cheeke to decke,
    The deaw no more will sleepe,
   Nuzzel'd in the Lillies necke.
  Much rather would it tremble heere,
  And leave them both to bee thy Teare.

8   Not the soft Gold which
   Steales from the Amber-weeping Tree,
    Makes sorrow halfe so Rich,
   As the drops distil'd from thee.
  Sorrowes best Iewels lye in these
  Caskets, of which Heaven keeps the Keyes.

9   When sorrow would be seene
   In her brightest Majesty,
    (For shee is a Queen)
   Then is shee drest by none but thee.
  Then, and onely then shee weares
  Her richest Pearles, I meane thy Teares.

5·3 soft] sacred *48 52* 5·5 Musicke,] musick. *52 T* : Musicke ; *A3*
5·6 this] his *48* *st. 6 is st. 12 in 48 52* 6·4 their Bottles] Crystall
Voyalls *48 52* 6·5 these] those *A3* 6·6 *A3 distinguishes* their
own wine. *st. 7 is st. 8 in 48 52* 7·2 cheeke] cheekes *A3* 7·5–
6 tremble heere . . . Teare] *See 52, st. 8* *st. 8 not in 48 52*. *A3 re-
verses sts. 8 and 9* *st. 9 is st. 7 in 48 52* 9·6 richest] proudest *48 52*

10   Not in the Evenings Eyes
            When they red with weeping are,
            For the Sun that dyes,
            Sits sorrow with a face so faire.
        Nowhere but heere did ever meet
        Sweetnesse so sad, sadnes so sweet.

11   Sadnesse all the while
            Shee sits in such a Throne as this,
            Can doe nought but smile,
            Nor beleeves shee sadnesse is.
        Gladnesse it selfe would bee more glad
        To bee made so sweetly sad.

12   There is no need at all
            That the Balsame-sweating bough
            So coyly should let fall,
            His med'cinable Teares ; for now
        Nature hath learn't t' extract a dew,
        More soveraigne and sweet from you.

13   Yet let the poore drops weepe,
            Weeping is the ease of woe,
            Softly let them creepe
            Sad that they are vanquish't so,
        They, though to others no releife
        May Balsame bee for their own grief.

14   Golden though hee bee,
            Golden *Tagus* murmurs though,
            Might hee flow from thee
            Content and quiet would he goe,
        Richer far does he esteeme
        Thy silver, then his golden streame.

st. 10 is st. 6 in 48 52   ¯10·1 Eyes] eye *R*   *st. 11 not in 48
52*   11·1 Sadnesse] Sadnes, *T*   11·4 beleeves] beleeue *A 3 R*
is. *A 3 S :* is *46 :* is : *70*   11·5 selfe] self, *R*   *st. 12 is st. 9 in
48 52*   12·1 There is] There 's *T A 3 R*   12·2 bough] tree *R*
12·6 and sweet] and more sweet *T R*   *st. 13 is st. 10 in 48 52*   13·2
ease *48 52 A 3 T R :* case *46S* (*T brackets the line*)   13·6 May Balsame
bee] Balsom may be *48 52*   *st. 14 is st. 13 in 48 52*   14·3–6.
See 52   14·2 murmurs though,] murmurs, though *Phillips* (1785) :
murmurs ; though *Turnbull* (1858). *But cf. p. 338, l. 10, below*   14·4
would he] he would *48 52 T*

15 Well does the *May* that lyes
  Smiling in thy cheekes, confesse,
   The *April* in thine eyes,
  Mutuall sweetnesse they expresse.
No *April* e're lent softer showres,
Nor *May* returned fairer flowers.

16 Thus dost thou melt the yeare
  Into a weeping motion,
   Each minute waiteth heere ;
  Takes his teare and gets him gone ;
By thine eyes tinct enobled thus
Time layes him up : he 's pretious.

17 Time as by thee he passes,
  Makes thy ever-watry eyes
   His Hower-Glasses.
  By them his steps he rectifies.
The sands he us'd no longer please,
For his owne sands hee'l use thy seas.

18 Does thy song lull the Ayre ?
  Thy teares just Cadence still keeps time.
   Does thy sweet breath'd *Prayer*
  Vp in clouds of Incense climbe ?
Still at each sigh, that is each stop :
A bead, that is a teare doth drop.

19 Does the Night arise ?
  Still thy teares doe fall, and fall.
   Does night loose her eyes ?
  Still the fountaine weeps for all.
Let night or day doe what they will
Thou hast thy taske, thou weepest still.

---

st. 15 is st. 14 in 48 52   15·3 thine] *thy T* 15·5–6.
See 52 *st. 15 is followed by st. 20 in T* *st. 16 is st. 25 in 48 52*
st. 16·1–3. See 52 *st. 17 not in R 48 52* 17·6 seas]
teares *T* *st. 18 is st. 24 in 48 52* 18·2. *See 52* 18·5
is] is, *48 52 A3 R* 18·6 teare] TEAR, *52 R T. A3 distinguishes*
Teare *st. 19 is st. 23 in 48 52*

20   Not, so long she liv'd,
            Will thy tombe report of thee
               But *so long she greiv'd*,
           Thus must we date thy memory.
Others by Dayes, by Monthes, by Yeares
Measure their Ages, Thou by Teares.

21   Say watry Brothers
            Yee simpering sons of those faire eyes,
               Your fertile Mothers.
           What hath our world that can entice
You to be borne ? what is't can borrow
You from her eyes swolne wombes of sorrow.

22   Whither away so fast ?
            O whither ? for the sluttish Earth
               Your sweetnesse cannot tast
           Nor does the dust deserve your Birth.
Whither hast ye then ? o say
Why yee trip so fast away ?

23   We goe not to seeke
            The darlings of *Aurora's* bed,
               The Roses modest cheeke
           Nor the Violets humble head.
No such thing ; we goe to meet
A worthier object, *Our Lords* feet.

---

st. 20 is st. 26 in 48 52. Not in R   st. 20. A 3 distinguishes ll. 1 and 3 and punctuates as follows :

               Not. So long shee liu'd,
               But. So long shee grieu'd

20·2 *Bracketed in* T   *st. 21 is st. 28 in 48 52, with many differences. See 52*   21·3 fertile] fruitfull *48 52* T *A 3* R   21·6 eyes] eyes, T *(comma doubtful in A 3)* eys ? R   *st. 22 is st. 29 in 48 52*   22·2, 5. *See 52*   22·2 sluttish] sordid *48 52* thirsty R   *st. 23 is expanded into sts. 30 and 31 in 48 52, q. v.*   23·2 darlings] darling T R 23·5 thing ;] thing. *A* T   23·6 worthier] worthy *48 52 A* T R   Lords] Lord Jesus T R

Crashaw — worships Mary — remorse
an example v mother figure —
worships God
he chose Mary.

The Teare ✓

wonder
awe

1. WHat bright soft thing is this ?
    Sweet *Mary* thy faire Eyes expence ?
      A moist sparke it is,
    A watry <u>Diamond</u> ; from whence
The very Terme, I think, was found
The water of a *Diamond*.

precious -ness v the te

Son Sunn

2.   O 'tis not a Teare,
      'Tis a starre about to drop
        From thine eye its spheare ;
      The <u>Sunne</u> will stoope and take it up.
Proud will his sister be to weare
This thine eyes Iewell in her Eare.

preciousness v tear

reverence to Mary
& her grief

3.   O 'tis a Teare,
      Too true a Teare ; for no sad eyne,
        How sad so e're
      Raine so true a Teare as thine ;
Each Drop leaving a place so deare,
Weeps for it selfe, is its owne Teare.

Mary — the
true exempla
v earth — the
mother figure

4.   Such a Pearle as this is,
    (Slipt from *Aurora's* dewy Brest)
      The Rose buds sweet lip kisses ;
    And such the Rose its selfe when vext
With ungentle flames, does shed,
Sweating in too warme a Bed.

tears ripen to blood ?

5.   Such the Maiden Gemme
    By the wanton Spring put on,
      Peeps from her Parent stemme,
    And blushes on the manly Sun :
This watry Blossome of thy Eyne
Ripe, will make the richer Wine.

marriage
symbol —
bride = soul
church = groom
Christ.

water — wine — blood

The Teare.   Also in 48 but not in 52. MSS. T A3 R S   1·1 bright
soft] bright=soft *T*   1·2 Eyes expence] eye expends *T R*   1·5
The very Terme, I think,] I thinke y^e very terme *S*   3·5 Drop]
place *R*   4·1 Pearle] pearle, *T*   4·2 *No brackets T R*   4·4 its] it
48   when] that's *R T A3*   4·6 too warme a] a too warme *R T :*
R omits st. 5, which is a variant of st. 11 of ' The Weeper' in 48 52, q.v.
p. 310, below. The stanza is thus practically given twice in 48   5·4
manly *T A3 :* watry *46 48*

grief for her son — indeed, for all mankind —
who must die to be saved.

titude – awe/wonder / reverence at her / if – at the / life v tears.

gr. respect + rev. for the V. mother / v Christ – next to Jesus, she / is a gr. obj. v worship

6
    Faire Drop, why quak'st thou so ?
  'Cause thou streight must lay thy Head
      In the Dust ? ô no ;
    The Dust shall never bee thy Bed :
A pillow for thee will I bring,
Stuft with Downe of Angels wing.

angels down – a / pillow for the tear.

7
    Thus carryed up on high,
  (For to Heaven thou must goe) –
    Sweetly shalt thou lye,
  And in soft slumbers bath thy woe ;
Till the singing Orbes awake thee,
And one of their bright *Chorus* make thee.

tears/ remorse – go to / heaven – God hears / man's contrition = / mercy v God.

8
    There thy selfe shalt bee
An eye, but not a weeping one,
    Yet I doubt of thee,
  Whither th'hadst rather there have shone
An eye of Heaven ; or still shine here
In th'Heaven of *Mary's* eye, a *Teare.*

mercy's tear / becomes an / eye v heaven – / a star? still / wd rather be a / tear

Divine Epigrams.

v is he worshipping? / not ?

symbol v baptism / sp cleansing –

On the water of our Lords *Baptisme.*

EAch blest drop, on each blest limme,
  Is washt it selfe, in washing him :
Tis a Gemme while it stayes here,
While it falls hence 'tis a Teare.

cleansing / water, tears.

yet Christ is more / pure than the / water wh. "cleanses" / his soul – ie He / cleanses the water.

Act. 8

On the baptized Æthiopian.

LEt it no longer be a forlorne hope
      To wash an Æthiope :
He 's washt, His gloomy skin a peacefull shade
      For his white soule is made :
And now, I doubt not, the Eternall Dove,
      A black-fac'd house will love.

6·3 ô] Ah *R*   8·1 shalt] shall *R*   8·4 th'hadst] thou'dst *S* :
th'adst *R*
   On the water &c.] MSS. *T A3 S. Heading in T :* Upon the water, w^ch
baptiz'd Christ.
   Act. 8 &c.] *MSS. T A3. Heading in T :* Acts. 8. *Upon the Æthiopian.*
Act.] Acts. *48*

On the miracle of multiplyed loaves.

SEe here an easie Feast that knowes no wound,
　That under Hungers Teeth will needs be sound :
A subtle Harvest of unbounded bread,
　What would ye more ? Here food it selfe is fed.

Vpon the Sepulchre of our Lord.

HEre, where our Lord once laid his Head,
　Now the Grave lies buried.

The Widowes Mites.

TWo Mites, two drops, (yet all her house and land)
　Falls from a steady Heart, though trembling hand :
The others wanton wealth foams high, and brave,
The other cast away, she onely gave.

Luk. 15.
On the Prodigall.

TEll me bright Boy, tell me my golden Lad,
　Whither away so frolick ? why so glad ?
What all thy Wealth in counsaile ? all thy state ?
Are Husks so deare ? troth 'tis a mighty rate.

On the still surviving markes of
our Saviours wounds.

WHat ever story of their crueltie,
　Or Naile, or Thorne, or Speare have writ in Thee,
　　Are in another sence
　　　Still legible ;
　　Sweet is the difference :
　　　Once I did spell

On the miracle &c.] MSS. T A3 S. Heading in T : John 6. *Upon the five loaves.* 2 sound] found *48* 4 ye] you *A3*
　Vpon the Sepulchre &c.] MSS. T A3. Heading in T : *On our Saviours Sepulcher.*
　The Widowes Mites.] MSS. T A3. Heading in T : *The Widdowes two mites.* 4 cast] threw *T*
　Luk. 15. &c.] MSS. T A3. Heading in T : Luke 15. 13. *Upon the rich young man.* Luk. 15.] *Not in 48* 3 What] What ! *T*
　On the Still &c.] MSS. T A3. Heading in T : *Upon the print of Christs wounds.* Joh. 20. 20. 3 in another sence] *bracketed T*

Every red letter
A wounded of thine,
Now, (what is better)
Balsome for mine.

Christ's sacrifice gives
mankind hope

Act. 5.

The sicke implore St. Peter'*s shadow.*

VNder thy shadow may I lurke a while,
Death's busie search I'le easily beguile :
Thy shadow *Peter*, must shew me the Sun,
My light's thy shadowes shadow, or 'tis done.

Mar. 7.

The dumbe healed, and the people
enjoyned silence.

CHrist bids the dumbe tongue speake, it speakes, the sound
Hee charges to be quiet, it runs round,
If in the first he us'd his fingers Touch :
His hands whole strength here, could not be too much.

Mat. 28.

Come see the place where the Lord lay.

SHow me himselfe, himselfe (bright Sir) O show
Which way my poore Tears to himselfe may goe,
Were it enough to show the place, and say,
Looke, *Mary*, here see, where thy Lord once lay,
Then could I show these armes of mine, and say
Looke, *Mary*, here see, where thy Lord once lay.

Act. 5. *&c.*] *MS. T. Heading in T :* Acts. 5. *The sick crave the shadow of Peter. In 48 the positions of this and of the preceding epigram are reversed.* Act.] Acts. *48* 3 shadow] shaddow, *48* T
Mar. 7 *&c.*] *MSS. T A3. Heading in T : Upon the tongue.* Mar.]
Mark. *48* 1 speakes,] speakes. *T A3* 2 round,] round : *48 :*
round. *T A3 T adds after l. 4 :*
Oh wild fire ! oh rude tongue ! if nought will shame thee,
Hell hath a wilder fire, and that shall tame thee.
Mat. 28 *&c.*] *MSS. T A3. Heading in T :* Mat. 28 *Mary to the Angell, shewing her the place, where Jesus lay.* 2 goe,] goe ; *48 A3 :*
goe. *T* 4 *Mary*, here see,] Mary here, see *48 :* Mary, here ; see *T :*
Mary, here see *A3* 6 here see,] here, see *48 :* heere, see *T :* here see *A3*

To Pontius *washing his hands.*

THy hands are washt, but ô the waters spilt,
  That labour'd to have washt thy guilt :
The flood, if any can, that can suffice,
  Must have its Fountaine in thine Eyes.

To the Infant Martyrs.

GOe smiling soules, your new built Cages breake,
  In Heav'n you'l learne to sing ere here to speake,
Nor let the milky fonts that bath your thirst,
          Bee your delay ;
The place that calls you hence, is at the worst
          Milke all the way.

christ — proves himself
phys. & sp. — bread &
life & bread & soul

tone = enthusiasm
image = bread — food

On the Miracle of Loaves.

NOw Lord, or never, they'l beleeve on thee,
  Thou to their Teeth hast prov'd thy Deity.

symbol & communion
suggested

Marke 4.

Why are yee afraid, O yee of little faith ?

AS if the storme meant him ;
  Or, 'cause Heavens face is dim,
  His needs a cloud.
Was ever froward wind
That could be so unkind,
  Or wave so proud ?
The Wind had need be angry, and the Water black,
That to the mighty *Neptune's* self dare threaten wrack.   8

There is no storme but this
Of your owne Cowardise

To Pontius *&c.*] *MSS. T A3. Heading in T : Pilate washes his hands.*
3 any can, *48 and* (?) *B.M. copy of 46 :* can *Bdl. copy of 46.* T *brackets*
if any can *and A3 places a single bracket after* can   4 its] his *T*
thine] thy *T A3*
  To the Infant Martyrs.] *MSS. T A3*   *To*] Upon *T*   2
speake,] speake : *48 :* speake. *T*
  On the Miracle &c.] *MS. T. Heading in T : On Christ's miracle at
the supper.*
  Marke 4. *&c.*] *MSS. T A3. Heading in T : Upon the disciples
awaking Christ in the storme.*   2 'cause] cause *B.M. copy of 1646.*
No break between ll. 8 and 9 in 48   9 storme] storme, *T*

That braves you out ;
You are the storme that mocks
Your selves ; you are the Rocks
Of your owne doubt :
Besides this feare of danger, there 's no danger here
And he that here feares Danger, does deserve his Feare. 16

On the Blessed Virgins bashfulnesse.

THat on her lap she casts her humble Eye ;
'Tis the sweet pride of her Humility.
The faire starre is well fixt, for where, ô where
Could she have fixt it on a fairer Spheare ?
'Tis Heav'n 'tis Heaven she sees, Heavens God there lyes
She can see heaven, and ne're lift up her eyes :
This new Guest to her Eyes new Lawes hath given,
'Twas once *looke up*, 'tis now *looke downe* to Heaven.

Vpon Lazarus *his Teares.*

RIch *Lazarus* ! richer in those Gems, thy Teares,
Then *Dives* in the Roabes he weares :
He scornes them now, but o they'l sute full well
With th'Purple he must weare in Hell.

Two went up into the Temple to pray.

TWo went to pray ? ô rather say
One went to brag, th'other to pray :
One stands up close and treads on high,
Where th'other dares not send his eye.

One neerer to Gods Altar trod,
The other to the Altars God.

12 storme] storme, *T*
On the Blessed &c.] MSS. *T A3* Dobell (ll. 5–8 only). *Heading in T:*
Upon the Virgins looking on our Saviour.   3 fixt,] fixt: *T*: fixt. *A3*
5 Heav'n 'tis] heaven, 'tis *48 T*   7 given,] given: *T*   *In Dobell the*
last four lines run as follows:

This new guest to our eys new laws hath giuen
Twas once looke up tis now looke downe to heauen
Tis heauen tis heauen we see, heau'ns god here lyes
We can see heauen & nere lift up our eys.

Vpon Lazarus *&c.*] *MSS. T A3*   Vpon] On *T*   1 thy
Teares, *48 A3* : thy Teares. *46* : those teares, *T*
Two went &c.] *MSS. T A3. Heading in T: Upon the Pharisee, &*
the Publicane. Not in couplets in 48   1 Two] Two men *A3*
4 send] lend *70*

Vpon the Asse that bore our Saviour.

HAth onely Anger an Omnipotence
   In Eloquence ?
Within the lips of Love and Ioy doth dwell
   No miracle ?
Why else had *Baalams* Asse a tongue to chide
   His Masters pride ?
And thou (Heaven-burthen'd Beast) hast ne're a word
   To praise thy Lord ?
That he should find a Tongue and vocall Thunder,
   Was a great wonder. 10
But ô me thinkes 'tis a farre greater one
   That thou find'st none.

Matthew 8.

I am not worthy that thou should'st come under my roofe.

THy God was making hast into thy roofe,
 Thy humble faith and feare keepes him aloofe :
Hee'l be thy Guest, because he may not be,
Hee'l come—into thy house ? no, into thee.

I am the Doore.

ANd now th'art set wide ope, The Speare's sad Art,
 Lo ! hath unlockt thee at the very Heart :
Hee to himselfe (I feare the worst)
  And his owne hope
Hath *shut* these Doores of Heaven, that durst
  Thus set them *ope*.

suffering
worships Christ in
his pain &
suffering —
Christ the door

symbol —

Vpon the Asse &c.] MSS. *T A3. Heading* in *T* : *Upon ye Asse that carried or Saviour.* 11 ô me thinkes] oh, (me thinkes,) *T*
 Matthew 8. *&c.*] MSS. *T A3. Heading* roofe.] roofe. &c. *T* 2 faith] faith, *48 T* feare] feare, *48* 4 come—] come *T* : come ; *A3* no,] No. *A3*
 46 next prints the epigram ' *Vpon the Powder Day* ' *removed in 48 to the* ' *Delights of the Muses* '. *See p. 185, below, and p. xlv, above.*
 I am the Doore.] MSS. *T A3* 2 Lo !] (Lord) *T*

Matthew. 9.

The blind cured by the word of our Saviour.

THou speak'st the word (thy word's a Law)
Thou spak'st and streight the blind man saw.

To speake and make the blind man see,
Was never man Lord spake like Thee.

To speake thus, was to speake (say I)
Not to his Eare, but to his Eye.

Matthew. 27.

And he answered them nothing.

O Mighty *Nothing* ! unto thee,
Nothing, wee owe all things that bee.
God spake once when hee all things made,
Hee sav'd all when hee *Nothing* said.
The world was made of *Nothing* then ;
'Tis made by *Nothyng* now againe.

To our Lord, upon the Water made Wine.

THou water turn'st to Wine (faire friend of Life)
Thy foe to crosse the sweet Arts of thy Reigne
Distills from thence the Teares of wrath and strife,
And so turnes wine to Water backe againe.

Matthew. 9. &c.] *MSS. T A 3. Heading in T : Upon Christs restoring
sight only by his word. Not in couplets in 48*   Matthew. 9.]
Matthew. 10. 46 &c.   1 speak'st] spak'st *T A 3*   3 see,]
see ? *T A 3*   4 No italics in 48. A 3 distinguishes the line*
Matthew. 27. &c.] *MSS. T A 3. Heading in T : Christ accused
answered nothing.*   3 spake once when] spake once, when *48 :
spake, when first T A 3*   4 all] all, *T*   5 Nothing then ;]
nothing ; then *T*
To our Lord &c.] *MSS. T A 3. Heading in T : Christ turnes water
into wine.*   1 turn'st] turn'dst *T*   2 Arts] acts *T A 3*

[handwritten marginalia: enthusiasm / worships Christ / & his conquest / over the priests / who question / him. / Christ's wisdom = / light, breaks / nets)]

Matthew. 22.

Neither durst any man from that Day aske him any more Questions.

Midst all the darke and knotty Snares,
    Blacke wit or malice can or dares,
Thy glorious wisdome breakes the Nets,
And treads with uncontrouled steps.
Thy quel'd foes are not onely now
Thy triumphes, but thy Trophies too :
They, both at once thy Conquests bee,
And thy Conquests memorye.
Stony amazement makes them stand
Waiting on thy victorious hand,   10
Like statues fixed to the fame
Of thy renoune, and their owne shame.
As if they onely meant to breath,
To bee the Life of their owne Death.
'Twas time to hold their Peace when they,
Had nere another word to say :
Yet is their silence unto thee,
The full sound of thy victory.
Their silence speakes aloud, and is
Thy well pronounc'd *Panegyris*.   20
While they speake nothing, they speake all
Their share, in thy Memoriall.
While they speake nothing, they proclaime
Thee, with the shrillest Trumpe of fame.
    To hold their peace is all the waies,
    These wretches have to speake thy praise.

Matthew. 22. *&c.*] *MS. A3*   2 Blacke] *So Bdl. copy of 46 :*
B.M. copy reads Blake   2 can] can,   *48 A3*   5, 6] *So Bdl. copy*
of 46. B.M. copy reads :

             Thy quell'd foes not onely now
             Thy quell'd foes are not onely two

9 Stony] *So Bdl. copy of 46 :* Strony *B.M. copy*   16 nere] not *A3*
17 thee,] thee *B.M. copy*   19 speakes] speake *A3*   is *48 A3 :*
is. *46*   22 share,] *So Bdl. copy of 46 :* share *B.M. copy of 46 48 A3*
24 Thee,] *So Bdl. copy of 46 :* Thee *B.M. copy*

Vpon our Saviours Tombe wherein never man was laid.

HOw Life and Death in Thee
           Agree ?
Thou had'st a virgin Wombe
           And Tombe.
A *Joseph* did betroth
           Them both.

tomb image
death/life cycle.

It is better to go into Heaven with one eye, &c.

ONe Eye ? a thousand rather, and a Thousand more
    To fix those full-fac't Glories, ô he 's poore
    Of Eyes that has but *Argus* store,
Yet if thou'lt fill one poore Eye, with thy Heaven and Thee,
    O grant (sweet Goodnesse) that one Eye may be
    All, and every whit of me.

— worships Christ /
God — his mercy
— enthusiasm /
— sight here =
sp. sight.

fill me with your goodness.

Luk. 11.

Vpon the dumbe Devill cast out, and the slanderous Jewes put to silence.

TWo Devills at one blow thou hast laid flat,
  A *speaking* Divell this, a *dumbe* one that.
Wa'st thy full victories fairer increase,
    That th'one spake, or that th'other held his peace ?

worships Christ
enthusiasm

Vpon our Saviours Tombe &c.] MSS. T A3 A2. Heading in T : In
Sepulcrum Domini. (Luke 23. *where was new man laid*)   Heading
in A3 : *Vpon our Sauiours Tombe ; (Wherin never was man laid.)*
Heading in A2 : *Crosh : In sepulchrū domini.* See also p. 279, below.
   It is better &c.] MSS. T A3. Heading in T : *It is better to enter into
the kingdom of God with one Eye &c.* Heading in A3 : *It is better to goe
into Heauen with one Eye. &c.*   3 store,] store. 48 A3 : store !
T.   *Space between ll. 3 and 4 in A3*   4 Heaven] heaven, 48 T
6 me] thee T
   Luk. 11. &c.] MSS. T A3. Heading in T : *Christ casteth out 2 divells
at once.*   Luk.] Luke. 48

Luke 10.

And a certaine Priest comming that way looked on him and passed by.

WHy dost Thou wound my wounds, ô Thou that passest by
Handling & turning them with an unwounded eye ?
The calm that cools thine eye does shipwrack mine, for ô !
Vnmov'd to see one wretched, is to make him so.

Luke 11.

Blessed be the paps which Thou hast sucked.

SVppose he had been Tabled at thy Teates,
Thy hunger feeles not what he eates :
Hee'l have his Teat e're long (a bloody one)
The Mother then must suck the Son.

To Pontius *washing his blood-stained hands.*

IS murther no sin ? or a sin so cheape,
That thou need'st heape
A Rape upon't ? till thy Adult'rous touch
Taught her these sullied cheeks this blubber'd face,
She was a Nimph, the meadowes knew none such,
Of honest Parentage of unstain'd Race,
The Daughter of a faire and well-fam'd Fountaine
As ever Silver-tipt, the side of shady mountaine.   8

See how she weeps, and weeps, that she appeares
Nothing but Teares ;
Each drop 's a Teare that weeps for her own wast ;
Harke how at every Touch she does complaine her :
Harke how she bids her frighted Drops make hast,
And with sad murmurs, chides the Hands that stain her.

Luke 10 *&c.*] *MSS. T A3. Heading in T : To them, yᵗ passed by at
oʳ Savioʳˢ passion.*   1 by] by, *48* : by ? *T*   3 *space (? intentional)
between ll. 2 and 3 in A3*
  Luke 11. *&c.*] *MSS. T A3. Heading in T : Blessed is —— & the
papps, wᶜʰ thou hast suckt &c.*
  To Pontius *&c.*] *MSS. T A3. Heading in T : On Pilate washing his
hands.*   1 Is] 'S *48*   2 need'st] did'st *48*   4 cheeks]
cheeks, *48 T A3*   6 Parentage] parentage, *48 T A3*   8
Silver-tipt,] Silver-tipt *48 T A3*   11 her] its *A3*   14 murmurs,]
murmur *T*   Hands] hand, *T :* hand *A3.*   stain] staines *T A3*

Leave, leave, for shame, or else (Good judge) decree,   15
What water shal wash this, when this hath washed thee.

Matthew 23.
Yee build the Sepulchres of the Prophets.

THou trim'st a Prophets Tombe, and dost bequeath
   The life thou took'st from him unto his *Death*.
Vaine man ! the stones that on his Tombe doe lye,
   Keepe but the score of them that made him dye.

Vpon the Infant Martyrs.

TO see both blended in one flood
   The Mothers Milke, the Childrens blood,
Makes me doubt if Heaven will gather,
Roses hence, or *Lillies* rather.

Joh. 16.
Verily I say unto you, yee shall weep and lament.

WElcome my Griefe, my Ioy ; how deare 's
   To me my Legacy of Teares !
I'le weepe, and weepe, and will therefore
Weepe, 'cause I can weepe no more :
   Thou, thou (Deare Lord) even thou alone,
Giv'st joy, even when thou givest none.

Joh. 15.
Vpon our Lords last comfortable discourse with his Disciples.

ALL *Hybla's* honey, all that sweetnesse can
   Flowes in thy Song (ô faire, ô dying Swan !)
Yet is the joy I take in't small or none ;
It is too sweet to be a long-liv'd one.

15 Leave, leave,] Oh, leave *T*
   Matthew 23. *&c.*] *MSS. T A3.   Heading in T : Ye build the sepul-chres &c.*   4 them] him, *T*
   Vpon the *&c.*] *MSS. T A3 S.   No heading in S*   2 *A3 distin-guishes* milke *and* blood   3 gather,] gather *48 T A3*   4 *A3 distinguishes* Roses *and* Lillies   hence] heere *T*
   Joh. 16. *&c.*] *MSS. T A3   (Heading)* yee] you *A3*   weep] weepe, *T*   3-4 *See note to heading of ' The Weeper ', p. 79, above.*
5 even] ô *A3* : oh *T*   6 givest none] giv'st us none *T*
   Joh. 15. *&c.*] *MSS. T A3.   No heading in T*

Luke 16. Dives *asking a drop.*

A Drop, one drop, how sweetly one faire drop
 Would tremble on my pearle-tipt fingers top ?
My wealth is gone, ô goe it where it will,
 Spare this one Iewell ; I'le be *Dives* still.

Marke 12.

(Give to Cæsar ----)
(And to God ------)

A LL we have is God's, and yet
 Cæsar challenges a debt,
Nor hath God a thinner share,
What ever *Cæsar's* payments are ;
All is God's ; and yet 'tis true
All wee have is *Cæsar's* too ;
All is *Cæsar's* ; and what ods
So long as *Cæsar's* selfe is Gods ?

But now they have seen, and hated.

S Eene ? and yet hated thee ? they did not see,
 They saw Thee not, that saw and hated thee :
No, no, they saw the not, ô Life, ô Love,
 Who saw ought in thee, that their hate could move.

Vpon the Thornes taken downe from our Lords head bloody.

K Now'st thou this, Souldier ? 'tis a much chang'd plant,
        (which yet
      Thy selfe did'st set,
'Tis chang'd indeed, did Autumn e're such beauties bring
      To shame his Spring ?

Luke 16. *&c.*] *MSS. T A3* 1 Drop, one drop,] *So Bdl. copy of 46 :* Drop ! one drop ! *B.M. copy T A3* 2 my] thy *A3*
 Marke *12. &c.*] *MSS. T A3. Heading in T : Upon paying tribute to Cæsar. Interspaced couplets in A3* 2 debt,] debt. *T A3*
 But now *&c.*] *MSS. T A3. T adds &c. to heading. A3 puts* Joh: *before heading* 1 *A distinguishes* Seene 4 thee] *So Bdl. copy of 46 :* htee *B.M. copy*
 Vpon the Thornes *&c.*] *MSS. T A3. Heading in 70 : Upon the Crown of Thorns taken from our Blessed Lords Head all bloody. For collation with version in 48 see notes to similar version in 52, p. 290, below* 1 this, *TA3 :* this *46*

O ! who so hard an husbandman could ever find
A soyle so kind ?
Is not the soile a kind one (thinke ye) that returnes
Roses for *Thornes* ?

Luc. 7.

She began to wash his feet with teares and
wipe them with the haires of her head.

HEr eyes flood lickes his feets faire staine,
Her haires flame lickes up that againe.
This flame thus quench't hath brighter beames :
This flood thus stained fairer streames.

On *St.* Peter *cutting of* Malchus *his eare.*

WEll *Peter* dost thou wield thy active sword,
Well for thy selfe (I meane) not for thy Lord.
To strike at eares, is to take heed there bee
No witnesse *Peter* of thy perjury.

Joh. 3.

But men loved darknesse rather then Light.

THe worlds light shines, shine as it will,
The world will love its Darknesse still :
I doubt though when the World's in Hell,
It will not love its Darknesse halfe so well.

---

5 an] a *T A3*   7 *(thinke ye)*] *T substitutes commas for brackets.*
Luc. 7. *&c.*] *MSS. T A3.   Heading in T : Upon Mary Magdalene.*
Luc.] *Luke 48 and catchword 46*   haires] *hayre A3*   1 Her]
Heer 46   4 stained] *stained, 48 A3 T*
  On St. Peter *&c.*] *MSS. A3 S (ll. 3 and 4 only and without heading).*
  Joh. 3. *&c.*] *MSS. T A3.   Heading in T : Joh. 3. 19. Light is come*
into the world &c.   1 shines,] *shines. T*   2 its] *his T A3*
3 Hell,] *Hell. 48*   4 It] *Hee T A3*   its] *his T A3*

Act. 21.

I am ready not onely to be bound but to dye.

COme death, come bands, nor do you shrink, my eares,
  At those hard words mans cowardise calls feares.
Save those of feare, no other bands feare I ;
Nor other death then this ; the feare to dye.

On St. Peter *casting away his Nets at our Saviours call.*

THou hast the art on't *Peter* ; and canst tell
  To cast thy Nets on all occasions well.
When Christ calls, and thy Nets would have thee stay :
To cast them well's to cast them quite away.

Our Lord in his Circumcision *to his Father.*

TO thee these first fruits of my growing death
  (For what else is my life ?) lo I bequeath.
Tast this, and as thou lik'st this lesser flood
Expect a Sea, my heart shall make it good.
Thy wrath that wades heere now, e're long shall swim
The flood-gate shall be set wide ope for him.
Then let him drinke, and drinke, and doe his worst,
To drowne the wantonnesse of his wild thirst.   8
Now's but the Nonage of my paines, my feares
Are yet but in their hopes, not come to yeares.
The day of my darke woes is yet but morne,
My teares but tender and my death new-borne.

Act. 21. *&c.*] *MSS. T A3. Heading in T : Pauls resolution.*   1
Come death, come bands] Come bonds, come death *T*   2 words]
names, *T*   3 bands] bonds *T*   4 Nor] No *48*   death]
feare *48*   this] that *T*
    On *St.* Peter *casting &c.*] *MSS. T S (no heading). Heading in T :*
On Peters casting the nett.   4 well's] well, 's *T*
    Our Lord *&c.*] *MSS. T A3. Couplets interspaced T A3. (Heading)*
Our Lord] Our B. Lord *48*   6 flood-gate] floodgates *T*
7]   Then shall hee drinke : & drinke shall doe his worst *T*
9 Now's] No'ws *46*
9, 10]   My paines are in their Nonage : my young feares
              Are yet but hopes ; weak, as my infant yeeres, *T*
10 but *T A3* : both *46 48*   11 woes] woe *48*   12 but] are *T*
A3 distinguishes death new borne.

Yet may these unfledg'd griefes give fate some guesse,
These Cradle-torments have their towardnesse.
These purple buds of blooming death may bee,
Erst the full stature of a fatall tree.   16
And till my riper woes to age are come,
This knife may be the speares *Prœludium.*

On the wounds of our crucified Lord.

O These wakefull wounds of thine !
    Are they Mouthes ? or are they eyes ?
Be they Mouthes, or be they eyne,
    Each bleeding part some one supplies.

Lo ! a mouth, whose full-bloom'd lips
    At too deare a rate are roses.
Lo ! a blood-shot eye ! that weepes
    And many a cruell teare discloses.

O thou that on this foot hast laid
    Many a kisse, and many a Teare,   10
Now thou shal't have all repaid,
    Whatsoe're thy charges were.

This foot hath got a Mouth and lippes,
    To pay the sweet summe of thy kisses :
To pay thy Teares, an Eye that weeps
    In stead of Teares such Gems as this is.

The difference onely this appeares,
    (Nor can the change offend)
The debt is paid in *Ruby*-Teares,
    Which thou in Pearles did'st lend.   20

14 their] a *T*   18 This] The *T*   18 *A3 distinguishes* Knife
and Speares.
    On the wounds &c.] *MSS. T A3. Not in stanzas in T.*   2 *A3 dis-
tinguishes* Mouthes *and* Eyes.   5 *A3 distinguishes* Mouth.   6 too]
two *46*   10 Teare,] *So Bdl. copy of 46* : Teare *B.M. copy*   13
lippes,] *So Bdl. copy of 46* : lippes *B.M. copy*   14 kisses :] *So Bdl.
copy of 46* : kisses *B.M. copy*   19 The] Thy *T*   19, 20 *T
distinguishes* Ruby (*no hyphen*) *and* Pearles.

On our crucified Lord Naked, and bloody.

TH' have left thee naked Lord, O that they had ;
This Garment too I would they had deny'd.
Thee with thy selfe they have too richly clad,
Opening the purple wardrobe of thy side.
    O never could bee found Garments too good
    For thee to weare, but these, of thine owne blood.

Easter day.

RIse, Heire of fresh Eternity,
    From thy Virgin Tombe :
Rise mighty man of wonders, and thy world with thee
    Thy Tombe, the universall East,
    Natures new wombe,
Thy Tombe, faire Immortalities perfumed Nest.

Of all the Gloryes Make Noone gay
    This is the Morne.
This rocke buds forth the fountaine of the streames of Day.
    In joyes white Annals live this houre,   10
    When life was borne,
No cloud scoule on his radiant lids no tempest lowre.

Life, by this light's Nativity
    All creatures have.
Death onely by this Dayes just Doome is forc't to Dye ;
    Nor is Death forc't ; for may hee ly
    Thron'd in thy Grave ;
Death will on this condition be content to Dy.

On our &c.] *MS. A3. For altered version with different heading in 52 (following 48) see p. 290, below.* 1 Th'] They 48   Lord,] Lord. 48   Lord, . . . had ;] *So Bdl. copy of 46 :* Lord ! . . . had ! *B.M. copy.* 2 too] too, 48   4 *Single bracket before* Opening *A3*   5] O never could there be garment to good 48   6 these] this 48
    Easter Day.] *MSS.* T *A3* S (*st. 3, ll. 3–6*). *Heading in 48 :* Vpon Easter Day. *Heading in* T: Upon Christs resurrection. *No heading in* S. 3 wonders,] *So Bdl. copy of 46 :* wonders ! *B.M. copy*   thee] thee, 48 *A3* : thee. T   6 perfumed] perfum'd *A3*   Nest. 48 T *A3* : Nest, 46   10 live] lives 48   15 this] *So Bdl. copy of 46 :* his *B.M. copy*   17 Grave ;] *So Bdl. copy of 46 :* Grave. *B.M. copy*

On the bleeding wounds of our crucified Lord

IEsu, no more, it is full tide
　From thy hands and from thy feet,
From thy head, and from thy side,
　All thy *Purple Rivers* meet.

Thy restlesse feet they cannot goe,
　For us and our eternall good
As they are wont ; what though ?
　They swim, alas ! in their owne flood.

Thy hand to give thou canst not lift ;
　Yet will thy hand still giving bee ;　　　10
It gives, but ô it self's the Guift,
　It drops·though bound, though bound 'tis free.

But ô thy side ! thy deepe dig'd side
　That hath a double *Nilus* going,
Nor ever was the *Pharian* tide
　Halfe so fruitfull, halfe so flowing.

What need thy faire head beare a part
　In Teares ? as if thine eyes had none ?
What need they helpe to drowne thine heart,
　That strives in Torrents of its owne ?　　　20

Water'd by the showres they bring,
　The thornes that thy blest browes encloses
(A cruell and a costly spring)
　Conceive proud hopes of proving Roses.

On the &c.] *MSS. T (sts. 1–5) A3. Heading in T : Upon our Saviours*
wounds.　　　*wounds*] *body 48*　　　*For altered version with different*
heading in 52 (following 48) see p. 288 below. Order of stanzas in 48
and 52 : 1, 5, 2, 3, 4, 7, 8, 9, 10 (6 omitted). T and A3 generally follow 46.
1 more,] *So Bdl. copy of 46 :* more, ! *B.M. copy*　　　2 hands] head
48 52　　　3 head] hands *48 52*　　　4 thy] the *48 52*　　　5 they]
now *48 52*　　　goe,] *So Bdl. copy of 46 :* goe *B.M. copy*　　　7 are
wont] were ever wont *48 52 T :* were wont *A 3*　　　8 swim,]
swimme. *52*　　　flood] blood *48 A3*　　　9 hand] hands *48 52*　　　11
gives,] gives. *A3*　　　self's] *So Bdl. copy of 46 :* selfe's *B.M. copy*
12 drops] gives *48 52*　　　18 Teares] showers *48 52*　　　19 thine]
thy *48 52*　　　20 strives] streames *48*

Not a haire but payes his River
  To this *Red Sea* of thy blood,
Their little channels can deliver
  Something to the generall flood.

But while I speake, whither are run
  All the Rivers nam'd before ?   30
I counted wrong ; there is but one,
  But ô that one is one all o're.

Raine-swolne Rivers may rise proud
  Threatning all to overflow,
But when indeed all's overflow'd
  They themselves are drowned too.

This thy Bloods deluge (a dire chance
  Deare Lord to thee) to us is found
A deluge of deliverance,
  A deluge least we should be drown'd.   40

Nere was't thou in a sence so sadly true,
The well of living Waters, Lord, till now.

Sampson *to his* Dalilah.

COuld not once blinding me, cruell, suffice ?
  When first I look't on thee, I lost mine eyes.

Psalme 23.

HAppy me ! ô happy sheepe !
  Whom my God vouchsafes to keepe
Even my God, even he it is,
That points me to these wayes of blisse ;
On whose pastures cheerefull spring,
All the yeare doth sit and sing,

25 Not a haire] No Haire so small *48 52*   26 blood] *Blood 48.*
A3 distinguishes Red Sea   32 all o're] all'ore *46*   34] *See 52*
  Sampson *&c.*] *MS. A3*
  Psalme 23. *MSS. T5 T6 A3 A2. Heading in T5 :* Ps. 23. (Para-
phrasticè.) *Heading in T6 :* ψ. 23. *At end in T6 :* R. Crashaw.
poem p. 25. (*the page-number in 46*) *Heading in A2 :* Psalme. 23. a
Periphrastique.   2 keepe ; *48* : keepe *46* keepe, *A3 70*   3 Ev'en
. . . ev'en] *So Bdl. copy of 46 :* Even . . . even *B.M. copy*   is,]
So Bdl. copy of 46 : is *B.M. copy*   4 wayes] paths *T5 A3 A2*
5 On *48 &c. :* One *46*

And rejoycing smiles to see
Their greene backs were his liverie :
Pleasure sings my soule to rest,
Plenty weares me at her brest,   10
Whose sweet temper teaches me
Nor wanton, nor in want to be.
At my feet the blubb'ring Mountaine
Weeping, melts into a Fountaine,
Whose soft silver-sweating streames
Make high Noone forget his beames :
When my waiward breath is flying,
Hee calls home my soule from dying,
Strokes and tames my rabid Griefe,
And does woe me into life :   20
When my simple weaknesse strayes,
(Tangled in forbidden wayes)
Hee (my Shepheard) is my Guide,
Hee's before me, on my side,
And behind me, he beguiles
Craft in all her knotty wiles :
Hee expounds the giddy wonder
Of my weary steps, and under
Spreads a Path cleare as the Day,
Where no churlish rub saies nay   30
To my joy-conducted Feet,
Whil'st they Gladly goe to meet
Grace and peace, to meet new laies
Tun'd to my great Shepheards praise.
Come now all yee terrors, sally
Muster forth into the valley,
Where triumphant darknesse hovers
With a sable wing, that covers
Brooding Horror. Come thou Death,
Let the damps of thy dull Breath   40
Overshadow even the shade,
And make darknesse selfe afraid ;

16 Make] Makes *T5*   20 woe] wooe *48* : woo *T A2*   21 When
my] And when *A3*   25 me,] me. *T5 A2* : me ; *T6*   26 knotty] subtile
A2   27 giddy] weary *T5 A3 A2*   28 weary] giddy *T5 A3 A2*
29 cleare as the] as cleare as *48*   33 meet] learne *T5 A3 A2*   35 yee]
you *A3*   36 into] in *A2*   38 that] and *A3*   39 Horror] horrors
A2   39 thou] thou, *T5 T6*   40 damps] lampe *A2*   41 the]
that *T5*

There my feet, even there shall find
Way for a resolved mind.
Still my Shepheard, still my God
Thou art with me, Still thy rod,
And thy staffe, whose influence
Gives direction, gives defence.
At the whisper of thy Word
Crown'd abundance spreads my Bord :   50
While I feast, my foes doe feed
Their rank malice not their need,
So that with the self-same bread
They are starv'd, and I am fed.
How my head in ointment swims !
How my cup orelooks her Brims !
So, even so still may I move
By the Line of thy deare Love ;
Still may thy sweet mercy spread
A shady Arme above my head,   60
About my Paths, so shall I find
The faire Center of my mind
Thy Temple, and those lovely walls
Bright ever with a beame that falls
Fresh from the pure glance of thine eye,
Lighting to Eternity.
There I'le dwell for ever, there
Will I find a purer aire
To feed my Life with, there I'le sup
Balme and Nectar in my Cup,   70
And thence my ripe soule will I breath
Warme into the Armes of Death.

Psalme 137.

O N the proud bankes of great Euphrates flood,   [1]
   There we sate, and there we wept :
Our Harpes that now no Musicke understood,
   Nodding on the Willowes slept,
     While unhappy captiv'd wee
     Lovely Sion thought on thee.

56 her] his *T5*   60 above] about *T5*   62 mind] mind, *T5 T6 A2*
66 Lighting] Lightning *A2*   67 dwell for ever,] dwell, for ever *48*
  Psalme 137.] *MSS. T5 T6 A3. Heading in T5 :* Ps. 137. (Para-
phrasi Poëticâ.) *Heading in T6 :* ψ. 137. *At end in T6 :* R. Crashaw.
p. 27. (*the page-number in 46*)   1·4] On the willowes nodding slept. *T5*

They, they that snatcht us from our Countries brest [2]
    Would have a Song carv'd to their Eares
In Hebrew numbers, then (ô cruell jest !)
    When Harpes and hearts were drown'd in Teares :
      Come, they cry'd, come sing and play
      One of Sions songs to day.

Sing ? play ? to whom (ah) shall we sing or play, [3]
    If not *Jerusalem* to thee ?
Ah thee *Jerusalem* ! ah sooner may
    This hand forget the mastery
      Of Musicks dainty touch, then I
      The Musicke of thy memory.

Which when I lose, ô may at once my Tongue [4]
    Lose this same busie speaking art
Vnpearcht, her vocall Arteries unstrung,
    No more acquainted with my Heart,
      On my dry pallats roofe to rest
      A wither'd Leafe, an idle Guest.

No, no, thy good, Sion, alone must crowne [5]
    The head of all my hope-nurst joyes.
But *Edom* cruell thou ! thou cryd'st downe, downe
    Sinke Sion, downe and never rise,
      Her falling thou did'st urge and thrust,
      And haste to dash her into dust.

Dost laugh ? proud *Babels* Daughter ! do, laugh on, [6]
    Till thy ruine teach thee Teares,
Even such as these, laugh, till a venging throng
    Of woes, too late doe rouze thy feares.
      Laugh, till thy childrens bleeding bones
      Weepe pretious Teares upon the stones.

   2·3 then (ô] (then ô *A3*   2·4 Harpes] harpe *A3*   2·6 One
48 &c. : On *46*   3·1 shall] should *A3*   or] & *T5 T6*   4·2 art]
art, *48 A3 T6* : art : *T5*   5·3 downe,] ddowne, *46*   5·4 never]
neuer neuer *A3*

A Hymne of the Nativity, sung by the Shepheards.

Chorus.   COme wee Shepheards who have seene   [1]
        Dayes King deposed by Nights Queene.
      Come lift we up our lofty song,
      To wake the Sun that sleeps too long.

      Hee in this our generall joy,   [2]
        Slept, and dreampt of no such thing
      While we found out the fair-ey'd Boy,
        And kist the Cradle of our King ;
      Tell him hee rises now too late,
      To shew us ought worth looking at.

      Tell him wee now can shew him more   [3]
        Then hee e're shewd to mortall sight,
      Then hee himselfe e're saw before,
        Which to be seene needs not his light :
      Tell him *Tityrus* where th'hast been,
      Tell him *Thyrsis* what th'hast seen.

Tityrus.   Gloomy Night embrac't the place   [4]
        Where the noble Infant lay :
      The Babe lookt up, and shew'd his face,
        In spight of Darknesse it was Day.
      It was thy Day, Sweet, and did rise,
      Not from the East, but from thy eyes.

Thyrsis.   Winter chid the world, and sent   [5]
        The angry North to wage his warres :
      The North forgot his fierce intent,
        And left perfumes, in stead of scarres :
      By those sweet Eyes persuasive Powers,
      Where he meant frosts, he scattered Flowers.

A Hymne &c.] MSS. T S (*st. 4, ll. 5, 6 ; st. 6 ; st. 12, ll. 1–4*). *For altered version in 52 with longer title and choric repetitions see p. 248 below. Order of stanzas in 52 : 1, 2, 3, 4, 5, 6, two extra stanzas, 7, 8, 9, 6, 10, 11, 13, 14, 15. 52 follows 48 with exceptions given in footnotes ad loc. T follows 46.*   ll. 1–7 See 52   1.4 sleeps] lyes T (*as 48 52*)   2.2 thing] thing ; *48* T: thing. *52*   4.1 *Tityrus*] *Tytirus 46*   5.1 the world] aloud *48 52*   5.6 frosts] frost T

Both.   We saw thee in thy Balmy Nest,   [6]
    Bright Dawne of our *Eternall Day* ;
Wee saw thine Eyes break from the East,
    And chase the trembling shades away :
Wee saw thee (and wee blest the sight)
Wee saw thee by thine owne sweet Light.

Tityrus.   I saw the curl'd drops, soft and slow   [7]
    Come hovering o're the places head,
Offring their whitest sheets of snow,
    To furnish the faire Infants Bed.
Forbeare (said I) be not too bold,
Your fleece is white, but 'tis too cold.

Thyrsis.   I saw th'officious Angels bring,   [8]
    The downe that their soft brests did strow,
For well they now can spare their wings,
    When Heaven it selfe lyes here below.
Faire Youth (said I) be not too rough,
Thy Downe though soft's not soft enough.

Tityrus.   The Babe no sooner 'gan to seeke,   [9]
    Where to lay his lovely head,
But streight his eyes advis'd his Cheeke,
    'Twixt Mothers Brests to goe to bed.
Sweet choise (said I) no way but so,
Not to lye cold, yet sleepe in snow.

All.   Welcome to our wondring sight   [10]
    Eternity shut in a span !
Summer in Winter ! Day in Night !
Chorus.   Heaven in Earth ! and God in Man !
Great litle one, whose glorious Birth,
Lifts Earth to Heaven, stoops heaven to earth.

Welcome, though not to Gold, nor Silke,   [11]
    To more then *Cæsars* Birthright is.
Two sister-Seas of virgins Milke,
    With many a rarely-temper'd kisse,
That breathes at once both Maid and Mother,
Warmes in the one, cooles in the other.

6·2 Bright] Young *52*   6·3 thine] thy *T*   Eyes break] Eyes-
break *46* : eyes breake *T 48 52*   the] their *48 52 T*   7·3 whitest]
white *T*   8·1, 2 See *52*   8·4 When] Since *48 52*   8·5, 6 *See*
52   9·1–6 See *52*   9·4 'Twixt] 'Twixts *T* (as *48 52*)   10·1
and 5 See 52   11·1 nor] or *T*   11·3 virgins] Virgin *48 52*

Shee sings thy Teares asleepe, and dips   [12]
   Her Kisses in thy weeping Eye,
Shee spreads the red leaves of thy Lips,
   That in their Buds yet blushing lye.
Shee 'gainst those Mother-Diamonds tryes
The points of her young Eagles Eyes.

Welcome, (though not to those gay flyes   [13]
   Guilded i'th' Beames of Earthly Kings
Slippery soules in smiling eyes)
   But to poore Shepheards, simple things,
That use no varnish, no oyl'd Arts,
But lift clean hands full of cleare hearts.

Yet when young *Aprils* husband showres,   [14]
   Shall blesse the fruitfull *Maia's* Bed,
Wee'l bring the first-borne of her flowers,
   To kisse thy feet, and crowne thy head.
To thee (Dread Lambe) whose Love must keepe
The Shepheards, while they feed their sheepe.

To thee meeke Majesty, soft King   [15]
   Of simple Graces, and sweet Loves,
Each of us his Lamb will bring,
   Each his payre of silver Doves.
At last, in fire of thy faire Eyes,
Wee'l burne, our owne best sacrifice.

12 *omitted in 52 but not in 48*   13·4 simple] home-spun *48 52*
13·5, 6 *See 52*   14·6 *See 52*   14·6 their] the *T*   15·5, 6 *See 52*

Sospetto d' Herode.

Libro Primo.

Argomento.

Casting the times with their strong signes,
Death's Master his owne death divines.
Strugling for helpe, his best hope is
Herod's suspition may heale his.
Therefore he sends a fiend to wake
The sleeping Tyrant's fond mistake ;
Who feares (in vaine) that he whose Birth
Meanes Heav'n, should meddle with his Earth.

1

MVse, now the servant of soft Loves no more,
Hate is thy Theame, and *Herod*, whose unblest
Hand (ô what dares not jealous Greatnesse ?) tore
A thousand sweet Babes from their Mothers Brest :
The Bloomes of Martyrdome. O be a Dore
Of language to my infant Lips, yee best
Of Confessours : whose Throates answering his swords,
Gave forth your Blood for breath, spoke soules for words.

2

Great *Anthony* ! *Spains* well-beseeming pride,
Thou mighty branch of Emperours and Kings.
The Beauties of whose dawne what eye may bide,
Which with the Sun himselfe weigh's equall wings.

Sospetto d' Herode &c.] *MS. T6 (two separate copies, here distin-*
guished as A and B. In the footnotes T, alone, stands for both copies.
TA or TB represents one or the other separate copy. In TB the
punctuation &c., seems occasionally to have been corrected in a different
hand. 'TB corr.' in the footnotes refers to these corrections.) Separate
title-page in TA : La Strage De Gli Innocentj Del Caualier Marino
Nouember 25th 1637. *Same in TB with punctuation and '* Translated
by R. C.' *added in another hand.* Argomento 1. 2 *Master*] monarch *T*
4 Herod's] Hero'ds 46   5 wake *T : wake, 46 48 70*   6 *sleeping*]
sleepy *T*   1·3 ô] so *70*   1·7 Throates] throat *corr.* to throat, *TB*
answering] answ'ring *TB corr.*

Mappe of Heroick worth ! whom farre and wide
To the beleeving world Fame boldly sings :
   Deigne thou to weare this humble Wreath that bowes,
   To be the sacred Honour of thy Browes.

3.

Nor needs my Muse a blush, or these bright Flowers
Other then what their owne blest beauties bring.
They were the smiling sons of those sweet Bowers,
That drinke the deaw of Life, whose deathlesse spring,
Nor *Sirian* flame, nor *Borean* frost deflowers :
From whence Heav'n-labouring Bees with busie wing,
   Suck hidden sweets, which well digested proves
   Immortall Hony for the Hive of Loves.

4.

Thou, whose strong hand with so transcendent worth,
Holds high the reine of faire *Parthenope,*
That neither *Rome,* nor *Athens* can bring forth
A Name in noble deedes Rivall to thee !
Thy Fames full noise, makes proud the patient Earth,
Farre more then matter for my Muse and mee.
   The *Tyrrhene* Seas, and shores sound all the same,
   And in their murmures keepe thy mighty Name.

5.

Below the Botome of the great Abysse,
There where one Center reconciles all things ;
The worlds profound Heart pants ; There placed is
Mischifes old Master, close about him clings
A curl'd knot of embracing Snakes, that kisse
His correspondent cheekes : these loathsome strings
   Hold the perverse Prince in eternall Ties
   Fast bound, since first he forfeited the skies,

2·5 farre] far, *T*B *corr.*   2·7 Wreath that bowes,] wreath, that bowes *48 T*   3·1 Flowers] Flowers, *T*B *corr.*   3·4 Life,] life ; *T*   spring,] springes *T*   3·6 wing,] winges *T*   4·3 *Rome,*] Rome *T*A : Rome, *T*B *corr.*   4·5 noise,] noyse *T*   4·6 Muse] Muse, *T*B *corr.*   5·2 There] There, *T*B *corr.*   5·5 curl'd] cursed *T*   embracing] 'mbracing *T*B *corr.*   5·8 skies. *T 70* : skies, *46 48*

6.

The Iudge of Torments, and the King of Teares :
Hee fills a burnisht Throne of quenchlesse fire :
And for his old faire Roabes of Light, hee weares
A gloomy Mantle of darke flames, the Tire
That crownes his hated head on high appeares ;
Where seav'n tall Hornes (his Empires pride) aspire.
  And to make up Hells Majesty, each Horne
  Seav'n crested *Hydra's* horribly adorne.

7.

His Eyes, the sullen dens of Death and Night,
Startle the dull Ayre with a dismall red :
Such his fell glances as the fatall Light
Of staring Comets, that looke Kingdomes dead.
From his black nostrills, and blew lips, in spight
Of Hells owne stinke, a worser stench is spread.
  His breath Hells lightning is : and each deepe grone
  Disdaines to thinke that Heav'n Thunders alone.

8.

His flaming Eyes dire exhalation,
Vnto a dreadfull pile gives fiery Breath ;
Whose unconsum'd consumption preys upon
The never-dying Life, of a long Death.
In this sad House of slow Destruction,
(His shop of flames) hee fryes himselfe, beneath
  A masse of woes, his Teeth for Torment gnash,
  While his steele sides sound with his Tayles strong lash.

9

Three Rigourous Virgins waiting still behind,
Assist the Throne of th' Iron-Sceptred King.
With whips of Thornes and knotty vipers twin'd
They rouse him, when his ranke Thoughts need a sting.
Their lockes are beds of uncomb'd snakes that wind
About their shady browes in wanton Rings.
  Thus reignes the wrathfull King, and while he reignes
  His Scepter and himselfe both he disdaines.

6·1 Teares] feares *T*B   6·4 flames, the] flames. yᵉ *T*   7·1
Death] death, *T*B *corr.*   7·3 glances] glances, *T*B *corr.*   8·4 Life,]
life *48 T*   8·7 woes,] woes. *T*B   9·1 Virgins] virgins, *T*B *corr.*
9·5 snakes] snakes, *T*A *T*B *corr.*

10

Disdainefull wretch ! how hath one bold sinne cost
Thee all the Beauties of thy once bright Eyes ?
How hath one blacke Eclipse cancell'd, and crost
The glories that did guild thee in thy Rise ?
Proud Morning of a perverse Day ! how lost
Art thou unto thy selfe, thou too selfe-wise
   Narcissus ? foolish *Phaeton* ? who for all
   Thy high-aym'd hopes, gaind'st but a flaming fall.

11

From Death's sad shades, to the Life-breathing Ayre,
This mortall Enemy to mankinds good,
Lifts his malignant Eyes, wasted with care,
To become beautifull in humane blood.
Where *Iordan* melts his Chrystall, to make faire
The fields of *Palestine*, with so pure a flood,
   There does he fixe his Eyes : and there detect
   New matter, to make good his great suspect.

12

He calls to mind th'old quarrell, and what sparke
Set the contending Sons of Heav'n on fire :
Oft in his deepe thought he revolves the darke
Sibills divining leaves : hee does enquire
Into th'old Prophesies, trembling to marke
How many present prodigies conspire,
   To crowne their past predictions, both hee layes
   Together, in his pondrous mind both weighes.

13.

Heavens Golden-winged Herald, late hee saw
To a poore *Galilean* virgin sent :
How low the Bright Youth bow'd, and with what awe
Immortall flowers to her faire hand present.
Hee saw th'old *Hebrewes* wombe, neglect the Law
Of Age and Barennesse, and her Babe prevent
   His Birth, by his Devotion, who began
   Betimes to be a Saint, before a Man.

10·2 thy once] thine owne *T*   10·3 cancell'd] conceal'd *T*   10·6
selfe,] selfe ? *T*   10·8 high-aym'd] high mind *T*   11·3 care,] care
*T*A care, *T*B *corr.*   12·2 on fire] a fire *T*B   12·7 predictions,]
predictions. *T*

14.

Hee saw rich Nectar thawes, release the rigour
Of th'Icy North, from frost-bount *Atlas* hands
His Adamantine fetters fall : greene vigour
Gladding the *Scythian* Rocks, and *Libian* sands.
Hee saw a vernall smile, sweetly disfigure
Winters sad face, and through the flowry lands
  Of faire *Engaddi* hony-sweating Fountaines
  With *Manna*, Milk, and Balm, new broach the Mountaines.

15.

Hee saw how in that blest Day-bearing Night,
The Heav'n-rebuked shades made hast away ;
How bright a Dawne of Angels with new Light
Amaz'd the midnight world, and made a Day
Of which the Morning knew not : Mad with spight
Hee markt how the poore Shepheards ran to pay
  Their simple Tribute to the Babe, whose Birth
  Was the great businesse both of Heav'n and Earth.

16.

Hee saw a threefold Sun, with rich encrease,
Make proud the Ruby portalls of the East.
Hee saw the Temple sacred to sweet Peace,
Adore her Princes Birth, flat on her Brest.
Hee saw the falling Idols, all confesse
A comming Deity. Hee saw the Nest
  Of pois'nous and unnaturall loves, Earth-nurst ;
  Toucht with the worlds true *Antidote* to burst.

17.

He saw Heav'n blossome with a new-borne light,
On which, as on a glorious stranger gaz'd
The Golden eyes of Night : whose Beame made bright
The way to *Beth'lem*, and as boldly blaz'd,
(Nor askt leave of the Sun) by Day as Night.
By whom (as Heav'ns illustrious Hand-maid) rais'd
  Three Kings (or what is more) three Wise men went
  Westward to find the worlds true *Orient*.

14·1 thawes,] thawes *48 T*   14·2 bount] bound *T*   16·7 Earth-
nurst ;] earth nurst *T*   17·7 (or what is more)] or (wch is more) *T*

18.

Strucke with these great concurrences of things,
Symptomes so deadly, unto Death and him ;
Faine would hee have forgot what fatall strings,
Eternally bind each rebellious limbe.
Hee shooke himselfe, and spread his spatious wings :
Which like two Bosom'd sailes embrace the dimme
    Aire, with a dismall shade, but all in vaine,
      Of sturdy Adamant is his strong chaine.

19.

While thus Heav'ns highest counsails, by the low
Footsteps of their Effects, hee trac'd too well,
Hee tost his troubled eyes, Embers that glow
Now with new Rage, and wax too hot for Hell.
With his foule clawes hee fenc'd his furrowed Brow,
And gave a gastly shreeke, whose horrid yell
    Ran trembling through the hollow vaults of Night,
      The while his twisted Tayle hee gnaw'd for spight.

20.

Yet on the other side, faine would he start
Above his feares, and thinke it cannot be.
Hee studies Scripture, strives to sound the heart,
And feele the pulse of every Prophecy.
Hee knowes (but knowes not how, or by what Art)
The Heav'n expecting Ages, hope to see
    A mighty Babe, whose pure, unspotted Birth,
      From a chast Virgin wombe, should blesse the Earth.

21.

But these vast Mysteries his senses smother,
And Reason (for what's Faith to him ?) devoure.
How she that is a maid should prove a Mother,
Yet keepe inviolate her virgin flower ;
How Gods eternall Sonne should be mans Brother,
Poseth his proudest Intellectuall power.
    How a pure Spirit should incarnate bee,
      And life it selfe weare Deaths fraile Livery.

    18·6 sailes] snailes *T*A : sailes *T*B *corr.*   18·7 Aire,] Ayre *T*
shade,] shade : *T*   19·2 too] soe *T*   19·3 Embers] embres, *T*A *T*B
corr.   20·5 or] *à T*   20·8 Virgin] virgins *T*

22.

That the Great Angell-blinding light should shrinke
His blaze, to shine in a poore Shepheards eye.
That the unmeasur'd God so low should sinke,
As Pris'ner in a few poore Rags to lye.
That from his Mothers Brest hee milke should drinke,
Who feeds with Nectar Heav'ns faire family.
  That a vile Manger his low Bed should prove,
  Who in a Throne of stars Thunders above.

23.

That hee whom the Sun serves, should faintly peepe
Through clouds of Infant flesh : that hee the old
Eternall Word should bee a Child, and weepe.
That hee who made the fire, should feare the cold ;
That Heav'ns high Majesty his Court should keepe
In a clay-cottage, by each blast control'd.
  That Glories selfe should serve our Griefs, & feares :
  And free Eternity, submit to yeares.

24.

And further, that the Lawes eternall Giver,
Should bleed in his owne lawes obedience :
And to the circumcising Knife deliver
Himselfe, the forfeit of his slaves offence.
That the unblemisht Lambe, blessed for ever,
Should take the marke of sin, and paine of sence.
  These are the knotty Riddles, whose darke doubt
  Intangles his lost Thoughts, past getting out.

25.

While new Thoughts boyl'd in his enraged Brest,
His gloomy Bosomes darkest Character,
Was in his shady forehead seen exprest.
The forehead's shade in Griefes expression there,
Is what in signe of joy among the blest
The faces lightning, or a smile is here.
  Those stings of care that his strong Heart opprest,
  A desperate, *Oh mee*, drew from his deepe Brest.

22·5 hee] hee, *T*A *T*B *corr.*   23·1 hee] he, *T*B *corr.*   23·4
hee] he, *T*B *corr.*

26.

Oh mee ! (thus bellow'd hee) *oh mee* ! what great
Portents before mine eyes their Powers advance ?
And serves my purer sight, onely to beat
Downe my proud Thought, and leave it in a Trance ?
Frowne I ; and can great Nature keep her seat ?
And the gay starrs lead on their Golden dance ?
   Can his attempts above still prosp'rous be,
    Auspicious still, in spight of Hell and me ?

27.

Hee has my Heaven (what would he more ?) whose bright
And radiant Scepter this bold hand should beare.
And for the never-fading fields of Light
My faire Inheritance, hee confines me here,
To this darke House of shades, horrour, and Night,
To draw a long-liv'd Death, where all my cheere
   Is the solemnity my sorrow weares,
    That Mankinds Torment waits upon my Teares.

28.

Darke, dusty Man, he needs would single forth,
To make the partner of his owne pure ray :
And should we Powers of Heav'n, Spirits of worth
Bow our bright Heads, before a King of clay ?
It shall not be, said I, and clombe the *North*,
Where never wing of *Angell* yet made way
   What though I mist my blow ? yet I strooke high,
    And to dare something, is some victory.

29.

Is hee not satisfied ? meanes he to wrest
Hell from me too, and sack my Territories ?
Vile humane Nature means he now t'invest
(O my despight !) with his divinest Glories ?

26·4 Thought] thoughts *T*B   it] me *T*B   26·5 I ;] I ! *T*A
26·6 gay] golden *T*B   27·3 light *T*A : Light. *46 48* : light,
*T*B   27·6 Death,] death : *T*   27·7 weares] beares *T*   27·8
Torment waits] torments wait *T*B   28·1 dusty *T* : dusky *46 48*
28·5 clombe] climbe *T*B   28·6 way] way. *T*   29·2 too,] too ? *T*
29·3 now *T* : not *46 48*

And rising with rich spoiles upon his Brest,
With his faire Triumphs fill all future stories ?
  Must the bright armes of Heav'n, rebuke these eyes ?
  Mocke me, and dazle my darke Mysteries ?

30.

Art thou not *Lucifer ?* hee to whom the droves
Of Stars, that guild the Morne in charge were given ?
The nimblest of the lightning-winged Loves ?
The fairest, and the first-borne smile of Heav'n ?
Looke in what Pompe the Mistresse Planet moves
Rev'rently circled by the lesser seaven,
  Such, and so rich, the flames that from thine eyes,
  Oprest the common-people of the skyes.

31.

Ah wretch ! what bootes thee to cast back thy eyes,
Where dawning hope no beame of comfort showes ?
While the reflection of thy forepast joyes,
Renders thee double to thy present woes.
Rather make up to thy new miseries,
And meet the mischiefe that upon thee growes.
  If Hell must mourne, Heav'n sure shall sympathize
  What force cannot effect, fraud shall devise.

32.

And yet whose force feare I ? have I so lost
My selfe ? my strength too with my innocence ?
Come try who dares, *Heav'n, Earth,* what ere dost boast,
A borrowed being, make thy bold defence.
Come thy Creator too, what though it cost
Mee yet a second fall ? wee'd try our strengths.
  Heav'n saw us struggle once, as brave a fight
  Earth now should see, and tremble at the sight.

29·5 with rich] rich w^th *T*B   30·1 thou not] not thou *T*   30·2
Stars,] stars *T*   30·7 flames . . . eyes,] flames, . . . eyes *T*B
31·1 thy] thyne *T*   31·7 Heav'n sure shall sympathize] sure
Heavn must sympathise *corr. to* Heavn sure, shall sympathise *T*B
sympathize] sympathize ; 70   32·3 dares, *Heav'n, Earth,*] dares ?
Heav'n ? Earth ? *T*A   boast,] boast *T*   32·5 too,] too ? *T*A

33.

Thus spoke th'impatient Prince, and made a pause,
His foule Hags rais'd their heads, & clapt their hands.
And all the Powers of Hell in full applause
Flourisht their Snakes, and tost their flaming brands.
Wee (said the horrid sisters) wait thy lawes,
Th'obsequious handmaids of thy high commands.
   Be it thy part, Hells mighty Lord, to lay
   On us thy dread commands, ours to obey.

34.

What thy *Alecto*, what these hands can doe,
Thou mad'st bold proofe upon the brow of Heav'n,
Nor should'st thou bate in pride, because that now,
To these thy sooty Kingdomes thou art driven.
Let Heav'ns Lord chide above lowder then thou
In language of his Thunder, thou art even
   With him below : here thou art Lord alone
   Boundlesse and absolute : Hell is thine owne.

35.

If usuall wit, and strength will doe no good,
Vertues of stones, nor herbes : use stronger charmes,
Anger, and love, best hookes of humane blood.
If all faile wee'l put on our proudest Armes,
And pouring on Heav'ns face the Seas huge flood
Quench his curl'd fires, wee'l wake with our Alarmes
   Ruine, where e're she sleepes at Natures feet ;
   And crush the world till his wide corners meet.

36.

Reply'd the proud King, O my Crownes Defence ?
Stay of my strong hopes, you of whose brave worth,
The frighted stars tooke faint experience,
When 'gainst the Thunders mouth wee marched forth :
Still you are prodigal of your Love's expence
In our great projects, both 'gainst Heav'n and Earth.
   I thanke you all, but one must single out,
   Cruelty, she alone shall cure my doubt.

33·1 pause,] pause ; *48* : pause *T*A : pause : *T*B   33·2 rais'd]
vayl'd *T*   33·8 ours] ours, *T*A   34·1 what these] with
these *T*B *corr.*   34·4 these] these, *T*A   34·8 Bound-
lesse] Boundlesse, *T*B   36·4 mouth] mouth, *T*A   36·8 my]
this *T*

37.

Fourth of the cursed knot of Hags is shee,
Or rather all the other three in one ;
Hells shop of slaughter shee do's oversee,
And still assist the Execution.
But chiefly there do's shee delight to be,
Where Hells capacious Cauldron is set on :
   And while the black soules boile in their owne gore,
    To hold them down, and looke that none seethe o're.

38.

Thrice howl'd the Caves of Night, and thrice the sound,
Thundring upon the bankes of those black lakes
Rung, through the hollow vaults of Hell profound :
At last her listning Eares the noise o'retakes,
Shee lifts her sooty lampes, and looking round
A gen'rall hisse, from the whole Tire of snakes
   Rebounding, through Hells inmost Cavernes came,
    In answer to her formidable Name.

39.

Mongst all the Palaces in Hells command,
No one so mercilesse as this of hers.
The Adamantine Doors, for ever stand
Impenetrable, both to prai'rs and Teares,
The walls inexorable steele, no hand
Of *Time*, or Teeth of hungry *Ruine* feares.
   Their ugly ornaments are the bloody staines,
    Of ragged limbs, torne sculls, & dasht out Braines.

40.

There has the purple *Vengeance* a proud seat,
Whose ever-brandisht Sword is sheath'd in blood.
About her *Hate*, *Wrath*, *Warre*, and *slaughter* sweat ;
Bathing their hot limbs in life's pretious flood.
There rude impetuous Rage do's storme, and fret :
And there, as Master of this murd'ring brood,
   Swinging a huge Sith stands impartiall *Death*,
    With endlesse businesse almost out of Breath.

38·3 Rung,] Rung *T*   38·4 Eares] eare *T*B   o'retakes,] oretakes. *T*
38·7 Rebounding,] Rebounding *T*   39·2 No] Not *T*B   prai'rs]
prayers, *T*   39·5 walls] wall *T*B   39·8 out *48 T* : our *46*
40·7 impartiall] imperiall *T*

41.

For Hangings and for Curtaines, all along
The walls, (abominable ornaments !)
Are tooles of wrath, Anvills of Torments hung ;
Fell Executioners of foule intents,   ·
Nailes, hammers, hatchets sharpe, and halters strong,
Swords, Speares, with all the fatall Instruments
 Of sin, and Death, twice dipt in the dire staines
 Of Brothers mutuall blood, and Fathers braines.

42.

The Tables furnisht with a cursed Feast,
Which *Harpyes*, with leane *Famine* feed upon,
Vnfill'd for ever.   Here among the rest,
Inhumane *Erisi-cthon* too makes one ;
Tantalus, Atreus, Progne, here are guests :
Wolvish *Lycaon* here a place hath won.
 The cup they drinke in is *Medusa's* scull,
 Which mixt with gall & blood they quaffe brim full.

43.

The foule Queens most abhorred Maids of Honour
Medæa, Jezabell, many a meager Witch
With *Circe, Scylla,* stand to wait upon her.
But her best huswifes are the *Parcæ,* which
Still worke for her, and have their wages from her.
They prick a bleeding heart at every stitch.
 Her cruell cloathes of costly threds they weave,
 Which short-cut lives of murdred *Infants* leave.

44.

The house is hers'd about with a black wood,
Which nods with many a heavy headed tree.
Each flowers a pregnant poyson, try'd and good,
Each herbe a Plague.   The winds sighes timed-bee
By a black Fount, which weeps into a flood.
Through the thick shades obscurely might you see
 Minotaures, Cyclopses, with a darke drove
 Of *Dragons, Hydraes, Sphinxes,* fill the Grove.

44·4 timed-bee] *So 46 48* : timed bee *T* 44·5 black] bleake *T*

45.

Here *Diomed's* Horses, *Phereus* dogs appeare,
With the fierce Lyons of *Therodamas.*
Busiris ha's his bloody Altar here,
Here *Sylla* his severest prison has.
The *Lestrigonians* here their Table reare ;
Here strong *Procrustes* plants his Bed of Brasse.
   Here cruell *Scyron* boasts his bloody rockes,
   And hatefull *Schinis* his so feared Oakes.

46.

What ever Schemes of Blood, fantastick frames
Of Death *Mezentius,* or *Geryon* drew ;
Phalaris, Ochus, Ezelinus, names
Mighty in mischiefe, with dread *Nero* too,
Here are they all, Here all the swords or flames
Assyrian Tyrants, or *Egyptian* knew.
   Such was the House, so furnisht was the Hall,
   Whence the fourth *Fury,* answer'd *Pluto's* call.

47.

Scarce to this Monster could the shady King,
The horrid summe of his intentions tell ;
But shee (swift as the momentary wing
Of lightning, or the words he spoke) left Hell.
Shee rose, and with her to our world did bring,
Pale proofe of her fell presence. Th'aire too well
   With a chang'd countenance witnest the sight,
   And poore fowles intercepted in their flight.

48.

Heav'n saw her rise, and saw Hell in the sight.
The field's faire Eyes saw her, and saw no more,
But shut their flowry lids for ever. Night,
And Winter strow her way ; yea, such a sore
Is shee to Nature, that a generall fright,
An universall palsie spreading o're
   The face of things, from her dire eyes had run,
   Had not her thick Snakes hid them from the Sun.

47·6 presence. *T* : presence, *46*   47·7 sight] Fight *70*   48·3
ever. *T* : ever *46 48*

49.

Now had the Night's companion from her den,
Where all the busie day shee close doth ly,
With her soft wing, wipt from the browes of men
Day's sweat, and by a gentle Tyranny,
And sweet oppression, kindly cheating them
Of all their cares, tam'd the rebellious eye
Of sorrow, with a soft and downy hand,
Sealing all brests in a *Lethæan* band.

50.

When the *Erinnys* her black pineons spread,
And came to *Bethlem*, where the cruell King
Had now retyr'd himselfe, and borrowed
His Brest a while from care's unquiet sting.
Such as at *Thebes* dire feast shee shew'd her head,
Her sulphur-breathed Torches brandishing,
Such to the frighted Palace now shee comes,
And with soft feet searches the silent roomes.

51

By *Herod* leige to Cesar now was borne
The Scepter, which of old great *David* swaid.
Whose right by *David's* linage so long worne,
Himselfe a stranger to, his owne had made :
And from the head of *Iudahs* house quite torne
The Crowne, for which upon their necks he laid
A sad yoake, under which they sigh'd in vaine,
And looking on their lost state sigh'd againe.

52

Vp, through the spatious Pallace passed she,
To where the Kings proudly-reposed head
(If any can be soft to *Tyranny*
And selfe-tormenting sin) had a soft bed.
She thinkes not fit such he her face should see,
As it is seene by Hell ; and seene with dread.
To change her faces stile she doth devise,
And in a pale Ghost's shape to spare his Eyes.

50·4 Brest] brests *T*A : brest *T*B *corr.*   from] for *T*A : from *corr.*
to for *T*B   51·1 Herod leige to Cesar *T*A : Herod——*46 48 70* : Herod,
Leige to Cæsar, *T*B *corr. (adding commas)*   51·3 linage *T 70* :
image *46 48*   51·5 head] house *T*   house] head *T*   51·6 laid
48 T : laid. *46*   51·8 state] state, *T*

53

Her selfe a while she layes aside, and makes
Ready to personate a mortall part.
Ioseph the Kings dead Brothers shape she takes,
What he by Nature was, is she by Art.
She comes toth' King and with her cold hand slakes
His Spirits, the Sparkes of Life, and chills his heart,
 Lifes forge ; fain'd is her voice, and false too, be
 Her words, sleep'st thou fond man? sleep'st thou? (said she)

54

So sleeps a Pilot, whose poore Barke is prest
With many a mercylesse o're mastring wave ;
For whom (as dead) the wrathfull winds contest,
Which of them deep'st shall digge her watry Grave.
Why dost thou let thy brave soule lye supprest,
In Death-like slumbers ; while thy dangers crave
 A waking eye and hand ? looke up and see
 The fates ripe, in their great conspiracy.

55

Know'st thou not how of th' Hebrewes royall stemme
(That old dry stocke) a despair'd branch is sprung
A most strange Babe ! who here conceal'd by them
In a neglected stable lies, among
Beasts and base straw : Already is the streame
Quite turn'd : th' ingratefull Rebells this their young
 Master (with voyce free as the Trumpe of *Fame*)
 Their new King, and thy Successour proclaime.

56

What busy motions, what wild Engines stand
On tiptoe in their giddy Braynes ? th' have fire
Already in their Bosomes ; and their hand
Already reaches at a sword : They hire
Poysons to speed thee ; yet through all the Land
What one comes to reveale what they conspire ?
 Goe now, make much of these ; wage still their wars
 And bring home on thy Brest more thanklesse scarrs.

53·4 is she] she is *T*B   53·5 slakes] shakes *corr. to* slakes *T*B
53·7 too,] too *T* 53·8 (said she)] (said she *46* (said she. *48 70*   55·5
Beasts] Beasts, *T*   55·6 turn'd] *48* : turn'd *46*   55·7 free]
free, *T*B 55·8 proclaime. *48 T* : proclaime *46*

57.

Why did I spend my life, and spill my Blood,
That thy firme hand for ever might sustaine
A well-pois'd Scepter ? does it now seeme good
Thy Brothers blood be-spilt life spent in vaine ?
'Gainst thy owne sons and Brothers thou hast stood
In Armes, when lesser cause was to complaine :
   And now crosse Fates a watch about thee keepe,
   Can'st thou be carelesse now ? now can'st thou sleep ?

58.

Where art thou man ? what cowardly mistake
Of thy great selfe, hath stolne King *Herod* from thee ?
O call thy selfe home to thy selfe, wake, wake,
And fence the hanging sword Heav'n throws upon thee.
Redeeme a worthy wrath, rouse thee, and shake
Thy selfe into a shape that may become thee.
   Be *Herod*, and thou shalt not misse from mee
   Immortall stings to thy great thoughts, and thee.

59.

So said, her richest snake, which to her wrist
For a beseeming bracelet shee had ty'd
(A speciall Worme it was as ever kist
The foamy lips of *Cerberus*) shee apply'd
To the Kings Heart, the Snake no sooner hist,
But vertue heard it, and away shee hy'd,
   Dire flames diffuse themselves through every veine,
   This done, Home to her Hell shee hy'd amaine.

60.

Hee wakes, and with him (ne're to sleepe) new feares :
His Sweat-bedewed Bed had now betrai'd him,
To a vast field of thornes, ten thousand Speares
All pointed in his heart seem'd to invade him :
So mighty were th'amazing Characters
With which his feeling Dreame had thus dismay'd him,
   Hee his owne fancy-framed foes defies :
   In rage, *My armes, give me my armes*, hee cryes.

57·4 be-spilt] be spilt *T*   57·7 thee] yea *T*A : you *T*B   59·1
richest snake, *48 70 T* : richest, *46*   59·7 diffuse] diffused *T*
59·8 amaine] agayne *T*B   60·2 him,] him *T*

61.

As when a Pile of food-preparing fire,
The breath of artificiall lungs embraves,
The Caldron-prison'd waters streight conspire,
And beat the hot Brasse with rebellious waves :
He murmures, and rebukes their bold desire ;
Th'impatient liquor, frets, and foames, and raves ;
    Till his o'reflowing pride suppresse the flame,
    Whence all his high spirits, and hot courage came.

62.

So boyles the fired *Herods* blood-swolne brest,
Not to be slakt but by a Sea of blood.
His faithlesse Crowne he feeles loose on his Crest,
Which on false Tyrants head ne're firmly stood.
The worme of jealous envy and unrest,
To which his gnaw'd heart is the growing food
    Makes him impatient of the lingring light.
    Hate the sweet peace of all-composing Night.

63.

A Thousand Prophecies that talke strange things,
Had sowne of old these doubts in his deepe brest.
And now of late came tributary Kings,
Bringing him nothing but new feares from th'East,
More deepe suspicions, and more deadly stings,
With which his feav'rous cares their cold increast.
    And now his dream (Hels firebrand) stil more bright,
    Shew'd him his feares, and kill'd him with the sight.

64.

No sooner therefore shall the Morning see
(Night hangs yet heavy on the lids of Day)
But all his Counsellours must summon'd bee,
To meet their troubled Lord without delay.
Heralds and Messengers immediately
Are sent about, who poasting every way
    To th'heads and Officers of every band ;
    Declare who sends, and what is his command.

61·6 liquor,] liquor *T*   62·2 slakt] slak'd, *T*B *corr*.   by] in *T*
62·6 food] floud *T*   62·7 light.] light, *T*A   63·5 stings,
48 : stings. *46* : stings *T*   64·4 Lord *T* : Lord : *46 48*   delay.
*T*B : delay *T*A *46 48*   64·7 band ;] band *T*

65.

Why art thou troubled *Herod* ? what vaine feare
Thy blood-revolving Brest to rage doth move ?
Heavens King, who doffs himselfe weake flesh to weare,
Comes not to rule in wrath, but serve in love.
Nor would he this thy fear'd Crown from three Teare,
But give thee a better with himselfe above.
    Poore jealousie ! why should he wish to prey
Vpon thy Crowne, who gives his owne away ?

66

Make to thy reason man ; and mocke thy doubts,
Looke how below thy feares their causes are ;
Thou art a Souldier *Herod* ; send thy Scouts
See how hee's furnish't for so fear'd a warre.
What armour does he weare ? A few thin clouts.
His Trumpets ? tender cryes, his men to dare
    So much ? rude Shepheards. What his steeds ? alas
Poore Beasts ! a slow Oxe, and a simple Asse.

Il fine del libro primo.

On a prayer booke sent
to *Mrs.* M.R.

LOe here a little volume, but large booke,
   (Feare it not, sweet,
     It is no hipocrit)
Much larger in it selfe then in its looke.

    It is in one rich handfull, heaven and all
       Heavens royall Hoasts incampt, thus small ;
      To prove that true, schooles use to tell,
    A thousand Angells in one point can dwell.

65·6 better] better, *T*B   66·3 Scouts] Scouts, *48 T* : scouts ; *T*B
corr.   66·4 See] See, *T*B *corr.*   66·6 cryes,] cries ; *48 T*B : cryes. *T*A
   On a prayer booke &c. MS. A 34. Separate title-page in A 34 : [*Emblem*]
Live Iesu Live *&c.* (*see p. 78, above*) Verses :|Vpon the Book of Common
Prayer.| *Poem begins on following page without further heading, and is
followed by the words ' R: Crashaw | Coll: Petren: '. For altered and
extended version in 48 52, with different heading, see 52, p. 328, below.
A 34 generally agrees with 46, with exceptions given below.* 1 large] great
48 52 70   2–4 *See 52, ll. 2–10*   4, 5 *N.B. punctuation 52*
5 rich] choice *48 52*   7 true, *48* : true *46 52*   8 A] Ten *48 52*

It is loves great Artillery,
Which here contracts it selfe and comes to lye   10
Close coucht in your white bosome, and from thence
As from a snowy fortresse of defence
Against the ghostly foe to take your part :
And fortifie the hold of your chast heart.

It is the Armory of light,
Let constant use but keep it bright,
   Youl find it yeelds
To holy hands, and humble hearts,
   More swords and sheilds
Then sinne hath snares, or hell hath darts.   20

    Onely bee sure,
    The hands bee pure,
That hold these weapons and the eyes
Those of turtles, chast, and true,
    Wakefull, and wise
Here is a friend shall fight for you,
Hold but this booke before your heart,
Let prayer alone to play his part.

But o', the heart
That studyes this high art,   30
Must bee a sure house keeper,
And yet no sleeper.

Deare soule bee strong,
Mercy will come ere long,
And bring her bosome full of blessings,
Flowers of never fading graces ;
To make immortall dressings
For worthy souls whose wise embraces
Store up themselves for him, who is alone
The spouse of Virgins, and the Virgins son.   40

  10 it] its *A34*   13 the ghostly foe] their ghostly foes *52* (their *by
misreading of ' y ' as elsewhere in 52*) : your ghostly ffoes *A34*   15
is the] is an *48 52*   18 hands *48 52 A34* : hand *46*   23 hold] holds
A34   28 his] its *48*   35 her] its *48* : his *52 A34*   full of]
fraught with *52*   37 dressings *48 52 A34* : dressings. *46*   40
A34 distinguishes the line.

But if the noble Bridegrome when hee comes
    Shall find the wandring heart from home,
       Leaving her chast abode,
        To gad abroad :

Amongst the gay mates of the god of flyes ;
    To take her pleasures, and to play
    And keep the divells holy day.
To dance in the Sunneshine of some smiling
        but beguiling
Spheare of sweet, and sugred lies,   50
    Some slippery paire,
    Of false perhaps as faire
Flattering but forswearing eyes

Doubtles some other heart
    Will git the start,
    And stepping in before,
Will take possession of the sacred store
    Of hidden sweets, and holy joyes,
    Words which are not heard with eares,
(These tumultuous shops of noise)   60
    Effectuall whispers whose still voyce,
The soule it selfe more feeles then heares.

Amorous Languishments, Luminous trances,
    Sights which are not seen with eyes,
Spirituall and soule peircing glances.
    Whose pure and subtle lightning, flies
Home to the heart, and setts the house on fire ;
And melts it downe in sweet desire :
        Yet doth not stay
To aske the windowes leave, to passe that way.   70

41 comes] come *48 52*   42 wandring] loyt'ring *48 52*   43 her]
its *48*   45 flyes; *48 52 A34*: flyes *46*   46 pleasures] pleasure
48 52 A34   47 in the] ith' *48*: th' *52*   49 beguiling *48 52 A34*:
beguiling. *46*   50 Spheare] Spheares *52 A34*   56 And] Meanwhile,
& *52 A34*   57 of the] of that *52 A34*   60 These] those *48 52*
tumultuous] tumultous *46*   61 still] st ll *46*   63 *A34 distinguishes*
Languishments *and* Trances   69 doth] does *52 A34*

Delicious deaths, soft exhalations
Of soule ; deare, and divine annihilations.
    A thousand unknowne rites
    Of joyes, and rarifyed delights.

An hundred thousand loves and graces,
    And many a misticke thing,
    Which the divine embraces
Of the deare spowse of spirits with them will bring.
    For which it is no shame,
That dull mortality must not know a name.   80

Of all this hidden store
Of blessings, and ten thousand more ;
    If when hee come
Hee find the heart from home,
    Doubtles hee will unload
Himselfe some other where,
      And powre abroad
      His precious sweets,
On the faire soule whom first hee meets.

O faire ! ô fortunate ! ô rich ! ô deare !   90
    O happy and thrice happy shee
    Deare silver breasted dove
      Who ere shee bee,
      Whose early Love
      With winged vowes,
Makes haste to meet her morning spowse :
And close with his immortall kisses.
    Happy soule who never misses,
    To improve that precious houre :
      And every day,   100
      Seize her sweet prey ;
All fresh and fragrant as hee rises,
Dropping with a balmy showre
A delicious dew of spices.

71–2 *A34 distinguishes* Deaths Exhalations *and* Annihilations   *72*
soule ; *48 52* : soule *46*   75] *See 52 l. 81* An hundred thousand]
A hundred *A34*   78 spirits] spitits *46*   80 mortality] mortallists
A34   81 this hidden] this *48 52*   83–4 *bracketed 48 52 A34*   *92*
Deare silver breasted] Selected *48 52*   95 winged] mingled *A34*
97 his] her *A34*   98 soule] indeed *48 52*

O let that happy soule hold fast
Her heavenly armefull, shee shall tast
At once, ten thousand paradises
    Shee shall have power,
    To rifle and deflower,
The rich and roseall spring of those rare sweets,   110
Which with a swelling bosome there shee meets,
Boundlesse and infinite————————
————————————bottomlesse treasures,
      Of pure inebriating pleasures,
Happy soule shee shall discover,
    What joy, what blisse,
    How many heavens at once it is,
To have a God become her lover.

On *Mr.* G. Herberts *booke intitu-*
led the Temple of Sacred Po-
ems, sent to a Gentle-
woman.

KNow you faire, on what you looke ;
  Divinest love lyes in this booke :
Expecting fire from your eyes,
To kindle this his sacrifice.
When your hands unty these strings,
Thinke you have an Angell by th' wings.
One that gladly will bee nigh,
To wait upon each morning sigh.
To flutter in the balmy aire,
Of your well perfumed prayer.   10
These white plumes of his heele lend you,
Which every day to heaven will send you :
To take acquaintance of the spheare,
And all the smooth faced kindred there.

105 that happy soule] the happy Soule *A34*: the blisseful *Heart 48 52*
112 *Blanks in 48 as in 46. Space before l. 115 in A34.*   115 soule]
proofe 48 52   118 a God] *her God 48 52 A34 distinguishes* Lover.
  On *Mr.* G. Herberts *booke &c. MS. T. Heading in T :* Vpon
Herberts Temple sent to a gentlewoman. R. Cr. *Mr.* G.] *Mr.* George *48*
1 faire,] (Faire) *T*   looke ;] looke ? *T*   3 your eyes,] your faire
eyes *T*   5 hands unty] hand vnties *T*   6 you have] yo'
have *48* you've *T*   7 will] would *T*   8 upon each] on your chast
T   10 perfumed *48 T*: prefumed *46*   12 which] That *T*   you :]
you, *T*   13 the] each *T*   14 the] your *T*

And though *Herberts* name doe owe
These devotions, fairest ; know
That while I lay them on the shrine
Of your white hand, they are mine.

In memory of the Vertuous and Learned Lady Madre de Teresa that sought an early Martyrdome.

Love thou art absolute, sole Lord
  Of life and death—To prove the word,
Wee need to goe to none of all
Those thy old souldiers, stout and tall
Ripe and full growne, that could reach downe,
With strong armes their triumphant crowne :
Such as could with lusty breath,
Speake lowd unto the face of death
Their great Lords glorious name, to none
Of those whose large breasts built a throne   10
For love their Lord, glorious and great,
Weell see him take a private seat,
And make his mansion in the milde
And milky soule of a soft childe.

  Scarce had shee learnt to lisp a name
  Of Martyr, yet shee thinkes it shame
  Life should so long play with that breath,
  Which spent can buy so brave a death.

Shee never undertooke to know,
What death with love should have to doe   20
Nor hath shee ere yet understood
Why to show love shee should shed blood,

15–18 *indented in 46 and 48, but not in T*   16 devotions, fairest;
know] devotions; Fairest, knowe, *T*   17 That while I] While I thus
T   18 *T distinguishes* mine
  *In memory &c. For altered version with separate title-page in 52
(generally following 48) and MS. Dobell see p. 315, sqq. As the number of
lines is the same in both 46 and 52, comparison is easy ; the verbal variants
are not given in the footnotes here, which only refer to doubtful readings or
misprints in 46. For differences between 52 and 48 see footnotes to 52.
Heading in 70 as title-page in 52.*   5 full grown 70 : full, grown 46
21 understood 52 : understood. 46 48

Yet though shee cannot tell you why,
Shee can love and shee can dye.

Scarce had shee blood enough, to make
A guilty sword blush for her sake ;
Yet has shee a heart dares hope to prove,
How much lesse strong is death then love.

Bee love but there, let poore sixe yeares,
Bee posed with the maturest feares   30
Man trembles at, wee straight shall find
Love knowes no nonage, nor the mind.
Tis love, not yeares, or Limbes, that can
Make the martyr or the man.
Love toucht her heart, and loe it beats
High, and burnes with such brave heats :
Such thirst to dye, as dare drinke up,
A thousand cold deaths in one cup.
Good reason for shee breaths all fire,
Her weake breast heaves with strong desire,   40
Of what shee may with fruitlesse wishes
Seeke for, amongst her mothers kisses.

Since tis not to bee had at home,
Sheel travell to a martyrdome.
No home for her confesses shee,
But where shee may A martyr bee.
Sheel to the Moores, and trade with them,
For this unvalued Diadem,
Shee offers them her dearest breath,
With Christs name int in change for death.   50
Sheel bargain with them, and will give
Them God, and teach them how to live
In him, or if they this denye,
For him sheel teach them how to dye.
So shall shee leave amongst them sowne,
Her Lords blood, or at lest her owne.

Farewell then all the world, adeiu,
Teresa is no more for you :
Farewell all pleasures, sports and joyes,
Never till now esteemed toyes.   60

38 cold *48 52* : coled *46*

Farewell what ever deare may bee,
Mothers armes, or fathers knee.
Farewell house, and farwell home :
Shees for the Moores and Martyrdome.

    Sweet not so fast, Loe thy faire spouse,
    Whom thou seek'st with so swift vowes
    Calls thee back, and bids thee come,
    T'embrace a milder Martyrdome.

Blest powers forbid thy tender life,
Should bleed upon a barbarous knife.   70
Or some base hand have power to race,.
Thy Breasts chast cabinet ; and uncase
A soule kept there so sweet. O no,
Wise heaven will never have it so.
Thou art Loves victim, and must dye
A death more misticall and high.
Into Loves hand thou shalt let fall,
A still surviving funerall.

    His is the dart must make the death
    Whose stroake shall taste thy hallowed breath ;   80
    A dart thrice dipt in that rich flame,
    Which writes thy spowses radiant name
    Vpon the roofe of heaven where ay
    It shines, and with a soveraigne ray,
    Beats bright upon the burning faces
    Of soules, which in that names sweet graces,
Find everlasting smiles. So rare,
So spirituall, pure and faire,
Must be the immortall instrument,
Vpon whose choice point shall be spent,   90
A life so loved, and that there bee
Fit executioners for thee,
The fairest, and the first borne sons of fire,
Blest Seraphims shall leave their quire,
And turne Loves souldiers, upon thee,
To exercise their Archerie.

<hr />

82 Name *52* : name. *46* : *Name,* *48*   92 thee, *M* : thee. *46 48*
52   93 sons *48 52* : Loves *46*   95 souldiers, *52* : *Souldiers, 48* :
souldiers *46*

O how oft shalt thou complaine
Of a sweet and subtile paine ?
Of intollerable joyes ?
Of a death in which who dyes   100
Loves his death, and dyes againe,
And would for ever so be slaine !
And lives and dyes, and knowes not why
To live, but that he still may dy.

How kindly will thy gentle heart,
Kisse the sweetly—killing dart :
And close in his embraces keep,
Those delicious wounds that weep
Balsome, to heale themselves with————
————————————————— thus   110
When these thy deaths so numerous,
Shall all at last dye into one,
And melt thy soules sweet mansion :
Like a soft lumpe of Incense, hasted
By too hot a fire, and wasted,
Into perfuming cloudes. So fast
Shalt thou exhale to heaven at last,
In a disolving sigh, and then
    O what ! aske not the tongues of men,
Angells cannot tell, suffice,   120
Thy selfe shalt feel thine owne full joyes.
And hold them fast for ever. There,
So soone as thou shalt first appeare,
The moone of maiden starres ; thy white
Mistresse attended by such bright
Soules as thy shining selfe, shall come,
And in her first rankes make thee roome.
Where mongst her snowy family,
Immortall wellcomes wait on thee.
O what delight when shee shall stand,   130
And teach thy Lipps heaven, with her hand,
On which thou now maist to thy wishes,
Heap up thy consecrated kisses.
What joy shall seize thy soule when shee
Bending her blessed eyes on thee

109 with———— ————]with. *48* : with *52*   122 ever. There *48* : ever
there, *46* : ever there *52*   123 appeare, *48 52* : appeare. *46*
135 eyes on thee *48 52* : eyes, on thee *46*

Those second smiles of heaven shall dart,
Her mild rayes, through thy melting heart :

Angells thy old friends there shall greet thee,
Glad at their owne home now to meet thee.
All thy good workes which went before,   140
And waited for thee at the doore :
Shall owne thee there : and all in one
Weave a Constellation
Of Crownes, with which the King thy spouse,
Shall build up thy triumphant browes.

All thy old woes shall now smile on thee,
And thy pains set bright upon thee.
All thy sorrows here shall shine,
And thy sufferings bee devine.
Teares shall take comfort, and turne Gems.   150
And wrongs repent to diadems.
Even thy deaths shall live, and new
Dresse the soule, which late they slew.
Thy wounds shall blush to such bright scarres,
As keep account of the Lambes warres

Those rare workes, where thou shalt leave writ,
Loves noble history, with witt
Taught thee by none but him, while here
They feed our soules, shall cloath thine there.
Each heavenly word, by whose hid flame   160
Our hard hearts shall strike fire, the same
Shall flourish on thy browes ; and bee
Both fire to us, and flame to thee :
Whose light shall live bright, in thy face
By glory, in our hearts by grace.

Thou shalt looke round about, and see
Thousands of crownd soules, throng to bee
Themselves thy crowne, sonnes of thy vowes :
The Virgin births with which thy spowse
Made fruitfull thy faire soule ; Goe now   170
And with them all about thee, bow

136 Those second smiles of heaven *bracketed 48 52*   139 thee.
48 52 : thee *46*   141 thee at the doore :] thee at the doore, *48* :
thee, at the door, *52*   167 Thousands *48 52* : Thousand *46*
168 vowes *48 52* : nowes *46*

To him, put on (heel say) put on
My Rosy Love, that thy rich Zone,
Sparkeling with the sacred flames,
Of thousand soules whose happy names,
Heaven keeps upon thy score (thy bright
Life, brought them first to kisse the light
That kindled them to starres,) and so
Thou with the Lambe thy Lord shall goe.
And where so e're hee sitts his white   180
Steps, walke with him those wayes of Light.
Which who in death would live to see,
Must learne in life to dye like thee.

An Apologie for the precedent Hymne.

THus have I back againe to thy bright name
Faire sea of holy fires transfused the flame
I tooke from reading thee. 'Tis to thy wrong
I know that in my weak and worthlesse song
Thou here art set to shine, where thy full day
Scarce dawnes, ô pardon, if I dare to say
Thine own deare books are guilty, for from thence
I learnt to know that Love is eloquence.
That heavenly maxim gave me heart to try
If what to other tongues is tun'd so high,   10
Thy praise might not speak English too, forbid
(by all thy mysteries that there lye hid ;)
Forbid it mighty Love, let no fond hate
Of names and words so farre prejudicate ;
Soules are not Spaniards too, one frendly flood
Of Baptisme, blends them all into one blood.
Christs Faith makes but one body of all soules,
And loves that bodies soule ; no Law controules

176–8 *Brackets adopted from* 48 52. *No brackets in* 46, *in which also a space is left between ll.* 176 *and* 177.   177 light 48 52 : light. 46
180 sitts] sets 48 52
An Apologie &c. For slightly altered version in 52 (*generally following* 48) *with fuller heading, see p.* 322, *below. Heading in* 70 *as in* 52 *except that '* a Protestant ' *replaces* ' among the protestantes '. *In* 48 *the* ' Apologie' *refers to both the preceding poem and* ' The Flaming Heart' *which it follows.*   3 thee. 'Tis] Thee. 'Tis 48 : thee 'tis 46
eloquence. 48 52 : eloquence 46   10 high, 48 52 : high. 46 : high 70
14 prejudicate : 48 : prejudicate 46 : præiudicate. 52

Our free trafick for heaven, we may maintaine,
Peace sure with piety, though it dwell in *Spaine*.　　20
What soule soever in any Language can·
Speake heaven like hers, is my soules country-man.
O 'tis not Spanish, but 'tis heaven she speakes,
'Tis heaven that lies in ambush there, and breakes
From thence into the wondring readers breast,
Who finds his warme heart, hatcht into a nest
Of little Eagles, and young Loves, whose high
Flights scorne the lazie dust, and things that dye.
There are enow whose draughts as deep as hell
Drinke up all *Spaine* in Sack, let my soule swell　　30
With thee strong wine of Love, let others swimme
In puddles, we will pledge this Seraphim
Bowles full of richer blood then blush of grape
Was ever guilty of, change wee our shape,
My soule, some drinke from men to beasts ; ô then,
Drinke wee till we prove more, not lesse then men :
And turne not beasts, but Angels.　Let the King,
Mee ever into these his Cellars bring ;
Where flowes such Wine as we can have of none
But him, who trod the Wine-presse all alone :　　40
Wine of youths Life, and the sweet deaths of Love,
Wine of immortall mixture, which can prove
Its tincture from the Rosie Nectar, wine
That can exalt weak earth, and so refine
Our dust, that in one draught, Mortality
May drinke it selfe up, and forget to dy.

On a Treatise of Charity.

RIse then, immortall maid ! *Religion* rise !
　Put on thy selfe in thine own looks : t' our eyes
Be what thy beauties, not our blots, have made thee,
Such as (e're our dark sinnes to dust betray'd thee)
Heav'n set thee down new drest ; when thy bright birth
Shot thee like lightning, to th'astonisht earth.

19 heaven,] *comma in 48 only*
On a Treatise &c.　First published in Five Pious And Learned Dis-
courses, . . . By Robert Shelford of *Ringsfield* in *Suffolk* Priest. . . .
Cambridge. 1635.　*Heading in 1635* : Upon the ensuing Treatises.
Signed Rich. Crashaw, Aul. Penb. A.B.　*MS. Sloane 1925 gives ll. 57–8
without heading.*

From th' dawn of thy faire eye-lids wipe away
Dull mists and melancholy clouds : take day
And thine owne beames about thee : bring the best
Of whatsoe're perfum'd thy *Eastern nest.*   10
Girt all thy glories to thee : then sit down,
Open this booke, faire Queen, *and take thy crown.*
These learned leaves shall vindicate to thee
Thy holyest, humblest, handmaid Charitie.
Sh'l dresse thee like thy selfe, set thee on high
Where thou shalt reach all hearts, command each eye.
Lo where I see thy offrings wake, and rise
From the pale dust of that strange sacrifice
Which they themselves were ; each one putting on
A majestie that may beseem thy throne.   20
The holy youth of heav'n, whose golden rings
Girt round thy awfull Altars, with bright wings
Fanning thy faire locks (which the world beleeves
As much as sees) shall with these sacred leaves
Trick their tall plumes, and in that garb shall go
If not more glorious, more conspicuous tho.
                    ——— Be it enacted then
By the faire lawes of thy firm-pointed pen,
Gods services no longer shall put on
A *sluttishnesse*, for *pure religion :*   30
No longer shall our Churches frighted stones
Lie scatter'd like the burnt and martyr'd bones
Of dead Devotion ; nor faint marbles weep
In their sad ruines ; nor Religion keep
A melancholy mansion in those cold
Vrns.   Like Gods Sanctuaries they lookt of old :
Now seem they Temples consecrate to *none,*
Or to a *new* God *Desolation.*
No more the hypocrite shall th'*upright* be
Because he's stiffe, and will confesse no knee :   40
While others bend their knee, no more shalt thou
(Disdainfull dust and ashes) bend thy brow ;
Nor on Gods Altar cast *two scorching eyes*
Bak't in hot scorn, for *a burnt sacrifice :*
But (for a *Lambe*) thy tame and tender *heart*
New struck by love, still trembling on his dart ;

12 this] thy *48*   16 shalt] shall *48*   17 offrings] *Altars 1635*
30 *A*] Pure *1635*

Or (for two *Turtle doves*) it shall suffice
To bring a paire of meek and humble *eyes.*
This shall from hence-forth be the masculine theme
Pulpits and pennes shall sweat in ; to redeem   50
Vertue to action, that life-feeding flame
That keeps Religion warme : not swell *a name*
Of faith, *a mountaine word*, made up of aire,
With those deare spoiles that wont to dresse the faire
And fruitfull Charities full breasts (of old)
Turning her out to tremble in the cold.
What can the poore hope from us, when we be
Vncharitable ev'n to *Charitie.*

On the Assumption.

Harke shee is called, the parting houre is come,
Take thy farewel poore world, heaven must go home.
A peece of heavenly Light purer and brighter
Then the chast stars, whose choice Lamps come to light her.
While through the christall orbs clearer then they
Shee climbes, and makes a farre more milky way ;
Shee's call'd againe, harke how th'immortall Dove
Sighs to his silver mate : rise up my Love,
Rise up my faire, my spotlesse one,
The Winter's past, the raine is gone :   10
The Spring is come, the Flowers appeare,
No sweets since thou art wanting here.

After l. 58 1635 continues :
> *Nor shall our zealous ones still have a fling*
> *At that most horrible and horned thing,*
> *Forsooth* the Pope : *by which black name they call*
> *The Turk, the Devil, Furies, Hell and all,*
> *And something more.   O he is Antichrist :*
> *Doubt this, and doubt (say they) that Christ is Christ.*
> *Why, 'tis a point of Faith.   What e're it be,*
> *I'm sure it is no point of Charitie.*
> *In summe, no longer shall our people hope,*
> *To be a true Protestant, 's but to hate the Pope.*

Rich. Crashaw, *Aul. Penb. A.B.*

On the Assumption. MSS. T A34 A1. Heading in T : On the
Assumption of the Virgin Marie. *For altered version with different
heading in 52 (generally following 48) see p. 304, below.   T and A34
generally agree with 46 ; A1 with 52, with exceptions given in footnotes
ad loc.*   3 Light] Earth, *48 :* earth ; *52 T*   4 her.] her, *48
A34 :* her *52*   7] *See 52*   9 faire, my] faire, & *T*   12 since
thou art] but thou are *48 52 :* save you, are *T*

Come away my Love,
Come away my Dove
   cast off delay :
The Court of Heav'n is come,
To wait upon thee home ;
   Come away, come away.

Shee's call'd againe, and will shee goe ;
When heaven bids come, who can say no ?   20
Heav'n calls her, and she must away,
Heaven will not, and she cannot stay.
Goe then, goe (glorious) on the golden wings
Of the bright youth of Heaven, that sings
Vnder so sweet a burden : goe,
Since thy great Sonne will have it so :
And while thou goest, our song and wee,
Will as wee may reach after thee.
Haile holy Queen of humble hearts,
Wee in thy praise will have our parts.   30
And though thy dearest looks must now be light
To none but the blest heavens, whose bright
Beholders lost in sweet delight
Feed for ever their faire sight
With those divinest eyes, which wee
And our darke world no more shall see.
Though, our poore joyes are parted so,
Yet shall our lips never let goe
Thy gracious name, but to the last,
Our Loving song shall hold it fast.   40

   Thy sacred Name shall bee
   Thy selfe to us, and wee
   With holy cares will keepe it by us,
      Wee to the last,
      Will hold it fast,
   And no Assumption shall deny us.

18 Come away, come away.] Come, come away. *48*: Come come away !
52: Come. come away *T*   *After l. 18, 48 52 and A1 insert 16 ll.*
See 52.   25 sweet] great *48*   26 great] dread *48 52*   27
song] song, *T*   *ll. 31–40 omitted in 52 and A1, but not in 48 70.*
31 be light] give light *T* : take its' flight *A34*   33 delight *48 T A34* :
delight ; *46*   37 joyes] eyes *T*   39 Thy] The *A34*   to]
for *A34*   41 sacred] precious *48 52*   43 cares] care *48 52 T*

All the sweetest showers,
Of our fairest Flowers,
Will wee strow upon it :
Though our sweetnesse cannot make   50
It sweeter, they may take
Themselves new sweetnesse from it.

Mary, men and Angels sing,
Maria Mother of our King.
Live rarest Princesse, and may the bright
Crown of an incomparable Light
Embrace thy radiant browes, ô may the best
Of everlasting joyes bath thy white brest.
Live our chaste love, the holy mirth
Of heaven, and humble pride of Earth :   60
Live Crowne of Women, Queen of men :
Live Mistris of our Song, and when
Our weak desires have done their best ;
Sweet Angels come, and sing the rest.

An Himne for the Circumcision
day of our Lord.

*R*Ise thou first and fairest morning,
   Rosie with a double red :
With thine owne blush thy cheekes adorning,
   And the deare drops this day were shed.

All the purple pride of Laces,
   The crimson curtaines of thy bed ;
Guild thee not with so sweet graces ;
   Nor sets thee in so rich a red.

Of all the faire cheekt flowers that fill thee,
   None so faire thy bosome strowes ;   10
As this modest Maiden Lilly,
   Our sinnes have sham'd into a Rose.

50 sweetnesse] sweets *48 52 T*   51 may] can *48 52 T*   53
Mary] Maria *48 52 T*   54 of] to *T*   55 rarest] Rosie *48 52 T*
Princesse, and] Princesse, live, and *48*: princesse, L*ive*. And *52*:
Princesse, Live ! & *T*   56 an] a most *48 52 T*   60 and] the
48 52 A 34   pride] bragg *T*   61 Crowne] Praise *T*   Queen]'
Pride *T*

   *An Himne &c. For altered version in 52 (generally following 48) see
p. 251, below.*

Bid the golden god the Sunne,
  Burnisht in his glorious beames :
Put all his red eyed rubies on,
  These Rubies shall put out his eyes.

Let him make poore the purple East,
  Rob the rich store her Cabinets keep,
The pure birth of each sparkling nest,
  That flaming in their faire bed sleep.   20

Let him embrace his owne bright tresses,
  With a new morning made of gems ;
And weare in them his wealthy dresses,
  Another day of Diadems.

When he hath done all he may,
  To make himselfe rich in his rise,
All will be darknesse, to the day
  That breakes from one of these faire eyes.

And soone the sweet truth shall appeare,
  Deare Babe e're many dayes be done :   30
The Moone shall come to meet thee here,
  And leave the long adored Sunne.

Thy nobler beauty shall bereave him,
  Of all his Easterne Paramours :
His Persian Lovers all shall leave him,
  And sweare faith to thy sweeter powers.

Nor while they leave him shall they loose the Sunne,
  But in thy fairest eyes find two for one.

On Hope,

By way of Question and Answer, betweene
A. Cowley, *and* R. Crashaw.

Cowley.

HOpe, whose weake being ruin'd is
   Alike, if it succeed, and if it misse.
Whom Ill, and Good doth equally confound,
And both the hornes of Fates dilemma wound.
   Vaine shadow ! that doth vanish quite
   Both at full noone, and perfect night.
   The Fates have not a possibility
      Of blessing thee.
If things then from their ends wee happy call,
'Tis hope is the most hopelesse thing of all.   10

Crashaw.

Deare Hope ! Earths dowry, and Heavens debt,
The entity of things that are not yet.
Subt'lest, but surest being ! Thou by whom
Our Nothing hath a definition.
   Faire cloud of fire, both shade, and light,
   Our life in death, our day in night.
   Fates cannot find out a capacity
      Of hurting thee.
From thee their thinne dilemma with blunt horne
Shrinkes, like the sick Moone at the wholsome morne.   20

Cowley.

   Hope, thou bold taster of delight,
Who, in stead of doing so, devour'st it quite.
Thou bring'st us an estate, yet leav'st us poore,
By clogging it with Legacies before.

On Hope *&c. MS. H. Heading in H :* Upon Hope : . . . The
Answer. *For much altered version of Crashaw's part in 52, see p. 345,
below. 48 and H generally agree with 46, with exceptions given below,
but H resembles 52 in giving the poems by Cowley and Crashaw separately,
with headings :* Upon Hope : *and* The Answer :   10 of] at *48*
12 things] those *H*

The joyes, which wee intire should wed,
Come deflour'd virgins to our bed.
Good fortunes without gaine imported bee,
 So mighty Custome's paid to thee.
For joy, like Wine kept close doth better taste :
If it take ayre before, its spirits waste.   30

Crashaw.

Thou art Loves Legacie under lock
Of Faith : the steward of our growing stocke.
Our Crown-lands lye above, yet each meale brings
A seemly portion for the Sons of Kings.
 Nor will the Virgin-joyes wee wed
 Come lesse unbroken to our bed,
 Because that from the bridall cheeke of Blisse,
  Thou thus steal'st downe a distant kisse,
Hopes chaste kisse wrongs no more joyes maidenhead,
Then Spousall rites prejudge the marriage-bed.   40

Cowley.

Hope, Fortunes cheating Lotterie,
Where for one prize an hundred blankes there bee.
Fond Archer Hope, who tak'st thine ayme so farre,
That still, or short, or wide thine arrowes are.
 Thine empty cloud the eye, it selfe deceives
 With shapes that our owne fancie gives :
 A cloud, which gilt, and painted now appeares,
  But must drop presently in teares.
When thy false beames o're Reasons light prevaile,
By *ignes fatui*, not North starres we sayle.   50

Crashaw.

Faire *Hope* ! our earlier Heaven ! by thee
Young *Time* is taster to Eternity.
The generous wine with age growes strong, not sower ;
Nor need wee kill thy fruit to smell thy flower.
 Thy golden head never hangs downe,
 Till in the lap of Loves full noone

It falls, and dyes : oh no, it melts away
  As doth the dawne into the day :
As lumpes of Sugar lose themselves, and twine
Their subtile essence with the soule of Wine.   60

Cowley.

Brother of Feare ! more gaily clad
The merrier Foole o'th' two, yet quite as mad.
Sire of Repentance ! Child of fond desire,
That blows the Chymicks, and the Lovers fire,
  Still leading them insensibly on,
  With the strange witchcraft of *Anon.*
By thee the one doth changing Nature through
  Her endlesse Laborinths pursue,
And th' other chases woman, while she goes
More wayes, and turnes, then hunted Nature knowes.   70

Crashaw.

Fortune alas above the worlds law warres :
Hope kicks the curl'd heads of conspiring starres.
Her keele cuts not the waves, where our winds stirre,
And *Fates* whole Lottery is one blanke to her.
  Her shafts, and shee fly farre above,
  And forrage in the fields of light, and love.
Sweet *Hope !* kind cheat ! faire fallacy ! by thee
  Wee are not where, or what wee bee,
But what, and where wee would bee : thus art thou
Our absent presence, and our future now.   80

Crashaw.

Faith's Sister ! Nurse of faire desire !
Feares Antidote ! a wise, and well stay'd fire
Temper'd 'twixt cold despaire, and torrid joy :
Queen Regent in young Loves minoritie.
  Though the vext Chymick vainly chases
  His fugitive gold through all her faces,
And loves more fierce, more fruitlesse fires assay
  One face more fugitive then all they,
True *Hope's* a glorious Huntresse, and her chase
The God of Nature in the field of Grace.   90

60 subtle] supple *52 H*   63 Child *H 52* : shield *46 48*   87 fierce,
more] fierce and *H*   88 then all] then *H*   90 field] fields *H*

917·9   L

THE
DELIGHTS
OF THE
MUSES.
OR,
Other Poems written on
severall occasions.

By Richard Cra∫haw, *∫ometimes of* Pembroke *Hall, and late Fellow of* St. Peters *Colledge in* Cambridge.

Mart. *Dic mihi quid melius de∫idio∫us agas.*

LONDON,
Printed by *T.W.* for *H. Mo∫eley,* at
the Princes Armes in S. *Pauls*
Churchyard, 1646.

Musicks Duell.

NOw Westward *Sol* had spent the richest Beames
Of Noons high Glory, when hard by the streams
Of *Tiber*, on the sceane of a greene plat,
Vnder protection of an Oake ; there sate
A sweet Lutes-master : in whose gentle aires
Hee lost the Dayes heat, and his owne hot cares.
  Close in the covert of the leaves there stood
A Nightingale, come from the neighbouring wood :
(The sweet inhabitant of each glad Tree,
Their Muse, their *Syren*. harmlesse *Syren* shee)   10
There stood she listning, and did entertaine
The Musicks soft report : and mold the same
In her owne murmures, that what ever mood
His curious fingers lent, her voyce made good :
The man perceiv'd his Rivall, and her Art,
Dispos'd to give the light-foot Lady sport
Awakes his Lute, and 'gainst the fight to come
Informes it, in a sweet *Præludium*
Of closer straines, and ere the warre begin,
Hee lightly skirmishes on every string   20
Charg'd with a flying touch : and streightway shee
Carves out her dainty voyce as readily,
Into a thousand sweet distinguish'd Tones,
And reckons up in soft divisions,
Quicke volumes of wild Notes ; to let him know
By that shrill taste, shee could doe something too.
  His nimble hands instinct then taught each string
A capring cheerefullnesse ; and made them sing
To their owne dance ; now negligently rash
Hee throwes his Arme, and with a long drawne dash   30
Blends all together ; then distinctly tripps
From this to that ; then quicke returning skipps

Musicks Duell. MSS. T A3 A2 S. Heading in T : Fidicinis, &
Philomelæ | Bellum Musicum. *Heading in A2 :* Fidicinis et Philomelæ
bellū Musicum.   18 it,] yᵐ *A2*   19 warre] waıres *T A3*
27 His] It's *catchword 46*

And snatches this againe, and pauses there.
Shee measures every measure, every where
Meets art with art ; sometimes as if in doubt
Not perfect yet, and fearing to bee out
Trayles her playne Ditty in one long-spun note,
Through the sleeke passage of her open throat :
A cleare unwrinckled song, then doth shee point it
With tender accents, and severely joynt it   40
By short diminutives, that being rear'd
In controverting warbles evenly shar'd,
With her sweet selfe shee wrangles ; Hee amazed
That from so small a channell should be rais'd
The torrent of a voyce, whose melody
Could melt into such sweet variety
Straines higher yet ; that tickled with rare art
The tatling strings (each breathing in his part)
Most kindly doe fall out ; the grumbling Base
In surly groanes disdaines the Trebles Grace.   50
The high-perch't treble chirps at this, and chides,
Vntill his finger (Moderatour) hides
And closes the sweet quarrell, rowsing all
Hoarce, shrill, at once ; as when the Trumpets call
Hot Mars to th' Harvest of Deaths field, and woo
Mens hearts into their hands ; this lesson too
Shee gives him backe ; her supple Brest thrills out
Sharpe Aires, and staggers in a warbling doubt
Of dallying sweetnesse, hovers ore her skill,
And folds in wav'd notes with a trembling bill,   60
The plyant Series of her slippery song.
Then starts shee suddenly into a Throng
Of short thicke sobs, whose thundring volleyes float,
And roule themselves over her lubricke throat
In panting murmurs, still'd out of her Breast
That ever-bubling spring ; the sugred Nest
Of her delicious soule, that there does lye
Bathing in streames of liquid Melodie ;

33 and pauses] y^n pauses *A2*   35 doubt] doubt; *48 A3*: doubt, *T*
38 sleeke] slick *T*   throat :] throat, *48 T S*: throate. *A3*: throate
A2   42 shar'd] shear'd *A3*   43 wrangles ;] wrangles. *48 A3 S*
46 melt] meete *A2*   47 that] & *A2*   48 each breathing in his]
each breath in his owne *A2*   56 into] in *A2*   57 thrills] shrills
A2   66 the] y^t *A2*   67 Of] O *A2*   68 streames] floods *A3*

Musicks best seed-plot, whence in ripend Aires
A Golden-headed Harvest fairely reares   70
His Honey-dropping tops, plow'd by her breath
Which there reciprocally laboureth
In that sweet soyle. It seemes a holy quire
Founded to th' Name of great *Apollo's* lyre.
Whose sylver-roofe rings with the sprightly notes
Of sweet-lipp'd Angell-Imps, that swill their throats
In·creame of Morning *Helicon,* and then
Preferre soft Anthems to the Eares of men,
To woo them from their Beds, still murmuring
That men can sleepe while they their Mattens sing :   80
(Most divine service) whose so early lay,
Prevents the Eye-lidds of the blushing day.
There might you heare her kindle her soft voyce,
In the close murmur of a sparkling noyse.
And lay the ground-worke of her hopefull song,
Still keeping in the forward streame, so long
Till a sweet whirle-wind (striving to gett out)
Heaves her soft Bosome, wanders round about,
And makes a pretty Earthquake in her Breast,
Till the fledg'd Notes at length forsake their Nest ;   90
Fluttering in wanton shoales, and to the Sky
Wing'd with their owne wild Eccho's pratling fly.
Shee opes the floodgate, and lets loose a Tide
Of streaming sweetnesse, which in state doth ride
On the wav'd backe of every swelling straine,
Rising and falling in a pompous traine.
And while shee thus discharges a shrill peale
Of flashing Aires ; shee qualifies their zeale
With the coole Epode of a graver Noat,
Thus high, thus low, as if her silver throat   100
Would reach the brasen voyce of warr's hoarce Bird ;
Her little soule is ravisht : and so pour'd

69 plot,] plot ; *70*   whence *T A3 A2* : when *46 48*   *72*
laboureth *T A3 A2* : laboureth. *46 48*   73 soile. it *T* : soyle. It *A3* :
soyle, It *A2* : soyle it *46 48*   74 of great] of *A2*   75 sylver-roofe]
siluer roofe *T A3*   sprightly] shrilly *A2*   ·78 men, *48 T A3 A2*
S : men. *46*   83 might you] you might *48*   84 noyse.] noyse,
48 A3 A2 S   92 Eccho's] echoes *A3 A2*   93 lets] lett
T   a] yᵉ *A2 S*   99 graver *48 T A3* (*A2 omits the line*):
grave *46*   99 Noat,] note. *T* : note *A3*   101 Bird ;] bird *A2*
102 ravisht :] ravisht, *A2*

Into loose extasies, that shee is plac't
Above her selfe, Musicks *Enthusiast.*
    Shame now and anger mixt a double staine
In the Musitians face ; yet once againe
(Mistresse) I come ; now reach a straine my Lute
Above her mocke, or bee for ever mute.
Or tune a song of victory to mee,
Or to thy selfe, sing thine owne Obsequie ;   110
So said, his hands sprightly as fire hee flings,
And with a quavering coynesse tasts the strings.
The sweet-lip't sisters musically frighted,
Singing their feares are fearfully delighted.
Trembling as when *Appollo's* golden haires
Are fan'd and frizled, in the wanton ayres
Of his owne breath : which marryed to his lyre
Doth tune the *Sphœares,* and make Heavens selfe looke higher.
From this to that, from that to this hee flyes
Feeles Musicks pulse in all her Arteryes,   120
Caught in a net which there *Appollo* spreads,
His fingers struggle with the vocall threads,
Following those little rills, hee sinkes into
A Sea of *Helicon* ; his hand does goe
Those parts of sweetnesse which with *Nectar* drop,
Softer then that which pants in *Hebe's* cup.
The humourous strings expound his learned touch,
By various Glosses ; now they seeme to grutch,
And murmur in a buzzing dinne, then gingle
In shrill tongu'd accents : striving to bee single.   130
Every smooth turne, every delicious stroake
Gives life to some new Grace ; thus doth h'invoke
Sweetnesse by all her Names ; thus, bravely thus
(Fraught with a fury so harmonious)
The Lutes light *Genius* now does proudly rise,
Heav'd on the surges of swolne Rapsodyes.

104 *Enthusiast.*] *Enthusiast 46* : *Enthusiasts 48*   *T distinguishes*
also Musicks   111 So] This *A2*   118 and make] make *A2*
higher. *T S A2* : higher *46 48 A3*   124 hand does] hands doe *A2*
128 By] Wth *A2*   grutch] crouch *S* : grudge *A2*   130 accents :]
accents, *48 T S* : accents *A3 A2*   131 turne] tongue *A2*   132
Giues Life to some grace. Thus doth he inuoke *A3*   doth h']
does he *T*   133 thus, bravely thus] thus brauely, thus *T A2*
134 Fraught] Rapt *A2*   135 light . . . rise,] proud Genius proudly
now doth rise *A2*

Whose flourish (Meteor-like) doth curle the aire
With flash of high-borne fancyes : here and there
Dancing in lofty measures, and anon
Creeps on the soft touch of a tender tone :   140
Whose trembling murmurs melting in wild aires
Runs to and fro, complaining his sweet cares
Because those pretious mysteryes that dwell,
In musick's ravish't soule hee dare not tell,
But whisper to the world : thus doe they vary
Each string his Note, as if they meant to carry
Their Masters blest soule (snatcht out at his Eares
By a strong Extasy) through all the sphæares
Of Musicks heaven ; and seat it there on high
In th' *Empyræum* of pure Harmony.   150
At length (after so long, so loud a strife
Of all the strings, still breathing the best life
Of blest variety attending on
His fingers fairest revolution
In many a sweet rise, many as sweet a fall)
A full-mouth *Diapason* swallowes all.
    This done, hee lists what shee would say to this,
And shee although her Breath's late exercise
Had dealt too roughly with her tender throate,
Yet summons all her sweet powers for a Noate   160
Alas ! in vaine ! for while (sweet soule) shee tryes
To measure all those wild diversities
Of chatt'ring stringes, by the small size of one
Poore simple voyce, rais'd in a Naturall Tone ;
Shee failes, and failing grieves, and grieving dyes.
Shee dyes ; and leaves her life the Victors prise,
Falling upon his Lute ; ò fit to have
(That liv'd so sweetly) dead, so sweet a Grave !

---

140 on] in *A2*   141 murmurs] murmure *T*   melting]
meeting *A2*   wild] mild *T*   143 dwell,] dwell *T A2 S*   144
dare] dares *48 T A3 S*   146 his] its *A2*   147 at] of *A2*
148 sphæares] spheares—— *T*   151 so loud] & lowd *T A2*   155
many as] as *A2*   156 full-mouth] full mouth'd *T*   157 lists]
lists, *T*   158 late] last *A2*   160 Noate] note. *T*: noate, *A2 S*
163 chatt'ring] chatting *T*   166 life] self *S*   167 Lute ;] Lute.
T (which distinguishes o fit ... Grave !)

Principi recèns natæ omen maternæ indolis.

CResce, ô dulcibus imputanda Divis,
　O cresce, & propera, puella Princeps,
In matris propera venire partes.
Et cùm par breve fulminum minorum,
Illinc Carolus, & Jacobus indè,
In patris faciles subire famam,
Ducent fata furoribus decoris ;
Cùm terror sacer, Anglicique magnum
Murmur nominis increpabit omnem
Latè Bosporon, Ottomannicásque   10
Non picto quatiet tremore Lunas ;
Te tunc altera, nec timenda paci,
Poscent prælia. Tu potens pudici
Vibratrix oculi, pios in hostes
Latè dulcia fata dissipabis.
O cùm flos tener ille, qui recenti
Pressus sidere jam sub ora ludit,
Olim fortior omne cuspidatos
Evolvet latus aureum per ignes ;
Quíque imbellis adhuc, adultus olim,   20
Puris expatiabitur genarum
Campis imperiosior Cupido ;
O quàm certa superbiore pennâ
Ibunt spicula, melleæque mortes,
Exultantibus hinc & indè turmis,
Quoquò jusseris, impigrè volabunt !
O quot corda calentium deorum
De te vulnera delicata discent !
O quot pectora Principum magistris
Fient molle negotium sagittis !   30
Nam quæ non poteris per arma ferri,
Cui matris sinus atque utrumque sidus
Magnorum patet officina Amorum ?

Principi recèns &c.   First published in ΣΥΝΩιΔίA, Sive Musarum Cantabrigiensium Concentus Et Congratulatio, Ad Serenissimum Britanniarum Regem Carolum, De quinta sua sobole, clarissima Principe, sibi nuper felicissimè nata . . . 1637. The poem is there followed by the signature : Ric. Crashaw, A.B. Coll. S. Pet. Soc.   Heading in 70L : Natalis Principis Mariæ.   10 Ottomannicásque 1637 48 : Ottomanìcásque 46

Hinc sumas licet, ô puella Princeps,
Quantacunque opus est tibi pharetrâ.
Centum sume Cupidines ab uno
Matris lumine, Gratiásque centum,
Et centum Veneres : adhuc manebunt
Centum mille Cupidines ; manebunt
Ter centum Venerésque Gratiæquĕ   40
Puro fonte superstites per ævum.

Out of Virgil,
In the praise of the Spring.

ALL Trees, all leavy Groves confesse the Spring
 Their gentlest friend, then, then the lands begin
To swell with forward pride, and seed desire
To generation ; Heavens Almighty Sire
Melts on the Bosome of his Love, and powres
Himselfe into her lap in fruitfull showers.
And by a soft insinuation, mixt
With earths large Masse, doth cherish and assist
Her weake conceptions ; No loane shade, but rings
With chatting Birds delicious murmurings.   10
Then *Venus* mild instinct (at set times) yeilds
The Herds to kindly meetings, then the fields
(Quick with warme *Zephires* lively breath) lay forth
Their pregnant Bosomes in a fragrant Birth.
Each body's plump and jucy, all things full
Of supple moisture : no coy twig but will
Trust his beloved bosome to the Sun ·
(Growne lusty now ;) No Vine so weake and young
That feares the foule-mouth'd Auster, or those stormes
That the Southwest-wind hurries in his Armes,   20
But hasts her forward Blossomes, and layes out
Freely layes out her leaves : Nor doe I doubt
But when the world first out of *Chaos* sprang
So smil'd the Dayes, and so the tenor ran
Of their felicity.   A spring was there,
An everlasting spring, the jolly yeare

37 *ceutum*] *centum 46*
Out of Virgil, *&c.   MSS. T A3.   Heading in T :* E Virg. Georg:
particula In laudem Veris. R. Cr.   2 gentlest] gentle *48*   3
seed] feed *T*   8 doth] does *A3*   10 Birds *48 70 T A3* :
Birds, *46*   13 *Zephires*] Zephyrus *T*   17 beloved] most loued *T*

Led round in his great circle ; No winds Breath
As then did smell of Winter, or of Death.
When Lifes sweet Light first shone on Beasts, and when
From their hard Mother Earth, sprang hardy men,   30
When Beasts tooke up their lodging in the Wood,
Starres in their higher Chambers : never cou'd
The tender growth of things endure the sence
Of such a change, but that the Heav'ns Indulgence
Kindly supplies sick Nature, and doth mold
A sweetly temper'd meane, nor hot nor cold.

With a Picture sent to a Friend.

I Paint so ill, my peece had need to bee
  Painted againe by some good Poesie.
I write so ill, my slender Line is scarce
  So much as th' Picture of a well-lim'd verse :
Yet may the love I send be true, though I
  Send nor true Picture, nor true Poesie.
Both which away, I should not need to feare,
  My Love, or *Feign'd* or *painted* should appeare.

In praise of Lessius *his rule of health.*

G Oe now with some dareing drugg,
  Baite thy disease, and while they tugg
Thou to maintaine their cruell strife,
Spend the deare treasure of thy life :

28 Death.] death : *T*   32 Chambers :] chambers. *T*   34 the
Heav'ns] heauens *T*
  *With a Picture &c. MSS. T A3. ll. 1–8 parallel in T, ll. 7, 8 only indented
A3   6 Send nor true] Send no true A3 : Send not true 70   7
should] shall T A3*
  In praise of Lessius *&c. MSS. T (ll. 1–15) A3 A2 (ll. 1–14) Bodl. 31037
(beginning at l. 15). First printed (ll. 15–end only) in* Hygiasticon : Or,
The right course of preserving Life and Health unto extream old Age :
Together with sound-nesse and integritie of the Senses, Judgement, and
Memorie.—Written in Latine by *Leonard Lessius,* And now done into
English. *The second Edition. . . . 1634. The version in 52 (see p. 342,
below), omitting ll. 11, 12 and adding 8 lines at the end, generally agrees
with Hygiasticon and 48. T and A2, which agree rather with 46, are
collated here ; Hygiasticon 48 A3 and Bodl. 31037, which conform rather
to 52, are collated with that text. Heading in T :* Upon Lessius his
Hygeiasticon. *T ends at l. 15 :* Reader. *and adds :* yͤ Rest I suppose
printed in Lessius. *Heading in A2 :* On taking Physicke.   4
treasure] treasures *T A2 (as 52)*

Goe take phisicke, doat upon
Some bigg-named composition,
The oraculous doctors mistick bills,
Certain hard words made into pills ;
And what at length shalt get by these ?
Onely a costlyer disease.   10
Goe poore man thinke what shall bee,
Remedie against thy remedie.
That which makes us have no need
Of Phisick thats Phisick indeed.

   Harke hether, Reader, wouldst thou see
Nature her owne Physitian bee.
Wouldst see a man all, his owne wealth,
His owne Physick, his owne health ?
A man whose sober soule can tell,
How to weare her garments well ?   20
Her garments that upon her sit,
As garments should doe close and fit ?
A well cloathed soule thats not opprest,
Nor choakt with what shee should bee drest ?
A soule sheathed in a christall shrine,
Through which all her bright features shine ?
As when a peece of wanton lawne,
A thinne aiereall vaile is drawne
O're beauties face, seeming to hide
More sweetly showes the blushing bride.   30
A soule whose intelectuall beames
No mistes doe maske no lazy steames ?
A happy soule that all the way,
To heaven, hath a summers day ?
Would'st thou see a man whose well warmed blood,
Bathes him in a genuine flood ?
A man whose tuned humours bee,
A set of rarest harmony ?
Wouldst see blith lookes, fresh cheeks beguile
Age, wouldst see *December* smile ?   40
Wouldst see a nest of Roses grow
In a bed of reverend snow ?
Warme thoughts free spirits, flattering
Winters selfe into a spring ?

5 Goe] Goe, *T A2*   11 Goe poore man] Goe, poore man, *T A2*
12 against] 'gainst *T A2*   14 Of Phisick] Of Physick, *T A2*

In summe, wouldst see a man that can
Live to bee old and still a man ?

The beginning of Heliodorus.

THe smiling Morne had newly wak't the Day,
 And tipt the mountaines in a tender ray :
When on a hill (whose high Imperious brow
Lookes downe, and sees the humble Nile below
Licke his proud feet, and hast into the seas
Through the great mouth thats nam'd from *Hercules*)
A band of men, rough as the Armes they wore
Look't round, first to the sea, then to the shore.
The shore that shewed them what the sea deny'd,
Hope of a prey. There to the maine land ty'd   10
A ship they saw, no men shee had ; yet prest
Appear'd with other lading, for her brest
Deep in the groaning waters wallowed
Vp to the third Ring ; o're the shore was spread
Death's purple triumph, on the blushing ground
Lifes late forsaken houses all lay drown'd
In their owne bloods deare deluge, some new dead,
Some panting in their yet warme ruines bled :
While their affrighted soules, now wing'd for flight
Lent them the last flash of her glimmering light.   20
Those yet fresh streames which crawled every where
Shew'd, that sterne warre had newly bath'd him there :
Nor did the face of this disaster show
Markes of a fight alone, but feasting too,
A miserable and a monstrous feast,
Where hungry warre had made himself a Guest :
And comming late had eat up Guests and all,
Who prov'd the feast to their owne funerall, &c.

The beginning &c. MSS. T A3. Heading in T : The Faire Æthiopian. R. Cr. *Both 46 and 48 read* ' Helidorus ' *for* ' Heliodorus '.
2 in *46 A3 and editor's copy of 48 :* with *T and B.M. copy of 48*   6
the] that *T*   7 they *48 T A3 :* thy *46*   14 to the] to her *A3*
16 drown'd] drown'd— *T*   17 deluge, *48 A3 :* deluge. *T :* deluge *46*
20 her] their *T*   25 monstrous] monstruous *48*   28 funerall,
&c.] funerall. &c. &c. &c. *T*

Out of the Greeke
Cupid's *Cryer.*

LOve is lost, nor can his Mother
 Her little fugitive discover :
Shee seekes, shee sighs, but no where spyes him ;
Love is lost ; and thus shee cryes him.
 O yes ! if any happy eye,
This roaving wanton shall descry :
Let the finder surely know
Mine is the wagge ; Tis I that owe
The winged wand'rer, and that none
May thinke his labour vainely gone,   10
The glad descryer shall not misse,
To tast the *Nectar* of a kisse
From *Venus* lipps. But as for him
That brings him to mee, hee shall swim
In riper joyes : more shall bee his
(*Venus* assures him) then a kisse ;
But least your eye discerning slide
These markes may bee your judgements guide ;
His skin as with a fiery blushing
High-colour'd is ; His eyes still flushing   20
With nimble flames, and though his mind
Be ne're so curst, his Tongue is kind :
For never were his words in ought
Found the pure issue of his thought.
The working Bees soft melting Gold,
That which their waxen Mines enfold,
Flow not so sweet as doe the Tones
Of his tun'd accents ; but if once
His anger kindle, presently
It boyles out into cruelty,   30
And fraud : Hee makes poore mortalls hurts,
The objects of his cruell sports.
With dainty curles his froward face
Is crown'd about ; But ô what place,
What farthest nooke of lowest Hell
Feeles not the strength, the reaching spell

Out of the Greeke &c. MS. A3.   16 then] than *B.M. copy of 48*
17 least] lest *B.M. copy of 48*   18 guide ; *48* : guide *46 A3*

Of his small hand ?   Yet not so small
As 'tis powerfull therewithall.
Though bare his skin, his mind hee covers,
And like a saucy Bird he hovers   40
With wanton wing, now here, now there,
'Bout men and women, nor will spare
Till at length he perching rest,
In the closet of their brest.
His weapon is a little Bow,
Yet such a one as (*Jove* knowes how)
Ne're suffred, yet his little Arrow,
Of Heavens high'st Arches to fall narrow.
The Gold that on his Quiver smiles,
Deceives mens feares with flattering wiles.   50
But ô (too well my wounds can tell)
With bitter shafts 'tis sauc't too well.
Hee is all cruell, cruell all ;
His Torch Imperious though but small
Makes the Sunne (of flames the sire)
Worse then Sun-burnt in his fire.
Wheresoe're you chance to find him
Cease him, bring him, (but first bind him)
Pitty not him, but feare thy selfe
Though thou see the crafty Elfe,   60
Tell down his Silver-drops unto thee,
They'r counterfeit, and will undoe thee.
With baited smiles if he display
His fawning cheeks, looke not that way
If hee offer sugred kisses,
Start, and say, The Serpent hisses.
Draw him, drag him, though hee pray
Wooe, intreat, and crying say
Prethee, sweet now let me goe,
Here's my Quiver Shafts and Bow,   70
I'le give thee all, take all, take heed
Lest his kindnesse make thee bleed.
   What e're it be Love offers, still presume
   That though it shines, 'tis fire and will consume.

42 'Bout] 'Boat *editor's copy of 48* : 'Bout *B.M. copy*   47 suffred,]
suffer'd *A3* 70   50 feares] feare *A3*   59 not him] him not *A3*
69 now] now, *A3*   71 take all, take] take all. take *A3*   74
shines] shine *A3*

HIgh mounted on an Ant *Nanus* the tall
   Was throwne alas, and got a deadly fall.
Vnder th'unruly Beasts proud feet he lies
All torne ; with much adoe yet ere he dyes,
Hee straines these words ; Base Envy, doe, laugh on.
Thus did I fall, and thus fell *Phaethon.*

Vpon Venus *putting on* Mars
his Armes.

WHat ? *Mars* his sword ? faire *Cytherea* say,
   Why art thou arm'd so desperately to day ?
Mars thou hast beaten naked, and ô then
What need'st thou put on armes against poore men ?

Vpon the same.

PAllas saw *Venus* arm'd, and streight she cry'd,
   Come if thou dar'st, thus, thus let us be try'd.
Why foole ! saies *Venus*, thus provok'st thou mee,
That being nak't, thou know'st could conquer thee ?

In Serenissimæ Reginæ partum
hyemalem.

SErta, puer : (quis nunc flores non præbeat hortus ?)
   Texe mihi facili pollice serta, puer.
Quid tu nescio quos narras mihi, stulte, Decembres ?
   Quid mihi cum nivibus ? da mihi serta, puer.
Nix ? & hyems ? non est nostras quid tale per oras ;
   Non est : vel si sit, non tamen esse potest.
Ver agitur : quæcunque trucem dat larva Decembrem,
   Quid fera cunque fremant frigora, ver agitur.
Nónne vides quali se palmite regia vitis
   Prodit, & in sacris quæ sedet uva jugis ?   10

High mounted &c. MSS. T A3 A2. Heading in 48 : On Nanus
mounted upon an Ant. Heading in A3 : Out of the Greeke. *Heading in
A2 :* On Nanus.   2 throwne] throwne downe A2   a deadly]
a A2   fall. T : fall 46 48   6 thus fell] so fell A2
   Vpon Venus &c. MSS. T A3. A3 adds to heading : Out of Ausonius.
No heading in T.   I faire] Sweet T A3
   Vpon the same. MSS. T A3. No heading in T.   2 dar'st]
darest A3   thus, thus let us] thus, lett vs thus T
   In Serenissimæ &c. First published in Carmen Natalitium Ad cunas
Illustrissimæ Principis Elisabethæ decantatum intra Nativitatis Dom.
solennia per humiles Cantabrigiæ Musas. . . . 1635. The poem is there
signed R. Crashaw, Coll. S. Pet. Socius.   Serenissimæ] Senerissimæ
46 48   9 vides] vide editor's copy of 48 : vides other copies

Tam lætis quæ bruma solet ridere racemis ?
Quas hyemis pingit purpura tanta genas ?
O Maria ! O divûm soboles, genitrixque Deorum !
Siccine nostra tuus tempora ludus erunt ?
Siccine tu cum vere tuo nihil horrida brumæ
Sydera, nil madidos sola morare notos ?
Siccine sub mediâ poterunt tua surgere brumâ,
Atque suas solùm lilia nosse nives ?
Ergò vel invitis nivibus, frendentibus Austris,
Nostra novis poterunt regna tumere rosis ?   20
O bona turbatrix anni, quæ limite noto
Tempora sub signis non sinis ire suis !
O pia prædatrix hyemis, quæ tristia mundi
Murmura tam dulci sub ditione tenes !
Perge precor nostris vim pulchram ferre Calendis :
Perge precor menses sic numerare tuos.
Perge intempestiva atque importuna videri ;
Inque uteri titulos sic rape cuncta tui. ·
Sit nobis sit sæpe hyemes sic cernere nostras
Exhæredatas floribus ire tuis.   30
Sæpe sit has vernas hyemes Maiosque Decembres
Has per te roseas sæpe videre nives.
Altera gens varium per sydera computet annum,
Atque suos ducant per vaga signa dies.
Nos deceat nimiis tantum permittere nimbis ?
Tempora tam tetricas ferre Britanna vices ?
Quin nostrum tibi nos omnem donabimus annum :
In partus omnem expende, Maria, tuos.
Sit tuus ille uterus nostri bonus arbiter anni :
Tempus & in titulos transeat omne tuos.   40
Nam quæ alia indueret tam dulcia nomina mensis ?
Aut qua tam posset candidus ire toga ?
Hanc laurum Janus sibi vertice vellet utroque,
Hanc sibi vel tota Chloride Majus emet.
Tota suam (vere expulso) respublica florum
Reginam cuperent te, sobolemve tuam.
O bona sors anni, cum cuncti ex ordine menses
Hic mihi Carolides, *hic* Marianus *erit !*   .

22 *sub signis non sinis*] *signis non subsinis editor's copy of 48 : other*
copies as 46   29 *nobis*] *nobis 48*

In Picturam Reverendissimi Epis-
copi, *D. Andrews.*

H*Æc charta monstrat, Fama quem monstrat magis,*
Sed & ipsa necdum fama quem monstrat satis,
Ille, ille totam solus implevit Tubam,
Tot ora solus domuit & famam quoque
Fecit modestam : mentis igneæ pater
Agilique radio Lucis æternæ vigil,
Per alta rerum pondera indomito Vagus
Cucurrit Animo, quippe naturam ferox
Exhausit ipsam mille Fœtus Artibus,
Et mille Linguis ipse se in gentes procul   10
Variavit omnes et fuit toti simul
Cognatus orbi : sic sacrum & solidum jubar
Saturumque cœlo pectus ad patrios Libens
Porrexit ignes : hac eum (*Lector*) *vides*
Hac (*ecce*) *charta O Vtinam & audires quoque.*

Vpon Bishop Andrewes *his*
Picture before his
Sermons.

T His reverend shadow cast that setting Sun,
Whose glorious course through our Horrizon run,
Left the dimme face of this dull Hemisphæare,
All one great eye, all drown'd in one great Teare.
Whose faire illustrious soule, led his free thought
Through Learnings Vniverse, and (vainely) sought

In Picturam &c. *MS. T* (*heading p. 374 below*)   2 *necdum fama*
quem] *quem dum fama quem non 48*   3 *totam solus*] *solus totam 48*
    Tubam 48 T : Tubani 46   8 *ferox 46 T : ferax conj. Garrod*   10
in gentes T ingentes *46 48*   11 *omnes, & fuit T :* omnes fuitq;
46 48   12 *orbi :* sic sacrum] orbi. mox sacrum, *T*   13 pectus ad
patrios] pectus ætherijs *T*   14 *ignes :*] astris. *T*   15 *Hac T :* Haec
46   charta O Vtinam & audires quoque] chartâ. cæteris audies quocȝ.
T (*final stop omitted in 46*)
Vpon Bishop &c. MSS. T A3 A2. Collated with version in : XCVI.
Sermons By . . . Lancelot Andrewes, Late Lord Bishop of Winchester. . . .
MDCXLI, *to which ' 1641 ' in footnotes refers. First published in the second*
edition of that work, 1631. Heading in T : Upon B^p Andrewes picture
before his booke. R. Cr. *Heading in A3 :* Vpon Bishop Andrewes
Heading in A2 : Crosh: on ye Picture of Bishoppe Andrewes before
his booke. *Heading* (*46*) : Andrewes *his*] Andrews *48*   1 This reverend
shadow cast that] *See heer a* Shadow *from that 1641*   2 our]
this 1641   through our] our *A2*   2 *bracketed in A2*   3 this]
our 1641   5 *indented 1641*   faire illustrious] rare industrious
1641

Roome for her spatious selfe, untill at length
Shee found the way home, with an holy strength
Snatch't her self hence, to Heaven : fill'd a bright place,
Mongst those immortall fires, and on the face   10
Of her great maker fixt her flaming eye,
There still to read true pure divinity.
And now that grave aspect hath deign'd to shrinke
Into this lesse appearance ; If you thinke,
Tis but a dead face, art doth here bequeath :
Looke on the following leaves, and see him breath.

Epitaphium in Dominum Herrisium.

SIste te paulum (viator) ubi Longum Sisti
Necesse erit, huc nempe properare te scias
            quocunque properas.
        Moræ prætium erit
        Et Lacrimæ,
        Si jacere hic scias
        Gulielmum
Splendidæ Herrisiorum familiæ
    Splendorem maximum :
Quem cum talem vixisse intellexeris,   10
        Et vixisse tantum ;
        Discas licet
        In quantas spes possit
        Assurgere mortalitas,
        De quantis cadere.

Quem { *Infantem, Essexia ——* } *vidit*
         { *Juvenem, Cantabrigia* }
        Senem, ah infælix utraque
        Quod non vidit.
                Qui   20

8 home,] home ; *T* : home : *1641*   an] a *A3*   9 Snatch't]
Snathc't *46*   place,] place *T A2*   10 Mongst] 'Midst *1641*
11 *indented 1641* .   her] a *1641 T*   12 There still to read] Where
still she reads *1641*   true pure divinity] true-pure-divinity *T*
    Epitaphium *&c.   There is a monument to Herris at Pembroke College,
Cambridge, comprising this epitaph.   MS. A2 (ll. 1–38 only).   Heading
in A2* : Epitaphium Gulielmi Herisij socij Aulæ Pemb: Crosh.   2
Necesse 48 : Nescese 46   erit] 'rit *A2 (which ends l. 1 here)*   10 *intellexeris 48* : *intelexeris 46* : intellexis *A2*   13 *quantas 48 A2* : *quantus 46*

Collegii Christi Alumnus,
Aulæ Pembrokianæ socius,
Vtrique, ingens amoris certamen fuit.
Donec
Dulciss. Lites elusit Deus,
Eumque cœlestis Collegii
Cujus semper Alumnus fuit
socium fecit ;
Qui & ipse Collegium fuit,
In quo   30
Musæ omnes & gratiæ,
Nullibi magis sorores,
Sub præside religione
In tenacissimum sodalitium coaluere.

Quem { Oratoria   Poetam
       Poetica   Oratorem
       Vtraque   Philosophum } Agnovere.
       Christianum Omnes

Qui { Fide   Mundum
      Spe   Cœlum   40
      Charitate   Proximum } Superavit.
      Humilitate Seipsum

Cujus
Sub verna fronte senilis animus,
Sub morum facilitate, severitas virtutis ;
Sub plurima indole, pauci anni ;
Sub majore modestia, maxima indoles
adeo se occuluerunt
ut vitam ejus
Pulchram dixeris & pudicam dissimulationem :   50
Imo vero & mortem,
Ecce enim in ipso funere
Dissimulari se passus est,
Sub tantillo marmore tantum hospitem,
Eo nimirum majore monumento
quo minore tumulo.

22 *Aulæ Pembrokianæ*] Pembrochiani (*bracketed with* Christi *l. 21*) *A2*
29 *ipse*] ipsũ *A2*   35 Oratoria *A2* : *Oratoriæ 46 48*   37
Vtraque Philosophum] Philosophia Utrumq̃ *A2*   44 *fronte senilis*
48 : *fronte-senilis 46*   47 *indoles 70L* : *indoles- 46* : *indoles. 48*

Eo ipso die occubuit quo Ecclesia
Anglicana ad vesperas legit,
Raptus est ne malitia mutaret Intellectum ejus ;
Scilicet Id. Octobris, Anno S 1631.   60

Vpon the Death of a Gentleman.

Faithlesse and fond Mortality,
  Who will ever credit thee ?
Fond and faithlesse thing ! that thus,
In our best hopes beguilest us.
What a reckoning hast thou made,
Of the hopes in him we laid ?
For Life by volumes lengthened,
A Line or two, to speake him dead.
For the Laurell in his verse,
The sullen Cypresse o're his Herse.   10
For a silver-crowned Head,
A durty pillow in Death's Bed.
For so deare, so deep a trust,
Sad requitall, thus much dust !
Now though the blow that snatcht him hence,
Stopt the Mouth of Eloquence,
Though shee be dumbe e're since his Death,
Not us'd to speake but in his Breath,
Yet if at least shee not denyes,

57–60 *omitted in* 70L   60 *Id.* 48 : Id 46   S] *Sal.* 48
Vpon the Death of a Gentleman. MSS. T *A3 A226* (*ll. 1–30*) H.
Heading in T : Ad exequias | In obitum desideratissimi Mʳˡ Chambers, |
Coll: Reginal. Socij. R. Cr. *Marginal note in* T : The title & Name not
in yᵉ print. *Heading in A3* : Vpon the Death of Mʳ Chambers | Fellow
of Queens Colledge | in Cambridge *Heading in A226* : An Elegie on
a Scholler. *Heading in H:* On a Gentlemans death.   4 In
our best hopes] Of oʳ ioyes *A226*   hopes] joyes T   beguilest] beguy-
leth *A3*   5 What a] What H   6 we] were *A226*   *After l. 10*
T *inserts :*

  ō printed { For soe many hoped yeares
            { Of fruit, soe many fruitles teares.

A226 also inserts this couplet.   12 durty pillow in] dreary pillow on *A226*
14 thus] so *A226*   16 Stopt] Did stop *A226*   *After l. 18* T *inserts :*

  ō printed { Leaving his death vngarnished
            { Therefore, because hee is dead,

19 Yet if] If yet *T A226*

The sad language of our eyes,   20
Wee are contented : for then this
Language none more fluent is.
Nothing speakes our Griefe so well
As to speake Nothing, Come then tell
Thy mind in Teares who e're Thou be,
That ow'st a Name to misery.
Eyes are vocall, Teares have Tongues,
And there be words not made with lungs ;
Sententious showers, ô let them fall,
Their cadence is Rhetoricall.   30
Here's a Theame will drinke th'expence,
Of all thy watry Eloquence,
Weepe then, onely be exprest
Thus much, *Hee's Dead,* and weepe the rest.

Vpon the Death of Mr. Herrys.

A Plant of noble stemme, forward and faire,
As ever whisper'd to the Morning Aire
Thriv'd in these happy Grounds, the Earth's just pride,
Whose rising Glories made such haste to hide
His head in Cloudes, as if in him alone
Impatient Nature had taught motion
To start from Time, and cheerfully to fly
Before, and seize upon Maturity.
Thus grew this gratious plant, in whose sweet shade
The Sunne himselfe oft wisht to sit, and made   10
The Morning Muses perch like Birds, and sing
Among his Branches : yea, and vow'd to bring
His owne delicious Phœnix from the blest
Arabia, there to build her Virgin nest,
To hatch her selfe in, 'mongst his leaves the Day
Fresh from the Rosie East rejoyc't to play.

20 The] Thee the *H*   sad] sad, sad *A226*   20 our] her *A226*
24 Nothing,] Nothing. *T*   nothing : 70 *A226*   26 a] thy *A226*   28
be] are *A226*   29 Sententious] Contentious *A226*
   *Vpon the Death of Mr. Herrys. MSS. T A3 S (ll. 15–21). Heading in
T, where it follows 'His Epitaph' (see p. 172, below) : In ejusdem præ-
matuꝛ obitu⁹. Allegoricum.* R. Cr. *Heading in A3* : Vpon the Death
of Mʳ Herris | Fellow of Pembroke Hall | in Cambridge.   3
happy] haphy *46*   9 plant] tree *T*   15 in,] in ; *48* : in.
T   leaves] Leaves : *70*   in, 'mongst his leaves] in 'mongst his
leaves ; *A3*   *S begins* : Amongst

To them shee gave the first and fairest Beame
That waited on her Birth : she gave to them
The purest Pearles, that wept her Evening Death,
The balmy *Zephirus* got so sweet a Breath　　　　20
By often kissing them, and now begun
Glad Time to ripen expectation.
The timourous Maiden-Blossomes on each Bough,
Peept forth from their first blushes : so that now
A Thousand ruddy hopes smil'd in each Bud,
And flatter'd every greedy eye that stood
Fixt in Delight, as if already there
Those rare fruits dangled, whence the Golden Yeare
His crowne expected, when (ô Fate, ô Time
That seldome lett'st a blushing youthfull Prime　　30
Hide his hot Beames in shade of silver Age ;
So rare is hoary vertue) the dire rage
Of a mad storme these bloomy joyes all tore,
Ravisht the Maiden Blossoms, and downe bore
The trunke.　Yèt in this Ground his pretious Root
Still lives, which when weake Time shall be pour'd out
Into Eternity, and circular joyes
Dance in an endlesse round, againe shall rise
The faire son of an ever-youthfull Spring,
To be a shade for Angels while they sing,　　　　40
Meane while who e're thou art that passest here,
O doe thou water it with one kind Teare.

Vpon the Death of the most desired Mr. Herrys.

DEath, what dost ? ô hold thy Blow,
What thou dost, thou dost not know.
Death thou must not here be cruell,
This is Natures choycest Iewell.
This is hee in whose rare frame,
Nature labour'd for a Name,

18 Birth : *48 (stop doubtful in 46)*: Birth, 70　　21 them,] yᵐ ;
&c. S *(ending here)*　　24 forth from] out of T　·　25 in] on
T　　31 shade] th' shade *A3*　　33 bloomy] blooming T *A3*　　34
Ravisht] Lauish't *A3*
　　*Vpon the Death of the most &c.　MSS. T A3 S (ll. 27–30).　Heading
in T* : An Elegie on Mʳ Herris.　R: Cr.　*Heading in A3* : Vpon the same.
5 hee] he, *T*

And meant to leave his pretious feature,
The patterne of a perfect Creature.
Ioy of Goodnesse, Love of Art,
Vertue weares him next her heart.   10
Him the Muses love to follow,
Him they call their vice-*Apollo*.
Apollo golden though thou bee,
Th'art not fairer then is hee.
Nor more lovely lift'st thy head,
Blushing from thine Easterne Bed.
The Gloryes of thy Youth ne're knew,
Brighter hopes then he can shew.
Why then should it e're be seene,
That his should fade, while thine is Greene ?   20
And wilt Thou, (ô cruell boast !)
Put poore Nature to such cost ?
O 'twill undoe our common Mother,
To be at charge of such another.
What ? thinke we to no other end,
Gracious Heavens do use to send
Earth her best perfection,
But to vanish and be gone ?
Therefore onely give to day,
To morrow to be snatcht away ?   30
I've seen indeed the hopefull bud,
Of a ruddy Rose that stood
Blushing, to behold the Ray
Of the new-saluted Day ;
(His tender toppe not fully spread)
The sweet dash of a shower now shead,
Invited him no more to hide
Within himselfe the purple pride
Of his forward flower, when lo
While he sweetly 'gan to show   40
His swelling Gloryes, *Auster* spide him,
Cruell *Auster* thither hy'd him,
And with the rush of one rude blast,
Sham'd not spitefully to wast

16 Blushing] (Blushing) *T A3*   thine] thy *T A3*   18 he]
his *T*   19 should it] should *A3*   21 Thou,] thou Death *A3*
25 we] wee, *T*   26 send] lend *T*   29 give] giuen *T*
A3   33 Blushing,] Blushing *T*   36 now] new *T A3*   37
hide *48 T A3* : hide. *46*

All his leaves, so fresh, so sweet,
And lay them trembling at his feet.
I've seene the Mornings lovely Ray,
Hover o're the new-borne Day :
With rosie wings so richly Bright,
As if he scorn'd to thinke of Night,   50
When a ruddy storme whose scoule,
Made Heavens radiant face looke foule ;
Call'd for an untimely Night,
To blot the newly blossom'd Light.
But were the Roses blush so rare,
Were the Mornings smile so faire
As is he, nor cloud, nor wind
But would be courteous, would be kind.
    Spare him Death, ô spare him then,
Spare the sweetest among men.   60
Let not pitty with her Teares,
Keepe such distance from thine Eares.
But ô thou wilt not, canst not spare,
Haste hath never time to heare.
Therefore if hee needs must go,
And the Fates will have it so,
Softly may he be possest,
Of his monumentall rest.
Safe, thou darke home of the dead,
Safe ô hide his loved head.   70
For Pitties sake ô hide him quite,
From his Mother Natures sight :
Lest for Griefe his losse may move,
All her Births abortive prove.

Another.

IF ever Pitty were acquainted
With sterne Death, if e're he fainted,
Or forgot the cruell vigour,
Of an Adamantine rigour,

    50 he] she *T*   51 ruddy] rugged *A3*   59 *not indented T*
him Death] then Death *A3*   ô] ah, *T*   61 Let] And lett *T*   *After*
l. 70 *T inserts :*
        not printed { Keepe him close, close in thine armes,
                    { Seal'd vpp with a thousand charmes.

    Another. MSS. T A3   Marginal heading in T : Another, in yᵉ print.
Heading in A3 : Vpon the same.   1 were] was *T*

Here, ô here we should have knowne it,
Here or no where hee'd have showne it.
For hee whose pretious memory,
Bathes in Teares of every eye :
Hee to whom our sorrow brings,
All the streames of all her springs :
Was so rich in Grace and Nature,
In all the gifts that blesse a Creature.
The fresh hopes of his lovely Youth,
Flourisht in so faire a grouth.
So sweet the Temple was, that shrin'd
The Sacred sweetnesse of his mind.
That could the Fates know to relent ?
Could they know what mercy meant ;
Or had ever learnt to beare,
The soft tincture of a Teare :
Teares would now have flow'd so deepe,
As might have taught Griefe how to weepe.
Now all their steely operation,
Would quite have lost the cruell fashion.
Sicknesse would have gladly been,
Sick himselfe to have sav'd him :
And his Feaver wish'd to prove
Burning, onely in his Love.
Him when wrath it selfe had seene,
Wrath its selfe had lost his spleene.
Grim Destruction here amaz'd,
In stead of striking would have gaz'd.
Even the Iron-pointed pen,
That notes the Tragicke Doomes of men
Wet with teares still'd from the eyes,
Of the flinty Destinyes ;
Would have learn't a softer style,
And have been asham'd to spoyle
His lives sweet story, by the hast,
Of a cruell stop ill plac't.

10

20

30

40

7 hee] he, *T*   9 Hee] He, *T*   12 Creature.] creature ; *T* : Creature,
A3   14 grouth.] growth ; *T* : growth *A3*   16 mind.] mind ;
T (*line omitted in A3*)   17 relent ?] relent ; *T* : relent ; 48 70 : relent, *T* : relent
A3   30 its] it *A3* : itselfe *T*   his] its *T*   34 notes]
quotes *T A3*   35 eyes,] Eyes *A3*   39 lives] Lifes
A3   story] stoty 46

In the darke volume of our fate,
Whence each leafe of Life hath date,
Where in sad particulars,
The totall summe of Man appeares,
And the short clause of mortall Breath,
Bound in the period of Death,
In all the Booke if any where
Such a tearme as this, *spare here*
Could have been found 'twould have been read,
Writ in white Letters o're his head :   50
Or close unto his name annext,
The faire glosse of a fairer Text.
In briefe, if any one were free,
Hee was that one, and onely he.
    But he, alas ! even hee is dead
And our hopes faire harvest spread
In the dust. Pitty now spend
All the teares that griefe can lend.
Sad mortality may hide,
In his ashes all her pride ;   60
With this inscription o're his head
All hope of never dying, here lyes dead.

His Epitaph.

PAssenger who e're thou art,
    Stay a while, and let thy Heart
Take acquaintance of this stone,
Before thou passest further on.
This stone will tell thee that beneath,
Is entomb'd the Crime of Death ;
The ripe endowments of whose mind,
Left his Yeares so much behind,

42 leafe] lease *T*   44 appeares, *T* : appeares. *46 48* : appeares
A3   46 Death,] death ; *T* Death : *70* death *A3*   49 Could have
been] Could bin *T*   50 Writ] Wrote *T*   55 *not indented T A3*
62 *T and A3 distinguish the whole line, which is also set out in A3*
62 lyes] is *T A3*   dead.] *dead 46*
  His Epitaph. MSS. T A3 S (ll. 7–10 and 23–4). Heading in T :
Epitaphium in eundem. R. Cr.   4 Before] Ere *A3*

That numbring of his vertues praise,
Death lost the reckoning of his Dayes ;   10
And believing what they told,
Imagin'd him exceeding old.
In him perfection did set forth,
The strength of her united worth.
Him his wisdomes pregnant growth
Made so reverend, even in Youth,
That in the Center of his Brest
(Sweet as is the Phænix nest)
Every reconciled Grace,
Had their Generall meeting place.   20
In him Goodnesse joy'd to see
Learning, learne Humility.
The splendor of his Birth and Blood,
Was but the Glosse of his owne Good :
The flourish of his sober Youth,
Was the Pride of Naked Truth.
In composure of his face,
Liv'd a faire, but manly Grace.
His Mouth was Rhetoricks best mold,
His Tongue the Touchstone of her Gold.   30
What word so e're his Breath kept warme,
Was no word now but a charme.
For all persuasive Graces thence
Suck't their sweetest Influence.
His vertue that within had root,
Could not chuse but shine without.
And th'heart-bred lustre of his worth,
At each corner peeping forth,
Pointed him out in all his wayes,
Circled round in his owne Rayes :   40
That to his sweetnesse, all mens eyes
Were vow'd Loves flaming Sacrifice.
   Him while fresh and fragrant Time
Cherisht in his Golden Prime ;
E're *Hebe's* hand had overlaid
His smooth cheekes, with a downy shade :
The rush of Death's unruly wave,
Swept him off into his Grave.

9 That] That, *T*   20 place. *48 T A3* : place *46*   42 vow'd] vow'd, *T*
43 *not indented T*   46 with a] with *T*   47 unruly] vntimely *T*

Enough, now (if thou canst) passe on,
For now (alas) not in this stone   50
(Passenger who e're thou art)
Is he entomb'd, but in thy Heart.

An Epitaph

Vpon Husband and Wife, which died, and were buried together.

TO these, Whom Death again did wed,
  This Grave's the second Marriage-Bed.
For though the hand of Fate could force,
'Twixt Soule and body a Divorce :
It could not sever Man and Wife,
Because they both liv'd but one Life.
Peace, good Reader, doe not weepe ;
Peace, the Lovers are asleepe :
They (sweet Turtles) folded lye,
In the last knot that love could tye.   10
Let them sleepe, let them sleepe on,
Till this stormy night be gone.
And th' eternall morrow dawne,
Then the Curtaines will bee drawne,
And they waken with that Light,
Whose day shall never sleepe in Night.

49 Enough,] Enough. *T A3*   52 entomb'd,] entomb'd ; *T*
An Epitaph &c.   MSS. T A3 A1 H.   Heading in T : Epitaphium
            ⎧ mortuorū. ⎫
Conjugu⁹ unâ ⎨   &   ⎬ R. Cr. *Heading in A1* : An Epitaph of
           ⎩ sepultorū. ⎭
a yonge Maried | Cupple dead and buried | togeather . . . *Heading in H* :
On A man and his wife who dyed together, and were so buried. *For
extended and altered version in 52 (generally following 48) see p. 339, below.
T A3 and H generally agree with 46 ; A1 verbatim with 52.*   2 the]
their *T A3 H*   5 sever] sunder *T A3 H*   6 Because they both
liv'd] Cause they both liued *T* : because they lived *H*   7 *indented
A3*   12 gone.] gone, *T 48*   13 morrow] morning *H*   15, 16
indented A3

An Epitaph.
Vpon Doctor Brooke.

A *Brooke* whose streame so great, so good,
Was lov'd was honour'd as a flood :
Whose Bankes the Muses dwelt upon,
More then their owne Helicon ;
Here at length, hath gladly found
A quiet passage under ground ;
Meane while his loved bankes now dry,
The Muses with their teares supply.

Vpon Mr. Staninough's *Death.*

D Eare reliques of a dislodg'd soule, whose lacke
Makes many a mourning Paper put on blacke ;
O stay a while e're thou draw in thy Head,
And wind thy selfe up close in thy cold Bed :
Stay but a little while, untill I call
A summons, worthy of thy Funerall.
    Come then youth, Beauty, and Blood, all ye soft powers,
Whose silken flatteryes swell a few fond houres
Into a false Eternity, come man,
(Hyperbolized nothing !) know thy span.   10
Take thine owne measure here, downe, downe, and bow
Before thy selfe in thy Idæa, thou
Huge emptinesse contract thy bulke, and shrinke
All thy wild Circle to a point ! ô sinke
Lower, and lower yet ; till thy small size,
Call Heaven to looke on thee with narrow eyes ;
Lesser and lesser yet, till thou begin
To show a face, fit to confesse thy kin

An Epitaph. &c.   MSS. T A3 H.   Heading in T : In obitum
D^{ris} Brooke. R. Cr. *Heading in A3 :* An Epitaph | Vpon the reverend
Dr Brooke. *Heading in H :* Epitaph on doctor Brooke :   7, 8
indented A3   7 bankes] banck, *T*
    Vpon Mr. Staninough's *Death. MS. A3. Heading in A3 :* Vpon the
Death of Mr Stanninough | Fellow of Queens Colledge in | Cambridge.
For slightly altered version in 52 (generally following 48) see p. 340, below.
A3 agrees rather with 46.   8 houres *48 52 A3 :* houres. *46*   12
thy Idæa] thine *Idæa A3*   13 emptinesse] emptinesse ! *A3*   14
wild] wide *48 A3*   18 kin] Kin, *A3*

Thy neighbour-hood to nothing ! here put on
Thy selfe in this unfeign'd reflection ;   20
Here gallant Ladyes, this unpartiall glasse
(Through all your painting) showes you your own face.
These Death-seal'd Lipps are they dare give the lye,
To the proud hopes of poor Mortality.
These curtain'd windowes, this selfe-prison'd eye,
Out-stares the Liddes of large-look't Tyranny.
This posture is the brave one : this that lyes
Thus low stands up (me thinkes) thus, and defyes
The world——All daring Dust and Ashes ; onely you
Of all interpreters read nature true.   30

Vpon the Duke of Yorke *his Birth A Panegyricke.*

BRittaine, the mighty Oceans lovely Bride,
Now stretch thy self (faire Ile) and grow, spread wide
Thy bosome and make roome ; Thou art opprest
With thine owne Gloryes : and art strangely blest
Beyond thy selfe : for lo ! the Gods, the Gods
Come fast upon thee, and those glorious ods,
Swell thy full gloryes to a pitch so high,
As sits above thy best capacitye.
  Are they not ods ? and glorious ? that to thee
Those mighty *Genii* throng, which well might bee   10
Each one an Ages labour, that thy dayes
Are guilded with the Vnion of those Rayes,
Whose each divided Beame would be a Sun,
To glad the Spheare of any Nation.

  19 *indented 48*   21 unpartiall] impartiall *70*   25 These]
Those *48 A3*   29 Ashes ;] *So Bodl. copy of 46* : Ashes, *B.M. copy*
  Vpon the Duke of Yorke *&c. MSS. T A3 A2. First printed in* Voces
Votivæ Ab Academicis Cantabrigiensibus, Pro novissimo Caroli &
Mariæ Principe Filio emissæ. . . . Cantabrigiæ. . . . MDCXL. *The poem is
there signed* R. Crashaw. Coll. S. Pet. *and the divisions of the poem are
marked by marginal headings, as follows* : The Prince. The D. of York.
L. Mary. L. Elizab. The new-born Prince. To the Queen. *The text in*
Voces Votivæ *generally agrees with 48, with the exceptions noted. Heading
in 48* : To the Queen, | Vpon her numerous Progenie, | A Panegyrick.
*48 gives separate headings for the different divisions of the poem. Heading
in T* : A Panegyrick. | Upon the birth of the Duke of Yorke. *Heading in
A2* : Crosh : On yᵉ new borne Prince | a Panegericke.   7 gloryes]
honours *48 T A2*   13 would] should *A2*

O if for these thou mean'st to find a seat,
Th'ast need ô *Brittaine* to be truly Great.
And so thou art, their presence makes thee so,
They are thy Greatnesse ; Gods where e're they go
Bring their Heaven with them, their great footsteps place
An everlasting smile upon the face,   20
Of the glad Earth they tread on. While with thee
Those Beames that ampliate Mortalitie,
And teach it to expatiate, and swell
To Majesty, and fulnesse, deigne to dwell ;
Thou by thy selfe maist sit, (blest Isle) and see
How thy Great Mother Nature doats on thee :
Thee therefore from the rest apart she hurl'd,
And seem'd to make an Isle, but made a world.

   Great *Charles* ! thou sweet Dawne of a glorious day,
Center of those thy Grandsires, shall I say   30
Henry and *James*, or *Mars* and *Phœbus* rather ?
If this were Wisdomes God, that Wars sterne father,
'Tis but the same is said, *Henry* and *James*
Are *Mars* and *Phœbus* under divers Names.
O thou full mixture of those mighty soules,
Whose vast intelligences tun'd the Poles
Of Peace and Warre ; Thou for whose manly brow
Both Lawrels twine into one wreath, and wooe
To be thy Garland : see (sweet Prince) ô see
Thou and the lovely hopes that smile in thee   40
Are ta'ne out and transcrib'd by thy Great Mother,
See, see thy reall shadow, see thy Brother,
Thy little selfe in lesse, read in these Eyne
The beames that dance in those full starres of thine.

---

15 O] Sure *48*   16 Th'ast] Th'hast *48 A3* : Th'hadst *T*   17
indented 48   makes] make *A3*   19 Bring their] Bring there *A3*
20 face,] face *48 70 A3*   21 on. *48 T A3* : on, *46 A2*   24
fulnesse, *48 T A2* : fulnesse *46 A3*   dwell ; *T A2* : dwell, *48* : dwell *A3*
25 blest] glad *A2*   *After l. 28 and a line space 48 inserts four lines :*

     Time yet hath dropt few plumes since Hope turn'd Ioy,
      And took into his armes the princely Boy,
      Whose birth last blest the bed of his sweet Mother,
      And bad us first salute our Prince a brother.

After this, separate heading in 48 : The Prince and Duke of York.
29 Great] Bright *48 T A3 A2*   30 shall–34 Names *bracketed in 48*
32–4 *bracketed A2*   35 mighty] two greate *A2*   40 lovely]
liuely *A3*   read] trace *48 T A2*   these] those *T* : his *A2*

From the same snowy Alablaster Rocke
These hands and thine were hew'n, these cherryes mocke
The Corall of thy lips. Thou art of all
This well-wrought Copy the faire Principall.

Iustly, Great Nature, may'st thou brag and tell
How even th'ast drawne this faithfull Paralell,   50
And matcht thy Master-Peece : ô then go on
Make such another sweet comparison.
See'st thou that *Mary* there ? ô teach her Mother
To shew her to her selfe in such another :
Fellow this wonder too, nor let her shine
Alone, light such another starre, and twine
Their Rosie Beames, so that the Morne for one
Venus, may have a Constellation.

So have I seene (to dresse their Mistresse *May*)
Two silken sister flowers consult, and lay   60
Their bashfull cheekes together, newly they
Peep't from their buds, shew'd like the Gardens eyes
Scarce wakt : like was the Crimson of their joyes,
Like were the Pearles they wept, so like that one
Seem'd but the others kind reflection.

45 snowy] white *A2*   46 These hands] Those hands *48 T*   these
cherryes mocke *A2 A3 70* : these Cherrimock *46* : those cherries mock
48 T   47 art] wert *48 T*   48 This] The *A3*   the faire] y^e *A2*
After l. 48, heading in 48 : Lady Mary.   49 may'st] didst *48 T*
50 th'ast] th' hadst *48 T*   this] that *48 T*   57 so that] that so
48 T A2   *After l. 58 heading in 48 :* Lady Elizabeth. *and six
lines inserted :*
 These words scarce waken'd Heaven, when (lo) our vows
 Sat crown'd upon the noble Infants brows.
 Th'art pair'd, sweet Princesse : In this well-writ book
 Read o're thy self ; peruse each line, each look.
 And when th'hast summ'd up all those blooming blisses,
 Close up the book, and clasp it with thy kisses.
59–61 *bracketed in T*   62 shew'd like] & seem'd *A2*   63 Scarce]
Halfe *A2*   64 Pearles] tears *48*   they] that *A3*   *After
l. 65 heading in 48 :* The new-borne Prince *and thirty-nine lines inserted :*
 And now 'twere time to say, Sweet Queen, no more. [ro say *48*]
 Fair source of Princes, is thy pretious store
 Not yet exhaust ? O no. Heavens have no bound,
 But in their infinite and endlesse Round
 Embrace themselves. Our measure is not theirs ; [Embraee *48*]
 Nor may the pov'rtie of mans narrow prayers
 Span their immensitie. More Princes come :
 Rebellion, stand thou by ; Mischief, make room :

But stay, what glimpse was that ? why blusht the day ?
Why ran the started aire trembling away ?
Who's this that comes circled in rayes, that scorne
Acquaintance with the Sunne ? what second Morne
At mid-day opes a presence which Heavens eye   70
Stands off and points at ? is't some Deity
Stept from her Throne of starres deignes to be seene ?
Is it some Deity ? or is't our Queene ?
'Tis shee, 'tis shee : her awfull Beauties chase
The Dayes abashed Glories, and in face
Of Noone weare their owne Sunshine, ô thou bright
Mistresse of wonders ! *Cynthia's* is the Night,
But thou at Noone dost shine, and art all Day,
(Nor does the Sunne deny't) our *Cynthia,*

War, Bloud, and Death (Names all averse from Ioy)
Heare this, We have another bright-ey'd Boy :
That word's a warrant, by whose vertue I
Have full authority to bid you Dy.
      Dy, dy, foul misbegotten Monsters ; Dy :
Make haste away, or e'r the world's bright Eye
Blush to a cloud of bloud. O farre from men
Fly hence, and in your Hyperborean den
Hide you for evermore, and murmure there
Where none but Hell may heare, nor our soft aire
Shrink at the hatefull sound. Mean while we bear
High as the brow of Heaven, the noble noise
And name of these our just and righteous joyes,
Where Envie shall not reach them, nor those eares
Whose tune keeps time to ought below the spheres.
      But thou, sweet supernumerary Starre,
Shine forth ; nor fear the threats of boyst'rous Warre.
The face of things has therefore frown'd a while
On purpose, that to thee and thy pure smile
The world might ow an universall calm ;
While thou, fair Halcyon, on a sea of balm
Shalt flote ; where while thou layst thy lovely head,
The angry billows shall but make thy bed :
Storms, when they look on thee, shall straight relent ;
And Tempests, when they tast thy breath, repent
To whispers soft as thine own slumbers be,
Or souls of Virgins which shall sigh for thee.
      Shine then, sweet supernumerary Starre ;
Nor feare the boysterous names of Bloud and Warre :
Thy Birthday is their Death's Nativitie ;
They've here no other businesse but to die.

Before l. 66, heading in 48 : To the Queen.   72 starres] starres, *48 A3*
her] yᵉ *A2*   74 *indented 48*   'Tis shee] Tis so *A2*   76 their
owne] there one *A2*   Sunshine, ô] Sunshine. O *48 T A3*   79
the] thy *48*   *Cynthia,*] Cynthia. *48 T A3*

N 2

Illustrious sweetnesse ! In thy faithfull wombe,   80
That Nest of *Heroes*, all our hopes finde roome.
Thou art the Mother *Phœnix*, and thy Breast
Chast as that Virgin honour of the East,
But much more fruitfull is ; nor does, as shee,
Deny to mighty Love a Deity.
Then let the Easterne world bragge and be proud
Of one coy *Phœnix*, while we have a brood
A brood of *Phœnixes* ; while we have Brother
And Sister *Phœnixes*, and still the Mother ;
And may we long ; long may'st thou live, t'encrease   90
The house and family of *Phœnixes*.
Nor may the light that gives their Eye-lids light,
E're prove the dismall Morning of thy Night :
Ne're may a Birth of thine be bought so deare,
To make his costly cradle of thy Beere.
O mayst thou thus make all the yeare thine owne,
And see such Names of joy sit white upon
The brow of every Moneth ; and when that's done
Mayest in a son of his find every son
Repeated, and that son still in another,   100
And so in each child often prove a Mother :
Long mayest thou laden with such clusters leane
Vpon thy Royall Elme (faire Vine) and when
The Heavens will stay no longer, may thy glory
And Name dwell sweet in some eternall story !
Pardon (bright excellence) an untun'd string,
That in thy Eares thus keeps a murmuring.
O speake a lowly Muses pardon ; speake
Her pardon or her sentence ; onely breake
Thy silence ; speake ; and she shall take from thence   110
Numbers, and sweetnesse, and an influence
Confessing thee : or (if too long I stay)
O speake thou and my Pipe hath nought to say :
For see *Appollo* all this while stands mute,
Expecting by thy voyce to tune his Lute.

80 *indented 48*   83 Virgin honour] virgin-hono^r *T*   85 Deity.
48 T A3 : Deity · *46*   90 *indented 48*   we long ;] they live *A2*
92 the light] the life *48 T*   93 thy] y^e *A2*   96 *indented 48*
all] still *A2*   98 that's] th'hast *48 T* : th'ast *A2*   102–5 *omitted*
A2   103 thy] the *48* : thy *Voces Votivæ*   105 story ! *48* : story *46*
space after l. 105 in T   106 *indented 48 A3*   107 murmuring.
48 T A3 A2 : murmuring *46*   113 say] playe *A2*   115 *space
after l. 114 in T*

But Gods are gratious : and their Altars, make
Pretious their offerings that their Altars take.
Give then this rurall wreath fire from thine eyes.
This rurall wreath dares be thy sacrifice.

Vpon Ford's *two Tragedyes*

Loves Sacrifice

and

The Broken Heart.

THou cheat'st us *Ford*, mak'st one seeme two by Art.
What is *Loves Sacrifice*, but *the broken Heart* ?

On a foule Morning, being then to take a journey.

WHere art thou Sol, while thus the blind-fold Day
Staggers out of the East, looses her way
Stumbling on Night ? Rouze thee Illustrious Youth,
And let no dull mists choake the Lights faire growth.
Point here thy Beames ; ô glance on yonder flockes,
And make their fleeces Golden as thy lockes.
Vnfold thy faire front, and there shall appeare
Full glory, flaming in her owne free spheare.
Gladnesse shall cloath the Earth, we will instile
The face of things, an universall smile.   10
Say to the Sullen Morne, thou com'st to court her ;
And wilt command proud *Zephirus* to sport her
With wanton gales : his balmy breath shall licke
The tender drops which tremble on her cheeke ;

116 *indented 48*   Altars,] Altars *48 T A3 A2*   117 their
offerings] there offringes *A3* : the offerings *48 A2*   118 then] yᵐ
A2 : them *70*   eyes.] eyes, *48 A3* : eyes ; *T*
Vpon Ford's *two Tragedyes, &c. MSS. T A3*
On a foule Morning, &c. MSS. T A3 A2 H S (*ll. 35–8*). *Heading in
T :* An Invitation to faire weather. In itinere cum vrgeretur matutinum
cœlum, tali carmine invitabatur serenitas. R. Cr. *Heading in A2 :*
Crosh : on yᵉ morning yᵗ was Clowdye when he was to take a iourney.
Heading in H : On A foule morning :   4 no] not *A2*   the]
thy *H*   5 yonder] yond faire *H*   7 faire front] front *H*   there] then
there *H*   12 proud] smooth *T* : sweete *A2*   13 balmy] wanton *A2*
14 The] Those *T A2*   which] that *T*   her] thy *A3 H*

Which rarifyed, and in a gentle raine
On those delicious bankes distill'd againe
Shall rise in a sweet Harvest ; which discloses
Two euer blushing beds of new-borne Roses.
Hee'l fan her bright locks teaching them to flow,
And friske in curl'd *Mæanders* : Hee will throw　　　20
A fragrant Breath suckt from the spicy nest
O'th pretious *Phœnix*, warme upon her Breast.
Hee with a dainty and soft hand, will trim
And brush her Azure Mantle, which shall swim
In silken Volumes ; wheresoe're shee'l tread,
Bright clouds like Golden fleeces shall be spread.
　　Rise then (faire blew-ey'd Maid) rise and discover
Thy silver brow, and meet thy Golden lover.
See how hee runs, with what a hasty flight
Into thy Bosome, bath'd with liquid Light.　　　30
Fly, fly prophane fogs, farre hence fly away,
Taint not the pure streames of the springing Day,
With your dull influence, it is for you,
To sit and scoule upon Nights heavy brow ;
Not on the fresh cheekes of the virgin Morne,
Where nought but smiles, and ruddy joyes are worne.
Fly then, and doe not thinke with her to stay ;
Let it suffice, shee'l weare no maske to day.

　　15–18 *not in A2*.　　　16 those] these *H*　　17 Shall] Will
T　　　Harvest ;] harvest, *T*　　　which discloses] and disclose *H*
18 Two euer blushing beds *T* : To every blushing Bed *46 48 A3 H*
new-borne] new blowne *T A3*　　　of new-borne Roses] the new-
borne Rose *H*　　22 O'th] Of th *A2*　　her] yᵉ *A2*　　23 dainty
and soft] soft & dainty *T A2*　　25 Volumes ; *48* : volumes. *T* :
uolumes : *A3 A2* : Volumes, *46*　　26 like] in *H*　　clouds] clouds, *T*
fleeces] fleeces, *T*　　27 *not indented T*.　　28 and] to *H*　　lover]
Mother *A3*　　29, 30 *not in A2*.　　29 hee] shee *A3*　　hasty] holy *H*
flight] flight, *48 T*　　30 with] in *T A3* Light] Night *A3*　　31 hence
fly away] hence away *A2*　　35 *S begins at* The fresh　　36
joyes are] joy is *T*　　38 *T distinguishes* Shee'l *&c.*

Vpon the faire Ethiopian sent to a Gentlewoman.

LO here the faire *Chariclia* ! in whom strove
So false a Fortune, and so true a Love.
Now after all her toyles by Sea and Land,
    O may she but arrive at your white hand,
Her hopes are crown'd, onely she feares that than,
    Shee shall appeare true Ethiopian.

On Marriage.

I Would be married, but I'de have no Wife,
I would be married to a single Life.

To the Morning.
Satisfaction for sleepe.

WHat succour can I hope the Muse will send
    Whose drowsinesse hath wrong'd the Muses friend ?
What hope *Aurora* to propitiate thee,
Vnlesse the Muse sing my Apology ?
    O in that morning of my shame ! when I
Lay folded up in sleepes captivity ;
How at the sight did'st Thou draw back thine Eyes,
Into thy modest veyle ? how did'st thou rise
Twice di'd in thine owne blushes, and did'st run
To draw the Curtaines, and awake the Sun ?   10
Who rowzing his illustrious tresses came,
And seeing the loath'd object, hid for shame
His head in thy faire Bosome, and still hides
Mee from his Patronage ; I pray, he chides :

Vpon the faire Ethiopian, &c. MSS. T A3.   3 and] by *A3*
4 your] her *A3*   hand, *48 T A3* : hand. *46*   5 crown'd, onely]
crown'd : Only *T* : crown'd. only *A3*
    On Marriage. MSS. T A3 A2 S.   Heading in T : Marriage.   1
but I'de] yett would *A2*
    To the Morning, &c. MSS. T A3 A2 H.   Heading in T : Ad Auroram.
Somnolentiæ expiatio. R. Cr. *Heading in A2 :* Crosh : To yᵉ Deane
on occasion of sleeping chappell.   *Heading in H :* To the morning a
Satisfaction for sleepe :   1 the] my *A2 H*   2 the] my *A2 H*
4 the] my *A2*   my] myne *A2*   5 *not indented T*   7
draw] call *T A2*   thine] thy *A3 H*   Eyes,] eyes *T A2*
13 and] which *A3*

And pointing to dull *Morpheus*, bids me take
My owne *Apollo*, try if I can make
His *Lethe* be my *Helicon* : and see
If *Morpheus* have a Muse to wait on mee.
Hence 'tis my humble fancy finds no wings,
No nimble rapture starts to Heaven and brings   20
Enthusiasticke flames, such as can give
Marrow to my plumpe *Genius*, make it live
Drest in the glorious madnesse of a Muse,
Whose feet can walke the milky way, and chuse
Her starry Throne ; whose holy heats can warme
The Grave, and hold up an exalted arme
To lift me from my lazy Vrne, to climbe
Vpon the stooped shoulders of old Time ;
And trace Eternity—But all is dead,
All these delicious hopes are buried,   30
In the deepe wrinckles of his angry brow,
Where mercy cannot find them : but ô thou
Bright Lady of the Morne, pitty doth lye
So warme in thy soft Brest it cannot dye.
Have mercy then, and when he next shall rise
O meet the angry God, invade his Eyes,
And stroake his radiant Cheekes ; one timely kisse
Will kill his anger, and revive my blisse.
So to the treasure of thy pearly deaw,
Thrice will I pay three Teares, to show how true   40
My griefe is ; so my wakefull lay shall knocke
At th' Orientall Gates ; and duly mocke
The early Larkes shrill Orizons to be
An Anthem at the Dayes Nativitie.
And the same rosie-fingerd hand of thine,
That shuts Nights dying eyes, shall open mine.

---

16 My] Mine *T A3 A2*   18 have] hath *A2*   19 Hence 'tis]
Since this *H*   wings] winge *T A2*   20 rapture starts *48 A3*
H : raptures, starts *46* : raptures start *T A2*   brings] bringe
T A2   24 can] may *H*   way] path *A2*   25 Her] His *A3*
26 hold] lift *A3*   27 lift] rayse *A3*   to] and *70 A3 A2*   28
stooped] stooping *48 T A3 A2 H*   29 Eternity—] æternity. *T A2*
30 these] those *A2*   32 mercy] pitty *A3*   35 Have mercy] Bee
gentle *T A2*   when he next shall] next time hee doth *A3*   37
Cheekes] face *T A2*   38 my] thy *A2*   39 So to] Goe too, *A2*
treasure] treasures *T A2*   40 Thrice] There *A2*   show] till
T A2   41 lay] clay *A2*   42 duly] duty *H (?)*   43
Orizons] Orizons, *T A3* : horizons, *A2*   45 the] that *H*

But thou, faint God of sleepe, forget that I
Was ever knowne to be thy votery.
No more my pillow shall thine Altar be,
Nor will I offer any more to thee   50
My selfe a melting sacrifice ; I'me borne
Againe a fresh Child of the Buxome Morne,
Heire of the Suns first Beames ; why threat'st thou so ?
Why dost thou shake thy leaden Scepter ? goe,
Bestow thy Poppy upon wakefull woe,
Sicknesse, and sorrow, whose pale lidds ne're know
Thy downy finger, dwell upon their Eyes,
Shut in their Teares ; Shut out their miseryes.

Vpon the Powder Day.

HOw fit our well-rank'd Feasts doe follow,
All mischiefe comes after *All Hallow.*

Loves Horoscope.

LOve, brave vertues younger Brother,
Erst hath made my Heart a Mother,
Shee consults the conscious Spheares,
To calculate her young sons yeares.
Shee askes if sad, or saving powers,
Gave Omen to his infant howers,
Shee asks each starre that then stood by,
If poore Love shall live or dy.

Ah my Heart, is that the way ?
Are these the Beames that rule thy Day ?
Thou know'st a Face in whose each looke,
Beauty layes ope loves Fortune-booke,
On whose faire revolutions wait
The obsequious motions of Loves fate,

47 *not indented* T   But] And *A2*   49 thine] thy *A3 H*
54 dost thou shake] shakest thou *A3*   58 miseries. *48 &c.* : miseryes
46
Vpon the Powder Day. MSS. T A3. Heading in T : In conjura-
tionem sulphuream.   1 follow,] follow ! *T* : follow ? *A3*   2 *T dis-*
tinguishes All=Mischiefe *and* All=Hallow.
Loves Horoscope. MSS. T A3.   1·8 shall] should *A3*   2·6
Loves] mans *T A3*

Ah my Heart, her eyes and shee,
Have taught thee new Astrology.
How e're Loves native houres were set,
What ever starry Synod met,
'Tis in the mercy of her eye,
If poore Love shall live or dye.

If those sharpe Rayes putting on
Points of Death bid Love be gone
(Though the Heavens in counsell sate,
To crowne an uncontrouled Fate,
Though their best Aspects twin'd upon
The kindest Constellation,
Cast amorous glances on his Birth,
And whisper'd the confederate Earth
To pave his pathes with all the good
That warmes the Bed of youth and blood)
Love ha's no plea against her eye
Beauty frownes, and Love must dye.

But if her milder influence move ;
And guild the hopes of humble Love :
(Though heavens inauspicious eye
Lay blacke on loves Nativitye ;
Though every Diamond in *Ioves* crowne
Fixt his forehead to a frowne,)
Her Eye a strong appeale can give,
Beauty smiles and love shall live.

O if Love shall live, ô where
But in her Eye, or in her Eare,
In her Brest, or in her Breath,
Shall I hide poore Love from Death ?
For in the life ought else can give,
Love shall dye although he live.

Or if Love shall dye, ô where,
But in her Eye, or in her Eare,
In her Breath, or in her Breast,
Shall I Build his funerall Nest ?
While Love shall thus entombed lye,
Love shall live, although he dye.

Ad Reginam.

E*T verò jam tempus erat tibi, maxima Mater,*
    Dulcibus his oculis accelerare diem :
Tempus erat, nè qua tibi basia blanda vacarent ;
    Sarcina ne collo sit minùs apta tuo.
Scilicet ille tuus, timor & spes ille suorum,
    Quo primum es felix pignore facta parens,
Ille ferox iras jam nunc meditatur & enses :
    Jam patris magis est, jam magis ille suus.
Indolis O stimulos ! Vix dum illi transiit infans ;
    Jamque sibi impatiens arripit ille virum.   10
Improbus ille suis adeò negat ire sub annis :
    Jam nondum puer est, major & est puero.
Si quis in aulæis pictas animatus in iras
    Stat leo, quem docta cuspide lusit acus,
Hostis (io !) est ; neque enim ille alium dignabitur hostem ;
    Nempe decet tantas non minor ira manus.
Tunc hasta gravis adversum furit ; hasta bacillum est :
    Mox falsum vero vulnere pectus hiat.
Stat leo, ceu stupeat tali bene fixus ab hoste ;
    Ceu quid in his oculis vel timeat vel amet,   20
Tam torvum, tam dulce micant : nescire fatetur
    Márs *ne sub his oculis esset, an esset* Amor.
Quippe illîc Mars *est, sed qui bene possit amari ;*
    Est & Amor *certe, sed metuendus Amor :*
Talis Amor, *talis* Mars *est ibi cernere ; qualis*
    Seu puer hic esset, sive vir ille deus.
Hic tibi jam scitus succedit in oscula fratris,
    Res (ecce !) in lusus non operosa tuos.
Basia jam veniant tua quantacunque caterva ;
    Jam quocunque tuus murmure ludat amor.   30
En ! Tibi materies tenera & tractabilis hic est :
    Hic ad blanditias est tibi cera satis.
Salve infans, tot basiolis, molle argumentum,
    Maternis labiis dulce negotiolum,
O salve ! Nam te nato, puer aurëe, natus
    Et Carolo *&* Mariæ *tertius est oculus.*

Ad Reginam. *First published in* Ducis Eboracensis Fasciæ A Musis
Cantabrigiensibus raptim contextæ. . . . Cantabrigiæ, . . . 1633. *The
poem is there signed :* Crashaw, Aul. Pembr. *Heading in* 70L: Natalis
Ducis Eboracensis.   16 tantas 48 70L: *tantus 46*   22 Márs *ne*]
Mársne 1633   23 *est, sed*] *1633 48* 70 : *est. sed 46*   29 *quanta-
cunque*] *quatacunque 46*   33 *basiolis,*] basiolis 70L

Out of Martiall.

FOure Teeth thou had'st that ranck'd in goodly state
Kept thy Mouthes Gate.

The first blast of thy cough left two alone,
The second, none.

This last cough *Ælia*, cought out all thy feare,
Th'hast left the third cough now no businesse here.

Out of the Italian.
A Song.

*To thy Lover
Deere, discover
That sweet blush of thine that shameth
(When those Roses
It discloses)
All the flowers that Nature nameth.*

*In free Ayre,
Flow thy Haire ;
That no more Summers best dresses,
Bee beholden
For their Golden
Lockes, to* Phœbus *flaming Tresses.*

*O deliver
Love his Quiver,
From thy Eyes he shoots his Arrowes,
Where* Apollo
*Cannot follow :
Featherd with his Mothers Sparrowes.*

*O envy not
(That we dye not)
Those deere lips whose doore encloses
All the Graces
In their places,
Brother Pearles, and sister Roses.*

Out of Martiall. *MSS.* T A3 *Add. MS.* 11258. *No heading in* T.
Heading in A3 *:* Vpon Ælia. | Out of Martiall. (*See also index to 48, p. 229,
below. Heading in text of 48 as 46.) Couplets not interspaced in* T *and*
A3.   6 here] there A3
Out of the Italian. MS. A3.

From these treasures
Of ripe pleasures
One bright smile to cleere the weather.
Earth and Heaven
Thus made even,
Both will be good friends together.

The aire does wooe thee,
Winds cling to thee,
Might a word once flye from out thee ;
Storme and Thunder
Would sit under,
And keepe silence round about Thee.

But if Natures
Common Creatures,
So deare Glories dare not borrow :
Yet thy Beauty
Owes a Duty,
To my loving, lingring sorrow.

When to end mee
Death shall send mee
All his Terrors to affright mee :
Thine eyes Graces,
Guild their faces,
And those Terrors shall delight mee.

When my dying
Life is flying ;
Those sweet Aires that often slew mee ;
Shall revive mee,
Or reprive mee,
And to many Deaths renew mee.

5·1 these] those *A3*   5·3 weather.] weather *A3*   5·5 Thus]
So *A3*   5·6 together] for euer *A3*   7·6 lingring] lingring, *48*
9·3 mee ;] mee *48 A3*

Out of the Italian.

LOve now no fire hath left him,
We two betwixt us have divided it.
Your Eyes the Light hath reft him.
The heat commanding in my *Heart* doth sit,
O ! that poore Love be not for ever spoyled,
Let my *Heat* to your *Light* be reconciled.

So shall these flames, whose worth
Now all obscured lyes
(Drest in those Beames) start forth
And dance before your eyes.

Or else partake my flames
(I care not whither)
And so in mutuall Names
Of Love, burne both together.

Out of the Italian.

WOuld any one the true cause find
How Love came nak't, a Boy, and blind ?
'Tis this ; listning one day too long,
To th' Syrens in my Mistresse Song,
The extasie of a delight
So much o're-mastring all his might,
To that one Sense, made all else thrall,
And so he lost his Clothes, eyes, heart and all.

In faciem Augustiss. Regis à mor-
billis integram.

MVsa redi ; vocat alma parens Academia : Noster
En redit, ore suo noster Apollo redit.
Vultus adhuc suus, & vultu sua purpura tantum
Vivit, & admixtas pergit amare nives.
Tune illas violare genas ? tune illa profanis,
Morbe ferox, tentas ire per ora notis ?

Out of the Italian. *MS. A3. Heading in A3 :* Italian.   3 hath]
haue *A3*   12 whither] wether *A3*
Out of the Italian. *MS. A3. Heading in A3 :* Italian. *Last line
set out A3.*
In faciem, *&c. First published in :* Anthologia in Regis Exanthemata :
Seu Gratulatio Musarum Cantabrigiensium de felicissimè conservata
Regis Caroli valetudine. . . . MDCXXXII. *The poem is there signed :*
Crashaw, Pembr.   6 *tentas 1632, 48 : tantas 46*

Tu Phœbi faciem tentas, vanissime? Nostra
  Nec Phœbe maculas novit habere suas.
Ipsa sui vindex facies morbum indignatur ;
  Ipsa sedet radiis ô bene tuta suis :   10
Quippe illic deus est, cœlûmque & sanctius astrum ;
  Quippe sub his totus ridet Apollo genis.
Quòd facie Rex tutus erat, quòd cætera tactus :
  Hinc hominem Rex est fassus, & inde deum.

On the Frontispiece of Isaacsons
Chronologie explained.

LEt hoary *Time's* vast Bowels be the Grave
  To what his Bowels birth and being gave ;
Let Nature die, if (*Phœnix*-like) from death
Revived Nature take a second breath ;
If on *Times* right hand, sit faire *Historie* ;
If, from the seed of empty Ruine, she
Can raise so faire an *Harvest* : Let Her be
Ne're so farre distant, yet *Chronologie*
(Sharpe sighted as the *Eagles* eye, that can
Out-stare the broad-beam'd Dayes Meridian)   10
Will have a *Perspicill* to find her out,
And, through the *Night* of error and dark doubt,
Discerne the *Dawne* of Truth's eternall ray,
As when the rosie *Morne* budds into Day.
  Now that *Time's* Empire might be amply fill'd,
Babels bold *Artists* strive (below) to build
Ruine a Temple ; on whose fruitfull fall
History reares her *Pyramids* more tall
Then were th' *Ægyptian* (by the life, these give,
Th' *Egyptian Pyramids* themselves must live :)   20
On these she lifts the *World* ; and on their base
Shewes the two termes and limits of *Time's* race :
That, the *Creation* is ; the *Judgement*, this ;
That, the World's *Morning*, this her *Midnight* is.

On the Frontispiece, &c. MS. T. Also in Satvrni Ephemerides Sive
Tabula Historico-Chronologica . . . By Henry Isaacson Londoner . . .
1633, *and not signed. Heading in T :* Vpon the Frontispeace of
Mr Isaackson's Chronologie. R. Cr. *In 46 and 48 the poem follows
that beginning* ' If with distinctive Eye ' (*see p. 410, below*) *and the
heading is* ' Or Thus '.   3 die, if *1633 T* : die, *46 48*   4 take]
takes *48*   5 Historie ;] Historie. *48* : History, *T*   18 Pyramids]
Pyramids, *T*

An Epitaph

Vpon Mr. Ashton *a conformable Citizen.*

THe modest front of this small floore
   Beleeve mee, Reader can say more
Then many a braver Marble can ;
Here lyes a truly honest man.
One whose Conscience was a thing,
That troubled neither Church nor King.
One of those few that in this Towne,
Honour all Preachers ; heare their owne.
Sermons he heard, yet not so many,
As left no time to practise any.   10
Hee heard them reverendly, and then
His practice preach'd them o're agen.
His *Parlour-Sermons* rather were
Those to the Eye, then to the Eare.
His prayers tooke their price and strength
Not from the lowdnesse, nor the length.
Hee was a Protestant at home,
Not onely in despight of *Rome.*
Hee lov'd his *Father* ; yet his zeale
Tore not off his Mothers veile.   20
To th'Church hee did allow her Dresse,
True *Beauty*, to true *Holinesse.*
Peace, which hee lov'd in Life, did lend
Her hand to bring him to his end ;
When Age and Death call'd for the score,
No surfets were to reckon for.
Death tore not (therefore) but sans strife
Gently untwin'd his thread of Life.
What remaines then, but that Thou
Write these lines, Reader, in thy Brow,   30

An Epitaph, &c. MS. A3. Heading in A3 : An Epitaph | Vpon
the Death of Mr Ashton | Citizen of London.   *4 A3 also distinguishes.*
8 *A3 distinguishes* heare their owne.   *After l. 12 A3 inserts :*
       For euery day his deedes put on
       His Sundayes *repetition*
19, 20 *A3 distinguishes* Father . . . Mothers   19 his] in *A3*   23
hee lov'd in Life] in Life he lou'd *A3*   24 bring] lead *A3*

And by his faire Examples light,
Burne in thy Imitation bright.
So while these Lines can but bequeath
A Life perhaps unto his Death.
His better Epitaph shall bee,
His Life still kept alive in Thee.

Rex Redux.

*I*Lle redit, redit. *Hoc populi bona murmura volvunt ;*
   Publicus hoc (audin' ?) plausus ad astra refert :
Hoc omni sedet in vultu commune serenum ;
   Omnibus hinc una est lætitiæ facies.
Rex noster, lux nostra redit ; redeuntis ad ora
   Arridet totis Anglia læta genis :
Quisque suos oculos oculis accendit ab istis ;
   Atque novum sacro sumit ab ore diem.
Forte roges tanto quæ digna pericula plausu
   Evadat Carolus, quæ mala, quósve metus :   10
Anne pererrati male fida volumina ponti
   Ausa illum terris pene negare suis :
Hospitis an nimii rursus sibi conscia, tellus
   Vix bene speratum reddat Ibera caput.
Nil horum ; nec enim male fida volumina ponti
   Aut sacrum tellus vidit Ibera caput.
Verus amor tamen hæc sibi falsa pericula fingit :
   (Falsa peric'la solet fingere verus amor)
At Carolo qui falsa timet, nec vera timeret :
   (Vera peric'la solet temnere verus amor)   20
Illi falsa timens, sibi vera pericula temnens,
   Non solum est fidus, sed quoque fortis amor.
Interea nostri satis ille est causa triumphi :
   Et satis (ah !) nostri causa doloris erat.
Causa doloris erat Carolus, sospes licet esset ;
   Anglia quod saltem dicere posset, Abest.
Et satis est nostri Carolus nunc causa triumphi ;
   Dicere quod saltem possumus, Ille redit.

32 *A 3 distinguishes* light   34 Death.] Death ; 48
*Rex Redux. First published in : Rex Redux, Sive Musa Cantabrigiensis
voti damnas De incolumitate & felici reditu Regis Caroli post receptam
Coronam, Comitiaq; peracta in Scotia. . . .* MDCXXXIII. *The poem is
signed : Rich. Crashaw, Aul. Pemb.*   6 *Arridet 48 : Aridet 46*   11
pererrati 48 : pererrati 46   26 *dicere 1633 48 : discere 46*

Out of Catullus.

COme and let us live my Deare,
Let us love and never feare,
What the sowrest Fathers say :
Brightest *Sol* that dyes to day
Lives againe as blith to morrow,
But if we darke sons of sorrow
Set ; ô then, how long a Night
Shuts the Eyes of our short light !
Then let amorous kisses dwell
On our lips, begin and tell   10
A Thousand, and a Hundred, score
An Hundred, and a Thousand more,
Till another Thousand smother
That, and that wipe of another.
Thus at last when we have numbred
Many a Thousand, many a Hundred ;
Wee'l confound the reckoning quite,
And lose our selves in wild delight :
While our joyes so multiply,
As shall mocke the envious eye.   20

Ad Principem nondum natum.

NAscere nunc ; ô nunc ! quid enim, puer alme, moraris ?
Nulla tibi dederit dulcior hora diem.
Ergone tot tardos (ô lente !) morabere menses ?
Rex redit. Ipse veni, & dic bone, Gratus ades.
Nam quid Ave nostrum ? quid nostri verba triumphi ?
Vagitu melius dixeris ista tuo.
At maneas tamen : & nobis nova causa triumphi
Sic demum fueris ; nec nova causa tamen :
Nam, quoties Carolo novus aut nova nascitur infans,
Revera toties Carolus ipse redit.

Out of Catullus. *MSS. T A3. Heading in T :* Catull. | Vivamus,
mea Lesbia &c R. Cr.   4 Brightest] Blithest *T A3*   9 amorous]
numerous *T A3*   10 On] Vpon *A3*   11 hundred, *T :* hundred :
A3 : Hundred *46 48*   score] score, *48*   12 An] a *T A3*   17 the]
our *T A3*   20 eye.] eye, *46*
Ad Principem, *&c.* (*Heading*) natum.] natum, Reginâ gravidâ *70L*

Wishes.

To his (supposed) Mistresse.

WHo ere shee bee,
   That not impossible shee
That shall command my heart and mee ;

Where ere shee lye,
Lock't up from mortall Eye,
In shady leaves of Destiny :

Till that ripe Birth
Of studied fate stand forth,
And teach her faire steps to our Earth ;

Till that Divine   10
Idæa, take a shrine
Of Chrystall flesh, through which to shine :

Meet you her my wishes,
Bespeake her to my blisses,
And bee yee call'd my absent kisses.

I wish her Beauty,
That owes not all his Duty
To gaudy Tire, or glistring shoo-ty.

Something more than
Taffata or Tissew can,   20
Or rampant feather, or rich fan.

More then the spoyle
Of shop, or silkewormes Toyle
Or a bought blush, or a set smile.

A face thats best
By its owne beauty drest,
And can alone commend the rest.

*Wishes. &c. First published in Witt's Recreations (1641) in the shorter
form given in the Commentary, p. 443, below. MSS. A3 H S (stanzas 10,
15–18, 35). Heading in H* : Wishes to A supposed mistrisse :   9 to]
tread *H*   13 Meet you] Meete *H*   15 yee] you *A3 H*
A3 distinguishes absent *and perhaps* kisses.   17 his] its *70*
18 Tire] fan *A3*   24 bought] bowe, *H*   27 commend *A3 H* :
command *46 48*

A face made up
Out of no other shop,
Then what natures white hand sets ope.   30

A cheeke where Youth,
And Blood, with Pen of Truth
Write, what the Reader sweetly ru'th.

A Cheeke where growes
More then a Morning Rose :
Which to no Boxe his being owes.

Lipps, where all Day
A lovers kisse may play,
Yet carry nothing thence away.

Lookes that oppresse   40
Their richest Tires but dresse
And cloath their simplest Nakednesse.

Eyes, that displaces
The Neighbour Diamond, and out faces
That Sunshine by their owne sweet Graces.

Tresses, that weare
Iewells, but to declare
How much themselves more pretious are.

Whose native Ray,
Can tame the wanton Day   50
Of Gems, that in their bright shades play.

Each Ruby there,
Or Pearle that dare appeare,
Bee its owne blush, bee its owne Teare.

A well tam'd Heart,
For whose more noble smart,
Love may bee long chusing a Dart.

Eyes, that bestow
Full quivers on loves Bow ;
Yet pay lesse Arrowes then they owe.   60

33 the] their *H*   36 owes. *48 A3* : owes : *H* : owes *46*   41 Tires]
Tires, *48 H* : Tires: *A3*   42 And cloath their simplest] themselves in
simple *H*   43 displaces] displace *H*   44 out faces] outface *H*
45 Graces.] grace *H*   53 dare] dares *A3 H*

Smiles, that can warme
The blood, yet teach a charme,
That Chastity shall take no harme.

Blushes, that bin
The burnish of no sin,
Nor flames of ought too hot within.

Ioyes, that confesse,
Vertue their Mistresse,
And have no other head to dresse.

Feares, fond and flight,   70
As the coy Brides, when Night
First does the longing lover right.

Teares, quickly fled,
And vaine, as those are shed
For a dying Maydenhead.

Dayes, that need borrow,
No part of their good Morrow,
From a fore spent night of sorrow.

Dayes, that in spight
Of Darkenesse, by the Light   80
Of a cleere mind are Day all Night.

Nights, sweet as they,
Made short by lovers play,
Yet long by th'absence of the Day.

Life, that dares send
A challenge to his end,
And when it comes say *Welcome Friend.*

Sydnæan showers
Of sweet discourse, whose powers
Can Crowne old Winters head with flowers,   90

Soft silken Houres,
Open sunnes ; shady Bowers,
Bove all ; Nothing within that lowres.

68 Mistresse] Misteresse *A3*   70 flight] sleight *H*   74 vaine]
fond *A3 H*   81 *A3 distinguishes* day all night   82] Nights sweet
as they *A3*   85 send *48 H A3* : send, *46* : *H puts ll. 88–96 before
ll. 79–87*   91 Houres] Houers *46*   92 sunnes] sunne *H* : sunnes,
48   Bowers,] Bowers ; *48*   93 all ;] all, *48 H*

What ere Delight
Can make Dayes forehead bright;
Or give Downe to the Wings of Night.

In her whole frame,
Have Nature all the Name,
Art and ornament the shame.

Her flattery,   100
Picture and Poesy,
Her counsell her owne vertue bee.

I wish, her store
Of worth, may leave her poore
Of wishes; And I wish —— No more.

Now if Time knowes
That her whose radiant Browes,
Weave them a Garland of my vowes;

Her whose just Bayes,
My future hopes can raise,   110
A trophie to her present praise;

Her that dares bee,
What these Lines wish to see:
I seeke no further, it is shee.

'Tis shee, and heere
Lo I uncloath and cleare,
My wishes cloudy Character.

May shee enjoy it,
Whose merit dare apply it,
But Modesty dares still deny it.   120

Such worth as this is,
Shall fixe my flying wishes,
And determine them to kisses.

Let her full Glory,
My fancyes, fly before yee,
Bee ye my fictions; But her story.

Imprimatur
Na: Brent.

F I N I S.

99 and] and all *A3*   102 counsell] counsayle, *A3*   104 worth,]
worth *48*   105 And I wish —— No more.] —— And I wish no more.
S   110 hopes can raise,] hopes, can rayse *A3*   119 dare] dares *A3*
120 But] Yet *A3*   126 her] she my *H*

THE TABLE.

---

21 *Asse*] *Asses 46*   39 *Yee*] *To 46*

24 Staninoughs] Stannoughs *46*   44 and] an *46*   48 Virgil]
Yirgil *46*

FINIS.

5 Serenissimæ Reginæ] Senerissimæ Regine 46

Poems added in 1648 and
not included in 1652

STEPS
TO THE
TEMPLE
By
R. C. Cantabr.

J. Crofs Sculpt:

STEPS

TO THE

TEMPLE,

Sacred Poems.

WITH
The Delights of the Muses.

By RICHARD CRASHAW, *sometimes of* Pembroke *Hall, and
late fellow of* S. Peters *Coll.
in* Cambridge.

*The second Edition wherein are added divers
pieces not before extant.*

LONDON,
Printed for *Humphrey Moseley,* and are to be
sold at his Shop at the Princes Armes
in St. *Pauls* Church-yard.
1 6 4 8.

Votiva Domus Petrensis Pro
Domo Dei.

UT *magìs in Mundi votis, Aviúmque querelis*
  Jam veniens *solet esse* Dies, *ubi cuspide primâ*
Palpitat, & roseo Lux prævia *ludit ab* ortu ;
Cùm nec abest Phœbus, *nec Eois lætus habenis*
Totus adest, volucrúmque procul vaga murmura mulcet :

Nos *ità ; quos nuper radiis afflavit honestis*
Relligiosa Dies ; *nostríque per atria Cœli*
(Sacra Domus nostrum *est* Cœlum) *jam* luce tenellâ
Libat adhuc trepidæ *Fax nondum firma* Diei :
Nos *ità jam exercet nimii impatientia* Voti,   10
Spéque sui propiore *premit.*————
                    ———— Quis *pectora tanti*
Tendit amor Cœpti ! Desiderio *quàm* longo
Lentæ spes *inhiant !* Domus *ô dulcissima rerum !*
Plena Deo Domus ! *Ah,* Quis erit, Quis (*dicimus*) Ille,
(*O Bonus, ô Ingens meritis, ô Proximus* ipsi,
Quem vocat in sua *Dona,* Deo !) *quo vindice totas*
Excutiant Tenebras *hæc* Sancta Crepuscula ?————
                    ———— Quando,

Quando *erit, ut tremulæ* Flos *heu* tener *ille* Diei,   20
Qui velut ex Oriente *suo jam* Altaria *circûm*
Lambit, & ambiguo *nobis procul annuit* astro,
Plenis *se pandat* foliis, *&* Lampade totâ
Lætus (*ut è medio cûm* Sol *micat aureus axe*)
Attonitam *penetrare* Domum *bene possit* adulto
Sidere, *nec dubio* Pia Mœnia *mulceat ore ?*

Quando *erit, ut* Convexa *suo quoque pulchra sereno*
Florescant, roseóque tremant Laquearia *risu ?*
Quæ *nimiùm* informis *tanquam sibi conscia* frontis
Perpetuis jam se lustrant lacrymantia *guttis.*   30

Quando *erit, ut claris meliori* luce Fenestris
Plurima per vitreos *vivat* Pia Pagina vultus ?

Quando *erit, ut* Sacrum *nobis* celebrantibus Hymnum
Organicos *facili, & nunquam fallente susurro*

Votiva Domus, *&c. MS. T.*   20 *tremulæ*] teneræ *T and 70L*
27–30 *separate section thus in T and 70L. No space after l. 26 in 48.*
29 *tanquam*] tanqnam *48*

Nobile murmur agat nervos ; *pulmonis iniqui*
Fistula *nec monitus faciat male-fida sinistros ?*

Denique, *quicquid id est, quod* Res *hîc* Sacra *requirit,*
Fausta illa, & felix (sitque ô Tua) Dextra, *suam cui*
Debeat hæc Aurora Diem. Tibi *supplicat* Ipsa,
Ipsa Tibi *fàcit* Ara preces. Tu *jam* Illius *audi,*   40
Audiet Illa tuas. *Dubium est (modò porrige* dextram)
Des *magìs, an* capias : *aude tantùm esse* beatus,
Et damnum hoc lucrare Tibi.———

———*Scis Ipse volucres*
Quæ Rota *volvat* opes; *has ergò hîc* fige *perennis*
Fundamenta Domûs Petrensi *in* Rupe ; *suámque*
Fortunæ *sic deme* Rotam. *Scis Ipse procaces*
Divitias *quàm prona vagos vehat* ala *per Euros,*
Divitiis *illas, agè, deme volucribus* alas,
Fácque suus Nostras *illis sit nidus ad* Aras :   50
Remigii ut tandem pennas melioris *adeptæ,*
Se rapiant Dominúmque suum *super æthera* secum.

Felix ô qui sic potuit bene providus uti
Proverb. 23. 5. Fortunæ pennis *& opum levitate* suarum,
Divitiisque suis Aquilæ sic *addidit* Alas.

E J U S D E M

In cæterorum Operum difficili Parturitione

G E M I T U S.

O *Felix nimis* Illa, *& nostræ nobile Nomen*
Invidiæ Volucris ! *facili quæ* funere *surgens*
Mater *odora sui* nitidæ *nova fila* juventæ,
Et festinatos *peragit sibi fata per* ignes.
Illa, *haud natales tot* tardis *mensibus horas*
Tam miseris tenuata moris, saltu *velut* uno
In nova secla rapit *sese, &* caput omne *decoras*
Explicat in frondes, roseóque repullulat *ortu.*

36 faciat *T* : nec faciat *48*   43 damnum *T : danum 48*   45
volvat] volvet *T 70L*   53–5 *not indented in T and 70L and no reference*
to Proverb. 23. 5.   53 ô] ô, *T*   ,55 Divitiisque *T* : Devitiis-
que *48*   Alas.] alas ! *T ·*
Ejusdem, &c. MS. *T.*   *70L omits* Ejusdem.   2 quæ
qnæ *48*   6 saltu *T 70L* : salutu *48*

Cinnameos simul Illa *rogos conscenderit, omnem*
Læta bibit Phœbum, *& jam jam victricibus alis*   10
Plaudit humum, Cinerésque suos.————
————————Heu ! dispare *Fato*
Nos ferimur ; Seniorque suo *sub* Apolline Phœnix
Petrensis Mater, dubias *librata per* auras
Pendet adhuc, quærítque sinum *in quo ponat* inertes
Exuvias, *spoliisque* suæ Reparata Senectæ
Ore Pari *surgat,* Similique *per omnia* Vultu.
At nunc heu nixu *secli melioris in* ipso
Deliquium patitur !—
At nunc heu Lentæ longo *in molimine* Vitæ   20
Interea moritur ! Dubio *stant* Mœnia vultu
Parte sui Pulchra, *& fratres in fœdera* Muros
Invitant frustrà, nec respondentia Saxis
Saxa *suis. Mœrent* Opera *intermissa,* manúsque
Implorant.————
————————Succurre Piæ, *succurre* Parenti,
O Quisquis pius *es.* Illi *succurre* Parenti,
Quam *sibi tot sanctæ* Matres *habuere* Parentem.
Quisquis es, ô Tibi, *crede,* Tibi *tot* hiantia *ruptis*
Mœnibus Ora *loqui !* Matrem Tibi, *crede,* verendam   30
Muros *tam longo* laceros *senióque sitúque*
Ceu Canos *monstrare suos. Succurre roganti.*
Per Tibi Plena *olim, per jam* Sibi Sicca *precatur*
Vbera, *nè desis* Senio. *Sic* longa Iuventus
Te *foveat, querulæ nunquam cessura* Senectæ.

Fides quæ sola justificat, non est sine Spe & Dilectione.

NAm neque tam sola est. *O quis malè censor amarus*
    Tam socias negat in mutua sceptra manus ?
Deme Fidem ; nec aget, nec erit jam nomen Amoris :
    Et vel erit, vel aget quid sine Amore Fides ?
Ergò Amor, I, morere ; I magnas, Puer alme, per umbras :
    Elysiis non tam numen inane locis.
O bene, quòd pharetra *hoc saltem tua præstat &* arcus,
    Nè tibi in extremos sit pyra nulla rogos !
O bene, quòd tuus has saltem tibi providet ignis,
    In tua quas possis funera ferre, faces !   10

23 *frustrà*] *frnstrà 48*

Durus es, ah, quisquis tam dulcia vincula solvis ;
  Quæ ligat, & quibus est ipse ligatus Amor.
O bene junctarum divortia sæva sororum,
  Tam penitus mixtas quæ tenuêre manus !
Nam quæ (tam varia) in tam mutua viscera vivunt ?
  Aut ubi, quæ duo sunt, tam propè sunt eadem ?
Alternis sese circùm amplectuntur in ulnis :
  Extráque & suprà, subter & intus eunt.
Non tam Nympha tenax, Baccho jam mista marito,
  Abdidit in liquidos mascula vina sinus.   20
Compare jam dempto, saltem sua murmura servat
  Turtur ; & in viduos vivit amara modos.
At Fidei sit demptus Amor ; non illa dolebit,
  Non erit impatiens, ægráque : jam moritur.
Palma, marem cui tristis hyems procul abstulit umbram,
  Protinus in viridem procubuit faciem ?
Undique circumfert caput, omnibus annuit Euris ;
  Siqua maritalem misceat aura comam :
Ah misera, expectat longùm, lentúmque expirat,
  Et demum totis excutitur foliis.   30
At sine Amore Fides, nec tantum vivere perstat
  Quo dici possit vel moritura Fides.
Mortua jam nunc est : nisi demum mortua non est
  Corporea hæc, animâ deficiente, domus.
Corpore ab hoc Fidei hanc animam si demis Amoris,
  Jam tua sola quidem est, sed malè sola Fides.
Hectore ab hoc, currus quem jam nunc sentit Achillis,
  Hectora eum speres quem modò sensit herus ?
Tristes exuvias, Oetæi frusta furoris,
  (Vanus) in Alcidæ nomen & acta vocas ?   40
Vel satis in monstra hæc, plùs quàm Nemeæa, malorum
  Hoc Fidei torvum & triste cadaver erit ?
Immo, Fidem usquè suos velut ipse Amor ardet amores ;
  Sic in Amore fidem comprobat ipsa Fides.

ERGO

Illa Fides vacuâ quæ sola superbiet aulâ,
  Quam Spes desperet, quam nec amabit Amor ;
Sola Fides hæc, tam miserè, tam desolatè
  Sola, (quod ad nos est) sola sit usque licet.
A sociis quæ sola suis, à se quoque sola est.
  Quæ sibi tam nimia est, sit mihi nulla Fides.   50

45 *superbiet*] *suberbiet* 48

Baptismus non tollit futura peccata.

* Ecclesia.

Q*Visquis es ille tener modò quem tua * mater Achilles*
  In Stygis æthereæ provida tinxit aquis,
Sanus, sed non securus dimitteris illinc :
  In nova non tutus vulnera vivis adhuc.
Mille patent aditus ; & plùs quàm calce petendus
  Ad nigri metues spicula mille dei.
Quòd si est vera salus, veterem meminisse *salutem ;*
  Si nempe hoc verè est esse, fuisse *pium ;*
Illa tibi veteres navis quæ vicerat Austros,
  Si manet in mediis usquè superstes aquis ;   10
Ac dum tu miseros in littore visis amicos,
  Et peccatorum triste sodalitium,
Illa tibi interea tutis trahet otia velis,
  Expectans donec tu rediisse queas :
Quin igitur da vina, puer ; da vivere *vitæ ;*
  Mitte suum senibus, mitte supercilium ;
Donemus timidæ, ô socii, sua frigora brumæ :
  Æternæ teneant hîc nova regna rosæ.
Ah non tam tetricos sic eluctabimur Euros ;
  Effractam *non est sic revocare* ratem.   20

Has undas aliis decet ergò extinguere in undis ;
  Naufragium hoc alio immergere naufragio :
Possit ut ille malis oculus modò naufragus undis,
  Jam lacrymis meliùs naufragus esse suis.

THE TABLE

11 Æthiopian] Æthiopan 48   36 It is] It it 48

FINIS.

8 his] bis 48

THE
DELIGHTS
OF THE
MUSES:
OR,

Other Poems written on
severall occasions.

By Richard Craſhaw, *ſometimes of* Pembroke *Hall, and late Fellow of St.*Peters *Colledge in* Cambridge.

Mart. *Dic mihi quid melius deſidioſus agas.*

LONDON,

Printed by *T.W.* for *H.Moſeley,* at
the Princes Armes in S.*Pauls*
Church-yard, 1648.

In Eundem Scazon.

HUc hospes, oculos flecte, sed lacrimis cæcos,
 Legit optime hæc, Quem legere non sinit fletus.
Ars nuper & natura, forma, virtusque
Æmulatione fervidæ, paciscuntur
Probare in uno juvene quid queant omnes,
Fecere. tantæ terra impar fuit liti,
Ergo hic ab ipso Judicem manent cœlo.

Ad Reginam,
Et sibi & Academiæ parturientem.

HUc ô sacris circumflua cœtibus,
 Huc ô frequentem, Musa, choris pedem
Fer, annuo doctum labore
 Purpureas agitare cunas.
Fœcunditatem provocat, en, tuam
Maria partu nobilis altero,
 Prolémque Musarum ministram
 Egregius sibi poscit Infans.
Nempe Illa nunquam pignore simplici
Sibíve soli facta puerpera est :   10
 Partu repercusso, vel absens,
 Perpetuos procreat gemellos.
Hos Ipsa partus scilicet efficit,
Inque ipsa vires carmina suggerit,
 Quæ spiritum vitámque donat
 Principibus simul & Camœnis.
Possit Camœnas, non sine Numine,
Lassare nostras Diva puerpera,
 Et gaudiis siccare totam
 Perpetuis Heliconis undam.   20

In Eundem Scazon. *Follows the poem* ' *Vpon the death of Mr.* Herrys;
see pp. 167–8 above. MS. T, with ' *not printed* ' *added in margin ;*
1–2 *written as separate couplet* (*ll. 3–7 indented*) *with space between*
ll. 2 and 3. 2 *fletus* T : *flectus* 48   6 *Fecere.* T : *Fuere* 48
impar T : *nuper* 48   *liti,* T : *liti* 48
 Ad Reginam, *&c. First published in* Voces Votivæ (*see footnote to*
p. 176, above). (*Heading*) Ad] In *VV*   *parturientem*] *paturientem*
48 : *semper parturientem VV*

Quin experiri pergat, & in vices
Certare sanctis conditionibus.
  Lis dulcis est, nec indecoro
    Pulvere, sic potuisse vinci.

Alternis Natura Diem meditatur & umbras,
  Hinc atro, hinc albo pignore facta parens.
Tu melior Natura tuas, dulcissima, servas
  (Sed quam dissimili sub ratione !) vices.
Candida Tu, & partu semper Tibi concolor omni :
  Hinc Natam, hinc Natum das ; sed utrinque Diem. 30

To the Queen

An Apologie for the length of the fol-
lowing Panegyrick.

WHen you are Mistresse of the song,
  Mighty Queen, to thinke it long,
Were treason 'gainst that Majesty
Your vertue wears. Your modesty
Yet thinks it so. But ev'n that too
(Infinite, since part of You)
New matter for our Muse supplies,
And so allowes what it denies.
Say then Dread Queen, how may we doe
To mediate 'twixt your self and You ?   10
That so our sweetly temper'd song
Nor be to short, nor seeme to long.
  Needs must your Noble prayses strength
  That made it long excuse the length.

To the Queen, &c. See p. 176 sqq. above. First published in Voces
Votivæ (see footnote to p. 176, above).   7 for] to VV

Bulla.

Q Vid tibi vana suos offert mea bulla tumores ?
Quid facit qd vestrum pondus inane meum ?
Expectat nostros humeros toga fortior ; ista
En mea bulla, lares en tua dextra mihi.

Quid tu ? quæ nova machina,
Quæ tam fortuito globo
In vitam properas brevem ?
Qualis virgineos adhuc
Cypris concutiens sinus,
Cypris jam nova, jam recens,   10
Et spumis media in suis,
Promsit purpureum latus ;
Conchâ de patriâ micas,
Pulchroque exsilis impetu ;
Statim & millibus ebria
Ducens terga coloribus
Evolvis tumidos sinus
Sphærâ plena volubili.
Cujus per varium latus,
Cujus per teretem globum   20
Iris lubrica cursitans
Centum per species vagas,
Et picti facies chori

*Bulla. MS. T. First published at the end of D. Heynsii Crepundia
Siliana. Ejusdem Dissertatio De veræ Criticæ apud Veteres ortu, pro-
gressu, usúque, cùm in cæteris disciplinis, tum in sacris : et Exercitatio
critica, Demonstrans omnem ferè Ægyptiorum, Græcorum, & Latinorum
Religionem ex Oriente fluxisse. In quibus diversi autorum loci tam
Græcorum, quàm Latinorum, emendantur, illustrantur, & explicantur.
Cantabrigiæ : Ex Officina R. Daniel, Almæ Academiæ Typographi. 1646.
Text and pagination end p. 305, followed by Index. On verso of last page
of index, without fresh pagination or marks :* Lector ; nè detur vacuum,
hem tibi Bullam verè auream ; Quæ nunc primùm audet in apertum
aerem. Argumenti certè non ità dissimilis, seu crepundia respicias,
seu Heinsii * guttulam. Quid enim aliud Bulla, quàm puerorum orna-
mentum, aut guttulæ commentarius ? Tam nil quousque intumuit !
Huic autem libro assuendam curavimus, nè à sociis suis derelicta
(reliqua enim ejusdem Poetæ nuper prodiêre) ludibrium ventis &
deberet, & solveret. *Heading follows in Heinsius :* Bulla. *Ri. Cr.*
Cantabrigiensis. *In Heinsius there are spaces after ll. 18, 34, 47, 58, 73
(end of page), 87, 99, 112, 120, 137, 144, 151, and the succeeding initial
lines are indented. 4 mihi] mei Heinsius T   lares] Lares Heinsius*

_____

* p. 73.

Circum regnat, & undique
Et se Diva volatilis
Jucundo levis impetu
Et vertigine perfidâ
Lascivâ sequitur fugâ
Et pulchrè dubitat ; fluit
Tam fallax toties novis,   30
Tot se per reduces vias,
Errorésque reciprocos
Spargit vena Coloribus ;
Et pompâ natat ebriâ.
Tali militiâ micans
Agmen se rude dividit ;
Campis quippe volantibus,
Et campi levis æquore
Ordo insanus obambulans
Passim se fugit, & fugat ;   40
Passim perdit, & invenit.
· Pulchrum spargitur hîc Chaos.
Hîc viva, hîc vaga flumina
Ripâ non propriâ meant,
Sed miscent socias vias,
Communique sub alveo
Stipant delicias suas.
Quarum proximitas vaga
Tam discrimine lubrico,
Tam subtilibus arguit   50
Juncturam tenuem notis,
Pompa ut florida nullibi
Sinceras habeat vias ;
Nec vultu niteat suo.
Sed dulcis cumulus novos
Miscens purpureos sinus
Flagrat divitiis suis,
Privatum renuens jubar.
Floris diluvio vagi,
Floris Sydere publico   60
Latè ver subit aureum,

24] *Circum regnat ; & undique.* Heinsius (*full-stop also in* T)   27
perfidâ] *persidâ* 48   37 *Campis*] Castris T   42 *Chaos.*] chaos,
Heinsius   56 *purpureos* Heinsius : *purpureus* 48   57 *flagrat*
Heinsius : *flagrant* 48

Atque effunditur in suæ
Vires undique Copiæ.
Nempe omnis quia cernitur,
Nullus cernitur hîc color,
Et vicinia contumax
Allidit species vagas.
Illîc contiguis aquis
Marcent pallidulæ faces.
Undæ hîc vena tenellulæ,   70
Flammis ebria proximis
Discit purpureas vias,
Et rubro salit alveo.
Ostri Sanguineum jubar
Lambunt lactea flumina ;
Suasu cærulei maris
Mansuescit seges aurea ;
Et lucis faciles genæ
Vanas ad nebulas stupent ;
Subque uvis rubicundulis   80
Flagrant sobria lilia.
Vicinis adeo rosis
Vicinæ invigilant nives,
Vt sint & niveæ rosæ,
Vt sint & roseæ nives,
Accenduntque rosæ nives,
Extinguuntque nives rosas.
Illîc cum viridi rubet,
Hîc & cum rutilo viret
Lascivi facies chori.   90
Et quicquid rota lubrica
Caudæ stelligeræ notat,
Pulchrum pergit in ambitum.
Hîc cœli implicitus labor,
Orbes orbibus obvii ;
Hîc grex velleris aurei
Grex pellucidus ætheris ;
Qui noctis nigra pascua
Puris morsibus atterit ;
Hîc quicquid nitidum et vagum   100
Cæli vibrat arenula

84 *and* 85 sint] sunt *T*   85 *roseæ* Heinsius *T* : *rosæ 48*   93] *in*
Heinsius *T* : & *in 48*

Dulci pingitur en joco.
Hîc mundus tener impedit
Sese amplexibus in suis.
Succinctique sinu globi
Errat per proprium decus.
Hîc nictant subitæ faces,
Et ludunt tremulum diem.
Mox se surripiunt sui &
Quærunt tecta supercilî ;   110
Atque abdunt petulans jubar,
Subsiduntque proterviter.
Atque hæc omnia quam brevis
Sunt mendacia machinæ !
Currunt scilicèt omnia
Sphærâ, non vitreâ quidem,
(Ut quondam siculus globus)
Sed vitro nitidâ magis,
Sed vitro fragili magis,
Et vitro vitreâ magis.   120

    Sum venti ingenium breve
Flos sum, scilicet, aëris,
Sidus scilicet æquoris ;
Naturæ jocus aureus,
Naturæ vaga fabula,
Naturæ breve somnium.
Nugarum decus & dolor ;
Dulcis, doctaque vanitas.
Auræ filia perfidæ ;
Et risus facilis parens.   130
Tantùm gutta superbior,
Fortunatius & lutum.
    Sum fluxæ pretium spei ;
Una ex Hesperidum insulis.
Formæ pyxis, amantium
Clarè cæcus ocellulus ;
Vanæ & cor leve gloriæ.
    Sum cæcæ speculum Deæ.
Sum fortunæ ego tessera,

---

102 *en Heinsius* : *in* 48 T   109 *surripiunt*] *recipiunt Heinsius*
117 *siculus*] *Siculus Heinsius*   121 *breve*] *breve. Heinsius*   126
somnium.] *somnium, Heinsius*   133 *not indented in Heinsius.*

Quam dat militibus suis ;   140
Sum fortunæ ego symbolum,
· Quo sancit fragilem fidem
Cum mortalibus Ebriis
Obsignatque tabellulas.
    Sum blandum, petulans, vagum,
Pulchrum, purpureum, et decens,
Comptum, floridulum, et recens,
Distinctum nivibus, rosis,
Vndis, ignibus, aëre,
Pictum, gemmeum, & aureum,   150
O sum, (scilicet, O nihil.)

Si piget, et longam traxisse in tædia pompam
    Vivax, & nimiùm Bulla videtur anus ;
Tolle tuos oculos, pensum leve defluet, illam
    Parca metet facili non operosa manu.
Vixit adhuc. Cur vixit ? adhuc tu nempe legebas ;
    Nempe fuit tempus tum potuisse mori.

Vpon two greene Apricockes sent to Cowley *by Sir* Crashaw.

TAke these, times tardy truants, sent by me,
  To be chastis'd (sweet friend) and chidd by thee.
Pale sons of our *Pomona* ! whose wan cheekes
Have spent the patience of expecting weekes,
Yet are scarce ripe enough at best to show
The redd, but of the blush to thee they ow.
By thy comparrison they shall put on
More summer in their shames reflection,
Than ere the fruitfull *Phœbus* flaming kisses
Kindled on their cold lips.   O had my wishes   10
And the deare merits of your Muse, their due,
The yeare had found some fruit early as you ;
Ripe as those rich composures time computes
Blossoms, but our blest tast confesses fruits.
How does thy April-Autumne mocke these cold

150 & aureum] aureum Heinsius   151] O sum, scilicet o nihil.
Heinsius : O sum, scilicet, ô *Nihil* T   153 T *distinguishes*
Bulla.   157 Nempe *Heinsius* T : Tempe 48   mori.] mori ? T
After l. 157 Heinsius adds FINIS.
  Vpon two &c   2 chidd] chide 48

Progressions 'twixt whose termes poor time grows old ?
With thee alone he weares no beard, thy braine
Gives him the morning worlds fresh gold againe.
'Twas only Paradice, 'tis onely thou,
Whose fruit and blossoms both blesse the same bough.   20
Proud in the patterne of thy pretious youth,
Nature (methinks) might easily mend her growth.
Could she in all her births but coppie thee,
Into the publick yeares proficiencie,
No fruit should have the face to smile on thee
(Young master of the worlds maturitie)
But such whose sun-borne beauties what they borrow
Of beames to day, pay back againe to morrow,
Nor need be double-gilt. How then must these,
Poore fruites looke pale at thy Hesperides !   30
Faine would I chide their slownesse, but in their
Defects I draw mine owne dull character.
Take them, and me in them acknowledging,
How much my summer waites upon thy spring.

Thesaurus malorum fæmina

QVis deus, O quis erat qui te, mala fœmina, finxit ?
Proh ! Crimen superûm, noxa pudenda deûm !
Quæ divùm manus est adeo non dextera mundo ?
In nostras clades ingeniosa manus !
Parcite ; peccavi : nec enim pia numina possunt
Tam crudele semel vel voluisse nefas.
Vestrum opus est pietas ; opus est concordia vestrum :
Vos equidem tales haud reor artifices.
Heus inferna cohors ! fœtus cognoscite vestros.
Num pudet hanc vestrum vincere posse scelus ?   10
Plaudite Tartarei Proceres, Erebique potentes
(Næ mirum est tantum vos potuisse malum)
Jam vestras Laudate manus. Si forte tacetis,
Artificum laudes grande loquetur opus.
Quàm bene vos omnes speculo contemplor in isto ?
Pectus in angustum cogitur omne malum.

Thesaurus, &c. MS. T. Heading in T : Thesaurus malorum mala
fæmina.   9 cognoscite] agnoscite T

Quin dormi Pluto. Rabidas compesce sorores,
    Jam non poscit opem nostra ruina tuam.
Hæc satis in nostros fabricata est machina muros,
    Mortales Furias Tartara nostra dabunt.   20

In Apollinem depereuntem Daphnen.

S *Tulte Cupido,*
  Quid tua flamma parat ?
Annon sole sub ipso
Accensæ pereunt faces ?
Sed fax nostra potentior istis,
Flammas inflammare potest, ipse uritur ignis,
Ecce flammarum potens
Majore sub flammâ gemit.
Eheu ! quid hoc est ? En Apollo
Lyrâ tacente (ni sonet dolores)   10
Comâ jacente squallet æternus decor
Oris, en ! dominæ quò placeat magis,
Languido tardum jubar igne promit.
Pallente vultu territat æthera.
Mundi oculus lacrymis senescit,
Et solvit pelago debita, quodque hauserat ignibus,
His lacrymis rependit.
Noctis adventu properans se latebris recondit,
Et opacas tenebrarum colit umbras,
Namque suos odit damnans radios, nocensque lumen.   20
An lateat tenebris dubitat, an educat diem,
Hinc suadet hoc luctus furens, inde repugnat amor.

Æneas Patris sui bajulus.

M *Ænia Trojæ*
  Hostis & ignis habet.
Hostes inter & ignes
Æneas spolium pium,

20 *Mortales*] *Mortalcs 48*
In Apollinem, *&c. MS. T. Heading in T :* In Phæbum amantem.
5 *indented in T   nostra*] *nostra, T*   12] Oris (ni Dominæ
quo placeat magis) *T   13 promit.*] promit *T*
Æneas, *&c. MS. T.   1–4 Thus T.   48 prints as follows :*
          Mænia Troiae—— *Hostis & ignis*
          Hostes inter & ignes —— *Æneas spolium pium*
T puts a comma after Hostis (l. 2) and inter (l. 3)

Atque humeris venerabile pondus
Excipit, & sævæ nunc ô nunc parcite flammæ,
Parcite haud (clamat) mihi,
Sacræ favete sarcinæ,
Quod si negatis, nec licebit
Vitam juvare, sed juvabo funus ;   10
Rogusque fiam patris ac bustum mei.
His dictis acies pervolat hostium,
Gestit, & partis veluti trophæis
Ducit triumphos.   Nam furor hostium
Jam stupet & pietate tantâ
Victor vincitur ; imò & moritur Troja libentius
Funeribusque gaudet,
Ac faces admittit ovans, ne lateat tenebras
Per opacas opus ingens pietatis.
Debita sic patri solvis tua, sic pari rependis   20
Officio.   Dederat vitam tibi, tu reddis huic,
Felix ! parentis qui pater diceris esse tui.

In Pigmaliona.

P*Ænitet Artis*
  Pigmaliona suæ.
Quod felix opus esset
Infelix erat artifex.
Sentit vulnera, nec videt ictum.
Quis credit ? gelido veniunt de marmore flammæ.
Marmor ingratum nimis
Incendit autorem suum.
Concepit hic vanos furores ;
Opus suum miratur atque adorat.   10
Prius creavit, ecce nunc colit manus,
Tentantes digitos molliter applicat ;
Decipit molles caro dura tactus.
An virgo vera est, an sit eburnea ;
Reddat an oscula quæ dabantur
Nescit.   Sed dubitat, Sed metuit, munere supplicat,
Blanditiasque miscet.
Te, miser, pœnas dare vult, hos Venus, hos triumphos

11 *ac*] & T   16–17 *So* T. 48 *divides the lines between* moritur *and*
Troja *and reads* libenter   21 *tibi,*] tibi ; T   huic,] huic. T
  In Pigmaliona. MS. T. *Heading in* T : Pigmalion.   16 *Sed*
dubitat, Sed metuit, munere] sed dubitat. sed metuit. munere T

Capit à te, quòd amorem fugis omnem.
Cur fugis heu vivas ? mortua te necat puella.　　　　20
Non erit innocua hæc, quamvis tuâ fingas manu,
Ipsa heu nocens erit nimis, cujus imago nocet.

Arion.

SQuammea vivæ
Lubrica terga ratis
Jam conscendit Arion.
Merces tam nova solvitur
Navis quàm nova scanditur.   Illa
Aërea est merces, hæc est & aquatica navis.
Perdidére illum viri
Mercede magnâ, servat hic
Mercede nullâ piscis : & sic
Salute plus ruina constat illi ;　　　　10
Minoris & servatur hinc quàm perditur.
Hic dum findit aquas, findit hic aëra :
Cursibus, piscis ; digitis, Arion :
Et sternit undas, sternit & aëra :
Carminis hoc placido Tridente
Abjurat sua jam murmura, ventusque modestior
Auribus ora mutat :
Ora dediscit, minimos & metuit susurros.
(Sonus alter vetat, ut sit sonus illis)
Aura strepens circum muta it lateri adjacente pennâ,　　20
Ambit & ora viri, nec vela ventis hîc egent ;
Attendit hanc ventus ratem : non trahit, at trahitur.

Phænicis { Genethliacon & Epicedion.

PHænix alumna mortis,
Quàm mira tu puerpera !
Tu scandis haud nidos, sed ignes.
Non parere sed perire ceu parata :
Mors obstetrix ; atque ipsa tu teipsam paris,

20 vivas *T* : *vivos 48*　　22 *heu*] (heu !) *T*
　Arion. *MS. T.*　　19 *vetat T* : *restat 48*　　sit *T* : *fit 48*
20 *it, T* : *sit 48*
　Phænicis, *&c. MS. T.*　(*Heading*) & Epicedion.] vel Epicedium *T*
1 *Phænix*] Phænix, *T*　　4 *Non*] Haud *T*

  Tu Tuique mater ipsa es,
   Tu tuique filia.
Tu sic odora messis
Surgis tuorum funerum ;
Tibique per tuam ruinam   10
Reparata, te succedis ipsa. Mors ô
Fœcunda ! Sancta ô Lucra pretiosæ necis !
  Vive (monstrum dulce) vive
   Tu tibique suffice.

Elegia.

I Te meæ lacrymæ (nec enim moror) ite. Sed oro
 Tantùm ne miseræ claudite vocis iter.
O liceat querulos verbis animare dolores,
 Et saltem ah periit dicere noster amor.
Ecce negant tamen, ecce negant, lacrymæque rebelles
 Indomitâ pergunt, præcipitantque viâ.
Visne (ô care) igitur Te nostra silentia dicant ?
 Vis fleat assiduo murmure mutus amor ?
Flebit, & urna suos semper bibet humida rores,
 Et fidas semper, semper habebit aquas.   10
Interea, quicunque estis ne credite mirum
 Si veræ lacrymæ non didicére loqui.

Epitaphium.

Q Uisquis nectareo serenus ævo,
 Et spe lucidus aureæ juventæ
Nescis purpureos abire soles,
Nescis vincula, ferreamque noctem
Imi carceris, horridumque Ditem,
Et spectas tremulam procul senectam,
Hinc disces lacrymas, & huc repones.
Hic, ô scilicet hic brevi sub antro

---

11 *te*] tu *T*
 Elegia. *MS. T. No heading in T. Heading in 70L (where it follows*
Epitaphium in Guilielmum Herrisium) : In Eundem.   1 *Sed oro*]
sed, oro, *T*   4 *T distinguishes* Ah periit *and* noster amor.
6 *Indomitâ pergunt*] Pergunt indomitâ 70L   8 *Vis*] Vis, *T*   12 *T*
distinguishes the line.
 Epitaphium. *MS. T. No heading in T.*   6 *senectam,*] senectam ; *T*   7 *huc repones. T : hinc repones.* 48

Spes & gaudia mille, mille longam
(Heu longam nimis) induére noctem.   10
Flammantem nitidæ facem juventæ,
Submersit Stygiæ paludis unda.
Ergo si lacrymas neges doloris
Huc certè lacrymas feres timoris.

Damno affici sæpe fit lucrum.

*D**Amna adsunt multis taciti compendia lucri*
  Felicique docent plus properare morâ,
Luxuriem annorum positâ sic pelle redemit
  Atque sagax serpens in nova sæcla subit.
Cernis ut ipsa sibi replicato suppetat ævo,
  Seque iteret, multâ morte perennis avis.
Succrescat generosa sibi, facilesque per ignes
  Perque suos cineres, per sua fata ferax.
Quæ sollers jactura sui ? quis funeris usus ?
  Flammarumque fides, ingeniumque rogi ?   10
Siccine fraude subis ? pretiosaque funera ludis ?
  Siccine tu mortem, ne moriaris, adis ?
Felix cui medicæ tanta experientia mortis,
  Cui tam Parcarum est officiosa manus.

Humanæ vitæ descriptio.

*O**Vita, tantum lubricus quidam furor*
  Spoliumque vitæ ! scilicet longi brevis
Erroris hospes ! Error ô mortalium !
O certus error ! qui sub incerto vagum
Suspendit ævum, mille per dolos viæ
Fugacis, & proterva per volumina
Fluidi laboris, ebrios lactat gradus ;
Et irretitos ducit in nihilum dies.
O fata ! quantum perfidæ vitæ fugit
Umbris quod imputemus atque auris, ibi   10

10 *Heu*] Heu ! *T*   13 *neges*] negas *T*   Damno affici, *&c. MS. T.*
6 *avis,*] avis ? *T*   7 *Succrescat*] Succrescit *T*   13 *Felix*]
Felix ! *T*
    Humanæ, *&c. MS. T. Heading in T* : Turbæ rerum humanarum per
errorᵭ insidias.   10 *Umbris . . . auris,*] Umbris, quod imputemus,
atᵯ auris ! *T*

Et umbra & aura serias partes agunt
Miscentque scenam, volvimur ludibrio
Procacis æstus, ut per incertum mare
Fragilis protervo cymba cum nutat freto.
Et ipsa vitæ fila, quêis nentes Deæ
Ævi severa texta producunt manu,
Hæc ipsa nobis implicant vestigia
Retrahunt trahuntque donec everso gradu
Ruina lassos alta deducat pedes.
Felix, fugaces quisquis excipiens dies
Gressus serenos fixit, insidiis sui
Nec servit ævi, vita inoffensis huic
Feretur auris, atque claudâ rariùs
Titubabit horâ : vortices anni vagi
Hic extricabit, sanus Assertor sui.

20

Tranquillitas animi, similitudine ductâ ab ave captivâ & canorâ tamen.

VT cùm delicias leves, loquacem
Convivam nemoris, vagamque musam
Observans dubiâ viator arte
Prendit desuper : horridusve ruris
Eversor, malè perfido paratu
(Heu durus !) rapit, atque io triumphans
Vadit ; protinus & sagace nisu
Evolvens digitos, opus tenellum
Ducens pollice lenis erudito,
Virgarum implicat ordinem severum,
Angustam meditans domum volucri.
Illa autem, hospitium licet vetustum
Mentem sollicitet nimis nimisque
Et suetum nemus, hinc opaca mitis
Umbræ frigora, & hinc aprica puri
Solis fulgura, Patriæque sylvæ

10

11 *umbra*] umbra, *T*   15 vitæ *T* : *vitæ, 48*   17 *vestigia*]
vestigia, *T*   20 Indented in *T.*   22 *ævi,*] ævi ; *T*
Tranquillitas, *&c. MS. T.* (*Heading*) similitudine . . . tamen.]
bracketed in *T*   captivâ] captiva, *T*   5 perfido *T* : *persido 48*

Q 2

Nunquam muta quies ; ubi illa dudum
Totum per nemus, arborem per omnem,
Hospes libera liberis querelis
Cognatum benè provocabat agmen :   20
Quanquam ipsum nemus, arboresque alumnam
Implorant profugam, atque amata multùm
Quærant murmura, lubricumque carmen
Blandi gutturis & melos serenum :
Illa autem, tamen, illa jam relictæ
(Simplex !) haud meminit domus, nec ultrà
Sylvas cogitat ; at brevi sub antro,
Ah pennâ nimium brevis recisâ,
Ah ritu viduo, sibique sola,
Privata heu fidicen ! canit, vagoque   30
Exercens querulam domum susurro
Fallit vincula, carceremque mulcet ;
Nec pugnans placidæ procax quieti
Luctatur gravis, orbe sed reducto
Discursu vaga saltitans tenello,
Metitur spatia invidæ cavernæ.
Sic in se pia mens reposta, secum
Altè tuta sedet, nec ardet extrà,
Aut ullo solet æstuare fato :
Quamvis cuncta tumultuentur, atræ   40
Sortis turbine non movetur illa :
Fortunæ furias onusque triste
Non tergo minus accipit quieto,
Quàm vectrix Veneris columba blando
Admittit juga delicata collo.
Torvæ si quid inhorruit procellæ,
Si quid sæviat & minetur, illa
Spernit, nescit, & obviis furorem
Fallit blanditiis, amatque & ambit
Ipsum, quo malè vulneratur, ictum.   50
Curas murmure non fatetur ullo ;
Non lambit lacrymas dolor, nec atræ
Mentis nubila frons iniqua prodit.
Quod si lacryma pervicax rebelli
Erumpit tamen evolatque guttâ.
Invitis lacrymis, negante luctu,
Ludunt perspicui per ora risus.

THE TABLE,

To the Delights of the Muses.

5 a Friend] Friend 48   7 Heliodorus] Helidorus 48   37 of the]
of 48

FINIS.

CARMEN
DEO NOSTRO,
TE DECET HYMNVS
SACRED POEMS,
COLLECTED,
CORRECTED,
AVGMENTED,
Moſt humbly Preſented.

TO
MY LADY
THE COVNTESSE OF
DENBIGH
BY
Her moſt deuoted Seruant.
R.   C.
IN hearty acknowledgment of his immortall
obligation to her Goodnes & Charity.

✤

AT PARIS,
By PETER TARGA, Printer to the Arch-
biſhope of Paris, in S. Victors ſtreete at
the golden ſunne.

M.   DC.   LII.

11 COVNTESSE] COVNTSSE 52   16 hearty] heaty 52
20 of Paris] ef Paris 52

CRASHAWE

THE

ANAGRAMME.

HE WAS CAR.

Was Car then Crashawe ; or Was Crashawe Car,
   Since both within one name combined are ?
Yes, Car's Crashawe, he Car ; t'is loue alone
Which melts two harts, of both composing one.
So Crashawe's still the same : so much desired
By strongest witts ; so honor'd so admired.
Car Was but He that enter'd as a friend
With whom he shar'd his thoughts, and did commend
(While yet he liu'd) this worke ; they lou'd each other :
Sweete Crashawe was his friend ; he Crashawes brother. 10
So Car hath Title then ; t'was his intent
That what his riches pen'd, poore Car should print
Nor feares he checke praysing that happie one
Who was belou'd by all ; dispraysed by none.
To witt, being pleas'd with all things, he pleas'd all.
Nor would he giue, nor take offence ; befall
What might ; he would possesse himselfe : and liue
As deade (deuoyde of interest) t'all might giue
Desease t'his well composed mynd ; forestal'd
With heauenly riches : which had wholy call'd   20
His thoughtes from earth, to liue aboue in'th aire
A very bird of paradice. No care
Had he of earthly trashe. What might suffice
To fitt his soule to heauenly exercise,
Sufficed him and may we guesse his hart
By what his lipps brings forth, his onely part
Is God and godly thoughtes. Leaues doubt to none
But that to whom one God is all ; all's one.

6 admired.] admired *52*   24 exercise,] exercise. *52*

What he might eate or weare he tooke no thought.
His needfull foode he rather found then sought.   30
He seekes no downes, no sheetes, his bed's still made.
If he can find a chaire or stoole, he's layd,
When day peepes in, he quitts his restlesse rest.
And still, poore soule, before he's vp he's dres't,
Thus dying did he liue, yet liued to dye
In th'virgines lappe, to whom he did applye
His virgine thoughtes and words, and thence was styld
By foes, the chaplaine of the virgine myld
While yet he liued without : His modestie
Imparted this to some, and they to me.   40
Liue happie then, deare soule ; inioy the rest
Eternally by paynes thou purchacedest,
While Car must liue in care, who was thy friend
Nor cares he how he liue, so in the end,
He may inioy his dearest Lord and thee ;
And sitt and singe more skilfull songs eternally.

31 made.] made *52*   32 find] find, *52*   36 th'virgines]
th-virgines *52*

A N

EPIGRAMME

*Vpon the pictures in the following Poemes which the
Authour first made with his owne hand, admirably
well, as may be seene in his Manuscript dedicated
to the right Honorable Lady the L. Denbigh.*

Twixt pen and pensill rose a holy strife
 Which might draw vertue better to the life.
Best witts gaue votes to that : but painters swore
They neuer saw peeces so sweete before
As thes : fruites of pure nature ; where no art
Did lead the vntaught pensill, nor had part
In th'worke.
The hand growne bold, with witt will needes contest.
Doth it preuayle ? ah no : say each is best.
This to the eare speakes wonders ; that will trye   10
To speake the same, yet lowder, to the eye.
Both their aymes are holy, both conspire
To wound, to burne the hart with heauenly fire.
This then's the Doome, to doe both parties right :
This, to the eare speakes best ; that, to the sight.

         THOMAS CAR.

  7 th'worke] th'-worke *52*   9 no] wo *52*

NON VI.

'Tis not the work of force but skill
To find the way into man's will.
'Tis loue alone can hearts vnlock.
Who knowes the WORD, *he needs not knock.*

TO THE

Noblest & best of Ladyes, the Countesse of Denbigh.

Perswading her to Resolution in Religion, & to render her selfe without further delay into the Communion of the Catholick Church.

WHat heau'n-intreated HEART is This?
  Stands trembling at the gate of blisse;
Holds fast the door, yet dares not venture
Fairly to open it, and enter.
Whose DEFINITION is a doubt
Twixt life & death, twixt in & out.
Say, lingring fair! why comes the birth
Of your braue soul so slowly forth?
Plead your pretences (o you strong
In weaknes! why you choose so long   10

Non Vi. &c. This poem appeared for the first time in 52. See, however, the different version below, p. 348, printed separately 1653. That version prints ll. 7–12 after l. 20 and from l. 26 to l. 56 differs widely from 52.

In labor of your selfe to ly,
Nor daring quite to liue nor dy ?
Ah linger not, lou'd soul ! a slow
And late consent was a long no,
Who grants at last, long time tryd
And did his best to haue deny'd.
What magick bolts, what mystick Barres
Maintain the will in these strange warres !
What fatall, yet fantastick, bands
Keep The free Heart from it's own hands !   20
So when the year takes cold, we see
Poor waters their owne prisoners be.
Fetter'd, & lockt vp fast they ly
In a sad selfe-captiuity.
The' astonisht nymphs their flood's strange fate deplore,
To see themselues their own seuerer shore.
Thou that alone canst thaw this cold,
And fetch the heart from it's strong Hold ;
Allmighty Love ! end this long warr,
And of a meteor make a starr.   30
O fix this fair INDEFINITE.
And 'mongst thy shafts of soueraign light
Choose out that sure decisiue dart
Which has the Key of this close heart,
Knowes all the corners of't, & can controul
The self-shutt cabinet of an vnsearcht soul.
O let it be at last, loue's houre.
Raise this tall Trophee of thy Powre ;
Come once the conquering way ; not to confute
But kill this rebell-word, IRRESOLVTE   40
That so, in spite of all this peeuish strength
Of weaknes, she may write RESOLV'D AT LENGTH,
Vnfold at length, vnfold fair flowre
And vse the season of loue's showre,
Meet his well-meaning Wounds, wise heart !
And hast to drink the wholsome dart.
That healing shaft, which heaun till now
Hath in loue's quiuer hid for you.
O Dart of loue ! arrow of light !
O happy you, if it hitt right,   50

16 deny'd. *53* : deny'd, *52*   40 word] wotd *52*

It must not fall in vain, it must
Not mark the dry regardles dust.
Fair one, it is your fate ; and brings
Æternall worlds vpon it's wings.
Meet it with wide-spread armes ; & see
It's seat your soul's iust center be.
Disband dull feares ; giue faith the day.
To saue your life, kill your delay
It is loue's seege ; and sure to be
Your triumph, though his victory.
'Tis cowardise that keeps this feild
And want of courage.not to yeild.
Yeild then, ô yeild, that loue may win
The Fort at last, and let life in.
Yeild quickly. Lest perhaps you proue
Death's prey, before the prize of loue.
This Fort of your fair selfe, if't be not won,
He is repulst indeed ; But you'are vndone.

60

Numifma   Vrbani 6

TO
THE NAME
ABOVE EVERY NAME,

THE
NAME OF
IESVS

A HYMN.

I Sing the NAME which None can say
But touch't with An interiour RAY :
The Name of our New PEACE ; our Good :— *hope*
Our Blisse : & Supernaturall Blood :
The Name of All our Liues & Loues.
Hearken, And Help, ye holy Doues !
The high-born Brood of Day ; you bright
Candidates of blissefull Light,
The HEIRS Elect of Loue ; whose Names belong
Vnto The euerlasting life of Song ;   10
All ye wise SOVLES, who in the wealthy Brest
Of This vnbounded NAME build your warm Nest.

anthusiasm

To the Name, &c. First printed in 48, with heading : On the name of
Jesus.   7 you] the 48

Awake, My glory. Sovl, (if such thou be,
And That fair Word at all referr to Thee)
   Awake & sing
   And be All Wing ;
Bring hither thy whole Self ; & let me see
What of thy Parent Heavn yet speakes in thee.
   O thou art Poore
   Of noble Powres, I see,   20
And full of nothing else but empty Me,
Narrow, & low, & infinitely lesse
Then this Great mornings mighty Busynes.
   One little World or two
   (Alas) will neuer doe.
   We must haue store.
Goe, Sovl, out of thy Self, & seek for More.
   Goe & request
Great Natvre for the Key of her huge Chest
Of Heauns, the self inuoluing Sett of Sphears 30
(Which dull mortality more Feeles then heares)
   Then rouse the nest
Of nimble Art, & trauerse round
The Aiery Shop of soul-appeasing Sound :
And beat a summons in the Same
   All-soueraign Name
To warn each seuerall kind
And shape of sweetnes, Be they such
   As sigh with supple wind
   Or answer Artfull Touch,   40
That they conuene & come away
To wait at the loue-crowned Doores of
   This Illustrious Day.
Shall we dare This, my Soul ? we'l doe't and bring
No Other note for't, but the Name we sing
   Wake Lvte & Harp
   And euery sweet-lipp't Thing
   That talkes with tunefull string ;
Start into life, And leap with me
Into a hasty Fitt-tun'd Harmony.   50
   Nor must you think it much
   T'obey my bolder touch ;

17 see 48 : see. 52 24 World] word 48 43 This 48 : Thas 52
45 sing] sing. 48 50 hasty Fitt-tun'd] habit fit of self-tun'd 48

I haue Authority in LOVE's name to take you
And to the worke of Loue this morning wake you
       Wake ; In the Name
Of HIM who neuer sleeps, All Things that Are,
      Or, what's the same,
      Are Musicall ;
      Answer my Call
      And come along ;
Help me to meditate mine Immortall Song.   60
Come, ye soft ministers of sweet sad mirth,
Bring All your houshold stuffe of Heaun on earth;
O you, my Soul's most certain Wings,
Complaining Pipes, & prattling Strings,
      Bring All the store
Of SWEETS you haue ; And murmur that you haue no more.
      Come, nere to part,
      NATVRE & ART !
      Come ; & come strong,   70
To the conspiracy of our Spatious song.
      Bring All the Powres of Praise
Your Prouinces of well-vnited WORLDS can raise ;
Bring All your LVTES & HARPS of HEAVN & EARTH;
What e're cooperates to The common mirthe
      Vessells of vocall Ioyes,
Or You, more noble Architects of Intellectuall Noise,
Cymballs of Heau'n, or Humane sphears,
Solliciters of SOVLES or EARES ;
      And when you'are come, with All   80
That you can bring or we can call ;
      O may you fix
      For euer here, & mix
      Your selues into the long
And euerlasting series of a deathlesse SONG ;
Mix All your many WORLDS, Aboue,
And loose them into ONE of Loue.
      Chear thee my HEART !
      For Thou too hast thy Part
      And Place in the Great Throng   90
Of This vnbounded All-imbracing SONG.

---

54 wake you] wake you ; *48*   63 houshold stuffe] Houshold-
stuffe *48*   73 Prouinces] powers *48*   74 your *48* : yours *52*
75 e're] ére *52*

Powres of my Soul, be Proud !
    And speake lowd
To All the dear-bought Nations This Redeeming Name,
And in the wealth of one Rich WORD proclaim
New Similes to Nature.
    May it be no wrong
Blest Heauns, to you, & your Superiour song,
That we, dark Sons of Dust & Sorrow,
    A while Dare borrow   100
The Name of Your Delights & our Desires,
And fitt it to so farr inferior LYRES.
Our Murmurs haue their Musick too,
Ye mighty ORBES, as well as you,
    Nor yeilds the noblest Nest
Of warbling SERAPHIM to the eares of Loue,
A choicer Lesson then the ioyfull BREST
    Of a poor panting Turtle-Doue.
And we, low Wormes haue leaue to doe
The Same bright Busynes (ye Third HEAVENS) with you. 110
Gentle SPIRITS, doe not complain.
    We will haue care
    To keep it fair,
And send it back to you again.
Come, louely NAME ! Appeare from forth the Bright
    Regions of peacefull Light
Look from thine own Illustrious Home,
Fair KING of NAMES, & come.
Leaue All thy natiue Glories in their Gorgeous Nest,
And giue thy Self a while The gracious Guest   120
Of humble Soules, that seek to find
    The hidden Sweets
    Which man's heart meets
When Thou art Master of the Mind.
Come, louely Name ; life of our hope !
Lo we hold our HEARTS wide ope !
Vnlock thy Cabinet of DAY
Dearest Sweet, & come away.

---

93 lowd] aloud *48*   101 Delights] Dilights *52*   105 yeilds]
yeild *48*   106 SERAPHIM] *Seraphins 48*   107 ioyfull] Loyall
48   115 from forth] forth from *48*   119 Gorgeous] Georgeous *52*
120 guest *48* : Guest. *52*

Lo how the thirsty Lands
Gasp for thy Golden Showres ! with long stretch't Hands 130
Lo how the laboring EARTH
That hopes to be
All Heauen by THEE,
Leapes at thy Birth.
The'attending WORLD, to wait thy Rise,
First turn'd to eyes ;
And then, not knowing what to doe ;
Turn'd Them to TEARES, & spent Them too.
Come ROYALL Name, & pay the expence
Of All this Pretious Patience.   140
O come away
And kill the DEATH of This Delay.
O see, so many WORLDS of barren yeares
Melted & measur'd out in Seas of TEARES.
O see, The WEARY liddes of wakefull Hope
(LOVE'S Eastern windowes) All wide ope
With Curtains drawn,
To catch The Day-break of Thy DAWN.
O dawn, at last, long look't for Day !
Take thine own wings, & come away.   150
Lo, where Aloft it comes ! It comes, Among
The Conduct of Adoring SPIRITS, that throng
Like diligent Bees, And swarm about it.
O they are wise ;
And know what SWEETES are suck't from out it.
It is the Hiue,
By which they thriue,
Where All their Hoard of Hony lyes.
Lo where it comes, vpon The snowy DOVE'S
Soft Back ; And brings a Bosom big with Loues.   160
WELCOME to our dark world, Thou
Womb of Day !
Vnfold thy fair Conceptions ; And display
The Birth of our Bright Ioyes.
O thou compacted
Body of Blessings : spirit of Soules extracted !
O dissipate thy spicy Powres
(Clowd of condensed sweets) & break vpon vs

130 Hands] hands ! *48*   133 Heauen] heavens *48*   139 the] th'
48   140 this] thy *48*   150 *line space after l. 150 in 48*

R 2

In balmy showrs ;
O fill our senses, And take from vs   170
All force of so Prophane a Fallacy
To think ought sweet but that which smells of Thee.
Fair, flowry Name ; In none but Thee
And Thy Nectareall Fragrancy,
          Hourly there meetes
An vniuersall SYNOD of All sweets ;
By whom it is defined Thus
          That no Perfume
          For euer shall presume
To passe for Odoriferous,   180
But such alone whose sacred Pedigree
Can proue it Self some kin (sweet name) to Thee.
SWEET NAME, in Thy each Syllable
A Thousand Blest ARABIAS dwell ;
A Thousand Hills of Frankincense ;
Mountains of myrrh, & Beds of spices,
And ten Thousand PARADISES
The soul that tasts thee takes from thence.
How many vnknown WORLDS there are
Of Comforts, which Thou hast in keeping !   190
How many Thousand Mercyes there
In Pitty's soft lap ly a sleeping !
Happy he who has the art
          To awake them,
          And to take them
Home, & lodge them in his HEART.
O that it were as it was wont to be !
When thy old Freinds of Fire, All full of Thee,
Fought against Frowns with smiles ; gaue Glorious chase
To Persecutions ; And against the Face   200
Of DEATH & feircest Dangers, durst with Braue
And sober pace march on to meet A GRAVE.
On their Bold BRESTS about the world they bore thee
And to the Teeth of Hell stood vp to teach thee,
In Center of their inmost Soules they wore thee,
Where Rackes & Torments striu'd, in vain, to reach thee.
          Little, alas, thought They
Who tore the Fair Brests of thy Freinds,

186 spices *48* : species *52*   188 soul that] soules tastes *48*
thence. *48* : thence *52*   203 bore] bare *48*   205 wore] ware *48*

Their Fury but made way
For Thee ; And seru'd therein Thy glorious ends.   210
What did Their weapons but with wider pores
Inlarge thy flaming-brested Louers
      More freely to transpire
      That impatient Fire
The Heart that hides Thee hardly couers.
What did their Weapons but sett wide the Doores
For Thee : Fair, purple Doores, of loue's deuising ;
The Ruby windowes which inrich't the EAST
Of Thy so oft repeated Rising.
Each wound of Theirs was Thy new Morning ;   220
And reinthron'd thee in thy Rosy Nest,
With blush of thine own Blood thy day adorning,
It was the witt of loue o'reflowd the Bounds
Of WRATH, & made thee way through All Those WOVNDS.
Wellcome dear, All-Adored Name !
      For sure there is no Knee
      That knowes not THEE.
Or if there be such sonns of shame,
      Alas what will they doe
      When stubborn Rocks shall bow   230
And Hills hang down their Heaun-saluting Heads
      To seek for humble Beds
Of Dust, where in the Bashfull shades of night
Next to their own low NOTHING they may ly,
And couch before the dazeling light of thy dread majesty.
They that by Loue's mild Dictate now
      Will not adore thee,
Shall Then with Iust Confusion, bow
      And break before thee.

210 therein *48* : them in *52*   ends. *48* ends *52*   223 o'reflowd]
óreflowd *52*   228 Or] Oh *48*   235 majesty.] Majesty ? *48*
239 thee. *48* : thee *52*

IN

THE HOLY

NATIVITY

OF

OVR LORD GOD

A

HYMN

SVNG AS BY THE

SHEPHEARDS.

In the Holy Nativity &c. For version in 1646 and collation with MSS. see p. 106, above. 52 generally follows 48, with exceptions given below. Heading in 48 : An Hymne of the Nativity, sung as by the Shepheards.

Ton Createur te fuict voir sa naissance,
Daignant souffrir pour toy des son enfance.

Quem vidistis Pastores? &c.

Natum vidimus &c.

THE
HYMN.

CHORVS.

COme we shepheards whose blest Sight
Hath mett loue's Noon in Nature's night ;
   Come lift we vp our loftyer Song
And wake the Svn that lyes too long.

To all our world of well-stoln joy
   He slept ; and dream't of no such thing.
While we found out Heaun's fairer ey
   And Kis't the Cradle of our King.
Tell him He rises now, too late
To show vs ought worth looking at.   10

Tell him we now can show Him more
   Then He e're show'd to mortall Sight ;
Then he Himselfe e're saw before ;
   Which to be seen needes not His light.
Tell him, Tityrus, where th'hast been
Tell him, Thyrsis, what th'hast seen.

Tityrus. Gloomy night embrac't the Place
   Where The Noble Infant lay.
The Babe look't vp & shew'd his Face ;
   In spite of Darknes, it was Day.   20
It was Thy day, Sweet ! & did rise
Not from the East, but from thine Eyes.

        Chorus   It was Thy day, Sweet

Thyrs. Winter chidde aloud ; & sent
   The angry North to wage his warres.
The North forgott his feirce Intent ;
   And left perfumes in stead of scarres.
By those sweet eyes' persuasiue powrs
Where he mean't frost, he scatter'd flowrs.

        Chorus   By those sweet eyes'   30

---

2 Noon] noone, *48*   4 *After this, 52 indents ll. 1, 3, and 5 of each stanza*
16 Thyrsis *48* : Thysis *52*   th'hast] th-hast *52*   23 Sweet] sweet,
&c. 48   28 eyes'] eyes *48* : eye's *52* (*cp. l. 30*)   30 eyes']
Eyes, *&c. 48*

Both. We saw thee in thy baulmy Nest,
 Young dawn of our æternall DAY !
We saw thine eyes break from their EASTE
 And chase the trembling shades away.
We saw thee ; & we blest the sight
We saw thee by thine own sweet light.

Tity. Poor WORLD (said I.) what wilt thou doe
 To entertain this starry STRANGER ?
Is this the best thou canst bestow ?
 A cold, and not too cleanly, manger ?   40
Contend, ye powres of heau'n & earth.
To fitt a bed for this huge birthe.

 Cho.   Contend ye powers

Thyr. Proud world, said I ; cease your contest
 And let the MIGHTY BABE alone.
The Phænix builds the Phænix' nest.
 Love's architecture is his own.
The BABE whose birth embraues this morn,
Made his own bed e're he was born.

 Cho.   The BABE whose.   50

Tit. I saw the curl'd drops, soft & slow,
 Come houering o're the place's head ;
Offring their whitest sheets of snow
 To furnish the fair INFANT's bed
Forbear, said I ; be not too bold.
Your fleece is white But t'is too cold.

 Cho.   Forbear, sayd I

Thyr. I saw the obsequious SERAPHIMS
 Their rosy fleece of fire bestow.
For well they now can spare their wings   60
 Since HEAVN itself lyes here below.

  32 Young] Bright *48*   33 EASTE] EATE *52*   41 ye *48* : the
52   earth.] earth *48*   43 ye *48* : the *52*   powers] Powers,
&c. 48   44 *Thyr.*] *Thyt. 52*   47 Love's] Lov's *52*   47
his own.] all one *48*   48 morn,] morn. *52 morne, 48*   50
BABE whose.] Babe *&c. 48*   51 *Tit.*] *Tir. 52*   54 bed] Bed :
48   56 cold. *48* : cold *52*   57 sayd I] (said I,) *&c. 48*
58 SERAPHIMS] *Seraphins 48*   60 wings *48* : wing. *52*

Well done, said I : but are you sure
Your down so warm, will passe for pure ?

   Cho. Well done sayd I

Tit. No no. your KING's not yet to seeke
 Where to repose his Royall HEAD
See see, how soon his new-bloom'd CHEEK
 Twixt's mother's brests is gone to bed.
Sweet choise, said we ! no way but so
Not to ly cold, yet sleep in snow.   70

   Cho. Sweet choise, said we.

Both. We saw thee in thy baulmy nest,
 Bright dawn of our æternall Day !
We saw thine eyes break from their EAST
 And chase the trembling shades away.
We saw thee : & we blest the sight.
We saw thee, by thine own sweet light.

   Cho. We saw thee, &c.

   FVLL CHORVS.

Wellcome, all WONDERS in one sight !
 Æternity shutt in a span.   80
Sommer in Winter. Day in Night.
 Heauen in earth, & GOD in MAN.
Great little one ! whose all-embracing birth
Lifts earth to heauen, stoopes heau'n to earth.

WELLCOME. Though nor to gold nor silk.
 To more then Cæsar's birthright is ;
Two sister-seas of Virgin-Milk,
 With many a rarely-temper'd kisse
That breathes at once both MAID & MOTHER,
Warmes in the one, cooles in the other.   90

WELCOME, though not to those gay flyes.
 Guilded ith' Beames of earthly kings ;
 Slippery soules in smiling eyes ;
 But to poor Shepheards, home-spun things :

 64 sayd I] (said we,) *&c. 48* 69 we] I *48* 70 sleep *48* : slep
52 71 choise, said we.] choice, *&c. 48* 74 their] thir *52* 85
nor to] not to *48* silk.] silke, *48* 89 breathes] brearhes *52*
After stanza ending at l. 90, 48 inserts that beginning She sings thy
Teares a sleep *as in 46.* 91–108 *in three stanzas of six lines each
in 48*

Whose Wealth's their flock ; whose witt, to be
  Well read in their simplicity.
Yet when young April's husband showrs
  Shall blesse the fruitfull Maja's bed
We'l bring the First-born of her flowrs
  To kisse thy FEET & crown thy HEAD. 100
To thee, dread lamb ! whose loue must keep
  The shepheards, more then they the sheep.
To THEE, meek Majesty ! soft KING
  Of simple GRACES & sweet LOVES.
Each of vs his lamb will bring
  Each his pair of sylver Doues ;
Till burnt at last in fire of Thy fair eyes,
  Our selues become our own best SACRIFICE.

NEW YEAR'S

DAY.

RIse, thou best & brightest morning !
  Rosy with a double Red ;
  With thine own blush thy cheeks adorning
    And the dear drops this day were shed.

All the purple pride that laces
  The crimson curtains of thy bed,
Guilds thee not with so sweet graces
  Nor setts thee in so rich a red.

Of all the fair-cheek't flowrs that fill thee
  None so fair thy bosom strowes, 10
As this modest maiden lilly
  Our sins haue sham'd into a rose.

Bid thy golden GOD, the Sun,
  Burnisht in his best beames rise,
Put all his red-ey'd Rubies on ;
  These Rubies shall putt out their eyes.

102 the sheep] their sheepe *48*   104 LOVES.] *Loves ; 48*
  New Year's Day. For different version in 46 see p. 141, above.
Heading in 48 as 46 except ' A Hymne' for ' An Himne' ; otherwise 48
generally agrees with 52. 52 indents ll. 1 and 3 of each stanza.   10
strowes] showes *48*   12 rose. *48* : rose *52*   16 These] Those *48*

Let him make poor the purple east,
 Search what the world's close cabinets keep,
Rob the rich births of each bright nest
 That flaming in their fair beds sleep,   20

Let him embraue his own bright tresses
 With a new morning made of gemmes ;
And wear, in those his wealthy dresses,
 Another Day of Diadems.

When he hath done all he may
 To make himselfe rich in his rise,
All will be darknes to the Day
 That breakes from one of these bright eyes.

And soon this sweet truth shall appear
 Dear BABE, ere many dayes be done,   30
The morn shall come to meet thee here,
 And leaue her own neglected Sun.

Here are Beautyes shall bereaue him
 Of all his eastern Paramours.
His Persian Louers all shall leaue him,
 And swear faith to thy sweeter Powres.

---

21 embraue] embrace *48*   31 morn] Moon *48* to] and *48*
After l. 36 48 adds the concluding couplet given in 46.

IN

THE GLORIOVS

EPIPHANIE

OF OVR LORD

GOD,

A HYMN.

SVNG AS BY THE

THREE KINGS

In the Glorious &c. First printed in 48, with heading : A Hymne for the Epiphanie. *Sung as by the three Kings.*

(1. *K I N G E.*)

B Right BABE ! Whose awfull beautyes make
The morn incurr a sweet mistake ;
(2.) For whom the'officious heauns deuise
To disinheritt the sun's rise,
(3.) Delicately to displace
The Day, & plant it fairer in thy face ;
[1.] O thou born KING of loues,
            [2.] Of lights,
            [3.] Of ioyes !
(*Cho.*) Look vp, sweet BABE, look vp & see   10
            For loue of Thee
            Thus farr from home
            The EAST is come
To seek her self in thy sweet Eyes
(1.) We, who strangely went astray,
            Lost in a bright
            Meridian night,
(2.) A Darkenes made of too much day,
            (3.) Becken'd from farr
            By thy fair starr,   20
Lo at last haue found our way.
(*Cho.*) To THEE, thou DAY of night ! thou east of west !
Lo we at last haue found the way.

ll. 1–6 not assigned to the three separate kings in 48   23 way.] way : *48*

To thee, the world's great vniuersal east.
The Generall & indifferent DAY.
(1.) All-circling point. All centring sphear.
The world's one, round, Æternall year.
(2.) Whose full & all-vnwrinkled face
Nor sinks nor swells with time or place ;
(3.) But euery where & euery while   30
Is One Consistent solid smile ;
   (1.) Not vext & tost
   (2.) 'Twixt spring & frost,
(3.) Nor by alternate shredds of light
Sordidly shifting hands with shades & night.
(*Cho.*) O little all ! in thy embrace
The world lyes warm, & likes his place.
Nor does his full Globe fail to be
Kist on Both his cheeks by Thee.
Time is too narrow for thy YEAR   40
Nor makes the whole WORLD thy half-sphear.
   (1.) To Thee, to Thee
   From him we flee
(2.) From HIM, whom by a more illustrious ly,
The blindnes of the world did call the eye ;
(3.) To HIM, who by These mortall clouds hast made
Thy self our sun, though thine own shade.
(1.) Farewell, the world's false light.
   Farewell, the white
   Ægypt ! a long farewell to thee   50
   Bright IDOL ; black IDOLATRY.
The dire face of inferior DARKNES, kis't
And courted in the pompous mask of a more specious mist.
   (2.) Farewell, farewell
   The proud & misplac't gates of hell,
   Pertch't, in the morning's way
And double-guilded as the doores of DAY.
The deep hypocrisy of DEATH & NIGHT
More desperately dark, Because more bright.
   (3.) Welcome, the world's sure Way ! 60
   HEAVN'S wholsom ray.
   (*Cho.*) Wellcome to vs ; and we
   (SWEET) to our selues, in THEE.

41 sphear] spear *52* *l.* 48 (1)] (2.) *52* 1. *48* world's] wold's *52*
53 pompous *48*: pompus *52*

(1.) The deathles HEIR of all thy FATHER's day !
　　　(2.) Decently Born.
Embosóm'd in a much more Rosy MORN,
The Blushes of thy All-vnblemish't mother.
　　　(3.) No more that other
　　　Aurora shall sett ope
Her ruby casements, or hereafter hope　　　　　　　　70
　　　From mortall eyes
To meet Religious welcomes at her rise.
(*Cho.*) We (Pretious ones !) in you haue won
A gentler MORN, a iuster sun.
(1.) His superficiall Beames sun-burn't our skin ;
　　　(2.) But left within
(3.) The night & winter still of death & sin.
(*Cho.*) Thy softer yet more certaine DARTS
Spare our eyes, but peirce our HARTS.
(1.) Therefore with His proud persian spoiles　　　80
(2.) We court thy more concerning smiles.
　　　(3.) Therfore with his Disgrace
We guild the humble cheek of this chast place ;
(*Cho.*) And at thy FEET powr forth his FACE.
(1.) The doating nations now no more
Shall any day but THINE adore.
(2.) Nor (much lesse) shall they leaue these eyes
For cheap Ægyptian Deityes.
(3.) In whatsoe're more Sacred shape　　　　　　　90
Of Ram, He-goat, or reuerend ape,
Those beauteous rauishers opprest so sore
The too-hard-tempted nations.
　　　(1.) Neuer more
By wanton heyfer shall be worn
(2.) A Garland, or a guilded horn.
The altar-stall'd ox, fatt OSYRIS now
　　　With his fair sister cow,
(3.) Shall kick the clouds no more ; But lean & tame,
(*Cho.*) See his horn'd face, & dy for shame.　　　100
And MITHRA now shall be no name.
(1.) No longer shall the immodest lust
Of Adulterous GODLES dust

[handwritten margin note: Christ new sun — loue not visuall but internal]

---

　83 this] thy *48*　　　95 worn *48 :* worn. *52*　　99–101 *48 places 3
before* But lean and tame *which has a separate line, and l. 101 only is
assigned to the Chorus.*

(2.) <u>Fly in the face of heau'n</u> ; As if it were
The poor world's Fault that he is fair.
(3.) Nor with peruerse loues & Religious RAPES
Reuenge thy Bountyes in their beauteous shapes ;
And <u>punish Best</u> Things worst ; <u>Because they stood</u>
<u>Guilty of being much for them too Good.</u>
[I.] Proud sons of death ! that durst compell   110
Heau'n it self to find them hell ;
[2.] And by strange witt of madnes wrest
From this world's EAST the other's WEST.
[3.] <u>All-Idolizing wormes</u> ! that thus could crowd
And <u>vrge Their sun into</u> thy cloud ;
Forcing his sometimes eclips'd face to be
A long deliquium to the light of thee.
[*Cho.*] Alas with how much heauyer shade
The shamefac't lamp hung down his head
     For that one eclipse he made   120
     Then all those he suffered !
[1.] For this he look't so bigg ; & euery morn
With a red face confes't this scorn.
Or hiding his vex't cheeks in a hir'd mist
Kept them from being so vnkindly kis't.
[2.] It was for this the day did rise
     So oft with blubber'd eyes.
For this the euening wept ; and we ne're knew
     But call'd it deaw.
     [3.] This dayly wrong   130
Silenc't the morning-sons, & damp't their song
[*Cho.*] Nor was't our deafnes, but our sins, that thus
Long made th'Harmonious orbes all mute to vs
     [1.] Time has a day in store
     When this so proudly poor
And self-oppressed spark, that has so long
By the loue-sick world bin made
Not so much their sun as SHADE,
     Weary of this Glorious wrong
From them & from himself shall flee   140
For shelter to the shadow of thy TREE ;

104 ' *2* ' *begins at* As if *48*   112 witt] will *48*   123 this] his
48   131 morning-sons,] morning *Suns* ; *48*   song] song ; *48*   133
vs] us. *48*   134 [1.] *So 48* : [2.] *52*   137 loue-sick *48* : loue-sick, *52*
  917·9   S

[*Cho.*] Proud to haue gain'd this pretious losse
And chang'd his false crown for thy CROSSE.
[2.] That dark Day's clear doom shall define
Whose is the Master FIRE, which sun should shine.
That sable Iudgment-seat shall by new lawes
Decide & settle the Great cause
   Of controuerted light,
[*Cho.*] And na'tur's wrongs rejoyce to doe thee Right.
[3.] That forfeiture of noon to night shall pay   150
All the idolatrous thefts done by this night of day ;
And the Great Penitent presse his own pale lipps
With an elaborate loue-eclipse
   To which the low world's lawes
   Shall lend no cause
[*Cho.*] Saue those domestick which he borrowes
From our sins & his own sorrowes.
[1.] Three sad hour's sackcloth then shall show to vs
His penance, as our fault, conspicuous.
[2.] And he more needfully & nobly proue   160
The nation's terror now then erst their loue.
[3.] Their hated loues changd into wholsom feares,
[*Cho.*] The shutting of his eye shall open Theirs.
[1.] As by a fair-ey'd fallacy of day
Miss-ledde before they lost their way,
So shall they, by the seasonable fright
Of an vnseasonable night,
Loosing it once again, stumble'on true LIGHT
[2.] And as before his too-bright eye
Was Their more blind idolatry,   170
So his officious blindnes now shall be
Their black, but faithfull perspectiue of thee ;
   [3.] His new prodigious night,
Their new & admirable light ;
The supernaturall DAWN of Thy pure day.
   While wondring they
(The happy conuerts now of him
Whom they compell'd before to be their sin)
   Shall henceforth see

---

144 clear] deere *48* 146 Iudgment] ludgment *52* 156
domestick] domesticks *48* 158 sad hour's] sad-houres *48*
162 loues] love's *48* 164 [1.] *So 48* : [2.] *52* 168 LIGHT]
light. *48* 171 blindnes] blindines *52* 175 day.] day, *48*

To kisse him only as their rod   180
Whom they so long courted as GOD,
[*Cho.*] And their best vse of him they worship't be
To learn of Him at lest, to worship Thee.
[1.] It was their Weaknes woo'd his beauty ;
            But it shall be
Their wisdome now, as well as duty,
To'injoy his Blott ; & as a large black letter
Vse it to spell Thy beautyes better ;
And make the night it self their torch to thee.
[2.] By the oblique ambush of this close night   190
            Couch't in that conscious shade
The right-ey'd Areopagite
Shall with a vigorous guesse inuade
And catche thy quick reflex ; and sharply see
            On this dark Ground
            To descant THEE.
[3.] O prize of the rich SPIRIT ! with what feirce chase
            Of his strong soul, shall he
            Leap at thy lofty FACE,
And seize the swift Flash, in rebound   200
From this obsequious cloud ;
            Once call'd a sun ;
            Till dearly thus vndone,
[*Cho.*] Till thus triumphantly tam'd (o ye two
Twinne SVNNES !) & taught now to negotiate you.
[1.] Thus shall that reuerend child of light,
[2.] By being scholler first of that new night,
Come forth Great master of the mystick day ;
[3.] And teach obscure MANKIND a more close way
By the frugall negatiue light   210
Of a most wise & well-abused Night
To lead more legible thine originall Ray,
[*Cho.*] And make our Darknes serue THY day ;
Maintaining t'wixt thy world & ours
A commerce of contrary powres,

---

182 their] the *48*   183 learni *48* : learn, *52*   lest,] least *48*
184 [1.] *So 48* : [2.] *52*   188 Vse it] Vse *48*   189 it *48* : in *52*
torch *48* : rorch *52*   191 that] the *48*   195 Ground] Grouud *52*
196 descant *48* : dscant *52*   197 what *48* : that *52*   198 his *48* :
this *52*   200 seize] scize *52*   201 obsequious] ohsequious *52*
205 you : *48* you *52*   209 *48 places* ' 3 ' *before l.* 208   210
negatiue] negat ne *52*

A mutuall trade
'Twixt sun & SHADE,
By confederat BLACK & WHITE
Borrowing day & lending night.
[1.] Thus we, who when with all the noble powres   220
That (at thy cost) are call'd, not vainly, ours
            We vow to make braue way
Vpwards, & presse on for the pure intelligentiall Prey;
            [2.] At lest to play
            The amorous Spyes
And peep & proffer at thy sparkling Throne;
[3.] In stead of bringing in the blissfull PRIZE
            And fastening on Thine eyes,
            Forfeit our own
            And nothing gain   230
But more Ambitious losse, at lest of brain;
[*Cho.*] Now by abased liddes shall learn to be
Eagles; and shutt our eyes that we may see.

The Close.

Therfore to THEE & thine Auspitious ray
            (Dread sweet!) lo thus
            At lest by vs,
The delegated EYE of DAY
Does first his Scepter, then HIMSELF in solemne Tribute pay.
            Thus he vndresses
            His sacred vnshorn tresses;   240
At thy adored FEET, thus, he layes down
            [1.] His gorgeous tire
            Of flame & fire,
[2.] His glittering ROBE, [3.] his sparkling CROWN,
[1.] His GOLD, [2.] his MIRRH, [3.] his FRANKINCENCE,
[*Cho.*] To which He now has no pretence.
For being show'd by this day's light, how farr
He is from sun enough to make THY starr,
His best ambition now, is but to be
Somthing a brighter SHADOW [sweet] of thee.   250

---

    223 for *48*: for, *52*   240 tresses *48*: treses *52*   242 gorgeous]
glorious *48*   245 [1.] His *48*: [3.] His *52*   245 *is printed in 48*:
1. His *Gold,* His (2.) *Myrrh,* (3.) *Frankincense,*

Or on heaun's azure forhead high to stand
Thy golden index ; with a duteous Hand
Pointing vs Home to our own sun
The world's & his HYPERION.

TO THE

QVEEN'S

MAIESTY.

MADAME.
'Mongst those long rowes of crownes that guild your race,
These Royall sages sue for decent place.
The day-break of the nations ; their first ray ;
When the Dark WORLD dawn'd into Christian DAY
And smil'd i'th' BABE's bright face, the purpling Bud
And Rosy dawn of the right Royall blood ;
Fair first-fruits of the LAMB. Sure KINGS in this ;
They took a kingdom while they gaue a kisse.
But the world's Homage, scarse in These well blown,
We read in you (Rare Queen) ripe & full-grown.   10
For from this day's rich seed of Diadems
Does rise a radiant croppe of Royalle stemms,
A Golden haruest of crown'd heads, that meet
And crowd for kisses from the LAMB's white feet.
In this Illustrious throng, your lofty floud
Swells high, fair Confluence of all highborn Bloud !
With your bright head whole groues of scepters bend
Their wealthy tops ; & for these feet contend.
So swore the LAMB's dread sire. And so we see't.
Crownes, & the HEADS they kisse, must court these FEET. 20

To the Qveen's Maiesty. *First printed in 48 with heading : To the*
Queenes Majestie upon his dedicating to her the foregoing Hymne. Heading
in 70 : To the Queen's Majesty on Twelfth Day.   1 crownes *48* :
cownes *52*   race, *48* : race. *52*   4 DAY] DAY. *52* : day *48*
5 face, the *48* : face. the *52*   6 dawn] down *48*   10 read] wade
48   Rare] deare *48*   13 Golden] Royall *48*   17 whole
48 : whose *52*   19 dread] great *48*

Fix here, fair Majesty ! May your Heart ne're misse
To reap new CROWNES & KINGDOMS from that kisse.
Nor may we misse the ioy to meet in you
The aged honors of this day still new.
May the great time, in you, still greater be
While all the YEAR is your EPIPHANY,
While your each day's deuotion duly brings
Three K I N G D O M E S to supply this day's three KINGS.

THE

OFFICE

OF

THE HO

L Y

CROSSE

The Office, &c. First published in 48 in a compressed form, omitting all
the versicles and responses with their repetitions, and giving (first) only the
' Hymns' for each service arranged in consecutive stanzas. There follow
(1) The last Antiphon, headed The Antiphona. (O Save us then, &c.)
(2) The Recommendation, headed The recõmendation of the precedent
Poems. (3) The Prayer, headed A Prayer. (4) The Antiphons for the
third, sixth, and ninth hours with the heading Christs victory. General
heading for the hymn stanzas : Vpon our B. Saviours Passion. MS. A1.
Heading in A1 : The office of the Holy Crosse | ffor the Houre of
Matines

Tradidit semetipsum pro nobis oblationem, et
hostiam Deo in odorem Suauitatis.   ad Ephi. 5

THE

HOWRES

FOR THE HOVR OF

MATINES.

The Versicle.

LORD, by thy Sweet & Sauing SIGN,

The Responsory.

Defend us from our foes & Thine.

℣. Thou shalt open my lippes, O LORD.

℟. And my mouth shall shew forth thy Prayse.

℣. O GOD make speed to saue me.

℟. O LORD make hast to help me.

GLORY be to the FATHER,
      and to the SON,
      and to the H. GHOST.

  As it was in the beginning, is now, & euer shall be, world
without end.   Amen.

THE HYMN.

THe wakefull Matines hast to sing
    The vnknown sorrows of our king,
The FATHER's word & wisdom, made
MAN, for man, by man's betraid ;
The world's price sett to sale, & by the bold
Merchants of Death & sin, is bought & sold.
Of his Best Freinds (yea of himself) forsaken,
By his worst foes (because he would) beseig'd & taken.

  3–11 ℣. *Thou shalt . . .* Amen. *omitted in A1.*   3 shalt] shallt *52*
4 shew forth] declare *70*   *Hymn.* 1 Matines] dawning *48* : minuits
A1   hast] hast's *48*   sing *48 A1*: sing, *52*   3 FATHER'S] FATHER'
52 A1: Fathers *48*   8 beseig'd] betrayd *48*

The Antiphona.

All hail, fair TREE.
Whose Fruit we be.
What song shall raise
Thy seemly praise.
Who broughtst to light
Life out of death, Day out of night.

The Versicle.

Lo, we adore thee,
Dread LAMB ! And bow thus low before thee,

The Responsor.

'Cause, by the couenant of thy CROSSE,
Thou'hast sau'd at once the whole world's losse.

The Prayer.

O Lord I E S V - C H R I S T, son of the liuing GOD ! inter-
pose, I pray thee, thine own pretious death, thy CROSSE
& Passion, betwixt my soul & thy iudgment, now & in the
hour of my death.   And vouchsafe to graunt vnto me thy
grace & mercy ; vnto all quick & dead, remission & rest ; to
thy church peace & concord ; to vs sinners life & glory euerlasting.   Who liuest and reignest with the FATHER, in the
vnity of the HOLY GHOST, one GOD, world without end.
Amen.

The Antiphona.] *The Antiphon. 70. The variants in 70 given here apply
also to the subsequent repetitions.*   The Prayer *omitted in A1.*   1
O Lord] O My Lord *70*   IESV-] *Jesus 48*   4 vnto me] me *70*
5 mercy . . . remission] *mercie, remission 48*   vnto all quick
& dead] to the living and dead *70*   6–7 to thy] *To the 48*

FOR THE HOVR OF
PRIME.

The Versicle.

Lord by thy sweet & sauing SIGN.

The Responsor.

Defend vs from our foes & thine.

℣. Thou shalt open.

℟. And my mouth.

℣. O GOD make speed.

℟. O LORD make hast.

Glory be to.

As it was in.

THE HYMN.

THe early PRIME blushes to say
  She could not rise so soon, as they
Call'd Pilat vp ; to try if He
Could lend them any cruelty.
  Their hands with lashes arm'd, their toungs with lyes,
And loathsom spittle, blott those beauteous eyes,
The blissfull springs of ioy ; from whose all-chearing Ray
The fair starrs fill their wakefull fires the sun himselfe drinks
    Day.

The Antiphona.

Victorious S I G N
That now dost shine,
Transcrib'd aboue
Into the land of light & loue ;
O let vs twine
Our rootes with thine,
That we may rise
Vpon thy wings, & reach the skyes.

For the Hovr of Prime. A1 begins at l. 1 of the Hymn, omitting Versicles and Responses. 70 completes the sentences assigned to the ℣ and ℟. Hymn. 1 PRIME] Morne *48*   2 She] It *48*   5 lyes, *48* : lyes. *52* : lyes *A1*   6 spittle, blott] spittle blotts *48*   8 himselfe] himfelfe *52*   *Antiphona*] *Antiphoua 52*

The Versicle.

Lo we adore thee
Dread LAMB ! and fall
Thus low before thee

The Responsor.

'Cause by the Conuenant of thy CROSSE
Thou'hast sau'd at once the whole world's losse.

The Prayer.

O Lord I E S V - C H R I S T son of the liuing GOD ! inter-
pose, I pray thee, thine own pretious death, thy CROSSE
& Passion, betwixt my soul & thy iudgment, now & in the
hour of my death. And vouchsafe to graunt vnto me thy
grace & mercy ; vnto all quick & dead, remission & rest ; to
thy church peace & concord ; to vs sinners life & glory euerlasting. Who liuest and reignest with the FATHER, in the
vnity of the HOLY GHOST, one GOD, world without end.
Amen.

THE THIRD.

The Versicle.

Lord, by thy sweet & sauing SIGN

The Responsor.

Defend vs from our foes & thine.
℣. Thou shalt open.
℟. And my mouth.
℣. O GOD make speed.
℟. O LORD make hast.
℣. Glory be to.
℟. As it was in the.

THE HYMN.

THe Third hour's deafen'd with the cry
Of crucify him, crucify.
So goes the vote (nor ask them, Why ?)
Liue Barabbas ! & let GOD dy.

Responsor 2 losse.] losse *52*   *Prayer*] *Prayer 52*   *The Prayer omitted
in A1.*   1 Lord] Lrod*52*   GOD] OOD *52*
    The Third.] The Third Howre *A1, followed immediately by* The Hymne
Hymn. 3 goes] goeth *A1*

But there is witt in wrath, and they will try
A HAIL more cruell then their crucify.
For while in sport he weares a spitefull crown,
The serious showres along his decent
   Face run sadly down.

The Antiphona.

CHRIST when he dy'd
Deceiud the CROSSE ;
And on death's side
Threw all the losse.
The captiue world awak't, & found
The prisoners loose, the Iaylor bound.

The Versicle.

Lo we adore thee
Dread L A M B, & fall
  thus low before thee

The Responsor.

'Cause by the conuenant of thy C R O S S E
Thou'hast sau'd at once the whole world's losse.

The Prayer.

O Lord I E S V-C H R I S T, son of the liuing GOD ! inter-
pose, I pray thee, thine own pretious death, thy CROSSE
& Passion, betwixt my soul & thy iudgment, now & in the
hour of my death. And vouchsafe to graunt vnto me thy
grace & mercy ; vnto all quick and dead, remission & rest ;
to thy church peace & concord ; to vs sinners life & glory euerlasting. Who liuest and reignest with the FATHER, in the
vnity of the HOLY GHOST, one GOD, world without end.
Amen.

---

6 then *48* : them *52* 8 The serious . . . sadly down *As one
line in 48 A1* *The Antiphona.* 2 the] rhe *52* side *48 A1* :
side. *52* Iaylor *48 A1* : Ialyor *52* *Resp.* 2 world's] word's *52*
The Prayer omitted in A1. 8 world] vorld *52*

THE SIXT.

The Versicle.

Lord by thy sweet & sauing SIGN,

The Responsor.

Defend vs from our foes & thine.

℣. Thou shalt open.

℟. And my mouth.

℣. O GOD make speed.

℟. O LORD make hast.

℣. Glory be

℟. As it was in

THE HIMN.

NOw is The noon of sorrow's night ;
  High in his patience, as their spite.
Lo the faint LAMB, with weary limb
Beares that huge tree which must bear Him.
That fatall plant, so great of fame
For fruit of sorrow & of shame,
Shall swell with both for HIM ; & mix
All woes into one CRVCIFIX.
Is tortur'd Thirst, it selfe, too sweet a cup ?
GALL, & more bitter mocks, shall make it vp.
Are NAILES blunt pens of superficiall smart ?
Contempt & scorn can send sure wounds to search the inmost
    Heart.

The Antiphona.

O deare & sweet Dispute
'Twixt death's & Loue's farr different FRVIT !
    Different as farr
As antidotes & poysons are.
    By that first fatall TREE
    Both life & liberty
    Were sold and slain ;
By this they both look vp, & liue again.

The Sixt.] The sixt Howre *A1, followed immediately by* The Hymne
Hymn. 3 Lo] For *48*   4 which] must *A1*   6 For] The *48*
   Ant. 2 death's] death *A1*   5 that] the *48 A1*

The Versicle.

Lo we adore thee
Dread LAMB ! & bow thus low before thee ;

The Responsor.

'Cause by the conuenant of thy CROSSE.
Thou'hast sau'd the world from certain losse.

The Prayer.

O Lord I E S V-C H R I S T, son of the liuing GOD ! inter-
pose, I pray thee, thine own pretious death, thy CROSSE
& Passion, betwixt my soul & thy iudgment, now & in the
hour of my death. And vouchsafe to graunt vnto me thy
grace & mercy ; vnto all quick & dead, remission & rest ; to
thy church peace & concord ; to vs sinners life & glory euerlasting. Who liuest and reignest with the FATHER, in the
vnity of the HOLY GHOST, one GOD, world without end.
Amen.

THE NINTH.

The Versicle.

Lord by thy sweet & sauing SIGN.

The Responsor.

Defend vs from our foes & thine.
℣. Thou shalt open.
℟. And my mouth.
℣. O GOD make speed.
℟. O LORD make hast.
　　Glory be to.
　　As it was in.

THE HYMN.

THe ninth with awfull horror hearkened to those groanes
Which taught attention eu'n to rocks & stones.
Hear, FATHER, hear ! thy LAMB (at last) complaines.
Of some more painfull thing then all his paines.
Then bowes his all-obedient head, & dyes
His own loue's, & our sin's GREAT SACRIFICE.

The Prayer omitted in A1
The Ninth.] The Ninth Howre *A1 followed immediately by* The Hymne
Hymn 2 rocks] roeks *52*　　4 painfull] painsull *52*　　6 loue's]
lou's *52*　　sin's GREAT] great sins *48*

The sun saw That ; And would haue seen no more ;
The center shook.   Her vselesse veil th'inglorious Temple
   tore.

The Antiphona.

O strange mysterious strife
Of open DEATH & hidden LIFE !
When on the crosse my king did bleed,
LIFE seem'd to dy, DEATH dy'd indeed.

The Versicle.

Lo we adore thee
Dread LAMB ! and fall
   thus low before thee

The Responsor.

'Cause by the conuenant of thy C R O S S E
Thou'hast sau'd at once the whole world's losse.

The Prayer.

O Lord I E S V-C H R I S T, son of the liuing GOD ! inter-
pose, I pray thee, thine own pretious death, thy CROSSE
& Passion, betwixt my soul & thy iudgment, now & in the
hour of my death.   And vouchsafe to graunt vnto me thy
grace & mercy ; vnto all quick and dead, remission & rest ;
to thy church peace & concord ; to vs sinners life & glory euerlasting.   Who liuest and reignest with the FATHER, in the
vnity of the HOLY GHOST, one GOD, world without end.
Amen.

7 no more ; *48* no more *52*   · 8 veil] veile, 48   *Vers.* 2 Dread]
Deard *52*   *Resp.* 2 world's] word's *52*.   *The Prayer omitted in A1*

EVENSONG.

The Versicle.

Lord, by thy sweet & sauing SIGN

The Responsor.

Defend vs from our foes & thine.

℣. Thou shalt open.

℟. And my mouth.

℣. O GOD make speed.

℟. O LORD make hast.

℣. Glory be to.

℟. As it was in the.

THE HYMN.

BVt there were Rocks would not relent at This.
Lo, for their own hearts, they rend his.
Their deadly hate liues still ; & hath
A wild reserue of wanton wrath ;
Superfluous SPEAR ! But there's a HEART stands by
Will look no wounds be lost, no deaths shall dy.
Gather now thy Greif's ripe FRVIT. Great mother-maid !
Then sitt thee down, & sing thine Eu'nsong in the sad TREE'S
  shade.

The Antiphona.

O sad, sweet TREE !
Wofull & ioyfull we
Both weep & sing in shade of thee.
When the dear NAILES did lock
And graft into thy gracious Stock
The hope ; the health,
The worth, the wealth
Of all the ransom'd WORLD, thou hadst the power
(In that propitious Hour)
To poise each pretious limb,
And proue how light the World was, when it weighd with HIM.
Wide maist thou spred
Thine Armes ; And with thy bright & blisfull head

EVENSONG] The Euensonge *A1 followed immediately by* The Hymne
Hymn. 1 would] could *48* 8 thine] thy *A1*

O'relook all Libanus.   Thy lofty crown
The king himself is ; Thou his humble THRONE.
Where yeilding & yet conquering he
Prou'd a new path of patient Victory.
When wondring death by death was slain,
And our Captiuity his Captiue ta'ne.

The Versicle.

Lo we adore thee
Dread LAMB ! & bow thus low before thee ;

The Responsor.

'Cause by the conuenant of thy CROSSE.
Thou'hast sau'd the world from certain losse.

The Prayer.

O lord I E S V-C H R I S T, son of the liuing, &c. 272.

COMPLINE.

The Versicle.

Lord by thy sweet & sauing SIGN,

The Responsor.

Defend vs from our foes & thine.
℣. Thou shalt open.
℟. And my mouth.
℣. O GOD make speed.
℟. O LORD make hast.
℣. Glory be
℟. As it was in

THE HIMN.

THe Complin hour comes last, to call
Vs to our own LIVE's funerall.
Ah hartlesse task ! yet hope takes head ;
And liues in Him that here lyes dead.

*The Prayer omitted in A1. Prayer &c. 272] 42 is the original page
number given in 52*
Compline.] The Compline *A1 followed immediately by* The Hymne
Hymn. 1 Complin] Nightening *48*   3 Ah] A *48*   takes] taike (?)
A1

Run, MARY, run ! Bring hither all the BLEST
ARABIA, for thy Royall Phœnix' nest ;
Pour on thy noblest sweets, Which, when they touch
This sweeter BODY, shall indeed be such.
But must thy bed, lord, be a borow'd graue
Who lend'st to all things All the LIFE they haue.
O rather vse this HEART, thus farr a fitter STONE,
'Cause, though a hard & cold one, yet it is thine owne.   Amen.

The Antiphona.

O saue vs then
Mercyfull KING of men !
Since thou wouldst needs be thus
A SAVIOVR, & at such a rate, for vs ;
Saue vs, o saue vs, lord.
We now will own no shorter wish, nor name a narrower word.
Thy blood bids vs be bold.
Thy Wounds giue vs fair hold.
Thy Sorrows chide our shame.
Thy Crosse, thy Nature, & thy name
Aduance our claim
And cry with one accord
Saue them, o saue them, lord.

7 touch *48* : touch. *52*   11 HEART, *48* : HEART. *52*   12
hard] hard, *48*
Ant. 4 such a rate] such rate *48*   *A1 adds the prayer with*
heading : The Prayer wch ought to | be read after every | office

T 2

EXPOSTVLATIO IESV XPI. CVM MVNDO INGRATO.

SVM pulcher: at nemo tamen me diligit.
Sum nobilis, nemo est mihi qui seruiat:
Sum diues: a me nemo quacquam postulat:
Et cuncta possum: nemo me tamen timet:
Æternus ecce sto: quæror a paucissimis.
Prudensque sum: sed me quis est qui consulit:
Et sum via: at per me quotuscunque ambulat:
Sum veritas: quare mihi non creditur:
Sum vita: verum rarus est qui me petit.
Sum veri lux: videre me nemo cupit.
Sum misericors: nullus fidem in me collocat.
TV si peris, non id mihi imputes, Homo:
Salus tibi est a me parata: hac vtere. L. Vusteger excud.

THE
RECOMMENDATION.

THese Houres, & that which houer's o're my E N D,
Into thy hands, and hart, lord, I commend.

Take Both to Thine Account, that I & mine
In that Hour, & in these, may be all thine.

That as I dedicate my deuoutest BREATH
To make a kind of LIFE for my lord's DEATH,

So from his liuing, & life-giuing DEATH,
My dying LIFE may draw a new, & neuer fleeting BREATH.

The Recommendation. *No space between couplets in 48.* MS. A1
2 I] I, *52*   8 BREATH. 48 : BREATH *52*

VPON
THE
H. SEPVLCHER.

Here where our LORD once lay'd his Head,
Now the graue lyes Buryed.

VEXILLA REGIS,
THE
HYMN
OF THE HOLY
CROSSE.

I.

LOok vp, languishing Soul! Lo where the fair
  BADG of thy faith calls back thy care,
    And biddes thee ne're forget
    Thy life is one long Debt
Of loue to Him, who on this painfull TREE
Paid back the flesh he took for thee.

grief at
mon ('s)
inadequacy
his guilt

II.

  Lo, how the streames of life, from that full nest
  Of loues, thy lord's too liberall brest,

Vpon the H. Sepvlcher. *Also in 46 q.v., p. 86, above. MS. A1*
Vexilla Regis, *&c. First published in 48 (except st. 7, ll. 1–6) with*
heading Vexilla Regis. *MS. A1.* *Heading* 2 The] Or the *A1*
1·1 languishing] languisting *52* 1·5 loue] love, *48* 1·6 for]
from *A1* 2·2 thy] the *48*

Flow in an amorous floud
Of WATER wedding BLOOD.
With these he wash't thy stain, transfer'd thy smart,
And took it home to his own heart.

III.

But though great LOVE, greedy of such sad gain
Vsurp't the Portion of THY pain,
 And from the nailes & spear
 Turn'd the steel point of fear,
Their vse is chang'd, not lost ; and now they moue
Not stings of wrath, but wounds of loue.

IV.

Tall TREE of life ! thy truth makes good
What was till now ne're vnderstood,
 Though the prophetick king
 Struck lowd his faithfull string,
It was thy wood he meant should make the THRONE
For a more then SALOMON.

V.

Larg throne of loue ! Royally spred
With purple of too Rich a red.
 Thy crime is too much duty ;
 Thy Burthen, too much beauty ;
Glorious, or Greiuous more ? thus to make good
Thy costly excellence with thy KING'S own BLOOD.

VI.

Euen ballance of both worlds ! our world of sin,
And that of grace heaun way'd in HIM,
 Vs with our price thou weighed'st ;
 Our price for vs thou payed'st ;

3·5 move *48* : moue. *52* 3·6 wrath] warth *52* 4·4 string, *48* :
string. *52* 4·5 the] a *48* THRONE] TRHONE *52* 5·6 excel-
lence] crueltie *48* 6·2 way'd] wag'd *48* 6·3] Both with one
price were weighed, *48* 6·4 Both with one price were paid, *48*

Soon as the right-hand scale reioyc't to proue
How much Death weigh'd more light then loue.

VII.

Hail, our alone hope ! let thy fair head shoot
Aloft ; and fill the nations with thy noble fruit.
  The while our hearts & we
  Thus graft our selues on thee ;
Grow thou & they. And be thy fair increase
The sinner's pardon & the iust man's peace.

  Liue, o for euer liue & reign
The LAMB whom his own loue hath slain !
And let thy lost sheep liue to'inherit
That KINGDOM which this CROSSE did merit.
  A M E N.

[handwritten marginalia: ex halata, taxe for mon thru chris Ms. sacrifice]

TO OVR B. LORD

VPON THE CHOISE OF HIS

Sepulcher.

  How life & death in Thee
    Agree !
  Thou hadst a virgin womb,
    And tomb.
  A IOSEPH did betroth
    Them both.

7·1–6 *omitted in* 48   7·9 to'] *for* to 48 7·10 this
CROSSE] thy blessed death 48   To our B. Lord, &c. *Also in* 46
q.v., p. 93, above.

CHARITAS
NIMIA.
OR
THE
DEAR BARGAIN.

LOrd, what is man ? why should he coste thee
  So dear ? what had his ruin lost thee ?
Lord what is man ? that thou hast ouerbought
  So much a thing of nought ?

Loue is too kind, I see ; & can
Make but a simple merchant man.
'Twas for such sorry merchandise
Bold Painters haue putt out his Eyes.

Alas, sweet lord, what wer't to thee
If there were no such wormes as we ?   10
Heau'n ne're the lesse still heaun would be,
    Should Mankind dwell
    In the deep hell.
What haue his woes to doe with thee ?

    Let him goe weep
    O're his own wounds ;
    SERAPHIMS will not sleep
Nor spheares let fall their faithfull rounds.

    Still would The youthfull SPIRITS sing ;
And still thy spatious Palace ring.   20
Still would those beauteous ministers of light
        Burn all as bright,

And bow their flaming heads before thee
Still thrones & Dominations would adore thee

Charitas Nimia, &c. *First published in 48, with same heading, but without division into stanzas ; a space, however, precedes the last four lines.* 1 *and* 2 thee] you *48*   7 merchandise *48* : merchandise. *52* 13 hell.] hell, *48*   20 thy] the *48*   23 thee] thee ; *48*

Still would those euer-wakefull sons of fire
> Keep warm thy prayse
> Both nights & dayes,
And teach thy lou'd name to their noble lyre.

Let froward Dust then doe it's kind ;
And giue it self for sport to the proud wind.   30
Why should a peice of peeuish clay plead shares
In the Æternity of thy old cares ?
Why shouldst thou bow thy awfull Brest to see
What mine own madnesses haue done with me ?

Should not the king still keepe his throne
Because some desperate Fool's vndone ?
Or will the world's Illustrious eyes ·
Weep for euery worm that dyes ;

> Will the gallant sun
> E're the lesse glorious run ?   40
Will he hang down his golden head
Or e're the sooner seek his western bed,
> Because some foolish fly
> Growes wanton, & will dy ?

If I were lost in misery,
What was it to thy heaun & thee ?
What was it to thy pretious blood
If my foul Heart call'd for a floud ?

> What if my faithlesse soul & I
> Would needs fall in   50
> With guilt & sin,
What did the Lamb, that he should dy ?
What did the lamb, that he should need,
When the wolf sins, himself to bleed ?

> If my base lust,
Bargain'd with Death & well-beseeming dust

25 euer-wakefull] wakefull *48*   29 Let] Ler *52*   33 thou
48 *70* : you *52*   45 were] was *48*   47 thy] the *48*   53
need, *48* : need ? *52*

Why should the white
Lamb's bosom write
The purple name
Of my sin's shame ?

60

Why should his vnstaind brest make good
My blushes with his own heart-blood ?

O my SAVIOVR, make me see
How dearly thou hast payd for me

That lost again my LIFE may proue
As then in DEATH, so now in loue.

SANCTA MARIA

DOLORVM

OR

THE MOTHER

OF

SORROWS.

A
Patheticall descant vpon the
deuout Plainsong

OF

*STABAT MATER
DOLOROSA.*

Sancta Maria, &c. *First published in 48, with heading : The Mother
of Sorrowes. and without stanzas 7 and 8. MS. A1, stanzas 1–6 only.
Heading in A1 :* Sancta Maria dolorum | Or the Mother of | sorrowes.

SANCTA MARIA

DOLORVM.

I.

IN shade of death's sad TREE
    Stood Dolefull SHEE.
Ah SHE ! now by none other
Name to be known, alas, but SORROW'S MOTHER.
        Before her eyes
    Her's, & the whole world's ioyes,
    Hanging all torn she sees ; and in his woes
    And Paines, her Pangs & throes.
    Each wound of His, from euery Part,
    All, more at home in her owne heart.

II.

    What kind of marble than
    Is that cold man
    Who can look on & see,
Nor keep such noble sorrowes company ?
        Sure eu'en from you
        (My Flints) some drops are due

1·4 MOTHER] NOTHER *52*   1·10 All,] Are *48*   owne *48* : one *52*

To see so many vnkind swords contest
    So fast for one soft Brest.
While with a faithfull, mutuall, floud
Her eyes bleed Teares, his wounds weep Blood.

III.

    O costly intercourse
    Of deaths, & worse,
    Diuided loues. While son & mother
Discourse alternate wounds to one another ;
    Quick Deaths that grow
    And gather, as they come & goe :
His Nailes write swords in her, which soon her heart
    Payes back, with more then their own smart
Her Swords, still growing with his pain,
Turn Speares, & straight come home again.

IV.

    She sees her son, her God,
    Bow with a load
    Of borrowd sins ; And swimme
In woes that were not made for Him.
    Ah hard command
    Of loue ! Here must she stand
Charg'd to look on, & with a stedfast ey
    See her life dy :
Leauing her only so much Breath
As serues to keep aliue her death.

[handwritten marginal note: the agony ✓ marg — the suffering — he wants it]

V.

    O Mother turtle-doue !
    Soft sourse of loue
    That these dry lidds might borrow
Somthing from thy full Seas of sorrow !
    O in that brest
    Of thine (the noblest nest
Both of loue's fires & flouds) might I recline
    This hard, cold, Heart of mine !
The chill lump would relent, & proue
Soft subject for the seige of loue.

3·2 worse, *48* : worse *52*   3·3 loues.] loves, *48 A1*   3·8 smart]
smart ; *48*   3·9 growing] growingt *52*   3·10 again. *48* : again *52*
5·6 noblest] nobest *52*

VI.

O teach those wounds to bleed
In me ; me, so to read
This book of loues, thus writ
In lines of death, my life may coppy it
With loyall cares.
O let me, here, claim shares ;
Yeild somthing in thy sad præerogatiue
(Great Queen of greifes) & giue
Me too my teares ; who, though all stone,
Think much that thou shouldst mourn alone.

VII.

Yea let my life & me
Fix here with thee,
And at the Humble foot
Of this fair TREE take our eternall root.
That so we may
At least be in loues way ;
And in these chast warres while the wing'd wounds flee
So fast 'twixt him & thee,
My brest may catch the kisse of some kind dart,
Though as at second hand, from either heart.

VIII.

O you, your own best Darts
Dear, dolefull hearts !
Hail ; & strike home & make me see
That wounded bosomes their own weapons be.
Come wounds ! come darts !
Nail'd hands ! & peirced hearts !
Come your whole selues, sorrow's great son & mother !
Nor grudge a yonger-Brother
Of greifes his portion, who (had all their due)
One single wound should not haue left for you.

IX.

Shall I, sett there
So deep a share
(Dear wounds) & onely now
In sorrows draw no Diuidend with you ?

6·3 loues] love *48*   6·4 it] it. *48*   6·5 cares.] cares *48*
6·7 in] to *48*   6·9 Me] Oh give me *48*   7·4 eternall] etertall *52*
9·1 I,] I in sins *48*

O be more wise
If not more soft, mine eyes !
Flow, tardy founts ! & into decent showres
    Dissolue my Dayes & Howres.
And if thou yet (faint soul !) deferr
To bleed with him, fail not to weep with her.

X.

    Rich Queen, lend some releife ;
    At least an almes of greif
    To'a heart who by sad right of sin
Could proue the whole summe (too sure) due to him.
    By all those stings
    Of loue, sweet bitter things,
Which these torn hands transcrib'd on thy true heart
    O teach mine too the art
To study him so, till we mix
Wounds ; and become one crucifix.

XI.

    O let me suck the wine
    So long of this chast vine
    Till drunk of the dear wounds, I be
A lost Thing to the world, as it to me.
    O faithfull freind
    Of me & of my end !
Fold vp my life in loue ; and lay't beneath
    My dear lord's vitall death.
Lo, heart, thy hope's whole Plea ! Her pretious Breath
Powr'd out in prayrs for thee ; thy lord's in death.

9·6 If *48* : Is *52*   soft] just *48*   10·1 Rich Queen,] Lend,
O *48*   10·9 him] thee *48*   11·3 the] thy *48*   11·4 world,]
world,, *52*   11·7 Let my life end in love, and lye beneath *48*
11·8 My dear lord's] Thy deare lost *48*   11·10 thee ; thy lord's in]
thee, in thy Lords *48*

VPON

THE

BLEEDING

CRVCIFIX

A

SONG.

I.

IEsu, no more !   It is full tide.
From thy head & from thy feet,
From thy hands & from thy side
All the purple Riuers meet.

II.

What need thy fair head bear a part
In showres, as if thine eyes had none ?
What need They help to drown thy heart,
That striues in torrents of it's own ?

III.

Thy restlesse feet now cannot goe
For vs & our eternall good,
As they were euer wont.   What though ?
They swimme.   Alas, in their own floud.

IV.

Thy hands to giue, thou canst not lift ;
Yet will thy hand still giuing be.
It giues but ô, it self's the gift.
It giues though bound ; though bound 'tis free.

Vpon the bleeding Crvcifix, &c. *First published in 46. See p. 101,
above. Heading in 48*: *On the bleeding body of our crucified Lord.
Lines 2 and 4 of each stanza indented in 48.*   2·4 striues] streames *48*
3·2 good, *48* : good. *52*   3·4 swimme.] swim, *48*   floud] blood
48 A3   4·3 giues but ô,] gives, But ô *48*

V.

But ô thy side, thy deep-digg'd side !
That hath a double Nilus going.
Nor euer was the pharian tide
Half so fruitfull, half so flowing.

VI.

No hair so small, but payes his riuer
To this red sea of thy blood
Their little channells can deliuer
Somthing to the Generall floud.

VII.

But while I speak, whither are run
All the riuers nam'd before ?
I counted wrong.   There is but one ;
But ô that one is one all ore.

VIII.

Rain-swoln riuers may rise proud,
Bent all to drown & ouerflow.
But when indeed all 's ouerflow'd
They themselues are drowned too.

IX.

This thy blood's deluge, a dire chance
Dear LORD to thee, to vs is found
A deluge of Deliuerance ;
A deluge least we should be drown'd.

N'ere wast thou in a sense so sadly true,
The WELL of liuing WATERS, Lord, till now.

5·3 pharian] *Pharian 48*   9·4 drown'd. *48* : drown'd *52*

VPON
THE CROWNE OF THORNS
TAKEN DOWNE
From the head of our Bl. LORD,
all Bloody.

Now'st thou This, Souldier ? 'Tis a much-chang'd plant which yet
　　Thy selfe didst sett.
O who so hard a Husbandman did euer find
　　A soile so kind ?
Is not the soile a kind one, which returnes
　　Roses for Thornes ?

VPON
THE BODY OF OVR
BL. LORD,
NAKED
AND
BLOODY.

Hey 'haue left thee naked, LORD, O that they had !
　This garment too I would they had deny'd.
　Thee with thy self they haue too richly clad ;
Opening the purple wardrobe in thy side.
　　O neuer could there be garment too good
　　For thee to wear, But this, of thine own Blood.

Vpon the Crowne &c. *First published in 46 in a longer form. The present form follows that of 48 with the exceptions given below. For collation of 46 with MSS. see p. 96, above.* (Heading) all Bloody] *bloody 48* 1 yet 46 48 &c. : yet. 52 2–3 and 4–5 *No division by spaces in 48.* 3 find 46 : find ; 52 find, 48 6 Thornes 46 48 &c. : Thrones 52

Vpon the Body &c. *First published in 46. See p. 100, above. The present form follows that of 48 with the exceptions given below. Heading in 48 :* On our crucified Lord, naked and bloody. 2 too] too, 48 2–3 and 4–5 *No division by spaces in 48.* 4 in] of 48

THE
HYMN
OF
SAINTE THOMAS
IN
ADORATION OF
THE
BLESSED
SACRAMENT.

The Hymn &c.   First published in 48 with heading : A Hymne to Our Saviour by the Faithfull Receiver of the Sacrament.   No division into stanzas in 48.   (Heading) SAINTE] SANITE 52

E cce panis Angeloru̇.

ADORO

TE

WIth all the powres my poor Heart hath
  Of humble loue & loyall Faith,
Thus lowe (my hidden life !) I bow to thee
Whom too much loue hath bow'd more low for me.
Down down, proud sense ! Discourses dy.
Keep close, my soul's inquiring ey !
Nor touch nor tast must look for more
But each sitt still in his own Dore.

    Your ports are all superfluous here,
Saue That which lets in faith, the eare.   10
Faith is my skill.   Faith can beleiue
As fast as loue new lawes can giue.
Faith is my force.   Faith strength affords
To keep pace with those powrfull words.
And words more sure, more sweet, then they
Loue could not think, truth could not say.

    O let thy wretch find that releife
Thou didst afford the faithfull theife.
Plead for me, loue ! Alleage & show
That faith has farther, here, to goe   20

And lesse to lean on. Because than
Though hidd as GOD, wounds writt thee man,
Thomas might touch ; None but might see
At least the suffring side of thee ;
And that too was thy self which thee did couer,
But here eu'n That's hid too which hides the other.

   Sweet, consider then, that I
Though allow'd nor hand nor eye
To reach at thy lou'd Face ; nor can
Tast thee GOD, or touch thee MAN   30
Both yet beleiue ; and wittnesse thee
My LORD too & my GOD, as lowd as He.

   Help lord, my Faith, my Hope increase ;
And fill my portion in thy peace.
Giue loue for life ; nor let my dayes
Grow, but in new powres to thy name & praise.

   O dear memoriall of that Death
Which liues still, & allowes vs breath !
Rich, Royall food ! Bountyfull BREAD !
Whose vse denyes vs to the dead ;   40
Whose vitall gust alone can giue
The same leaue both to eat & liue ;
Liue euer Bread of loues, & be
My life, my soul, my surer selfe to mee.

   O soft self-wounding Pelican !
Whose brest weepes Balm for wounded man.
Ah this way bend thy benign floud
To'a bleeding Heart that gaspes for blood.
That blood, whose least drops soueraign be
To wash my worlds of sins from me.   50
Come loue ! Come LORD ! & that long day
For which I languish, come away.
When this dry soul those eyes shall see,
And drink the vnseal'd sourse of thee.
When Glory's sun faith's shades shall chase,
And for thy veil giue me thy FACE.

A M E N

26 eu'n] e'en *48*   33 my Faith, my Hope *48* : my Hope *52*
36 to thy name & praise.] to name thy Praise. *70*   37–8 *omitted in 48*
44 surer selfe] surer-selfe *48*   50 worlds of sins] worlds-of-sins *48*
AMEN.] *omitted in 48*

LAVDA SION SALVATOREM.

THE HYMN.

FOR

THE BL.

SACRAMENT.

I.

R Ise, Royall SION ! rise & sing
Thy soul's kind shepheard, thy hart's KING.
Stretch all thy powres ; call if you can
Harpes of heaun to hands of man.
This soueraign subject sitts aboue
The best ambition of thy loue.

II.

Communior

Lo the BREAD of LIFE, this day's
Triumphant Text, prouokes thy prayse.
The liuing & life-giuing bread,
To the great twelue distributed
When LIFE, himself, at point to dy
Of loue, was his own LEGACY.

III.

Come, loue ! & let vs work a song
Lowd & pleasant, sweet & long ;
Let lippes & Hearts lift high the noise
Of so iust & solemn ioyes,
Which on his white browes this bright day
Shall hence for euer bear away.

Lavda Sion &c. *First published in 48 with heading : A Hymne on the*
B. Sacrament. 1·3 you] thou *48* (you can *omitted in copy*
of 52 used by Waller) 1·4 to] and *48* 1·6 ambition] ambitions
48 2·1 LIFE] LIEE *52* 2·5 dy] dye, *48* 2·6 loue,] *Love 48*
3·3 the] their *48*

IV.

Lo the new LAW of a new LORD
With a new Lamb blesses the Board.
The aged Pascha pleads not yeares
But spyes loue's dawn, & disappeares.
Types yeild to TRVTHES ; shades shrink away ;
And their NIGHT dyes into our Day.

V.

But lest THAT dy too, we are bid
Euer to doe what he once did.
And by a mindfull, mystick breath
That we may liue, reuiue his DEATH ;
With a well-bles't bread & wine
Transsum'd, & taught to turn diuine.

Communion

VI.

The Heaun-instructed house of FAITH
Here a holy Dictate hath
That they but lend their Form & face,
Themselues with reuerence leaue their place
Nature, & name, to be made good
By' a nobler Bread, more needfull BLOOD.

VII.

Where nature's lawes no leaue will giue,
Bold FAITH takes heart, & dares beleiue.
In different species, names not things
Himself to me my SAVIOVR brings,
As meat in That, as Drink in this ;
But still in Both one CHRIST he is.

VIII.

The Receiuing Mouth here makes
Nor wound nor breach in what he takes.

4·1 LORD] LORD. *52* *Law 48* 5·1 bid *48* : bid. *52* 5·5
wine] wine. *52* : *Wine 48* 6·4 place] place, *48* 6·5 good *48* :
good. *52* 7·2 beleiue.] belieue *52* : Believe *48* 7·3 different species]
different-species *48* Names *48* : name *52* 8·2 Nor *48* :
Non *52*

Let one, or one THOVSAND be
Here Diuiders, single he
Beares home no lesse, all they no more,
Nor leaue they both lesse then before.

IX.

Though in it self this SOVERAIN FEAST
Be all the same to euery Guest,
Yet on the same (life-meaning) Bread
The child of Death eates himself Dead.
Nor is't loue's fault, but sin's dire skill
That thus from LIFE can DEATH distill.

X. •

When the blest signes thou broke shall see,
Hold but thy Faith intire as he
Who, howsoe're clad, cannot come
Lesse then whole CHRIST in euery crumme.
In broken formes a stable FAITH
Vntouch't her pretious TOTALL hath.

XI.

Lo the life-food of ANGELLS then
Bow'd to the lowly mouths of men !
The children's BREAD ; the Bridegroom's WINE.
Not to be cast to dogges, or swine.

XII.

Lo, the full, finall, SACRIFICE
On which all figures fix't their eyes.
The ransom'd ISACK, & his ramme ;
The MANNA, & the PASCHAL Lamb.

XIII.

IESV MASTER, Iust & true !
Our FOOD, & faithfull SHEPHARD too !
O by thy self vouchsafe to keep,
As with thy selfe thou feed'st thy SHEEP.

9·6 LIFE] *Life, 48*   11·3 WINE.] *Wine, 48*   12·1 SACRIFICE]
SACRIEICE *52*

XIV.

O let that loue which thus makes thee
Mix with our low Mortality,
Lift our lean Soules, & sett vs vp
Convictors of thine own full cup,
Coheirs of SAINTS. That so all may
Drink the same wine ; and the same WAY.
Nor change the PASTVRE, but the PLACE
To feed of THEE in thine own FACE.

A M E N.

14·3 lean] meane *48*   14·4 Convictors] *Con-victors 48*   14·7
change] chang *52*   14·9 AMEN.] *omitted in 48*

DIES IRÆ DIES ILLA.

Dies Iræ &c. First published in 48, with heading : A Hymne in
meditation of the day of judgement. First lines not indented in 48.
MS. A1 with heading as in 52, but with no punctuation.

THE
HYMN.
OF THE
CHVRCH,
IN MEDITATION OF
THE DAY OF
IVDGMENT.

I.

HEars't thou, my soul, what serious things
Both the Psalm and sybyll sings
Of a sure iudge, from whose sharp Ray
The world in flames shall fly away.

II.

O that fire ! before whose face
Heaun & earth shall find no place.
O those eyes ! whose angry light
Must be the day of that dread Night.

III.

O that trump ! whose blast shall run
An euen round with the circling Sun.
And vrge the murmuring graues to bring
Pale mankind forth to meet his king.

IV.

Horror of nature, hell & Death !
When a deep Groan from beneath
Shall cry we come, we come & all
The caues of night answer one call.

1·1 what *48* : with *52*   2·3 those] these *70*   3·1 run] rnn
52   4·3 come &] come, and *48*   4·4 call. *48* : call *52* A*1*

V.

O that Book ! whose leaues so bright
Will sett the world in seuere light.
O that Iudge ! whose hand, whose eye
None can indure ; yet none can fly.

VI.

Ah then, poor soul, what wilt thou say ?
And to what Patron chuse to pray ?
When starres themselues shall stagger ; and
The most firm foot no more then stand.

VII.

But thou giu'st leaue (dread Lord) that we
Take shelter from thy self, in thee ;
And with the wings of thine own doue
Fly to thy scepter of soft loue.

VIII.

Dear, remember in that Day
Who was the cause thou cams't this way.
Thy sheep was stray'd ; And thou wouldst be
Euen lost thy self in seeking me.

IX.

Shall all that labour, all that cost
Of loue, and eu'n that losse, be lost ?
And this lou'd soul, iudg'd worth no lesse
Then all that way, and wearynesse ?

X.

Iust mercy then, thy Reckning be
With my price, & not with me
'Twas pay'd at first with too much pain,
To be pay'd twice ; or once, in vain.

5·3 that] the *48*   5·4 flye. *48 A1* : fly *52*   6·1 Ah] O *A1*
10·2 me] me : *48*

XI.

Mercy (my iudge) mercy I cry
With blushing Cheek & bleeding ey,
The conscious colors of my sin
Are red without & pale within.

Sinful nature
vmon

XII.

O let thine own soft bowells pay
Thy self ; And so discharge that day.
If sin can sigh, loue can forgiue.
O say the word my Soul shall liue.

XIII.

Those mercyes which thy MARY found
Or who thy crosse confes't & crown'd,
Hope tells my heart, the same loues be
Still aliue ; and still for me.

XIV.

Though both my Prayres & teares combine,
Both worthlesse are ; For they are mine.
But thou thy bounteous self still be ;
And show thou art, by sauing me.

inadequacy
vmon

XV.

O when thy last Frown shall proclaim
The flocks of goates to folds of flame,
And all thy lost sheep found shall be,
Let come ye blessed then call me.

XVI.

When the dread ITE shall diuide
Those Limbs of death from thy left side,
Let those life-speaking lipps command
That I inheritt thy right hand.

XVII.

O hear a supliant heart ; all crush't
And crumbled into contrite dust.
My hope, my fear ! my Iudge, my Freind !
Take charge of me, & of my END.

12·4 word] word, *48*   15·4 *48 distinguishes : come yee Blessed,*
16·4 thy] the *48*   17·4 *A1 adds* Amen

THE

HIMN

O GLORIOSA DOMINA.

HAil, most high, most humble one !
Aboue the world ; below thy SON
Whose blush the moon beauteously marres
And staines the timerous light of starres.
He that made all things, had not done
Till he had made Himself thy son
The whole world's host would be thy guest
And board himself at thy rich BREST.
O boundles Hospitality !
The FEAST of all things feeds on the.   10
  The first Eue, mother of our FALL,
E're she bore any one, slew all.
Of Her vnkind gift might we haue
The inheritance of a hasty GRAVE ;

THE HIMN &c.   First printed in 48 with heading : The Virgin-Mother.
2 thy SON] the Son, 48   4 Starres 48 : stares 52   10 things 48 :
thing 52

Quick burye'd in the wanton TOMB
    Of one forbidden bitt ;
Had not a Better FRVIT forbidden it.
        Had not thy healthfull womb
    The world's new eastern window bin
And giuen vs heau'n again, in giuing HIM.   20
Thine was the Rosy DAWN that sprung the Day
Which renders all the starres she stole away.
    Let then the Aged world be wise, & all
Proue nobly, here, vnnaturall.
'Tis gratitude to forgett that other
And call the maiden Eue their mother.
    Yee redeem'd Nations farr & near,
Applaud your happy selues in her,
(All you to whom this loue belongs)
And keep't aliue with lasting songs.   30
    Let hearts & lippes speak lowd ; and say
Hail, door of life : & sourse of day !
The door was shutt, the fountain seal'd ;
Yet LIGHT was seen & LIFE reueald.
The door was shutt, yet let in day,
The fountain seald, yet life found way.
    Glory to thee, great virgin's son
In bosom of thy FATHER's blisse.
    The same to thee, sweet SPIRIT be done ;
As euer shall be, was, & is.   40

A M E N.

21 sprung] *Spring 48, with comma after Rosie-dawn*   26 their]
your *48*   mother] morher *52*   35 *supplied from 48 : not in 52*

IN THE
GLORIOVS
ASSVMPTION
OF
OVR BLESSED
LADY.

THE HYMN.

Hark ! she is call'd, the parting houre is come.
Take thy Farewell, poor world ! heavn must goe home.
A peice of heau'nly earth ; Purer & brighter
Then the chast starres, whose choise lamps come to light her
While through the crystall orbes, clearer then they
She climbes ; and makes a farre more milkey way.
She's calld. Hark, how the dear immortall doue
Sighes to his syluer mate rise vp, my loue !
Rise vp, my fair, my spottlesse one !
The winter 's past, the rain is gone.   10
    The spring is come, the flowrs appear
No sweets, but thou, are wanting here.
       Come away, my loue !
       Come away, my doue ! cast off delay,
       The court of heau'n is come
       To wait vpon thee home ; Come come away !
       The flowrs appear.
Or quickly would, wert thou once here.

In the Gloriovs Assvmption &c. *For earlier version in 46 and collation
see p. 139, above. 48 and MS. A1 generally agree with 52 ; exceptions are
noted here. Title in 48 : On the assumption.*   1 come. 48 : come 52
9 fair, my] faire and A1   14 cast off delay] *separate line in 48*
16 Come come away] *separate line in 48*   17 appear.] appeare, 48
Space after l. 17 in A1   18 wert] were 48   here. 48 : here 52

The spring is come, or if it stay,
'Tis to keep time with thy delay.   20
The rain is gone, except so much as we
Detain in needfull teares to weep the want of thee.
   The winter 's past.
   or if he make lesse hast,
His answer is, why she does so.
If sommer come not, how can winter goe.
   Come away, come away.
The shrill winds chide, the waters weep thy stay ;
The fountains murmur ; & each loftyest tree
Bowes low'st his heauy top, to look for thee.   30
   Come away, my loue.
   Come away, my doue &c.
She 's call'd again. And will she goe ?
When heaun bidds come, who can say no ?
Heaun calls her, & she must away.
Heaun will not, & she cannot stay.
Goe then ; goe Gloriovs.
   On the golden wings
Of the bright youth of heaun, that sings
Vnder so sweet a Burthen. Goe,   40
Since thy dread son will haue it so.
And while thou goest, our song & we
Will, as we may, reach after thee.
Hail, holy Queen of humble hearts !
We in thy prayse will haue our parts.
   Thy pretious name shall be
   Thy self to vs ; & we
   With holy care will keep it by vs.
   We to the last
   Will hold it fast   50
   And no Assvmption shall deny vs.
   All the sweetest showres
   Of our fairest flowres
   Will we strow vpon it.

21 so] as *48* *Space after l. 22 in A1* 23 past.] past *48*
25 does] doth *48*   *Space after . l. 26 in A1* 29
loftyest] loftie *A1* tree] three. 52 : Tree, *48* 30 heauy] leauy
48 : heauiest *A1* 37 Goe . . . wings] *single line in 48* Gloriovs.]
(*glorious*) *48* 40 Sweet] great *48* *Between ll. 45 and 46 the 48*
edition inserts ten lines corresponding to ll. 31–40 of 46 edition. 46
be *48* : be. *52*

Though our sweets cannot make
It sweeter, they can take
Themselues new sweetnes from it.
M A R I A, men & Angels sing
M A R I A, mother of our KING.
    LIVE, rosy princesse, LIVE. And may the bright   60
Crown of a most incomparable light
Embrace thy radiant browes. O may the best
Of euerlasting ioyes bath thy white brest.
LIVE, our chast loue, the holy mirth
Of heaun ; the humble pride of earth.
Liue, crown of woemen ; Queen of men.
Liue mistresse of our song. And when
Our weak desires haue done their best,
Sweet Angels come, and sing the rest.

66 crown] ctown *52*   68 best, *48 &c.* : brest *52*

SAINTE

MARY

MAGDALENE

OR

THE WEEPER.

Loe where a WOVNDED HEART with Bleeding EYES conspire.
Is she a FLAMING Fountain, or a Weeping fire !

Sainte Mary &c. The couplet first published in 48 under the heading of
The Weeper as an introduction to that poem. MS. A1.
SAINTE] SANITE 52 On St A1

X 2

THE
WEEPER.

I.

HAil, sister springs !
Parents of syluer-footed rills !
    Euer bubling things !
        Thawing crystall ! snowy hills,
Still spending, neuer spent ! I mean
Thy fair eyes, sweet MAGDALENE !

II.

        Heauens thy fair eyes be ;
    Heauens of euer-falling starres.
        'Tis seed-time still with thee
        And starres thou sow'st, whose haruest dares
Promise the earth to counter shine
Whateuer makes heaun's forhead fine.

The Weeper. *MS. Dobell. For earlier version in 46, and collation with other MSS., see p. 79, above. 52 generally follows 48 ; exceptions noted here. 48 indents first and third lines of each stanza, as 46.* 1·2 footed] forded *48* 2·2 starres.] starres., *52*

III.

But we'are deceiued all.
Starres indeed they are too true ;
For they but seem to fall,
    As Heaun's other spangles doe.
It is not for our earth & vs
To shine in Things so pretious.

IV.

Vpwards thou dost weep.
Heaun's bosome drinks the gentle stream.
Where th'milky riuers creep,
    Thine floates aboue ; & is the cream.
Waters aboue th' Heauns, what they be
We' are taught best by thy TEARES & thee.

V.

Euery morn from hence
A brisk Cherub somthing sippes
Whose sacred influence
    Addes sweetnes to his sweetest Lippes.
Then to his musick. And his song
Tasts of this Breakfast all day long.

VI.

Not in the euening's eyes
When they Red with weeping are
For the Sun that dyes,
    Sitts sorrow with a face so fair,
No where but here did euer meet
Sweetnesse so sad, sadnesse so sweet.

VII.

When sorrow would be seen
In her brightest majesty
(For she is a Queen)
    Then is she drest by none but thee.
Then, & only then, she weares
Her proudest pearles ; I mean, thy TEARES.

3·1 we'are] we are *48*   5·5 And] thus *Dobell*   5·6 this]
his *48*

VIII.

The deaw no more will weep
The primrose's pale cheek to deck,
The deaw no more will sleep
Nuzzel'd in the lilly's neck ;
Much reather would it be thy TEAR,
And leaue them Both to tremble here.

IX.

There's no need at all
That the balsom-sweating bough
So coyly should let fall
His med'cinable teares ; for now
Nature hath learn't to'extract a deaw
More soueraign & sweet from you.

X.

Yet let the poore drops weep
(Weeping is the ease of woe)
Softly let them creep,
Sad that they are vanquish't so.
They, though to others no releife,
Balsom maybe, for their own greife.

XI.

Such the maiden gemme
By the purpling vine put on,
Peeps from her parent stemme
And blushes at the bridegroome sun.
This watry Blossom of thy eyn,
Ripe, will make the richer wine.

XII.

When some new bright Guest
Takes vp among the starres a room,
And Heaun will make a feast,
Angels with crystall violls come
And draw from these full eyes of thine
Their master's Water : their own Wine.

8·5 TEAR, *48* : TEAR. *52*   9·1 There's] There is *48*   9·6
soueraign] soveraigne, *48*   10·4 they *48* : they, *52*   11 *Cp.*
stanza 5 of ' The Teare ' in 46, p. 84, above.   11·3 parent stemme]
steme, *48*   11·4 Bridegroome *48* : bridegroomes *52*   11·5
Blossom] Balsome *48*   12·5 draw *48* : deaw *52*   12·6 Water]
Waters *48*

XIII.

Golden though he be,
Golden Tagus murmures tho ;
Were his way by thee,
Content & quiet he would goe.
So much more rich would he esteem
Thy syluer, then his golden stream.

XIV.

Well does the May that lyes
Smiling in thy cheeks, confesse
The April in thine eyes.
Mutuall sweetnesse they expresse.
No April ere lent kinder showres,
Nor May return'd more faithfull flowres.

XV.

O cheeks ! Bedds of chast loues
By your own showres seasonably dash't
Eyes ! nests of milky doues
In your own wells decently washt,
O wit of loue ! that thus could place
Fountain & Garden in one face.

XVI.

O sweet Contest ; of woes
With loues, of teares with smiles disputing !
O fair, & Freindly Foes,
Each other kissing & confuting !
While rain & sunshine, Cheekes & Eyes
Close in kind contrarietyes.

XVII.

But can these fair Flouds be
Freinds with the bosom fires that fill thee
Can so great flames agree
Æternall Teares should thus distill thee !

14·6 faithfull] fragrant *Dobell*   15 *to end : 52 abandons indention*
of first lines.   15·1 cheeks] ckeeks *52*   15·3 Doves *48* : doues. *52*
XVI.] *Number missing in 52*   16·1 Contest ;] contest *48*   woes *48* :
woes. *52*   16·2 of teares with] and tears, and *48*   17·2 bosom]
balsome *48* thee *48* : you *52*   17·3 Can so] Cause *48*

O flouds, o fires ! o suns ô showres !
Mixt & made freinds by loue's sweet powres.

XVIII.

Twas his well-pointed dart
That digg'd these wells, & drest this Vine ;
And taught the wounded HEART
The way into these weeping Eyn.
Vain loues auant ! bold hands forbear !
The lamb hath dipp't his white foot here.

XIX.

And now where're he strayes,
Among the Galilean mountaines,
Or more vnwellcome wayes,
He's follow'd by two faithfull fountaines ;
Two walking baths ; two weeping motions ;
Portable, & compendious oceans.

XX.

O Thou, thy lord's fair store !
In thy so rich & rare expenses,
Euen when he show'd most poor,
He might prouoke the wealth of Princes.
What Prince's wanton'st pride e're could
Wash with Syluer, wipe with Gold.

XXI.

Who is that King, but he
Who calls't his Crown to be call'd thine,
That thus can boast to be
Waited on by a wandring mine,
A voluntary mint, that strowes
Warm syluer shoures where're he goes !

XXII.

O pretious Prodigall !
Fair spend-thrift of thy self ! thy measure
(Mercilesse loue !) is all.
Euen to the last Pearle in thy treasure.

18·2 Vine *48 Dobell* : wine *52*　　　18·3 the] that *48 Dobell*　　　18·4
these] those *48*　　　20·2 rare] large *48*　　　20·4 wealth] wrath *48*
21·2 calls't] *blank space 48*　　　21·6 he] it *Dobell*　　　22·4 to the]
to thy *48*　treasure] threasure *52*

All places, Times, & obiects be
Thy teare's sweet opportunity.

XXIII.

Does the day-starre rise ?
Still thy starres doe fall & fall
Does day close his eyes ?
Still the FOVNTAIN weeps for all.
Let night or day doe what they will,
Thou hast thy task ; thou weepest still.

XXIV.

Does thy song lull the air ?
Thy falling teares keep faith full time.
Does thy sweet-breath'd praire
Vp in clouds of incense climb ?
Still at each sigh, that is, each stop,
A bead, that is, A TEAR, does drop.

XXV.

At these thy weeping gates,
(Watching their watry motion)
Each winged moment waits,
Takes his TEAR, & gets him gone.
By thine Ey's tinct enobled thus
Time layes him vp ; he's pretious.

XXVI.

Not, so long she liued,
Shall thy tomb report of thee ;
But, so long she greiued,
Thus must we date thy memory.
Others by moments, months, & yeares
Measure their ages ; thou, by TEARES.

XXVII.

So doe perfumes expire.
So sigh tormented sweets, opprest
With proud vnpittying fire.
Such Teares the suffring Rose that's vext

22·6 opportunity. *48* : opportunity *52*   24·3 praire] paire *52*
24·6 does] doth *48*   drop.] drop, *52* drop *48*   25·3 waits, *48* :
waits. *52*   26·5 years *48* : yeares. *52*   27·3 fire *48* : fires *52*

With vngentle flames does shed,
Sweating in a too warm bed.

XXVIII.

Say, ye bright brothers,
The fugitiue sons of those fair Eyes
Your fruitfull mothers !
What make you here ? what hopes can tice
You to be born ? what cause can borrow
You from Those nests of noble sorrow ?

XXIX.

Whither away so fast ?
For sure the sordid earth
Your Sweetnes cannot tast
Nor does the dust deserue your birth.
Sweet, whither hast you then ? o say
Why you trip so fast away ?

XXX.

We goe not to seek,
The darlings of Auroras bed,
The rose's modest Cheek
Nor the violet's humble head.
Though the Feild's eyes too WEEPERS be
Because they want such TEARES as we.

XXXI.

Much lesse mean we to trace
The Fortune of inferior gemmes,
Preferr'd to some proud face
Or pertch't vpon fear'd Diadems.
Crown'd Heads are toyes. We goe to meet
A worthy object, our lord's FEET.

28·1 ye *48*: the *52*   29·4 your *48*: their *52*   29·6 Why you
trip] Why 'tis you trip *Dobell*

A HYMN

to the name < and honour of
the renowned

S. TERESIA

Foundres of the Reformation of the Order of
barefoote Carmelites;

A Woman

for Angelicall height of Contemplation,
for Masculine courage of Performance;
more then a woman.

Who yet a Child
outranne Maturity.
& durst plott a Martyrdome;
but was reserved by God
to dy the liuing death of the life of his loue.
of whose great impressions
as her noble heart had most high experiment,
so hath she in her life most heroically exprest them,
in her Spirituall posterity most fruitfully propagated them,
and in these her heaunly Writings
most sublimely, most sweetly
taught them to y' world.

—

LOVE thou art absolute. sole Lord.
Of life & Death. To proue the word
Wee'l now to none of y' all

Thos:

TITLE OF THE HYMN IN HONOUR OF ST. TERESA
From a manuscript in the Pierpont Morgan Library, New York

A HYMN
TO
THE NAME AND HONOR
OF
THE ADMIRABLE
SAINTE
TERESA,
FOVNDRESSE
of the Reformation of the Discalced
CARMELITES, both
men & Women;

A

WOMAN
for Angelicall heigth of speculation, for
Masculine courage of performance,
more then a woman.

WHO
Yet a child, out ran maturity, and
durst plott a Martyrdome;

A Hymn &c. For earlier version in 46 see p. 131, above. 52 generally
follows 48 with exceptions noted below. MS Dobell (30 lines only, corresponding to ll. 69–96 and 149–50)   SAINTE] SANITE 52
Heading in 48 as 46

Le Vray portraict de S.ᵉᵉ Terese, Fondatrice
des Religieuses, & r Religieux reformez de
l'ordre de N.Dame du mont Carmel. Dœdœ
le 4 Octo. 1582. Canonisee le 12 Mars 1622.
J. Meßager excudit.

THE
HYMNE.

LOue, thou art Absolute sole lord
 Of LIFE & DEATH.   To proue the word,
Wee'l now appeal to none of all
Those thy old Souldiers, Great & tall,
Ripe Men of Martyrdom, that could reach down
With strong armes, their triumphant crown ;
Such as could with lusty breath
Speak lowd into the face of death
Their Great LORD's glorious name, to none
Of those whose spatious Bosomes spread a throne   10
For LOVE at larg to fill : spare blood & sweat ;
And see him take a priuate seat,
Making his mansion in the mild
And milky soul of a soft child.
 Scarse has she learn't to lisp the name
Of Martyr ; yet she thinks it shame
Life should so long play with that breath
Which spent can buy so braue a death.
She neuer vndertook to know
What death with loue should haue to doe ;   20
Nor has she e're yet vnderstood
Why to show loue, she should shed blood
Yet though she cannot tell you why,
She can LOVE, & she can DY.
 Scarse has she Blood enough to make
A guilty sword blush for her sake ;
Yet has she'a HEART dares hope to proue
How much lesse strong is DEATH then LOVE.
 Be loue but there ; let poor six yeares
Be pos'd with the maturest Feares   30
Man trembles at, you straight shall find
LOVE knowes no nonage, nor the MIND.
'Tis LOVE, not YEARES or LIMBS that can
Make the Martyr, or the man.

2 word, *48* : word. *52*   9 name,] name ; *48*   11 fill : *48* :
fill, *52*   sweat ;] sweat, *48*   14 child. *48* : child *52*   15
has] hath *48*   21 has] hath *48*   25 has] hath *48*   27
has] hath *48*   dares] dare *48*   31 straight] staight *52*   33 or] nor *48*

Love touch't her Heart, & lo it beates
High, & burnes with such braue heates ;
Such thirsts to dy, as dares drink vp,
A thousand cold deaths in one cup.
Good reason.   For she breathes All fire.
Her weake brest heaues with strong desire   40
Of what she may with fruitles wishes
Seek for amongst her Mother's kisses.
    Since 'tis not to be had at home
She'l trauail to a Martyrdom.
No home for hers confesses she
But where she may a Martyr be.
    Sh'el to the Moores ; And trade with them,
For this vnualued Diadem.
She'l offer them her dearest Breath,
With Christ's Name in't, in change for death.   50
Sh'el bargain with them ; & will giue
Them God ; teach them how to liue
In him : or, if they this deny,
For him she'l teach them how to Dy.
So shall she leaue amongst them sown
Her Lord's Blood ; or at lest her own.
    Farewel then, all the world !   Adieu.
Teresa is no more for you.
Farewell, all pleasures, sports, & ioyes,
(Neuer till now esteemed toyes)   60
Farewell what ever deare may bee,
Mother's armes or Father's knee
Farewell house, & farewell home !
She 's for the Moores, & Martyrdom.
    Sweet, not so fast ! lo thy fair Spouse
Whom thou seekst with so swift vowes,
Calls thee back, & bidds thee come
T'embrace a milder Martyrdom.
    Blest powres forbid, Thy tender life
Should bleed vpon a barborous knife ;   70
Or some base hand haue power to race
Thy Brest's chast cabinet, & vncase

---

40 weake *48*: what *52*   42 kisses *48*: hisles *52*   44
to] for *48*   Martyrdom] Maryrdom *52*   ·   47 trade] try *48*   52
God ; teach] God, and teach *48*   54 him] him, *48*   61 *So*
48. Line missing in 52.   64 Martyrdom. *48*: Martyrdom *52*
Space after l. 64 in 48   72 chast] soft *48*

A soul kept there so sweet, ô no ;
Wise heaun will neuer haue it so
THOV art love's victime ; & must dy
A death more mysticall & high.
Into loue's armes thou shalt let fall
A still-suruiuing funerall.
His is the DART must make the DEATH
Whose stroke shall tast thy hallow'd breath ;   80
A Dart thrice dip't in that rich flame
Which writes thy spouse's radiant Name
Vpon the roof of Heau'n ; where ay
It shines, & with a soueraign ray
Beates bright vpon the burning faces
Of soules which in that name's sweet graces
Find euerlasting smiles. So rare,
So spirituall, pure, & fair
Must be th'immortall instrument
Vpon whose choice point shall be sent   90
A life so lou'd ; And that there be
Fitt executioners for Thee,
The fair'st & first-born sons of fire
Blest SERAPHIM, shall leaue their quire
And turn loue's souldiers, vpon THEE
To exercise their archerie.
   O how oft shalt thou complain
Of a sweet & subtle PAIN.
Of intolerable IOYES ;
Of a DEATH, in which who dyes   100
Loues his death, and dyes again.
And would for euer so be slain.
And liues, & dyes ; and knowes not why
To liue, But that he thus may neuer leaue to DY.

74 so] so. *48*   79 make the] make your *Dobell*   87–98 *Dobell reads:*

> Find euerlasting smiles: when Tombs
> Give up their throbbing Martyrdoms
> Tears shall take Comfort & turn gems
> And wrongs repent to Diadems
> But no Grosse-moulded dust can bee
> fit executioner for thee
> The fairst and first Borne sonns of fire
> Blest Seraphims shall leaue their quire
> And turne loues soldiers upon thee
> To exercize their archery
> And After thou shalt kisse ye light
> That kindled the A star so bright

92 thee, *46 48*: Thee. *52*   94 SERAPHIM] *Seraphims 48*

How kindly will thy gentle HEART
Kisse the sweetly-killing DART !
And close in his embraces keep
Those delicious Wounds, that weep
Balsom to heal themselues with.   Thus
When These thy DEATHS, so numerous,   110
Shall all at last dy into one,
And melt thy Soul's sweet mansion ;
Like a soft lump of incense, hasted
By too hott a fire, & wasted
Into perfuming clouds, so fast
Shalt thou exhale to Heaun at last
In a resoluing SIGH, and then
O what ?   Ask not the Tongues of men.
Angells cannot tell, suffice,
Thy selfe shall feel thine own full ioyes   120
And hold them fast for euer.   There
So soon as thou shalt first appear,
The MOON of maiden starrs, thy white
MISTRESSE, attended by such bright
Soules as thy shining self, shall come
And in her first rankes make thee room ;
Where 'mongst her snowy family
Immortall wellcomes wait for thee.
    O what delight, when reueal'd LIFE shall stand
And teach thy lipps heau'n with his hand ;   130
On which thou now maist to thy wishes
Heap vp thy consecrated kisses.
What ioyes shall seize thy soul, when she
Bending her blessed eyes on thee
(Those second Smiles of Heau'n) shall dart
Her mild rayes through thy melting heart !
    Angels, thy old freinds, there shall greet thee
Glad at their own home now to meet thee.
    All thy good WORKES which went before
And waited for thee, at the door,   140
Shall own thee there ; and all in one
Weaue a constellation

[marginalia, handwritten]
"The key images comprising this emblem are all traditional symbols. incense symbolizes consecration to God; the hot fire symbolizes spiritual ardor; the perfume stands for acceptability to God. Teresa, consecrated to God, dies because of excessive spiritual ardor (Neoplatonic notion) and enjoys forever the Beatific Vision. All of this has been expressed by means of an emblematic picture constructed from three traditional symbols." Bertonasco Crashaw and the Baroque // 26-7.

Of CROWNS, with which the KING thy spouse
Shall build vp thy triumphant browes.
   All thy old woes shall now smile on thee
And thy paines sitt bright vpon thee
All thy sorrows here shall shine,
All thy SVFFRINGS be diuine.
TEARES shall take comfort, & turn gemms
And WRONGS repent to Diademms.   150
Eu'n thy DEATHS shall liue ; & new
Dresse the soul that erst they slew.
Thy wounds shall blush to such bright scarres
As keep account of the LAMB's warres.
   Those rare WORKES where thou shalt leaue writt,
Loue's noble history, with witt
Taught thee by none but him, while here
They feed our soules, shall cloth THINE there.
Each heaunly word by whose hid flame
Our hard Hearts shall strike fire, the same   160
Shall flourish on thy browes. & be
Both fire to vs & flame to thee ;
Whose light shall liue bright in thy FACE
By glory, in our hearts by grace.
   Thou shalt look round about, & see
Thousands of crown'd Soules throng to be
Themselues thy crown.   Sons of thy vowes
The virgin-births with which thy soueraign spouse
Made fruitfull thy fair soul, goe now
And with them all about thee bow   170
To Him, put on (hee'l say) put on
(My rosy loue) That thy rich zone
Sparkling with the sacred flames
Of thousand soules, whose happy names
Heau'n keeps vpon thy score.   (Thy bright
Life brought them first to kisse the light
That kindled them to starrs.) and so
Thou with the LAMB, thy lord, shalt goe ;
And whereso'ere he setts his white
Stepps, walk with HIM those wayes of light   180
   Which who in death would liue to see,
   Must learn in life to dy like thee.

147 *So 48. Line missing in 52.*   148 All] And *48*   151 DEATHS]
Deat'hs 48 DEATH *52*   155 writt, *48*: writt. *52*   163 bright] bright,
48   169 soul, goe] soule. Goe *48*   175 keeps *46 48*: keep *52*

AN

APOLOGIE.

FOR

THE FORE-GOING HYMNE
as hauing been writt when the author was yet among the
protestantes.

THus haue I back again to thy bright name
  (Fair floud of holy fires !) transfus'd the flame
I took from reading thee, tis to thy wrong
I know, that in my weak & worthlesse song
Thou here art sett to shine where thy full day
Scarse dawnes.   O pardon if I dare to say
Thine own dear bookes are guilty.   For from thence
I learn't to know that loue is eloquence.   *St Francis de Sale*
That hopefull maxime gaue me hart to try
If, what to other tongues is tun'd so high,   10
Thy praise might not speak English too ; forbid
(By all thy mysteryes that here ly hidde)
Forbid it, mighty Loue ! let no fond Hate
Of names & wordes, so farr præiudicate.
Souls are not SPANIARDS too, one freindly floud
Of BAPTISM blends them all into a blood.
CHRIST'S faith makes but one body of all soules
And loue's that body's soul, no law controwlls
Our free traffique for heau'n, we may maintaine
Peace, sure, with piety, though it come from SPAIN.   20
What soul so e're, in any language, can
Speak heau'n like her's is my souls country-man.

An Apologie &c.   *For earlier version in 46 see p.* 136, *above.   52 general-
ly follows 48 with exceptions noted below.   Heading in 48, where it follows
' The flaming Heart ',* : *An Apologie for the precedent Hymnes on* Teresa.
(*Heading*) HYMNE] HYMEN *52*   3 thee, tis] Thee. 'Tis *48*
8 learn't] learn'd *48*   12 thy] the *48*   18 And] Aud *52*   19
Heav'n, *48* : heau'n *52*

O 'tis not spanish, but 'tis heau'n she speaks !
'Tis heau'n that lyes in ambush there, & breaks
From thence into the wondring reader's brest ;
Who feels his warm HEART hatch'd into a nest
Of little EAGLES & young loues, whose high
Flights scorn the lazy dust, & things that dy.

    There are enow, whose draughts (as deep as hell)
Drink vp al SPAIN in sack. Let my soul swell   30
With thee, strong wine of loue ! let others swimme
In puddles ; we will pledge this SERAPHIM
Bowles full of richer blood then blush of grape
Was euer guilty of, Change we too 'our shape
(My soul,) Some drink from men to beasts, o then
Drink we till we proue more, not lesse, then men,
And turn not beasts, but Angels. Let the king
Me euer into these his cellars bring
Where flowes such wine as we can haue of none
But HIM who trod the wine-presse all alone   40
Wine of youth, life, & the sweet Deaths of loue ;
Wine of immortall mixture ; which can proue
It's Tincture from the rosy nectar ; wine
That can exalt weak EARTH ; & so refine
Our dust, that at one draught, mortality
May drink it self vp, and forget to dy.

25 the] a *48*   26 hatch'd *48* : *omitted in 52*   29 enow *48*
now *52*   37 And] 'And *52*   40 alone] alone. *48*   45 at] in *48*

THE

FLAMING HEART

VPON THE BOOK AND

Picture of the seraphicall saint

TERESA,

(AS SHE IS VSVALLY EX-
pressed with a SERAPHIM
biside her.)

WEll meaning readers ! you that come as freinds
  And catch the pretious name this peice pretends ;
Make not too much hast to' admire
That fair-cheek't fallacy of fire.
That is a SERAPHIM, they say
And this the great TERESIA.
Readers, be rul'd by me ; & make
Here a well-plac't & wise mistake
You must transpose the picture quite,
And spell it wrong to read it right ;   10
Read HIM for her, & her for him ;
And call the SAINT the SERAPHIM.
    Painter, what didst thou vnderstand
To put her dart into his hand !
See, euen the yeares & size of him
Showes this the mother SERAPHIM.
This is the mistresse flame ; & duteous he
Her happy fire-works, here, comes down to see.
O most poor-spirited of men !
Had thy cold Pencil kist her PEN   20
Thou couldst not so vnkindly err
To show vs This faint shade for HER

The Flaming Heart &c. First published in 48 (ll. 1–84 only) with
heading : The flaming Heart. Vpon the booke and picture of Teresa.
As she is usually expressed with a Seraphim beside her. Lines 85–108
added in 52.   3 too] so 48   8 mistake] mistake. 48   11 Read]
And 48   16 Showes] Shew 48   18 happy] happier 48 see.
48 : see 52   22 HER] Her. 48

Why man, this speakes pure mortall frame ;
And mockes with female FROST loue's manly flame.
One would suspect thou meant'st to paint
Some weak, inferiour, woman saint.
But had thy pale-fac't purple took
Fire from the burning cheeks of that bright Booke
Thou woûldst on her haue heap't vp all
That could be found SERAPHICALL ;   30
What e're this youth of fire weares fair,
Rosy fingers, radiant hair,
Glowing cheek, & glistering wings,
All those fair & flagrant things,
But before all, that fiery DART
Had fill'd the Hand of this great HEART.
   Doe then as equall right requires,
Since HIS the blushes be, & her's the fires,
Resume & rectify thy rude design ;
Vndresse thy Seraphim into MINE.   40
Redeem this iniury of thy art ;
Giue HIM the vail, giue her the dart.
   Giue Him the vail ; that he may couer
The Red cheeks of a riuall'd louer.
Asham'd that our world, now, can show
Nests of new Seraphims here below.
   Giue her the DART for it is she
(Fair youth) shootes both thy shaft & THEE
Say, all ye wise & well-peirc't hearts
That liue & dy amidst her darts,   50
What is't your tastfull spirits doe proue
In that rare life of Her, and loue ?
Say & bear wittnes. Sends she not
A SERAPHIM at euery shott ?
What magazins of immortall ARMES there shine !
Heaun's great artillery in each loue-spun line.
Giue then the dart to her who giues the flame ;
Giue him the veil, who kindly takes the shame.
   But if it be the frequent fate
Of worst faults to be fortunate ;   60

25 paint *48* : print *52*   28 cheeks] checks *52*   30 found]
form'd *48*   31 What] But *48* weares] wore *48*   33
cheek] cheekes *48*   34 those] those, *48* flagrant] fragrant
Grosart   36 Had] She *48*   48 shaft] shafts *48*   58 kindly
takes *48* : giues *52*

If all 's præscription ; & proud wrong
Hearkens not to an humble song ;
For all the gallantry of him,
Giue me the suffring SERAPHIM.
His be the brauery of all those Bright things,
The glowing cheekes, the glistering wings ;
The Rosy hand, the radiant DART ;
Leaue HER alone THE FLAMING HEART.
 Leaue her that ; & thou shalt leaue her
Not one loose shaft but loue's whole quiuer.   70
For in loue's feild was neuer found
A nobler weapon then a WOVND.
Loue's passiues are his actiu'st part.
The wounded is the wounding heart.
O HEART ! the æquall poise of lou'es both parts
Bigge alike with wounds & darts.
Liue in these conquering leaues ; liue all the same ;
And walk through all tongues one triumphant FLAME
Liue here, great HEART ; & loue and dy & kill ;
And bleed & wound ; and yeild & conquer still.   80
Let this immortall life wherere it comes
Walk in a crowd of loues & MARTYRDOMES.
Let mystick DEATHS wait on't ; & wise soules be
The loue-slain wittnesses of this life of thee.
O sweet incendiary ! shew here thy art,
Vpon this carcasse of a hard, cold, hart,
Let all thy scatter'd shafts of light, that play
Among the leaues of thy larg Books of day,
Combin'd against this BREST at once break in
And take away from me my self & sin,   90
This gratious Robbery shall thy bounty be ;
And my best fortunes such fair spoiles of me.
O thou vndanted daughter of desires !
By all thy dowr of LIGHTS & FIRES ;
By all the eagle in thee, all the doue ;
By all thy liues & deaths of loue ;
By thy larg draughts of intellectuall day,
And by thy thirsts of loue more large then they ;

(handwritten marginalia:) St. Francis de Sales / Traité de l'Amour de Dieu (Paris 1925) II 238–44.

---

64 suffring] suffting] *52*   65 things, *48* : things. *52*   66 glistering] glittering *48*   74 heart. *48* : heart *52*   76 wounds *48* : wound *52*   darts.] darts, *48*   *ll. 85–108 not in 48*   98 thirsts] thrists *52 (a possible form, however ; see O.E.D. art.* 'thirst')

By all thy brim-fill'd Bowles of feirce desire
By thy last Morning's draught of liquid fire ;   100
By the full kingdome of that finall kisse
That seiz'd thy parting Soul, & seal'd thee his ;
By all the heau'ns thou hast in him
(Fair sister of the SERAPHIM !
By all of HIM we haue in THEE ;
Leaue nothing of my SELF in me.
Let me so read thy life, that I
Vnto all life of mine may dy.

A SONG.

LOrd, when the sense of thy sweet grace
    Sends vp my soul to seek thy face.
Thy blessed eyes breed such desire,
I dy in loue's delicious Fire.
    O loue, I am thy SACRIFICE.
Be still triumphant, blessed eyes.
Still shine on me, fair suns ! that I
Still may behold, though still I dy.

Second part.

    Though still I dy, I liue again ;
Still longing so to be still slain,   10
So gainfull is such losse of breath,
I dy euen in desire of death.
    Still liue in me this louing strife
Of liuing DEATH & dying LIFE.
For while thou sweetly slayest me
Dead to my selfe, I liue in Thee.

A Song. *First published in 48 with heading :* A Song of divine Love.
MS. *A1. Heading in A1 :* A Songe   1 grace] geace 52   8–9 Second]
The second 48   11 *breath,* 48 : breath. 52   13 louing]
longing 48

PRAYER.

AN ODE, WHICH WAS
Præfixed to a little Prayer-book
giuen to a young

GENTLE-WOMAN.

LO here a little volume, but great Book !
A nest of new-born sweets ;
  Whose natiue fires disdaining
  To ly thus folded, & complaining
  Of these ignoble sheets,
  Affect more comly bands
  (Fair one) from thy kind hands
  And confidently look
  To find the rest
Of a rich binding in your BREST.   10
It is, in one choise handfull, heauenn ; & all
Heaun's Royall host ; incamp't thus small
To proue that true, schooles vse to tell,
Ten thousand Angels in one point can dwell.
It is loue's great artillery
Which here contracts it self, & comes to ly
Close couch't in your white bosom : & from thence
As from a snowy fortresse of defence,
Against your ghostly foes to take your part,
And fortify the hold of your chast heart. 20
It is an armory of light
Let constant vse but keep it bright,
   You'l find it yeilds
To holy hands & humble hearts
   More swords & sheilds
Then sin hath snares, or Hell hath darts.

Prayer. &c. For earlier version in 46 and collation see p. 126, *above.*
52 generally follows 48, with exceptions noted below. (*Heading*)
giuen] *giuin 52* young] *young. 52* *48 omits the words* Prayer
and little. *7* thy *48 :* the *52* *11 48 conforms to punctuation of 46,*
q.v. *13* true, *48 :* true *52 46* *16* it] il *52* *17* your *48 :*
their *52* *19* your ghostly foes] *the* Ghostly foe *48 :* their ghostly
foes *52* your part *48 :* their part *52* *20* your *48 :* their *52*
(*probably* yʳ *in Crashaw's MS. in each of these instances*)

Only be sure
The hands be pure
That hold these weapons ; & the eyes
Those of turtles, chast & true ;   30
Wakefull & wise ;
Here is a freind shall fight for you,
Hold but this book before your heart
Let prayer alone to play his part,
But ô the heart
That studyes this high ART
Must be a sure house-keeper ;
And yet no sleeper.
Dear soul, be strong.
MERCY will come e're long   40
And bring his bosom fraught with blessings,
Flowers of neuer fading graces
To make immortall dressings
For worthy soules, whose wise embraces
Store vp themselues for HIM, who is alone
The SPOVSE of Virgins & the Virgin's son.
But if the noble BRIDEGROOM, when he come,
Shall find the loytering HEART from home ;
Leauing her chast aboad
To gadde abroad   50
Among the gay mates of the god of flyes ;
To take her pleasure & to play
And keep the deuill's holyday ;
To dance ith' sunshine of some smiling
But beguiling
Spheares of sweet & sugred Lyes,
Some slippery Pair
Of false, perhaps as fair,
Flattering but forswearing eyes ;
Doubtlesse some other heart   60
Will gett the start
Mean while, & stepping in before
Will take possession of that sacred store
Of hidden sweets & holy ioyes.

33 your *48* : their *52*   38 sleeper] fleeper *52*   41 his] its *48*
bosom] besom *52*   49 her] its *48*   51 Among] Amongst *48*   54
ith' *48* : th' *52*   56 Spheares] Spheare *48*   62 Mean while,] *omitted
in 48*   63 that] the *48*   64 ioyes.] joyes, *48*

WORDS which are not heard with EARES
(Those tumultuous shops of noise)
Effectuall wispers, whose still voice
The soul it selfe more feeles then heares ;
Amorous languishments ; luminous trances ;
SIGHTS which are not seen with eyes ;   70
Spirituall & soul-peircing glances
Whose pure & subtil lightning flyes
Home to the heart, & setts the house on fire
And melts it down in sweet desire
          Yet does not stay
To ask the windows leaue to passe that way ;
Delicious DEATHS ; soft exalations
Of soul ; dear & diuine annihilations ;
          A thousand vnknown rites
Of ioyes & rarefy'd delights ;   80
A hundred thousand goods, glories, & graces,
          And many a mystick thing
          Which the diuine embraces
Of the deare spouse of spirits with them will bring
          For which it is no shame
That dull mortality must not know a name.
          Of all this store
Of blessings & ten thousand more
          (If when he come
          He find the Heart from home)   90
          Doubtlesse he will vnload
          Himself some other where,
          And poure abroad
          His pretious sweets
On the fair soul whom first he meets.
O fair, ô fortunate !   O riche, ô dear !
O happy & thrice happy she
          Selected doue
          Who ere she be,
          Whose early loue   100
          With winged vowes
Makes hast to meet her morning spouse
And close with his immortall kisses.
Happy indeed, who neuer misses

75 does] doth *48*

To improue that pretious hour,
  And euery day
  Seize her sweet prey
All fresh & fragrant as he rises
Dropping with a baulmy Showr
A delicious dew of spices ;   110
O let the blissfull heart hold fast
Her heaunly arm-full, she shall tast
At once ten thousand paradises ;
  She shall haue power
  To rifle & deflour
The rich & roseall spring of those rare sweets
Which with a swelling bosome there she meets
  Boundles & infinite
  Bottomles treasures
Of pure inebriating pleasures.   120
Happy proof ! she shal discouer
  What ioy, what blisse,
How many Heau'ns at once it is
To haue her GOD become her LOVER.

TO
THE SAME PARTY
COVNCEL
CONCERNING HER
CHOISE.

DEar, heaun-designed SOVL !
  Amongst the rest
Of suters that beseige your Maiden brest,
  Why may not I
  My fortune try
And venture to speak one good word
Not for my self alas, but for my dearer LORD ?

117 meets] meets. *48*   118 *See note to l. 112 in 46.*
 To the same *&c.* *First published in 48 with same heading.* MS. *A1.*
Heading in A1 : Good Councell to a yonge Gentlewoman. 4 may
48 : my *52*

You'aue seen allready, in this lower sphear
Of froth & bubbles, what to look for here.
Say, gentle soul, what can you find　　　　　　　　10
　　　　But painted shapes,
　　　　Peacocks & Apes,
　　　　Illustrious flyes,
Guilded dunghills, glorious L Y E S,
　　　　Goodly surmises
　　　　And deep disguises,
Oathes of water, words of wind ?
TRVTH biddes me say, 'tis time you cease to trust
Your soul to any son of dust.
'Tis time you listen to a brauer loue,　　　　　　20
　　　　Which from aboue
　　　　Calls you vp higher
　　　　And biddes you come
　　　　And choose your roome
Among his own fair sonnes of fire,
　　　　Where you among
　　　　The golden throng
That watches at his palace doores
　　　　May passe along
And follow those fair starres of yours ;　　　　　30
Starrs much too fair & pure to wait vpon
The false smiles of a sublunary sun.
Sweet, let me prophesy that at last t'will proue
　　　　Your wary loue
Layes vp his purer & more pretious vowes,
And meanes them for a farre more worthy SPOVSE
Then this world of Lyes can giue ye
'Eun for Him with whom nor cost,
Nor loue, nor labour can be lost ;
Him who neuer will deceiue ye.　　　　　　　40
Let not my lord, the Mighty louer
Of soules, disdain that I discouer
　　　　The hidden art
Of his high stratagem to win your heart,

9 here.] here, *48*　　　14 L Y E S,] lyes. *48*　　　18 cease] leaue
A1　　　30 follow] fellow *48*　　　31 too fair &] to faire a *A1*　　　*Space
after l. 32 in 48.*　　　35 purer] purer, *48*　　　35 more] most *48*
37 *Indented 48* ye] you *A1*　　　38 'Eun] Ene *A1* nor] no *A1*
41 *Space after l. 40, which is also indented, in 48.*

It was his heaunly art
Kindly to crosse you
In your mistaken loue,
That, at the next remoue
Thence he might tosse you
And strike your troubled heart   50
Home to himself ; to hide it in his brest
The bright ambrosiall nest,
Of loue, of life, & euerlasting rest.
Happy Mystake !
That thus shall wake
Your wise soul, neuer to be wonne
Now with a loue below the sun.
Your first choyce failes, ô when you choose agen
May it not be amongst the sonnes of Men.

Space after l. 53 in 48.   *56–7 Slightly indented in 48.*

ALEXIAS

THE

COMPLAINT

OF

THE FORSAKEN WIFE

OF SAINTE ALEXIS.

THE FIRST ELEGIE.

I late the roman youth's lou'd prayse & pride,
    Whom long none could obtain, though thousands try'd,
Lo here am left (alas), For my lost mate
T'embrace my teares, & kisse an vnkind FATE.
Sure in my early woes starres were at strife,
And try'd to make a WIDOW ere a WIFE.
Nor can I tell (and this new teares doth breed)
In what strange path my lord's fair footsteppes bleed.
O knew I where he wander'd, I should see
Some solace in my sorrow's certainty   10
I'd send my woes in words should weep for me.
(Who knowes how powrfull well-writt praires would be ?)
Sending's too slow a word, my selfe would fly.
Who knowes my own heart's woes so well as I ?
But how shall I steal hence ? ALEXIS thou
Ah thou thy self, alas, hast taught me how.
Loue too, that leads the way, would lend the wings
To bear me harmlesse through the hardest things.
And where loue lends the wing, & leads the way,
What dangers can there be dare say me nay ?   20
If I be shipwrack't, Loue shall teach to swimme.
If drown'd ; sweet is the death indur'd for HIM,

Alexias &c. *First published in 48 among ' The Delights of the Muses ',*
with heading verbally the same as here omitting the word ' Sainte '.
52 generally follows 48, with exceptions noted here.   COMPLAINT]
COMPLAINT. *52*   SAINTE] SANITE *52*   1 lou'd] loud *48*   9
should] would *48*   10 certainty] certainty. *48*   11 me.]
me, *48*   17 the way *48* : the *52*

The noted sea shall change his name with me ;
I, 'mongst the blest STARRES a new name shall be.
And sure where louers make their watry graues
The weeping mariner will augment the waues.
For who so hard, but passing by that way
Will take acquaintance of my woes, & say
Here 't was the roman MAID found a hard fate
While through the world she sought her wandring mate. 30
Here perish't she, poor heart, heauns, be my vowes
As true to me, as she was to her spouse.
O liue, so rare a loue ! liue ! & in thee
The too frail life of femal constancy.
Farewell ; & shine, fair soul, shine there aboue
Firm in thy crown, as here fast in thy loue.
There thy lost fugitiue thou'hast found at last.
Be happy ; and for euer hold him fast.

THE

SECONDE ELEGIE.

THough All the ioyes I had fleed hence with Thee
Vnkind ! yet are my TEARES still true to me
I'am wedded ore again since thou art gone ;
Nor couldst thou, cruell, leaue me quite alone.
ALEXIS' widdow now is sorrow's wife.
With him shall I weep out my weary life.
Wellcome, my sad sweet Mate ! Now haue I gott
At last a constant loue that leaues me not.
Firm he, as thou art false, Nor need my cryes
Thus vex the earth & teare the beauteous skyes.   10
For him, alas, n'ere shall I need to be
Troublesom to the world, thus, as for thee.
For thee I talk to trees ; with silent groues
Expostulate my woes & much-wrong'd loues.
Hills & relentlesse rockes, or if there be
Things that in hardnesse more allude to thee ;
To these I talk in teares, & tell my pain ;
And answer too for them in teares again.

23 his] its *48*   25 where] when *48*   graues *48* : graues. *52*
37 thou'hast] th'hast *48*
  1 fleed] fled *48*   3 I'am] I'm *48*   10 the beauteous *48* : the *52*

How oft haue I wept out the weary sun !
My watry hour-glasse hath old times outrunne.   20
O I am learned grown, Poor loue & I
Haue study'd ouer all astrology.
I'am perfect in heaun's state, with euery starr
My skillfull greife is grown familiar.
Rise, fairest of those fires ; whate're thou be
Whose rosy beam shall point my sun to me.
Such as the sacred light that erst did bring
The EASTERN princes to their infant king.
O rise, pure lamp ! & lend thy golden ray
That weary loue at last may find his way.   30

THE
THIRD ELEGIE.

RIch, churlish LAND ! that hid'st so long in thee,
My treasures, rich, alas, by robbing mee.
Needs must my miseryes owe that man a spite
Who e're he be was the first wandring knight.
O had he nere been at that cruell cost
NATVRE's virginity had nere been lost.
Seas had not bin rebuk't by sawcy oares
But ly'n lock't vp safe in their sacred shores.
Men had not spurn'd at mountaines ; nor made warrs
With rocks ; nor bold hands struck the world's strong barres.
Nor lost in too larg bounds, our little Rome   11
Full sweetly with it selfe had dwell't at home.
My poor ALEXIS, then in peacefull life,
Had vnder some low roofe lou'd his plain wife.
But now, ah me, from where he has no foes
He flyes ; & into willfull exile goes.
Cruell return.   Or tell the reason why
Thy dearest parents haue deseru'd to dy.
And I, what is my crime I cannot tell.
Vnlesse it be a crime to' haue lou'd too well.   20

20 Times *48* : time *52*   23 I'am] I'm *48*
  5 cost] eost *52*   7 by] with *48*   11 Nor] Not *48*
13 ALEXIS] ALEYIS *52*   ALEXIS, then] *Alexis* then, *48*   14
wife. *48* : wife *52*   16 exile] exiles *48*   17 Or] O *48*   19
tell.] tell, *48*   20 to'have] t'have *48*

If Heates of holyer loue & high desire
Make bigge thy fair brest with immortall fire,
What needes my virgin lord fly thus from me,
Who only wish his virgin wife to be ?
Wittnesse, chast heauns ! no happyer vowes I know
Then to a virgin GRAVE vntouch't to goe.
Loue's truest Knott by Venus is not ty'd ;
Nor doe embraces onely make a bride.
The QVEEN of angels, (and men chast as You)
Was MAIDEN WIFE & MAIDEN MOTHER too.   30
CECILIA, Glory of her name & blood
With happy gain her maiden vowes made good.
The lusty bridegroom made approach : young man,
Take heed (said she) take heed, VALERIAN !
My bosome's guard, a SPIRIT great & strong,
Stands arm'd, to sheild me from all wanton wrong.
My Chastity is sacred ; & my sleep
Wakefull, her dear vowes vndefil'd to keep.
PALLAS beares armes, forsooth, and should there be
No fortresse built for true VIRGINITY ?   40
No gaping gorgon, this. None, like the rest
Of your learn'd lyes. Here you'l find no such iest.
I'am yours, O were my GOD, my CHRIST so too,
I'd know no name of loue on earth but you.
He yeilds, and straight Baptis'd, obtains the grace
To gaze on the fair souldier's glorious face.
Both mixt at last their blood in one rich bed
Of rosy MARTYRDOME, twice Married.
O burn our hymen bright in such high Flame.
Thy torch, terrestriall loue, haue here no name.   50
How sweet the mutuall yoke of man & wife,
When holy fires maintain loue's Heaunly life !
But I, (so help me heaun my hopes to see)
When thousands sought my loue, lou'd none but Thee.
Still, as their vain teares my firm vowes did try,
ALEXIS, he alone is mine (said I)
Half true, alas, half false, proues that poor line.
ALEXIS is alone ; But is not mine.

29 QVEEN of angels] Blessed Virgin *48*   33 approach : *48* :
approach *52*   41 gaping] facing *48*   50 haue] hath *48*   51
sweet] sweet's *48*   54 thousands *48* : thousand *52*   56 I)]
I.) *48*

DESCRIPTION

OF

A RELIGIOVS HOVSE

AND CONDITION

OF LIFE

(OVT OF BARCLAY.)

NO roofes of gold o're riotous tables shining
　　Whole dayes & suns deuour'd with endlesse dining ;
No sailes of tyrian sylk proud pauements sweeping ;
Nor iuory couches costlyer slumbers keeping ;
False lights of flairing gemmes ; tumultuous ioyes ;
Halls full of flattering men & frisking boyes ;
Whate're false showes of short & slippery good
Mix the mad sons of men in mutuall blood.
But WALKES & vnshorn woods ; and soules, iust so
Vnforc't & genuine ; but not shady tho.　　　　　　　　10
Our lodgings hard & homely as our fare.
That chast & cheap, as the few clothes we weare.
Those, course & negligent, As the naturall lockes
Of these loose groues, rough as th'vnpolish't rockes.
A hasty Portion of præscribed sleep ;
Obedient slumbers ? that can wake & weep,
And sing, & sigh, & work, and sleep again ;
Still rowling a round sphear of still-returning pain.
Hands full of harty labours ; Paines that pay
And prize themselves ; doe much, that more they may,　　20
And work for work, not wages ; let to morrow's
New drops, wash off the sweat of this daye's sorrows.
A long & dayly-dying life, which breaths
A respiration of reuiuing deaths.

Description &c.　*First published in 48 with heading : Description
of a religious house.*　　DESCRIPTION]　DESCRIPTION.　*52*
4 costlyer] costly *48*　　　6 frisking *48* : frishing *52*　　　7 slippery
48 : flippery *52*　　　11 fare.] fare ; *48*　　　17 sing, &] sing, &, & *52*
18 *Spheare 48* : spear *52*　　　19–20 Paines . . . themselves] *Supplied
from 48, missing in 52*　　23 dying *48* : ding *52*

· But neither are there those ignoble stings
That nip the bosome of the world's best things,
And lash Earth-laboring souls.
No cruell guard of diligent cares, that keep
Crown'd woes awake ; as things too wise for sleep.
But reuerent discipline, & religious fear,   30
And soft obedience, find sweet biding here ;
Silence, & sacred rest ; peace, & pure ioyes ;
Kind loues keep house, ly close, and make no noise,
And room enough for Monarchs, while none swells
Beyond the kingdomes of contentfull Cells.
The self-remembring SOVL sweetly recouers
Her kindred with the starrs ; not basely houers
Below : But meditates her immortall way
Home to the originall sourse of LIGHT & intellectuall Day.

AN

EPITAPH

VPON

A YOVNG MARRIED COVPLE

DEAD AND BVRYED

TOGETHER.

TO these, whom DEATH again did wed,
This GRAVE's their second Marriage-bed.
For though the hand of fate could force
'Twixt SOVL & BODY a Diuorce,
It could not sunder man & WIFE,
'Cause They Both liued but one life.
Peace, good Reader.   Doe not weep.
Peace, The Louers are asleep.
They, sweet Turtles, folded ly
In the last knott loue could ty.   10

30 reuerent] reverend *48*   33 and make] make *52* and keep *48*
An Epitaph *&c. For earlier version in 46 and collation with MSS. see*
p. 174 above.   52 generally follows 48, with exceptions given below.
MS. A1 agrees with 52.   5 WIFE] WIEE *52*

And though they ly as they were dead,
Their Pillow stone, their sheetes of lead,
(Pillow hard, & sheetes not warm)
Loue made the bed ; They'l take no harm
Let them sleep : let them sleep on.
Till this stormy night be gone,
Till the' Æternall morrow dawn ;
Then the curtaines will be drawn
And they wake into a light,
Whose day shall neuer dy in Night.   2

DEATH'S LECTVRE

AT THE

FVNERAL

OF

A YOVNG GENTLEMAN.

Dear Reliques of a dislodg'd SOVL, whose lack
     Makes many a mourning paper put on black !
O stay a while, ere thou draw in thy head
And wind thy self vp close in thy cold bed.
Stay but a little while, vntill I call
A summons worthy of thy funerall.
Come then, YOVTH, BEAVTY, & blood !
          All ye soft powres,
Whose sylken flatteryes swell a few fond howres
Into a false æternity.   Come man ;   10
Hyperbolized NOTHING ! know thy span ;
Take thine own measure here : down, down, & bow
Before thy self in thine idæa ; thou

---

14 harm] harme. *48*   17 Till] And *48*   19 And] 'And *52*
a] that *48* light, *48* : light. *52*
     Death's Lecture *&c.   For version in 46, and collation with MS., see*
p. 175 above.   52 generally agrees with 48, with exceptions given below.
Heading in 48 : At the Funerall of a young Gentleman.   (*Heading*)
AT THE] AND THE *52*   7 come . . . powres *as one line 48*   8 ye
48 : the *52*   powers, *48* : powres. *52*   12 here : *48* : here *52*

Huge emptynes ! contract thy self ; & shrinke
All thy Wild circle to a Point. O sink
Lower & lower yet ; till thy leane size
Call heaun to look on thee with narrow eyes.
Lesser & lesser yet ; till thou begin
To show a face, fitt to confesse thy Kin,
Thy neigbourhood to NOTHING. 20
Proud lookes, & lofty eyliddes, here putt on
Your selues in your vnfaign'd reflexion,
Here, gallant ladyes ! this vnpartiall glasse
(Though you be painted) showes you your true face.
These death-seal'd lippes are they dare giue the ly
To the lowd Boasts of poor Mortality
These curtain'd windows, this retired eye
Outstares the liddes of larg-look't tyranny.
This posture is the braue one this that lyes
Thus low, stands vp (me thinkes,) thus & defies 30
The world. All-daring dust & ashes ! only you
Of all interpreters read Nature True.

15 Wild] wide *48*   17 narrow] norrow *52*   20 *indented 48*   26
Mortality] Mortalitie. *48*   27 These] Those *48*   29 one] one. *48*
31 world.] world—— *48 continuing* All &c. *on next line indented.*

TEMPERANCE.

OR THE

CHEAP PHYSITIAN

VPON

THE TRANSLATION OF

L E S S I V S.

G Oe now ; and with some daring drugg
    Bait thy disease.   And whilst they tugge,
Thou to maintain their pretious strife
Spend the dear treasures of thy life.
Goe, take physick Doat vpon
Some big-nam'd composition.
Th'Oraculous DOCTOR's mystick bills ;
Certain hard WORDS made into pills,
And what at last shalt' gain by these ?
Only a costlyer disease.   10
That which makes vs haue no need
Of physick, that's PHYSICK indeed.
Hark hither, Reader ! wilt thou see
Nature her own physitian be ?

Temperance &c. *For version in 46 and collation with some MSS.
see p. 156 above. 52 agrees generally with Hygiasticon, 48, and MSS. A 3
and Bodl. 31037, with exceptions given below. Lines 1–12 are missing
in Hygiasticon and in MS. Bodl. 31037. Heading in Hygiasticon :* To
the Reader, upon this Books intent. *Heading in 48 as 46. Heading
in A 3 :* Vpon Lessius. *Heading in Bodl. 31037 :* To yᵉ reader on
Lessius hygiasticon.   (*Heading*) OR THE] OF THE *52*   1 and
with] with *A 3* ·   2 whilst] while *48 A 3*   3 pretious] cruell *A 3*
4 treasures] treasure *48*   6 big-nam'd composition] *A 3 distinguishes*   7 mystick bills] *A 3 distinguishes*   8 hard WORDS]
A 3 distinguishes   9 last shalt' gain] last shall gaine *48* : length shalt
gett *A 3*   *After l. 10 A 3 (cp. 46) inserts the couplet :*
       Goe poore man thinke what shall bee
       Remedy 'gainst thy remedy
13 hither, *Hyg 48* : hither. *52*   wilt] wouldst *Hyg A 3 Bodl. 31037*

Wilt' see a man, all his own wealth,
His own musick, his own health ;
A man whose sober soul can tell
How to wear her garments well.
Her garments, that vpon her sitt
As garments should doe, close & fitt ;   20
A well-cloth'd soul ; that's not opprest
Nor choak't with what she should be drest.
A soul sheath'd in a christall shrine ;
Through which all her bright features shine ;
As when a peice of wanton lawn
A thinne, aeriall veil, is drawn
Or'e beauty's face ; seeming to hide
More sweetly showes the blushing bride.
A soul, whose intellectuall beames
No mists doe mask, no lazy steames.   30
A happy soul, that all the way
To HEAVN rides in a summer's day.
Wouldst' see a man, whose well-warm'd blood
Bathes him in a genuine flood !
A man, whose tuned humors be
A set of rarest harmony ?
Wouldst' see blith lookes, fresh cheekes beguil
Age ? wouldst see december smile ?
Wouldst' see nests of new roses grow
In a bed of reuerend snow ?   40
Warm thoughts, free spirits flattering
Winter's selfe into a SPRING.
In summe, wouldst see a man that can
Liue to be old, and still a man ?
Whose latest & most leaden houres
Fall with soft wings, stuck with soft flowres ;
And when life's sweet fable ends,

15 Wilt'] Wouldst *Hyg A3 Bodl. 31037*   man, all] man all, *48*
16 musick] Physick *48*   21 oppreṣt] oppest *52*   23 A soul]
Whose soul's *Hyg Bodl. 31037*   24 bright] fayre *A3*   27
face ; *Hyg Bodl. 31037* : face *52 48 A3*   seeming . . . bride.] *A3*
distinguishes   31 way *Hyg A3* : way. *52* : way, *48 Bodl. 31037*
all... (32) day.] *A3 distinguishes*   32 rides in] hath *A3*   36 set]
all versions except 52 which reads seat   39 nests of new] a nest of
Hyg a bed of *A3 Bodl. 31037*   roses] *A3 distinguishes*   40 bed]
nest *A3*   of reuerend] nf renerend *52*   reuerend snow] *A3*
distinguishes   42 SPRING] SRING *52*   43-4 *Couplet indented 48*
47 fable] *A3 distinguishes*

Soul & body part like freinds ;
No quarrells, murmurs, no delay ;
A KISSE, a SIGH, and so away.   50
This rare one, reader, wouldst thou see ?
Hark hither ; and thy self be HE.

HOPE.

HOpe whose weak beeing ruin'd is
        Alike if it succeed or if it misse !
Whom ill or good does equally confound
And both the hornes of fate's dilemma wound.
            Vain shadow ; that dost vanish quite
            Both at full noon & perfect night !
The starres haue not a possibility
            Of blessing Thee.
If thinges then from their end we happy call,
'Tis hope is the most hopelesse thing of all.   10
    Hope, thou bold Taster of delight !
Who instead of doing so, deuourst it quite.
Thou bringst vs an estate, yet leau'st vs poor
By clogging it with legacyes before.
            The ioyes which we intire should wed
            Come deflour'd-virgins to our bed.
Good fortunes without gain imported be
            Such mighty custom's paid to Thee.
For ioy like wine kep't close, does better tast ;
If it take air before his spirits wast.   20
    Hope fortun's cheating lottery
Where for one prize, an hundred blankes there be.
Fond archer, hope.   Who tak'st thine aime so farr
That still or short or wide thine arrowes are
            Thinne empty cloud which th'ey deceiues
            With shapes that our own fancy giues.
A cloud which gilt & painted now appeares
            But must drop presently in teares

---

48 Soul] His soul *Hyg Bodl. 31037*   50 A KISSE, a SIGH] A sigh,
a kisse, *A3*

    Hope. *See 46, p. 143 above, where the poem is printed with the succeed-*
ing poem by Crashaw, in alternating stanzas.   16 bed. *46* : bed, *48* :
bed *52*   18 Thee. *46 48* : Thee *52*

When thy false beames o're reason's light prevail,
By IGNES FATVI for north starres we sail. 30
  Brother of fear more gayly clad.
The merryer fool oth two, yet quite as mad.
Sire of repentance, child of fond desire
That blow'st the chymick & the louer's fire.
    Still leading them insensibly'on
    With the strong witchcraft of Anon.
By thee the one does changing nature through
    Her endlesse labyrinth's pursue,
And th'other chases woman ; while she goes
More wayes & turnes then ·hunted nature knowes. 40

            M. COWLEY.

M. CRASHAWS
ANSWER
FOR HOPE.

DEar hope ! earth's dowry, & heaun's debt !
   The entity of those that are not yet.
Subtlest, but surest beeing ! Thou by whom
Our nothing has a definition !
    Substantiall shade ! whose sweet allay
    Blends both the noones of night & day.
Fates cannot find out a capacity
    Of hurting thee.
From Thee their lean dilemma, with blunt horn,
Shrinkes, as the sick moon from the wholsome morn. 10
  Rich hope ! loue's legacy, vnder lock
Of faith ! still spending, & still growing stock !
Our crown-land lyes aboue yet each meal brings
A seemly portion for the sonnes of kings.
    Nor will the virgin ioyes we wed
    Come lesse vnbroken to our bed,

33 repentance] repenrance 52
M. CRASHAWS &c. For earlier version in 46 and collation see
p. 143 above.   CRASHAWS] CRASHAWS. 52   10 morn.]
morn 52

Because that from the bridall cheek of blisse
  Thou steal'st vs down a distant kisse.
Hope's chast stealth harmes no more ioye's maidenhead
Then spousall rites preiudge the marriage bed.   20
  Fair hope ! our earlyer heau'n by thee
Young time is taster to eternity
Thy generous wine with age growes strong, not sowre.
Nor does it kill thy fruit, to smell thy flowre.
   Thy golden, gròwing, head neuer hangs down
   Till in the lappe of loues full noone
It falls ; and dyes ! o no, it melts away
  As does the dawn into the day.
As lumpes of sugar loose themselues ; and twine
Their supple essence with the soul of wine.   30
  Fortune ? alas, aboue the world's low warres
Hope walks ; & kickes the curld heads of conspiring starres.
Her keel cutts not the waues where These winds stirr
Fortune's whole lottery is one blank to her.
   Her shafts, and shee fly farre above,
   And forrage in the fields of light and love.
Sweet hope ! kind cheat ! fair fallacy by thee
We are not WHERE nor What we be,
But WHAT & WHERE we would be.   Thus art thou
Our absent PRESENCE, and our future Now.
  Faith's sister ! nurse of fair desire !   40
Fear's antidote ! a wise & well-stay'd fire !
Temper twixt chill despair, & torrid ioy !
Queen Regent in yonge loue's minority !
   Though the vext chymick vainly chases
   His fugitiue gold through all her faces ;
Though loue's more feirce, more fruitlesse, fires assay
   One face more fugitiue then all they ;
True hope's a glorious hunter & her chase,
The GOD of nature in the feilds of grace.   50

VIVE IESV.

  17 cheek] ckeek *52*   35–6 *Not in 52. Restored from 48.* 36
indented in 52. 40 *not indented in 52.* 41 antidote] antitode *52*

A LETTER

FROM

M.r CRASHAW,

to the

Countess of DENBIGH,

Against Irresolution and Delay in matters of RELIGION.

LONDON.

Against Irresolution and Delay in matters of RELIGION.

WHat Heav'n-besieged Heart is this
   Stands Trembling at the Gate of Blisse :
Holds fast the Door, yet dares not venture
Fairly to open and to enter ?
Whose Definition is, A Doubt
'Twixt Life and Death, 'twixt In and Out.
Ah ! linger not, lov'd Soul : A slow
And late Consent was a long No.
Who grants at last, a great while try'de,
And did his best to have Deny'de.   10
   What Magick-Bolts, what mystick Barrs
Maintain the Will in these strange Warrs ?
What Fatall, yet fantastick, Bands
Keep the free Heart from his own Hands ?
Say, lingring Fair, why comes the Birth
Of your brave Soul so slowly forth ?
Plead your Pretences, (O you strong
In weaknesse) why you chuse so long
In Labour of your self to ly,
Not daring quite to Live nor Die.   20
   So when the Year takes cold we see
Poor Waters their own Prisoners be :
Fetter'd and lock'd up fast they lie
In a cold self-captivity.
Th'astonish'd Nymphs their Floud's strange Fate deplore,
To find themselves their own severer Shoar.
   Love, that lends haste to heaviest things,
In you alone hath lost his wings.
Look round and reade the World's wide face,
The field of Nature or of Grace ;   30
Where can you fix, to find Excuse
Or Pattern for the Pace you use ?

Against Irresolution &c. Cp. the widely different version first published in 52, p. 236 above.

Mark with what Faith Fruits answer Flowers,
And know the Call of Heav'n's kind showers :
Each mindfull Plant hasts to make good
The hope and promise of his Bud.
Seed-time's not all ; there should be Harvest too.
Alas ! and has the Year no Spring for you ?
 Both Winds and Waters urge their way,
And murmure if they meet a stay.   40
Mark how the curl'd Waves work and wind,
All hating to be left behind.
Each bigge with businesse thrusts the other,
And seems to say, Make haste, my Brother.
The aiery nation of neat Doves,
That draw the Chariot of chast Loves,
Chide your delay : yea those dull things,
Whose wayes have least to doe with wings,
Make wings at least of their own Weight,
And by their Love controll their Fate.   50
So lumpish Steel, untaught to move,
Learn'd first his Lightnesse by his Love.
 What e're Love's matter be, he moves
By th'even wings of his own Doves,
Lives by his own Laws, and does hold
In grossest Metalls his own Gold.
 All things swear friends to Fair and Good,
Yea Suitours ; Man alone is wo'ed,
Tediously wo'ed, and hardly wone :
Only not slow to be undone.   60
As if the Bargain had been driven
So hardly betwixt Earth and Heaven ;
Our God would thrive too fast, and be
Too much a gainer by't, should we
Our purchas'd selves too soon bestow
On him, who has not lov'd us so.
When love of Us call'd Him to see
If wee'd vouchsafe his company,
He left his Father's Court, and came
Lightly as a Lambent Flame,   70
Leaping upon the Hills, to be
The Humble King of You and Me.
Nor can the cares of his whole Crown
(When one poor Sigh sends for him down)

Detain him, but he leaves behind
The late wings of the lazy Wind,
Spurns the tame Laws of Time and Place,
And breaks through all ten Heav'ns to our embrace.
    Yield to his Siege, wise Soul, and see
Your Triumph in his Victory.   80
Disband dull Feares, give Faith the day :
To save your Life, kill your Delay.
'Tis Cowardise that keeps this Field ;
And want of Courage not to Yield.
    Yield then, O yield, that Love may win
The Fort at last, and let Life in.
Yield quickly, lest perhaps you prove
Death's Prey, before the Prize of Love.
This Fort of your Fair Self if't be not wone,
He is repuls'd indeed, but You'r undone.   90

F I N I S.

POEMS FROM MSS.

POEMS FROM MSS., INCLUDED IN PREVIOUS MODERN EDITIONS.

I. Bodl. MS. Tanner 465.

Ps. 1.

O te te nimis, & nimis beatum !
Quem non lubricus implicavit error ;
Nec risu misero procax tumultus.
Tu cùm grex sacer vndique execrandis
Strident consilijs, nec aure (felix !)
(Felix !) non animo, vel ore mixtus,
Haud intelligis impios susurros.
Sed tu delicijs ferox repôstis
Cultu simplice, sobriâque curâ
Legem numinis usque, & vsque voluis.   10
   Læta sic fidas colit arbor undas :
   Quam nec immiti violentus aurâ
   Seirius frangit, neque contumacis
      Ira procellæ.
At tu, profane pulvis, & lusus sacer
Cujusvis auræ ; fronte quâ tandem feres
Vindex tribunal ? quanta tum, & qualis tuæ
Moles procellæ stabit ? ô quàm ferreo
Frangêre nutu, præda frontis asperæ,
Sacrique fulminandus ah procul, procul   20
A luce vultûs, aureis procul à locis,
Vbi longa gremio mulcet æterno pios
Sincera semper pax, & vmbrosâ super
Insurgit alâ, vividique nectaris
Imbres beatos rore perpetuo pluit.
   Sic ille sic ô vindice stat vigil,
   Et stabit irâ torvus in impios,
     Seseque sub mentes bonorum
     Insinuat facili favore.

Ps. 1. *Also in T6, with heading* Ψ. 1.   *T6 gives verse numbers preceding ll. 1, 8, 11, 12, 15, 16, 26 ; it also indents ll. 11, 12, 13, which are not indented in T5. At end in T6 :* R. Crashaw, MS.
  12 Quam *T6 :* Quem *T5*

Acts 28. 3.

Paule, nihil metuas. non fert hæc vipera virus :
　Virtutem vestræ vult didicisse manûs.
Oscula, non morsus ; supplex, non applicat hostis.
　Nec metuenda venit, sed miseranda magìs.

Joh. 6. 14. 26.

Jam credunt. Deus es. (Deus est, qui teste palato,
　Quique ipso demum est judice dente Deus.)
Scilicet hæc sapiunt miracula : de quibus alvus
　Proficere, & possit pingue latus fluere.
Hæc sua fecisti populo miracula. credunt.
　Gens pia ! & in ventrem relligiosa suum !

In lacrymas Christi patientis.

Sæve dolor ! potes hoc ? oculos quoque perpluis istos ?
　O quàm non meritas hæc arat vnda genas !
O lacrymas ego flere tuas, ego dignior istud,
　Quod tibi cunque cadit roris, habere meum.
Siccine ? me tibi flere tuas ? ah, mi bone Jesu,
　Si possem lacrymas vel mihi flere meas !
Flere meas ? immò immò tuas. hoc si modò possem :
　Non possem lacrymas non ego flere meas.
Flere tuas est flere meas. tua lacryma, Christe,
　Est mea. vel lacryma est si tua, causa mea est.　　10

Joh. 19. In Sepulchrum Domini.

Jam cedant, veteris cedant miracula saxi,
　Vnde novus subito fluxerat amne latex.
Tu, felix rupes, vbi se lux tertia tollet,
　Flammarum sacro fonte superba flues.

Joh. 13. 34. vbi amorem præcipit.

Sic magis in numeros, morituraque carmina vivit
　Dulcior extremâ voce caducus olor ;
Vt tu inter strepitus odii, & tua funera, Jesu,
　Totus amor liquido totus amore sonas.

4 *Also in A4. Spaced in two couplets.*　　5 *(Heading)* 34.] 14 *T*

Act. 12. 23.

Euge Deus ! (pleno populus fremit vndique plausu.)
  Certè non hominem vox sonat. euge Deus !
Sed tamen iste Deus qui sit, vos dicite, vermes,
  Intima turba illi ; vos fovet ille sinu.

Bonum est nobis esse hîc.

Cur cupis hîc adeo, dormitor Petre, manere ?
  Somnia non alibi tam bona, Petre, vides.

Mat. 6. 29.   Videte lilia agrorum—nec Solomon &c.

Candide rex campi, cui floris eburnea pompa est,
  Deque nivis fragili vellere longa toga ;
Purpureus Solomon impar tibi dicitur.   esto.
  Nempe (quod est melius) par fuit ille rosis.

Marc. 7. 33. & 36.

Voce, manuque simul linguæ tu, Christe, ciendæ :
  Sistendæ nudis vocibus vsus eras.
Sanè at lingua equus est pronis effusus habenis :
  Vox ciet, at sistit non nisi tota manus.

In Beatæ Virginis verecundiam.

Non est hoc matris, sed (crede) modestia nati,
  Quòd virgo in gremium deijcit ora suum.
Illîc jam Deus est.   oculus jam Virginis ergò,
  Vt cælum videat, deijciendus erit.

Mitto vos, sicut agnos in medio luporum.

Hos quoque ? an hos igitur sævi lacerabitis agnos ?
  Hîc saltem, hîc vobis non licet esse lupis.
At sceleris nulla est clementia. at ergò scietis,
  Agnus qui nunc est, est aliquando Leo.

1·1 Deus !] *Stop uncertain ; perhaps full-stop.*   plausu.] *stop
uncertain : perhaps colon*   3 *Also in A4. Spaced in two couplets.*

Mat. 4. *Christus à dæmone vectus.*

Ergò ille, Angelicis ô sarcina dignior alis,
  Præpete sic Stygio sic volet ille vehi ?
Pessime ! nec lætare tamen. tu scilicet inde·
  Non minùs es Dæmon, non minùs ille Deus.

Joh. 1. 23.

Vox ego sum, dicis. tu vox es, sancte Johannes ?
  Si vox es, sterilis cur tibi mater erat ?
Quàm fuit ista tuæ mira infæcundia matris !
  In vocem sterilis rarior esse solet.

Vox Joannes ; X^{us} Verbum.

Monstrat Joannes Christum. haud res mira videtur :
  Vox vnus, verbum scilicet alter erat.
Christus Joanne est prior. hæc res mira videtur :
  Voce suâ verbum non solet esse prius.

In natales Domini Pastoribus nuntiatos.

Ad te sydereis, ad te, Bone Tityre, pennis
  Purpureus juvenis gaudia tanta vehit.
O bene te vigilem, cui gaudia tanta feruntur,
  Vt neque, dum vigilas, te vigilare putes.
Quem sic monstrari voluit pastoribus æther,
  Pastor, an Agnus erat ? Pastor, & Agnus erat.
Ipse Deus cùm Pastor erit, quis non erit agnus ?
  Quis non pastor erit, cùm Deus Agnus erit ?

Apocal. xii. 7.

Arma, viri ! (ætheriam quocunque sub ordine pubem
  Siderei proceres ducitis) Arma viri !
Quæque suis, (nec queîs solita est) stet dextra sagittis,
  Stet gladij sævâ luce corusca sui.
Totus adest, totisque movet se major in iris.
  Fertque Draco, quicquid vel Draco ferre potest.
Quas secum facies (imæ mala pignora noctis) !
  Quot secum nigros ducit in arma Deos !

1 *Also in A4. Spaced in two couplets.*   5 *Also in A4. Spaced in couplets. Heading in A4 :* Revel: 12. 7 | Et factum est prælium in cælo | Michael et Angeli ejus. &c.

Jam pugnas parat (heu sævus !) jam pugnat.   & ecce
   Vix potui, *Pugnat,* dicere.   jam cecidit.   10
His tamen ah nimium est quòd frontibus addidit iras ;
   Quòd potuit rugas his posuisse genis :
Hoc torvum decus est, tumidique ferocia fati,
   Quòd magni sceleris mors quoque magna fuit.
Quòd neque, si victus, jaceat victoria vilis :
   Quòd meruit multi fulminis esse labor.
Quòd queat ille suas hoc inter dicere flammas,
   Arma tuli frustra : sed tamen arma tuli.

Act. 17.   In Atheniensem merum.

Ipsos naturæ thalamos sapis, imaque rerum
   Concilia, & primæ quicquid agunt tenebræ.
Quid dubitet refluum mare.   quid vaga sydera volvant.
   Christus at est studijs res aliena tuis.
Sic scire, est tantùm nescire loquaciùs illa.
   Qui nempe illa sapit sola, nec illa sapit.

Joh. 15.   Ego vitis vera.

Credo quidem.   sed & hoc hostis te credidit ipse
   Caiaphas, & Judas credidit ipse, reor.
Vnde illis, Jesu, vitis nisi vera fuisses,
   Tanta tui potuit sanguinis esse sitis ?

Abscessum Christi queruntur discipuli.

Ille abijt.   jamque ô quæ nos mala cunque manetis,
   Sistite jam in nostras tela parata neces.
Sistite.   nam quibus hæc vos olim tela paratis,
   Abscessu Domini jam periêre sui.

In descensum Spiritûs Sancti.

Quæ vehit auratos nubes dulcissima nimbos ?
   Quis mitem pluviam lucidus imber agit ?
Agnosco.   nostros hæc nubes abstulit ignes :
   Hæc nubes in nos jam redit igne pari.

1·10 cecidit] *A4 distinguishes*   1·18 *A4 also distinguishes the line*   2
and 3 also in A4, in reverse order.   Couplet spacing.   2 (*Heading*)
Act. 17.] Act. *A4*   2·3 'mare.] mare, *A4*   2·4 at *A4* : et *T*   3
(*Heading*) 15.] 14. *T*

O nubem gratam, & memorem ! quæ noluit ultrà
    Tam sævè de se nos potuisse queri !
O bene ! namque alio non posset rore rependi,
    Cælo exhalatum quod modò terra dedit.

Act. x. 39.

Quis malus appendit de mortis stipite vitam ?
    O malus Agricola ! hoc inseruisse fuit ?
Immò quis appendit vitæ hac ex arbore mortem ?
    O bonus Agricola ! hoc inseruisse fuit.

Joh. 10.   Ego sum ostium.

Jamque pates. cordisque seram gravis hasta reclusit,
    Et clavi claves undique te reserant.
Ah, vereor, sibi ne manus impia clauserit illas,
    Quæ cæli has ausa est sic aperire fores.

In spinas demtas è Christi capite cruentatas.

Accipe (an ignoscis ?) de te sata germina, Miles.
    Quàm segeti est messis discolor illa suæ !
O quæ tam duro gleba est tam grata colono ?
    Inserit hic spinas : reddit & illa rosas.

Joh. iii.

Nox erat, & Christum (Doctor malè docte) petebas,
    In Christo tenebras depositure tuas.
Ille autem multo dum te bonus irrigat ore,
    Atque per arcanas ducit in alta vias,
Sol venit, & primo pandit se flore diei,
    Ludit et in dubijs aureus horror aquis.
Sol oritur. sed adhuc, & adhuc tamen (ô bone) nescis.
    Sol oritur. tecum nox tamen est & adhuc.

    Non cæli illa fuit ; nox fuit illa tua.

Luc. xv.

O ego vt Angelicis fiam bona gaudia turmis !
    Me quoque sollicito quære per arva gradu.
Mille tibi tutis ludunt in montibus agni,
    Quos potes haud dubiâ dicere voce tuos :

---

6 *(Heading) xv.] ix. T Also published in 70L with several variants.
See p. 70 above.*

Vnus ego erravi, quò me meus error abegit :
  Vnus ego fuerim gaudia plura tibi.
Gaudia non faciunt, quæ nec fecere timorem,
  Et plus, quæ donant ipsa perîcla, placent.
Ex his, quos retines, fuerit tibi latior vsus :
  Ex me, quem recipis, dulcior vsus erit.   10

In Baptistam Vocem.

Tantum habuit Baptista loqui, tot flumina rerum,
  Vt bene Vox fuerit, prætereaque nihil.
Ecce autem *Verbum* est vnum tantùm ille loquutus :
  Vno sed *Verbo* cuncta loquutus erat.

Act. 12. 6, 7.   In D. Petrum ab Angelo solutum.

Mors tibi, & Herodes instant : cùm nuncius ales
  Gaudia fert, quæ tu somnia ferre putas.
Quid tantum dedit ille (rogo) tibi ?   Vincula solvit.
  Mors tibi, & Herodes nonne dedisset idem ?

Luc. 5.   Relictis omnibus sequuti sunt eum.

Ad nutum Domini abjecisti retia, Petre.
  Tam bene non vnquam jacta fuere priùs.
Scilicet hoc rectè jacere est tua retia, Petre,
  Nimirum, Christus cùm jubet, abijcere.

Joh. 1   Agnus Dei, qui tollit peccata mundi.

Ergò tot heu (torvas facies) tot in ora leonum,
  In tot castra lupûm qui meat, Agnus erit ?
Hic tot in horribiles, quot sunt mea crimina, pardos ?
  Hic tot in audaces vngue, vel ore feras ?
Ah melius ! pugiles quis enim commiserit istos ?
  Quos sua non faciunt arma, vel ira pares.

Marc. 8.   Pisces multiplicati.

Quæ secreta meant taciti tibi retia uerbi,
  Queîs non tam pisces, quàm capis Oceanum ?

1·8 ipsa perîcla,] ipsa, perîcla *T*   3 (*Heading*) *The MS. reads* Act. 3.
The correct figures 12. 6, 7 *are inserted above the* 3.

Joh. 13.   *Domine, non solùm pedes, sed & caput, &c.*

En caput ! atque suis quæ plus satìs ora laborant
    Sordibus ! huc fluvios huc (ais) adde tuos.
Nil opus est.   namque hæc (modò tertius occinat ales)
    E fluvijs fuerint, Petre, lavanda suis.

Joh. 12. 37.   *Cùm tot signa edidisset, non credebant.*

Quantâ amor ille tuus se cunque levauerit alâ,
    Quo tua cunque opere effloruit alta manus ;
Mundus adest, contráque tonat.   signisque reponit
    Signa.   (adeo sua sunt numina vel sceleri.)
Imò (ô nec nimij vis sit temeraria verbi)
    Ille vno sensu vel tua cuncta premit.
Tot, tantisque tuis mirâclum hoc objicit vnum,
    Tot tantisque tuis non adhibere fidem.

Act. 1.   *In nubem, quæ Dnū abstulit.*

O Nigra hæc !   Quid enim mihi candida pectora monstrat ?
    Pectora Cygnǽis candidiora genis.
Sit verò magis alba, suo magis aurea Phæbo,
    Quantumcunque sibi candida ;   nigra mihi est.
Nigra mihi nubes ! et quâ neque nigrior Austros,
    Vel tulit irati nuncia tela Dei.
Nigra ! licèt nimbos, noctem neque detulit ullam.
    Si noctem non fert, at rapit, ecce, diem.

Luc. 19.   *Vidit urbem, & flevit super eam.*

Ergò meas spernis lacrymas, urbs perfida ?   Sperne.
    Sperne meas.   quas ô sic facis esse tuas.
Tempus erit, lacrymas poterit cùm lacryma demum
    Nostra (nec immeritò) spernere spreta tuas.

Luc. 18.   *Nec sicut iste Publicanus.*

Tu quoque dum istius miseri peccata fateris,
    Quæ nec is irato mitiùs vngue notat ;
Hic satis est gemino bonus in sua crimina telo.
    Interea quid erit, mi Pharïsæe, tuis ?

2 (*Heading*) 37.] 19. T

Mat. 8.—& accedentes discipuli excitavérunt eum.

Ah, quis erat furor hos (tam raros) soluere somnos ?
  O vos, queîs Christi vel sopor invigilat !
Illum si somnus tenuit, vos somnia terrent,
  Somnia tam vanos ingeminata metus.
Nil Christi nocuit somnus (mihi credite.)   Somnus,
  Qui nocuit, vestræ somnus erat fidei.

Mat. 15.   In mulierem Canaanæam cum Dn° decertantem.

Cedit jo.   jam, jamque cadet.   modò fortiter vrge.
  Jam, tua nî desit dextera, jamque cadet.
Nimirum hoc velit ipse.   tuo favet ipse triumpho :
  Ipse tuas tacitus res tuus hostis agit.
Quas patitur, facit ille manus.   ictu ille sub omni est ;
  Atque in te vires sentit, amatque suas,
Vsque adeò haud tuus hic ferus est, neque ferreus hostis !
  Vsque adeò est miles non truculentus Amor !   ·
Illo quàm facilis victoria surgit ab hoste,
  Qui, tantùm vt vinci possit, in arma venit !   10

Mat. 9.   Quare comedit Magister vester
cum peccatoribus &c.

Siccine fraternos fastidis, improbe, morbos,
  Cùm tuus, (& gravior) te quoque morbus habet ?
Tantum ausus medicum morbus sibi quærere, magnus ;
  Tantum ausus medicum spernere, Major erat.

Marc. 1. & Luc. 14.   In $\begin{cases} febricitantem \\ \& \\ hydropicum \end{cases}$ *sanatos.*

Nuper lecta gravem extinxit pia pagina febrem :
  Hydropi siccos dat modò lecta sinus.
Hæc vice fraternâ quàm se miracula tangunt,
  Atque per alternum fida juvamen amant !
Quippe ignes istos his quàm bene mersit in undis !
  Ignibus his illas quàm bene vicit aquas !

In S. Lucam Medicum.

Hanc, mihi quam miseram faciunt mea crimina vitam,
    Hanc, medici, longam vestra medela facit.
Hocné diu est vixisse ? diu (mihi credite) non est
    Hoc vixisse ; diu sed timuisse mori.
Tu folijs, Medice alme, tuis medicamina præbes,
    Et medicaminibus (quæ mala summa) malis.
Hoc mortem bene vitare est ; vitare ferendo.
    Et vixisse diu est hoc ; citò posse mori.

Tollat crucem suam—&c.

Ergò tuam pone ; vt nobis sit sumere nostram :
    Si nostram vis nos sumere, pone tuam.
Illa illa, ingenti quæ te trabe duplicat, illa
    Vel nostra est, nostras vel tulit illa cruces.

In (Joh. 17.) Cygnæam D̃ Jesû cantionem.

Quæ mella, ô quot, Christe, favos in carmina fundis !
    Dulcis, & (ah furias !) ah moribundus olor !
Parce tamen ; minus hæ si sunt mea gaudia voces :
    Voce quidem dulci, sed moriente canis.

Et conspuebant illum.

Quid non tam fœdè sævi maris audeat ira !
    Conspuit ecce oculos (sydera nostra) tuos.
Forsan & hîc aliquis sputo te excæcat, Jesu,
    Qui debet sputo, quòd videt ipse, tuo.

Joh. 4. Rogavit eum, vt descenderet, & sanaret filium suum.

Ille vt eat tecum, in natique, tuique salutem ?
    Qui petis ; ah nescis (credo) quòd Ales Amor.
Ille vt eat tecum ? quàm se tua vota morantur !
    Ille vt eat ? tantò seriùs esset ibi.
Ne tardus veniat, Christus tecum ire recusat :
    Christi nempe ipsum hoc ire moratur iter.

Christi nempe vijs perit hoc quodcunque meatur :
   Christi nempe vijs vel properare mora est.
Hîc est, cui tu vota facis tua, Christus : at idem
   (Crede mihi) dabit hæc qui rata, Christus ibi est.   10

Luc. 5. 9.   Pavor enim occupauerat eum super capturam piscium.

Dum nimiùm in captis per te, Petre, piscibus hæres,
   Piscibus (ut video) captus es ipse tuis.
Rem scio.   te prædam Christus sibi cepit : & illi
   Vna in te ex istis omnibus esca fuit.

Joh. 15. 24.   vidérunt, & odérunt me.

Vidit ? & odit adhuc ?   Ah, te non vidit, Jesu.
   Non vidit te, qui vidit, & odit adhuc.
Non vidit, te non vidit (dulcissime rerum)
   In te qui vidit quid, quod amare neget.

Luc. 18. 39.

Tu mala turba tace. mihi tam mea vota propinquant,
   Tuque in me linguam vis tacuisse meam ?
Tunc ego, tunc taceam, mihi cùm meus Ille loquetur.
   Si nescis, oculos vox habet ista meos.
O noctis miserere meæ.   miserere, per illam,
   Quæ tam læta tuo ridet in ore diem.
O noctis miserere meæ.   miserere, per illam
   Quæ, nisi te videat, nox velit esse, diem.
O noctis miserere meæ.   miserere, per illam,
   Hæc mea quam (fidei) nox habet ipsa, diem.   10
Illa dies animi (Jesu) rogat hanc oculorum.
   Illam (oro) dederis ; hanc mihi ne rapias.

Mat. 22.   In Pharisæos Christi uerbis insidiantes.

O quàm te miseri ludunt vaga tædia voti,
   Ex ore hoc speras qui, Pharisæe, malum !
Sic quis ab Auroræ noctem speraverit ulnis,
   Vnde solet primis Sol tener ire rosis ?
Sic Acheronta petas illinc, vnde amne corusco
   Lactea sydereos Cynthia lavit equos.

---

3 Joh. 15. 24.] Joh. *T*   4 *Also published in 70L with several variants. See p. 69 above.*

Sic violas aconita roges : sic toxica nympham,
　Garrula quæ vitreo gurgite vexat humum.
Denique (ut exemplo res hæc propiore patescat)
　A te sic speret quis (Pharisæe) bonum.　　　　10

Mat. 9.

Falleris.　& nudum malè ponis (Pictor) Amorem :
　Non nudum facis hunc, cùm sine veste facis.
Nonne hic est (dum sic digito patet ille fideli)
　Tunc, cùm vestitus, tunc quoque nudus amor ?

[*Without heading*]

Tolle oculos, tolle ô tecum (tua sydera) nostros.
　Ah quid enim, quid agant hîc sine sole suo ?
Id, quod agant sine sole suo tua sydera, Cælum :
　Id terræ hæc agerent hîc sine sole suo.
Illa suo sine sole suis cæca imbribus essent :
　Cæca suis lacrymis hæc sine sole suo.

Act. 21.　Nam ego non solum vinciri—&c.

Quid mortem objicitis nostro, quid vinĉla timori ?
　Non timor est illinc, non timor inde meus.
Vincula, quæ timeam, sunt vincula sola timoris :
　Sola timenda mihi est mors, timuisse mori.

Mat. 11.　-Legatio Baptistæ ad Christum.

Oro, quis es ? legat ista suo Baptista Magistro.
　Illi quæ referant, talia Christus habet.
Cui cæcus cernit, mutus se in verba resoluit,
　It claudus, vivit mortuus ; Oro, quis est ?

[*Without heading*]

Ergò veni ; quicunque ferant tua signa timores :
　Quæ nos cunque vocant tristia, Christe, veni.
Christe, veni.　suus avulsum rapiat labor axem,
　Nec sinat implicitas ire redire vias.
Mutuus attonito titubet sub fædere mundus,
　Nec Natura vagum dissona volvat opus.
Christe, veni.　roseos ultrà remeare per ortus
　Nolit, & ambiguos Sol trahat æger equos.

Christe, veni. ipsa suas patiatur Cynthia noctes,
  Plus quàm Thessalico tincta tremore genas.   10
Astrorum mala cæsaries per inane dolendùm
  Gaudeat, horribili flore repexa caput.
Sole sub invito subitæ vis improba noctis
  Corripiat solitam, non sua jura, diem.
Importuna dies, nec Eöi conscia pacti,
  Per desolatæ murmura noctis eat.
Christe, veni. tonet Oceanus pater ; & sua nolit
  Claustra. vagi montes sub nova sceptra meent.
Christe, veni. quodcunque audet metus, audeat ultrà.
  Fata id agant, quod agent. tu modò, Christe, veni.   20
Christe, veni. quâcunque venis mercede malorum.
  Quanti hoc constiterit cunque venire, veni.
Teque, tuosque oculos tanti est potuisse videre !
  Oh tanti est te vel sic potuisse frui !
Quicquid id est, Pater, omne tuo pensabitur ore ;
  Quicquid id est, veniat : *Tu modò, Christe, veni.*

[*Without heading*]

Felices ! properâstis jo, properâstis. & altam
  Vicistis gyro sub breviore viam.
Vos per non magnum vestri mare sanguinis illuc
  Cymba tulit nimijs non operosa notis ;
Quò nos tam lento sub remigio luctantes
  Ducit inexhausti vis malè fida freti.
Nos mora, nos longi consumit inertia lethi.
  In ludum mortis, luxuriemque sumus.
Nos ævo, & senio, & latis permittimur undis.
  Spargimur in casus,—porrigimur furijs.   10
Nos miseri sumus ex amplo ; spatioque perimus.
  In nos inquirunt fata ; probantque manus.
Ingenium fati sumus, ambitioque malorum ;
  Conatus mortis, consiliumque sumus.
In vitæ multo multæ patet area mortis

Non vitam nobis numerant, quot viximus, anni :
  Vita brevis nostra est ; sit licèt acta diu.
Viuere non longum est, quod longam ducere vitam :
  Res longa est vitâ sæpe peracta brevi.   20

---

2 *might be headed* Ad Infantes Martyres (*cp. p. 24, above*)   2·16
omitted in T   2·20 *The MS. reads :* Res longa vitâ sæpe peracta
brevi est.

Nec vos tam vitæ Deus in compendia misit,
    Quàm vetuit vestræ plus licuisse neci.
Accedit vitæ quicquid decerpitur ævo.
    Atque illò breviùs, quò citiùs morimur.

Domitiano. · *De S. Johanne ad portam Lat.*

Ergò vt inultus eas ?   Sed nec tamen ibis inultus,
    Sic violare ausus meque, meosque Deos.
Vre oleo, Lictor.   Oleo parat vrere Lictor :
    Sed quem vri Lictor credidit, unctus erat.
Te quoque sic olei virtus malefida fefellit ?
    Sic tua te Pallas, Domitiane, juvat ?

Εἰς τὸν τοῦ Στεφάνου στέφανον.

Ecce tuos lapides ! nihil est pretiosius illis ;
    Seu pretium capiti dent, capiantúe tuo.
Scilicet hæc ratio vestri diadematis : hoc est,
    Vnde coronatis uos decet ire comis.
Quisque lapis quantò magis in se vilis habetur,
    Ditior hôc capiti est gemma futura tuo.

[*Without heading*]

Ah ferus, ah culter ! qui tam bona lilia primus
    In tam crudeles jussit abire rosas.
Virgineüm hoc qui primus ebur violavit ab ostro ;
    Inque sui instituit muricis ingenium.
Scilicet hinc olim quicunque cucurrerit amnis,
    Ex hoc purpurei germine fontis erit.
Scilicet hunc mortis primum puer accipit vnguem :
    Inijciunt hodie fata, furorque manus.
Ecce illi sanguis fundi jam cæpit ; & ecce,
    Qui fundi·possit, vix bene sanguis erat.   10
Excitat è dolio vix dum bene musta recenti,
    Atque rudes furias in nova membra vocat.
Improbus ! vt nimias jam nunc accingitur iras !
    Armaque non molli sollicitanda manu !
Improbus ! vt teneras audet jam ludere mortes !
    Et vitæ ad modulum, quid puerile mori !

3·4 uos *conj. Garrod :* nos *T*   4 *might be headed In Christi circum-
cisionem (cp. p. 38, above).*   .

Improbus ! ut tragici impatiens præludia fati
   Ornat, & in socco jam negat ire suo !
Scilicet his pedibus manus hæc meditata cothurnos !
   Hæc cum blanditijs mens meditata minas ?   20
Hæc tam dura brevem decuêre crepundia dextram ?
   Dextra Gigantæis hæc satis apta genis ?
Sic cunis miscere cruces ? cumque vbere matris
   Commisisse neces, & scelus, & furias ?
Quo ridet patri, hoc tacite quoque respicit hastam ;
   Quoque oculo matrem mulcet, in arma redit.
Dij Superi ! furit his oculis ! hoc asper in ore est !
   Dat Marti vultus, quos sibi mallet Amor.
Deliciæ irarum ! torvi, tenera agmina, risus !
   Blande furor ! terror dulcis ! amande metus !   30
Præcocis in pænas pueri lascivia tristis !
   Cruda rudimenta ! & torva tyrocinia !
Jam parcum, breviusque brevi pro corpore vulnus,
   Proque brevi brevior vulnere sanguis eat :
Olim, cùm nervi, vitæque ferocior haustus
   Materiam morti, luxuriemque dabunt ;
Olim maturos vltrò conabitur imbres ;
   Robustum audebit tunc, solidumque mori.
Ergò illi, nisi qui in sævos concreverit vsus,
   Nec nisi quem possit fundere, sanguis erit ?   40
Euge puer trux ! Euge tamen mitissime rerum !
   Quique tibi tantùm trux potes esse, puer !
Euge tibi trux ! Euge mihi mitissime rerum !
   Euge Leo mitis ! trux sed & Agne tamen !
Macte puer ! macte hoc tam duræ laudis honore !.
   Macte ô pænarum hac indole, & ingenio !
Ah ferus ah culter ! sub quo, tam docte dolorum,
   In tristem properas sic, puer, ire virum.
Ah ferus, ah culter ! sub quo, puer auree, crescis
   Mortis proficiens hac quasi sub ferulâ.   50

[*Without heading*]

Ne, pia, ne nimium, Virgo, permitte querelis :
   Haud volet, haud poterit natus abesse diu.
Nam quid eum teneat ? vel quæ magis oscula vellet ?
   Vestri illum indigenam quid vetet esse sinûs ?

1·47 Ah ferus] At ferus *T*

Quippe illis quæ labra genis magis apta putentur ?
　Quæúe per id collum dignior ire manus ?
His sibi quid speret puer ambitiosiùs ulnis ?
　Quóve sub amplexu dulciùs esse queat ?
O quæ tam teneram sibi vitis amicior vlmum
　Implicet, alternis nexibus immoriens ?　　　　　10
Cui circum subitis eat impatientior vlnis ?
　Aut quæ tam nimijs vultibus ora notet ?
Quæ tam prompta puer toties super oscula surgat ?
　Quâ signet gemmâ nobiliore genam ?
Illa ubi tam vernis adolescat mitiùs auris,
　Tamúe sub apricis pendeat vua jugis ?
Illi quâ veniat languor tam gratus in umbrâ ?
　Commodiùs sub quo murmure somnus agat ?
O vbi tam charo, tam casto in carcere regnet,
　Maternoque simul, virgineoque sinu ?　　　　　20
Ille vt ab his fugiat ? nec tam bona gaudia vellet ?
　Ille vt in hos possit non properare sinus ?
Ille sui tam blanda sinûs patrimonia spernet ?
　Hæres tot factus tam bene delicijs ?
Ne tantum, ne, Diva, tuis permitte querelis :
　Quid dubites ? *Non est hic fugitivus Amor.*

[*Without heading*]

Accipe dona, Puer ; parvæ libamina laudis.
　Accipe, non meritis accipienda suis.
Accipe dona, Puer dulcis. dumque accipis illa,
　Digna quoque efficies, quæ, puer, accipias.
Siue oculo, siue illa tuâ dignabere dextrâ ;
　Dextram, oculumque dabis posse decere tuum.
Non modò es in dantes, sed & ipsa in dona benignus ;
　Nec tantùm donans das, sed & accipiens.

In partum B. Virg⁵ non difficilem.

Nec facta est tamen illa Parens impunè ; quòd almi
　Tam parcens uteri venerit ille Puer.
Vna hæc nascentis quodcunque pepercerit hora,
　Toto illum vitæ tempore parturijt.
Gaudia parturientis erat semel ille parenti ;
　Quotidie gemitus parturientis erat.

2·4 accipias *conj. Garrod* : accipies *T*

[Without heading]

Circulus hic similem quàm par sibi pergit in orbem !
  Principiumque suum quàm bene finis amat !
Virgineo thalamo quàm pulchrè conuenit ille
  (Quo nemo jacuit) virgineus tumulus !
Vndique vt hæc æquo passu res iret ; & ille
  Josepho desponsatus, & ille fuit.

In Sanctum igneis linguis descendentem Spiritum.

Absint, qui ficto simulant pia pectora vultu,
  Ignea quos luteo pectore lingua beat.
Hoc potius mea vota rogant, mea thura petessunt,
  Vt mihi sit mea mens ignea, lingua luti.

Cùm horum aliqua dedicâram Præceptori meo colendissimo, Amico amicissimo, R. Brooke.

En tibi Musam, (Præceptor colendissime) quas ex tuis modò scholis, quasi ex Apollinis officinâ, accepit, alas timidè adhuc, nec aliter quàm sub oculis tuis jactitantem.

Qualiter è nido multâ jam floridus alâ
Astra sibi meditatur avis, pulchrosque meatus
Aërios inter proceres ; licèt æthera nunquam
Expertus, rudibusque illi sit in ardua pennis
Prima fides ; micat ire tamen, quatiensque decorâ
Veste leues humeros, querulumque per aëra ludens
Nil dubitat vel in astra vagos suspendere nisus.   10
At verò simul immensum per inane profundis
Exhaustus spatijs, vacuoque sub æthere pendens,
Arva procul, sylvasque suas, procul omnia cernit,
Cernere quæ solitus ; tum verò victa cadit mens,
Spesque suas, & tanta tímens conamina, totus
Respicit ad matrem, pronisque revertitur auris.

Quòd tibi enim hæc feram (Vir ornatissime) non ambitio dantis est, sed justitia reddentis : neque te libelli mei tam elegi patronum, quàm dominum agnosco. Tua sanè sunt hæc, et mea. neque tamen ita mea sunt, quin si quid in illis boni est, 20 tuum hoc sit totum : neque interim in tantum tua, vt quantumcunque est in illis mali illud non sit ex integro meum. ita medio quodam, & misto jure vtriusque sunt. ne vel mihi, dum

me in societatem tuarum laudum elevarem, invidiam facerem ;
vel injuriam tibi, vt qui te in tenuitatis meæ consortium
deducere conarer. Ego enim de meo nihil ausim boni mecum
agnoscere, nedum profiteri palàm, præter hoc vnum (quo
tamen nihil melius) animum nempe non ingratum, tuorumque
beneficiorum historiam religiosissimâ fide in se reponentem.
hoc quibuscunque testibus coram, hoc palàm in os cœli, 30
meæque conscientiæ meum jactó. effero me in hoc ultra
æmuli patientiam. Enim vero elegantiore obsequio venerentur
te (& venerantur, scio) tuorum alij : nemo me sincero magis,
vel ingenuo poterit. Horum denique rivulorum, tenuium
vtcunque, nulliusque nominis, hæc saltem laus erit propria,
quòd *suum nempe nôrint Oceanum.*

Hymnus Veneri.
dum in illius tutelam transëunt virgines.

Tu tuis adsis, Venus alma, sacris :
Rideas blandùm, Venus, & benignùm,
Quale cùm Martem premis, aureoque
    Frangis ocello.

Rideas. ô tum neque flamma Phæbum,
Nec juvent Phœben sua tela. gestat
Te satis contra tuus ille tantùm
    Tela Cupido.

Sæpe in ipsius pharetrâ Dianæ
Hic suas ridens posuit sagittas.   10
Ausus et flammæ Dominum magistris
    Vrere flammis.

Virginum te orat chorus (esse longùm
Virgines nollent) modò servientûm
Tot columbarum tibi, passerumque au-
    gere catervam.

Dedicant quicquid labra vel rosarum,
Colla vel servant tibi liliorum :
Dedicant totum tibi ver genarum,
    Ver oculorum.   20

Hymnus Veneri. 10 Hic] Hîc *T*

Hinc tuo sumas licet arma nato,
Seu novas his ex oculis sagittas ;
Seu faces flamma velit acriori
    Flare comatas.

Sume. et ô discant, quid amica ; quid nox,
Quid bene, & blandè vigilata nox sit ;
Quid sibi dulcis furor, & protervus
    Poscat amator.

Sume. per quæ tot tibi corda flagrant.
Per quod arcanum tua cestus halat.   30
Per tuus quicquid tibi dixit olim, aut
    Fecit Adonis.

Spes Diva, salue. Diva auidam tuo
Necessitatem numine prorogans ;
    Vindicta fortunæ furentis ;
      Vna salus medijs ruinis.

Regina quamvis, tu solium facis
Depressa parvi tecta tugurij
    Surgunt jacentes inter ; illic
      Firma magis tua regna constant.

Cantus catenis, carmina carcere,
Dolore ab ipso gaudiaque exprimis.   10
    Scintilla tu vivis sub imo
      Pectoris, haud metuens procellas.

Tu regna servis ; copia pauperi :
Victis triumphus : littora naufrago :
    Ipsisque damnatis patrona :
      Anchora sub medio profundo.

Quin ipse alumnus sum tuus. vbere
Pendemus isto ; & hinc animam traho.
    O, Diva nutrix, ô fouentes
      Pande sinus. sitiens laboro.   20

Non accipimus brevem vitam, sed facimus.

Ergò tu luges nimiùm citatam
Circulo vitam properante volvi ?
Tu Deos parcos gemis, ipse cùm sis
        Prodigus ævi ?

Ipse quod perdis, quereris perire ?
Ipse tu pellis, sed et ire ploras ?
Vita num servit tibi ? servus ipse
        Cedet abactus.

Est fugax vitæ (fateor) fluentum :
Prona sed clivum modò det voluptas,   10
Amne proclivi magis, & fugace
        Labitur undâ.

Fur Sopor magnam hinc (oculos recludens)
Surripit partem. ruit inde partem
Temporis magnam spolium reportans
        Latro voluptas.

Tu creas mortes tibi mille. & æva
Plura quò perdas, tibi plura poscis.

     Pulchra non diuturna.

Eheu ver breve, & invidum !
Eheu floriduli dies !
Ergò curritis. improbâ
Et quæ nunc face fulgurat,
Dulcis forma tenacibus
Immiscebitur infimæ
Heu ! noctis nebulis ; amor
Fallax, umbraque somnij.
Quin incumbitis. (invida
Sic dictat colus, & rota   10
Cani temporis incito
Currens orbe volubilis)
O deprendite lubricos
Annos ; et liquidum jubar
      B b 2

Verni syderis, ac novi
Floris fulgura, mollibus
Quæ debetis amoribus,
Non impendite luridos
In manes, avidum & Chaos.
   Quanquam sydereis genis,   20
Quæ semper nive sobriâ
Synceris spatijs vigent,
Floris germine simplicis,
Flagrant ingenuæ rosæ :
   Quanquam perpetuâ fide
Illic mille Cupidines,
Centum mille Cupidines,
Pastos nectareâ dape
Blandis sumptibus educas ;
Istis qui spatijs vagi,   30
Plenis lusibus ebrij,
Vdo rore beatuli,
Vno plus decies die
Istis ex oculis tuis
Istis ex oculis suas
Sopitas animant faces,
Et languentia recreant
Succo spicula melleo ;
Tum flammis agiles novis
Lascivâ volitant face,   40
Tum plenis tumidi minis,
Tum vel sydera territant,
Et cælum, & fragilem Jovem :
   Quanquam fronte sub arduâ
Majestas gravis excubans,
Dulces fortiter improbis
Leges dictat amoribus :
   Quanquam tota, per omnia,
Cælum machina præferat,
Tanquam pagina multiplex   50
Vivo scripta volumine
Terris indigitans polos,
Et compendia syderum :
   Istis heu tamen heu genis,
Istis purpureis genis,
Oris sydere florido,

Regno frontis amabili,
Mors heu crastina forsitan
Crudeles faciet notas,
Naturæque superbiam   60
Damnabit tumuli specu.

Veris descriptio.

Tempus adest, placidis quo Sol novus auctior horis
Purpureos mulcere dies, & sydere verno
Floridus, augusto solet ire per æthera vultu,
Naturæ communis amor ; spes aurea mundi ;
Virginëum decus ; & dulcis lascivia rerum,
Ver tenerum, ver molle subit ; jam pulchrior annus
Pube novâ, roseæque recens in flore juuentæ
Felici fragrat gremio, & laxatur odorâ
Prole parens ; per aquas, perque arva, per omnia latè
Ipse suas miratur opes, miratur honores.   10
Jam Zephyro resoluta suo tumet ebria tellus,
Et crebro bibit imbre Jovem.   Sub frondibus altis
Flora sedens, audit (fælix !) quo murmure lapsis
Fons patrius minitetur aquis, quæ uertice crispo
Respiciunt tantùm, & strepero procul agmine pergunt.
Audit & arboreis siquid gemebunda recurrens
Garriat aura comis.   audit quibus ipsa susurris
Annuit, & facili cervice remurmurat arbor.
Quin audit querulas, audit quodcunque per vmbras
Flebilibus Philomela modis miserabile narrat.   20
Tum quoque præcipuè blandis Cytheræa per orbem
Spargitur imperijs ; molles tum major habenas
Incutit increpitans, cestus magis ignea rores
Ingeminat, tumidosque sinus flagrantior ambit ;
Nympharum incedit latè, charitumque coronâ
Amplior, & plures curru jam nectit olores :
Quin ipsos quoque tum campis emittit apricis
Læta parens, gremioque omnes effundit Amores.
Mille ruunt equites blandi, peditumque protervæ
Mille ruunt acies : levium pars terga ferarum   30
Insiliunt, gaudentque suis stimulare sagittis ;
Pars optans gemino multum properare volatu
Aërios conscendit equos ; hic passere blando
Subsiliens leue ludit iter ; micat huc, micat illuc

Hospitio levis incerto, & vagus omnibus umbris :
Verùm alter gravidis insurgens major habenis
Maternas molitur aues : ille improbus acrem
Versat apem similis, seseque agnoscit in illo.
Et brevibus miscere vias, ac frangere gyris :
Pars leviter per prata vagi sua lilia dignis   40
Contendunt sociare rosis ; tum florëus ordo
Consilio fragrante venit : lascivit in omni
Germine læta manus : nitidis nova gloria pennis
Additur ; illustri gremio sedet aurea messis ;
Gaudet odoratas coma blandior ire sub vmbras.
Excutiunt solitas (immitia tela) sagittas,
Ridentesque aliis pharetræ spectantur in armis.
Flore manus, & flore sinus, flore omnia lucent.
Vndique jam flos est.   vitreas hic pronus ad vndas
Ingenium illudentis aquæ, fluitantiaque ora,   50
Et vaga miratur tremulæ mendacia formæ.
Inde suos probat explorans, & judice nymphâ
Informat radios, ne non satis igne protervo
Ora tremant, agilesque docet nova fulgura vultus,
Atque suo vibrare jubet petulantiùs astro.

[*On Bp Andrew's's picture.*]

Hæc est, quæ sacrâ didicit florere figurâ,
  Non nisi per lachrymas charta videnda tuas.
Scilicet ah dices, hæc cùm spectaveris ora,
  Ora sacer sic, ô sic tulit ille pater.
Sperabis solitas illinc, pia fulmina, voces ;
  Sanctaque tam dulci mella venire viâ.
Sic erat illa, suas Famæ cùm traderet alas,
  Ad calamum (dices) sic erat illa manus.
Tale erat & pectus, celsæ domus ardua mentis,
  Tale suo plenum sydere pectus erat.   10
O bene fallacis mendacia pulchra tabellæ !
  Et, qui tam simili vivit in ære, labor !
Cùm tu tot chartis vitam, Pater alme, dedisti ;
  Hæc meritò vitam charta dat vna tibi.

Hæc est &c.] *In T this poem immediately follows the lines on Bishop
Andrews's picture,* 'Haec charta monstrat' (*see* p. 163, *above*). *No
separate heading to second set of verses in T.*

In Natales Mariæ Principis.

Parce tuo jam, bruma ferox, ô parce furori.
Pone animos. ô pacatæ da spiritus auræ
Afflatu leuiore grauem demulceat annum.
Res certè, & tempus meruit. Licèt improbus Auster
Sæviat, & rabido multùm se murmure volvat ;
Imbriferis licèt impatiens Notus ardeat alis ;
Hîc tamen, hîc certè, modò tu non (sæva) negares,
Nec Notus impatiens jam, nec foret improbus Auster.
Scilicet hoc decuit ? dum nos tam lucida rerum
Attollit series, adeò commune serenum   10
Lætitiæ, vernisque animis micat alta voluptas ;
Jam torvas acies, jam squallida bella per auras
Volvere ? & hybernis annum corrumpere nimbis ?
Ah melius ! quin luce novæ reparata juuentæ
Ipsa hodie vernaret hyems ; pulchroque tumultu
Purpureas properaret opes ; effunderet omnes
Læta sinus, nitidumque diem fragrantibus horis
Æternùm migrare velit ; florumque beatâ
Luxurie tanta ô circum cunabula surgat,
Excipiatque novos, & molliter ambiat artus.   20
    Quippe venit. sacris iterum vagitibus ingens
Aula sonat. venit en roseo decus addita fratri
Blanda soror. tibi se brevibus, tibi porrigit vlnis,
Magne puer ! facili tibi torquet hiantia risu
Ora ; tibi molles lacrymas, & nobile murmur
Temperat, inque tuo ponit se pendula collo.
Tale decus ; juncto veluti sub stemmate cùm quis
Dat socijs lucere rosis sua lilia. talis
Fulget honos ; medio cùm se duo sydera mundo
Dulcibus intexunt radijs. nec dignior olim   30
Flagrabat nitidæ fælix consortio formæ,
Tunc cùm sydereos inter pulcherrima fratres
Erubuit primùm, & Ledæo cortice rupto
Tyndarida explicuit teneræ nova gaudia frontis.
    Sic socium ô miscete jubar, tu, candide frater,
Tuque serena soror. sic ô date gaudia patri,
Sic matri. cùmque ille olim, subeüntibus annis,
Ire inter proprios magnâ cervice triumphos
Egregius volet, atque suâ se discere dextrâ ;
Te quoque tum pleno mulcebit sydere & alto   40

Flore tui, dulcesque oculos maturior ignis
Indole divinâ, & radijs intinget honoris.
Tunc ô te quoties (nisi quòd tu pulchrior illâ)
Esse suam Phæben falsus jurabit Apollo !
Tunc ô te quoties (nisi quòd tu castior illâ)
Esse suam Venerem Mavors jurabit inanis !
Felix ah ! et cui se non Mars, non aureus ipse
Credet Apollo parem ! tantâ qui conjuge celsus
In pulchros properare sinus, & carpere sacras
Delicias, oculosque tuos, tua basia solus   50
Tum poterit dixisse sua ; & se nectare tanto
Dum probat esse Deum, superas contemnere mensas.

Honoratiss° D° Rob° Heath, summo Justit.
de com. Banco.   Gratulatio.

Ignitum latus, & sacrum tibi gratulor ostrum,
   O amor ; atque tuæ gloria magna togæ !
Nam video.   Themis ecce humeris, Themis ardet in istis,
   Inque tuos gaudet tota venire sinus.
O ibi purpureo quàm se bene porrigit astro !
   Et docet hîc radios luxuriare suos !
Imò eat æternâ sic ô Themis aurea pompâ !
   Hîc velit ô sydus semper habere suum !
Sic flagret, & nunquam tua purpura palleat intus.
   O nunquam in vultus digna sit ire tuos.   10
Sanguine ab innocuo nullos bibat illa rubores.
   Nec tam crudeli murice proficiat.
Quæque tibi est (nam quæ non est tibi ?) candida virtus
   Fortunam placidè ducat in alta tuam.
Nullius viduæ lacrymas tua marmora sudent.
   Nec sit, quæ inclamet te, tibi fracta domus.
Non gemat vlla suam pinus tibi scissa ruinam,
   Ceu cadat in domini murmure mæsta sui.
Fama suas subter pennas tibi sternat eünti ;
   Illa tubæ faciat te melioris opus.   20
Thura tuo (quacunque meat) cum nomine migrent ;
   Quæque vehit fælix te, vehat aura rosas.

<hr>

1·48 qui] cui *T*   2·16 fracta *conj. Garrod* : facta *T*

Vive tuis (nec enim non sunt æquissima) votis
  Æqualis, quæ te sydera cunque vocant.
Hæc donec niveæ cedat tua purpura pallæ,
  Lilium ubi fuerit, quæ rosa vestis erat.

Serenissimæ Reginæ librum suum commendat Academia.

Hunc quoque maternâ (nimium nisi magna rogamus)
  Aut aviæ saltem sume, Maria, manu.
Est Musâ de matre recens rubicundulus infans,
  Cui pater est partus (quis putet ?) ille tuus.
Vsque adeo impatiens amor est in virgine Musâ :
  Jam nunc ex illo non negat esse parens.
De nato quot habes olim sperare nepotes,
  Qui simul & pater est, & facit esse patrem !

Horatii Ode.
Ille & nefasto te posuit die &c.

Ἑλληνιϛί.

Ὤρᾳ σε κεῖνος θῆκεν ἀποφράδι
Ὁ πρῶτος ὅστις, χειρί τε βώμακι
  Ἔθρεψε, δένδρον, τῆς τε κώμης
    Αἴτιον, ἐσσομένων τ᾽ ἔλεγχος.

Κεῖνος τοκῆος θρύψε καὶ αὐχένα,
Κεῖνός γε (φαίην) αἵματι ξεινίῳ
  Μυχώτατον κοιτῶνα ῥαῖνε
    Νύκτιος, ἀμφαφάασκε κεῖνος

Τὰ δῆτα Κόλχων φάρμακα, καὶ κακοῦ
Πᾶν χρῆμα, δώσας μοι ἐπιχώριον   10
  Σὲ στυγνὸν ἔρνος, δεσπότου σε
    Ἔμπεσον ἐς κεφαλὴν ἀεικῶς.

Πάσης μὲν ὥρης πᾶν ἐπικίνδυνον.
Τίς οἶδε φεύγειν ; δείδιε Βοσφόρον
  Λιβὺς ὁ πλωτὴρ, οὐδ᾽ ἀνάγκην
    Τὴν κρυφίην ἑτέρωθεν ὀκνεῖ.

3·8 ἀμφαφάασκε] ἀμφαφάασε *T*   9 Κόλχων] κόλχων *T*   15 ἀνάγκην]
ἀναίκην *T*.

Πάρθων μάχημων Ῥωμάϊκος φυγήν,
Καὶ τόξα·   Πάρθος Ῥωμαίκην βίαν,
Καὶ δεσμὰ·   λάους ἀλλὰ μοίρας
Βάλλε, βαλεῖ τ' ἀδόκητος ὁρμή.   20

Σχέδον σχέδον πῶς Περσεφόνης ἴδον
Αὔλην μελαίνην, καὶ κρίσιν Αἰακοῦ,
Καλήν τ' ἀπόστασιν μακαίρων,
Αἰολίαις κινύρην τε χορδαῖς

Σαπφὼ πατρίδος μεμφομένην κόραις,
Ἠχοῦντα καί σε πλεῖον ἐπιχρύσῳ,
Ἀλκαῖε, πλήκτρῳ σκληρὰ νῆος,
Σκληρὰ φυγῆς, πολέμου τε σκληρά.

Ευφημέουσαι δ' ἀμφοτέρων σκιαὶ
Κλύουσι θάμβει, τὰς δὲ μαχὰς πλεόν,   30
Ἀναστάτους τε μὲν τυράννους
Ὠμιὰς ἔκπιεν ὦσι λᾶος.

Τί θαῦμ'; ἐκείναις θὴρ ὅτε τρίκρανος
Ακην ἀοιδαῖς, οὔατα κάββαλε,
Ἐριννύων τ' ἡδυπαθοῦσι
Βόστρυχες, ἡσυχίων ἐχιδνῶν.

Καὶ δὴ Προμηθεύς, καὶ Πέλοπος πατὴρ
Εὔδουσιν ἠχεῖ τῷ λαθικήδεϊ :
Ἄγειν λέοντας Ὠρίων δὲ
Οὐ φιλέει, φοβεράς τε λύγκας.   40

In reũ. D^{ris} Brooke.
Epitaphium.

Posuit sub istâ (non gravi) caput terrâ
Ille, ipsa quem mors arrogare vix ausa
Didicit vereri, plurimumque suspenso
Dubitavit ictu, lucidos procul vultus,
Et sydus illud oris acre prospectans.
Cui literarum fama cùm dedit lumen,
Accepit, atque est ditior suis donis.
Cujus serena facilitas graves mores

---

17 μάχημων] μάχημον T   24 χορδαῖς] χορδαῖς. T
2·5 sydus illud oris acre *conj. Bensly :* sydus oris acre procul T Cp.
p. 2, *l. 21, above.*   8 facilitas graves *conj. Bensly :* gravitas faciles T

Mulcere novit ; cujus in senectute
Famaeque viguit, & juventa fortunæ.   10
Ita brevis ævi, vt nec videri festinus ;
Ita longus, vt nec fessus.   Et hunc mori credis ?

In obitum Rev. V. D^{ris} Mansell Coll. Regin. M^{ri} qui reu. D^s Brooke interitum proximè secutus est.

Ergo iterum in lacrymas, & sævi murmura planctûs
   Ire jubet tragicâ mors iterata manu ?
Scilicet illa novas quæ jam fert dextra sagittas,
   Dextra priore recens sanguine stillat adhuc.
Vos ô, quos sociâ Lachesis propè miscuit vrnâ,
   Et vicina colus vix sinit esse duos ;
Ite ô, quos nostri jungunt consortia damni ;
   Per nostras lacrymas ô nimis ite pares !
Ite per Elysias felici tramite valles,
   Et socijs animos conciliate vijs.   10
Illic ingentes vltrò confundite manes,
   Noscat & æternam mutua dextra fidem.
Communes eadem spargantur in otia curæ,
   Atque idem felix poscat vtrumque labor.
Nectareæ simul ite vagis sermonibus horæ :
   Nox trahat alternas continuata vices.
Vna cibos ferat, vna suas vocet arbor in vmbras.
   Ambobus faciles herba det vna toros.
Certum erit interea quanto sit major habenda,
   Quàm quæ per vitam est, mortis amicitia.   20

Luke 2.   Quærit Jesum suum Maria.

And is he gone, whom these armes held but now ?
       Their hope, their vow ?
Did ever greife, & joy in one poore heart
       Soe soone change part ?
Hee's gone.   the fair'st flower, that e're bosome drest,
       My soules sweet rest.
My wombes chast pride is gone, my heau'en=borne boy ;
       And where is joy ?

1·11 videri] redire *or* venire *conj. Bensly*   12 hunc mori] mori hunc
conj. Bensly   2·9 valles,] valles. *T*
(*Heading*) *Maria.*] *followed by* &c. *erased.*

Hee's gone.   & his lou'd steppes to wait upon,
    My joy is gone.   10
My joyes, & hee are gone ; my greife, & I
    Alone must ly.
Hee's gone.   not leaving with me, till he come,
    One smile at home.
Oh come then.   bring thy mother her lost joy :
    Oh come, sweet boy.
Make hast, & come, or e're my greife, & I
    Make hast, & dy.
Peace, heart ! the heauens are angry.   all their sphæres
    Rivall thy teares.   20
I was mistaken.   some faire sphære, or other
    Was thy blest mother.
What, but the fairest heauen, could owne the birth
    Of soe faire earth ?
Yet sure thou did'st lodge heere.   this wombe of mine
    Was once call'd thine.
Oft haue these armes thy cradle envied,
    Beguil'd thy bed.
Oft to thy easy eares hath this shrill tongue
    Trembled, & sung.   30
Oft haue I wrapt thy slumbers in soft aires,
    And stroak't thy cares.
Oft hath this hand those silken casements kept,
    While their sunnes slept.
Oft haue my hungry kisses made thine eyes
    Too early rise.
Oft haue I spoild my kisses daintiest diet,
    To spare thy quiet.
Oft from this breast to thine my loue=tost heart
    Hath leapt, to part.   40
Oft my lost soule haue I bin glad to seeke
    On thy soft cheeke.
Oft haue these armes (alas !) show'd to these eyes
    Their now lost joyes.
Dawne then to me, thou morne of mine owne day,
    And lett heauen stay.
Oh, would'st thou heere still fixe thy faire abode,
    My bosome God :
What hinders, but my bosome still might be
    Thy heauen to thee ?   50

Math. 16 . 25 . *Whosoeuer shall loose his life &c.*

Soe I may gaine thy death, my life I'le giue.
(My life's thy death, & in thy death I liue.)
Or else, my life, I'le hide thee in his graue,
By three daies losse æternally to saue.

In cicatrices Domini Jesu.

Come, braue soldjers, come, & see
Mighty loue's Artillery.
This was the conquering dart ; & loe
There shines his quiuer, there his bow.
These the passiue weapons are,
That made great Loue a man of warre.
The quiver, that he bore, did bide
Soe neare, it prov'd his very side.
In it there sate but one sole dart ;
A peircing one.   his peirced heart.   10
His weapons were nor steele, nor brasse :
The weapon, that he wore, he was.
For bow his vnbent hand did serue,
Well strung with many a broken nerue.
Strange the quiuer, bow, & dart !
A bloody side, & hand, & heart !
But now the feild is wonne : & they
(The dust of Warre cleane wip'd away)
The weapons now of triumph be,
That were before of Victorie.   20

In amorem divinum.   (Hermannus Hugo.)

Æternall loue ! what 'tis to loue thee well,
None, but himselfe, who feeles it, none can tell.
But oh, what to be lou'd of thee as well,
None, not himselfe, who feeles it, none can tell.

Petronij

Ales Phasiacis petita Colchis &c. R. Cr.

The bird, that's fetch't from Phasis floud,
Or choicest hennes of Africk=brood ;
These please our palates. & why these ?
'Cause they can but seldome please.
Whil'st the goose soe goodly white,
And the drake yeeld noe delight,
Though his wings conceited hewe
Paint each feather, as if new.
These for vulgar stomacks be,
And rellish not of rarity.   10
But the dainty Scarus, sought
In farthest clime ; what e're is bought
With shipwracks toile, Oh, that is sweet,
'Cause the quicksands hanselld it.
The pretious Barbill, now groune rife,
Is cloying meat. How stale is Wife ?
Deare wife hath ne're a handsome letter,
Sweet mistris sounds a great deale better.
Rose quakes at name of Cinnamon.
Vnlesse't be rare, what's thought upon ?   20

Horatij

Ille & nefasto te posuit die &c. R. Cr.

Shame of thy mother soyle ! ill=nurtur'd tree !
Sett to the mischeife of posteritie !
That hand, (what e're it were) that was thy nurse,
Was sacrilegious, (sure) or somewhat worse.
Black, as the day was dismall, in whose sight
Thy rising topp first staind the bashfull light.
That man (I thinke) wrested the feeble life
From his old father.   that mans barbarous knife
Conspir'd with darknes 'gainst the strangers throate ;
(Whereof the blushing walles tooke bloody note)   10

Petronij. *Also in A3, with heading :* Out of Petronius.   6 the]
dayntyest *A3*   7–8 *not in A3*   11 dainty] pretious *A3*
15 The pretious Barbill,] the Barbill too is *A3*   rife,] rife *A3*
16 Is] And *A3*   17–18] *A3 distinguishes* Deare Wife *and* Sweet
Mistresse

Huge high-floune poysons, eu'n of Colchos breed,
And whatsoe're wild sinnes black thoughts doe feed,
His hands haue padled in ; his hands, that found
Thy traiterous root a dwelling in my ground.
Perfidious totterer ! longing for the staines
Of thy kind Master's well=deseruing braines.
Mans daintiest care, & caution cannot spy
The subtile point of his coy destiny,
W^{ch} way it threats.   With feare the merchants mind
Is plough'd as deepe, as is the sea with wind,   20
(Rowz'd in an angry tempest) ; Oh the sea !
Oh ! that's his feare ; there flotes his destiny :
While from another (unseene) corner blowes
The storme of fate, to wch his life he owes.
By Parthians bow the soldjer lookes to die,
(Whose hands are fighting, while their feet doe flie.)
The Parthian starts at Rome's imperiall name,
Fledg'd with her Eagles wing ; the very chaine
Of his captivity rings in his eares.
Thus, ô thus fondly doe wee pitch our feares   30
Farre distant from our fates.   our fates, that mocke
Our giddy feares with an unlook't for shocke.
    A little more, & I had surely seene
Thy greisly Majesty, Hell's blackest Queene ;
And Æacus on his Tribunall too,
Sifting the soules of guilt ; & you, (oh you !)
You euer=blushing meads, where doe the Blest
Farre from darke horrors home appeale to rest.
There amorous Sappho plaines upon her Lute
Her loues crosse fortune, that the sad dispute   40
Runnes murmuring on the strings.   Alcæus there
In high=built numbers wakes his golden lyre,
To tell the world, how hard the matter went,
How hard by sea, by warre, by banishment.
There these braue soules deale to each wondring eare
Such words, soe precious, as they may not weare
Without religious silence ;   aboue all
Warres ratling tumults, or some tyrants fall.
The thronging clotted multitude doth feast.
What wonder ?   when the hundred=headed beast   50

21 tempest) ;] *The semi-colon is uncertain ; possibly a comma*
45 eare,] *comma uncertain*   48 fall.] *full-stop uncertain*

Hangs his black lugges, stroakt with those heavenly lines ;
The Furies curl'd snakes meet in gentle twines,
And stretch their cold limbes in a pleasing fire.
Prometheus selfe, & Pelops sterved Sire
Are cheated of their paines ; Orion thinkes
Of Lions now noe more, or spotted Linx.

On ye Gunpowder-Treason.

I sing Impiety beyond a name :
Who stiles it any thinge, knowes not the same.

Dull, sluggish Ile ! what more than Lethargy
Gripes thy cold limbes soe fast, thou canst not fly,
And start from of thy center ? hath heauens loue
Stuft thee soe full with blisse, thou can'st not moue ?
If soe, oh Neptune, may she farre be throune
By thy kind armes to a kind world vnknowne :
Lett her surviue this day, once mock her fate,
And shee's an Island truely fortunate.   10
Lett not my suppliant breath raise a rude storme
To wrack my suite.   oh   keepe pitty warme
In thy cold breast, & yearely on this day
Mine eyes a tributary streame shall pay.
Do'st thou not see an exhalation
Belch'd from the sulph'ry lungs of Phlegeton ?
A living Comet, whose pestiferous breath
Adulterates the Virgin aire ? with death
It labours.   Stif'led nature's in a swound,
Ready to dropp into a chaos, round   20
About horror's displai'd ; It doth portend,
That earth a shoure of stones to heauen shall send,
And crack the Christall globe ; the milky streame
Shall in a siluer raine runne out, whose creame
Shall choake the gaping earth, wch then shall fry
In flames, & of a burning feuer dy.
That wonders may in fashion be, not rare,
A winters thunder with a groane shall scare,
And rouze the sleepy ashes of the dead,
Making them skip out of their dusty bed.   30
Those twinckling eyes of heauen, wch eu'n now shin'd,
Shall with one flash of lightning be struck blind.

The sea shall change his youthfull greene, & slide
Along the shore in a graue purple tide.
It does præsage, that a great Prince shall climbe,
And gett a starry throne before his time.
To vsher in this shoale of Prodigies,
Thy infants, Æolus, will not suffice.
Noe, noe, a giant wind, that will not spare
To tosse poore men like dust into the aire ;   40
Justle downe mountaines : Kings courts shall be sent,
Like bandied balles, into the firmament.
Atlas shall be tript upp, Joue's gate shall feele
The weighty rudenes of his boysterous heele.
All this it threats, & more   Horro^r, that flies
To th' Empyræum of all miseries.
Most tall Hyperbole's cannot descry it ;
Mischeife, that scornes expression should come nigh it.
All this it only threats.   the Meteor ly'd ;
It was exhal'd, a while it hung, & dy'd.   50
Heauen kickt the Monster doune. doune it was throune,
The fall of all things it præsag'd, its owne
It quite forgott.   the fearfull earth gaue way,
And durst not touch it, heere it made noe stay.
At last it stopt at Pluto's gloomy porch ;
He streightway lighted vpp his pitchy torch.
Now to those toiling soules it giues its light,
W^{ch} had the happines to worke i'th' night.
They banne the blaze, & curse its curtesy,
For lighting them vnto their misery.   60
Till now hell was imperfect ; it did need
Some rare choice torture ; now 'tis hell indeed.
Then glutt thy dire lampe with the warmest blood,
That runnes in violett pipes : none other food
It can digest.   then watch the wildfire well,
Least it breake forth, & burne thy sooty cell.

---

54 it,] *comma uncertain ; perhaps full-stop*   58 i'th'] *perhaps* ith'

Upon the gunpowder treason.

Reach me a quill, pluckt from the flaming wing
Of Pluto's Mercury, that I may sing
Death to the life.　My inke shall be the blood
Of Cerberus, or Alecto's viperous brood.
Vnmated malice !　Oh vnpeer'd despight !
Such as the sable pinions of the night
Neuer durst hatch before : Extracted see
The very Quintessence of villanie.
I feare to name it ; least that he, wch heares,
Should haue his soule frighted beyond the sphæres.　　10
Heauen was asham'd, to see our mother Earth
Engender with the Night, & teeme a birth
Soe foule, one minutes light had it but seene,
The fresh face of the morne had blasted beene.
Her rosy cheekes you should haue seene noe more
Dy'd in vermilion blushes, as before :
But in a vaile of clouds mufling her head
A solitary life she would haue led.
Affrighted Phæbus would haue lost his way,
Giving his wanton palfreys leaue to play　　20
Olympick games in the' Olympian plaines,
His trembling hands loosing the golden raines.
The Queene of night gott the greene sicknes then,
Sitting soe long at ease in her darke denne,
Not daring to peepe forth, least that a stone
Should beate her headlong from her jetty throne.
Joues twinckling tapers, that doe light the world,
Had beene puft out, & from their stations hurl'd.
Æol kept in his wrangling sonnes, least they
With this grand blast should haue bin bloune away.　　30
Amazed Triton with his shrill alarmes
Bad sporting Neptune to pluck in his armes,
And leaue embracing of the Isles, least hee
Might be an actor in this Tragædy :
Nor should wee need thy crisped waues, for wee
An Ocean could haue made t' haue drowned thee.
Torrents of salt teares from our eyes should runne,
And raise a deluge, where the flaming sunne

8 villanie.] *perhaps no stop in MS.*

Should coole his fiery wheeles, & neuer sinke
Soe low to giue his thirsty stallions drinke.　　40
Each soule in sighes had spent its dearest breath,
As glad to waite vpon their King in death.
Each winged Chorister would swan=like sing
A mournfull Dirge to their deceased King.
The painted meddowes would haue laught noe more
For joye of their neate coates ; but would haue tore
Their shaggy locks, their floury mantles turn'd
Into dire sable weeds, & sate, & mourn'd.
Each stone had streight a Niobe become,
And wept amaine ; then rear'd a costly tombe,　　50
T' entombe the lab'ring earth.　for surely shee
Had died just in her deliuery.
But when Joues winged Heralds this espied,
Vpp to th' Almighty thunderer they hied,
Relating this sad story.　streightway hee
The monster crusht, maugre their midwiferie.
And may such Pythons neuer liue to see
The light's faire face, but still abortiue bee.

Upon the gunpowder treason.

Grow plumpe, leane Death ; his Holinesse a feast
Hath now præpar'd, & you must be his guest.
Come grimme destruction, & in purple gore
Dye seu'n times deeper than they were before
Thy scarlet robes.　for heere you must not share
A common banquett.　noe, heere's princely fare.
And least thy bloodshott eyes should lead aside
This masse of cruelty, to be thy guide
Three coleblack sisters, (whose long sutty haire,
And greisly visages doe fright the aire ;　　10
When Night beheld them, shame did almost turne
Her sable cheekes into a blushing morne,
To see some fowler than herselfe) these stand,
Each holding forth to light the aery brand,
Whose purer flames tremble to be soe nigh,
And in fell hatred burning, angry dy.
Sly, lurking treason is his bosome freind,
Whom faint, & palefac't feare doth still attend.

These need noe invitation.   onely thou,
Black dismall horro^r, come ; make perfect now   2Q
Th' Epitome of hell : oh lett thy pinions
Be' a gloomy Canopy to Pluto's minions.
In this infernall Majesty close shrowd
Your selues, you Stygian states ; a pitchy clowd
Shall hang the roome, & for your tapers bright,
Sulphureous flames, snatch'd from æternall night.
But rest, affrighted Muse ; thy siluer wings
May not row neerer to these dusky Kings.
Cast back some amorous glances on the cates,
That heere are dressing by the hasty fates.   30
Nay.   stopp thy clowdy eyes.   it is not good,
To droune thy selfe in this pure pearly flood.
But since they are for fire workes, rather proue
A Phænix, & in chastest flames of loue
Offer thy selfe a Virgin sacrifice
To quench the rage of hellish deities.
    But dares destruction eate these candid breasts,
The Muses, & the Graces sugred neasts ?
Dares hungry death snatch of one cherry lipp ?
Or thirsty treason offer once to sippe   40
One dropp of this pure Nectar, wch doth flow
In azure channells warme through mounts of snow ?
The roses fresh, conserued from the rage,
And cruell ravishing of frosty age,
Feare is afraid to tast of : only this,
He humbly crau'd to banquett on a kisse.
Poore meagre horro^r streightwaies was amaz'd,
And in the stead of feeding stood, & gaz'd.
Their appetites were gone at th' uery sight ;
But yet their eyes surfett with sweet delight.   50
Only the Pope a stomack still could find ;
But yett they were not powder'd to his mind.
Forthwith each God stept from his starry throne,
And snatch'd away the banquett.   euery one
Convey'd his sweet delicious treasury
To the close closet of æternity :
Where they will safely keepe it, from the rude,
And rugged touch of Pluto's multitude.

30 fates.] *stop uncertain : perhaps comma.*

Upon the Kings coronation.

Sound forth, cælestiall Organs, lett heauens quire
Ravish the dancing orbes, make them mount higher
With nimble capers, & force Atlas tread
Upon his tiptoes, e're his siluer head
Shall kisse his golden burthen.   Thou, glad Isle,
That swim'st as deepe in joy, as Seas, now smile ;
Lett not thy weighty glories, this full tide
Of blisse, debase thee ; but with a just pride
Swell : swell to such an height, that thou maist vye
With heauen itselfe for stately Majesty.   10
Doe not deceiue mee, Eyes : doe I not see
In this blest earth heauens bright Epitome,
Circled with pure refined glory ? heere
I veiw a rising sunne in this our sphære,
Whose blazing beames, maugre the blackest night,
And mists of greife, dare force a joyfull light.
The gold, in wch he flames, does well præsage
A precious season, & a golden age.
Doe I not see joy keepe his revels now,
And sitt triumphing in each cheerfull brow ?   20
Vnmixt felicity with siluer wings
Broodeth this sacred place.   hither peace brings
The choicest of her oliue=crownes, & praies
To haue them guilded with his courteous raies.
Doe I not see a Cynthia, who may
Abash the purest beauties of the day ?
To whom heauens lampes often in silent night
Steale from their stations to repaire their light.
Doe I not see a constellation,
Each little beame of wch would make a sunne ?   30
I meane those three great starres, who well may scorne
Acquaintance with the Vsher of the morne.
To gaze upon such starres each humble eye
Would be ambitious of Astronomie.
Who would not be a Phænix, & aspire
To sacrifice himselfe in such sweet fire ?
Shine forth, ye flaming sparkes of Deity,
Yee perfect Emblemes of Divinity.

Fixt in your sphæres of glory, shed from thence
The treasures of our liues, your influence.   40
For if you sett, who may not justly feare,
The world will be one Ocean, one great teare.

Upon the Kings Coronation.

Strange Metamorphosis ! It was but now
The sullen heauen had vail'd its mournfull brow
With a black maske : the clouds with child by greife
Traueld th' Olympian plaines to find releife.
But at the last (having not soe much powe'r
As to refraine) brought forth a costly shower
Of pearly drops, & sent her numerous birth
(As tokens of her greife) unto the earth.
Alas, the earth, quite drunke with teares, had reel'd
From of her center, had not Joue vpheld   10
The staggering lumpe : each eye spent all its store,
As if heereafter they would weepe noe more.
Streight from this sea of teares there does appeare
Full glory flaming in her owne free sphære.
Amazed Sol throwes of his mournfull weeds,
Speedily harnessing his fiery steeds,
Up to Olympus stately topp he hies,
From whence his glorious rivall hee espies.
Then wondring starts, & had the curteous night
Withheld her vaile, h' had forfeited his sight.   20
The joyfull sphæres with a delicious sound
Affright th' amazed aire, & dance a round
To their owne Musick, nor (vntill they see
This glorious Phæbus sett) will quiet bee.
Each aery Siren now hath gott her song,
To whom the merry lambes doe tripp along
The laughing meades, as joyfull to behold
Their winter coates couer'd with flaming gold.
Such was the brightnesse of this Northerne starre,
It made the Virgin Phœnix come from farre   30
To be repaird : hither she did resort,
Thinking her father had remou'd his court.
The lustre of his face did shine soe bright,
That Rome's bold Eagles now were blinded quite,

4 reliefe.] *stop uncertain*

The radiant darts, shott from his sparkling eyes,
Made euery mortall gladly sacrifice
A heart burning in loue ; all did adore
This rising sunne. their faces nothing wore,
But smiles, & ruddy joyes, & at this day
All melancholy clowds vanisht away.   40

Upon the birth of the Princesse Elizabeth.

Bright starre of Majesty, oh shedd on mee
A precious influence, as sweet as thee.
That with each word, my loaden pen letts fall,
The fragrant spring may be perfum'd withall.
That Sol from them may suck an honied shower,
To glutt the stomack of his darling flower.
With such a sugred livery made fine,
They shall proclaime to all, that they are thine.
Lett none dare speake of thee, but such as thence
Extracted haue a balmy Eloquence.   10
But then, alas, my heart ! oh how shall I
Cure thee of thy delightfull tympanie ?
I cannot hold, such a spring tide of joy
Must have a passage, or 'twill force a way.
Yet shall my loyall tongue keepe this command :
But giue me leaue to ease it with my hand.
And though these humble lines soare not soe high,
As is thy birth ; yet from thy flaming eye
Drop downe one sparke of glory, & they'l proue
A præsent worthy of Apollo's loue.   20
My quill to thee may not præsume to sing :
Lett th' hallowed plume of a Seraphick wing
Bee consecrated to this worke, while I
Chant to my selfe with rustick melodie.
   Rich, liberall heauen, what, hath yor treasure store
Of such bright Angells, that you giue vs more ?
Had you, like our great Sunne, stamped but one
For earth, 't had beene an ample portion.
Had you but drawne one liuely coppy forth,
That might interpret our faire Cynthia's worth,   30
Y' had done enough to make the lazy ground
Dance, like the nimble sphæres, a joyfull round.

But such is the cælestiall Excellence,
That in the princely patterne shines, from whence
The rest pourtraicted are, that 'tis noe paine
To ravish heauen to limbe them o're againe.
Wittnesse this mapp of beauty ; euery part
Of wch doth show the Quintessence of art.
See ! nothing's vulgar, every atome heere
Speakes the great wisdome of th' artificer.   40
Poore earth hath not enough perfection,
To shaddow forth th' admired Paragon.
Those sparkling twinnes of light should I now stile
Rich diamonds, sett in a pure siluer foyle ;
Or call her cheeke a bed of new blowne roses ;
And say that Ivory her front composes ;
Or should I say, that with a scarlet waue
Those plumpe soft rubies had bin drest soe braue ;
Or that the dying lilly did bestow
Vpon her neck the whitest of his snow ;   50
Or that the purple violets did lace
That hand of milky doune : All these are base ;
Her glories I should dimme with things soe grosse,
And foule the cleare text with a muddy glosse.
Goe on then, Heauen, & limbe forth such another,
Draw to this sister miracle a brother ;
Compile a fift glorious Epitome
Of heauen, & earth, & of all raritie ;
And sett it forth in the same happy place,
And I'le not blurre it with my Paraphrase.   60

Ex Euphormione.   R. Cr.

O Dea syderei seu tu stirps alma Tonantis &c.

Bright Goddesse, (whether Joue thy father be ;
Or Jove a father will be made by thee)
Oh crowne these praie'rs (mov'd in a happy hower)
But with one cordiall smile. for (loe) that power
Of Loues all=daring hand, that makes me burne,
Makes me confess't. Oh, doe not thou with scorne,
Great Nymph, o'relooke my lownesse. heau'n you know,
And all their fellow Deities will bow

Even to the naked'st vowes. thou art my fate ;
To thee the Parcæ haue given up of late   10
My threds of life. if then I shall not live
By thee ; by thee yet lett me die. this giue,
High beauties soveraigne, that my funerall flames
May draw their first breath from thy starry beames.
The Phænix selfe shall not more proudly burne,
That fetcheth fresh life from her fruitfull urne.

Upon the death of a freind.

Hee's dead : Oh what harsh musicks there
Vnto a choyce, and curious eare !
Wee must that Discord surely call,
Since sighs doe rise, and teares doe fall.
Teares fall too low, sighes rise too high,
How then can there be Harmony ?
But who is he ? him may wee know,
That jarres, and spoiles sweet consort soe ?
O Death, 'tis thou : you false time keepe,
And stretch'st thy dismall voice too deepe.   10
Long time to Quavering age you giue,
But to Large youth short time to liue.
You take vpon you too too much,
In striking where you should not touch.
How out of tune the world now lies,
Since youth must fall, when it should rise !
Gone be all Consort, since alone
He, that once bore the best part,'s gone.
Whose whole life Musick was ; wherein
Each vertue for a part came in.   20
And though that Musick of his life be still,
The Musick of his name yett soundeth shrill.

1·9 Evèn] *second* e *uncertain ; perhaps erased*   *Upon the death &c.*
Also in R7   17 all Consort] oᵣ comfort R7

An Elegy upon the death of M͏ͬ Stanninow fellow of Queenes Colledge.

Hath aged winter, fledg'd with feathered raine,
To frozen Caucasus his flight now tane ?
Doth hee in downy snow there closely shrowd
His bedrid limmes, wrapt in a fleecy clowd ?
Is th' earth disrobed of her apron white,
Kind winter's guift, & in a greene one dight ?
Doth she beginne to dandle in her lappe
Her painted infants, fedd with pleasant pappe,
W^{ch} their bright father in a pretious showre
From heavens sweet milky streame doth gently poure ?   10
Doth blith Apollo cloath the heavens with joye,
And with a golden waue wash cleane away
Those durty smutches, wch their faire fronts wore,
And make them laugh, wch frown'd, & wept before ?
If heaven hath now forgot to weepe ; ô then
W^t meane these shoures of teares amongst us men ?
These Cataracts of greife, that dare eu'n vie
With th' richest clowds their pearly treasurie ?
If winter's gone, whence this vntimely cold,
That on these snowy limmes hath laid such hold ?   20
What more than winter hath that dire art found,
These purple currents hedg'd with violets round
To corrallize, wch softly wont to slide
In crimson waueletts, & in scarlet tide ?
If Flora's darlings now awake from sleepe,
And out of their greene mantletts dare to peepe :
O tell me then, what rude outragious blast
Forc't this prime flowre of youth to make such hast
To hide his blooming glories, & bequeath
His balmy treasure to the bedd of death ?   30
'Twas not the frozen zone ; One sparke of fire,
Shott from his flaming eye, had thaw'd it's ire,
And made it burne in loue : 'Twas not the rage,
And too vngentle nippe of frosty age :
'Twas not the chast, & purer snow, whose nest
Was in the modest Nunnery of his brest :

An Elegy &c.   Also in R7.   (Heading) upon] on *R7*   *Colledge.*]
Colledge. Camb. R7   8 infants] infant *R7*   22 round *R7* : round· *T*
24 tide] dide *R7*

Noe. none of these ravish't those virgin roses,
The Muses, & the Graces fragrant posies.
W^{ch}, while they smiling sate upon his face,
They often kist, & in the sugred place   40
Left many a starry teare, to thinke how soone
The golden harvest of our joyes, the noone
Of all our glorious hopes should fade,
And be eclipsed with an envious shade.
Noe. 'twas old doting Death, who, stealing by,
Dragging his crooked burthen, look't awry,
And streight his amorous syth (greedy of blisse)
Murdred the earth's just pride with a rude kisse.
A winged Herald, gladd of soe sweet a prey,
Snatch't vpp the falling starre, soe richly gay,   50
And plants it in a precious perfum'd bedd,
Amongst those Lillies, wch his bosome bredd.
Where round about hovers with siluer wing
A golden summer, an æternall spring.
Now that his root such fruit againe may beare,
Let each eye water't with a courteous teare.

An Elegie on the death of Dr Porter.

Stay, silver=footed Came, striue not to wed
Thy maiden streames soe soone to Neptunes bed :
Fixe heere thy wat'ry eyes vpon these towers,
Vnto whose feet in reuerence of the powers,
That there inhabite, thou on euery day
With trembling lippes an humble kisse do'st pay.
See all in mourning now ; the walles are jett,
With pearly papers carelesly besett.
Whose snowy cheekes, least joy should be exprest,
The weeping pen with sable teares hath drest.   10
Their wronged beauties speake a Tragædy,
Somewhat more horrid than an Elegy.
Pure, & unmixed cruelty they tell,
W^{ch} poseth mischeife's selfe to Parallel.

42–3 joyes, the noone . . . fade] ioyes should fade *R7*   54 an
æternall] a perpetuall *R7*   55 *indented R7*
   An Elegie &c. Also in R7.   4 powers,] powers *R7*   7 *Omitted
in R7*

Justice hath lost her hand, the law her head ;
Peace is an Orphan now ; her father's dead.
Honesties nurse, Vertues blest Guardian,
That heauenly mortall, that Seraphick man.
Enough is said.   now, if thou canst crowd on
Thy lazy crawling streames, pri'thee be gone,   20
And murmur forth thy woes to euery flower,
That on thy bankes sitts in a uerdant bower,
And is instructed by thy glassy waue
To paint its perfum'd face wth colours braue.
In vailes of dust their silken heads they'le hide,
As if the oft departing sunne had dy'd.
Goe learne that fatall Quire, soe sprucely dight
In downy Surplisses, & vestments white,
To sing their saddest Dir'ges, such as may
Make their scar'd soules take wing, & fly away.   30
Lett thy swolne breast discharge thy strugling groanes
To th' churlish rocks ; & teach the stubborne stones
To melt in gentle drops, lett them be heard
Of all proud Neptunes siluer=sheilded guard ;
That greife may crack that string, & now vntie
Their shackled tongues to chant an Elegie.
Whisper thy plaints to th' Oceans curteous eares,
Then weepe thyselfe into a sea of teares.
A thousand Helicons the Muses send
In a bright Christall tide, to thee they tend,   40
Leaving those mines of Nectar, their sweet fountaines,
They force a lilly path through rosy mountaines.
Feare not to dy with greife ; all bubling eyes
Are teeming now with store of fresh supplies.

32 teach] teare *R7*   35 that string] those strings *R7*

II. Brit. Mus. Add. MS. 33219.

At th' Iuory Tribunall of your hand
(Faire one) these tender leaues doe trembling stand.
Knowing 'tis in the doome of your sweet Eye
Whether the Muse they cloth shall liue or die.
Liue shee, or dye to Fame ; each Leafe you meet
Is her Lifes wing, or her death's winding-sheet.

Though now 'tis neither May nor June
And Nightingales are out of tune,
Yett in these leaues (Faire one) there lyes
(Sworne seruant to your sweetest Eyes)
A Nightingale, who may shee spread
In your white bosome her chast bed,
Spite of all the Maiden snow
Those pure untroden pathes can show,
You streight shall see her wake and rise
Taking fresh Life from your fayre Eyes.   10
And with clasp't winges proclayme a spring
Where Loue and shee shall sit and sing
For lodg'd so ne're your sweetest throte
What Nightingale can loose her noate ?
Nor lett her kinred birds complayne
Because shee breakes the yeares old raigne
For lett them know shee's none of those
Hedge-Quiristers whose Musicke owes
Onely such straynes as serue to keepe
Sad shades and sing dull Night asleepe.   20
No shee's a Priestesse of that Groue
The holy chappell of chast Love

Your Virgin bosome.   Then what e're
Poore Lawes diuide the publicke yeare,
Whose reuolutions wait upon
The wild turnes of the wanton sun ;
Bee you the Lady of Loues Yeere :
Where your Eyes shine his suns appeare :
There all the yeare is Loues long spring.
There all the yeare Loues Nightingales   30
    shall sitt and sing.

Out of Grotius his Tragedy of Christes sufferinges.

O thou the span of whose Omnipotence
Doth graspe the fate of thinges, and share th' euents
Of future chance ! the world's grand sire ; and mine
Before the world.   Obedient lo ! I joyne
An æquall pace thus farre ; thy word my deedes
Haue flow'd together. if ought further needes
I shrinke not. but thus ready stand to beare
(ffor else why came I ?) eu'n what e're I feare.
Yett o what end ? where does the period dwell
Of my sad labours ? no day yett could tell   10
My soule shee was secure.   Still haue I borne
A still increasing burden ; worse hath torne
His way through bad, to my successiue hurt.
I left my glorious Fathers star-pau'd Court
E're borne was banish't : borne was glad t' embrace
A poore (yea scarce a) roofe.   whose narrow place
Was not so much as cleane : a stable kind ;
The best my cradle and my birth could find.
Then was I knowne ; and knowne unluckily
A weake a wretched child ; eu'n then was I   20
For Juryes king an enemy, euen worth
His feare ; the circle of a yeares round growth
Was not yett full, (a time that to my age
Made litle, not a litle to his rage)
When a wild sword eu'n from their brests, did lop
The Mothers Joyes in an untimely crop.
The search of one child (cruell industry !)
Was losse of multitudes ; and missing mee

A bloud drunke errour spilt the costly ayme
Of their mad sin ; (how great ! and yett how uayne !) 30
I cal'd a hundred miracles to tell
The world my father. then does enuy swell
And breake upon mee : my owne uirtues height
Hurtes mee far worse then Herods highest spite ;
A riddle ! (father) still acknowledg'd thine
Am still refus'd ; before the Infant Shrine
Of my weake feet the Persian Magi lay
And left their Mithra for my star : this they.
But Isaacks issue the peculiar heyres,
Of thy old goodnesse, know thee not for theires, 40
Basely degenerous. Against mee flocke
The stiffe neck'd Pharisees that use to mocke
Sound goodnesse with her shadow which they weare,
And 'gainst religion her owne colours beare.
The bloud hound brood of Priests against mee draw
Those Lawlesse tyrant masters of the Law.
Profane Sadocus too does fiercely lead
His court-fed impes against this hated head.
What would they more ? th' aue seene when at my nod
Great Natures selfe hath shrunke and spoke mee god. 50
Drinke fayling there where I a guest did shine
The Water blush'd, and started into Wine.
Full of high sparkeling uigour : taught by mee
A sweet inebriated extasy.
And streight of all this approbation gate
Good wine in all poynts. but the easy rate ;
Other mens hunger with strange feasts I quell'd
Mine owne with stranger fastings, when I held
Twice twenty dayes pure abstinence, To feed
My minds deuotion in my bodyes need. 60
A subtle inundation of quicke food
Sprang in the spending fingers, and o'reflow'd
The peoples hunger, and when all were full
The broken meate was much more then the whole.
The Wind in all his roaring brags stood still
And listned to the whisper of my will ;
The wild waues couch'd ; the sea forgott to sweat
Vnder my feet, the waters to bee wett.

51 *indented in A3 (new page).*

In death-full desperate ills where art and all
Was nothing, there my uoyce was med'cinall.   70
Old clouds of thickest blindnesse fled my sight
And to my touch darke Eyes did owe the light.
Hee that ne're heard now speakes, and finds a tongue
To chaunt my prayses in a new-strung song.
Euen hee that belches out a foaming flood
Of hot defiance 'gainst what e're is good
Father and Heyre of darkenesse, when I chide
Sinkes into Horrours bosome, glad to hide
Himselfe in his owne hell ; and now lets loose
Mans brest (his tenement) and breakes up house.   80
Yett here's not all : nor was't enough for mee
To freind the liuing world euen death did see
Mee ranging in his quarters ; and the land
Of deepest silence answered my command.
Heau'n, Earth, and Sea, my triumphs. what remain'd
Now but the Graue ? the Graue it selfe I tam'd.

                           &c :.

SUPPLEMENTARY POEMS

FROM MSS., NOT INCLUDED IN PREVIOUS MODERN EDITIONS.

I. Bodl. MS. Tanner 465.

On the death of Wm Henshaw,
student in Emān. Coll.

See a sweet streame of Helicon,
Runne into death's black Ocean.
See his pretious siluer waue
I' th' jetty channele of a graue.
Hither, Muses, turne your eyes,
See where your Aqua=vitæ lies.
Angry heaven doth now bequeath
This living fountaine vnto death.
Come therefore now, & him interre,
Find him a glorious Sepulcher.   10
But trust him not vnto the earth,
She had him euer since his birth.
In yor breasts lett him haue roome,
In those snowy hills a tombe.
Come, weaue your locks, those threads of gold,
Make a winding sheet, t'enfold
His Ivory limbs ; & in this shrine,
Heauens milky way he shall outshine.
From the Alablaster banckes
Of your cheekes pluck all theranckes   20
Of those modest blushing roses,
And the Lillies : make you posies,
To deck his hearse ; & lett each were
The liquid jewell of a teare.
Your starry eyes, like tapers, burne,
That may conduct vs to his urne.

On the death of Wm Henshaw, &c. Also in R7, with Cornwallis *at foot.*
22 the] your *altered to* the *T* : yor *R7*

Where when our wat'ry eyes shall see
Our pictures of mortalitie,
There soe louely, faire, & bright,
And soe sumptuously dight,   30
(Narcissus=like) wee'l flame in loue,
And his funerall fewell proue.
For in this shape, that now Death is,
To entertaine him were a blisse.

P. *Cornwallis.*

An Elegy vpon the death of Mr Wm Carre, student in E͞man : Colledge.

Death hath drawne our golden Carre
Into the miry graue soe farre,
That there (alas !) it's like to stand,
Vntill some loving Angells hand
Out of this prison sett's it free,
And mount it on heavens axell tree.
Then each cælestiall precious stone,
From their Christall boxes gone,
Shall gladly runne to kisse his feete,
And smoothly paue the milky street,   10
W^{ch} leads vnto the rosy arbour,
Where Apollo's bride doth harbour.
There he shall leane his louely head,
Vpon her crimson veluet bedd ;
From whence this starre of excellence
Shall shed his precious influence ;
And in spite of the sick steames,
And lazy foggs of death, his beames
Shall smiling flow in a bright shower
From Aurora's guilded bower.   20
Th' Astronomer, that euery night
Studies by heauens candle light,
And reades the volumes of the sky
With a too=ambitious eye,
When his glory shall appeare,
Flaming in its owne free spheare,

30 sumptuously] triumphiously *R7*   34 ' her ' *altered to* ' him '
T : her *R7*
    An Elegy &c.   Also in R7 with Cornwallis *at foot.   (Heading) Carre,
. . . Colledge.]* Carre in Eman. Coll. *R7*   26 Flaming] Shining *R7*

Shall start, & thinke, that Charles his waine
Hath travelld o're th' Olympian plaine,
And in the chamber of the East
Taken vp his quiet rest.   30
In the meane time lett us try
The Rhetorick of a weeping eye.
Rigid death shall then be kind,
When an eye a tongue can find.
O, pri'thee death, release him then,
Release the sweetest among men !
But if thou turn'st away thine eares,
Wee'l drowne thee in a sea of teares.
Thou, & Apollo's bright Carre shall
Into a briny Ocean fall.   40

P. *Cornwallis.*

An Elegy on the death of the Lady Parker.

Can such Perfection fade ? can Vertue die,
And find a graue, & not an Elegie ?
Can such a flaming Constellation
Of heauens bright graces, sweetly mett in one,
In silence be eclips'd, & forc'd to shrowd
Their precious beames under a marble clowd,
Without a swanlike Dirge ? Should I in verse,
As broken as my heart, her worth rehearse,
The jarring accents of my ragged song
Her lifes melodious harmony would wrong.   10
Nor can my humble fancy soare soe high,
As was her Excellence.   Oh could I fly
Betwixt Seraphick pinions ! that I might
Towre vpp to th' loftiest spheare, & take the height
Of full growne goodnes, & exactly see
The perfect modell of bright Sanctity !
Then would I dare in order to repeate
Each Scæne of her pure life, & tell how great
Her glories were, & euery grace enrowle,
And make a mappe of her most Holy soule.   20
But oh, 'twere grosse impiety, I feare,
To lett my fancy climbe aboue thy beare.

An Elegy &c. Also in R7.   19 enrowle] unroule *R7*   22 thy]
her *R7*

D d 2

'Twill not aspire vnto a higher roome,
May it obtaine a lodging in thy tombe,
Whil'st others striue to hang a mournfull verse,
I'le pinne my saddest thoughts vpon thy hearse.
Heere shall my winged cogitations rest,
I'le lock the wanderers in this sable chest,
And gladly be a Her'mit, may I haue
A blessed mansion in this sacred graue.   30
There would I sitt, & study euery art,
That witty greife can learne me : How a heart
May with one groane be splitt ; & how I may
With a lowd sobb scare from their house of clay
My nimble spirits ; how my soule may fly
On a few winged sighes aboue the sky.
How through the open sluces of mine eyes
Each crimson streame may be lett out, wch lies
Warme in its violet channell ; & ô then
Faine would I learne an Epitaph to pen.   40
But greife forbids, & tell's me, shee'l take care,
That euery heart her Epitaph shall weare.

An Elegy upon the death of Mr Christopher Rouse Esquire.

Christopher Rouse. ⎱ Anagr.
Oh rich purest rose. ⎰

Rich, purest rose, prime flowre of blooming youth,
That once did'st flourish in a happy growth,
Soe sweetly loaden with perfumes, that low
The fragrant burthen made thy stalke to bow :
When amorous heav'en beheld it, straightway to it
Thousands of sacred Cupids came to woo it.
Like as I'ue seene the daily labouring Bee
Fly from her thatched cottage merrily
Vnto some honyed mine, & all along
The way singing a plaine melodious song,   10
Spying at length the lillies snowy breasts,
Or the pure sanguine roses cheekes, she rests,
And Siren=like pleasantly sings a while,
Vntill sh' hath flatter'd out her precious spoile,

Then to her waxen closets home she flies,
Bearing the liquid gold upon her thighes :
Just soe those heavenly Sirens, that doe swimme
In gulfes of deepest blisse, when they saw him,
Came singing divine Anthems, as they flew
Into the Paradise, where this rose grew.   20
Then on each part sate a cælestiall Bee,
That sung a sweet song for as sweet a fee ;
Thus heaven with earth did traffick, they did buy
The purest sweetnes for pure harmony.
But at the length into their starry hiue
They snatch't the rose itselfe ; thus they depriue
Earth of its most delicious influence,
Of all perfumes the very Quintessence ;
I meane that precious soule, where euery Grace
Tooke vpp its heauen on earth ; that glorious place,   30
Where each faire Virgin=vertue had her throne,
Each her embalmed habitation.
This was the Muses Helicon, the blest
Parnassus, where each had a Phœnix nest.
This haue they tooke, leaving the spoiled stemme,
I meane that corpes, the Caskett of that jemme,
W^{ch} earst wee had, sparkling with heavenly light,
With euery starre of excellencie dight ;
But now haue lost.   ô Sorrow, giue me leaue
To begg this boone of those, that did bereaue   40
Vs of our blisse, that from their wings soe bright
One golden quill may take an easy flight :
With wch these lines I may characterize
O're the blest place, where this rich relique lies.

An Epitaph.

Heere in deaths closett, Reader, know,
Lies a casket, wch did owe
The brightest gemme, that e're did shine,
W^{ch} now makes Abra'ms bosome fine.
Therefore its shrine desires supply
Of watry pearles from each kind eye.

An Epitaph.   Also in R7.   For order see p. lxxx, above.

II. Brit. Mus. MS. Harl. 6917.

Epithalamium :

1. Come virgin Tapers of pure waxe
   made in the Hiue of Loue, all white
as snow, and yet as cold, where lackes
   Hymens holy heate and light ;
      where blooming kisses
         their beds yet keepe
      and steepe their blisses
         in Rosy sleepe ;
where sister budds yet wanting brothers
kisse their owne lipps in Lieu of others ;   10
helpe me to mourne a matchlesse maydenhead
         that now is dead :

2. A fine thinn negatiue thing it was,
   a nothing with a dainty name,
which pruned her plumes in selfe loues glasse,
   made up of fancy and fond fame ;
      within the shade
         of its owne winge
      it sate and played
         a selfe crownd King ;   20
A froward flower, whose peevish pride
within it selfe, it selfe did hide,
flying all fingers, and euen thinking much
         of its owne touch :

3. This bird indeed the phænix was
   late chaced by loues revengefull arrowes,
whose warres now left the wonted passe
   and spared the litle liues of sparrowes ;
      to hunt this foole
         whose froward pride,
      Loues noble schoole,   30
         and Courts denyed,
And froze the fruite of faire desire
which flourisheth in mutuall fire,
'gainst nature, who 'mong all the webbs she spunn
         nere woue A Nunne :

4. She of Cupids shafts afraid
  left her owne balme-breathing East,
and in a westerne bosome made
  a softer, and a sweeter neast ;   40
   there did she rest
    in the sweet shade,
   of a soft breast,
    whose beauties made
Thames oft stand still, and lend a glasse
while in her owne she saw heauens face,
and sent him full of her faire names report
    to Thetis Court :

5. And now poore Loue was at a stand
  the Christall castle which she kept   50
was proofe against the proudest hand ;
  there in safest hold she slept ;
   his shafts expence
    left there noe smart,
   but bounding thence
    broached his owne heart ;
At length a fort he did devise
built in noble Brampstons eyes
and ayming thence this matchlesse maydenhead
    was soone found dead :   60

6. Yet Loue in death did wayte upon her,
  granting leaue she should expire
in her fumes, and haue the honour
  t' exhale in flames of his owne fire ;
   her funerall pyle
    the marriage bedd,
   in a sighed smile
    she vanished.
So rich a dresse of death nere famed
the Cradles where her kindred flamed ;   70
so sweet her mother phænixes of th' East
    nere spiced their neast :

7. With many pretty peevish tryalls
  of angry yeelding, faint denyings,
melting No's, and milde denyalls,
  dying liues, and short liued dyings ;

with doubtfull eyes,
   halfe smiles, halfe teares,
with trembling joyes,
   and jocund feares ;   80
Twixt the pretty twylight strife
of dying maide and dawning wife ;
twixt raine, and sun-shine, this sweet maydenhead
    alas is dead :

8. Happy he whose wakefull joyes
   kept the prize of this rich losse,
happy she whose watry eyes
   kisse noe worse a weeping Crosse ;
    thrice happy he
      partakes her store,   90
    thrice happy she
      hath still the more.
Thinke not sweet Bride, that faint shewer slakes
the fires he from thy faire eyes takes,
Thy dropps are salt, and while they thinke to tame,
    sharpen his flame :

9. Blessd Bridegroome ere the raine be layd
   use good weather while it proues,
those dropps that wash away the maide
   shall water your warme planted loues ;   100
    faire youth make haste
      ere it be drye
    the sweet brine taste
      from her moist eye ;
Thy lipps will finde such deaw as this is
best season for a louers kisses,
and those thy morning starres will better please
    bathed in those seas :

10. Nor may thy Vine, faire oake, embrace thee
   with ivy armes, and empty wishes,   110
but with full bosome enterlace thee,
   and reach her Clusters to thy kisses ;
    safe may she rest
      her laden boughes,
    on thy firme breast,
      and fill thy vowes,

up to the brimm, till she make euen
their full topps with the faire eyed heauen,
And heauen to guild those glorious Hero's birth
    stoope and kisse earth : 120

11. Long may this happy heauen tyed band
    exercise its most holy art,
  keeping her heart within his hand,
    keeping his hand upon her heart,
      but from her eyes
        feele he noe Charmes,
      finde she noe joy
        but in his armes ;
May each maintaine a well fledged neast
of winged loues in eithers breast, 130
Be each of them a mutuall sacrifice
    of eithers eyes :

12. May their whole life a sweet song proue
    sett to two well composed parts,
  by musickes noblest master, Loue,
    playd on the strings of both their harts ;
    whose mutuall sound
      may euer meete
    in a just round,
      not short though sweet ; 140
Long may heauen listen to the songe,
and thinke it short though it bee long ;
oh proue't a well sett song indeed, which showes
    sweet'st in the Close.

APPENDIX I.

POEMS PROBABLY SPURIOUS.

On the Frontispiece of Isaacsons *Chronologie explained.*

IF with distinctive Eye, and Mind, you looke
 Vpon the *Front*, you see more then one Booke.
Creation is *Gods Booke*, wherein he writ
Each Creature, as a Letter filling it.
History is *Creations* Booke ; which showes
To what effects the *Series* of it goes.
Chronologie's the Booke of *Historie*, and beares
The just account of *Dayes, Moneths*, and *Yeares*.
But *Resurrection*, in a Later Presse,
And *New Edition*, is the summe of these.   10
The Language of these Bookes had all been one,
Had not th' *Aspiring Tower of Babylon*
Confus'd the Tongues, and in a distance hurl'd
As farre the speech, as men, oth' new fill'd world.
    Set then your eyes in method, and behold
Times embleme, *Saturne* ; who, when store of Gold
Coyn'd the first age, *Devour'd* that *Birth*, he fear'd :
Till *History*, Times eldest Child appear'd ;
And *Phœnix*-like, in spight of *Saturnes* rage,
Forc'd from her *Ashes*, Heyres in every age.   20
From th'*rising Sunne*, obtaining by just Suit,
A *Springs Ingender*, and an *Autumnes Fruit.*
Who in those *Volumes* at her motion pen'd,
Vnto *Creations Alpha* doth extend.
Againe ascend, and view *Chronology*,
By *Optick Skill* pulling farre *History*
Neerer ; whose *Hand* the piercing *Eagles* Eye
Strengthens, to bring remotest Objects nigh.
Vnder whose *Feet*, you see the *Setting Sunne*,
From the darke *Gnomon*, o're her Volumes runne,   30
Drown'd in eternall Night, never to rise ;
Till *Resurrection*, show it to the eyes

On the Frontispiece &c. See Commentary, p. 463, below, and foot-note, p. 191, above.
. 1 distinctive] dictinctive *46*   8 *Moneths*] and Monthes *1633* : of Moneths *70*

Of *Earth*-worne men ; and her shrill Trumpets sound
Affright the *Bones* of Mortals from the ground.
The *Columnes* both are crown'd with either *Sphere*,
To show *Chronology* and *History* beare
No other *Culmen* ; then the double Art
Astronomy, *Geography*, impart.

Meliùs purgatur stomachus per vomitum,
quàm per secessum.

DUm vires refero vomitûs, & nobile munus,
  Da mihi de vomitu, grandis Homere, tuo.
Nempe olim, multi cùm carminis anxia moles
  Vexabat stomachum, magne Poëta, tuum ;
Ægraque jejuno tenuabat pectora morsu,
  Jussit & in crudam semper hiare famem :
Phæbus (ut est medicus) vomitoria pocula præbens
  Morbum omnem longos expulit in vomitus.
Protinus & centum incumbunt toto ore Poëtæ,
  Certantes sacras lambere relliquias.   10
Quod vix fecissent, (scio) si medicamen ineptum
  Venisset miserè posteriore viâ.
Quippe per amfractus, cæcique volumina ventris
  Sacra (putas) hostem vult medicina sequi ?
Tam turpes tenebras hæc non dignatur. at ipsum
  Sedibus ex imis imperiosa trahit
          Ergò
Per vomitum stomachus meliùs purgabitur. alvus
  Quàm quà secretis exit opaca vijs.

Priscianus verberans, & vapulans.

QUid facis ? ah ! tam perversâ quid volvitur irâ ?
  Quid parat iste tuus, posterus iste furor ?
Ah, truculente puer ! tam fædo parce furori.
  Nec rapiat tragicas tam gravis ira nates.
Ecce fremit, fremit ecce indignabundus Apollo.
  Castalides fugiunt, & procul ora tegunt.
Sic igitur sacrum, sic insedisse caballum
  Quæris ? & (ah) fieri tam malè notus eques ?

---

36 beare] beare, *46*   *Meliùs purgatur &c. See Introduction, p.*
lxiv, above.   *Priscianus verberans &c. See Introduction, p. lxiv, above.*

Ille igitur phaleris nitidus lucebit in istis ?
 Hæc erit ad solidum turpis habena latus ? 10
His ille (haud nimium rigidis) dabit ora lupatis ?
 Hæc fluet in miseris sordida vitta jubis ?
Sic erit ista tui, sic aurea pompa triumphi ?
 Ille sub imperijs ibit olentis heri ?
Ille tamen neque terribili stat spumëus irâ ;
 Vngula nec celso fervida calce tonat.
O meritò spectatur equi patientia nostri !
 Dicite Jö. tantum quis toleravit equus ?
Pegasus iste ferox, mortales spretus habenas,
 Bellerophontæâ non tulit ire manu. 20
Noster equus tamen exemplo non turget in isto :
 Stat bonus, & solito se pede certus habet.
Imò licèt tantos de te tulit ille pudores,
 Te tulit ille iterum. sed meliore modo.
Tunc rubor in scapulas ô quàm bene transijt iste,
 Qui satìs in vultus noluit ire tuos !
At mater centum in furias abit, & vomit iram
 Mille modis rabidam : jura, forumque fremit.
Quin fera tu, taceas ; aut jura, forumque tacebunt :
 Tu legi vocem non sinis esse suam. 30
O malè vibratæ rixosa volumina linguæ !
 Et satìs in nullo verba tonanda foro !
Causidicos (vesana !) tuos tua fulmina terrent.
 Ecce stupent miseri : ah ! nec meminêre loqui.
Hinc tua, (fæde puer) fædati hinc terga caballi
 Exercent querulo jurgia lenta foro.
Obscænas lites, & olentia jurgia ridet
 Turpiter in causam sollicitata Themis.
Juridicus lites quisquis tractaverit istas,
 Oh satis emunctâ nare sit ille, precor. 40
At tu de misero quid vis, truculente, caballo ?
 Cur premis insultans, sæue ! tyranne puer !
Tené igitur fugiet ? fugiet sacer iste caballus ?
 Non fugiet. sed (si vis) tibi terga dabit.

39–40 Also in Nisus verberans et vapulans.

Ad librum super hac re ab ipso ⎫ *Priscianus* ⎧ *verberans,*
ludi magistro editum, qui dr̈ ⎭   ⎨ *&*
                                          ⎩ *vapulans.*

S Ordes ô tibi gratulamur istas,
    O Musa aurea, blanda, delicata !
Sordes ô tibi candidas, suoque
Jam nec nomine, jam nec ore notas !
Sacro carmine quippe delinitæ
Se nunc ô bene nesciunt, novâque
Mirantur facie novum nitorem.
Ipsas tu facis ô nitere sordes.
Sordes ô tibi gratulamur ipsas !
Si non hic natibus procax malignis   10
Fædo fulmine turpis intonâsset :
Vnde insurgeret hæc querela vindex,
Docto & murmure carminis severi
Dulces fortiter aggregaret iras ?
Ipsæ ô te faciunt nitere sordes.
Sordes ô tibi gratulamur ipsas.
    Quàm pulchrè tua migrat Hippocrene !
Turpi quàm bene degener parenti !
Fædi filia tam serena fontis.
Has de stercore quis putaret undas ?   20
    Sic ô lactea surge, Musa, surge.
Surge inter medias serena sordes.
Spumis qualiter in suis Dione,
Cùm prompsit latus aurëum, atque primas
Ortu purpureo movebat undas.
Sic ô lactea surge, Musa, surge.
Enni stercus erit Maronis aurum.

Vpon a gnatt burnt in a candle.

L Ittle=buzzing=wanton elfe,
    Perish there, & thanke thy selfe.
Thou deseru'st thy life to loose,
For distracting such a Muse.

Ad librum &c. See Introduction, p. lxiv, above.
    Vpon a gnatt &c. Also in R7   I] Sylly Buzzing wanton Elfe *R7*
4 distracting] abusing *R7*

Was it thy ambitious aime
By thy death to purchase fame ?
Didst thou hope he would in pitty
Haue bestow'd a funerall ditty
On thy Ghoast ? & thou in that
To have outliued Virgills gnatt ?   10
No.   the treason, thou hast wrought,
Might forbid the such a thought.
If that night's worke doe miscarry,
Or a syllable but vary,
A greater foe thou shalt me find,
Then Domitian to thy kind.
Phæbus, to revenge thy fault,
In a fiery trapp thee caught ;
That thy winged mates might know it,
And not dare disturbe a Poët.   20
Deare, & wretched was thy sport,
Since thyselfe was crushed for't.
Scarcely had that life a breath,
Yet it found a double death ;
Playing in the golden flames,
Thou fell'st into an inky Thames ;
Scorch'd, & drown'd.   That petty sunne
A pretty Icarus hath undone.

5 thy] thine *R7*   13 doe] chance *R7*   14] Or but a syllable to
uarye *R7*   16 Then Domitian to *R7 :* The destruction of *T*
19 might] may *R7*   20 disturbe] t'enrage *R7*   22 thyselfe
was crushed] thy life was giuen *R7*   23 that] thy *R7*   26
Thames ;] *stop uncertain*

APPENDIX II.

BIOGRAPHICAL DOCUMENTS.

Memoires of the Lives, Actions, Sufferings & Deaths of those Noble, Reverend, and Excellent Personages, That Suffered . . . for the Protestant Religion, And the great Principle thereof, Allegiance to their Soveraigne, In our late Intestine Wars, . . . By Da: Lloyd, A.M. sometime of Oriel-Colledge in Oxon. London . . . MDCLXVIII.

(p. 618)

Mr. *Richard Crashaw*, his Father had done so well in the *Temple* where he was Preacher ; and he promised so much where he was a Scholar, that two great Lawyers, I think Sir *Henry Yelverton*, and Sir *Randolph Crew* took him to their care, the one paying for his *Diet*, the other for his *Cloaths*, Books, and Schooling till he was provided of both in the Royal Foundation at *Charter-House*, where his nature being leisurely advanced by Art, and his own pretty conceits improved by those of the choicest Orators and Poets, which he was not onely taught to understand, but imitate and make, not only their rich sense his own, but to smooth his soul as well as fill it, for things are rough without words, their expressions too ; the essays Mr. *Brooks* (his worthy Master still alive, whose even, constant, and pursuing diligence and industry, did wonders in that School) imposed upon him, on the Epistles and Gospels, at School, were the ground of that Divine fancy, so famous in (*a*) *Pembroke-hall*, where he was Scholar ; and *Peter-house*, where he was Fellow, in *Cambridge*, where he was esteemed the other (*b*) *Herbert* of our Church, for making Poetry, as

Marginal notes by Lloyd:
(*a*) *Whose way of versifying on sacred subjects was brought by Sir* R. Dallington, *sometimes Greek Scholar there, into the* Charter-house, *where he was Master and another* Justinian.
(*b*) *Mr.* Herbert *Brother to the Lord* Herbert *of* Cherbury, *Orator of the University of* Cambridge, *a Priest of the Church of* England, *whose Lyturgy he was ravished with, as all are with his Poems the* Temple.

Divine in its object, as in its Original, and setting wit disparaged in talking out most of its gallant Genius on Fables, Women, Drollery, or Flattery ; upon a matter and subject as noble as its nature, making his Verses not in his Study at St. *Peters-house*, but in his Devotions, wherein he spent many a night, at St. *Maries* Church ; warbling his Hymns for St. *Ambroses* his Saints, under *Tertullians* Roof of Angels ; having no other *Helicon*, than the *Jordan* of his eyes ; nor *Parnassus*, than the *Sion* where dwelled his thoughts, that made the Muses Graces, and taught Poems to do what they did of old, propagate Religion, and not so much Charm as Inspire the Soul. *Hebrew, Greek, Latine, Spanish, French, Italian*, were as familiar to him as *English*. Philosophy came as plausible from him as his Speeches or Sermons ; those thronged Sermons on each Sunday and Holiday, that ravished more like Poems, than both the Poet and Saint (two (*c*) of the most sacred names in heaven and earth) scattering not so much Sentences and [? read ' as '] Extasies, his soul brea[t]hing in each word, was the soul of the Assembly, as its original is of the World. Poetry, Musick, Drawing, Limning, Graving, (exercises of his curious Invention, and sudden Fancy) were the subservient recreations of his vacant hours, not the grand business of his soul; his diet was temperate, to a Lesson [read ' Lessian '] exactness, whence his memory was so clear, that he had ready at his service the choicest treasures of Greek and Latine Poets, those *Gibeonites* to draw water to the Tabernacle. This Divine Poet, that had set a Language (made up of the Quintessence of Fancy and Reason) for the Angels (as the Schoolmen state their way of discourse) to converse in ; seeing Atheism prevailing in *England*, embraced Popery in *Italy*, chusing rather to live in the Communion of that corrupt Church, in the practise of fundamental truths, confessed to be then mixed with some errors, than to stay here, where was hardly the face of any Church, after the overthrow of those to make way for all errors ; being resolved to any Religion, than that which taught a holy Rebellion (*d*) and Perjury, a pious Sacriledge, a godly Parracide, and made the very horrors of nature, the glory of Christianity. And died of a Feaver, the holy order of his soul over-heating his body, Canon of *Loretto*, whence he was carried to heaven, as that Church was brought thither by Angels, singing.

(*c*) A. C.   (*d*) *He was turned out for not taking the Covenant.*

Wood : *Fasti Oxonienses*

(In *Athenae Oxonienses*, 1691, 2, Vol. II, col. 688,
Incorporations for 1641.[1])

This year *Rich, Crashaw* of *Cambridge* was incorporated,
not that it appears so in the publick register, but in the
private observations of a certain Master of Arts that was
this year living in the University ; but in what degree he was
incorporated those observations mention not.   This person
who was the Son of an eminent Divine named *Will. Crashaw*,
was educated in Grammar learning in *Suttons Hospital* called
the *Charter-house* near to *London*, and in Academical, partly
in *Pemb*. Hall of which he was Scholar, and afterwards in
Peter House of which he was Fellow ; where, as in the former
House, his admirable faculty in Latin and English Poetry was
well known.   Afterwards he was Master of Arts, in which
degree, 'tis probable, he was incorporated : But being soon
after thrown out of his Fellowship, as many others of the said
University of *Cambridge* were, for denying the *Covenant* in the
time of the rebellion, he was for a time put to his shifts.   At
length upon an infallible foresight that the Church of *England*
would be quite ruined by the unlimited fury of the Presby-
terians, he changed his religion and went beyond the Seas,
and took up his abode for a time in the great City of *Paris* :
But being a meer Scholar and very shiftless, Mr. *Abr. Cowley*
the Poet, did, upon intimation of his being there, find him out
in a sorry condition, *an.* 1646 or thereabouts.   Whereupon
exhibiting to him, as much as laid in his power, for the present,
did afterwards obtain for him Letters of commendation from
Henrietta Maria Queen of *England*, then in those parts, and
some relief.   Afterwards he journied into *Italy*, and by virtue
of those Letters he became *Secretary to a Cardinal in Rome*,
and at length one of the Canons or Chaplains of the rich Church
of *our Lady at Loretto* some miles distant thence, where he died
and was buried about 1650.   Before he left *England* he wrot
certain Poems, which were intit. *Steps to the Temple*, because
in the Temple of God, under his wing, he led his life, in
S. *Maries* Church near to *Peter* House before mention'd.
There, as 'tis said, he lodged under *Tertullians* roof of
Angels.   There he made his nest more gladly than *Davids*

---

[1] Two unimportant notes by Wood have been omitted.

swallow near the House of God, where like a primitive Saint he offer'd more prayers in the night, than others usually offer in the day. There he pen'd the said Poems called *Steps to the Temple* for happy Souls to climb Heaven by. To the said *Steps* are joyned other Poems intit. *The delights of the Muses*, wherein are several Latin Poems ; which tho of a more humane mixture, yet they are sweet, as they are innocent. He hath also written *Carmen· Deo nostro*, being Hymns and other sacred Poems, addressed to the Countess of *Denbigh*. He was excellent in five Languages besides the Mother Tongue, viz. in Hebrew, Greek, Latin, Italian and Spanish ; the two last whereof tho he had little use, yet he had the knowledg of them, &c.

Documents from Peterhouse, Cambridge.

I. CRASHAW'S APPOINTMENT TO HIS FELLOWSHIP.[1]

(Autograph signature.)

Anno Domini millesimo sexcentissimo tricesimo sexto vicesimo die mensis Nouembris Richardus Crashaw admissus fuit a Reuerendo in Christo Patre ac Domino Domino Francisco Episcopo Eliensi ad locum siue societatem Magistri Simon Smeth legitimè vacantem in Collegio siue Domo Sancti Petri, & vicesimo secundo die ejusdem mensis coram Magistro & Socijs ejusdem Collegii personaliter constitutus, juramentum præstitit quod singulis ordinationibus & statutis Collegii (quantum in ipso est) reverenter obediret, & specialiter præter hoc de non appellando contra amotionem suam secundum modum & formam statutorum prædictorum, & de salvando cistam Magistri Thomæ de Castro-Bernardi & Magistri Thomæ Holbrooke (quantum in ipso est) indemnem, quo juramento præstito admissus fuit a Magistro Collegii in perpetuum socium eiusdem Collegii & in locum supradictum

Per me Richardum Crashaw Londinensem

II. THE LOAN TO THE KING.

(As quoted by T. A. Walker, in Peterhouse, 1906, p. 108.)

July 2, 1642.—It was ordered this day by ye M^r and all ye fellowes then att home y^t ye M^r lending one hundred pound

---

[1] The abbreviated words in this document are given in their extended forms.

for his M^{tyes} use, and ye College chest fourty, y^t threescore
pound borrowed for ye same use, in ye name of ye fellowes,
for wch ye present fellowes have given security, shall be payd
by all ye fellowes out of their next dividend. '

['signed by Cosin, by John Tolly, Richard Crashaw,
John Wilson, and Matthew Hanscomb.']

III. THE COLLEGE PLATE AND THE KING.
(*Autograph signature.*)

July 6, *1642*

Memorandum that it was this day decreed that the plate
of the Coll together wth that of the Chappel wch can bee spared
should bee in these dangerous times deposited in the kings
hand. in witnesse whereof wee al the fellows then present in
the Coll have heereto set our hands

> John Tolly   Præses
> Ri : Crashaw.
> Jo : Wilson   Proc jun /
> Matthew. Hanscomb.

IV. THE EJECTION OF CRASHAW AND OTHERS
FROM FELLOWSHIPS, AND APPOINTMENT OF
SUCCESSORS.

Whereas in pursuite of an ordinance of Parliam^t for regulating and reforming of ye Vniuersitie of Cambridge I haue
ejected Mr Beaumont, Mr Penniman, Mr Crashaw, Mr Holder,
Mr Tyringham late fellowes of Peter-house in Cambridge
And whereas Mr Charles Hotham, Robert Quarles, Howard
Becher, Walter Ellis, Edward Sammes haue beene examined
and approved by ye Assembly of Divines now sitting at
Westminster according to ye said ordinance as fitt to bee
ffellowes These are therefore to require you and every of you
to receiue the said Charles Hotham, Robert Quarles, Howard
Becher, Walter Ellis, Masters of Arts, & Edward Samês Bach^r
as ffellowes of your Colledge in roome of the said Mr Beaumont,
Mr Penniman, Mr Crashaw, Mr Holder, Mr Tyringham formerly
ejected and to giue them place according to theire seniority
in the Vniuersity in reference to all those that are or shall

hereafter bee putt in by mee accordinge to ye ordinance of Parliam^t aforesaid Given vnder my hand and seale the eleaventh day of June Anno 1644.

To the Master President and
ffellowes of Peter-house in
Cambridge

Manchester.

Documents from the Archives of the Santa Casa respecting Crashaw's appointment and death at Loreto.[1]

I. *Cardinal Pallotto's Letter of Appointment.*[2]

Ioannes Baptista Miseratione Diuina Tituli Sancti Siluestri de Capite Sanctæ Romanæ Ecclesiæ Presbiter Cardinalis Pallottus nuncupatus Almæ Domus, et Civitatis Lauretanæ Apostolica Auctoritate Comprotector. Dilecto Nobis in Christo Riccardo Croseo, Sacerdoti Anglo, familiari nostro, salutem in Domino sempiternam.

Uitæ ac morum honestas, aliaque laudabilia probitatis, et uirtutum merita super quibus apud nos fide digno commendaris testimonio et ⟨quæ⟩ sufficienter experti sumus nos inducunt ut tibi reddamur ad gratiam liberales. Cum itaque, sicut accepimus, Beneficiatus quem in Ecclesia Cathedrali Almæ Domus Lauretanæ dum uiueret obtinebat Petrus Paulus Massiccius, per obitum ipsius Petri Pauli de mense currenti, uacauerit et uacet ad præsens : Nos ad quos tamquam Comprotectorem præfatæ Almæ Domus Lauretanæ Apostolica auctoritate deputatum, ut in Litteris Apostolicis in ⟨forma⟩ breuis expeditis sub die 27 Septembris anni 1645, collatio provisio, et omnimoda alia dispositio dicti Beneficiatus, ut supra, et quorumcumque aliorum Beneficiorum in dicta Ecclesia existentium, dum illa in mensibus Sedi Apostolicæ reservatis uacent in uim indultorum Apostolicorum expectant et pertinent, Tibi de cuius idoneitate nobis legitime constat præmissorum meritorum intuitu specialem gratiam facere uolentes Beneficium prædictum, siue præmissis, siue alio quouis modo uacet, cum illi forsan annexis et· omnibus iuribus et pertinentiis suis, tibi,

[1] The abbreviated words in the original documents are here given in their extended forms.
[2] Documents Nos. I and III are from the *Archivio Storico del Pio Istituto di Santa Casa*, ' Registro di Lettere Apostoliche, Ordini, etc.', vol. iv (1645–72), fo. 25 v.–7 v.

in uim indultorum prædictorum, ac omnibus aliis melioribus, uia iure, et causa, et forma quibus possumus ac debemus tenore præsentium conferimus, et te de illo etiam prouidemus, mandantes propterea Reuerendis Dominis Capitularibus et Canonicis dictæ Ecclesiæ, ac Notariis, et Tabellionibus quibuscumque aliisque nobis uigore dictæ Comprotectionis subditis personis quatenus ipsi aut aliquis eorum per se uel alium seu alios fuerint requisiti seu requisitus, te, uel Procuratorem tuum, nomine tuo, in corporalem possessionem dicti Beneficiatus et illi annexorum Iurium et pertinentiarum predictarum inducant et inducat auctoritate nostra et defendant seu defendat inductum, amoto exinde quolibet illicito detemptore, facientes, seu faciens, te, uel pro te, Procuratorem tuum ad huiusmodi Benefitium, ut moris est, admitti, Tibique de illius et annexorum eorumdem fructibus, redditibus, prouentibus, iuribus, et obuentionibus uniuersis integre responderi, in contrarium facientibus non obstantibus quibuscumque. In quorum omnium et singulorum fidem præsentem manu nostra subscriptam fieri et per infrascriptum Secretarium nostrum subscribi, sigillique iussimus et fecimus impressione muniri.

Datum Romæ extra Portam Angelicam hac die Uigesima quarta Mensis Aprilis Millesimo Sexcentesimo quadragesimo nono, Pontificatus Sanctissimi in Christo Patris et Domini Nostri Domini Innocentii diuina prouidentia Papæ Decimi anno quinto.

Ioannes, Baptista, Cardinalis Pallottus Comprotector
Trolius de Troliis Secretarius
Omisso sigillo impresso in capsula stanea appenso cum Cordulis rubri coloris.

II. *Letter of Attorney appointing Crashaw's deputy for the ceremony of induction (' propter loci distantiam').*[1]

IN NOMINE DOMINI—AMEN.

Præsenti publico Instrumento cunctis ubique pateat euidenter, et notum sit quod Anno ab eiusdem Domini Nostri Jesu Christi Natiuitate, millesimo Sexcentesimo quadragesimo nono, Indictione secunda, Die uero uigesima quarta mensis Aprilis ; Pontificatus autem Sanctissimi in Christo Patris, et

---

l. 14 admitti] admicti *in the MS.*

[1] From *Archivio Storico*, Busta I, Tit. VIII, fascicolo I⁰—Capitolo e Clero an. 1507–1806. Docum. sciolti fo. 375–6.

Domini Nostri Domini Innocentij D⟨i⟩uina Prouidentia Papæ
decimi Anno eius quinto, In me Notarij publici Testibusque
infrascriptorum ad hæc omnia et singula uocatorum habitorum
specialiter, atque rogatorum præsentia præsens, et personaliter
Constitutus Illustris, Admodum Reverendus D. Riccardus
Crosius filius quondam Guglielmi sacerdos Anglus mihi Notario
cognitus asserens, et affirmans ipsum fuisse, et esse prouisum
de uno beneficiatu in Ecclesia Cathedrali, ac Alma Domo
Lauretana per obitum quondam Reverendi Domini Pauli
Massucij uacante, ab Eminentissimo et Reverendissimo Domino Ioanne Baptista Presbitero Cardinali Pallotto nuncupato
dictæ Almæ Domus Lauretanæ Apostolica auctoritate Com-
protectore, uolens igitur ipse Reverendus Dominus Constitutus
illius possessionem capere, et quia personaliter ad infrascripta
peragenda uacare non potest, propter loci distantiam suum
propterea decreuit, et deliberauit constituere Procuratorem.
Ideo citra reuocationem &c. sponte et ex certa eius Scientia,
spontaneaque, et deliberata uoluntate non per errorem aliquem
seductus, uel circumuero, sed omnibus meliori modo uia
Iure, titulo, et causa quibus magis melius ualidius, et efficacius
de Iure fieri potuit, et debuit ac potest, et debet fecit
constituit creauit, deputauit, et solemniter ordinauit suum
uerum, certum, legitimum, et indubitatum Procuratorem, acto-
rem Nuncium generalem, et specialem Itá tamen quod speciali-
tas generalitati non deroget nec é contra uidelicet PerIllustrem
et Admodum Reverendum Dominum Alessandrum Crucianum
in eadem Ecclesia Cathedrali Canonicum Thesaurarium absen-
tem &c. ad ipsius Reverendi Domini Constituentis nomine
et pro eo, ac eius parte, ueram, realem, actualem ciuilem, et
corporalem possessionem supradicti beneficiati, omniumque et
singulorum illius Iurium, membrorum, et pertinentiarum
quarumcumque capiendum, adipiscendum et apprehendendum,
captamque, adeptam, et apprehensam retinendum, et con-
tinuandum &c. et si necesse erit in dominio a quibus opus
fuerit recognosci faciendum &c., omnesque, et singulos alios
actus super premissis necessarios, et opportunos, et in supra-
dicta Cathedrali Ecclesia fieri solitos, et consuetos peragendum
&c., et generaliter omnia alia, et singula faciendum, dicendum,
gerendum, et exercendum in premissis necessaria, et oppor-
tuna, et quæ ipse Dominus constituens faceret ac facere posset
si predictis omnibus, et singulis præsens, et personaliter
Interesset etiam si talia forent, quæ mandatum exigerent

magis speciale, quam presentibus est expressus promittens
habere ratum &c. releuans &c. super quibus, omnibus, et
singulis prædictis petitum fuit à me Notario Publico Infra-
scripto ut unum uel plura, publicum, seu publica Instrumentum et Instrumenta conficerem, atque traderem, et pro ut
opus fuerit, et requisitus ero Actum Romæ In officio mei &c.
Regionis Pontis præsentibus ibidem audientibus, et Intelli-
gentibus his uidelicet PerIllustri et Admodum Reverendo
Domino Stephano Torretto filio quondam Augustini Cammeri-
neris, et Illustri et Reverendo Domino Ioanne Garcia de
Cortigera filio quondam Dedaci Burgero testibus ad prædicta
omnia et singula uocatis, habitis specialiter, atque rogatis

  Ego Augustinus Teulus Curiæ Cancellarius Cameræ
  Apostolicæ notarius de prædictis rogatis presens
  Instrumentum subscripsi et publicaui rogatus

III. *The certificate of induction.*

In Dei Nomine, Amen. Anno Domini Millesimo Sex-
centesimo quadragesimo nono Indictione secunda, die uero
Uigesima octaua Mensis Aprilis, Tempore Pontificatus
Sanctissimi in Christo Patris, et Domini Nostri Domini
Innocentii diuina providentia Papæ Decimi Anno quinto.

Cunctis ubique pateat euidenter et notum sit qualiter In
mei notarii publici testiumque infrascriptorum præsentia
præsens, et personaliter existens PerIllustris et admodum
Reverendus Dominus Gaspar Lusignanus Archidiaconus
Cathedralis Ecclesiæ Lauretanæ in Choro dictæ Ecclesiæ cum
maiori numero perIllustrium Dominorum Canonicorum,
Beneficiatorum, et Clericorum Capituli, hora Tertiarum in
executione supradictarum literarum a me Cancellario lectarum
et publicatarum in actualem realem, et corporalem possessionem dicti Beneficiatus et Prebendæ illiusque Iurium et pertinentiarum suarum posuit immisit, et introduxit PerIllustrem
et admodum Reverendum Dominum Alexandrum Crucianum
Canonicum Thesaurarium Ecclesiæ Lauretanæ Procuratorem
PerIllustris et admodum Reverendi Domini Riccardi Crosii
Angli, prout de dicto Mandato Procuræ constat sub rogitu
Domini Augustini Theuli Notarii Cameræ Apostolicæ sub
die 24 Aprilis 1649, ad quod &c. et eidem Domino Procuratori, ut moris est, genuflexo in Choro dictæ Ecclesiæ
birretum in capite imposuit, et alia gessit et fecit quæ in

similibus requiruntur, et Stallum in Choro assignauit, mandans de fructibus, prouentibus iuribus, et obuentionibus uniuersis dicto Domino Riccardo Croseo, siue eius Domino Procuratori in futurum per quos spectat integre responderi aliisque gestis, et obseruatis iuxta stilum ueram possessionem denotantibus, dictusque PerIllustris Dominus Alexander Crucianus Thesaurarius Procurator declarauit, et declarat se in dicta possessione pro dicto principali continuare uelle, et protestatus fuit quod per suum inde recessum non intendit huiusmodi possessionem dimittere, sed illam animo, et corpore retinere, et continuare donec &c. nemine contradicente, nec in aliquo se opponente &c. Super quibus &c.

Actum Laureti in Choro dictæ Ecclesiæ, præsentibus ibidem Reuerendo Domino Francisco Montano de Laureto et Domino Petro Guerrino Organista testibus ad prædicta &c.

Ego Jacobus Carrellus Notarius et Cancellarius rogatus &c.

IV. *The record of Crashaw's death.*[1]

Anno Domini 1649 die 21 Augusti

Reverendus Dominus Riccardus Crosius Beneficiatus Almæ Domus Lauretanæ de Anglia ætatis suæ annorum 36 circiter in Communione Sanctæ Matris Ecclesiæ Animam Deo reddidit, cuius confessionem audiuit Reuerendus P. Erigus Lindunus Pœnitentiarius, sed a Reverendo Domino Giorgio Tinto Curato roboratus fuit sacra Olei unctione, cuius corpus sepultum est in tumulo sacerdotum.

V. *A further note of Crashaw's appointment.*[2]

Riccardo Crashaw Inglese fu familiare del Card. Pallotto Protettore. Con Bolla 24 aprile 1649 ottenne il beneficio N° 7 le cui rendite consistevano in appezzamenti rustici e fruttavano scudi 96 : 46. oltre la porzione di pane e vino quotidiana e un assegno in danari.

---

[1] From the *Archivi Parrochiali di Loreto*, ' Liber Mortuorum ', vol. ii (1646–57), fo. 73. The date of the letter, similar to No. 1 above, appointing Crashaw's successor, is Aug. 25, 1649. (' Registro di Lettere, etc.' fo. 30 v.)

[2] From the *Archivio Capitolare di Loreto*, ' Libro di memorie ', fo. 280.

COMMENTARY.

THE MS. DEDICATION IN MS. ADDIT. 40176.

PAGE **2**, ll. 21–2. *sydus oris tui te plenissimi & virtutum tuarum.*
The mingled construction of ' plenus ' with the ablative ' te ' and
the genitive ' virtutum ', ' your countenance so full of yourself and
your virtues ', though curious, seems not impossible for a writer
of Renaissance Latin. It also avoids ' oris tui tui '.

l. 23. *modestiæ.* ' Modestia ' has been suggested and may have
been replaced by ' modestiæ ' owing to a slip in writing. If
' modestiæ ' is kept, the subject of ' dispensat ' must be an unex-
pressed pronoun standing for ' sydus '. This goes well enough
with ' minùs fervido . . . sed dulci . . . radio ', though not so well
with ' vmbram . . . offundens '; on the whole it seems best to
retain ' modestiæ '.

EPIGRAMMATUM SACRORUM LIBER.

[*Cross-references will be found in the Index of first lines showing
where Crashaw's Latin, Greek, and English epigrams correspond.*]

PAGE **6**, Heading] *Benjamino Lany.* See *D.N.B.*, art. ' Ben-
jamin Laney '. Laney, whose dates are 1591–1675, was Master of
Pembroke Hall from 1630 until his ejection in March 1643/4. The
High Church principles and practices for which Crashaw praises
him here and in the following poem caused him to be denounced
by Prynne as ' one of the professed Arminians, Laud's creatures
to prosecute his designs in the university of Cambridge ' (*Canter-
buries Doome*, 1646, p. 176). After the Restoration he became
bishop successively of Peterborough, Lincoln, and Ely.

PAGE **7**, l. 60. (*Non alio . . . &c.*) These words refer to ' plectra '
in the previous line, and a modernized text would require a stop
after the second bracket (or after ' Phœbo ' inside the bracket).

PAGE **8**, l. 70. *Majórque cerni.* The expression is copied from
maiorque videri, used of the Cumaean Sibyl in *Aeneid*, vi. 49.

l. 76. *comit.* Compare p. 64, l. 4 : ' Quæque comunt . . .' In
both places Crashaw treats the first syllable of the verb as if it
were short, and he seems to connect the word with *cŏma*, hair, in
accordance with a widespread error. Compare Cooper's *Thesaurus* (ed. 1573), art. ' Coma '.

l. 77. *ipse Deus, Deus.* Compare Virgil, *Eclogues*, 5, l. 64 :

> deus, deus ille, Menalca !

and Lucretius, 5, l. 8 :

> deus ille fuit, deus, inclute Memmi.

PAGE **9**, Heading] Magistro *Tournay.* ' Joannes Turney ' was
admitted to Pembroke Hall March 1, 1620, and took the degrees
of A.B. 1623–4 ; A.M. 1627 ; and S.T.B. (B.D.), 1634. On June
14, 1634, Dr. Samuel Ward wrote from ' Sidney College ' to James
Ussher : ' . . . We have had some doings here of late about one of
Pembroke-Hall, who preaching in St. Mary's, about the beginning
of Lent, upon that text, James, chap. ii. ver. 22. seemed to avouch
the insufficiency of faith to justification, and to impugn the
doctrine of our 11th article of justification by faith only ; for

which he was convented by the vice-chancellor, who was willing to
accept of an easy acknowledgment : but the same party preaching
his Latin sermon, pro gradu, the last week, upon Rom. chap. iii.
ver. 28. he said, he came not, palinodiam canere ; which moved
our vice-chancellor, Dr. Love, to call for his sermon ; which he
refused to deliver. Whereupon, upon Wednesday last, being
Barnaby day, the day appointed for the admission of the bachelors
of divinity, and the choice of the bachelors of divinity, which must
answer die comitiorum ; he was stayed by the major part of the
suffrages of the doctors of the faculty. And though sundry doctors
did favour him, and would have had him to be the man that
should answer die Comitiorum, yet he is put by, and one
Mr. Flatkers of our college chosen to answer. Whose first question is
  1. Sola fides justificat.
  2. Realis præsentia Christi in eucharistia non ponit transub-
stantiationem.
  The truth is, there are some heads among us, that are great
abettors of Mr. Tourney, the party above-mentioned, who are no
doubt backed by others.' (Elrington, *Works of Ussher*, 1847, vol. xv,
p. 579). Compare the title of Crashaw's Latin poem, p. 208, below,
' Fides quæ sola justificat, non est sine Spe & Dilectione '.
  l. 11. (*heu simili de prole puerpera*). Compare Horace, *Odes*,
IV. v. 23 :
Laudantur simili prole puerperæ,

  l. 16. (*Quàm primùm potuit dicere*) *dixit*, erit. Compare the
second line of the distich which Suetonius (' Domitianus ', 23)
records as having been composed as a comment on the raven's
remark, "Εσται πάντα καλῶς, a few months before Domitian's assassi-
nation :
Nuper Tarpeio quae sedit culmine cornix
Est bene non potuit dicere, dixit : *erit*.

  PAGE 10, Heading] *Magistro Brook*. Robert Brooke is described in *Alumni Carthusiani*, 1913 (B. Marsh and F. A. Crisp),
as ' Usher 27 October 1626, Schoolmaster 8 December 1628,
removed at the Assembly of 25 January 164$\frac{3}{4}$, after being se-
questered by a Committee of the House of Commons for refusing
the Solemn League and Covenant. He matriculated 27 June, 1623,
from Magdalen Hall, Oxford . . .' He received a pension after the
Restoration (24 Jan. 1664) and was still living when David Lloyd
wrote his account of Crashaw (q.v. App. II, p. 415, above).
  ll. 15–16. *Híc tuus inveniet, &c.* Crashaw may have remembered the lines in Hall's *Satires* (VI. i. 1–4), where marking with
the nail and placing an obelus in the margins to indicate dis-
approval are mentioned :
Labeo reserues a long nayle for the nonce
To wound my Margent through ten leaues at once,
Much worse then *Aristarchus* his blacke Pile,
That pierc'd olde *Homers* side.

  PAGE 11, l. 31. *Hæc coràm, atque oculis legeret Lucretia justis.*
Crashaw probably had in his mind the concluding lines (9–10) of
Martial, xi. 16 :
Erubuit posuitque meum Lucretia librum,
Sed coram Bruto ; Brute, recede : leget.

  PAGE 12, ll. 51–2. *Veronensi . . . Bilbilicisve.* The reference is
to Catullus and Martial, born at Verona and Bilbilis respectively.

PAGE **13,** l. 93. *sitit & bibit.* Compare p. 53, ll. 7–8.

l. 121. *amaverit undas.* The conjecture that ' ignes ' should replace ' undas ' might be adopted in view of (1) the weak antithesis in ' aquas ' and ' undas '; (2) the ' ille ignis ' of l. 123, apparently referring to the lines immediately preceding ; and (3) Crashaw's use of this kind of phrase in the same connexion in ' The Weeper ' (st. 17, p. 311, below) :

> But can these fair Flouds be
> Freinds with the bosom fires that fill thee

PAGE **14,**, l. 126. *testis* for *testis,.* The comma seems more likely to represent a printer's error than an intentional break in the sentence on Crashaw's part.

l. 9 (prose). *vendicant.* Cooper's *Thesaurus* (ed. 1573) in accordance with an opinion then general has ' vendico . . . *to vendicate :* *to clayme : to chalenge to himselfe* ' as well as the classical ' vindico ', to which is given the meaning : ' *To reuenge or punish : to defend or deliuer from danger or wrong : to restore to liberty.*'

l. 20 (prose). *Quanquam δ.* Compare Virgil, *Aeneid,* v. 194–5 :

> Non iam prima peto Mnestheus, neque vincere certo ;
> Quamquam o !

l. 25 (prose). *magistros Acygnianos.* See Biography, p. xxii, above. The following passage in Barclay's *Euphormionis Satyricon,* Pars III (' Apologia Euphormionis pro se ') is relevant to Crashaw's remarks : ' Quis captos Acignianorum artibus ignorat, qui cæterorum quidem tanquam barbara & incondita ingenia aspernati, apud Acignianos credunt Musas omnes felici facinore pæne in custodia haberi ? Majestas & moderatio incessus, & secretum ab externis penetrale, tum quorundam ingeniorum felicitas, quæ in illis viguerunt, eos ad tam immodicam scientiæ famam evexit.'

The spelling ' Acygnianos ' instead of ' Acignianos ', preferred by Barclay, probably refers to the derivation ἀ-κύκνος, which turns on the black dress of the Jesuits, as well as to the name of the society's founder.

PAGE **15,** l. 4. *Plus habet hic* templi ; *plus habet ille* Dei. This is an adaptation of the last line of Claudian's poem ' De sene Veronensi qui suburbium numquam egressus est ' (ed. Koch, 1893, *Carmina Minora,* xx. 22) :

> Plus habet hic vitæ, plus habet ille viæ.

l. 13. *Quis novus hic, &c.* Compare Virgil, *Aeneid,* iv. 10 :

> Quis novus hic nostris successit sedibus hospes !

PAGE **17,** l. 2. *Nec frustra Æthiopem nempe lavare fuit.* Compare the Greek proverb quoted by Lucian, ' Adversus indoctum ', cap. 28, Οἶδα ὡς μάτην ταῦτά μοι λελήρηται καὶ κατὰ τὴν παροιμίαν Αἰθίοπα σμήχειν ἐπιχειρῶ, and the epigram in the *Anthologia Palatina* (xi. 428), attributed to Lucian :

> Εἰς τί μάτην νίπτεις δέμας Ἰνδικόν ; ἴσχεο τέχνης·
> Οὐ δύνασαι δνοφερὴν νύκτα καθηλιάσαι.

The legend to Alciati's fifty-ninth ' Emblema ' is a translation of this Greek :

> Abluis Æthiopem quid frustra ? ah desine : noctis
> Illustrare nigræ nemo potest tenebras.

Erasmus in his ' Adagia ' (p. 320, col. 2, in the ' Adagia ' of J. J.
Grynæus) has *Æthiopem lavas : Æthiopem dealbas*, and quotes
Lucian κατὰ τὴν παροιμίαν, &c. (as above) with the translation
' Ac juxta proverbium, Æthiopem lavare conor '.

PAGE 18, ll. 7–8. *Cur tibi tota vagos, &c.* It looks as though
Crashaw had the Fourth Satire of Juvenal fresh in his memory, or
at least the earlier part ; compare ll. 25–6 :

> potuit fortasse minoris
> Piscator quam piscis emi.

and 29–31 :

> cum tot sestertia, partem
> Exiguam et modicae sumptam de margine cenae,
> Purpureus magni ructarit scurra Paleti.

and with Crashaw's line ending ' . . . patrimonia census ' compare
Juvenal, x. 13 :

> . . . cuncta exuperans patrimonia census.

PAGE 19, l. 5. (*sic, sic juvat ire sub umbras*) : from Virgil,
Aeneid, iv. 660.

PAGE 20, l. 14. *Inque* bonam *felix i fugitive* crucem. This is a
play on the common formula of objurgation :

> I in malam crucem.   Plautus, *Casina*, 977.

Compare :

> fugite hinc in malam crucem.   *Menaechmi*, 1017.
> Ei dierecte in maximam malam crucem.   *Poenulus*, 347.

PAGE 21, ll. 3–4.   *unus*
> *Iste oculus fiam* totus & omnis ego.

Compare Catullus, xiii. 13–14 :

> Quod tu cum olfacies, deos rogabis,
> Totum ut te faciant, Fabulle, nasum.

PAGE 23, l. 13. *Pellibus exiguis arctatur, &c.* This is a curious
adaptation of Martial, xiv. 190 :

> *Titus Livius in membranis.*
> Pellibus exiguis artatur Livius ingens,
> Quem mea non totum bibliotheca capit.

Crashaw would have found the abandoned spelling ' arctatur '.

PAGE 24, ll. 7–12. *Frustra illum, &c.* Compare Marino, *La Lira*,
Part III, p. 175 (ed. 1615), ' Nel Martirio di S. Stefano ', ll. 5–8 :

> Son ben per lui crudeli, e fieri ordigni
> La pietre sì ; ma 'l Martire dolente
> Più de le vostre colpe i colpi sente,
> Che 'l fulminar de' rigidi macigni.

PAGE 24, ll. 19–20. *Ah, redeas, &c.* Compare ll. 47–50 of the
English poem on the same text, p. 380, below.

PAGE 30, l. 5. *Vicinia sæva salutis, &c.* Compare p. 236, l. 2
sqq., ' Stands trembling at the gate of blisse', &c.

l. 6. *O quàm tu malus es proximitate boni !* Compare Ovid, *Ars
Amatoria*, ii. 662 :

> Et lateat vitium proximitate boni.

l. 7. *Ah ! portu qui teste perit, bis naufragus ille est.* Crashaw is
referring to a Latin proverbial saying. See A. Otto, *Die Sprichwörter und sprichwörtlichen Redensarten der Römer*, p. 284, where
' Navem in portu mergis ' is quoted from Seneca the rhetorician

(*Rhet. Controv.* ii. 6. 4), 'in portu, ut dicitur, naufragium' from St. Jerome, *Adv. Ioann. Hieros.* 37, and 'in Romano portu naufragium fecit' from Jerome's *In Rufinum* ii. 32.

PAGE 31, l. 10. *Dimidium fidei, qui bene nescit, habet.* This recalls :

Dimidium facti qui coepit habet. Horace, *Epistles*, i. ii. 40.

l. 16. *Non possum Autumno nobiliore frui.* This recalls a line in Martial (xi. 69. 12) which Crashaw probably had in his mind :

Non potui fato nobiliore mori.

PAGE 33, ll. 15–16.

An Saulus fuerit cæcus, vix dicere possum ;
Hoc scio, quòd captus lumine Saulus erat.

This couplet belongs to a class of which the earliest and best-known is Martial's epigram, i. 32 :

Non amo te, Sabidi, nec possum dicere quare :
Hoc tantum possum dicere, non amo te.

Cf. Martial, xi. 64 :

Nescio tam multis quid scribas, Fauste, puellis :
Hoc scio, quod scribit nulla puella tibi.

and John Owen, Bk. V (Renouard's edition), epigram 8 :

An Petrus fuerit Romæ, sub iudice lis est ;
Simonem Romæ nemo fuisse negat.

PAGE 34, l. 13. *Dicite, quæ tanta est sceleris fiducia vestri?* This recalls :

Tantane vos generis tenuit fiducia vestri ?
Virgil, *Aeneid*, i. 132.

PAGE 35, l. 14. *Dormit; nec dormit omnibus illa tamen.* 'Non omnibus dormio' was proverbial. See A. Otto, *Die Sprichwörter und sprichwörtlichen Redensarten der Römer*, p. 121. It is in Polydore Vergil's *Proverbiorum liber* and Erasmus's *Adagia.* Crashaw would probably have known it from Erasmus, if not from Cicero, *Epp. ad Fam.* vii. 24. 1. The story with which the origin of the proverb was connected is thus told by R. Y. Tyrrell in his note on the passage of Cicero, who attributes the saying to Cipius.

'The story about Cipius was that he was in the habit of pretending to be asleep, lest he should find himself forced to condemn something in the conduct of his wife ; but that on one occasion, when a slave, taking advantage of his apparent slumber, was making away with a stolen cup, he suddenly started up with the words, "I am not asleep to every one", and recovered his stolen property.'

PAGE 38, ll. 15–16. *Qui tanta negotia, &c.* Compare 'Sospetto d' Herode' st. 15, ll. 7–8 (p. 113, below)

whose Birth
Was the great businesse both of Heav'n and Earth.

l. 24. *Nympha pudica, &c.* For this line, the best-known of all Crashaw's Latin verses, Prof. E. Bensly points out in *Notes and Queries*, Tenth Series, x, Oct. 17, 1908 (p. 307) that the poet may have been indebted to Maximilianus Sandæus (van der Sandt, 1578–1656) : *Maria Flos mysticus siue Orationes Ad Sodales in festivitatibus deiparæ Habitæ desumpta materia a floribus cum figuris Ereis* [Mainz, 1629]. 'On p. 24 opposite the beginning of the first oration ("Maria in Purificatione Rosa"), is an emblem, a rose with a picture in its centre of the presentation in the Temple, and under it the distich,

> Vin' scire unde suum rosa candida traxerit ostrum ?
> Purgantem vidit Virginem, et erubuit.'

Compare also the translation from Grotius, p. 399, below, l. 52:

> The water blush'd, and started into wine.

Crashaw's three concluding words are also used by Cabilliau, *Magdalena* (Antwerp, 1625, p. 199), Magdalea Silva, lxiii, l. 2 :

> Monstrifero speculo vidit, & erubuit.

Vida's *Christiad*, ii. 431 :

> Pars Jedaba venere : Canam hi liquere modo atra
> Miratam puras in vína rubescere lymphas.

(See *Notes and Queries*, October 16, 1852, p. 358.)
Crashaw's epigram was remembered when its authorship was forgotten and it has been attributed to Dryden and to Addison. It was sometimes quoted (without original authority) with 'Lympha' for 'Nympha'. Grosart in his edition gives several translations into English by subsequent authors. See also *Notes and Queries*, Fourth Series, iv, p. 244 (1869).

PAGE 41, ll. 13–20. *Sive* oculos, *sive* ora, *&c.* Compare Marino, *La Lira*, Part II, p. 142 (ed. 1615), ' Alla piaga del costato ', ll. 1–3 :

> Piaga dolce d' Amore,
> Già tu piaga non sei,
> Ma bocca di quel core,

PAGE 42, l. 7. *antiqui agnosco vestigia patris.* The expression is apparently suggested by Virgil, *Aeneid*, iv. 23 :

> agnosco veteris vestigia flammea.

ll. 9–16. *Nasceris, en! &c.* Compare the poem 'Easter Day', which is a free version of this epigram, p. 100, below.

PAGE 45, ll. 5–6. *Verùm ubi composito, &c.* The language is reminiscent of the passage in *Aeneid*, ii. 682–4, where Virgil describes the sudden appearance of fire which plays harmlessly about Iulus' head :

> Ecce levis summo de vertice visus Iuli
> Fundere lumen apex, tactuque innoxia mollis
> Lambere flamma comas et circum tempora pasci.

PAGE 47, l. 17. *I lictor ; manibúsque audacibus injice vinc'la.* Compare Cicero, *pro C. Rabirio*, iv. 13, ' I, lictor, colliga manus ', and Livy, i. 26. 11, ' I, líctor, conliga manus '.

PAGE 48, l. 2. *Sic pugnum Logices stringere.* For the clenched fist as the symbol of Logic (and the open hand that of Rhetoric) compare Owen, *Epigrammata*, Lib. II. 61 :

> Parcus & Prodigus.
> Rhetoricæ studiosus ego sum, Prodigus inquit :
> Parcus ait, Logicæ sum studiosus ego.
> Semper clausa manus Logicam designat avari :
> Prodiga Rhetoricam semper aperta manus.

l. 15. *tumes* : ' tume ', which has been suggested, would no doubt give a more satisfactory sense, but as ' tumes ' has both manuscript support and a meaning it seems best to retain it.

Epigrammata Sacra. 431

PAGE 50, l. 4. *Cui* vitæ *ex ipso* fonte *sititur aqua!* Compare Ovid, *Epist. ex Ponto*, III. v. 18 :

> Gratius ex ipso fonte bibuntur aquae.

l. 5. *Felices animæ!* Compare Virgil, *Aeneid*, vi. 669, ' Dicite, felices animæ . . .', where Æneas is addressing the souls in Elysium.

l. 19. *Felix, qui potuit* . . . Compare Virgil, *Georgic*, ii. 490 :

> Felix, qui potuit rerum cognoscere causas.

PAGE 51, l. 5. Noli altum sapere (*hoc veteres voluêre magistri*). It is rather curious that Crashaw should give this as a precept of ' veteres magistri ', as it is a Biblical quotation, Rom. xi. 20 (Vulg.), ' Noli altum sapere, sed time ' (' Be not high-minded, but fear '). It seems possible that he was thinking for the moment of the printer's mark first adopted by Robert Étienne—the olive-tree bearing a scroll with ' Noli altum sapere sed time ', and a figure of an aged man pointing to these words.

PAGE 52, ll. 3, 4. *Domitiane.* Crashaw has treated the first syllable as though it were long. Compare p. 365, 2, l. 6. below.

l. 6. *possit ut ille mori.* Compare Lucan, *Belli Civilis*, Lib. II. 105–9, and especially l. 109 :

> Non senis extremum piguit vergentibus annis
> Præcepisse diem, nec primo in limine vitae
> Infantis miseri nascentia rumpere fata.
> Crimine quo parvi caedem potuere mereri ?
> Sed satis est iam posse mori.

PAGE 64, l. 2. *Heu cœli quantam hinc invidiam patimur!* Compare Virgil, *Georgics*, i. 503 seq., where Virgil is praying that Octavian may still remain on earth :

> Iam pridem nobis caeli te regia, Caesar,
> Invidet, atque hominum queritur curare triumphos.

ll. 5–6.   *tot pictæ vellera nubis ;*
> *Vellera, quæ roseâ Sol variavit acu.*

Virgil, *Georgics*, . 441, has :

> Ille ubi nascentem maculis variaverit ortum

of the sun's spotted disk at rising, and Martial, viii. 28. 18, has

> Texta, Semiramia quæ variantur acu,

of embroidery. But to combine the notions and to speak of the sun's *rosy needle* is curious, though no doubt the *fleeces of cloud* help to introduce the metaphor, and also *pictæ* ; Virgil, e.g., has ' pictus acu chlamydem ' (*Aeneid*, ix. 582), ' pictus acu tunicas ', &c. (*Aeneid*, xi. 777), and Ovid uses *pingere acu* for embroidering.

PAGE 65 [Title-page 1670]. Εἵνεκεν εὐμαθίης, &c. From *Anthologia Palatina*, vii. 22. 5–6 ; the poem is an epitaph on Sophocles. In the first line quoted Μελιχρὸς should be μελιχρὸς.

PAGE 68, l. 4. δασιόις. The coinage perhaps results from a confusion of δασύς and λάσιος.

STEPS TO THE TEMPLE.

Page 75, l. 1. *The Authors friend.* This, as suggested by A. Warren (*Richard Crashaw*, p. 220), may well have been Joseph Beaumont, Fellow of Peterhouse, 1636–44, and Master of the College after the Restoration. For Beaumont's witness to the friendship see p. xxxix. The florid style of the Preface can be paralleled from Beaumont's other writings.

l. 4. *Jamblicus* (*in vita Pythagoræ*). The reference should be not to Iamblichus' Life of Pythagoras but to Eunapius' Life of Iamblichus in *Vitæ Sophistarum* (ed. Boissonade, 1878, p. 458), where mention is made of the power of levitation attributed to Iamblichus : ' te inter fundendum preces videri ab humo plus-quam cubitos decem sublimem rapi atque attolli . . .'.

l. 21. Suarez *on the subject.* The reference is probably to Suarez's *Comm. et Disp. in Summam Theologicam S. Thomæ*, I, pars. ii, lib. 2, c. 26, where it is denied that angels use human language, though there is no special mention of poetry.

l. 27. *seven shares and a halfe.* Compare Ben Jonson, *Poëtaster*, Act III, Sc. i, ad fin., ' Commend me to seuen-shares and a halfe '. Theatrical performers were distinguished as whole-sharers, three-quarter-sharers, half-sharers, &c.

Page 76, l. 42. *St.* Maries *Church neere St.* Peters *Colledge.* The church of Little St. Mary's, adjoining Peterhouse, was used as the college chapel prior to the building of the new chapel (in use 1632, see Introduction, p. xxii, above). It was the latter, and not Little St. Mary's, that was famous for the sculptured angels afterwards pulled down by the Parliamentary Commissioners in 1643.

l. 43. Tertullian's *roofe of Angels.* Professor Souter suggests that this *may* refer to the passage in Tertullian's *Liber de Specta-culis*, c. xxvii (ed. Migne, I, col. 658), ' Dubitas enim illo momento, quo in diaboli Ecclesia fueris, omnes angelos prospicere de cælo, et singulos denotare, quis blasphemiam dixerit, &c.'. A writer in *Notes and Queries*, Fifth Series, vi, 1876, p. 233, E. Marshall, ob-serves that Tertullian (*De Anima*, c. ix) speaks of the soul ' con-versing with the angels ' in church and calls the church ' heaven ' in the *De Spectaculis*, c. xxv. It is also suggested that the phrase may refer to the interpretation which Tertullian gives of St. Paul's direction for the dress of women in public worship, who are ' to have power on the head because of the angels '; and the same writer notes Crashaw's own use of ' cœlum ' in connexion with Peter-house Chapel in ' Votiva Domus Petrensis pro Domo Dei ' (p. 206, ll. 7, 8, below) :　　　　*nostrique per atria Cœli*
(Sacra Domus nostrum *est* cœlum).

l. 52. *five Languages.* David Lloyd (see Appendix II, p. 416, above) includes French.

l. 62. (*almost Lessian temperance*). See on p. 156 the poem ' In praise of Lessius his rule of health '.

Page 77, l. 75. *his Poem upon Bishop* Andrews *Picture.* See p. 163, below.

Page 79. *The Weeper.* In this poem and in ' The Teare ' (p. 84, above) Crashaw appears to have been indebted to *Francisci Remondi Societatis Iesu Epigrammata et Elegiæ . . . Antverpiæ . . . M. DCVI.*, the work from which he translated his ' Alexias ' elegies (see note, pp. 450–2, below).   Epigram xxix, Lib. I, (p. 15) is as follows :

De lacrymis Sanctæ Mariæ Magdalenæ, quas
ad Christi pedes effudit.

Felices nimium gemini tua lumina fontes,
   Quæque venit trita sedula gutta via.
Se lacrymam esse tuam cuperet, dum vere tepenti
   Labitur in molles humida gemma rosas.
Si manare oculis posset Pactolus ab istis,
   Aurifer hac iret ditior amnis aqua.
Tam pretiosa pedes Domini nisi lamberet unda,
   Unda quid, ah ! quererer, tam pretiosa peris ?

Crashaw had also probably read some of Marino's verses on this subject : ' La Maddelena ai piedi di Christo | Madrigali ' (ed. Croce, 1913, p. 369), ' Maddalena di Tiziano ' (ed. cit., p. 242), ' Per la Maddelena alla Croce ' (ed. cit., p. 374).   Crashaw may also have been indebted to Marino for the form.   See the stanza quoted below, note to st. 14.   Marino often uses stanzas of similar form.   See also the notes to the longer version, pp. 448–9, below. Marvell's verses ' Eyes and Tears ' seem to show Crashaw's influence.

St. 1, ll. 1 and 3.   Compare *Baduini Cabilliavi e Soc. Jesu Magdalena*, Antwerp, 1625, Lib. II. Elegia xiv (p. 59) :

Magdalenæ lacrymæ gemmæ

Magdalis vt glacies Phœbeo saucia telo
Liquitur, & vernâ plus niue delacrymat.

St. 4, ll. 1–2.   *Vpwards thou dost weepe, &c.*   Compare Hermannus Hugo, *Pia Desideria*, Lib. I. viii, who quotes from Ecclesiasticus xxxv. 18 and 19 : ' Nonne lacrymæ viduæ ad maxillam descendunt ?   A maxilla enim ascendunt, usque ad cœlum.'

St. 4, l. 3.   *milky rivers.*   See note to p. 312, st. xix, ll. 4–6, below.

Page 80, St. 5, l. 6–st. 6, l. 6.   Compare Donne, ' Twicknam Garden ' (*Works*, ed. Grierson, vol. i, p. 29), ll. 19–22 :

Hither with christall vyals, lovers come,
   And take my teares, which are loves wine,
And try your mistresse Teares at home,
   For all are false, that tast not just like mine ;

It will be observed that the phrase ' crystall violls ' is used in the 1648 and 1652 versions of ' The Weeper ', see p. 310, st. xii, below.

St. 7, l. 2.   *The Primroses pale cheeke.*   Compare *Cymbeline*, iv. ii. 221 : ' The flower that 's like thy face, pale primrose '.

St. 7, l. 5.   *Much rather, &c.*   Compare the epigram by Remond quoted above, note to heading, l. 3, ' Se lachrymam esse tuam cuperet '.

St. 8, l. 2.   *the Amber-weeping Tree.*   Crashaw no doubt refers to the story of the Heliades.

Page 81, St. 14, ll. 1–6.   *Golden, &c.*   Compare the epigram by Remond quoted above in note to heading, ll. 5–6.   Compare also (for l. 6 especially) Marino, *op. cit.*, ed. Croce, p. 371 :

Dalla testa e da' lumi
e di chiome e di lagrime confonde,
sparse in lucide stille e 'n tepid' onde,
costei, torrenti e fiumi.
Oh richezza, oh tesoro !
Due piogge : una d'argento e l' altra d' oro.

F f

l. 2. *murmurs though*. See foot-notes. The use of ' though ' in
this way at the end of a sentence is paralleled in the verses ' On
a Treatise of Charity ' (p. 138, l. 26, below).

PAGE 83. *The Teare*. See note introductory to ' The Weeper '
pp. 432–3, above. ' The Teare ' probably represents material not
used in the longer poem. In the 1648 edition st. 5 of ' The Teare '
is given in both poems.

PAGE 84, St. 4. Compare Marino, *La Lira, Parte Seconda*, 1615,
p. 162, ' Nel medesimo suggetto ' (i.e. ' Lachrymis cepit rigare
pedes eius '), Mad. CLVI.

PAGE 85.   DIVINE EPIGRAMS.

[See the cross-references in the Index of first lines, showing where
Crashaw's English epigrams correspond to the Latin and Greek.
It will be noticed that with only three exceptions (p. 86·1, p. 100·1
and p. 102·2) Latin counterparts, more or less complete, of all the
epigrams in English given here were either published in 1634 or
exist in MS. Tanner 465; but many of those in Latin have no English
counterpart. It seems likely that the Latin epigrams were generally
written first, a selection being afterwards translated into English.]

ll. 1–4. *Each blest drop, &c.* Compare Joseph Beaumont, ' The
Waters of H. Baptisme ' (*Minor Poems*, ed. Robinson, pp. 38–9) :

> The Waves came crowding downe apace,
> Each one ambitious for yᵉ grace
> To touch that skin, a Purer Thing
> Then their owne Spring.
> Thus were They washed, (& not He
> Who came as clean as Puritie) . . .

ll. 5–10. *Let it no longer, &c.* Compare the Latin version of
this epigram in Stubbe's *Horæ Subsecivæ* (1651)—see Introduction,
p. xliv, above—which is as follows :

> *In Æthiopem baptizatum.* Act. 8. 38.
> Opus nè videatur impossibile, Æthiopem
> In-summo-nigricantem lavare.
> Lotus est enim, & cutis nigra umbrosum jam
> Animæ candidæ est velum.
> Nigram, puto, domum diliget perpetuò
> Immortalis post haec columba.

PAGE 86, ll. 5–6. *Here, where, &c.* Compare ll. 7–8 of the Latin
epigram *Nasceris, en !* &c., p. 42, above.

l. 11. *my golden Lad*. A similar expression is used by William
Crashaw in *The Iesuites Gospel* (1610), pp. 9 and 72 :

> I will not, oh I dare not, golden childe

translating :

> *Nolo tuas ô nolo tuas puer auree mammas :*

PAGE 89, ll. 19–20. *Two went, &c.* Compare the Latin version
of this epigram in Stubbe's *Horæ Subsecivæ* (1651)—see Introduction, p. xliv, above—which is as follows :

> *Duo homines ascenderunt in templum ad precandum.* Luc. 18. 10.
> Precaturi ibant duo, vel ut ità dicam :
> Ille precaturus, hic jactaturus.
> Hic grande incedens propè accessit, alter
> Quâ è regione non sustinuit prospicere.
> Unus quidem aram egregiam propè venit,
> Sed prope Deum, qui sortitus est aram, unus.

PAGE 96, l. 1. *A Drop, one drop, &c.* Compare William Crashaw, translating from Clarus Bonarscius (Carolus Scribanius) in *The Iesuites Gospel* (1610), p. 9 :

> But one, euen one poore drop I do implore
> from thy right hand, or side : I aske no more.

PAGE 100, ll. 1–6. *Th' have left thee naked, &c.* Compare Marino, *La Lira*, Part III, p. 190 (ed. 1615), ' Il sudore del sangue ' :

> *Suda sangue (ahi bontade)*
> *Rè, che prendendo la corona, e'l regno,*
> *Di rugiadosa porpora celeste*
> *Tesse a le membra sue la regia veste.*

PAGE 102. *Sampson, &c.* l. 1. *Could not once, &c.* Compare the Latin version of this epigram in Stubbe's *Horæ Subsecivæ* (1651)— see Introduction, p. **xliv**, above—which is as follows :

> *Samson excæcatus ad Dalilam.*
>
> Crudelis, nónne suffecit semel lumina aufferre ?
> Oculis captus eram ubi te primùm vidi.

Psalme 23. To some extent this poem resembles in spirit and rhythm a poem in William Crashaw's *A Manuall for True Catholickes. London, . . .* 1611. That book begins with some translations of ' holy meditations and Prayers. Gathered out of certaine ancient Manuscripts, written 300 yeares *ago, or more.*', and this section contains the poem in question, a translation of the verses beginning ' Hæc est fides orthodoxa ' and headed ' The conclusion with a deuout and holy prayer ' (p. 32).

ll. 5–6. *On whose pastures, &c.* Compare William Crashaw, *op. cit.*, p. 36 :

> Here the light doth neuer cease,
> Endlesse spring and endlesse peace.

PAGE 103, ll. 21–4. *When my simple, &c.* Compare William Crashaw, *op. cit.*, p. 34 :

> Oh doe thou stay my feete from treading
> In paths to hell and horror leading :

PAGE 105, St. 4, l. 3. *Vnpearcht.* Compare ' Musicks Duel ', p. 151, above, l. 51, ' The high-perch't treble '.

PAGE 109. *Sospetto d' Herode.* Comparison with the original, Marino's *La Strage de gli Innocenti* (? first published in 1610), will show that as usual Crashaw has given himself a very free hand, and that for many of the most striking phrases in the English translation there is no counterpart in the Italian.

Argomento, l. 2. *Death's Master.* In *T* the reading is ' Monarch'. Below, st. 40, l. 7, *T* reads ' imperiall ' for ' impartiall ' ; and in st. 51, l. 1, the blank in the printed texts following the word ' *Herod* ' is filled in *T* by the phrase ' leige to Cesar '. It seems worth suggesting that the changes in the printed text in these instances may have been the work of an unintelligent censor, who thought it his duty to delete such references to kingship as caught his eye in a hasty reading. Compare the story of censorial objection to Milton's metaphor of the eclipse (*Paradise Lost*, i. 594–9) which ' with fear of change Perplexes Monarchs '.

St. 2, l. 1. *Great Anthony.* The reference is to St. Anthony of Padua.

PAGE III, St. 7, l. 4. *looke Kingdomes dead.* Compare Lovelace, *Lucasta*, 1649, p. 127 :

> Finding she could not looke,
> She struck him·dead.

St. 8, l. 8. *While his steele sides, &c.* Compare Milton, *On the Morning of Christs Nativity*, l. 172 :

> Swindges the scaly Horrour of his foulded tail.

PAGE 112, St. 11, l. 3. *wasted with care.* Compare Milton, *Paradise Lost*, i. 601–2 : ' care Sat on his faded cheek'.

St. 11, l. 4. *To become beautifull in humane blood.* There appears to be nothing in the Italian original corresponding to this somewhat obscure line, which is probably to be taken with ' care ' in l. 3. Satan, who has lost ' all the Beauties of his once bright Eyes ' (st. 10, l. 2), has often experienced the desire ('care ') to regain his beauty through the shedding of human blood.

PAGE 113, St. 15, ll. 7–8. *whose Birth, &c.* See note to p. 38, ll. 15–16.

PAGE 114, St. 18, ll. 5–7. *and spread his spatious wings &c.* Compare Milton, *Paradise Lost*, ii. 927–8 :

> At last his Sail-broad Vannes
> He spreads for flight.

St. 18, l. 8. *Of sturdy Adamant . . . chaine.* Compare *Paradise Lost*, i. 48 : ' In Adamantine Chains'.

St. 19, ll. 6–7. *And gave a gastly shreeke, &c.* Compare Milton, *Paradise Lost*, i. 542–3 :

> A shout that tore Hells Concave, and beyond
> Frighted the Reign of *Chaos* and old Night.

PAGE 116, St. 28, l. 2. *To make the partner, &c.* Compare Milton, *Paradise Lost*, i. 653–4 :

> A generation, whom his choice regard
> Should favour equal to the Sons of Heaven :

St. 28, ll. 7–8. *What though I mist my blow, &c.* Compare Milton, *Paradise Lost*, i. 105 sqq. :

> What though the field be lost ?
> All is not lost ; the unconquerable Will, &c.

PAGE 117, St. 30, l. 8. *Oprest the common-people of the skyes.* Compare Sir Henry Wotton, ' *On his Mistris, the* Queen *of* Bohemia ', l. 4, ' You *Common-people* of the *Skies* ' (*Reliquiæ Wottonianæ*, 1651, p. 518).

St. 31, ll. 3–8. *the reflection of thy forepast joyes, &c.* Compare Middleton, *The Witch*, II. i. 218–21 :

> 'Tis not so much the horror of their pains,
> Though they be infinite, as the loss of joys ;
> It is that deprivation is the mother
> Of all the groans in hell, . . .

PAGE 130. *On Mr.* G. Herberts *booke intituled the Temple of Sacred Poems, sent to a Gentlewoman.* The Temple. Sacred Poems and Private Ejaculations *was first published in 1633.

ll. 11–12. *These white plumes, &c.* These two lines were printed

in the 1650 edition of *Recreation for Ingenious Head-peeces. Or,
A Pleasant Grove for their Wits to walke in,* and in the subsequent
editions of 1654, 1663, and 1667, in the course of a brief foreword
to ll. 11–28 of Vaughan's ' The Resolve ' : ' . . . I would commend
to thy sharpest view and serious consideration ; The Sweet
Cælestiall sacred Poems by Mʳ· *Henry Vaughan,* intituled *Silex
Scintillans.*

> There plumes from Angels wings, he'l lend thee,
> Which every day to heaven will send thee.
> (*Heare him thus invite thee home.*) '

PAGE 131. *In memory of the Vertuous and Learned Lady Madre
de Teresa, &c.* This poem was no doubt inspired by the auto-
biographical work, *La Vida de la Santa Madre Teresa de Jesus.*
An English translation of this (? by Toby Matthew) was published
in 1642 : *The Flaming Hart or the Life of the Glorious S. Teresa,
Foundresse of the Reformation, of the Order of the All-Immaculate
Virgin-Mother, our B. Lady, of Mount-Carmel . . . Antwerpe . . .
M. DC. XLII.* The translator signs himself 'M. T.'. Compare
the title of Crashaw's poem first published in 1648, *The Flaming
Heart, &c.* (see p. 324, below).

PAGE 133, ll. 79–80. *His is the dart.* The reference here and
elsewhere in this poem, and also in *The Flaming Heart* (see p. 325,
below), is to the incident recorded as follows in the 1642 translation of the biography, p. 419 :

' It pleased our Blessed Lord, that I should haue sometimes,
this following Vision. I saw an Angell very neer me, towards my
left side, and he appeared to me, in a Corporeall forme ; though
yet I am not wont to see anie thing of that kind, but very rarely.
For, though . . . But, in this Vision, our Lord was pleased, that
I should see this Angell, after this other manner. He was not
great ; but rather little ; yet withall, he was of very much beautie.
His face was so inflamed, that he appeared to be of those most
Superiour Angells, who seem to be, all in a fire ; and he well might
be of them, whome we call *Seraphins* ; but as for me, they neuer
tell me their names, or rankes ; yet howsoeuer, I see thereby, that
there is so great a difference in Heauen, between one Angell, and
another, as I am no way able to expresse. I saw, that he had a
long Dart of gold in his hand ; and at the end of the iron below,
me thought, there was a little fire ; and I conceaued, that he
thrust it, some seuerall times, through my verie Hart, after such
a manner, as that it passed the verie inwards, of my Bowells ;
and when he drew it back, me thought, it carried away, as much,
as it had touched within me ; and left all that, which remained,
wholy inflamed with a great loue of Almightye God. The paine
of it, was so excessiue, that it forced me to utter those groanes ;
and the suauitie, which that extremitie of paine gaue, was also
so very excessiue, that there was no desiring at all, to be ridd of it ;
nor can the Soule then, receaue anie contentment at all, in lesse,
then God Almightie himself.'

PAGE 134. ll. 101–2. *Loves his death, &c.* Compare *The Flaming
Hart* (1642), p. 417 : ' For, the Soule, as I was saying, would alwaies
be very glad, if she might be euer dying, of this Disease '.

PAGE 137. *On a Treatise of Charity.* Robert Shelford, the
author of the book in which this poem first appeared in 1635 (see
foot-notes), was an M.A. (1587) of Peterhouse. On the title-page

of *Five Pious and Learned Discourses, &c.*, he is described as ' of *Ringsfield* in *Suffolk* Priest'. James Ussher, writing to Dr. Samuel Ward of Sidney Sussex College, Cambridge, from Drogheda, Sept. 15, 1635, refers to Shelford and his book as follows : ' But while we strive here to maintain the purity of our ancient truth, how cometh it to pass that you in Cambridge do cast such stumbling blocks in our way ? by publishing unto the world such rotten stuff as Shelford hath vented in his five discourses ; wherein he hath so carried himself, ut Famosi Perni amanuensem possis agnoscere. The Jesuits of England sent over the book hither to confirm our papists in their obstinacy, and to assure them that we are now coming home unto them as fast as we can ; I pray God this sin be not deeply laid to their charge, who give an occasion to one blind thus to stumble' (Elrington, *Works of Ussher*, vol. xvi, p. 9).

PAGE **139.** *On the Assumption.* This poem was strangely treated by Tate, who in the second edition of his *Poems* (1684, p. 169) has ' An Attempt on the Ode of Assumption, By Mr Crashaw '—a mere transposition of Crashaw's words.

PAGE **141,** ll. 47–52. *All the sweetest showers, &c.* Compare Joseph Beaumont' Jesus inter Ubera Maria ' (read ' Mariæ ') (*Minor Poems*, ed. Robinson, p. 17) :

> True, He needs no Sweets, say They,
> But Sweets have need of Him, to keep them so.
>
> .   .   .   .   .   .
>   come strow
>   Your pious showres
>   Of Easterne Flowres.

The whole poem is very much in Crashaw's manner.

An Himne l. 6. *The crimson curtaines of thy bed.* Compare Milton, *On the Morning of Christs Nativity*, ll. 229–30 :

> So when the Sun in bed,
> Curtain'd with cloudy red,

ll. 11–12. *As this modest, &c.* Compare the Latin verses, ' Ah ferus &c.' p. 365, below, ll. 1–2.

PAGE **143.** *On Hope, &c.* Cowley's poem was first published in *The Mistresse* . . . 1647, p. 61. His own answer ' *For Hope* ' follows on p. 63.

THE DELIGHTS OF THE MUSES.

PAGE **147,** l. 11. *Dic mihi, &c.* Martial, *Epigrammata*, VIII. iii, l. 12, reading ' ages ' for ' agas '.

PAGE **149.** *Musicks Duell.* The Latin poem of which this is a free translation is by the Jesuit Famianus Strada (1572–1649) and appears to have been first published in *Prolusiones Academicæ, Oratoriæ, Historicæ, Poeticæ : R. P. Famiani Stradæ Romani è Societate Iesv . . . Coloniæ Agrippinæ, . . . Anno M. DC. XVII.* (Lib. II. Prolvs. VI. Poet. Academia. II. p. 351, *Claudiani stylus*) : The following is the original text. It will be noticed that ll. 57–156 of Crashaw's poem are an expansion of only fourteen lines (36–49) of the original.

> *IAM Sol à medio pronus deflexerat orbe*
> *Mitius è radijs vibrans crinalibus ignem.*
> *Cum Fidicen propter Tiberina fluenta, sonanti*
> *Lenibat plectro curas, æstumque leuabat*
> *Ilice defensus nigra scenaque virenti.*

Audijt hunc hospes siluæ Philomela propinquæ
Musa loci, nemoris Siren, innoxia Siren ;
Et propè succedens stetit abdita frondibus, alte
Accipiens sonitum, secumque remurmurat, & quos
Ille modos variat ligitis, hæc gutture reddit. 10
    Sensit se Fidicen Philomela imitante referri,
Et placuit ludum volucri dare. plenius ergò
Explorat citharam, tentamentumque futuræ
Præbeat vt pugnæ, percurrit protinus omnes
Impulsu pernice fides. Nec segnius illa
Mille per excurrens variæ discrimina vocis,
Venturi specimen præfert argutula cantus.
    Tunc Fidicen per fila movens trepidantia dextram,
Nunc contemnenti similis diuerberat vngue,
Depectitque pari chordas & simplice ductu : 20
Nunc carptim replicat, digitisque micantibus vrget
Fila minutatim, celsrique repercutit ictu.
Mox silet. Illa modis totidem respondet, & artem
Arte refert. Nunc ceu rudis aut incerta canendi
Proijcit in longum, nulloque plicatile flexu
Carmen init, simili serie, jugique tenore,
Præbet iter liquidum labenti è pectore voci :
Nunc cæsim variat, modulisque canora minutis.
Delibrat vocem, tremuloque reciprocat ore.
    Miratur Fidicen parvis è faucibus ire 30
Tàm varium tàm dulce melos : majoraque tentans
Alternat mira arte fides : dum torquet acutas,
Inciditque graues operoso verbere pulsat,
Permiscetque simul certantia rauca sonoris,
Ceu resides in bella viros clangore lacessat.
Hoc etiam Philomela canit dumque ore liquenti
Vibrat acuta sonum, modulisque interplicat æquis ;
Ex inopinato grauis intonat, & leue murmur
Turbinat introrsus, alternantique sonore
Clarat, & infuscat ceu martia classica pulset. 40
    Scilicet erubuit Fidicen, iraque calente,
Aut non hoc, inquit, referes Citharistria siluæ,
Aut fracta cedam cithara. Nec plura loquutus
Non imitabilibus plectrum concentibus vrget
Namque manu per fila volat, simul hos, simul illos
Explorat numeros, chordaque laborat in omni,
Et strepit, et tinnit, crescitque superbius, & se
Multiplicat relegens, plenoque choreumate plaudit.
Tum stetit expectans, si quid paret æmula contra.
Illa autem, quanquam vox dudum exercita fauces 50
Asperat, impatiens vinci simul aduocat omnes
Ne quidquam vires. Nam dum discrimina tanta
Reddere tot fidium natiua & simplice tentat
Voce, canaliculisque imitari grandia paruis ;
Impar magnanimis ausis, imparque dolori
Deficit & vitam summo in certamine linquens
Victoris cadit in plectrum, par nacta sepulcrum.
VSQVE adeò & tenues animas ferit æmula Virtus.

Strada's poem has been paraphrased by other English poets ;
among Crashaw's contemporaries, by John Ford in *The Lovers*

Melancholy (publ. 1629), Act i; Sc. i, by William Strode in *The
Academy of Pleasure* (1656, p. 123), ed. Dobell (1907), pp. 16–18 ;
by Vilvain, *Enchiridion Epigrammatum*, 1654, p. 177 ; and by
' Mʳ Wilson ' in *Poems by Several Hands, collected by N. Tate*,
1685, p. 405. There is an anonymous version, *Strada's Musical
Duel, . . . In Latine, Much Enlarg'd in English* . . . 1671. 4°.
Sig. A3 has a drop-title ' Strada's Musical Duel, In Latine ; First
imitated in English by Mr. Crashaw, then by Mr. Hinton ; and
now by a third Hand so enlarg'd, and the whole Frame of the
Poem so alter'd, that little of Strada is preserv'd, save only the
Scene and Issue of the Duel : All in a more familiar Style then that
of Claudian imitated by Strada '. There is a manuscript version in
the British Museum, Add. MS. 19268. Later versions were made
by Ambrose Phillips, by I. M. in the *Gentleman's Magazine*,
Aug. 1791, &c. Seventeenth-century allusions to contests between a nightingale and singers or musicians are numerous, as
in Coryat's *Crudities*, 1611, p. 253.

PAGE 152, l. 128. *grutch.* To murmur or complain. See art.
' grutch ' in *O.E.D.*

PAGE 154. *Principi recèns natæ, &c.* The collection in which
this poem appeared (see foot-note) was published in honour of
the birth of the Princess Anne, March 17, 1636/7, who died in 1640.

PAGE 155. *Out of* Virgil, *&c. Georgics*, ii. 323–45.
l. 3. *seed desire* : ' genitalia semina poscunt '.

PAGE 156. *In praise of* Lessius *his rule of health.* Léonard Leys,
or Lessius, theologian, was born near Antwerp in 1554 and died
in 1623. He became a Jesuit in 1572 and was professor of philosophy at Douai for seven years. *Hygiasticon, seu vera ratio valetu-
dinis bonæ et vitæ* . . . was published at Antwerp in 1613 and 1614.
For further details see *Biographie Nationale de Belgique*, art.
' Leys'. The translation published at Cambridge in 1634 has been
attributed to Nicholas Ferrar; but the evidence for this seems
hardly complete.

PAGE 157, l. 18. *His owne Physick.* Compare Donne, ' The
Cross ', l. 29 :

> Then are you your own physic or need none.

PAGE 158. *The beginning of* Heliodorus. *Heliodori Aethiopi-
corum Libri Decem* (Bibliotheca Teubneriana, 1855, p. 3). See
note to p. 183, below.

PAGE 159. *Out of the Greeke* Cupid's *Cryer. Moschi Reliquiæ*
(Bibliotheca Teubneriana, 1861, p. 108), ii, Ἔρως δραπέτης.

PAGE 161, l. 1. *High mounted, &c.* Ausonius, *Opuscula* (Bibliotheca Teubneriana, 1886, p. 428), Epig. xx [cxxii], ' In Faustulum
staturæ brevis'. And compare the Greek epigram by Lucilius,
Anth. Gr. xi. 104, there quoted. Crashaw's translation is referred to
by Samuel Wesley in his *Maggots : or Poems*, 1685, pp. 6 and 170.

Vpon Venus *putting on* Mars *his Armes. Anth. Gr.* Appendix
Planudea, Lib. IV (Tauchnitz edition, xvi. 171) :

> Ἄρεος ἔντεα ταῦτα τίνος χάριν, ὦ Κυθέρεια,
> ἐνδέδυσαι, κενεὸν τοῦτο φέρουσα βάρος ;
> αὐτὸν Ἄρη γυμνὴ γὰρ ἀφώπλισας· εἰ δὲ λέλειπται
> καὶ θεός, ἀνθρώποις ὅπλα μάτην ἐπάγεις.

This epigram is ascribed to Leonidas, apparently Leonidas of
Alexandria. It is thus rendered by Grotius :

> Martis hic ornatus ; cur hunc, Venus aurea, sumis ?
> Cur corpus tenerum tam grave portát onus ?
> Armis exueris Martem cum nuda, Deorum
> Maior in humanum cur capis arma genus ?

Vpon the same. l. 1. *Pallas saw, &c.* Ausonius : ' De Pallade volente certare armis cum Venere ' (*Opuscula*, Bibliotheca Teubneriana, 1886, p. 336, Epig. lxiii [xlii]).

In Serenissimæ, &c. The collection in which this poem first appeared was published in honour of the birth of the Princess Elizabeth, Dec. 28, 1635. See also the poem ' Upon the birth of the Princesse Elizabeth ', p. 391, below.

PAGE 162, l. 33. *Altera gens varium per sydera computet annum.* Crashaw probably recollected Claudian's poem on the old man of Verona (ed. Koch, *Carmina Minora*, xx), l. 11 of which is :

> Frugibus alternis non consule computat annum.

l. 34. *ducant.* The emendation to ' *ducat* ' is tempting, even with full allowance for the possibility that ' gens ' (l. 33) may be taken as a collective. It is awkward to pass from ' computet ' to ' ducant '.

PAGE 163. *In Picturam, &c.* Compare the Latin poem in MS. Tanner 465, ' Hæc est, &c.', p. 374, below.

l. 8. *ferox* : ' ferax ' is attractive, but since ' ferox ' has manuscript as well as printed authority and gives a possible sense it seems best to retain it.

Vpon Bishop Andrewes *his Picture, &c.* See *D.N.B.*, art. ' Lancelot Andrewes ', whose dates are 1555–1626, and who was for some time (*c.* 1589–1605) Master of Pembroke College.

PAGE 164. *Epitaphium in Dominum Herrisium.* The William Herrys, Fellow of Pembroke Hall, celebrated here and in several English elegiac poems matriculated from Christ's College, Cambridge in 1624. He took the degree of A.B. in 1627–8 and of A.M. in 1631. The family to which he belonged had its seat at Margaretting, Essex.

PAGE 166, ll. 57–9. *Eo ipso die . . . Intellectum ejus. The Booke of Common Prayer* (1604, The Hampton Court Book) prescribes as the first lesson at Evening Prayer on Oct. 15 the Book of Wisdom, chap. iv ; verse 11 of which is partially quoted here, viz. : ' Raptus est, ne malitia mutaret intellectum ejus, aut ne fictio deciperet animam illius ' (Vulgate). (Note kindly supplied by Mr. A. Attwater.)

Vpon the Death of a Gentleman. See headings in *T* and *A*3 quoted in the foot-notes. Michael Chambers entered Queens' College in 1625 and became Fellow of the same college in 1630. He was buried Feb. 16, 1633/4 in the college chapel. (Searle, *The History of The Queens' College*, 1871, p. 511.)

PAGE 167, ll. 27 sqq. *Eyes are vocall, &c.* Compare Milton, *The Passion*, st. vii :

> For sure so well instructed are my tears,
> That they would fitly fall in order'd Characters.

and E. Revett's Elegy on Lovelace (Hazlitt's edition, p. 286) :

> Why should some rude hand carve thy sacred stone,
> And there incise a cheap inscription ?
> When we can shed the tribute of our tears
> So long, till the relenting marble wears ;
> Which shall such order in their cadence keep,
> That they a native epitaph shall weep ;

442 *Commentary.*

PAGE **175.** *An Epitaph. Vpon Doctor* Brooke. See *D.N.B.*, art.
' Samuel Brooke ', who was Master of Trinity College, Cambridge,
from 1629 until his death on Sept. 16, 1631, just after his appointment to the Archdeaconry of Coventry.
Vpon Mr. Staninough's *Death.* James Stanenough entered
Queens' College in 1622, and afterwards became Fellow of the
same college. He was buried in the college chapel March 5,
1634/5.
PAGE **176.** *Vpon the Duke of* Yorke *his Birth A Panegyricke.*
See foot-notes recording the additions made to the earlier form
of the poem. The children of Charles I and Henrietta Maria
celebrated in the final form are Charles, born May 29, 1630 ;
Mary, born Nov. 4, 1631 ; James, born Oct. 14, 1633 ; Elizabeth,
born Dec. 28, 1635 ; Henry, born July 8, 1640. In the earlier
form of the poem only Charles, James, and Mary are mentioned.
PAGE **181.** *Vpon* Ford's *two Tragedyes, &c.* The two tragedies
in question were both published in 1633.
PAGE **183.** *Vpon the faire Ethiopian, &c.* The translation of
Heliodorus to which Crashaw appears to allude was : *The Faire
Æthiopian. Dedicated to the King and Queene. By their Maiesties
most humble Subiect and Seruant, William L'isle. . . . London . . .
1631.* Reissued 1638.
To the Morning. ll. 2–3. *the Muses friend . . . Aurora.* Crashaw
no doubt had in mind the saying ' Aurora Musis amica '.
PAGE **187.** *Ad Reginam.* The collection in which this poem
first appeared (see foot-note) was published in honour of the Duke
of York, afterwards James II.
PAGE **188.** *Out of* Martiall. *Epigrams*, Bk. I, No. xix, ' Si
memini, &c.'.
Out of the Italian. A Song. The original of this lyric is in
Rime d' Ansaldo Cebà . . . In Anversa, Appresso Martino Nutio,
M.D.XCVI., p. 25 verso, and is as follows :

Dispiegate
  Guance amate
  Quella porpora acerbetta ;
  Che perdenti
  Che dolenti
  Fian le rose in su l' herbetta

Deh scoprite,
  Deh partite
  Chiare stelle i vostri rai ;
  Che partendo
  Che scoprendo
  Fia men chiaro il sol d' assai.

Deh togliete
  Quella rete
  Auree chiome, aureo thesoro ;
  Ch'a toccarni
  Ch'a spiegarni
  Tornerà quest' aria d'oro.

Suela, suela
  Quel, che cela
  Dolce bocca il desir nostro ;

Ch' a suelarlo,
Ch' a mostrarlo
Perderan le perle, e l'ostro.

Apri o labro
Di cinnabro
Vu sorriso ancor tra 'l velo ;
Ch' ad aprirlo,
Ch' a scoprirlo
Riderà la terra, e 'l cielo.

Tocca, tocca
Bella bocca
L'aria homai di qualch' ac-
  cento ;
Che toccando,
Che parlando
Tacerà per l' aria il vento.

Ma se fuore
Tant' honore
Non sospinge il tuo sereno,
Tua vaghezza,
Tua bellezza
La pietà mi mostri almeno.

E la doue
  Morte moue
  A predarmi i suoi guerrieri,
  Lidia mia
  Tutta pia
  Volgi gli occhi lusinghieri.

Che se tocchi
  Co begli occhi
  Lo mio spirto fuggitiuo,
  La tu' aita
  La tua vita
  Mel terran nel petto viuo.

PAGE 190. *Out of the Italian.* ' Love now, &c.'. I am indebted to Professor H. J. C. Grierson for pointing out to me that the original of this lyric is in *La Lira, Rime del Cavalier Marino. Parte Seconda. Madriali & Canzoni. . . . In Venetia,* MDCXV., p. 14 :

Foco d' Amore diuiso.

MAD. XI.

Amor non hà più foco,
Che' l diuise frà noi :
Diede l' arsura à me, la luce à voi.
Donna gentil per Dio
Rendete il vostro lume à l' ardor mio,
Onde chiaro, e lucente à gli occhi vostri
(Qual' è nel cor) si mostri,
Ó pur' in voi la fiamma mia prendete,
E com' io ardo ardete.

Out of the Italian. ' Would any one, &c.' The original of this piece, also translated by Drummond (ed. Kastner, vol. I, p. 126), is given on p. xciv.

PAGE 191. *On the Frontispiece, &c.* See note to p. 410, below, where the reasons are given for regarding as spurious the poem which precedes this in the 1646 edition.

l. 11. *Perspicill.* An optic glass or telescope. See *O.E.D.* for further illustration.

PAGE 192. *An Epitaph Vpon Mr.* Ashton *a conformable Citizen.* The supplementary information in Add. MS. 33219 that the subject of this poem was a ' Citizen of London ' has so far not led to any certain identification.

PAGE 193. *Rex Redux.* The collection in which these verses first appeared was published in honour of Charles I's return from Scotland, where he went in 1633 to be crowned at Edinburgh.

PAGE 194. *Out of* Catullus. Carmen v.

Ad Principem nondum natum. The references to Charles I's return (presumably from Scotland ; see the poem *Rex Redux,* p. 193, above, and note *ad loc.*) make it probable that the unborn child in question was James (afterwards James II), born Oct. 14, 1633.

PAGE 195. *Wishes.* This poem had already appeared in a shorter form in *Witt's Recreations Augmented with Ingenious Conceites for the wittie, And Merrie Medecines for the Melancholie. . . .* 1641. The first edition, 1640, does not contain the poem, which in that of 1641 is on pp. V8ᵛ–XIᵛ (under separate division, entitled *Fancies and Fantastickes*) as follows :

Wishes to his supposed Mistresse.

Who e're she be,
That is the onely shee,
That shall command my heart and mee :

Might you heare my wishes,
Bespeake her to my blisses,
And be ye call'd my absent kisses.

I wish her beauty,
That owes not all his duty
To gawdie tyre, or some such folly.

A face that's best,
By it's owne beauty drest,
And can alone command the rest.

Joyes that confesse
Vertue her Mistresse,
And have no other head to dresse.

Life that dares send
A challenge to his end,
And when it's come say, welcome friend.

I wish her store
Of wealth may leave her poore
Of wishes : and I wish no more.

Now if time knowes
That her, whose radiant browes
Weave them a Garland of my woes ;

Her that dare be
What these lines wish to see,
I seeke no further, it is she.

Let her full glorie
(My fancies) fly before ye
Be ye my fection, but her my storie.

PAGE **197,** l. 70. *flight.* In the sense of ' fleeting '. See art.
' flight ' in *O.E.D.* There is no need to adopt the reading ' slight '.

POEMS ADDED IN 1648 AND NOT INCLUDED IN 1652.

PAGE **206.** *Votiva Domus Petrensis Pro Domo Dei.* In connexion
with Crashaw's interest in Matthew Wren's new chapel at Peterhouse see Introduction, p. xxii, above, and T. A. Walker's *Peterhouse* (1906).

ll. 20, 27, 31, 33. Quando *erit, ut . . .* Crashaw has taken the
phrase from Ovid, *Heroides,* vii. (Dido to Aeneas), 19–20 :

Quando erit, ut condas instar Carthaginis urbem,
      Et videas populos altus ab arce tuos ?

PAGE **208.** *Fides quæ sola justificat, non est sine Spe & Dilectione.*
See note to p. 9, above.

PAGE **209,** l. 45. *Illa Fides vacuâ quæ sola superbiet aulâ :* ' vacuâ
. . . aulâ ' may be an echo of Horace, *Odes,* III. xiv. 36 :

Et vacuam patefecit aulam.

PAGE **214.** *In Eundum Scazon.* This poem immediately follows
the elegy ' *Vpon the Death of Mr.* Herrys ' beginning ' A Plant of
noble stemme ' (see p. 167, above, and note to p. 164).

Ad Reginam, &c. The collection in which this and the following
poem, *To the Queen,* first appeared (see foot-note) was published
in honour of the birth of Prince Henry, July 8, 1640. In *48* they
immediately precede the poem *To the Queen, Vpon her numerous*

Progenie, A Panegyrick, i.e. the later and extended form of *Vpon the Duke of* Yorke *his Birth A Panegyricke* (see p. 176, above).
PAGE 215, ll. 23–4. *nec indecoro Pulvere.* From Horace, *Odes,* II. i. 22 :

Non indecoro pulvere sordidos.

PAGE 220. *Vpon two greene Apricockes, &c.* See Introduction, p. xxxiv, above.
PAGE 221. *Thesaurus malorum fœmina.* The full proverb is as in *T* (see foot-note). Erasmus, *Adagia* under ' Thesaurus malorum ' has : ' Extat inter Græcanicas sententias huiusmodi senarius :

Θησαυρός ἐστι τῶν κακῶν κακὴ γυνή.

Id est : Thesaurus est mulier malorum, si mala est.'
PAGE 222, l. 19. *Hæc satis in nostros fabricata est machina muros.* Compare Virgil, *Aeneid,* ii. 46 (of the Trojan horse) :

Aut hæc in nostros fabricata est machina muros.

In Apollinem depereuntem Daphnen. This piece and the three following are modelled metrically on the lines ' Pasiphaes Fabula ' to be found in several books printed by Crashaw's time, e.g. *Epigrammata et Poematia Vetera,* Paris, 1590 (ed. P. Pithou), p. 447. The twenty-two lines, each in a different metre, reproduce the various lines employed by Horace.

Æneas Patris, &c., ll. 1–2. *Mœnia Trojæ, &c.* Probably reminiscent of Virgil, *Aeneid,* ii. 289–90 :

' Heu fuge, nate dea, teque his ' ait ' eripe flammis.
Hostis habet muros, ruit alto a culmine Troia.'

PAGE 225, *Elegia.* l. 4. The meaning would no doubt be made clearer to the modern reader by printing :

Et saltem ' ah ! periit ' dicere ' noster amor '.

But Crashaw does not make a habit in his Latin verses of distinguishing speeches by means of inverted commas.
PAGE 226. *Damno affici sæpe fit lucrum.* ll. 3–4. *Luxuriem annorum, &c.* The wanton life (*luxuriem*) attributed to the serpent is illustrated by a remark in the notes to the 1621 edition of Alciatus' *Emblemata,* p. 36, on emblem 5, ' Serpentem quoque inter significationes alias turpium voluptatum, & mollium illecebrarum notam esse, aliunde didicimus ' (*nota* meaning practically ' symbol '). In Joachim Camerarius's *Emblemata,* centuria iv, no. 82, the serpent shedding its skin represents a man putting away sin, and a quotation from St. Basil is given, in which he exhorts men to be wise as serpents, and, as the serpent creeps through a narrow place to strip off its old skin, so to put off the old man by walking in the narrow way. Compare again Caussin, *Polyhistor Symbolicus* (1631), Lib. IX, no. 4.

CARMEN DEO NOSTRO.

PAGE 231. *The Countesse of Denbigh.* A good account of the life of Susan, first Countess of Denbigh, is given in *Royalist Father and Roundhead Son* (1912), by Cecilia, Countess of Denbigh. The first countess was the daughter of Sir George Villiers and sister of George, Duke of Buckingham. She appears ultimately to have subscribed to the Roman Catholic faith, her son, Basil, second

Earl of Denbigh, having made formal acknowledgement to this effect in 1651. See also A. Warren, op. cit., pp. 54–5 and 223.

PAGE 233. *The Anagramme. He was Car.* See note to p. 235, below.

PAGE 234, ll. 44–5.   *so in the end,*
        He may injoy his dearest Lord, &c.

Compare Sir T. Browne, *Religio Medici*, Part I, Section vii : ' so that I might ' (first, unauthorized, edition (1642) has ' so I might ') ' enjoy my Saviour at the last, I could with patience be nothing almost unto Eternity '.

PAGE 235. *Vpon the pictures, &c.* Search has been made for the manuscript in question, but vainly.

l. 16. *Thomas Car.* See *D.N.B.*, art. ' Thomas Carre ' (Miles Pinkney). His dates were 1599–1674. After studying at the English College at Douay he was ordained priest in 1625 and was afterwards appointed procurator of the college, holding the office till 1634. He was then for many years occupied in founding the monastery of canonesses of St. Augustin at Paris, where he died.

PAGE 236. *Emblem and verses, 'Tis not the work of force but skill,* &c. Dr. M. Praz calls my attention to the similarity between this emblem and one on p. 140 of *Af-beeldinghe van d'eerste eeuwe der Societeyt Iesu . . . T'Antwerpen . . . M. DC. XL.* The heart is enclosed in a heavy ornamental frame ; the hinge is on the left side and the lock on the right. Beneath the emblem are the words :

Tantùm opus est verbo $\begin{cases} \text{Men kan het van buyten} \\ \text{Met een vvoort ontslvyten.} \end{cases}$

Crashaw may have seen the volume while in Holland.

l. 2. *Stands trembling at the gate of blisse.* The main idea of this poem is anticipated in the Latin epigram beginning :

Penè ? *quid hoc* penè *est ? Vicinia sæva salutis !*

(see p. 30, above).

PAGE 237, l. 15. *long time.* Possibly the article ' a ' has been dropped before ' long '. Compare the second version of this poem, p. 348, above, l. 9, ' a great while try'de '.

ll. 15–16. It seems possible that these two lines are interrogative, with the sense ' Who can be said to grant at last when every effort has been made to combat persuasion ? ' In neither version does the punctuation lend any positive support to this view ; a full-stop was sometimes used in the seventeenth century after a question. But ' Who ' more probably refers to ' no '.

ll. 46–7. *And hast . . . That healing shaft.* Compare Joseph Beaumont ' Love ' (*Minor Poems*, ed. Robinson, p. 23) :

Soft as yᵉ Ray
Of this Sweet Day
Are all His healing Shafts where e'r they slay.

PAGE 243, l. 142. *And kill the Death of this Delay.* Compare p. 238, l. 58 :

To saue your life, kill your delay.

' of ' here signifies ' consisting in '.

PAGE 255. *In the Glorious Epiphanie, &c.* l. 41. *half-sphear.* The form ' spear ' for ' sphere ' (' spheare ' *48*), although already old-fashioned by 1650 is repeated in this 1652 edition (see below, p. 338, l. 18) and might justifiably have been retained in both places.

PAGE **258**, ll. 152–7. *And the Great Penitent, &c.* Crashaw perhaps visualizes the sun signifying by compression of its lips and by the ' loue-eclipse ' its renunciation of the love (compare l .161) or worship which it had formerly received. For this the laws of nature can offer no explanation, though the sun is acting in accordance with human domestic law, which it feels to be relevant to the sin of sun-worship and to the sorrow which it feels for having permitted it. Or, again, the sun's behaviour may be a mere gesture of sympathy and self-effacement; and the domestic laws those by which Christ was judged.

l. 162. *Their hated loues.* ' Hated ' because of the sun's own repentance.

ll. 165–8. *Miss-ledde before . . . stumble' on true Light.* Compare *King Lear,* IV. i. 18–21 :

> I have no way, and therefore want no eyes ;
> I stumbled when I saw. Full oft 'tis seen,
> Our means secure us, and our mere defects
> Prove our commodities.

PAGE **259**, l. 184. *at lest, to worship Thee.* The phrase ' at lest ' appears to go with ' worship ' and not with ' Him ' ; ' to *worship* Thee' is not the only thing which may be learnt. The comma has emphasizing value. Crashaw *may*, however, have written ' last '.

l. 192. *The right-ey'd Areopagite.* The reference is to the pseudo-Dionysius (not, as Grosart stated, to St. Paul) and to his doctrine of the ' via negativa ' (compare ll. 210–12, below). See S. Dionysius Areopagita, *De Mystica Theologia,* especially chaps. i and ii (ed. Migne, 1857, cols. 997–1032).

ll. 204–5. *o ye two Twinne Sunnes !* The reference is to the child's eyes. Compare Phineas Fletcher, *Poetical Miscellanies,* ' An Hymn ' (ed. Anderson in *Poets of Great Britain,* vol. iv, p. 471) st. 2, ll. 1–3 :

> Wake, O mine eyes ! awake, and view
> Those two twin lights, whence heavens drew
> Their glorious beams.

PAGE **260**, l. 236. *At lest by us.* This would seem to mean ' through our agency, at least ', if not in physical fact.

PAGE **263.** *The Office of the Holy Crosse.* The original of this Office is in many medieval manuscript Books of Hours and was published in the Sarum Primers which appeared in Queen Mary's reign. See, for example, *The Prymer in Englysshe and in Latin, sette out alonge, after the use of Sarum* (Rothom. . . . 1555). Compare also Maskell, *Monumenta Ritualia Ecclesiæ Anglicanæ,* 2nd edition, 1882, vol. iii, pp. x–xii. Crashaw's translation of the verse is, as usual, of the freest possible order.

PAGE **266.** *The Prayer,* l. 5. The omission in the text of *48* (see foot-notes), which eludes the charge of praying for the dead, may be due to some person who did not share Crashaw's Roman faith.

PAGE **277.** *Vexilla Regis.* The freedom of Crashaw's rendering of this and of other well-known Church hymns or sequences will be appreciated by comparison with the originals. In the present instance see Daniel, *Thesaurus Hymnologicus* (1855), vol. i, p. 160.

PAGE **284.** *Sancta Maria Dolorum*. Compare Daniel, *Thesaurus Hymnologicus* (1855), vol. ii, pp. 131-3 (Jacobus de Benedictis : ' Sequentia de Septem Doloribus Beatæ Virginis ').

PAGE **287,** st. xi, ll. 7-10. *Fold up my life, &c.* The variant reading of *48* makes the meaning clearer. The two final lines are perhaps ambiguous ; (i) ' thy lord's in death ' might go with ' prayers ' ; *sc.* that thou may'st be thy lord's in death ; (ii) more probably the concluding phrase parallels the preceding one ; *sc.* thy lord's breath poured out for thee in (his) death.

PAGE **291.** *The Hymn of Sainte Thomas*. Compare the original ' Adoro te devote, latens deitas ', given in Daniel, *Thesaurus Hymnologicus* (1855), vol. i, p. 255.

PAGE **294.** *Lauda Sion Salvatorem*. Compare Daniel, *Thesaurus Hymnologicus* (1855), vol. ii, p. 97 (S. Thomas Aquinas ' De venerabili Sacramento in festo Corporis Christi ').

PAGE **298.** *Dies Iræ*. Compare Daniel, *Thesaurus Hymnologicus* (1855), vol. ii, pp. 103-8 (Thomas de Celano, ' *Prosa de Mortuis* ').

PAGE **302.** *The Himn O Gloriosa Domina*. The original hymn is mentioned though not included in Daniel's *Thesaurus Hymnologicus* ; but is in Mone's *Lateinische Hymnen des Mittelalters* (1854), vol. ii, p. 129, with the heading ' Purificationis b. Mariæ v.' The text is as follows :

> O gloriosa femina
> excelsa supra sidera,
> qui te creavit provide,
> lactas sacrato ubere.
>
> Quod Eva tristis abstulit,
> tu reddis almo germine ;
> intrent ut astra flebiles,
> cœli fenestra facta es.
>
> Tu regis alti janua
> et porta lucis fulgida :
> vitam datam per virginem
> gentes redemptæ plaudite !
>
> Deo patri sit gloria etc.

PAGE **308.** *The Weeper*. See notes to version first published in 1646, pp. 432-4, above.

PAGE **311,** st. xvii. *But can these fair Flouds, &c.* Compare John Owen, *Epigrammata*, i. 74 (published in 1606) :

> *Nilo negli occhi, Ætna nel cuore*

> Frigidus ardentes intravit Nilus ocellos,
> Dum cor Ætnæo carpitur igne meum.
> Nec tantus fluvio lacrymarum extinguitur ardor,
> Nec tanti fletus flumina siccat amor.
> Sic sibi discordes, exercent vim tamen ambo,
> In me concordes, ignis et unda suam.

Compare also Green, *Never too Late*, ' Isabells Ode ', ll. 27-32 :

> Her eies carried darts of fire
> Featherd all with swift desire ;

> Yet foorth these fierie darts did passe
> Pearled teares as bright as glasse ;
> That wonder 'twas in her eine
> Fire and water should combine

PAGE 312, st. xix, ll. 4–6. *two faithfull fountaines ; Two walking baths, &c.* Many parallels to these much criticized lines might be quoted. Compare Hermannus Hugo, *Pia Desideria* (1624), Lib. I. viii :

> Quis dabit capiti meo aquam, et oculis meis
> fontem lacrymarum, et plorabo die ac nocte.
> (Jer. ix. 1.)

> Capta nec Andromache qua lumina proluit unda,
> Illa meis lacrymis unda sat esse potest,
> Nec tua, Jesside, lacrymati balnea lecti,
> Balnea nocturnis humida semper aquis.   (ll. 9–12.)

> Hos oculis voveam gravidis mihi currere nimbos ;
> Et caput hoc totus fiat ut Oceanus.   (ll. 27–8.)

Compare also Cabilliau, *Magdalena* (1625), Magdalea Silva, xlvii (p. 186), ll. 1–2 :

> Everris madido concinno sedula lymphas,
> Vnde Dei in castos balnea fusa pedes.

and xliv (p. 200), ll. 3–4 :

> Falleris, & nescis. nec falleris. alba gemello
> Te dare fonte putas balnea ? flendo capis.

Southwell uses in a similar connexion the metaphor of the bath ; see ' Saint Peter's Complaint ', lxiv, ll. 1–2 :

> O pooles of Hesebon ; the baths of grace,
> Where happie spirits diue in sweet desires,

Compare Gervase Markham, *Marie Magdalens Lamentations*, 1601 (ed. Grosart, ' The Conclusion,' st. 17, l. 4) :

> Thou letst me wash Thy feet in my teare bath :

There are also Elizabethan usages of ' cistern ' in similar connexions. Compare Greene, *Selimus*, ll. 1450–2 :

> for how can Aga weep ?
> Or run a brinish shower of pearled tears,
> Wanting the watery cisterns of his eyes ?

Compare also Marlowe, *Hero and Leander*, sestiad i, ll. 296–9 :

> Forth from those two tralucent cisterns brake
> A stream of liquid pearl, which down her face
> Made milk-white paths.

PAGE 315. *A Hymn to . . . Sainte Teresa.* See notes to pp. 131–3, above.

PAGE 318, l. 63. *Farewell house, & farewell home !* Compare Joseph Beaumont, ' House & Home ' (*Minor Poems*, ed. Robinson, p. 60) : ' What is House, & what is Home.'

PAGE 324. *The Flaming Heart.* This title appears to be borrowed from that of the English translation of the Life of S. Teresa, published in 1642 at Antwerp. See note to p. 131, above.

Page 333, ll. 49–51. *Thence he might tosse you, &c.* Compare
G. Herbert, ' The Pulley ', ll. 19–20 :

> If goodness lead him not, yet weariness
> May toss him to my breast.

Page 334. *Alexias.* The originals of these three elegies,
in *F. Remondi* . . . *Epigrammata et Elegiæ* . . . *Antverpiæ* 1606, were
published several times in the seventeenth century. The freedom
with which Crashaw treats them will be seen by comparison with
the following passages, which give all that seems obviously to
have been drawn upon. In Crashaw's ' second elegy ' only
ll. 19–30 appear to be based on Remond, and the original Latin
verses are found in Remond's ' Elegia Quinta '. Crashaw's
' third elegy ' refers to Remond's ' Elegia Secunda '.

Elegia Prima.

> Illa ego Romana virgo laus magna iuuentæ
> 　　Quæ toties fueram mille negata procis,
> En iaceo miseranda nouo sine coniuge coniux,
> 　　Pæne relicta priùs quàm bene iuncta viro.
> Succedit tantis etiam noua cura querelis,
> 　　Vulneret (heu !) teneros quo vagas orbe pedes.
> Si mihi nota foret regio qua liber oberrat,
> 　　Inciperet certus mitior esse dolor.
> Illi missa graues narraret epistola curas,
> 　　Audirét meas forsitan ille preces.
> Nectuntur scribendo moræ :　prior ipsa volarem,
> 　　Atque meæ fierem nuntia tristitiæ.
> Cedere nam didici furtim, te, ô Alexi, magistro,
> 　　Et fugere è patria sola puella domo.
> Ipse daret pedibus celeres amor anxius alas,
> 　　Præcipitíque irem per loca vasta fuga.
> Nulláque virgineos tardare pericula gressus,
> 　　Dicere nec possent, parua puella mane.
>
> 　　　(*Twenty-six lines not translated.*)
>
> Méque docebit amor, fuerit si fracta carina,
> 　　Indociles vndis arte mouere manus.
>
> 　　　(*Eighteen lines not translated.*)
>
> Si tamen in me eritis crudeles vos quoque pisces,
> 　　Naufraga si duro sum peritura mari,
> Me manibus perijsse tuis, amor alme, iuuabit :
> 　　Castus honorati funeris auctor eris.
> Déque meo pontus faciet sibi nomine nomen,
> 　　Et felix inter sidera sidus ero.
> Nauita præteriens illa plorabit in unda,
> 　　Firmabítque mea vota marina fide ;
> Et dicet, perijt quondam hîc Romana puella,
> 　　Dum toto amissum quæreret orbe virum.
> Viuat tantus amor :　semper sis, ô bona virgo,
> 　　Tam dilecta Deo, quàm bene fida viro.
>
> 　　　(*Sixteen lines not translated.*)

In ' The Seconde Elegie ', ll. 19–30 correspond to the following lines
in Remond's

Elegia Quinta.

> *Ast ego quot Soles numero ? si credis amanti,*
> 　　*Quolibet in spatio sæcula mille traho.*

Iam didici stellas, iam Lunæ tempora noui,
 Eois iam sum doctior Astrologis.
Surge, age, pacato sidus mihi noscere cælo,
 Æthereásque nouo lumine vince faces :
Quale Magos olim Christi ad cunabula reges
 Duxit, & optatam constitit ante casam :
Nascere, & ambiguum radijs mihi percute Alexim :
 Ibo nec incertas pes teret vsque vias.

'The Third Elegie' corresponds to Remond's

ELEGIA SECVNDA.

Crudelis regio, quæ te fouet vsque latentem :
 Illa meis facta est terra beata malis.
Ah ! percat quisquis, si fas est dicere, primus
 Inuiti docuit terga domare salis ;
Intactum qui fregit iter, montesque subegit,
 Virgineam pedibus qui violauit humum.
Septeni colles, & Tybridis Ostia, tutus
 Exigui limes tunc erat imperij.
Tunc erat Vrbs vix nota sibi, paruoque Quiriti
 Extremi Æthiopes porta Capena fuit.
Dictator numerabat oues pressoque senator
 Fessus aratro, humili sub lare iura dabat.
Nunc quoque sic vtinam, clausis regionibus, esses
 Mecum sub vili pauper Alexi casa ?
Cur fugis è patria non vllo pulsus ab hoste ?
 Si tibi cura mei est, ô fugitiue redi.
Si tibi cura mei nulla est, miserere parentum ;
 Quem trahis, ipse iubet spiritus esse pium.
Non hæc sperabant meritæ solatia vitæ
 Et pater infelix, & miseranda parens.
Immatura vtrique paras heu ! funera, iam iam
 In tumulum tristi cum patre mater abit.
Prompta tuæ tu solus habes medicamina culpæ ;
 Funera regressu sunt reuocanda tuo.
Vita veni, quid enim peccauimus omnes ?
 Totáne Roma potest esse nouerca tibi ?
Ast ego quid merui ? vel quo rea crimine dicor ?
 Nullum in me crimen, præter amare, vides.
Si tibi virginitas, iuuenis castissime, sancta est,
 Virgineo possum viuere nupta thoro.
Viuere si possum cum coniuge virgine virgo,
 Cur fugis aspectus dure marite meos ?
Este mihi testes Superi, nil firmius opto,
 Quàm vita exacta cælibe posse mori.
Connubij non vincla venus, non fœdera nectit ;
 Nec facit amplexus concubitusque virum.
Cælicolûm Regina potens, & gloria terræ
 Ipsa simul coniux, virgo parensque fuit.
Cæcilia antiquæ potuit noua gloria gentis
 O quàm dissimilem ducere virgo virum !
Coniugis in thalamum prima cùm nocte veniret,
 Protinus exclamat, Valleriane caue :
Valleriane caue, custos fortissimus adstat,
 Qui mihi libati corporis vltor erit.

Est mihi virginitas summo iurata Tonanti ;
    Peruigil in lectum fert sua vota sopor.
Gorgone tuta, meo caream Alite ? telaque vibrans,
    Fingitur à vobis Pallas, inermis ero ?
Crede mihi, Paridis non est hæc fabula vestri,
    Cùm Menelaæo rapta Lacena thoro est.
Sum tua, tu meus es, Christum cole ; sim modò virgo.
    Tu pater, &' coniux, & mihi frater eris.
Sic ait. Ille sacro lustratus fonte, meretur
    Optato ætherei militis ore frui.
Sanguis vtrumque iterum fœcunda in morte maritat :
    Ornat vtrique manum palma, corona caput,
Noster Hymen tali caleat face, teda iugalis
    Sentiet haud flammas dire Cupido tuas.
Femina, virque iugo sacri subiguntur amoris.
    O quanta existit vis in amore pari !
Ast ego te rerum pulcherrime, semper amaui :
    Sic placidi redeant in mea vota dies.
O ! quoties cùm me peteret malè sana procorum
    Turba, meus, dixi, solus Alexis erit.
Altera vera fuit, fuit, heu ! vox altera mendax ;
    Et solus, sed non diceris esse meus.

PAGE **338.** *Description of a Religious House.* Compare Barclay, *Argenis,* Lib. V (p. 613 in Leyden edition of 1630) :

Non isthic aurata domus, luxuque fluentes
Sunt epulæ, spondave sopor pretiosus eburna,
Aut in carbaseo Tyrius velamine murex.
Non gemma vibrante nitor, non persona cantu
Limina, non prono famulantum examina collo,
Atque avidas quicquid trahit in certamina gentes ;
Sed nemora, & nudæ rupes, neglectaque squalent
Confraga : Sunt epulæ viles, jussæque quietis
Hora brevis : Duro velantur corpora texto :
Et labor in pretio, & vitam mors longa fatigat.
At neque crudeles Diræ, vilique flagello
Sævit cura ferox : falso non abditus ore
Ipse sua insanus furit in præcordia livor.
Alma quies parvisque habitat concordia tectis,
Et semper niveo veri de pectore risus.
Ipsa suæ meminit stirpis, seseque Deisque
Meus fruitur fœlix, & novit in astra reverti.

l. 18. *sphear.* See note to p. 255, l. 41, above.

PAGE **339,** l. 35. *kingdomes of contentfull Cells.* Compare the phrase in the letter written by Crashaw in 1643, 'a little contenfull kingdom' (see Introduction, p. xxix, l. 32, above).

An Epitaph, &c. Printed as '*An Epitaph On Alcander, and Julietta his Wife, who died in one anothers Arms, two Days after Marriage. By R. S.*' In *New Miscellaneous Poems. With The Cavalier's Answers to the Nun's Five Love-Letters. In Verse.* London . . . 1716, p. 62. The appropriation (on p. 202) follows this, the longer, original version, and the variants are chiefly in ll. 1–6 :

    To these, whom Death again did wed,
    This Tomb's a second Marriage-bed ;

For tho' the cruel Hand of Fate
Could Soul and Body separate,
It could not Man and Wife divide,
They liv'd one Life, one Death they dy'd.

PAGE 340. *Death's Lecture, &c.* See note to p. 175, above.
PAGE 342. *Temperance.* See note to p. 156, above.
PAGE 344. *Hope.* See note to p. 143, above.

A LETTER FROM Mr· CRASHAW.

PAGES 348–50. See notes to pp. 236–7, above.

POEMS FROM MSS., INCLUDED IN PREVIOUS MODERN EDITIONS.

PAGE 352. *Ps. 1.* Crashaw's original MS. may have indicated by spaces after ll. 10, 14, and 25 the changes of metre, ll. 1–10 being Phalæcian hendecasyllables, ll. 11—14 a Sapphic stanza, ll. 15–25 six-footed iambics, and ll. 26–9 an Alcaic stanza.

PAGE 354. *Epig. 1*, l. 2. *Certè non hominem vox sonat. euge Deus!* Compare Virgil, *Aeneid*, i. 328 :

. . . nec vox hominem sonat : O, dea certe.

l. 3. *Sed tamen iste Deus qui sit, vos dicite, vermes.* Compare Virgil, *Eclogues*, i. 18 :   ,

Sed tamen, iste deus qui sit, da, Tityre, nobis.

PAGE 355. *Epig. 3*, ll. 1, 3. *Joannes . . . Joanne.* Here and in some other places though the MS. reads ' J ' the scansion is probably quadrasyllabic and would be clearer to the modern reader from the spelling with ' I '. ' J ' and ' I ', however, were hardly sufficiently differentiated in Crashaw's time to justify emendation.

Apocal. xii. 7. ll. 1, 2. *Arma, viri !* . . . A reminiscence, probably, of Aeneas's cry (*Aeneid*, ii. 668) :

Arma, viri, ferte arma.

PAGE 356. *Epig. 2, In Atheniensem merum.* The expression seems to have been suggested by Juvenal, *Sat.* vi. 187, where *mera Cecropis* is applied to the Roman lady who discards her Latin dialect and becomes ' a pure Athenian '. (In both cases ' a pure Athenian ' is applied not to a native of Athens but to one who has Athenian characteristics.) Compare Introduction, p. xxxi, l. 1, above.

PAGE 357. *Epig. 5*, l. 1. *Nox erat, & Christum (Doctor malè docte) petebas.* Compare Horace, *Epodes*, xv. 1 :

Nox erat, et caelo fulgebat luna sereno.

PAGE 358. *Epig. 2*, l. 2. *Vt bene Vox fuerit, prætereaque nihil.* Compare Erasmus, *Apophthegmata*, ii. i. 13: Alius [*sc.* Laco] cum in luscinia plumis revulsis minimum reperisset carnium : *Vox*, inquit, *tu es, præterea nihil.* The original, Φωνὰ τύ τις ἐσσί, καὶ οὐδὲν ἄλλο, is in Plutarch, *Moralia*, 233 A (*Apophthegmata Laconica*). Xylander's translation (1570) is

Vox tu es, & nihil præterea.

PAGE 360. *Epig. 1*, l. 3. *vos somnia terrent.* Compare Virgil, *Aeneid*, iv. 9 :

Anna soror, quae me suspensam insomnia terrent !

Epig. 2, l. 7. *Vsque adeò haud tuus hic ferus est, neque ferreus hostis !* The jingle is borrowed from Tibullus, i. x [xi in old edd.], 1–2 :

> Quis fuit, horrendos primus qui protulit enses ?
> Quam ferus et vere ferreus ille fuit !

or (less probably) from Cicero, *Ad Quintum Fratrem*, i. iii. 3 : Quem ego ferus ac ferreus e complexu dimisi meo.

PAGE 362. *Epig. 3*, l. 3. *Non vidit, te non vidit (dulcissime rerum).* From Horace, *Satires*, i. ix. 4 :

> Quid agis, dulcissime rerum ?

PAGE 363. *Epig. 5*, l. 1. *legat.* One of Crashaw's mistakes of quantity. He must mean the verb ' legare ', the first syllable of which is long.

Epig. 6, l. 1. *quicunque.* The meaning seems to be ' whatever terrors bring signs of thy coming '..

PAGE 364. *Felices ! &c.* In this piece Crashaw shows once more his interest in the Massacre of the Innocents as a poetic theme. Compare pp. 88 and 109 sqq., above. The central thought is summed up in the last two lines, where ' vita ' stands for true or eternal life and ' ævum ' for mortal life.

l. 15. *In vitæ multo.* The expression may be somewhat unusual, but with the meaning ' in a long extent of life, in a prolonged life ' exactly fits the sense of the passage, and the ' multo multæ ' is in keeping with the pointed style of the piece. Crashaw could, further, have adduced Tacitus, *Annals*, iv. 39 : ' nam sibi multum superque vitae fore, quod tali cum principe explevisset.'

patet area. The phrase was probably suggested by Ovid, *Epist. (Heroides)*, i. 72 :

> Et patet in curas area lata meas.

and *Tristia*, iv. iii. 84 :

> Et patet in laudes area magna tuas.

l. 20. *Res longa, &c.* The alteration is metrically necessary and Crashaw can hardly be thought responsible for the reading in the MS.

PAGE 365. *Epig. 2*, l. 6. *Sic tua te Pallas, Domitiane, juvat ?* ' *tua* Pallas ' (1) because Domitian affected a special cult of Minerva (' Minervam, quam superstitiose colebat ', Suetonius, *Domitianus*, 15), and (2) because Pallas was the creator of the olive-tree. *Pallas* is sometimes used in poetry as actually equivalent to *oil*, e.g. in Ovid, *Heroides*, xix (Hero to Leander), 44 :

> *Pallade* iam *pingui* tinguere membra putas ?

and *Tristia*, iv. v. 4 :

> Ut vigil infusa Pallade flamma solet.

With the treatment here of ' Domitiane ' as if the first syllable were long, compare that of *cōmit*, p. 8, l. 76, above, and see note thereon. See also note to p. 52, ll. 9–10, above.

Epig. 4, ll. 1–3 :

> *Ah ferus, ah culter ! qui tam bona lilia primus*
> *In tam crudeles jussit abire rosas.*
> *Virgineüm hoc qui primus ebur violavit ab ostro.*

Compare Virgil, *Aeneid*, xii. 67–9 :

> Indum sanguineo veluti violaverit ostro
> Si quis ebur, aut mixta rubent ubi lilia multa
> Alba rosa : talis virgo dabat ore colores.

PAGE 367. *Epig. 2*, ll. 3–4. Compare p. 181, ll. 116–17.

PAGE 368. *Cùm horum, &c.* l. 3. *R. Brooke.* See note to p. 10, above.

PAGE 369, l. 26. *Ego enim . . . mecum agnoscere, &c.* Crashaw is contrasting ' mecum agnoscere ' and ' profiteri palam ', and though ' mecum agnoscere ' is without satisfactory classical authority it seems best to keep it, in view of the ' secum cogitare ' found in classical Latin and in the Vulgate, and of the passage in Cicero's *De Finibus* (ii. 23. 76), by which Crashaw may have been influenced : ' Eamne rationem igitur sequere, qua tecum ipse et cum tuis utare, profiteri et in medium proferre non audeas ? '

PAGE 370. *Spes Diva.* l. 6. *tugurij.* The second syllable of this word, though short, is here treated as if it were long.

PAGE 371. *Non accipimus brevem vitam, sed facimus.* From Seneca, *Dialogorum*, Lib. X (' De Brevitate Vitæ '), cap. i. 4, ' Ita est : non accipimus brevem vitam sed facimus, nec inopes eius sed prodigi sumus '.

Pulchra non diuturna. l. 8. *umbraque somnij.* The ultimate origin of this phrase is in Pindar, *Pythia*, viii. 135 (95) sq., Ἐπάμεροι· τί δέ τις ; τί δ'οὔ τις ; σκιᾶς ὄναρ ἄνθρωπος, though in Crashaw the phrase is inverted, the ' dream of a shadow ', becoming the ' shadow of a dream '. Jean Passerat (1534–1602) begins an epitaph which he wrote for himself with the lines :

> Qui sim, viator, quæris ? ipse nescio :
> Nisi quod sepultus puluis, vmbræ somnium.

See *Delitiæ C. Poetarum Gallorum* (1609), Pars III, p. 171.

PAGE 373. *Veris descriptio.* l. 15. *strepero.* There is no classical authority for the adjective ' streperus ', but its existence in Crashaw's time is witnessed by the 1677 edition of Holyoke's Dictionary, where the meanings ' hoarse ' and ' jarring ' are assigned to it. It is also used by J. C. Scaliger, *Poemata*, Pars I (p. 77 in edition of 1574), ' Teretismata', i, l. 42 :

> Non gula : non strepero turris damnata fritillo.

PAGE 374, l. 55. *astro.* In late Latin ' iubere ' is commonly followed by the dative, and emendation to ' astrum ' seems therefore unnecessary.

PAGE 375. *In Natales Mariæ Principis.* l. 34. *Tyndarida.* The erroneous belief that ' Tyndarida ' could be used as a nominative singular still persisted in Crashaw's time and is even discussed by Bentley with a view to its extirpation in his Horace (1711), note on Sat. 1. i. 100. There is therefore no need to emend to ' Tyndaris ' in accordance with classical usage.

PAGE 376. *Honoratiss° D° Rob° Heath.* See article ' Robert Heath ' in *D.N.B.* Heath became Chief Justice of Common Pleas in 1631. l. 2. *tuæ gloria magna togæ !* Suggested by Martial, ii. 90, 2 :

> Gloria Romanae, Quintiliane, togae.

PAGE 377. *Serenissimæ Reginæ, &c.* l. 3. *Est Musâ de matre recens rubicundulus infans.* Juvenal, *Satires*, vii. 196, has :

> adhuc a matre rubentem.

Horatii Ode. Compare the English version, p. 382, below.

l. 13. ἐπικίνδυνον. Crashaw shortens the penultimate syllable, probably owing to his pronunciation of the Greek according to accent. Compare πατρίδος, l. 25, below, and τρίκρανος, l. 33, below; also ἐπιχρύσῳ, l. 26, below (nom. sing. ἐπίχρυσος).

l. 14. Βοσφόρον should strictly be accented on the first syllable and be spelt with a π, not φ. As spelt here it seems to be a back-formation from the Latin.

PAGE 378. *In reuerendum Doctorem Brooke.* See note to p. 175, above.

l. 5. *sydus illud oris acre prospectans.* The ' procul ' appears to have crept in from l. 4. Professor Bensly, in suggesting the emendation, points out other examples of the same phrase, in p. 8, l. 21, above : ' Sydus illud oris tui auspicatissimum ', and in the dedication in Add. MS. 40176, see p. 2, above, ll. 21–2.

l. 8. *Cujus serena facilitas graves mores.* Professor Bensly, in suggesting his emendation, points out that the manuscript reading does not scan and that the ' gravitas ' cannot strictly be said to ' mulcere mores '. The contrast between *gravitas* and *facilitas* is classical. Compare Cicero, *Pro Murena,* 31, 66 : ' si illius comitatem et facilitatem tuae gravitati severitatique asperseris.' Compare also p. 165, l. 45, above : ' Sub morum facilitate, severitas virtutis.'

PAGE 379, l. 11. *videri festinus.* ' fessus ', in l. 12, suggesting the metaphor of the journey of life, lends support to the emendations proposed, but uncertainty as to what word has in fact been replaced by ' videri ' seems to justify leaving the text open to conjecture.

l. 12. *hunc mori.* See foot-note. The metre could also be restored by deleting ' Et ' ; but ' Et ' seems to have a function and there are other instances of metrical licence in Crashaw's Latin works.

In obitum Rev. V. D^{ris} Mansell. John Mansel was President of Queens' College 1622–31, on Oct. 7 of which year he died. He entered the college in 1594 and was elected to a Fellowship June 31, 1600. (Searle, *The History of the Queens' College,* 1871, pp. 447–9.)

PAGE 380, ll. 47–50. *Oh, would'st thou, &c.* Compare the Latin epigram, p. 24, above, ' Ah, redeas, &c.'.

PAGE 381. *In amorem divinum. (Hermannus Hugo.)* The original is in *Pia Desideria . . . Antverpiæ M. DC. XXIII.* Liber Tertius, p. 287 :

> Quid totis Te, Dius amor, sit amare medullis,
> Expertus nisi sit, dicere nemo potest :
> Quid verò sit amare, iterumque abs te redamari,
> Sit licet expertus, dicere nemo potest ;

PAGE 382. *Petronij Ales Phasiacis, &c.* From *Titi Petroni Arbitri Satyricon,* 93 (p. 186 in Loeb Classics edition).

Horatij Ille & nefasto, &c. Compare the Greek version, p. 377, above.

PAGE 384. *On ye Gunpowder-Treason.* ll. 23–4. *the milky streame, &c.* Compare ' The Weeper ', st. 4, ll. 3–4, p. 79, above.

> Where th' milky rivers meet,
> Thine Crawles above and is the Creame.

ll. 28–30. *A winters thunder, &c.* See note to p. 404, ll. 32–6, below.

PAGE **385,** ll. 35–6. *a great Prince shall climbe, &c.* Compare Donne, *Sermons,* ed. Pearsall Smith, p. 50.

ll. 63–4. *the warmest blood . . . pipes.* See note to p. 404, ll. 38–9, below.

PAGE **386.** *Upon the gunpowder treason.* ll. 14–16. *The fresh face, &c.* Compare 'To the Morning. Satisfaction for sleepe', ll. 7–9, p. 183, above :

> How at the sight did'st Thou draw back thine Eyes,
> Into thy modest veyle ? how did'st thou rise
> Twice di'd in thine owne blushes, . . .

PAGE **388,** l. 53. *Forthwith, &c.* Compare ' Vpon the Duke of *Yorke* his Birth A Panegyricke ', ll. 71–2, p. 179, above :

> is't some Deity
> Stept from her Throne of starres . . .

PAGE **389.** *Ŭpon the Kings coronation.* ll. 2–3. *Ravish the dancing orbes, &c.* Compare ' Upon the birth of the Princesse Elizabeth ', p. 391, l. 32, below :

> Dance, like the nimble sphæres, a joyfull round.

l. 25. *Doe I not see a Cynthia.* Cynthia, or Henrietta Maria (compare ' Vpon the Duke of *Yorke* his Birth ', l. 79, p. 179, above), was not crowned with Charles I in Feb. 1626.

l. 26. *Abash the purest beauties of the day ?* Compare ' Vpon the Duke of *Yorke* his Birth ', ll. 74–5, p. 179, above :

> her awfull Beauties chase
> The Dayes abashed Glories, . . .

PAGE **390.** *Upon the Kings Coronation.* See the comparison of this poem with ' On a foule Morning, being then to take a journey ', pp. lxvi–lxx, above.

PAGE **391.** *Upon the birth of the Princesse Elizabeth.* See note to p. 161, above.

ll. 17–18. *And though . . . birth.* See note to p. 403, ll. 11–12, below.

ll. 22–3. *Lett th' hallowed plume, &c.* See note to p. 403, ll. 12–13, below.

l. 25. *Rich, liberall heauen.* On this form of compound phrase, see p. lxxiii, above.

l. 32. *Dance, &c.* See note to p. 389, ll. 2–3, above.

PAGE **392,** ll. 55–6. *Goe on then, Heauen, &c.* Compare ' Vpon the Duke of *Yorke* His Birth ', p. 178, ll. 53–4, above.

> See'st thou that *Mary* there ? ô teach her Mother
> To shew her to her selfe in such another.

Ex Euphormione. From *Euphormionis Lusinini Satyricon,* Part II (edition of 1628, Amsterdam, p. 134) :

> O dea, syderei seu tu stirps alma Tonantis,
> Seu patrem factura Iovem, da numine dextro
> Has movisse preces, placataque lumina flecte.
> Ecce ignes jussitque pati, jussitque fateri
> Nil non ausus amor.   Nec sortem despice nostram,
> Nympha potens, Cælum cognataque numina cernis
> ·Pauperibus votis & parco thure vocari,

Placarique tamen. Tibi jam sua stamina Parcæ
Concessere meæ. Vitam si sorte negabis,
Da saltem Regina mori ; da sydere flammæ
Nympha perire tuæ. Non dignius arserit ales,
Quæ super Eoos extincta renascitur ignes.

PAGE 394. *An Elegy upon the death of M*ʳ *Stanninow.* See note
to p. 175, above.

l. 10. *milky streame.* See note to p. 384, ll. 23–4, above.

ll. 22–4. *These purple currents, &c.* See note to p. 404, ll. 38–9,
below.

l. 28. *prime flowre of youth.* See p. 404, l. 1, below.

PAGE 395. *An Elegie on the death of D*ʳ *Porter.* George Porter,
Fellow of Queens' College, Cambridge, and Regius Professor of
Civil Law, died in 1635. See Searle, *History of the Queens' College,*
ii, p. 455.

l. 1. *silver-footed Came.* Compare ' The Weeper ', st. 1, l. 2,
p. 308, above, ' syluer-footed rills '. The expression is not, however, peculiar to Crashaw.

l. 3. *thy wat'ry eyes.* See p. 402, l. 27, below.

PAGE 396, l. 20. *crawling streames.* Compare ' The Weeper ',
st. 4, l. 4, p. 79, above, and ' The beginning of Heliodorus ', l. 21,
p. 158, above.

ll. 29–30. *such as may, &c.* See note to p. 404, ll. 32–6, below.

l. 34. *Neptunes silver-sheilded guard.* Crashaw is no doubt
thinking of classical allusions to the dumbness of fishes, e.g.
Horace, *Odes,* IV. iii. 19–20 :

O mutis quoque piscibus
Donatura cycni, si libeat, sonum.

For the epithet, compare that of Alexander's Persian guards,
ἀργυράσπιδες (Aelian, *Varia Historia,* ix. 3).

l. 38. *a sea of teares.* Compare ' To the Name . . . of Iesus ',
l. 144, p. 243, above, and ' An Elegy vpon the death of Mʳ Wᵐ
Carre ', l. 38, p. 403, below.

l. 43. *bubling eyes.* Compare ' The Weeper ', st. 1, l. 3, p. 79,
above : ' Ever bubling things ! ', and see note to p. 405, ll. 5–6,
below.

Add. MS. 33219.

PAGE 397, ll. 3–4. *'tis in the doome of your sweet Eye, &c.* Compare ' Loves Horoscope ', ll. 19–20, p. 186, above :

'Tis in the mercy of her eye,
If poore Love shall live or dye.

' Loves Horoscope ' is among the poems included in Add. MS.
33219.

Though now, &c. l. 5. *A Nightingale.* The reference is to
' Musicks Duell ' (pp. 142–53, above).

PAGE 398. *Out of Grotius.* The prologue to the *Christus Patiens.*
Compare the translation by George Sandys, first published in 1640.

l. 23 sqq. Compare p. 162, l. 33, above, ' *Altera gens* ', &c.

ll. 25–6. *eu'n from their brests, &c.* Compare ' Sospetto
d' Herode ', st. 1, ll. 3–4, p. 109, above :
tore
A thousand sweet Babes from their Mothers Brest :

PAGE 399, l. 52. *The water blush'd, &c.* Compare the Latin
epigram, ' Unde rubor vestris ', l. 4, p. 38, above.

POEMS FROM MSS. NOT INCLUDED IN PREVIOUS MODERN EDITIONS.

PAGE 401. BODLEIAN MS. TANNER 465.

See the preliminary discussion of these poems, pp. lxx–lxxiii, above.

Wm Henshaw. William Henshaw, of Emmanuel College, was buried at Great St. Andrew's, Cambridge, on Nov. 8, 1634. He was of Leicestershire, and was admitted to the college in 1631, matriculating in the Easter term of that year.

l. 14. *snowy hills.* Compare ' The Weeper ', st. 1, l. 4, p. 79, above: ' *Thawing Christall! Snowy Hills!* '

l. 18. *Heauens milky way he shall outshine.* Compare ' On the Assumption ', l. 6, p. 304, above: ' She climbes; and makes a farre more milkey way.'

l. 24. *The liquid jewell of a teare.* Compare ' The Teare ', sts. 1 and 2, p. 84, above: ' A watry Diamond ' and ' This thine eyes Iewell '.

PAGE 402, l. 27. *our wat'ry eyes.* Compare ' An Elegie on the death of Dr Porter ', l. 3, p. 395, above: ' Fixe heere thy wat'ry eyes '.

Mr Wm Carre. William Carre, or Carr, matriculated from Queens' College at Michaelmas, 1631, and went to Emmanuel in 1633. He was buried at Great St. Andrew's, Cambridge, on Nov. 12, 1634. He appears to have been of an Essex family.

ll. 15–16. *From whence, &c.* Compare ' Upon the birth of the Princesse Elizabeth ', ll. 1–2, p. 391, above :
> Bright starre of Majesty, oh shedd on mee
> A precious influence, as sweet as thee.

ll. 17–18. *And in spite, &c.* Compare ' In praise of *Lessius* his rule of health ', ll. 31–2, p. 157, above :
> A soule whose intelectuall beames
> No mistes doe maske no lazy steames ?

ll. 21–4. *Th' Astronomer, &c.* Compare ' Upon the Kings coronation ', ll. 33–4, p. 389, above :
> To gaze upon such starres each humble eye
> Would be ambitious of Astronomie.

ll. 25–6. *When his glory, &c.* Compare ' On a foule Morning, being then to take a journey ', ll. 7–8, p. 181, above :
> Vnfold thy faire front, and there shall appeare
> Full glory, flaming in her owne free spheare.

and ' Upon the Kings Coronation ', ll. 13–14, p. 390, above :
> Streight from this sea of teares there does appeare
> Full glory flaming in her owne free sphære.

PAGE 403, l. 32. *The Rhetorick of a weeping eye.* Compare ' Vpon the Death of a Gentleman ', l. 20, p. 167, above: ' The sad language of our eyes '. See also note thereto, p. 441, above.

l. 34. *When an eye a tongue can find.* Compare *loc. cit.*, ll. 27–8 :
> Eyes are vocall, Teares have Tongues,
> And there be words not made with lungs ;

ll. 35–6. *O, pri'thee death, &c.* Compare ' Vpon the Death of the most desired Mr. *Herrys* ', ll. 59–60, p. 170, above :
> Spare him Death, ô spare him then,
> Spare the sweetest among men.

PAGE 403. *the Lady Parker.* It has not been possible to identify the person in whose honour this poem was written ; if the poem is Crashaw's it cannot refer to the wife of William Parker, fourth Baron Monteagle and eleventh Baron Morley, as she died after Crashaw (*Parish Register, Great Hallingbury*) and in any case would have been referred to more naturally as Lady Monteagle. It seems possible, however, that the lady in question was William Parker's daughter Frances, of whom nothing appears to be recorded except that she ' died a Nun '. See art. ' William Parker ' in *D.N.B.*

ll. 3–4. *Can such, &c.* Compare the poem in memory of S. Teresa, ll. 140–4, p. 135, above :

> All thy good workes which went before
>   . . . and all in one
> Weave a Constellation
> Of Crownes, . . .

and ' His Epitaph ', ll. 17–20, p. 173, above :

> That in the Center of his Brest
>
>   .   .   .   .
> Every reconciled Grace,
> Had their Generall meeting place.

ll. 11–12. *Nor can . . . Excellence.* Compare ' Upon the birth of the Princesse Elizabeth ', ll. 17–18, p. 391, above :

> And though these humble lines soare not soe high,
> As is thy birth ;

and ' To the Morning ', ll. 19–20, p. 184, above :

> Hence 'tis my humble fancy finds no wings,
> No nimble rapture starts to Heaven . . .

ll. 12–13. *Oh could I fly Betwixt Seraphick pinions!* Compare ll. 22–3, p. 391, above :

> Lett th' hallowed plume of a Seraphick wing
> Bee consecrated to this worke,

PAGE 404, ll. 29–30. *And gladly, &c.* Compare ' Easter day ', ll. 16–18, p. 100, above :

>   for may hee ly
> Thron'd in thy Grave ;
> Death will on this condition be content to Dy.

ll. 32–6. *How a heart, &c.* Compare ' An Elegie on the death of Dr Porter ', ll. 29–30, p. 396, above :

> To sing their saddest Dir'ges, such as may
> Make their scar'd soules take wing, & fly away.

and ' On ye Gunpowder-Treason ', p. 384, above, ll. 28–30 :

> A winters thunder with a groane shall scare,
> And rouze the sleepy ashes of the dead,
> Making them skip out of their dusty bed.

l. 35. *My nimble spirits.* Compare ' To the Morning ', l. 20, quoted in note to ll. 11–12 of this poem, above.

ll. 38–9. *Each crimson streame, &c.* Compare ' An Elegy upon the death of Mr Stanninow ', ll. 22–4, p. 394, above :

> These purple currents hedg'd with violets round
> To corrallize, wch softly wont to slide
> In crimson waueletts, & in scarlet tide ?

and ' On yᵉ Gunpowder-Treason ', ll. 63–4, p. 385, above :

> the warmest blood,
> That runnes in violett pipes :

l. 42. *That euery heart, &c.* Compare ' His Epitaph ', ll. 50–2, p. 174, above :

> For now (alas) not in this stone
> (Passenger who e're thou art)
> Is he entomb'd, but in thy Heart.

Heading] *Mʳ Christopher Rouse.* A student of this name was admitted to Pembroke College (Crashaw's college) on April 19, 1621. He is described in the Admission Book as ' Johannis Equitis Aurati filius primogenitus Henham in agro Suffolcensi natus, 15 annos habens '. On March 2, 1623, ' Gratia ei conceditur ad respondend: quæstiones ' (*Pembroke Admission-Book*). As to his later career and the date of his death no particulars have been discovered.

l. 1. *Rich, purest rose.* See the note on Crashaw's fondness for the double adjective, Introduction, p. lxxiii, above.

prime flowre of blooming youth. Compare ' An Elegy upon the death of Mʳ Stanninow', l. 28, p. 394, above : ' this prime flowre of youth '.

ll. 14–16. *Vntill sh' hath flatter'd, &c.* Compare ' Cupid's *Cryer*', ll. 25–6, p. 159, above :

> The working Bees soft melting Gold,
> That which their waxen Mines enfold,

(for ' Mines ' in this connexion, compare l. 9, above).

PAGE 405, ll. 17–18. *that doe swimme In gulfes of deepest blisse.* Compare ' Cupid's *Cryer* ', ll. 14–15, p. 159, above :

> hee shall swim
> In riper joyes :

and ' Upon the Kings coronation ', ll. 5–6, p. 389 :

> Thou, glad Isle,
> That swim'st as deepe in joy, as Seas,

ll. 29 and 36. *I meane.* See the references quoted in the Introduction, pp. lxxii–lxxiii, above.

ll. 29–32. *where euery grace, &c.* Compare ' His Epitaph ', ll. 19–20, p. 173, above :

> Every reconciled Grace,
> Had their Generall meeting place.

See also note to p. 403, ll. 3–4, above.

ll. 41–2. *that from their wings, &c.* Compare ' Upon the birth of the Princesse Elizabeth ', ll. 22–3, p⸍ 391, above :

> Lett th' hallowed plume of a Seraphick wing
> Bee consecrated to this worke,

and see also note to p. 403, ll. 12–13, above.

An Epitaph. l. 3. *The brightest gemme, &c.* Compare ' Vpon the Death of the most desired Mr. *Herrys* ', l. 4, p. 168, above :

> This is Natures choycest Iewell.

l. 4. *Wᶜʰ now, &c.* Compare ' The Weeper ', st. 2, l. 6, p. 79, above :

> What ever makes Heavens fore-head fine.

ll. 5–6. *Therefore its shrine, &c.* Compare 'An Epitaph. Vpon Doctor *Brooke* ', ll. 7–8, p. 175, above :

> Meane while his loued bankes now dry,
> The Muses with their teares supply.

and ' An Elegie on the Death of Dr Porter ', ll. 43–4, p. 396, above :

> all bubling eyes
> Are teeming now with store of fresh supplies.

l. 6. *watry pearls.* Compare ' The Teare ', st. 1, l. 4, p. 83, above : ' A watry Diamond '.

PAGE 406. BRIT. MUS. MS. HARL. 6917.

See the preliminary discussion of this MS., pp. lxxvi–lxxviii, above.

PAGE 407. *Epithalamium*, l. 58. *noble Brampstons eyes.* It is impossible to be sure as to the identity of this Brampston, but it seems very likely that he was Sir John Bramston the younger (1611–1700), whose father was Chief Justice betweén 1632 and 1642, and whose autobiography was published in 1845 by the Camden Society. From this it appears that he married in 1635 Alice, eldest daughter of Anthony Abdy, alderman of London. The seat of the Bramstons was at Whitechapel, of which parish William Crashaw, the poet's father, was rector from 1618 to 1626, between Richard Crashaw's sixth and fourteenth years, and acquaintance may easily have begun then. John Bramston's brother, Moundeford, went to Queens' College, Cambridge, in 1632, the year after Crashaw's admission to Pembroke. The reference to the Thames in stanza 4 renders it scarcely possible that the poem was written for Moundeford's own wedding, which took place in 1639, as Moundeford married a Suffolk girl and left Cambridge to live in that county. See the Autobiography, p. 26.

l. 59. The sense is clearer if a comma is understood after ' thence '.

ll. 64–7. *t' exhale, &c.* Crashaw uses elsewhere the word ' exhale ' in connexion with the idea of death. Compare ' On a prayer booke ', ll. 71–2, p. 129, above :

> Delicious deaths, soft exhalations
> Of soule ; deare, and divine annihilations.

Compare also the verses on S. Teresa, ll. 113–17 (p. 134, above), where the exhalation is associated, as it is here, with fire and sighs :

> Like a soft lumpe of Incense, hasted
> By too hot a fire, and wasted,
> Into perfuming cloudes. So fast
> Shalt thou exhale to heaven at last,
> In a disolving sigh,

l. 71. *mother phænixes.* Compare ' Vpon the Duke of *Yorke* his Birth A Panegyricke ', ll. 82–3, p. 180, above :

> Thou art the Mother *Phænix*, and thy Breast
> Chast as that Virgin honour of the East,

PAGES 407–8, ll. 76 and 81–2. Compare ' A Song ', ll. 13–14, p. 327, above :

> Still liue in me this louing strife
> Of liuing DEATH & dying LIFE.

Compare also ' The Office of the Holy Crosse', *Antiphona*, ll. 1–2, p. 272, above:

> O strange mysterious strife
> Of open DEATH & hidden LIFE !

With this stanza, in general, compare ' Wishes. To his (supposed) Mistresse ', ll. 70-5, p. 197, above :

> Feares, fond and flight,
> As the coy Brides, when Night
> First does the longing lover right.
> Teares, quickly fled,
> And vaine, as those are shed
> For a dying Maydenhead.

PAGE **408,** l. 86. *this rich losse.* Compare ' In the Glorious Epiphanie ', l. 142, p. 258, above :

> Proud to haue gain'd this pretious losse.

l. 94. *the fires, &c.* Compare ' Vpon the Duke of *Yorke* his Birth A Paneygricke ', l. 118, p. 181, above :

> Give then this rurall wreath fire from thine eyes.

ll. 105-6. The rhyme ' this is ' and ' kisses ' is used elsewhere by Crashaw. Compare ' The Teare ', st. 4, ll. 1-3, p. 84, above, and ' Wishes. To his (supposed) Mistresse ', ll. 121-3, p. 198, above.

ll. 109-12. *Nor may thy Vine, &c.* The imagery and the phraseology are partially repeated in ' Vpon the Duke of *Yorke* his Birth A Panegyricke ', ll. 102-3, p. 180, above :

> Long mayest thou laden with such clusters leane
> Vpon thy Royall Elme (faire Vine)

PAGE **409,** l. 121. *heauen tyed.* This type of compound is not uncommon in Crashaw, especially with ' heaven ' as its first element, ' heau'n-intreated ' (p. 236, l. 1, above), ' Heaun-instructed ' (p. 295, st. 6, l. 1, above), ' heaun-designed ' (p. 331, l. 1, above).

l. 129. *neast.* This is one of Crashaw's favourite words. In the Hymn ' To the Name . . . of Iesus ', pp. 239-45, above, it occurs five times in the rhyming position. In this ' Epithalamium ' it also occurs three times at the end of a line.

APPENDIX I.
POEMS PROBABLY SPURIOUS.

PAGE **410.** *On the Frontispiece of* Isaacsons *Chronologie explained.* This poem is almost certainly the work of Edward Rainbow, D.D., who became Fellow of Magdalene College, Cambridge, in 1633 and afterwards Bishop of Carlisle.

In his biography, published in 1688, reference is made (p. 84) to ' a Paper of Verses upon the Frontispiece of Mr. *Henry Isaacson's* Chronology ; which acurate Chronologer was our Bishops particular Friend . . .', and the writer goes on ' Of the Honour of the former of these Poems, printed without the addition of any name in 1633, he was robbed by the Publisher of Mr. *Richard Crashaw's* Poems, Entituled, *Steps to the Temple*, and ascribed by him to that Ingenious *Epigrammatist.* But he having no Title to it, but what the modest silence of Mr. *Rainbow* gave him, I have recovered it to the true Owner by a *Melius inquirendum*, and subjoyned it here.'

PAGE **411.** *Melius purgatur, &c.* See the introductory notes on these verses, p. lxiv, above.

Priscianus verberans, &c. See the introductory notes on these verses, p. lxiv, above.

PAGE **413.** *Vpon a gnatt burnt in a candle.* See the introductory notes on these verses, p. lxv, above.

INDEX OF FIRST LINES.

Page numbers in italics refer to versions in another language of the poems in question.

917·9   H h

INDEX OF TITLES

(Excluding those of the Epigrammata Sacra, pp. 15–71 and 352–68; and of the Divine Epigrams, pp. 85–102 (see pp. 199–200) and 379–81.)